Bonds of Union

CIVIL WAR AMERICA

Peter S. Carmichael, Caroline E. Janney, and Aaron Sheehan-Dean, *editors*

This landmark series interprets broadly the history and culture of the Civil War era through the long nineteenth century and beyond. Drawing on diverse approaches and methods, the series publishes historical works that explore all aspects of the war, biographies of leading commanders, and tactical and campaign studies, along with select editions of primary sources. Together, these books shed new light on an era that remains central to our understanding of American and world history.

BRIDGET FORD

Bonds of Union

Religion, Race, and Politics in a
Civil War Borderland

The University of North Carolina Press
Chapel Hill

The paper in this book meets the guidelines for permanence
and durability of the Committee on Production Guidelines for
Book Longevity of the Council on Library Resources.

The University of North Carolina Press has been a member of the
Green Press Initiative since 2003.

Cover illustration: From Maria Goodell Frost, *Gospel Fruits; or, Bible Christianity Illustrated: A Premium Essay* (Cincinnati: American Reform Tract and Book Society, 1856), courtesy of the American Antiquarian Society.

Library of Congress Cataloging-in-Publication Data
Ford, Bridget, author.
Bonds of union : religion, race, and politics in a Civil War borderland / Bridget Ford.
pages cm—(Civil War America)
Includes bibliographical references and index.
ISBN 978-1-4696-2622-2 (cloth : alk. paper)—ISBN 978-1-4696-2623-9 (ebook)
1. Ohio—History—Civil War, 1861–1865—Social aspects. 2. Kentucky—History—Civil War, 1861–1865—Social aspects. 3. United States—History—Civil War, 1861–1865—Social aspects. I. Title. II. Series: Civil War America (Series)
E525.F675 2016
973.7′1—dc23
2015031950

Portions of this work appeared earlier in somewhat different form in Bridget Ford, "Black Spiritual Defiance and the Politics of Slavery in Antebellum Louisville," *Journal of Southern History* 78, no. 1 (February 2012): 69–106, and are reprinted here by permission of the publisher.

For Bonnie, my mother, and in memory of my father,
James T. Ford (1939–2004)

Contents

Preface

Abraham Lincoln spoke of "bonds of union" before audiences uneasy about the survival of the United States during tense moments in the 1850s. In the spring of 1854, adoption of the Kansas-Nebraska Act outraged Lincoln, for the new federal law would allow slavery's broad dispersion across new western states, despite long-standing political consensus that it should not. Although not an elected representative at the time, he took action, hoping to convince Illinois voters of the folly and injustice contained in Stephen Douglas's Nebraska legislation. A regular visitor to the state library in Springfield over a number of weeks, Lincoln studied "the general question of domestic slavery" from the time of America's founding. In the late summer and fall of 1854, Lincoln shared his conclusions in a public address that ran to some seventeen thousand words, judging from a published copy of the Peoria speech. None of Lincoln's other speeches rivaled it in length.[1]

Delivered to Illinois audiences, this passionate address represented new thinking for Lincoln. With congressional limits on slavery's extension legally in place before 1854, "the nation was looking to the forming of new bonds of Union," Lincoln asserted, "and a long course of peace and prosperity seemed to lie before us." But now, with slavery's perpetuity seemingly guaranteed by Douglas's retrograde legislation, Lincoln predicted "shocks, throes, and convulsions," or, in less metaphorical phrasing, "collision and violence." This was because an "eternal antagonism" existed between the "selfishness" inherent to mastery over other human beings and the "love of justice" propelling opponents of slavery to act. This irreconcilability, combined with Douglas's flawed "popular sovereignty" policy, meant that proslavery and antislavery partisans would bitterly contest every inch of new American territory. Lincoln recoiled at this future. In a year of dramatic shifts in voters' political allegiances as a consequence of the Kansas-Nebraska Act, the 1854 Peoria speech gave evidence of a kind of antislavery conversion for Lincoln personally. Determined to extricate Americans from the curse of slavery, he injected new "eloquence and moral power" into his speeches.[2] Evoking "bonds of union" untarnished by slavery's inherent violence was of a piece with that purposefulness.

The phrase "bonds of union" can sound stilted, if not archaic, to the modern ear. Today, elected leaders might draw on similar wording to add historical cachet, and wedding officiants can intone about the "bond of union" for solemn effect. Americans may recognize variants of the wording from the New Testament, for love is the "perfect bond of union" among believers in Christ.[3] But as a key to understanding some essential basis or character of the United States, the phrase has lost its rich nineteenth-century context. Even "Union," meaning the nation, is a nearly empty term for many today, one that perhaps conjures haunting photographs of Lincoln or calls to mind stagey annual State of the Union addresses, but little more.[4] This book tries to illuminate what Americans might have understood when Lincoln called on them to reflect on the "true bonds of union," as he did once again in his famous 1858 debate with Stephen Douglas.[5]

In the nineteenth century, Americans used the phrase "bonds of union" in very specific ways. Protestants were deeply familiar with the wording, for a bond of union defined "that invisible bond, connect[ing] each of them to Christ" within a community of faith.[6] The words also described family relations, for "every association of home, however humble, becomes linked to the heart with a bond of union that knows no separation."[7] The phrase entered into nineteenth-century Americans' political lexicon to address one of the lasting problems of the American nation from the time of its independence eighty years earlier: What could possibly hold together a vast continental republic comprising such diverse interests, peoples, and landscapes? Lincoln was therefore only one of many public figures to appeal to bonds of union. In 1845, when antislavery leader Salmon Chase spoke to Liberty Party activists in Cincinnati, he insisted that the "natural bond of union" for their third party was its dedication to "rights." In contrast to mainstream Whigs, whose "bond" was simply that of "interest," the Liberty Party would fight for "true Democracy" guided by a sense of "the brotherhood of the Human Family."[8] To be sure, each of these examples comes from formal rather than casual or everyday expression: a church manual in the first example, an antislavery tract in the second, and a major political speech in the last. If the phrase "bonds of union" sounds affected today, even in the Civil War era its direct use was reserved for considerations of great import: establishing religious and political communities and protecting family love.

When nineteenth-century Americans drew on the language of human and political "bonds," they clearly meant to call attention to serious matters requiring high resolve. Because Americans used the phrase as a summons to political purposefulness and careful thinking about human relations, it seemed to me a touchstone for understanding vitally important matters in the Civil War era. With rhetorical use of "bonds of union" as a starting point, then, I have tried to understand what Americans thought held them together in "union" when that relationship was severely tested.

But recall Lincoln's Peoria speech from 1854: Americans were "looking to the forming of new bonds of Union" before acts of Congress gravely threatened this ongoing work.[9] To Lincoln, Americans' bonds with each other were in gestation, still in process of realization. As a lawyer and then an elected leader, he looked to the Constitution and history to clarify Americans' "bonds of union." His conclusion: slavery's constitutional protection was emphatically not one of these bonds, and, in fact, wreaked havoc on Americans' ties with each other.[10] In 1858, during the Lincoln-Douglas debates, he prodded other citizens to study the nature of their political bonds, as he had: "I leave it to you to say whether, in the history of the Government, this institution of slavery has not always failed to be a bond of union, and, on the contrary, been an apple of discord and an element of division in the house."[11] Though couched in rhetoric, this prompting speaks to Lincoln's sincere sense that a moment of reckoning had arrived, and that Americans had the wherewithal to see slavery as alien both to their Constitution and to their history.

Lincoln's research at the Springfield library in 1854, combined with his office seeking, might seem the work of an unusually dedicated individual. But his quest to define the "true bonds of union" was not unique.[12] In fact, for almost three decades, from the 1840s to the end of the Civil War, diverse Americans labored mightily to comprehend what, if anything, held them together in one polity, a "union" no less. Their determined (if not stubborn) work to define Americans' bonds of union—without the bonds of slavery—is the subject of this book.

This book describes Americans' sustained efforts to imagine and foster bonds of union in an especially fractious region, the Ohio-Kentucky borderland. This region was riven by some of the country's worst religious conflicts and racial violence between 1840 and 1860.[13] Then, following the secession of southern states to form the Confederacy in the winter of 1860–61, this borderland area seemed on the brink of anarchy and civil dissolution even though the state of Kentucky remained loyal to the Union. But Confederate army advances, political party strife, and the chaotic unraveling of slavery in Kentucky severely tested white loyalties there. Though many Ohioans and Kentuckians inflamed hostility and distrust over and again throughout the era, some residents strained against the power of these animosities. This was particularly true in Cincinnati and Louisville, the two most significant cities in Ohio and Kentucky, respectively. Just under 150 miles distant from each other following the Ohio River, these two cities saw spectacular growth between 1840 and 1860. Amid the din of rapid urbanization, a remarkable set of individuals and societies created strong-enough bonds of union to weather the storms of religious, racial, and political violence. This book is foremost an effort to recover their work.

Fast-paced, crowded, and diverse, Cincinnati and Louisville were unique within the wider Ohio-Kentucky borderland. They also differed from other cities in the country in notable ways. First, the arrival of thousands of European Catholics, especially Germans, to the cities of the Ohio River valley in the 1840s and 1850s led to an entirely distinctive religious history, where immigrants and native-born Protestants both sought out "bonds of union" among believers and with Christ through intense devotional zeal—much of it imported by Catholic religious orders—not seen elsewhere in the United States. In the decade before the Civil War, Cincinnatians and Louisvillians bathed in mystical waters that brought forth rich articulations of union with the divine. These religious pursuits created a climate conducive to the exploration of human bonds of union in the here and now.

Next, arguably, the nation's most influential antislavery politics emerged from Cincinnati and Louisville. Cincinnatians played an essential role in the Republican Party's formation in the 1850s, and in 1849 the nation waited with bated breath to see whether Louisvillians could successfully press their case for emancipation in Kentucky, the only major slave state to consider abolishing the institution in the late antebellum era. Black Cincinnatians and Louisvillians could also be counted among the most organized political communities in the nation; in consequence, they elaborated basic conditions for a genuinely inclusive Union before the Civil War—as much, or more, than any other group of Americans at the time. Ahead of other states and regions of the country, they fought with unprecedented organization and energy for enlightened education for their children, seeking to establish a formal bond between the state and families of color through public schools. In response to these efforts, white Cincinnatians and Louisvillians came to hold an open-ended sense of African American potential that deserved cultivation and investment from the larger society. The belief in unlimited black ability coursed through literature and social movements unique to both cities.

Finally, when warfare came with a vengeance to the West, civilians in Louisville and Cincinnati were at the forefront of relief for soldiers, with the largest hospital and aid system in the country. Collecting and maintaining information about the health of hundreds of thousands of soldiers, Louisvillians communicated their fates to families throughout loyal Union states. They therefore explored the nature of bonds between those with utterly incompatible experiences of warfare undertaken in the name of union, and they did so on an unprecedented scale.

Through these varied prisms, this book explains how it was that Kentucky, a slave state, remained with the Union in 1861, despite great pressure outside of Louisville to renege on the federal compact formed in 1789. Kentucky's decision in favor of the Union was one of the most momentous of the Civil War. Without the state, Lincoln famously insisted—not without reason—Union military victory would be impossible. Louisvillians sustained Kentuckians' loyalties through the war; this consequence of bonds of union forged before 1861 was as significant as any.[14] By many Americans' logic at the time, the nation should have fractured along the Ohio River, the most obvious geographical fissure separating slave states from free states. The bonds holding Louisvillians, and the state of Kentucky, in the Union meant a messier break, one that precluded unity within the slave South.[15]

This book culminates with the end of slavery in Kentucky, which came about in a singular way, since the state had been exempt from the Emancipation Proclamation in 1863. On July 4, 1865, Louisvillians publicly declared slavery dead in Kentucky, in front of tens of thousands of bondsmen and bondswomen who had come to the city as refugees from violence in the interior of the state. Two African American leaders—Ohio's first black attorney, John Mercer Langston, and Louisville's leading black Baptist pastor, Henry Adams—presided over Kentucky's Emancipation Day. Both men had deep roots in Cincinnati and Louisville, and they brought more than two decades of experience thinking about, and organizing around, the promise of a more inclusive Union. Though Kentucky lurched violently toward emancipation, black Louisvillians and Cincinnatians like Adams and Langston carried the state's slaves over the threshold to freedom and offered hopeful reassurances about the future.

Some of the individuals discussed in this book are not well known today, though studies of antebellum Cincinnati and Louisville have demonstrated their importance.[16] People like William Gibson of Louisville and John Isom Gaines of Cincinnati deserve wide attention now. Working in concert with key white antislavery figures in Louisville and Cincinnati, they beat back the colonizationist enterprise in Ohio and Kentucky once and for all and compelled both states to invest in black lives, a radical historical shift in the Civil War era. Because they labored—unceasingly, it seemed—to establish conditions for African American rights and opportunities in these cities before the Civil War, a Union without slavery, and without racial separation via colonization, was more fully imaginable for white Ohioans and Kentuckians.

They also helped Louisville remain, by and large, a loyal city. The Louisvillians described in this book preserved allegiances to the Union while many white Kentuckians vacillated or broke faith.

William Gibson and John Gaines did not always talk about "bonds," or about "union," in express terms. In consequence, this book takes what might seem, on the surface, quite indirect investigations into ideas of union in the Civil War era. I also explore diverse topics that appear to be more in the realm of culture, disconnected from high politics, statecraft, and warfare. Among these topics are preaching styles and devotional literature; refinement and antislavery fiction; and poetry and historical writing. But through these varied cultural expressions, I argue, we can see how Americans in this Civil War borderland construed their connections to others and to things larger than themselves. However, the investigations here are not intended solely to reveal expressions and desires for bonds of union. Instead, I want to show how pursuits of union among diverse people became manifest in concrete action and real human relations. I also want to show how these actions took place within, but also dramatically altered, a larger political context. This book therefore examines culture in practice and in constant dialogue with unfolding events. Put another way, the absence of the precise phrase "bonds of union" in the historical evidence did not preclude me from examining how Americans checked the more divisive forces in their culture, and thereby helped to preserve the Union. By way of simple analogy, members of a family might not directly state their feelings toward each other, but they reveal desire for connection and security in their many daily actions.

I use the family comparison warily. For one, nations are not families, though nationalists can appropriate the language of family relations in order to make their state appear grounded in nature rather than history. Moreover, the individuals described here generally did not advocate a stronger union through interfaith or interracial marriage, for example, though such relationships (legal, loving, or otherwise) were realities in the Civil War era. One radical voice in this book, Mattie Griffith, suggested marriage as a means to ease the racial gulf, but this Louisvillian left Kentucky permanently before she did so. To have promoted interracial marriage in either Kentucky or Ohio would have invited violence, for the idea of "amalgamation" had a hoary history of use as psychic threat. White Kentuckians and Ohioans had no little experience exploiting dread fears of racial mixture as a means to provoke violence against African Americans and abolitionists.

But in other ways, an analogy to familial "bonds of union" may be apt. The language of sympathy and sentiment, derived from an idealized model of domestic or family relations, pervades the era and, to a certain extent, this book too. Antislavery writers drew heavily from this emotional language of love and loss to imagine how enslaved peoples experienced family rupture. Along with a new humanitarian impulse to meliorate pain and cruelty, the language of sympathy demanded that Americans "remember those who are in bonds, as bound with them."[17] Caution is in order here, though, before we assume that such language is evidence of a radical shift in white sensibilities. However much sentimental language encouraged identification with enslaved people's sufferings, its use also created distance. As many historians and literary scholars have noted, sentimentalism valorized the humane feelings of white Americans but did not also offer any concrete methods to alter the conditions producing that anguish. As the historian Margaret Abruzzo argues, "such sensitivities could be deeply self-referential."[18] And in any event, no one section or region of the country had a monopoly on sentimental or humanitarian claims. If both northerners and southerners insisted they wanted to improve the lives of enslaved peoples by reducing their pain, as Abruzzo shows for the antebellum era, then we have to look beyond humane language as an animating force behind emancipation. This demands a tricky balancing act for historians of the era: though we rely on textual evidence from the past, we must be careful in accepting expressions and desires unconditionally. In consequence, this book examines the interplay of cultural expression with action to understand how Americans living in this borderland rendered the bonds of slavery incompatible with the bonds of Union.

To understand how Americans defined their bonds of union in the Civil War era, we must also have a sense of the meaning of "union." Between adoption of the U.S. Constitution in 1789 and outbreak of civil war just over seventy years later, Americans' sense of connection to, and confidence in, their nascent nationhood usually drew on two rival concepts, "union" and its fragmented opposite, "disunion." It is difficult to recapture the diffusion of these terms through Americans' spoken and print expression from these first several generations of nationhood. Americans of every political stripe, from all manner of economic and cultural backgrounds, made "ardent use" of these ideas in the welter of nineteenth-century print literature, in the country's avid associational activity, and in every imaginable civic space, from U.S. Senate chambers to western agricultural fairs. Both words gave immediate shape to people's sense of confidence or unease in their futures, superficially akin to "right direction" or "wrong track" polling language today. But unlike the reductionism of modern surveys, "union" and "disunion" were richly invested, "potent" concepts in the imaginations of Americans two centuries ago.[19]

Not far removed from the founding generation, Americans living in the early republic better recalled the purpose behind the U.S. Constitution's preamble, which described the new government as consistent with the people's desire to "form a more perfect Union." Discord and impotence under the Articles of Confederation provoked many to wish for a stronger central administration ensuring greater unity among states, and this crisis in governance was not soon forgotten. But next-generation Americans added new layers of meaning to the term "union" through extensive reiteration and elaboration, thereby conjuring far more than the federal system of government. First, with unprecedented popular participation in elections and governance by 1840, the Union grew to signify a democracy directly empowering its people, unique in the annals of human history and therefore worthy of patriotic reverence. Second, as the political scientist Rogan Kersh has argued, union came to represent a desire for a "common identity," even an "inclusive hope," by affirming diverse Americans' "active sense of connection and attachment" alongside their commitment to self-government. In this way, union promoted "a sense of shared membership in a worthy polity" among Americans of different backgrounds and political persuasions.[20]

Insofar as the term "community" has supplanted "union" as the surest expression of citizens' emotional connections to each other today, our sense of government's role as an "integrative force" has diminished. Yet to Americans of the early republic, "affective ties" among diverse peoples—the imagined bonds between strangers who shared neither kinship nor cultural affinity—could not be disentangled from the efficient working of representative government. This conception of union may strike twenty-first-century Americans as surprising. In our more compartmentalized language, "community" and "government" tend to stand as separate rather than overlapping entities; in consequence, our own practice of citizenship or democracy can seem to have less of the spirit of mutual regard than was purveyed in the broad idea of union.[21]

Union thinking exerted force in the first half of the nineteenth century. Absent the idea's cohesive power before 1860, Kersh and other historians have posited, the United States could not have endured the Civil War with its constitution essentially intact and its people desirous of reconciliation after 1865. Of course, "disunion" stood as the destructive foil to "union" in nineteenth-century Americans' sensibilities, and it is entirely possible to argue that the language of fragmentation and alienation proved the more powerful historical force, as Elizabeth Varon has recently done. Slavery, not rhetoric, provoked the Civil War, but Americans also made incessant use of the "discourse of disunion" from the time of the United States' founding—so much so that prophecies, threats, accusations, and actual plans of division, as Varon classifies the unwieldy range of disunion speech, provided "the terms of the debate that pulled the Union apart."[22] From the vantage of our own century, it may seem beside the point to try to determine which of the two concepts—union or disunion—carried greater weight for nineteenth-century Americans. Of necessity, the concepts stood together as the two poles of understanding about the relative strength and fragility of the United States as an organized community. Human society routinely seeks order in such cognitive pairings: inclusion against exclusion, love against cruelty, civility against vulgarity, security against danger, purity against pollution, and so on. In the particular historical era of the United States between its founding and the Civil War, union and disunion described and arranged Americans' sense of outermost possibility about their compact with one another. Both concepts also drove individuals to act out of conviction, whether as a means to protect the federal Constitution and its promise of self-rule, or in pursuit of a separate nationhood to secure the perpetuity of a racial caste system.

That the United States finally did fragment into separate warring entities bespeaks the inordinate fear and loathing contained within disunion logic.[23] Because southern states' secession announced such an unmitigated rejection of the unionist construction of the U.S. Constitution, it is understandable that this shattering act remains the more salient event to explain among historians. Tracing the deepening hold of union ideas after 1789 appears to be a somewhat less enticing project. But it is an underlying argument of this book that many Americans invested a tremendous amount of imaginative work into their ideas of religious, racial, and political unions in the Civil War era, and that this work merits revisiting in our own historical moment. To a remarkable degree, the language of union in the nineteenth century fostered a sense of identification across human differences and lived experience, and understood those identifications as the lifeblood of enlightened self-government in ways that we sometimes seem at a loss to describe today. While accounting for the many divisive forces at work in nineteenth-century American life, this book hopes to recover an inclusive, wide-ranging understanding of union and seeks its origins among both northerners and some southerners.

At times in the writing of this book, it has seemed impossibly tragic that we have not met some of the most basic aspirations of the Civil War generation. Even so, I do not offer lessons, or a "usable past," since our own circumstances and immediate choices are so vastly different from those of the nineteenth century. But by paying attention to the practices of union undertaken more than 150 years ago, we gain perspective from the strenuous efforts to forge connections among people with different origins and histories, and to make those bonds a condition of the Union's persistence.

This argument returns us to the stock phrase deployed by Lincoln, "bonds of union." An odd redundancy appears evident here, for in a certain literal sense, he spoke of the "bonds of the bonds" holding the nation together, since union by itself suggests the "action of joining or uniting one thing to another or others."[24] Therein lies the immediate subject of this book: not union per se, but the imagined connections that seemed essential to join disparate parts into one whole. The book therefore describes bonds fashioned by Americans before 1865 to diminish seemingly stark divides in matters of faith, race, and law—not as abstractions, but in lived experience. The book contends that Americans elaborated these bonds in unlikely pursuits—while seeking piety, enlightenment, and relief from suffering—and in the least hospitable places. Lincoln's speeches of the 1850s as citizen and candidate assumed his western audience's ready familiarity with a phrase such as "bonds of union." But this book finds that residents of the Ohio River valley, especially those living in dynamic places such as Cincinnati and Louisville, carried on uniquely rich, if not painstaking, discussions of the "bonds of union" and that the region therefore deserves our focused attention. More importantly, they reimagined political "bonds" as a basis for freedom and human potential.

While distinctive, Louisville and Cincinnati represented American history writ large. Settled in the first blush of the nineteenth century, they grew rapidly from small, insignificant trading posts at the outer edge of the United States into awe-inspiring cities—for their time—situated in the geographical center of the country. Attracting the world's seekers, dreamers, and gawkers, the cities displayed all of the admirable haste and vitality of the first half of the nineteenth century.[25] Yet diverse groups also fought for primacy in these dynamic places. They did so with a full-tilt, rushing energy, and fierce clashes ensued over immediate questions about immigration and slavery. Longer-term tensions between Reformation and Counter-Reformation ideologies, between racist categorization and universalism within Enlightenment thinking, and between federal and state power in the U.S. Constitution made local conflicts in Cincinnati and Louisville ferocious. Residents played out these great tensions in close proximity to people who seemed to fall on the opposite side of unalterable divides. To diminish differences across faith, race, and section, some imagined and cultivated potent bonds of union. These bonds varied tremendously: they included union between humanity and the divine, between black and white families and the state, and between civilians and soldiers. This book describes these bonds and the individuals who invested in them, and seeks to show their power in holding together the Union and furthering emancipation during the American Civil War.

Acknowledgments

This book could not have been written without support from a number of institutions. I especially thank Stanford University and the American Antiquarian Society for generous fellowships that provided me with precious time to research and write. The Huntington Library and Yale University also offered critical support. I depended greatly on the exceptional staffs at several libraries, including the American Antiquarian Society, the Cincinnati History Library and Archives, the Public Library of Cincinnati and Hamilton County, the Filson Historical Society, and the Buswell Memorial Library Archives and Special Collections at Wheaton College. I would like to express my appreciation to the Union Baptist Church in Cincinnati, and in particular the Turner family, for sharing with me the church's remarkable nineteenth-century records.

My development as a historian is of a piece with this work. I thank my lucky stars for extraordinary teachers and mentors over the years: Mark Carnes, Karen Halttunen, Rosalind Rosenberg, Herbert Sloan, Alan Taylor, and Clarence Walker. Robert Gross, Anne Rose, and David Wills gave me important early guidance on this book. Bob Gross ultimately read the manuscript several times, offering apt and thoughtful suggestions each time. I am very much indebted to him for his unstinting effort to make this a better book. For their examples of scholarship and friendship, I thank Seth Rockman and Dee Andrews. At the California State University, the Department of History at East Bay has afforded me a happy professional home. Despite some truly dire financial straits in recent years, my department remained a model of integrity and dedication—with a healthy dose of gallows humor thrown in for good measure. I feel very fortunate to work among such exceptional historians. My colleague, Henry Reichman, a historian of Russia, generously read this book in its entirety, providing valuable comments and editorial suggestions. With unending commitment to our mission, Ms. Wanda Washington ensured that our department met its obligations to students and to the State of California. Karen Halttunen and Seth Rockman provided guidance as this book took its final form.

I would like to acknowledge the support of special individuals, including two amazing friends, Zabrae Valentine and Alycia Harshfield. I thank Charles

Thorpe and the entire Thorpe family of Sacramento. They have taught me about faith, family, and friendship and introduced me to the important historical scholarship of Earl E. Thorpe, Charles's brother. In addition, Charles helped me to connect with Cincinnati's Union Baptist Church. Kimberly Gonsalves provided editorial assistance and, at times, a critical lifeline for this project.

My greatest appreciation goes to my family. The Lamb-Sun-Blum-Cockcroft clan models dedication to family every single day. I thank Dr. Sheryl Sun for allowing us to lean on her generosity and expertise in more ways than I can count. Jennifer Cockcroft is aunt extraordinaire to my son, who cannot believe his good fortune in the Cousin Department. I offer deepest thanks to Lula Mae Lamb, who never once declined to care for my young son as I worked and who has provided unconditional love, wise insight, and delicious meals to her children and grandchildren for nearly sixty years.

My uncles Patrick and Terrence Ford have allowed me to hear the cadences of my father's inimitable style of speech, while also ensuring that we had a sense of a paterfamilias still available to us. My brother Dylan has provided me with sage counsel and unerring editorial skills time and again. I have counted on him to get me through more than a few rough patches in life. I thank him from the bottom of my heart for pulling us through all with extraordinary good humor and keen intelligence. This book is dedicated to my mother, Dr. Bonnie Ford, and my late father, Judge James Timothy Ford. One of the most brilliant and clear-thinking persons I have ever met, my mom earned her doctorate in history from the University of California at Davis just as I was entering my senior year in high school, and I returned to Davis for my own PhD less than a decade later. In this unusual family saga devoted to historical study, my mom has provided the lion's share of childcare for my son as I sought to earn tenure and then write this book. She therefore combined her unmatchable wit, intellectual gifts, and workaday teaching duties with family life for two generations. My father was an extraordinary judge who understood the meaning of justice through an acute sense of the past. I hope this book lives up to his memory, if only in small part.

More than any others, Bryan and Theo Lamb have lived with this book as a physical fact. Bryan, my husband, and my son, Theo, have given me space and quiet when I needed it on weekends and nights, and have operated under the firm belief that I could indeed make this book a reality. I am, and will be, forever grateful to them for their trust in me and their assumption that this was a valuable endeavor when so many other needs and opportunities beckoned. My bonds with them mean everything to me. Lastly, I thank my son's school, Commodore Sloat Elementary School in San Francisco, for helping me to see both the great promise in universal public education and the setbacks when state funding fails. I began this book in earnest when Theo entered school as a kindergartner. Four years later, I recognize the antecedents for his school's high aspirations, daunting challenges, and vigilant supporters in the era examined here.

This was the book I could write, under the circumstances in which I lived. It is very much my own work, and any errors, infelicities, or faulty judgments are therefore mine alone.

Bridget Ford
San Francisco, California

Bonds of Union

Adolphus Ranney, "Map of the United States" (New York, 1854). This map of the United States shows the geographical centrality of Cincinnati and Louisville at midcentury. It also shows the proximity of these two "western" cities, one in a free state and the other in a slave state, and the relative ease of river transport between the two. In consequence, people and ideas frequently circulated between the two dynamic urban environments.

(© Cartography Associates, David Rumsey Collection. Courtesy of the American Antiquarian Society)

Part I

Protestant and Catholic

CHAPTER ONE

Collision

In 1826, two occasions vied for Americans' attention: the fiftieth anniversary of the Declaration of Independence and Pope Leo XII's Holy Year of Jubilee in the United States. The civic celebration and the new pope's call to Catholics to revitalize their faith bore little outward resemblance to each other, but the special events did invigorate Americans' patriotism and Catholics' attachments to Rome. While American Protestants did not have a unique claim to civic loyalty over that of American Catholics, the evangelical revivalism taking shape in the 1820s, often denoted as the "Second Great Awakening," attached powerful providential understandings to the creation, survival, and expansion of the republic. In consequence, a supercharged Protestantism with a dawning perception of its "manifest destiny" collided with the new Catholic fervor emanating from Europe. The new states beyond the Allegheny Mountains, known in the first part of the nineteenth century as the Western Country, emerged as the critical battleground, where Americans at home and Europeans abroad believed the final "death struggle" between the two faiths would take place.[1]

In the renewed bid for spiritual supremacy over North America's interior, religious groups selected Cincinnati and Louisville as their headquarters after 1830. In these two fledgling cities, Protestants and Catholics built powerful churches, institutions, and organizations with the zeal and wealth to crusade throughout the Western Country. Inspired by transcendent purpose, missionaries supported by Cincinnati's and Louisville's religious societies competed fiercely for souls. This heady competition reawakened old Reformation and Counter-Reformation conflicts, and the soaring ambitions, ear-popping rhetoric, and paranoiac fantasies made for tense relations throughout the antebellum era. In this tinderbox environment, extreme religious violence erupted in Cincinnati and Louisville after the nation's two main political parties fractured in the mid-1850s, giving free rein to nativist furies around elections. Until that moment, though, Protestants and Catholics relied mostly on "soft power" to proselytize, convert, and seize ultimate victory for one faith or the other in the rapidly growing Western Country.

Ambitions

Searching for evidence of literary achievement among the Ohio River valley's earliest settlers, a beleaguered antiquarian by the name of William Henry Venable instead unearthed a stunning array of religious writings emanating from Cincinnati and Louisville in the decades before the Civil War. A prominent Ohio educator and man of letters by the 1870s, Venable began with an "incidental rummage through the alcoves of a dozen dusty libraries" in Cincinnati. Twenty years of laborious excavation later, Venable published his *Beginnings of Literary Culture in the Ohio Valley* in 1891.[2] Here he registered shock at the volume of propaganda by "new sects" of Protestants and "newly inspired older sects," who "wrought zealously to infuse their doctrines every-where" in the West. Venable expressed wonderment at these antebellum Protestants, whose "active energy might be likened to that force of chemical elements which scientists observe in substances just set free from combination, and existing in what is called the *nascent*, or new-born state. . . . The action and reaction of [these] colliding elements in the Ohio Valley struck out much intellectual heat and light."[3] As Venable discovered in his research, "every leading sect had its 'organ' or periodical" to propagate its views and announce the " 'good time coming' " to western readers.[4] These publications stand as a testament to the utterly fantastic ambitions of their authors, editors, and readers, for according to America's faithful at the time, the West was fast ripening for the biblical millennium. In somewhat more secular but no less optimistic terms, evangelical Protestants also insisted that the West's "character and destiny, is involved much in the happiness of our race."[5] A witness to this religious excitement, the Presbyterian minister (and first president of Oberlin College) Asa Mahan later wrote, "Never in the history of the world, as I believe, were Christians more sincere, ardent, and single-hearted."[6]

Surprisingly, those seeking to make the inland West the seedbed for a new millennium flocked to the region's cities. That Cincinnati and Louisville would wield such monumental influence over human and sacred history seemed unlikely, to say the least, in 1820: Cincinnati's diminutive congregations, struggling to survive without settled ministers, and Louisville's whist-loving, theater-going population hardly presented models for emulation, let alone ground for sowing a moral revolution. But after about 1830, these cities proved irresistible for ambitious ministers desiring headquarters for their labors. For one, the new wealth generated by early manufacturing enterprises and extensive commercial ties to interior towns and settlements in the West and South provided financial resources for bold missionary schemes.

Moreover, the two cities' growing significance as regional publishing and print distribution centers allowed a variety of Protestant groups to disseminate their particular religious messages cheaply and easily to widespread western audiences. After 1830, Protestant religious societies in Cincinnati and Louisville would harness the power of the transportation revolution to the cause of religion by raising funds and hiring evangelists who utilized road, river, and rail to hasten the arrival of a new heaven on earth.

Ministers from the East overcame misgivings about relocating to remote and unfinished Cincinnati and Louisville by imagining these cities' auspicious futures. "Generally I hate the thought of a city," Jonathan Blanchard wrote to his fiancée in Vermont. The native-born New Englander considered moving on "to some pleasant country place in Illinois," but felt it a duty to remain in Cincinnati where "I could do a great deal where a great deal needs to be done." The greater Ohio Valley was "to be the seat of *Empire*," he predicted, and with Cincinnati poised to reign as the commercial capital of this developing empire, Blanchard accepted the Sixth Street Presbyterian Church's call.[7] Louisville also attracted its share of ministers who believed that it offered "a wider field of activity and influence" than cities in the East.[8] William Jackson, an Episcopal minister born in 1793 in Tutbury, England, decided to leave his New York church, St. Stephen's, after receiving "a most unexpected call from the vestry of Christ Church, Louisville, Ky.," in 1837. Although health concerns, probably tuberculosis, helped persuade Jackson to move to Kentucky, his conviction that the Mississippi Valley was "whitening . . . for the harvest" led him to view the Louisville call as "providential." In justifying his decision to a brother in England, Jackson quoted a newspaper, the *New-York Observer*, on Louisville's religious significance: " 'This city is one of the most important in the valley of the Mississippi, and is a place where a powerful moral influence would reach further, and be more efficient, than at any point of that vast region.' "[9]

The Reverend Jackson's confidence in Louisville's virtuous potential marked a reversal from commentators' disparaging remarks about the city's irreverence two decades earlier. By the time Jackson decided to move west, Louisville's commercial importance and regional influence seemed all but assured. Moreover, by the mid-1830s, Protestant churches in Louisville as well as Cincinnati had sufficiently large congregations with financial means to support full-time ministers. Although eastern societies had supplied the Ohio River valley with itinerant preachers and temporary ministers from the late eighteenth century, Cincinnati's and Louisville's churches grew independent of this aid after a series of Protestant revivals in the late 1820s.[10]

Fortified by new members and converts, Protestant congregations in these two cities began to launch their own regional missionary enterprises, and by 1840 several had become powerhouses of western evangelism.

The shifting fortunes of Cincinnati and Louisville's Baptist churches illustrate local Protestants' increasing reliance on urban congregations for their western missionary work. In the early 1830s, both cities' First Baptist churches had barely survived schisms and crises produced by the "Christian Reform" movement. In Cincinnati, Alexander Campbell's preaching carried off some 118 members, leaving First Baptist with just 32 members and "so reduced as to be unable to sustain a pastor."[11] But in 1831, an ambitious minister from Philadelphia, Samuel W. Lynd, saw opportunity in Cincinnati's predicament. Known for his "eloquence in the pulpit" and "literary attainments," Lynd started with just 19 members but rapidly consolidated scattered Baptists in the city into his new Sixth Street Baptist Church.[12] Among the twenty-five churches reporting to the Miami Baptist Association in 1829, Cincinnati's First Baptist Church—the organization's only urban church—had ranked thirteenth in its number of members, reporting 32 adherents.[13] But by 1834, under Lynd's leadership, Sixth Street Baptist Church reported 259 members; the next largest, in Lebanon, claimed 150 members.[14] Although rural churches had dominated the regional Miami Baptist Association since its founding in 1798, Lynd would serve as the moderator of its annual meetings between 1836 and 1845 and Cincinnati's Baptist churches would direct the organization's busy missionary agenda for the remainder of the antebellum period.

At first, Lynd's ambitious schemes to establish the "empire of Immanuel" in the Ohio River valley engendered opposition from rural precincts.[15] "On us the latter days have fallen," Lynd had announced in 1832. Enlivened but agitated by this weighty responsibility, he urged his fellow ministers to hasten God's work. "If we pray 'thy kingdom come,' and do not exert ourselves to spread the knowledge of Christ in the world, our prayers will be sin."[16] Much to his disappointment, twenty churches (representing 706 rural Baptists in southwestern Ohio) decried such "human instrumentality" as rank "Arminianism, Missionism, and Meanism" and refused to associate with Lynd's faction.[17] Although the anti-mission or "Primitive" Baptist group survived into the twentieth century, its hard message that this world is an unrelenting "vale of sin and disappointment" and its declaration that the "Lord's people have always been a poor and afflicted people" found fewer and fewer adherents.[18] By 1856 the group represented just ten churches, and by 1917 only five churches remained, harboring a minuscule 112 members.[19]

Without this "hyper-Calvinism" constraining their activities, Lynd and his pro-mission party flew into action.[20] In "one of the signs of the approach of the millennium," Lynd had quoted prophecy in 1832, "Many shall run to and fro, and knowledge shall be increased." Lynd's own wearying travels across the state of Ohio must have looked like a sign that the Lord was "*now* fulfilling" his biblical promise.[21] In addition to his leadership in the Miami Baptist Association, by 1835 Lynd was president of both the Ohio Baptist Convention and the Western Baptist Education Society, a willing committeeman in the General Convention of Western Baptists, and a tireless promoter of all "the great objects of benevolence connected with the advancement of the Redeemer's Kingdom."[22] Lynd's field of missionary activity was the entire western valley, where he encouraged the work of "Village Missionaries," especially in Ohio.[23] Financially supported by congregations but hired by the Ohio Baptist Convention, these missionaries labored exclusively in rural settlements and "country" towns lacking permanent ministers.[24] To expand the supply of ministers in the West, Lynd also vigorously promoted educational enterprises, including seminaries in Ohio and Kentucky "destined to bless this land and the world," according to the Western Baptist Education Society.[25] Reversing three decades of rural predominance in the Ohio Valley's religious affairs, Lynd's Sixth Street Church members supported such missionary work far more than any other in southeastern Ohio. And by the mid-1840s, Cincinnati's four Baptist churches supplied more than 40 percent of all missionary funds collected by the nineteen churches belonging to the regional Miami Baptist Association.[26]

Between 1830 and 1840, Louisville's white Baptists also began to wield their urban advantages—their multiple transportation links to the Ohio Valley's agricultural hinterland and greater congregational wealth—to sponsor missionary work throughout Kentucky with an enthusiasm nearly matching that of Cane Ridge, the famed revival of 1801. As a result of "three great evangelistic preachers," all ministers at Louisville's First Baptist Church in the 1830s, Baptists became the most populous religious adherents in Kentucky by 1850, far outstripping Methodists, Presbyterians, and Roman Catholics.[27] That Louisville's Baptists would exercise such influence could not have been predicted in 1830, when "a large Majority" of First Baptist Church declared their support for Alexander Campbell's movement and accused their former brethren of "promot[ing] Hatred Varience [*sic*] Emulation wrath strife seditions Backbitings Swellings Enveyings & such like things."[28] Although reduced to fewer than two hundred members in 1831, the church nevertheless attracted several powerful missionary preachers who launched the longest running series of revivals in Kentucky's history, converting some eighteen thousand men and women between 1834 and 1843.[29]

The Rev. J. S. Willson, pastor at Louisville's First Baptist Church between 1834 and 1835, sparked this long revival after proposing a "visionary" scheme that divided Kentucky into three sectors to be visited by "Evangelical Bands" and "Helping Evangelists." Although one denominational leader later complained that Willson's administrative logic "defie[d] the comprehension of ordinary mortals," its immediate result was a legendary revival rippling out from Shelbyville, Kentucky, which left an estimated twenty-one hundred men and women basking in the "millennial glow."[30] As a consequence of Willson's work, some Baptists in Kentucky were persuaded that "the inhabitants of the earth are ripening fast for some general revolution."[31] Willson, for one, would not live to see this revolution: he collapsed and died in August 1835, after fifty straight days of arduous revival work.[32]

Willson's missionary plan expired with him, but Baptist leaders regrouped to form the General Association of Baptists in Kentucky at a meeting held in Louisville's First Baptist Church in 1837. The association's explicit purpose was to continue the revival work throughout the state.[33] For the next fifty years, Louisville's Baptist churches spearheaded the General Association's efforts, largely because of their greater financial resources. Kentucky's rural Baptists provided notoriously scant support for their ministers, few of whom could settle permanently or devote their full energies to preaching among the state's agricultural settlements. According to one Baptist minister, country churches adhered to this maxim: "The Lord keep our preachers humble, and we will keep them poor."[34] His recollection reveals the growing disparity between urban and rural churches. After about 1830, churches in commercial cities like Louisville provided the financial means and organizational leadership to proselytize in the backcountry. And judging from Louisville's Baptist church minutes, urban congregations trained, examined, and licensed a substantial number of preachers servicing rural Baptists before western colleges and seminaries began to provide adequate numbers of ministers. By 1888, fifty years after the General Association's founding, Kentucky's Baptist ministers reckoned their missionary success at fifty thousand souls saved, at a cost of roughly $200,000, paid largely by Louisville's churches.[35] As "the mother of the General Association" and with its generous "love for the whole State," First Baptist Church of Louisville would justifiably claim these fifty thousand conversions as its own work.[36]

Bringing Glad Tidings

Black Americans also imagined the West as a place of unique beauty overlaid with religious significance. As the freeborn William Gibson traveled from Baltimore to Louisville in 1847, the "picturesque scenery" of the Allegheny Mountains and the Ohio River "caused my imagination to reach out in wonder and amazement at the great and stupendous work of nature, and the possibility of these rocks and mountains fleeing away at the final consummation of all things."[37] Like white Protestants, blacks viewed Cincinnati and Louisville as important missionary fields because of their strategic locations in the West and, in the case of Cincinnati, the northern free city's proximity to the South. Black Methodists and Baptists imagined that Cincinnati had a peculiar religious mission to fulfill by providing a gateway to freedom—both physical and psychological—for slaves and recently freed blacks. A. R. Green, a minister stationed at Cincinnati's Allen Temple in the late 1840s, urged the importance of an African Methodist Episcopal Church presence in Ohio's southernmost city: "Now, the mere fact that we go in and out before those poor people, unfits them for slaves, and trains them for freedom."[38]

Green's statement suggests a distinction between black and white visions of the Ohio Valley's religious and moral promise. While white missionaries and ministers almost invariably faced west to confront impiety, black missionaries—even those born and raised in eastern states—ultimately turned south to confront the horrific consequences of slavery and caste prejudice. Particularly in the 1820s and 1830s, but even as late as 1850, travel narratives, local guides, and missionary literature produced by white authors dwelled on distinctions between the western and eastern United States, thereby slighting contrasts between northern free and southern slave states. By contrast, black migrants, even those from eastern states, oriented themselves along a North-South axis upon their arrival in places like Cincinnati and Louisville.

William Gibson provides an illustration. "At an early age" he had "manifested a desire to travel West." A student of future African Methodist Episcopal (AME) bishop Daniel Payne, Gibson was persuaded by leading black Methodists to organize an elementary school for enslaved and free black children in Louisville. At least at the outset of his journey, Gibson considered his migration from Baltimore to Louisville a fulfillment of his youthful desire to move west, even though both cities lay in the slave South. But after encountering white resistance to his school, he entertained second thoughts about his relocation to Kentucky. Indeed, within a few years of his arrival in the southern state, Gibson and several other free blacks from Louisville purchased land in southern Ontario, Canada, after learning that a bill before the Kentucky legislature sought to bind out all free black children away from their parents. The legislature eventually dropped consideration of the outrageous scheme, and Gibson decided to remain in Kentucky because, to him, Louisville constituted a "field of labor for such an one if desirous of benefiting his race." This missionary impulse sustained Gibson through the 1850s—harrowing years for free blacks in the South—as he helped strengthen Louisville's AME churches and schools and secretly carried Frederick Douglass's newspapers and speeches into the state. Although he once more resolved to abandon the city and even purchased property in Indianapolis at the end of the Civil War, friends again prevailed upon Gibson to remain in Louisville in order to run schools for freed men and women. As a "western" city, Louisville probably offered free blacks no more independence than an eastern (and Upper South) city like Baltimore. Yet for African Americans "imbued with the spirit of freedom," as Gibson was, the city constituted a crucial western arena in which to introduce and transmit ideas from northern free blacks to slaves in the South.[39]

William Gibson's personal experience reflected a broader pattern among Methodists who considered Ohio and Kentucky missionary fields. In the 1820s, AME church leaders such as Bishop Morris Brown had grown concerned for black townspeople and settlers in the West, especially Ohio, whose attendance at rural white churches and camp meetings was accompanied by "impositions and afflictions." Rev. David Smith later explained, "The Macedonian cry, 'come and help,' was heard on the west side of the Allegheny mountains." As Smith discovered while ministering throughout Ohio's hinterlands, black settlers were "devoured on every side by the wolves of slavery, prejudice, and ostracism."[40] Smith and a phalanx of ministers moved across western states setting up independent African Methodist Episcopal congregations, usually among black Methodists who had been deprived of the support and fellowship churches normally provide their members.

News of the formation of an independent black denomination seems to have reached Cincinnati only in 1823, some seven years after the AME Church's ecclesiastical organization in Philadelphia in 1816. According to an oral history related on the fiftieth anniversary of Allen Temple, Cincinnati's first independent African American church, black Methodists decided to break off from the white episcopacy after their preachers were denied the Lord's Supper at a camp meeting until all white participants had first enjoyed the sacrament. A missionary received the small group of thirty-three members into the African Methodist Episcopal connection in 1824. They initially met in their preacher's house cellar, which the congregation called "Jerico."[41] Fifty years later, Allen Temple's Rev. B. W. Arnett celebrated the arrival of AME Church missionaries in the West:

> This little band of hero warriors started with the strength of the God of Israel, and on they went from one city to another, preaching the gospel of freedom to soul, mind, and body; and everywhere they went they were received with open arms and a joyful heart. They crossed the Alleghany [*sic*] Mountains . . . and all along the great valley of the Monongahela the voice of the sons of God was heard calling on the people to arise and shine, for their lights had come, bringing glad tidings of great joy to all men, white and black.[42]

AME Church itinerants took this missionary zeal and redemptive message into Kentucky some ten years later. In the mid-1830s, Rev. David Smith went to Louisville but initially concluded it was too dangerous to establish an AME church in the city.[43] However, Smith married a free Louisville woman, made his home directly across the Ohio River in Jeffersonville, Indiana, and at the behest of a white minister took charge of two black churches in Louisville still connected with the white-led Methodist Episcopal Church. Secretly at first, Smith preached the AME gospel of independence at his relatives' home in Louisville, and the small band soon organized into a separate AME congregation around 1840. Louisville's authorities arrested the AME Church's leading western missionary and future bishop, Elder William P. Quinn, at one of these early meetings, but "finding that he had the proper papers for conducting the meetings," allowed the congregation to continue.[44] Shortly thereafter, the church began to meet openly and built a small frame meetinghouse.[45] By 1844, Reverend Quinn reported to the General Conference that "the church erected in the city of Louisville, Ky., is in a flourishing condition," and he emphasized its importance for the denomination's missionary cause west of the Alleghenies: "I am fully persuaded this mission, if faithfully conducted, will, at no distant period, accomplish wonders for our people settled in these western states in their moral and religious elevation. They need nothing more than proper encouragement and proper direction in order to attain an elevated position that will be truly enviable."[46] By midcentury, church leaders such as Bishops Quinn, Brown, and Payne considered Cincinnati and Louisville critical settings in which to encourage independent black churches because both cities cast so wide an influence over the Ohio and Mississippi Valleys.

More importantly, they realized, because the two cities lay on slavery's border, the congregations in Cincinnati and Louisville provided a unique link between free and enslaved blacks. In the northern city, "colored people flocked" to the AME Church on learning that its ministers "told the people how God had delivered the children of Israel." From the congregation's founding, Cincinnati's first AME Church made good on this promise directly by assisting fugitive slaves.[47] Black Louisvillians also instantly recognized the AME denomination as "an abolition church," according to William Gibson.[48] The arrival of AME Church missionaries in both Cincinnati and Louisville "stimulated the hope of the people, gave them glimpses of the freedom, the coming of which they could never fail to expect," recalled one prominent Cincinnati Methodist after the Civil War.[49]

Although black Baptists lacked the AME Church's centralized organization, they too made Cincinnati and Louisville hubs from which they evangelized the Ohio Valley. Cincinnati's first independent black Baptist church, known later as Union Baptist, organized in 1831 with just 14 men and women, but by 1840 counted a powerful 263-member congregation.[50] Already in the mid-1830s, the church spearheaded black Baptist missionary efforts, first by hiring its own traveling preacher who organized churches in the western part of Ohio and then by founding an "Association of Regular Baptist Churches of Color" whose primary purpose was to "support a missionary preacher of color" in the Ohio Valley. In his sermon before the association in 1837, Cincinnati's minister, Charles Satchell, quoted from Isaiah 28:16, "Therefore . . . saith the Lord God, Behold, I lay in Zion for a foundation a stone, a tried stone, a precious corner stone, a sure foundation," and thus set out the group's ambitious purpose not only to evangelize but also to raise permanent black churches in the West.[51]

As the wealthiest black congregation in Ohio, Cincinnati's Union Baptist Church provided the lion's share of the funding—more than 60 percent—for this work.[52] These missionary efforts bore fruit in Ohio's rural hinterlands. By 1840, eleven congregations besides Union Baptist sent delegates to the association's meeting in Chillicothe.[53] And during these years, the Cincinnati congregation's minister and elders traveled throughout western Ohio, even north of Columbus, to assist fledgling black churches in such remote places as Brush Creek, Lorrimy Creek, and Clear Creek.[54] Yet Satchell had still larger ambitions. A "vast field of operation . . . lies open before us, both at home and abroad," he wrote in his 1840 "Circular Letter" to participating churches. "Let us, therefore, give no rest to our hands, nor ease to our minds, until Satan's kingdom is completely inundated."[55]

For missionaries, Cincinnati and Louisville emerged as crucial religious centers from which to broadcast an evangelical message of the need for salvation. The Ohio Valley's cities offered dynamic settings—easily drawn crowds, financial support for ministers and itinerant preachers, rich print media resources to broadcast religious happenings, and bustling competition among denominations. As river steamboats increasingly connected East to West and North to South, white and black missionaries came to see Cincinnati and Louisville as launching points for a new religious millennium. Black Protestants also believed that Cincinnati and Louisville, as crossroads between North and South, would prove vital in transmitting a message of freedom to enslaved blacks. In 1840, blacks and whites living in these center points of the nation's commercial and cultural exchange believed they beheld a millennium of freedom.

These hopes appeared well founded, for in the late 1830s and early 1840s, evangelicals in Cincinnati and Louisville passed through an extraordinary season of religious renewal. Labeled by contemporaries as the "Great Western Revivals," this spiritual awakening led many Protestants to insist that their millennial hopes for the inland West had been realized. The western revivals, they also inferred, assured the primacy of Protestantism in the rapidly expanding American nation. With cities like Cincinnati and Louisville won over for Christ, Protestantism had shown its capacity to move in tandem with a restless population of ambitious men and women seeking new opportunities.

Studies of western revivalism usually begin and end with the remarkable frontier camp meeting held at Cane Ridge, Kentucky, where thousands of settler families gathered in 1801 to hear Presbyterian, Methodist, and Baptist preachers reclaim sinners for seven straight days. The rustic setting became synonymous with spiritual awakenings in the American West. Yet the burgeoning cities of early republic Ohio and Kentucky fostered a spiritual zeal with more far-reaching consequences: the energetic ministers who gravitated to these entrepôts built up widespread missionary enterprises and raised hopes for a "perfect" society on earth characterized by a constant state of revival, always converting and preparing humans for a "more glorious Paradise above," as Jonathan Blanchard described his congregation's relentless work of evangelism from its base in Cincinnati. In 1839, the Presbyterian minister sensed the dawning of this new social organization for perpetual awakening to Christ: "The world is on its way back to God!" he rejoiced, convinced that the inland West's cities had figured out means to achieve humanity's moral renovation.[56]

In the context of the United States' widespread religious awakenings of the nineteenth century, such fantastic ambitions were not entirely unique. But in the early republic era, both Ohio and Kentucky invited settlers to undertake fresh starts and cultivated reputations as places of swift renewal and rapid growth, notions that harmonized especially well with evangelicalism's newly bright message of redemption through humanity's own moral agency. However, by the 1840s, the very same cities that appeared poised to inaugurate a new heaven on earth, according to Protestants, had captured the full attentions of an old foe, the Roman Catholic Church.

Specters

After his consecration as bishop in 1833, John Baptist Purcell traveled from Baltimore to his see city, Cincinnati, in the Diocese of Ohio, which then included the entire state within its ecclesiastical boundaries. The Irish-born priest, just thirty-three years old and with a brief record as a college professor and administrator at Mount St. Mary's in Emmitsburg, Maryland, now had responsibility for sixteen churches, fourteen priests, and six or seven thousand Catholics spread throughout a large jurisdiction.[57] Arriving in Cincinnati in late 1833, he found his diocese, and especially his see city, in a deplorable condition. Cincinnati's ecclesiastical buildings—which then included just one church, a school, a seminary, and living quarters for about five priests—were decrepit: "ill-constructed & inconvenient, of wretched materials, half-finished, leaking, mill-dewed roofs & walls; . . . [and] full of filth" as Purcell recorded in his private journal. Moreover, in the fourteen-month interregnum between the death of his predecessor, Bishop Edward D. Fenwick, and Purcell's arrival in Cincinnati, priests and seminarians had lapsed into scandalous habits, such as frequenting whiskey shops and the theater. Purcell found another cleric in a perfect state of insanity. Even worse, he discovered "squires" performing marriage rites for Catholics and confusion among the laity about who could receive communion. After five months in his western diocese, Purcell privately vented, "O Jesu! O Potestas, O Patientia!!"[58]

Across the Ohio River in the Diocese of Bardstown, the aging Bishop Benedict Joseph Flaget, exile from the French Revolution, oversaw a sprawling jurisdiction that in 1833 included all of Kentucky, Tennessee, Indiana, and part of Illinois.[59] Born in 1763, Flaget had served as the diocese's first bishop since 1810; by the early 1830s, he was worn out from unceasing travel and pastoral labor throughout his immense diocese, which had originally included the entire valley between the Great Lakes and Tennessee and the Appalachian Mountains and the Mississippi River. Hard of hearing, impaired in his speech, and exhausted, Flaget offered his resignation to the Propaganda

Fide in Rome in 1832. However, he would continue to serve as bishop until his death in 1850 at the age of eighty-seven.[60]

Into these two impoverished western dioceses flowed thousands of Catholic faithful during the 1830s. Shifting diocesan boundaries before 1840 make it difficult to chart Catholic affiliation in the West, but rough estimates by Bishops Flaget and Purcell suggest that their dioceses experienced remarkable numerical growth even before European Catholic immigration to Ohio and Kentucky exploded in the 1840s and 1850s. While visiting Rome in 1836, Bishop Flaget estimated that in 1810, approximately 16,000 faithful had dwelled in his once-vast jurisdiction stretching from Tennessee to the border with British Canada; by 1836, Flaget counted 35,000 Catholics in a reduced diocese that included just the state of Kentucky.[61] In 1833, 6,000 to 7,000 Catholics reportedly lived in the Diocese of Ohio; a decade later the church claimed to have 50,000 believers under Bishop Purcell's care.[62] However, institutional growth in the West lagged far behind the needs of this rapidly growing number of faithful. In 1840, the Diocese of Bardstown encompassed just forty churches and chapels and forty-five priests.[63] If Flaget's estimates were accurate, each Kentucky priest cared for, on average, about 800 persons. At nearly the same time in Ohio, the ratio of clergy to faithful appeared far more disadvantageous: each of thirty-eight priests served roughly 1,315 Catholics.

Lacking funds to build churches and clergy to fill them, Bishops Flaget and Purcell and their missionaries incessantly worried that Catholics were "in great danger of falling away from the Church, for they hardly ever see a priest."[64] They also feared that Protestant ministers, especially Methodists, "lie in wait" for these unattended Catholics to lure them into sectarian heresy.[65] Letter after letter from Cincinnati beseeched Rome and various European religious orders for material aid and fresh laborers for the burdensome missionary work. In 1840, Purcell sent one of his seminarians, then studying in Rome, on an urgent visit to the minister-general of the Order of St. Francis: "[B]eg him, for the love of God," Ohio's bishop charged his representative, "to send us some other missionaries."[66]

For all of this internal fretting, Roman Catholics in Ohio and Kentucky exuded a public confidence out of proportion to their actual strength in the 1830s. Indeed, the church's minority status seems to have prompted an exaggerated display of Catholic belief and ritual.[67] In the early 1830s, for example, Catholics built a dramatic cathedral in Louisville, the city's largest church at the time. With a 115-foot nave, interior colonnades, exterior buttresses, and "the whole surmounted with minarets," the St. Louis Cathedral introduced a fascinating medieval pastiche to residents of the western commercial city.[68]

Also in the early 1830s, the Cincinnati diocese launched a weekly magazine that boldly asserted Catholic tenets and mocked Protestants' penchant for division, "clamorous egotism," and incessant need for "revivals" of faith.[69] In early volumes of the *Catholic Telegraph*, Catholics claimed to have protected "the sacred deposite of faith whole and entire" through eighteen long centuries. Writers boasted that the venerable church stood "flourishing and refulgent" in the Mississippi and Ohio Valleys.[70] With no little air of superiority, they predicted that Protestants would soon return to the "bosom of the One, Holy, Catholic and Apostolic Church" and joyfully reported new conversions, as when a Cincinnati priest "baptized five adult converts from the wanderings of indefinite Protestantism" in November 1831.[71] The magazine's illustrated masthead further displayed Catholic confidence: with the Latin rendering of Matthew 16:18 ("Thou art Peter, and upon this rock I will build my church; and the gates of hell shall not prevail against it") on either side of her, the Virgin Mary reclined against a globe depicting the western hemisphere. In the background loomed a dome resembling St. Peter's Basilica, thus suggesting the power of the church in "The Valley of the Mississippi" and Rome's unbroken ambitions to unite the New World under the banner of Catholicism.

Immigration from Catholic Europe and a resurgent Roman church caught Protestant Americans by surprise in the 1830s. Beginning slowly in the 1820s, then accelerating in the 1830s, foreign immigration shored up the Catholic Church's presence within the United States. In reaction, anti-Catholic sentiment erupted in dramatic fashion in Charlestown, Massachusetts, when a working-class mob burned an Ursuline convent to the ground in August 1834.[72] This first anti-Catholic riot in the United States laid bare class and ethnic rivalries between immigrant and native-born residents and reanimated archetypal images of Catholics as cruel inquisitors and morbid ascetics.[73] Protestant fears of Catholic encroachment in the Ohio and Mississippi Valleys in the early 1830s also turned on these issues and themes. But the rhetoric surrounding conflicts between Protestants and Catholics in the Western Country drew force from another highly charged theme: the security of the Union, and its commitments to self-government. With the discovery of transatlantic ties between the Cincinnati and Louisville dioceses and Catholic missionary societies in Europe, many Protestant Americans grew convinced that autocrats, in league with the pope, were plotting to destroy the United States from within and reclaim the spiritual descendants of Martin Luther and John Calvin.

Subserviency

A grave national crisis loomed in the Ohio River valley, according to Samuel F. B. Morse, who first alerted native Americans to foreign Catholics' designs on the United States. Most famous for his invention of the telegraph, Morse spent much of the 1830s fulminating against papal intrigue in the American West. About 1830, while visiting Italy, Morse discovered the existence of the Leopoldinen-Stiftung, or Leopoldine Foundation, an Austrian missionary society founded in 1829 to provide financial assistance to the Diocese of Cincinnati for the building of churches and support of priests. In 1828, Cincinnati's Bishop Fenwick had sent his vicar-general, the Right Reverend Frederic Résé, to Europe to solicit funds for the diocese. Though Résé had little success in Rome, he found a friendly audience in Austria, where he pleaded his cause before Emperor Francis I. Moved by the plight of Catholics in the Cincinnati diocese, the emperor established the Leopoldinen-Stiftung in the memory of his daughter, Leopoldina, the former empress of Brazil.[74] Throughout the Austrian empire, the society collected small weekly alms from Catholics to be distributed among American dioceses.

In the first ten years of the Leopoldine Foundation's existence, the Cincinnati diocese received the bulk of its assistance (approximately $48,000), although Bardstown also received significant sums before 1839.[75] The society funded priests' travel to the United States and shipped valuable accoutrements of the Mass, priests' apparel, and religious art to Bishops Fenwick, Purcell, and Flaget. In Résé's first report to the society, probably written about 1830, he described the early fruits of Austrian missionary aid: "150 Protestants were converted to Catholicism in this city [Cincinnati] alone, and hardly a day passes on which several persons do not present themselves to the bishop and ask instructions."[76] Austria's prime minister, the antidemocratic Prince Metternich, responded to such favorable news on behalf of the emperor. In a communication published in the society's reports, Metternich assured Bishop Fenwick that the "emperor, who, is steadfastly devoted to our holy Religion, has felt a vivid joy at the report, that the Truth is making rapid progress in the regions of North America."[77]

Morse used the Leopoldine Foundation's reports to produce a series of inflammatory anti-Catholic letters under the pen name "Brutus" for the *New-York Observer* in 1834. Published together as *Foreign Conspiracy Against the United States*, Morse's letters asserted that the Leopoldine Foundation constituted a "vigorous and unexampled effort . . . to cause Popery to overspread this country." But its object was only "ostensibly" religious, he argued. While admitting that evidence of Austrian despots' political motives failed to appear in the society's reports, Morse asked: "Is it credible that the manufacturers of chains for binding liberty in Europe, have suddenly become benevolently concerned only for the *religious welfare* of this republican people?" As proof of a conspiracy to undermine self-government in the United States, Morse offered this purported truism: "Popery, from its very nature, favor[s] despotism." Thus, if the Leopoldine Foundation "succeeds in fastening upon us the chains of papal bondage, she has a people as fit for any yoke she pleases to grace our necks, as any slaves over whom she now holds her despotic rod."[78]

Reprinted in seven editions before 1847, Morse's exposé of the Leopoldine Foundation aroused anti-Catholic sentiment and helped launch the first national anti-immigrant movement in the United States. In 1836, the Native American Democratic Association even made "Brutus" a candidate for New York City's mayoral race. As a third-party candidate, Morse failed to break political loyalties to the Whig and Democratic Parties, but his *Foreign Conspiracy Against the United States* succeeded in alarming the nation about the Roman Catholic Church's suspicious doings in a far-flung western diocese.[79]

The Presbyterian minister Lyman Beecher also described the spiritual perils lurking in America's great inland valley in his *Plea for the West*, a published version of his fund-raising speeches on behalf of Cincinnati's Lane Seminary in 1834.[80] Delivered before rapt New England audiences, Beecher's addresses evoked an incipient religious war in the West between "superstition" and "evangelical light." Like Morse, Beecher identified "powerful missionary societies" funded by European despots and the pope, laboring to "reduc[e] our western states to spiritual subserviency to the see of Rome."[81] Where Morse brought the Leopoldine Foundation's activities in the Diocese of Cincinnati to light, Beecher contributed new research into a French missionary association, the Society for the Propagation of the Faith, to expose another front for European designs on the American West.[82]

Founded in Lyons in 1822, the Society for the Propagation of the Faith took a special interest in the Catholic Church's American missions, especially the Diocese of Bardstown. Bishop Flaget's French origins perhaps account for his diocese's substantial aid from the society: between 1823 and 1869, the Bardstown diocese (later known as the Diocese of Louisville after a shift of the see city to Louisville in 1841) garnered about $160,000 of direct aid while the Cincinnati diocese received about $118,000 in the same period.[83] Beecher worried with Morse that European "potentates" had sent to the American West ignorant paupers and criminals who, on gaining the vote, would overthrow democratic government at the dictate of their Catholic priests.

But Beecher sensed an even more insidious scheme behind this French missionary society. Scrutinizing the Society for the Propagation of the Faith's *Annales*, Beecher found incriminating evidence that Catholic bishops planned to use their educational institutions—their multifarious convent schools, female academies, and seminaries—to convert Protestant youth to Catholicism and thereby subvert enlightened religion and liberal democratic government. Beecher singled out Bishop Flaget as especially guileful, for the Bardstown bishop wanted to lure Protestant children into Roman Catholic schools in order to effect a "most happy revolution"—to use Flaget's words. This revolution had commenced with Protestant children memorizing the catechism, lisping prayers to the Virgin Mary, and prostrating themselves before the priests and nuns who served as their instructors. With children under this powerful sway, all westerners became vulnerable to Catholic incursion: "I would compel all MY KENTUCKIANS to admire and love a religion so beneficent and generous, *and perhaps I should finish by converting them,*" Bishop Flaget wrote in the *Annales* and Beecher gravely quoted in his *Plea for the West*. In time, Americans would forsake the vigilance and vigor necessary to sustain free institutions and evangelical faith. Then the "wily minister Metternich" would enthrall America's citizens.[84]

Beecher's evocative, if paranoiac, contrast between "despotism" and "liberty" and between "superstition" and "evangelical light" drew its persuasive power from Reformation history and myth, not from the actual state of affairs in western states, for his dread of enslavement by a Catholic priesthood appears irrational given the fifty-three impoverished and overburdened clergymen laboring in Ohio and Kentucky in 1835.[85] Neither diocese had sufficient resources or priests to bring Ohio's one million and Kentucky's 700,000 residents under the pope's sway. Nor did the ten or so diocesan schools, seminaries, colleges, and female academies scattered across Ohio and Kentucky—most of them shoestring operations with brief and unstable histories—have any credible ambitions to convert western Protestants to the Catholic faith via their impressionable children.[86]

Because of this distance between argument and evidence, not all Protestants accepted Beecher's and Morse's conspiracy theories uncritically in the 1830s. In fact, some found their "dreams about Rome, and Vienna, and Metternich" absurd.[87] One prolific writer on the West's progress and future eminence, James Hall, ridiculed nativist logic as found in Beecher's *Plea*.[88] Born into a prominent Presbyterian family in Philadelphia, the Cincinnati-transplant maintained bona fides among both Protestants and westerners in the early 1830s. Writing in the *Western Monthly Magazine*, Hall considered the argument that Catholic priests could manipulate the complex and decentralized levers of American party politics an "amazing fatuity." "We can imagine no motive which could induce the pope to employ his clergy in so hopeless a task," Hall wrote.[89] As to the charge that American Catholics, even recent immigrants, would rush to support monarchical government, Hall asked, "Can it be credited that the Irish who have fled from the oppression of a ruthless tyranny, could be prevailed upon to forget their hatred of kings, and forge new chains for their own hands?" To the contrary, evidence suggested that Catholic immigrants "inclined to the most radical school of democracy."[90]

Hall even defended Catholics' "christian zeal" to promote their faith and to establish "liberal" institutions of learning in the American West as the harmless work of a permanent religious minority.[91] According to his own religious census, Catholics made up just one twenty-fifth of the American population; it therefore seemed a remote statistical possibility that Roman Catholic efforts to proselytize among Protestants would effect any radical or lasting shift in the balance between the faiths. Taking the side of an unfairly maligned minority faith, Hall declared it "vulgar prejudice" to rail against the "poor" Catholics: "The very fact that the Roman Catholics are, and can be with impunity, thus trampled upon . . . affords in itself the most conclusive evidence of the groundlessness of the fears."[92]

In the 1830s, it was possible for a number of Protestants to take a principled stand against religious "narrow-mindedness and bigotry."[93] The Roman Catholic Church's precarious foothold in the American West lent credence to Hall's position, and other Cincinnati commentators echoed his complaint against the shrill tone and wildly exaggerated perils found in most anti-Catholic pronouncements. Westerners familiar with the Roman Catholic Church's pecuniary difficulties and internal squabbling found little reason to emulate the Charlestown hysteria. And with the Great Western Revivals thundering to their climax in the second half of the 1830s, many Protestants believed they were poised to establish a permanent heaven on earth in the Ohio and Mississippi Valleys. It would have seemed a poor allocation of their resources and energies to worry overmuch about a relatively small number of misguided Catholics. Even Lyman Beecher appeared to view the Roman Catholic threat as a distant specter rather than an immediate danger in 1835. In his inimitable style, Beecher had combined dark forecasts of future enslavement by the pope with boisterous optimism that such an apocalyptic fate might be avoided through the proper "application of physical effort and pecuniary and moral power to evangelize the world."[94] Beecher urged the prompt construction of Protestant churches, common and Sabbath schools, and colleges, "which, like the great orbs of attraction and light, shall send forth at once their power and illumination."[95] Should westerners undertake such a building program, the specter of spiritual and political despotism under Catholic auspices would fast fade and the religious "emancipation of the world" soon commence in the American Middle West.[96] Beecher's eager acceptance of the presidency of Cincinnati's Lane Seminary in 1832 signaled his own genuine optimism about the West's future religious promise.

Fury

As it happened, Hall's evidence and Beecher's optimism, while applicable to conditions in the 1830s, misjudged trends for western cities like Cincinnati and Louisville. James Hall's principled defense of a minority faith had rested on statistical assumptions that the Catholic Church could never surpass Protestants in numbers or influence in the American West. But by the early 1850s, after a decade of unprecedented immigration from Europe, Roman Catholics were the single largest denomination in Cincinnati. In Louisville, Catholics ran a close second to Methodists before becoming the largest denomination during the 1860s.[97]

While Methodism remained the predominant faith in Ohio and Baptists claimed a majority of believers in Kentucky through the antebellum period, foreign immigration to western cities in the 1840s and 1850s transformed Cincinnati and Louisville into Catholic strongholds. Lured by new manufacturing jobs, Germans, Austrians, and the Irish constituted nearly 40 percent of Cincinnati's population by 1850; at the same time in Louisville, nearly 25 percent of the city's residents came from these predominantly Catholic regions of Europe. According to the 1860 census, Louisville's German and Irish immigrants approached 30 percent of the city's population. Because nearly all the Protestant denominations had made Cincinnati and Louisville headquarters for their evangelical labors throughout the Ohio and Mississippi Valleys, Protestants felt peculiar shock and disappointment in witnessing the surging growth of Catholicism on the banks of the Ohio River in the two decades before the Civil War. In 1851, Charles Cist offered his "fair estimate" that Roman Catholics made up 35 percent of Cincinnati's entire population, Protestants 62 percent, and Jews 3 percent.[98] Though he seems not to have considered that some among the city's residents might deny affiliation with any faith, Cist's relative proportions nonetheless offer a guide to religious adherence at midcentury. Most importantly, his ratios placed Catholics in the religious plurality if Cincinnati's Protestants were counted according to their separate denominational affiliations. At roughly the same time that Cist was producing his city guides, Bishop Purcell wrote to the Association of the Propagation of the Faith in Lyons that his see city contained more than twenty-five thousand Catholic parishioners.[99] For Louisville's Catholic population, Bishops Flaget and Martin John Spalding (Flaget's successor) provided the only comprehensive estimates. In 1841, Flaget claimed to oversee four thousand Catholic parishioners in his new see city. By 1863, Bishop Spalding counted Louisville's Catholic population at thirty thousand, representing a 650 percent increase in just two decades.[100]

The rapid influx of German and Irish immigrants into Cincinnati and Louisville between 1840 and 1860 not only exacerbated the difficulties faced by Bishops Purcell and Flaget to provide priests, churches, schools, and pastoral aid to the Catholic faithful, but also introduced entirely new problems to western dioceses. The Irish-born Purcell, who never learned to speak German, faced the thankless task of mediating bitter disputes between Tyrolean and Bavarian friars and between "Hoch-Deutsch" and "Platt-Deutsch" parishioners. Moreover, the numerous European religious communities arriving in the diocese to establish schools, orphanages, and convents after 1840 competed for property and resources. By 1860, Dominicans, Redemptorists, Jesuits, Franciscans, Lazarists, Benedictines, Sisters of Charity, Dominican nuns, Sisters of Notre Dame de Namur, Sisters of the Most Precious Blood, Ursulines, Sisters of the Good Shepherd, Sisters of Mercy, and Sisters of the Poor of St. Francis had arrived in the diocese, heeding Purcell's urgent plea for priests and sisterhoods.[101] As in Purcell's diocese, Kentucky's Sulpicians, Dominicans, Jesuits, Trappists, Xaverians, Ursulines, Sisters of Charity of Nazareth, Sisters of Loretto at the Foot of the Cross, and Sisters of the Good Shepherd tested the patience of Bishops Flaget and Spalding.

These growing pains notwithstanding, the orders represented an unprecedented transfer of European Catholic tradition into America's heartland: by 1860, twenty-two distinctive religious communities had built monasteries, friaries, convents, and even an abbey in the Dioceses of Cincinnati and Louisville. These orders operated a stunning array of academies, colleges, hospitals, orphanages, and asylums—a total of 113 institutions (not including some one hundred parish schools) in the two dioceses by 1860.[102] The thirty-odd institutions radiating out from Louisville have led American Catholics to label this part of Kentucky "The Holy Land."[103] European orders arriving in the Dioceses of Cincinnati and Louisville also introduced distinctive forms of religious expression—including dress, art, and cloistered living arrangements—that generated a complex mixture of fascination and revulsion in Protestants.[104] Hence, the unanticipated appearance of thousands of Catholic immigrants and exotic religious communities, along with their rapid institution building, redefined both Louisville's and Cincinnati's cultural and intellectual landscapes between 1840 and 1860. In consequence, a Protestant majority once confident of its ability to Christianize the world from its western missionary outposts grew skeptical of its providential assignment.

In the late 1840s, the Cincinnati minister Charles B. Boynton breathed new fury into Lyman Beecher's decade-old *Plea for the West*. Boynton had succeeded Jonathan Blanchard at the Sixth Street Presbyterian Church after the Presbyterian minister's unhappy departure from Cincinnati on failing to usher in his "Perfect State of Society." Preoccupied with prayer meetings and revivals while under Blanchard's care, members of the reorganized Vine Street Congregational Church appeared to favor the nativist agenda in the late 1840s and 1850s. In an oration delivered in 1847 before Cincinnati's "Native Americans," Boynton repeated many of the arguments found in *A Plea for the West* but evinced little of Beecher's abiding confidence in the American West's millennial promise. According to Boynton, Protestants now fought for mere survival: we are "brought to the final struggle—the death grapple—in which Romanism, or Protestantism and Liberty must die," he declaimed before his audience.[105]

Where Beecher had proposed a scheme to assimilate Catholics through common schools and "republican institutions" (with the ultimate object to convert them to Protestantism), Boynton urged purity and exclusion. This nation, he argued, "should be filled by a Protestant, an American people; a homogeneous mass, fused to a unit by all the proud and tender associations of a common birthright, and a common faith, and animated by one single soul. This—and not a State formed of an ill-cemented human conglomerate— was the idea of our fathers."[106] And while remarking on the stalled efforts to implement Beecher's vision for a massive school and institution-building program on evangelical principles, Boynton expressed bitterness. Paying homage to Beecher, in attendance that evening, he recriminated, "Here, by my side, is that bold, strong pioneer in education and religion in the West; who has grown gray, but not weak, in maintaining our fathers' faith. . . . Had he been sustained, as I think he might and should have been, a Catholic seminary would not have supplanted in this city one which he designed for the

Protestant education of our daughters."[107] In fact, it was Catharine Beecher, Lyman's daughter, who had established the ill-fated Western Female Institute shortly after the Beecher clan's arrival in 1832, and it was the Sisters of Charity who took over the institute's property in order to run an orphanage and day school. By 1846, not long before Boynton spoke, eight sisters cared for ninety-five orphans and two hundred pupils on the site of Beecher's defunct school; they would shortly make the property their motherhouse.[108] Infuriated, Boynton vowed that Catholics "shall not lead our children in captivity to Rome; they shall dig no dungeons in our soil; nor drive the stake, nor kindle the faggot here." The Congregational minister promised "a thousand Bunker Hills" to defend Americans against the Catholic scourge.[109]

Boynton's vitriol typified anti-Catholic feeling in Cincinnati and Louisville in the 1840s and 1850s.[110] Cincinnati publishers churned out sensational fiction by local authors, such as Isaac Kelso's *Danger in the Dark: A Tale of Intrigue and Priestcraft* (1854), which went through thirty-one editions within a year of its initial publication.[111] Numerous short treatises, pamphlets, and other ephemeral works appeared—one provocatively arguing that Pope Pius IX was the Antichrist and offering a portrait of him with a cloven foot.[112] More learned disquisitions by Cincinnati authors also found audiences, including Rev. Charles Elliott's *Delineation of Roman Catholicism, Drawn from the Authentic and Acknowledged Standards of the Church of Rome* (1841), a two-volume, one-thousand-page indictment of Catholic "idolatry" whose worshippers, Elliott argued, stood poised to "overturn the civil and religious liberties of the United States."[113]

In Louisville, prominent ministers formed a "Protestant League" in 1844 and published a weekly newspaper, the *True Catholic*. Editor George Prentice led the city's leading Whig newspaper, the *Louisville Journal*, down the path of virulent Know-Nothingism. In 1855, Prentice offered this inflammatory editorial: "Until the light of Protestantism shone in the world there was no religious freedom. Popery, with its iron heel, treads out the life of religious liberty. The Romish corporation . . . has ever been the prostitute of Satan. Millions have suffered martyrdom because they would not surrender their consciences. . . . Rally to put down an organization of Jesuit Bishops, Priests and other papists, who aim by secret oaths and horrid midnight plottings, to sap the foundations of all our political edifices."[114] Then he incited his readers, "Americans, are you all ready? We think we hear you shout 'Ready.' Well, fire! And may heaven have mercy on our foe."[115]

Anti-Catholic screeds like this had Catholics—both clergy and laity—living in fear through much of the 1840s and 1850s. During this time, Franciscans in Cincinnati and Louisville modified their traditional brown habits in order to move safely through the streets.[116] In 1844, "people threw wooden sticks at us and cursed us," one friar wrote after walking a short distance to the bishop's house.[117] About 1854, Purcell, now archbishop of his diocese, wrote in a private letter, "For many years I have never felt secure of my life in this city, a single night. The martyrdoms of our bodies will be a trifle."[118] A diary entry by a laywoman, Marianne Reilly, shows Catholics on edge in Cincinnati in the spring of 1853: "Poor Mr. [Rev. Whelan] accused me of being scared to death but I found he and all the others were not without apprehension."[119]

Serious violence erupted some eight months after Reilly's entry. In December 1853, Papal Nuncio Gaetano Bedini's visit to Cincinnati sparked a riot as radical German exiles from the European revolutions of 1848 protested Bedini's repression of Italian nationalists.[120] Here immigrant German atheists and native-born evangelical Christians converged in their political complaints against the Roman Catholic Church, and the two groups briefly allied to thwart Bedini's religious mission to Cincinnati. When city police moved to block armed protestors in their march toward the city's cathedral, a melee broke out and one protestor died; police arrested sixty for their participation in the riot.[121] Two weeks later, a crowd composed of five thousand mostly native-born Americans burned Bedini in effigy, although no violence took place.[122] These proved the worst disorders on Bedini's trouble-ridden tour through the United States, and the nuncio hastily returned to Europe within a month of the Cincinnati protests.[123]

Two years later, one of the country's most violent anti-Catholic riots took place in Louisville. Ranking alongside riots in Philadelphia (1844) and Baltimore (1856) in casualties and property damage, Louisville's 1855 election riots killed an estimated twenty-two and wounded many more. The mobs ransacked a German neighborhood and destroyed a row of tenements owned by an Irish businessman.[124] As in the Philadelphia riots, the mobs in Louisville believed that Roman Catholics stored gunpowder and munitions in their churches. After breaking into one church and finding nothing suspicious, the mob took cannon, muskets, and bayonets from the courthouse and began moving toward the Cathedral of the Assumption. In an effort to prevent the cathedral's destruction, Bishop Spalding entrusted the keys to Louisville's recently elected Know-Nothing mayor; city officials searched the building and assured the crowd that "neither men nor arms [were] concealed there."[125] Relenting in its attack on the cathedral, the mob rushed its cannon and arms toward a predominantly Irish ward, where rioters fired on a tenement, killing some twelve residents and setting a block of buildings ablaze.

Political volatility stemming from sectional conflicts over slavery and foreign immigration provided the backdrop to this anti-Catholic violence. In both Cincinnati and Louisville—as through most of the nation—the Whig Party had all but disintegrated by 1852 because of its inability to hold together northern and southern factions.[126] Its demise was a stunning reversal of fortune for party adherents in the two Ohio River cities: for two decades, through the 1830s and 1840s, Whig ideology—with its evangelical Protestant and commercial view of the world—had held sway in both Cincinnati and Louisville. The visible presence of the Beecher clan (including Lyman and his daughters Harriet and Catharine) symbolized Whig moral influence in Cincinnati through those decades. In Louisville, a city once described as "thoroughly Whig" in sentiment, the ambitious commercial classes embraced Henry Clay's "American System" of internal improvements and centralized banking through the 1830s and 1840s.[127]

But demographics conspired against the party's continuing hegemony in both cities. Immigration from Germany and Ireland contributed new voters to the Democratic Party through the 1840s, and by 1850 the party largely controlled city government in Cincinnati.[128] Emboldened by these political gains, Cincinnati's Catholic bishop even began to demand public tax monies for parochial schools. Surrendering to new political realities, the Beecher family had entirely decamped from the city by 1852. In the same year, Louisvillians elected their first Catholic (by conversion) mayor, James Stephens Speed. Although Speed belonged to the Whig Party, his election offered a symbolic concession to the city's growing number of Catholic voters.[129]

The anti-Catholic and nativist American (or Know-Nothing) Party experienced a swift rise and fall from power in both Cincinnati and Louisville in the mid-1850s. In Cincinnati, Know-Nothings won local elections in 1854 by winning over the city's key swing voters—non-Catholic German immigrants—on an exclusively anti-Catholic platform. To achieve their election victories, Know-Nothings temporarily stifled their anti-immigrant rhetoric in Cincinnati, but this political alliance between foreign-born and native-born Americans proved unsustainable.[130] In the following year's elections, local Know-Nothings alienated their German Protestant (and in not a few cases, atheist) erstwhile allies with unrestrained hostility toward the foreign born. This hostility, after all, was the party's raison d'être.[131] Anticipating losses to Democratic Party candidates, bands of Know-Nothing supporters roamed through predominantly Democratic wards destroying ballot boxes on Election Day.

In the rioting that ensued, Cincinnati resembled a war zone. Heavily armed Germans barricaded themselves in the "Over-the-Rhine" district; when Know-Nothings attempted to storm the barriers, two were mortally wounded in the attack. The mob then thought better of an invasion and withdrew.[132] Viewed as the aggressors in this rioting and losing credibility through their seizure of ballot boxes, Cincinnati's Know-Nothing Party collapsed after the 1855 elections. Thereafter, former Whigs, nativists, and non-Catholic Germans increasingly turned to the Republican Party in the city.[133] In Louisville, a bizarre mayoral race decided by the Kentucky Court of Appeals allowed a Know-Nothing Party candidate to unseat the city's Catholic mayor in 1855, just five months before the city's "Bloody Monday" riots. But as in Cincinnati, these riots proved a public relations disaster for the American Party and led to its swift unraveling in Louisville.[134]

By 1850, native-born Protestant Whigs had enjoyed political power in Cincinnati and Louisville for nearly two decades. Yet demographic shifts in these two cities, underway for more than a decade by midcentury, disabled Whig political power and helped forge novel political alignments. The Democratic Party won its first local offices in the early 1850s on the strength of its new voter base. Even the American Party implicitly acknowledged the political power of Catholic and foreign-born voters when it condoned its members' efforts to destroy ballot boxes and intimidate voters in predominantly Democratic wards in both cities' 1855 elections. American Party successes, as well as the extraordinary violence accompanying its electoral contests, register the profound frustration felt by native-born Protestants in the wake of European immigration to Whig political strongholds like Cincinnati and Louisville.

The election riots at midcentury drew animus from the combative religious environment pitting Protestant against Catholic in a rivalry for spiritual control of the American Middle West. Intensified by Reformation and Counter-Reformation history and memory, this rivalry was difficult to dispel amid frenzied economic growth and epic migration to new interior states. Participants in these religious conflicts perceived a foreshortening of time to accomplish great things: the mass evangelization of thousands of relocating peoples from Europe and eastern states who sought fresh starts in the Western Country. Black Protestant missionaries also raced against time to bring spiritual solace and some manner of physical security to rural settlers and city dwellers exposed to the hard hands of slavery and inequality. So much of human happiness and future reward appeared to hinge on the success of these evangelical efforts. Yet many of those engaged in this religious charge found it irresistible to graft seemingly ancient struggles over faith and practice onto their task. This grafted language from Reformation and Counter-Reformation eras sharpened the work of proselytization in the Western Country. Use of such language also instilled fear. When combined with political instability and rapidly shifting demographics, these fears manifested in deadly collisions on the eve of the Civil War.

CHAPTER TWO

Attraction

The friction between Catholics and Protestants in the Ohio River valley is not difficult to detect in historical records, despite their foreign appearance to the modern eye: crammed newspaper columns, old broadsides, and strange little pamphlets bristle with the era's religious slanders and calumnies. Interrogations of Catholicism also seeped into fictional writing that we might consider the highest art or literature representative of the period. Yet a quite opposite phenomenon is also evident, for in striking ways, between 1830 and 1860 Catholics and Protestants grew to resemble each other in both their outward guises and internal imperatives. For their part, Catholics cultivated a more personal speaking style following Protestants' model—one that evangelists had perfected through multiple cycles of revival in the first half of the nineteenth century. In pursuit of beauty to lessen the distance between human and divine, Protestants made an unlikely pivot toward medieval styles of architecture—a style very nearly synonymous with Catholicism.[1] These shifts are especially visible in urban settings like Cincinnati and Louisville, where Catholic orders could specialize in preaching and where Protestant congregations had the wherewithal to invest in costly sanctuaries.

That Catholic and Protestant religious societies began to sound and look alike before 1860 is perhaps not surprising, given that they so strenuously competed for followers. Such consuming rivalry can lead, unwittingly, to outright appropriation and copycat expressions. In scrutinizing each other's practices, Catholics and Protestants fixed on the sources of greatest strength within their competitors' arsenals. For Protestants, that strength was auditory, especially in preaching a highly personal message to spiritual seekers. For Catholics, power often resided in beauty, and in particular, an entirely distinctive architecture inseparable from devotional practices. In seeking to match each other's strengths in these two areas, Catholics and Protestants had to offer justification for obvious adjustments to their traditions. These justifications are illuminating, for they suggest the deeper imperatives common to both traditions: a desire to close, even eliminate, distances between preachers and seekers and between humanity and the divine. Although such aspirations might well define religious faith outside of any narrow time period, American Catholics and Protestants during these few decades labored to explain their swift adoption of, and vast financial outlays for, practices that seemed to go against their most fervent expressions of doctrinal difference in the very same moment. In the process of redefining the look and practice of their respective faiths, Catholics and Protestants dwelled sensitively on the best means to connect personally with disparate peoples and to elicit sympathetic responses from an urban populace with any number of decent (and indecent) reasons to ignore invitations to belonging.

Awakenings

Between 1820 and 1860, itinerant preachers and missionaries, along with more settled ministers and priests, labored to draw restless migrants into the organized practice of faith and into a vital congregational life. The strategies they used, whether Protestant or Catholic in origin, whether homegrown or recently imported from Europe, met their audience's need for a simple and direct explanation of central Christian ideas of sin and salvation, penitence and redemption. In personal, emotional language, preachers labored to recapture the gifts of Christ's apostles by offering the gospel with renewed clarity and force at special gatherings outside regular church meetings. Certainly, the perceived competition for souls energized Protestant and Catholic revivalists to reach out to audiences with great urgency about the need for personal conversion. But whether labeled "revivals" or "missions," as in the Catholic case, these popular gatherings also reflected Americans' desire for simplicity over didacticism, experience over reflection, and immanence over aloofness.[2] While we have separate studies of Catholic and Protestant revivalism demonstrating the evolution of a "fiercely evangelical and deeply individualistic" style of faith by the mid-nineteenth century, setting these histories side by side in the same narrative underscores the broader cultural, if not political, implications of this "strikingly American" practice of religion among natives and newcomers.[3]

In 1828, British traveler and writer Frances Trollope arrived in Cincinnati to discover the subject of " 'revival' talked of by every one we met throughout the town."[4] In the late 1820s, large outdoor camp meetings, prayer meetings, and protracted meetings consumed the energies of Protestant groups all at once, giving Cincinnatians and Louisvillians their first inklings of a widespread revival. Over the next two decades, the "Great Western Revivals," as they came to be known, transformed fledgling urban churches in Cincinnati and Louisville into powerful congregations with broad regional influence by enlisting thousands of new converts in the cause of Christ.[5] Between 1830 and 1840, Presbyterian, Methodist, and Baptist churches in Cincinnati added about 2,900 new members, a sure demonstration of revivalism's significance in driving Protestant growth before 1845. In Louisville, these same churches enrolled roughly 1,960 new members in the decade before 1840. And in a brief surge of activity—just four months between December 1839 and April 1840 in Cincinnati and several months in late 1842 and early 1843 in Louisville, urban churches in the Ohio River valley enjoyed a special "melting time."[6] The numbers are striking: Cincinnati's Methodist churches reported some 730 new members in a single year, representing a 40 percent increase between 1839 and 1840; Cincinnati's white Baptists invited over 200 religious seekers into their congregation in 1840, a 77 percent increase over the previous years' membership total; and between late 1842 and early 1843, Louisville's black and white Baptists offered 432 converts the "right hand of fellowship," a 47 percent increase.[7] As late as 1888, Cincinnati's participants recalled the Revival of 1840 as "an event the influence of which is still felt in this Church and city—aye! which will be felt throughout eternity."[8]

Even Methodists, who could reminisce over hundreds of memorable camp meeting revivals in Ohio and Kentucky between 1800 and 1845, commemorated Cincinnati's Revival of 1840 as especially remarkable. One participant and observer, the Reverend Maxwell Pierson Gaddis, traced the power of this urban revival to the arrival in Cincinnati of the legendary preacher John Newland Maffitt.[9] Judging from a book entitled *Pulpit Sketches*, which Maffitt wrote and published while residing in Louisville in early 1839, the Methodist preacher was primed for glory. Even on the printed page, Maffitt's power as an orator pulses through the work. In militant language, he prophesied that soon "America will be seen coming up out of the wilderness, terrible as an army with banners, travelling in the greatness of the strength of the Lord of Hosts." "Powerful and encouraging" signs of a "moral revolution" were now "spread before us," he insisted. Time was nigh, Maffitt claimed, for a "special out-pouring of the Holy Spirit" and "the consecration of this *western world* as a vast theatre of millennial piety and happiness."[10]

According to Gaddis, the opening scene of this new millennium on earth took place in a Cincinnati boardinghouse on December 5, 1839, five days after Maffitt began preaching in the city. On that evening, Gaddis arrived home from a Methodist class meeting and consecrated his "soul and body anew, a living sacrifice unto God." With everyone in the boardinghouse already gone to bed, Gaddis "felt my heart melt like wax before the fire, and my eyes suffused in tears of joy." He then conversed directly with the Holy Ghost, who asked him, "Do you give up all?" After he promised to do so, the

Holy Spirit "immediately whispered in my heart, in sweetest accents, 'Yes, I now receive you.' I instantly rose up from my prostrate position on the floor, and exclaimed with emphasis, 'I am the Lord's forever! I am the Lord's forever! I am the Lord's forever!'" Gaddis's cries of joy soon awakened the other boardinghouse residents, and four persons, including a servant woman, began struggling for their souls. Gaddis next ran down the street to another boardinghouse and roused its inhabitants to praying. "All language utterly fails to convey to the reader any adequate idea of the *power felt within me*," Gaddis wrote of that night. "It did seem to me that I had power and compass of voice to arouse the city of Cincinnati—yea, even a slumbering world."[11]

After the night of December 5, 1839, with both Maffitt and Gaddis in peak form, Cincinnatians were consumed by revival. By January 27, 1840, "thousands upon thousands" had witnessed Maffitt's preaching, and sinners "awakened and converted at every coming together." In the *Western Christian Advocate*, Gaddis boasted that "our love-feast may well be called the '*Centenary Mammoth Love-Feast.*'" In one evening alone, he wrote, "*one thousand* partook of the broken body and shed blood of the Son of God."[12] According to Wesley Chapel's membership records, at least 428 persons claiming salvation joined the Methodist church on a probationary basis in January 1840 and became full members of the church six months later.[13] Gaddis hazarded a guess that these converts constituted "a larger number, perhaps, than was ever received into full membership at any one time in America." Wesley Chapel's successes signaled a new Christian era: "God is setting the captive free," Gaddis exulted. It seemed a harbinger of genuine moral revolution that General William Henry Harrison, then a presidential candidate, attended Wesley Chapel every night for a week to sing and pray with the penitent. One evening, when Maffitt struck up a hymn, "To die on the field of battle / With glory in my soul," Harrison was moved to approach the pulpit, take Maffitt's hand, and join the chorus. According to Gaddis, the audience stood rapt as the revival preacher and war veteran sang together of a " 'bright glory' " shortly to come.[14]

The pattern of Cincinnati's urban awakening had roots in the eighteenth century, when large numbers of colonial Americans helped activate a long-running series of transatlantic religious revivals that stressed the role of human emotions in stimulating conversion. Collectively labeled by historians as the "Great Awakening," these geographically dispersed and episodic revivals promoted "heart religion" (or "experimental piety"), which demanded that sinners feel the operations of the Holy Spirit on their souls—from agonizing "self-abasement" in preparation for a new birth to "exaltation" on receiving grace and pardon.[15] In 1721, English theologian and hymn-writer Isaac Watts, whose emotional songs gave expression to heart religion in Britain and North America for more than a century after their introduction in 1708, contended that Christian conviction "is a witness that dwells more in the heart than in the head. It is a testimony known by being felt and practised, and not by mere reasoning, the greatest reasoners may miss of it, for it is a testimony written in the heart."[16] With this new emphasis on the emotions as a means to grace, ministers and laity alike were charged with arousing, calibrating, and channeling human feelings.[17] By the first decades of the nineteenth century, a new class of "populist preachers" with "the sheer talent of being able to move people" to cathartic public conversions had achieved a kind of cultural omnipresence throughout the United States.[18] Cincinnati's and Louisville's revivals of the 1830s and 1840s attest to the diminishing resistance to such emotional appeals among more sophisticated, urbane congregations, as well as to the growing influence of Baptists, Methodists, and other upstart denominations in the nation's cities.

Speech

The beginnings of Catholic revivalism in the urban West seem to have been nearly coincident with Protestants' upsurge in activity in the late 1820s, and many of the populist features of American Christianity in the nineteenth century connected to the widespread religious awakenings found their correlates among the Roman Catholic faithful of Ohio and Kentucky. The remarkable similarities in this region between Protestants and Catholics are perhaps not surprising, given the magnitude of the task they set for themselves, which was to win over souls in the American Middle West and claim a kind of final victory for one or the other faith in the North American heartland. Well into the 1840s, Ohio and Kentucky were still considered missionary fields by both Protestants and Catholics, and the region drew individuals from both faiths who had a particular zeal for preaching and itinerancy.[19] While settled ministers and priests eventually enjoyed the support of wealthy congregations and parishes, as well as the prestige connected with beautiful, durable churches in both Louisville and Cincinnati by the 1840s, the faithful still demanded the periodic revival of the spirit associated with mass awakenings led by inspiring preachers and missionaries. Although less widely known for their revivalism, Catholic priests and missionaries proved skillful adepts who adjusted their message and their style to audiences apparently requiring urgent, emotional appeals to conversion and repentance.

Although not susceptible to the same kind of splintering and division so strikingly apparent among Protestants in the first half of the nineteenth century, Roman Catholics nonetheless diversified to meet the needs of widely varying parishes and scattered flocks. Those European religious orders with the greatest emphasis on preaching and itinerancy—namely, the Jesuits, Franciscans, and Redemptorists—were urgently sought by the bishops in Cincinnati and Louisville. Bishops also showed great sensitivity to the vernacular of their parishes, seeking out missionaries who could speak the language of their communicants and care for those newcomers—whether German or Irish—who had endured the dislocations of migration. And, naturally, leaders of the Roman Catholic Church hoped to recall the wayward who had fallen into heresy. Toward that end, the church especially needed missionaries to defend the faith doctrinally but also to offer a "soul-stirring spectacle" appealing to potential converts who faced an abundance of religious choices in the first half of the nineteenth century.[20]

A small group of Catholic priests, refugees from the French Revolution, sought to reestablish diocesan control over the Old Northwest and Kentucky and Tennessee in 1811 when they traveled by flatboat down the Ohio River from Maryland to Kentucky. Among these priests was the Right Reverend John Baptist David, the first known Catholic revivalist in the United States, whose evangelizing to the faithful in Kentucky and building up of the Roman church rested on the strength of "retreats," as Catholic revivals were initially known.[21] Arriving in the United States in 1792, David recognized his special ability to preach in English to congregations in Maryland, where he led a number of retreats each year prior to his removal to Kentucky. "Zeal and earnestness" marked these early revivals, with David driven by the belief that "the conversion or spiritual profit of even *one* soul, was sufficient to enlist all the zeal, and to call forth all the energies of the preacher." Offering "plain" rather than complex discourses, David transformed congregations: "On his arrival among them, he found his congregations cold and neglectful of their Christian duties; he left them fervent and exemplary. Piety everywhere revived; the children and servants made their first communion; the older members of the congregations became regular communicants."[22] It was perhaps because of these special talents that the church selected David to be among the first Catholic priests to reorganize the West from a base in Kentucky.

Immediately upon his arrival in Bardstown, David set about establishing a seminary for the training of priests with similar zeal. The future bishop of the Dioceses of Louisville and Baltimore, Martin John Spalding, was a native Kentuckian drawn into the priesthood and trained by David at Saint Thomas

Seminary, just outside of Bardstown. Spalding recalled that David "often dwelt on the sublime grandeur of the ministry," and inspired his seminarians with a passage from Saint Luke, "I have come to cast fire upon the earth, and what will I but that it be kindled?" (Luke 12:49). Their sole purpose, David insisted, was "the salvation of souls," which priests and missionaries undertook in "cooperation with Christ." David seems not to have labored in Louisville, but rather worked to train priests and support Catholics in the neighborhood of Saint Thomas Seminary. He also prepared an important book of meditations to be used during retreats for both priests and the general public, called *A Spiritual Retreat of Eight Days*, which saw repeated publication in Louisville well into the 1860s. David's successful work training priests and leading retreats led Spalding to describe him as the *"Father of the Clergy of the West."*[23]

David's efforts at the seminary laid the groundwork for the first major Catholic revival in the American West following the proclamation of a jubilee to celebrate the accession of Pope Leo XII. Cincinnatians and Louisvillians celebrated the jubilee for nearly two years, with the bishops of Ohio and Kentucky traveling throughout their vast dioceses leading revivals. At least twenty took place in Kentucky, where aging French priests Flaget and David were joined by younger, native-born priests such as Robert A. Abell and Ignatius A. Reynolds, both of whom attended David's Saint Thomas Seminary.[24]

Born in 1792 in central Kentucky, Abell was among the first students at the seminary, arriving just after its opening in 1811. Having lost his father at the age of ten, Abell was reared by a devout but eccentric mother who took to wearing a "coarse cotton gown" without shoes or stockings, and "'lived . . . the life of a penitent'" following the "apostacy [*sic*]" from the church of "one or more of her children."[25] It seems possible that the young Abell siblings had met some of Kentucky's legendary Protestant revivalists of the first decade of the nineteenth century, and were drawn into new religious communities. Robert, though, followed his parents' faith into the priesthood, yet became a revivalist himself, not unlike the Peter Cartwrights or James McGreadys among Kentucky's Protestants. Having earned local fame as a gifted debater, despite a haphazard elementary education, the young Robert was sent to a newly opened Catholic school near Springfield, Kentucky, and from there he attended Saint Thomas Seminary in 1811. Ordained as a priest seven years later, and obtaining a "good horse" and "an otherwise slim outfit," Abell led missions throughout Kentucky, with stints in Illinois and Tennessee, as well as preaching tours in Philadelphia and Baltimore, until his death in 1873.[26]

Gaining renown as "the Kentucky Priest," Abell aspired to a style more commonly connected with Protestant revivalists. In ordinary language, he spoke of central Christian themes in his sermons: "God's love toward His fallen creatures; the beauty of holiness; the sufferings endured by the Son of God for sinners." "Appreciated by the people" more than "by the learned divines," Abell displayed a "rough-shod eloquence" in his preaching. When asked once about the books inspiring his sermons, Abell responded, only half in jest, " 'Why, my dear sir, we have no books in Kentucky! And having no books, we go to nature for inspiration! . . . And when, as some amongst us are called to do, we ascend the pulpit to instruct others in the ways of God, the Holy Ghost just tells us what to say, and we say it!' " Emotion and "pathos" in his sermons drew tears from his listeners, and he saw "constantly increasing numbers of the faithful" at his missions and churches, especially in Louisville, where he had charge of Saint Louis Church after 1823. But Abell never settled in a single parish for long, preferring a "missionary life" over regular ministerial work, and seemed just as content preaching out of doors as in churches, with an ingrained aversion to speaking from written notes, even, for example, while delivering the keynote speech at the consecration of the new Bardstown cathedral in 1819 before the bishop, senior clergy, and his former seminary professors.[27]

Because Reverend Abell left few, if any, written records, the story of his childhood and clerical life comes from his biographer and friend, Benedict J. Webb, who claimed to have written his expansive history, *The Centenary of Catholicity in Kentucky* (1884), chiefly for "the preservation of the well-earned fame" of the man he dubbed "the Kentucky Priest."[28] Webb's sprawling six-hundred-page book is drawn from personal memory as well as extensive correspondence with Catholics, both lay and clerical, throughout the state, and thus broadly reflects lay sentiment prior to the Civil War.[29] What stands out in Webb's extensive treatment of early Kentucky Catholicism is his close attention to the church's popular preachers and their distinctive speaking styles. In addition to Abell, Webb celebrated the pastoral labors of the Reverends Ignatius Aloysius Reynolds, John McGill, and Martin John Spalding, all native to Kentucky, as well as the preaching of the Reverend John Larkin, an English-born Jesuit.

During the 1830s and 1840s, these clerics each, in turn, served Saint Louis Church in Louisville, Webb's parish, so this would account for his close knowledge of the men's speaking styles.[30] Reynolds, later bishop of Charleston, attended Saint Thomas Seminary, and because of his "reputation for eloquence," was among the popular "preachers of the jubilee" in 1826, which typically marks the beginning of Catholic revivalism in the United States.

While Reynolds's "sermons were models of persuasive oratory, addressed to Catholics, and to the end of their sanctification," Reverend McGill displayed greater fervor: "His impassioned words fairly blistered themselves into the minds of his hearers," and as a consequence he drew "the estranged" back into the church with greater success than any of the other early priests. In contrast to McGill's fiery zeal, the Reverend John Larkin, a Jesuit who had charge of Saint Louis Church for four years, achieved "mastery over the pathetic in oratory," as Webb well recalled his sermons: "In depicting scenes of the passion of our Lord, for instance, he appeared to lose sight of himself and his surroundings in the contemplation of his Savior's sufferings. Nor was this mere acting. The tears he evoked by his pathetic delineations and pleadings had their primary fount in his own eyes." This was a lecturer who elicited cries of "Go on! go on!" from his audience after two full hours of "captivating" speaking. Webb also had a remarkable memory for speakers' diction and intonation: where Bishop Spalding's voice was "musical" and "of that full and rounded character that men listen to with pleasure the world over," Reverend Abell's voice was "husky" and lacking in Spalding's precise articulation, though nevertheless achieving "true *melliflua majestas*" in his preaching, which Webb lovingly evoked throughout his history.[31]

Webb thus attributed the foundation and growth of the Roman Catholic Church in Kentucky to the great clerical preachers of the first half of the nineteenth century. This prominent layman had comparatively little to say about architecture, art, ritual, beauty, incense, or any of the other sensory means through which Catholics were said to worship exclusively, at the expense of scriptural word. Certainly, Webb appreciated the value of a "magnificent temple" like that of the Cathedral of the Assumption in Louisville, dedicated in 1852, and he disparaged the "eyesore" of a building representing the church at Frankfort, but Webb made eloquent and popular speakers and preachers the true pillars of the early church in Kentucky.[32]

Well into the 1840s, the Roman Catholic Church struggled to find the resources, whether financial or material, to replicate the artful worship that defined Old World Catholicism. Lacking even the most basic accessories of Catholic worship, priests necessarily relied on direct explanations of the faith and celebrated a rudimentary form of Mass. The Franciscan missionary William Unterthiner, laboring among German Catholics in and around Cincinnati in the 1840s, explained to his superiors that he "rode an entire week from one settlement to another, having everything with me on the horse. The altar, in short, everything." He described his preparation for the Mass: "The altar consists of a portable crucifix, the cards for the Canon, chalice and everything that goes with it. I set it up in five minutes on a table or a box. I bake the hosts with a pressing iron and cut them out with scissors."[33] Lest his Roman correspondents speculate about his unfortunate conditions, Unterthiner hastened to add that the settlements he visited did not "suffer from hunger."[34] But under such diminished circumstances, exceptional persuasive abilities, not beautiful worship, coaxed German immigrants back into regular observance of their faith.

Magic Power of the Methodists

The rudimentary nature of worship during early years of settlement, however accurate, is a narrative staple in Protestant and Catholic histories of church beginnings in Kentucky and Ohio, and elsewhere, and the trope derives its power from scriptural accounts of the early Jews and Christ's disciples. Unencumbered by comfortable trappings, faith burned brightly among the apostles, sacred history reminds self-satisfied and complacent followers. But for Catholics in the Ohio River valley, the emphasis on eloquence and persuasive oratory had less to do with material deprivation, or a truer zeal, than with the nature of religious competition after 1820. Just as Protestants attempted to match the escalating grandeur of the Roman Catholic Church in the United States over the nineteenth century with their own beautiful worship spaces, Catholics had to fend off Protestant incursions, mostly among German immigrants, who seemed particularly susceptible to the blandishments of the Methodists.[35] A Franciscan priest, Rev. Francis Huber, writing to his minister-general from Cincinnati in 1840, reported that "a vast multitude of Methodist preachers . . . lie in wait not only for Lutherans and Calvinists, but also for German Catholics and try to lead them astray by gifts and words and ensnare them to their side." Huber therefore urged the Franciscan Order to send more German-speaking priests who could hear confessions and offer "the Word of God" to Cincinnati's immigrants.[36] According to Huber, speech and language, not architecture, art, or ritual per se, would prevent such embarrassing losses to the Protestants.

Despite his conspiratorial picture of Methodists' evangelization, Huber apprehended a real threat to the nascent Catholic Church in places like Cincinnati and Louisville. In the late 1830s, Cincinnati was the birthplace of a new, aggressively evangelical church, the German Methodist Episcopal Church, which became a distinctive branch of the national Methodist denomination and maintained its own districts, missions, and German-language press. The founder of the German Methodist Church, William Nast, converted from his native Lutheranism in 1835 after a long struggle against a peculiarly "desponding and self-despairing" perception of his sins, during which he once "held his finger in a burning candle till it burned into a crisp, in order to wake himself up to a sense of his lost condition." Born in Stuttgart, Nast immigrated to the United States in 1828 after declining to further his theological training for the Lutheran ministry, having become "lost in the labyrinth of Pantheism, the most modern form of German rationalism," during his university studies. After seven years as a peripatetic tutor and teacher of classics in Pennsylvania, New York, and Ohio, Nast attended a Methodist meeting in Knox County, Ohio, where he finally "obtained the long-sought witness of the Spirit, clearer than the light of the sun." His once-hopeless soul now "filled with joy unutterable and full of glory," Nast immediately grew "anxious to proclaim this salvation to his countrymen." "The Gospel word," wrote his biographer Adam Miller, was "like a fire shut up in his bones," and with his newfound confidence, Nast concluded he "must and would preach" to German immigrants like himself.[37]

In 1837, Nast chose Cincinnati as his headquarters for "combatting two bitter enemies, popery and infidelity," and as a special missionary to German-speaking immigrants, began to see conversions in 1838, when 22 members formally joined the city's German mission.[38] By 1840, the number had risen to 100, and the number of Methodist ministers laboring among the German population had grown to four within the Ohio Conference, while the mission also sent out preachers to neighboring districts, including Louisville, then part of the Kentucky Conference of Methodists. Louisville's German mission quickly posted gains of nearly 100 members by 1841, and the numbers of converts grew steadily in both cities through the first part of the 1840s. By 1850, Cincinnati counted three German congregations, with a total of some 484 members and probationers, and Louisville's German-speaking Methodists, who totaled over 200 members, had a choice of two congregations. Twenty years after "the first German sacramental meeting ever held among the foreign Germans in the Methodist Episcopal Church," Nast boasted of 20,000 members throughout the Midwest and New York, California, and Germany, "a net increase of 1,000 per year," along with 281 houses of worship.[39] By 1864, the earliest Methodist missions among German-speaking immigrants in Cincinnati and Louisville reported some 1,000 members, whose five congregations were now part of a larger "Central German Conference," with districts in Ohio, Michigan, Indiana, and Kentucky. Growing out of the original Cincinnati mission, this midwestern conference claimed upward of 9,000 members at the end of the Civil War.[40]

Most of these German-speaking Methodists converted from either Lutheranism or Roman Catholicism, predominant faiths of the German states, which makes the work of German Methodist preachers in missionary fields like Cincinnati and Louisville appear all the more impressive. Despite the decisive influence of German pietism on John Wesley in the eighteenth century, German Lutheran and Roman Catholic immigrants carried strong biases against the Methodist church with them to the United States in the nineteenth century.[41] Arriving in Cincinnati in 1839, the immigrant William Ahrens, born into a Lutheran family, sought boarding among "an acquaintance from my native place" of northern Germany but, to his horror, learned that the family had converted to Methodism. "These people have . . . gone over to Antichrist," he announced to his friend and fellow traveler, as Ahrens rushed them both out of the boardinghouse, convinced as he was that these Methodist converts would shortly "deliver them over to the devil" through "sorceries."[42] A Catholic from Bavaria, J. M. Winkler, also found himself boarding among Methodist converts and was warned by Catholic acquaintances that the German who owned the residence secretly filled a "certain flask" with "Methodist drops," which he sprinkled on his boarders during the night to make them abandon Catholicism. "For several nights I could not sleep," Winkler remembered, anxious about "Mr. Hawbold coming with his flask."[43]

Like Ahrens and Winkler, German immigrants alternately worried about and were seduced by the "magic power of the Methodists."[44] This power seemed to rest most obviously in German Methodist preachers' extraordinary speaking gifts, which Nast cultivated among early missionaries of the church. "Eccentric men," Nast insisted, had built up the original Methodist church, and now, he reasoned, the German missions would "require as much zeal, as much energy, as much power of God, to bring a German Methodist Church into successful operation." He therefore wanted to see "unusual and more sensible manifestations of the Divine Spirit" among his preachers, men eager to be "sent into battle" and psychologically skilled in "breaking down the carnal security of the German people."[45]

The German church discovered a good number of such preachers among Lutheran and Roman Catholic converts, men who would become "mighty instrument[s] in the salvation of sinners."[46] Nast, for one, knew whereof he spoke, and delivered sermons that immigrant Engelhardt Riemenschneider recalled "went like a two-edged sword through my soul," leaving him sleepless for days while "wrestling with God in prayer." Still unconverted, Riemenschneider attended another of Nast's meetings, where he "preached from the subject of Naaman's leprosy." The immigrant "was so affected that I suddenly fell from the bench and began to cry aloud to God for mercy." Three more weeks passed, during which Riemenschneider was "daily growing thinner and paler," and his health appeared grave, when finally "grace dawned in my heart," he wrote. As with Riemenschneider, German immigrants understood their conversions to Methodism to follow from powerful preaching. Nicholas Nuhfer, a Roman Catholic, remembered a German Methodist minister from 1842, the year of Nuhfer's conversion, whose speaking "made a deeper impression on my mind than any I had ever heard." For the first time in his life, Sebastian Barth "heard the language of Canaan, which was like a joyful sound to my inner nature," at a Methodist meeting in Louisville. In 1846, the Catholic J. M. Winkler converted to Methodism after "a true son of thunder" broke his resistance. Henry Kolbe, a self-declared infidel, visited a German Methodist church in Cincinnati where "the word preached sank deeply into my heart."[47]

The best preaching, according to Nast and his German-speaking preachers and exhorters, "humbles, convinces, melts, [and] renews" its listeners, and it did so by conveying an impression that the speaker understood the unique fear and despair of each seeker standing alone, disgraced, in the face of sin.[48] Converts recounted deeply personal responses to such proselytizing, even that offered at crowded meetinghouses. While at a protracted meeting in Louisville, J. H. Barth "saw how sin had deformed my moral nature" and "wondered how a stranger could be so well acquainted with the workings and feelings of my heart." But in preaching to audiences "a crucified Redeemer" and the means by which converts could "be delivered from the burden of [their] sins," ministers gave comfort.[49] "Lay aside every weight, despondency, gloom, [and] hard thoughts [sic]," urged the Methodist class leader George H. Buck in Cincinnati, for "Jesus intercedes" on your behalf. "Behold, wonder, believe and be saved!" Buck exhorted his class of German immigrants. Such preaching was "plain and powerful," but offered listeners a "foretaste of heaven" and a feeling of joy and release from their earthly burdens and personal failings.[50]

Friars

Catholic priests had to match this preaching prowess or lose a claim to the masses of Germans leaving Europe for America, and perhaps, ultimately, a claim to play a pivotal rather than inconsequential role in the religious life of the ascendant United States. In Cincinnati and Louisville, the responsibility for protecting Catholics' historical relevance fell to an order that had long specialized in itinerant preaching and converting, the Franciscans, following the example of its founder, Saint Francis of Assisi, who in fervent sermons to large crowds, it was said, "made a tongue out of his whole body."[51] Established amid a broader effort toward renewal of the Catholic Church in medieval Europe, the first Franciscans preached "in colourful, dramatic and intelligible terms," often as not on the streets of Italian cities in the first part of the thirteenth century. Modeling themselves after Christ and his apostles both in their poverty and in their zeal, the Franciscans exemplified a renewed fidelity to the Gospels, from which they preached in a more "exhortatory than doctrinal" fashion. Known as the "Order of Preachers," Franciscans spoke in the vernacular, with greater urgency about the need for repentance, the better to elicit conversions among the great crowds who sought out the inspired men.[52]

The friars who began arriving in Cincinnati and Louisville in the 1840s came largely under the auspices of a German-speaking province of the Franciscans established in the Austrian Tyrol, at Innsbruck, formally called the Order of Friars Minor of the Reformed Tyrolese Province of Saint Leopold. The province's first missionaries traveled to the United States assisted by funding from the Ludwig-Missionsverein, founded in 1838 by King Ludwig I of Bavaria to support German missions in North America.[53] By the late 1830s and early 1840s, leading Catholics in both Europe and the United States had grown alarmed at the absence of priests for the thousands of German-speaking immigrants arriving in places like the Ohio River valley. The plight of German Catholics had become a public scandal after a visit to the United States by Roman Catholic Canon Josef Salzbacher of Vienna in 1842, where he was chagrined to discover immigrants who "see no priest, attend no Mass, hear no sermon for many years" and thus fall into the hands of Protestants. With German-speaking missionaries, though, "thousands and thousands, who are now lost, could be saved."[54] In Salzbacher's publication, *Meine Reise nach Nordamerika im Jahre 1842*, Cincinnati had elicited particular attention for having more German Catholics than any other diocese in the United States. By 1840, some fourteen thousand Germans resided in the city, already about 30 percent of the city's total population, and the one parish designated for German-speaking Catholics by Bishop John Baptist Purcell (who never learned to speak German) claimed as many as ten thousand members that year.[55] Soon after Salzbacher's plea for missionaries to places like Cincinnati, members of religious orders, supported by Catholic societies in Europe, began to arrive in American dioceses to assist secular clergy and provide pastoral work in the German language.

Franciscans belonging to the Province of Saint Leopold took a special interest in the Ohio River valley, and particularly Cincinnati and Louisville, where they felt called to save "souls about to perish because of the lack of priests." In 1844, Father William Unterthiner had readied for a mission to the Holy Land, but the provincial definitorium (or council) concluded he should go to Cincinnati instead, for the thirty-four-year-old friar had proven himself "zealous for souls, sound in character . . . and skillful in public speaking and other gifts."[56] When Unterthiner died in Cincinnati after a grueling summer of preaching, his obituary in the local *Catholic Telegraph* recast the matter of his choice, declaring that the young friar was "inflamed with a holy desire of walking in the footsteps of the devoted missionaries of his Order who had evangelized the Tartars of Asia and the Indians of the New World," and thus had sought out the mission in the United States.[57] Whether the move was self-selected or by order of his province, Unterthiner achieved great success as a preacher and revivalist among German Catholics in Cincinnati and the greater Ohio River valley before his death in 1857, at the relatively young age of forty-eight. Even in the late 1850s, friars from Tyrol beseeched their superiors for an opportunity to join the American mission. Writing from Schwaz, in Tyrol, thirty-three-year-old Francis Jerome Holzer explained that "for a *long* time now I have had a strong desire to go across the sea solely to save souls," and "with all zeal and fervor" he hoped to "fulfill the inmost desires and wishes of my heart" to become a missionary in North America.[58] To the limited degree that friars had a choice of placement, the men from the Tyrolean province who labored in the United States' mission stations appear to have been particularly "dedicate[d] . . . to the salvation of others' souls," sometimes even at the expense of the Franciscan rule as it had developed over four centuries in primarily Catholic countries.[59]

Once in mission settings like Cincinnati and Louisville, the friars discovered a number of unusual circumstances requiring dispensations from their regular rule, and these local conditions underscored a peculiar American religious culture to which Catholics found themselves continually adjusting. First and foremost was the aggressive work of the Methodists who "move every stone so that Catholics may be led astray."[60] The friars therefore felt obligated to undertake nearly incessant missionary labor in and around population centers like Cincinnati, traveling to remote areas where Catholics more easily "fall away from the faith" without access to priests and working tirelessly within urban parishes providing pastoral care. In the cities, friars oversaw such diverse activities as regular divine services, revivals, schools, choirs, visitation of the sick, and building projects.[61] In America, "everything must be brought to the pastor," Father Unterthiner once complained to his superiors to underscore the difficulty of retiring to "a place for spiritual recovery," such as a cloister or friary.[62] Ambitious friars wanted to follow Catholic immigrants wherever fortune took them, and demands for greater mobility appeared to require a flexible interpretation of their order's rules. "With the lack of priests," explained Unterthiner, "one must again be on the move," and so "to do everything as in Catholic countries . . . is simply not possible," he argued to his superiors.[63] The friars in Cincinnati thus requested dispensations from rules governing dress, travel, money, fasts, and seclusion in order to accomplish the end of saving souls.[64] Tensions flared in the mid-1850s when it became clear to the delegate general in Rome that missionaries in Cincinnati had failed to establish a proper "friary well disciplined to return to when they need solitude, in order to meet their vowed obligations."[65] Until 1858, when the Franciscans established a friary at Cincinnati where the "monastic life could be observed," the missionaries risked recall to Europe for living too much in the world and outside the bonds of their sacred confraternity.[66]

If the friars in Cincinnati and Louisville acted the part of regular parish priests or lingered too long on missions without practicing regular vows in the cloister, they insisted to their European superiors that they were following the "seraphic" spirit of their founder, Saint Francis, as demonstrated by the success of their preaching and saving of souls. Here, credit for invigorating Catholic immigrants' faith and staving off the Methodists in Cincinnati may largely be given to Unterthiner, who eventually presided over the largest German parish, Saint John the Baptist, in the city's Over-the-Rhine district, led popular revivals in the Ohio River valley, and served as superior of the Tyrolese friars' American mission.[67] Unterthiner thus played a critical role in reshaping European religious practices to fit conditions in places like Cincinnati and Louisville, and helped his provincial administrators select talented young friars to labor in the North American mission.

Unterthiner stressed over and again to his own superiors that only men with powerful speaking skills would succeed in stemming losses to the Protestants and combating religious indifference among German immigrants, whom he characterized as a recalcitrant group: in his words, they were "perpetual dreamers" caught up in "the deception of freedom" in the United States.[68] Yet, as Unterthiner observed, "if someone finds one absurd thing and knows how to present it well, he finds a following" in places like Cincinnati and Louisville.[69] While critical of Americans' seeming gullibility, he nevertheless recognized certain advantages for his own order, which prided itself on gospel-inspired preaching. "The clear teaching of Christ," he wrote, should not be hidden behind "rationalistic verbiage" that confuses listeners. The First Epistle of Saint Paul to the Corinthians, Unterthiner wrote, was "written precisely for this country," with its injunctions against preaching the "wisdom of the wise" or relying on human eloquence or "signs" to elicit false conversions.[70] "But we preach Christ crucified," Paul exhorted his followers, and Unterthiner measured himself and the other German friars against this same "spirit of an apostle."[71] Do not send a "too eager tree-splitter," he urged his definitor, lest the misguided missionary put off immigrants too harried to worry about doctrinal fastidiousness or too bored by incessant hashing it out with the Protestants. Methodists' unsophisticated but effective preaching would sound all the more compelling in comparison to poorly delivered dogma. Besides affirming the value of a simple message, Unterthiner hoped to see rather more upbeat friars, possessing "a good sense of humor," who "take the more lenient way" with audiences and in the confessional. "Crabby" preaching, or "Jansenistic strictness" in conferring absolution, drove lay Catholics away "embittered," and straight into the hands of the Methodists, who quickly seized grace despite painful admission of one's sinful nature.[72]

Unterthiner therefore acted as a gatekeeper for the Franciscans in Tyrol, who were unfamiliar with American conditions, to prevent what he considered the wrong sorts—dour men, "hotheads," or "gluttons"—from becoming missionaries to the United States. While character mattered, the art of persuasion trumped all else in Unterthiner's vetting of missionaries. When a Father Accurs arrived in Cincinnati in 1850, Unterthiner reported a collective "shock" among the friars already stationed there, since "it is well known that he is no preacher." Unfortunately, Father Accurs lacked "delivery," and as Unterthiner took pains to explain to his Tyrolean definitorium, "in order to succeed here, one must have good delivery; otherwise it is over and finished."[73] In Cincinnati, Unterthiner coached the mission's friars to establish a personal connection with audiences. He thought that Father Sigismund "promises to do well," since he "practices preaching diligently, . . . and he has already improved a great deal in delivery." Writing two years later, in 1852, while requesting more friars to serve the American missions, Unterthiner offered this caveat: only send those men with "good voices."[74] The competitive environment in which the friars worked, where Methodists, Lutherans, and Baptists sought to build up their churches with immigrants unloosed from the parishes of Europe, compelled the Tyrolean friars to emphasize their roots as the Order of Preachers.

In the missions at Cincinnati and Louisville, the Franciscans greeted new kinds of audiences, "a grand mixture of all sorts of people," even though primarily German-speaking, with "a few Protestants . . . always coming."[75] To his dismay, Unterthiner recognized that immigrant Catholics had already become habituated to "rely[ing] on themselves alone," a troubling American trait in his view, so the mission required judicious and obliging priests to cope with the "unbelievable touchiness of the people."[76] To entice these diverse and often skeptical listeners back to the faith required a style of evangelical preaching that Unterthiner excelled at, as Father Arsacius Wieser underscored in a letter describing Cincinnati's Catholic revivals of the late 1840s:

> [I] had the good fortune to hear just as well as from the holy city [Unterthiner's] voice thundering with zeal and fire, which as they flock here in crowds from all parts of the city to hear the words of life, has moved the most obdurate to sorrow and penance, and no heart remains untouched and unconsoled. Full of joy and courage, with happy faces they go from that place; so also in the confessional, the Catholics themselves who for many years have not been to confession . . . and he led them back again on the road to correction.[77]

For his large immigrant audiences, Unterthiner perfected a hopeful message of salvation through perseverance, and he supercharged his revivals with the emotive power to move diverse people to seek out grace and penance as a matter of personal choice. As a consequence, the friars recognized Unterthiner "as the best preacher in Cincinnati."[78] And Bishop Purcell, frequently baffled by the deep social and cultural divisions among German immigrants, expressed great relief that Unterthiner "unites everyone in this area very well" through his preaching.[79]

As Unterthiner and others stressed over and over to their superiors, such preaching was difficult work. By 1848, Unterthiner's revivals had built up Saint John the Baptist church to five thousand regular communicants, with as many as eight thousand receiving the holy sacraments at Easter and fifteen thousand communions during Christmas services. While pleased by the success of his efforts, he continued to beg for additional missionaries: "Our church is too full," Unterthiner wrote to his superiors in Tyrol, and "preaching two or three times and saying two Masses on one day," as many of the friars did, was exhausting labor.[80] By 1850, Unterthiner was also undertaking regular missions, or revivals, beyond Cincinnati, but the exertion and risk remained great in the backcountry: "Whoever has not broken a leg or has never fallen into holes is no missionary," he observed.[81] Preaching missions in urban churches sapped energies too: in Louisville, for example, he delivered thirty sermons in ten days at the German church in 1849. Unterthiner's style of "zealous" labor in the service of saving souls made an indelible mark on the missions at Cincinnati and Louisville. In Louisville during the mid-1850s, Father David Widmann made his best effort to follow Unterthiner's example, but he lacked the requisite stamina, having "preached myself until my tongue was numbed and I was incapable of speech." Widmann therefore wanted to return home, believing "only Tyrolese air, water, and wine" could repair his broken missionary body.[82] Rather than keeping his vocation's religious vows sacred, Unterthiner's exclusive focus on saving souls ran afoul of his superiors in Europe and made the friars subject to recall until a proper cloister allowed the men to tend to their own spiritual souls in Cincinnati.

In all, twenty-two priests and brothers belonging to the Province of Saint Leopold served as missionaries in the Ohio River valley before 1860, with their two most prominent mission stations at Cincinnati and Louisville, where they were responsible for the leading German Catholic parishes in both cities. In addition to Saint John the Baptist church in Cincinnati and Saint Boniface's and Saint Martin's in Louisville, the friars cared for a number of congregations just outside of Cincinnati and labored in rural Butler and Licking Counties in Ohio.[83] Of course, Jesuits, Redemptorists, and Dominicans had their own star preachers in the Ohio River valley encouraging Catholics to renew their commitments to the church in a new land, but the Franciscans, more than any other religious order, drew German immigrants back into the church of their nativity, however far they had strayed while yet in Europe or in the process of migration. To combat spiritual indifference and the Methodist threat, Franciscan missionaries chose the parish revival as their foremost tool, and they drew on their vocation's tradition of powerful, emotional preaching to inject those revivals with a sense of urgency to confess one's moral lapses while also offering simple messages of consolation and salvation in a familiar tongue.

With so many religious order preachers laboring in the early American West to invigorate the Roman Catholic Church, revivals became a familiar part of the religious landscape on both sides of the Ohio River before the Civil War. First appearing in Kentucky in 1826, Catholic revivals, or missions, took place almost annually in parishes in Louisville and Cincinnati after 1840, and drew larger and larger crowds through the 1850s as church buildings grew in physical size and immigrants flocked to western metropolises. Jesuits, Franciscans, and Redemptorists appear to have enjoyed the most successful missions, and they regularly crisscrossed the Ohio River to preach at the large urban parishes in Louisville and Cincinnati. For example, Rev. John Larkin, a Jesuit widely known for his popular preaching in Louisville, led a "retreat," or revival, at Cincinnati's cathedral for two weeks in 1841, where some six hundred audience members were inspired to take communion to signal their recommitment of faith, and "several converts" announced intentions to join the church.[84] Father William Unterthiner conducted revivals in Cincinnati's and Louisville's German parishes through the second half of the 1840s, and famed itinerant preachers, Fathers F. X. Weninger, Arnold Damen, and Cornelius Smarius, all Jesuits, could be counted on to visit one of the two Ohio River cities regularly after 1848, when the Austrian-born Weninger offered a ten-day mission at Unterthiner's Saint John the Baptist church, during which five thousand "approach[ed] the Holy table," marking the largest Catholic revival yet in the city. Within two years of his first mission in Cincinnati, Weninger had presided over sixteen revivals in Ohio, Kentucky, and Missouri. A decade later, when the Rev. Arnold Damen arrived at Saint Francis Xavier Church in Cincinnati, the popularity of the revivals had grown well beyond the capacity of single parishes to conduct. With "crowds too big for the building" at Saint Francis Xavier, audiences spilled over to nearby Saint Thomas Church. In all, Damen inspired six thousand Cincinnatians to receive communion during the Lenten season of 1861. In Louisville six months later, Damen along with Smarius held missions at three churches, including the cathedral, and repeating Cincinnati's successes, saw some six thousand Catholics take the sacraments as a testament to their sense of saving faith, while fifty-one Protestants joined the ranks of the converted.[85]

These fierce Jesuit preachers, along with the more locally known Franciscans like Unterthiner in Louisville and Cincinnati, shaped a distinctively evangelical Catholicism throughout the American Middle West, as well as in the northern reaches of Kentucky. While Catholics' renewal of faith during the missions "necessarily had to be sealed by the reception of the sacraments of communion and confession," as Jay Dolan has explained, the religious order preachers of the era also drew on their Catholic European traditions to meet American audiences' insistence on immediacy, familiarity, and fervency.[86] Described as "a most eloquent, lucid, powerful and untiring preacher" in Cincinnati's *Catholic Telegraph*, Damen once explained the reason for his "great vehemence" as a speaker: "The more a preacher thunders from the pulpit the more the Irish and Americans like him."[87] Just as Unterthiner worked to prevent the uninspired from joining his order's American missions, Damen implored his father general to provide missionaries truly devoted to Jesuits' "sacred ministry," rather than add to the oversupply of college professors who engaged, at most, "but three or four pupils in their classes," ignoring the masses of Catholics needing spiritual sustenance.[88]

Defining the mission as an all-out "intense spiritual drive," Damen called for "robust" speakers who could "preach extempore" to rouse apostates toward recognition of their sinful natures and the need for saving grace.[89] Damen, missionary to English-speaking audiences, and Weninger and Unterthiner, reviving the faith among German immigrants, shaped the form and style of Catholic revivalism, particularly in places like Cincinnati and Louisville, where the three preached frequently and counseled the bishops and priests in both dioceses on the importance of the missions.[90]

Revivals led by men like Unterthiner, Weninger, and Damen contributed to the stunning growth of the Roman Catholic Church in the Ohio River valley in the two decades before the Civil War. The Cincinnati diocese reported 65,000 communicants in 1845, spread throughout the entire state of Ohio, but 160,000 parishioners by 1860 in an archdiocese overseeing just the southern half of the state. Louisville's diocese reported a Catholic population of 40,000 in all of Kentucky in 1845, and 60,000 in the western half of the state by 1860. Over the course of the 1850s, Roman Catholics built up far more church accommodations for the burgeoning Catholic parishes than did the Methodists in Cincinnati and its immediate environs in Hamilton County: whereas Methodist church growth reflected a near doubling of its churchgoing population, the Catholic population in Cincinnati claimed nearly 50,000 seats at their churches by 1860, reflecting growth of 157 percent over the previous decade. The sheer scope of the Roman Catholic Church's endeavors by 1860 was truly remarkable.[91] In addition to building up parishes, educational and charitable institutions run by the religious orders had become part of the warp and woof of urban life in places like Cincinnati and Louisville. While remaining distinctive, Catholic religious orders and the institutions they created nevertheless had adapted successfully to a competitive spiritual environment that prized a style of evangelization uniquely suited to zealous missionaries like the followers of Saint Francis and Ignatius of Loyola.

Beauty

In the 1840s, black and white evangelicals embarked on ambitious church building and beautification campaigns in both Cincinnati and Louisville. During the next twenty years, religious people in these two entrepôts reconfigured their cities' landscapes by constructing spectacular churches. This transformation was striking. Where wood-frame and brick meetinghouses with Greek Revival motifs had once easily blended with commercial counting houses adorned in the same classical style, new Gothic-inspired churches stood dramatically apart from the built environments of Louisville and Cincinnati. After 1840, spires, pinnacles, and buttresses soared over commercial and government buildings and dwarfed domestic architecture. At a minimum, these gracious stone churches conveyed durability, a quality lacking in evangelicals' fleeting revivals, however inspired and authentic they may have been. But while the new churches expressed strength, these edifices betrayed a seemingly opposite purpose: they reflected a hope that beauty softened hard hearts, rendering individuals more susceptible to moral renovation. Though Protestants and Catholics often sounded alarms about each other's cunning and deceit, and though they scrambled to build ever more attractive churches in an architectural game of one-upmanship, one consequence of their hard-edged competition was a contradictory emphasis on the pliability of the human senses and emotions.

Religious competition nevertheless hastened this rapid change in the look and feel of the urban environment. By the 1840s, Protestants rued their failure to invest in real estate and lay down more impressive stakes. In comparison, Catholics proved savvy urban developers, constructing churches in advance of each "swelling flood of business, wealth, and population" into Cincinnati's newest neighborhoods, observed one Methodist. With characteristic foresight, Catholics located St. Peter-in-Chains Cathedral on "the best site for such a edifice," though it initially stood outside the urban core. But the cathedral now occupied "a thriving portion of the city, and will soon occupy its centre."[92] In the church-building race, Protestants appeared to be falling behind. Thus in the 1840s and 1850s, Reformed congregations of every sort, even the fiercely evangelical Baptists and Methodists, launched new building campaigns or undertook costly renovations to offer visible evidence that Protestants had not yielded the West's most important commercial cities and missionary fields to the Church of Rome.

Extraordinary costs, real estate dealings, design decisions, and all manner of construction exigencies made these daunting projects for voluntary building committees. Protestants also had to reckon with a Reformation tenet that material objects could never express sacred attributes. Though a too-great emphasis on beautiful churches risked muddling this central theological point, Protestants wishing to prettify their devotion could devise creative workarounds. Many quietly elegant churches dotted the Eastern Seaboard by 1830. Still, a number of forces held in check cultural pressure to renovate church buildings—whether as a stimulus to faith or as a measure of refinement. Most importantly, participants in the religious revivals of the eighteenth and early nineteenth centuries insisted on an exclusive reliance on Christ's saving grace for a personal conversion experience. Baptists and Methodists—the fastest-growing Protestant denominations after 1750—succeeded in attracting thousands of revival converts without art or artifacts, and they chose humble settings over pleasing churches to express their faith. These popular denominations spurned such refinements as "Popish" contrivances well into the nineteenth century. In contrast to urbane Episcopalians, Congregationalists, and Presbyterians, Methodists preferred the great outdoors, cloth tents, and rough clearings for revival meetings; likewise, Baptists tended toward the unplastered and undistinguished in their meetinghouses.[93] It was possible to conclude that those denominations struggling to retain adherents—most notably Episcopalians in the aftermath of the Revolution and New England's Congregationalists in the first decades of the nineteenth century—resorted to aesthetic strategies to kindle faith. In any event, prior to 1840, the most popular Protestant sects in America did not refine their churches, and their restraint counteracted new pressures to adorn and aestheticize faith.

Thus when British traveler Frances Trollope arrived in Cincinnati in 1828, she met an "uninteresting mass of buildings" and could not detect any "attempt at beauty in any of [the city's] edifices." Of Cincinnati's two dozen Protestant churches, none stood out to her except an awkward structure dubbed the "two-horned church" because of its "two little peaked spires." In part, this early architectural indifference stemmed from the city's rushed growth at the nation's western edge. Yet the "flatness of reality" described by Trollope also suggested a lack of incentive among the Protestant faithful to distinguish their meetinghouses from the rest of the city's built environment.[94] Before 1840, Protestants had little reason to invest limited resources in dramatic church architecture. Consumed by revivalism and struggling to provide spiritual oversight to several thousand new members, white and black Protestants in Cincinnati and Louisville did not need beautiful churches to stimulate faith or spur conversions. Few, if any, evangelicals expressed self-consciousness about the common appearance of their meetinghouses. For many years, Congregationalists in Cincinnati found an Engine and Hose Company Hall entirely satisfactory for their religious meetings.

Roman Catholics first ushered the new standards for ecclesiastical design and aesthetics into the Ohio River valley. Cincinnati's Saint Peter's Cathedral and Louisville's Saint Louis Church, dedicated in 1826 and 1832, respectively, introduced Gothic decor and building principles to the provincial American landscape.[95] The historian Richard Bushman has argued that secular styles emanating from Europe's aristocratic courts inspired provincial Americans' aggressive pursuit of refinement in their manners, clothes, houses, gardens, and churches after 1690. On the American frontier, the Roman Catholic Church provided many native-born Protestants with their first taste of stately worship informed by aristocratic codes of behavior.[96] More than any other churches in the two cities, Saint Peter's Cathedral and Saint Louis Church (later Cathedral) represented direct connections to European courtly society, for aristocrats and ecclesiastics in France, Belgium, Holland, England, Italy, and Austria furnished the money and accoutrements to build these two richly appointed cathedrals.

The Leopoldinen-Stiftung in Vienna, for example, contributed a steady supply of valuable art and religious artifacts to adorn churches in the Diocese of Ohio and to ensure refined execution of the Roman Catholic liturgy. In 1832 alone, the missionary society sent 3,427 pictures, 19 large oil paintings, 45 smaller oil paintings, 126 altar cloths, 1,259 rosaries and crucifixes, 29 large crucifixes and statues, and over 500 books, along with censors, albs, vestments, linens, chalices, chasubles, laces, stoles, rochets, and a ciborium. Similar shipments arrived in 1831, 1833, and 1839.[97]

Bishops Fenwick and Purcell distributed these devotional objects throughout Ohio's Catholic communities, but they reserved the most spectacular works of art and most valuable instruments of the liturgy for Cincinnati's cathedral. In 1824, Cardinal Fesch, Napoleon's uncle, gave Bishop Fenwick thirteen oil paintings, including Bartolomé Murillo's "St. Peter Delivered," a seventeenth-century work seized from the Cathedral of Seville by French troops during the Peninsular War.[98] All thirteen paintings hung in Cincinnati's Saint Peter's Cathedral after 1826. This baroque art encircled a "splendid bronze tabernacle, surmounted by a beautiful crucifix, in the midst of ten superb candlesticks." On its exterior, Saint Peter's exhibited the defining element of Gothic architecture, the "pointed arch," in its "fine Gothic windows" illuminating the interior nave and delicate niches gracing the doorway. Next door, the bishop's residence offered a foretaste of embellishments popular in the 1830s and 1840s: quatrefoils, exotic ogee arches, and pinnacles. By European and later American standards, Saint Peter's must be considered primitive, but according to the *U.S. Catholic Miscellany*, its architecture and interior decor "impart[ed] an awful solemnity to the performance of the divine service."[99]

Louisville's first "chaste specimen of Gothic style," Saint Louis Church, acquainted inland America with buttresses and, incongruously, minarets in 1832.[100] Although it would not serve as the Kentucky diocese's cathedral until 1841, Louisville's Catholic church would eventually contain art and religious accoutrements donated by the king of Naples, Louis I of Bavaria, Ferdinand

II of the Kingdom of the two Sicilies, King Louis Philippe of France, and Popes Leo XII and Gregory XVI.[101]

After 1840, rapid growth in the number of Catholics in Cincinnati and Louisville fueled projects for more extravagant churches in both cities. Cincinnati's Catholics consecrated their new cathedral in 1845. After ten years of construction, the Diocese of Cincinnati had spent $120,000 on the new Saint Peter's, which city boosters proclaimed the "finest building in the west, and the most imposing, in appearance, of any of the cathedrals in the United States."[102] Though Catholics in Cincinnati chose Greek Revival over Gothic, an obviously baroque aesthetic reigned inside, where builders installed an "altar of the purest Carrara marble, made by Chiappri, of Genoa, . . . embellished with a centre piece, being a circle with rays, around which, wreaths and flowers are beautifully chiseled."[103] Angels carved in Italy stood on either side of this altar, and dramatic oil paintings from Spain and Germany further enriched the interior. In his 1851 guide to Cincinnati, Charles Cist offered a detailed description of the cathedral's "exquisite design" and "rich and expensive character" as well as a plate illustration of Saint Peter's, an honor he bestowed on no other local church.[104]

Dedicated in 1852, Louisville's new Cathedral of the Assumption was simply spectacular: its 287-foot steeple dwarfed every other building in the city and stood slightly taller than Trinity (Episcopal) Church in New York City, which had boasted the highest steeple in America. Ribbed vaulted ceilings, side aisles, and clerestory windows introduced new complexity to Gothic church architecture in Louisville, and the cathedral's interior decor surpassed in splendor any other civil or ecclesiastical space in the city. A breathtaking deep blue ceiling decorated with thousands of gold leaf stars surrounded a fresco of the Assumed Virgin; fresco medallions depicting the apostles graced nave arches. Behind the altar a hand-painted glass window, among the largest in the nation even today, depicts Mary's coronation by Christ.[105]

In 1819, the sum total of Catholic church property in Cincinnati had consisted of a small timber building constructed in eastern Kentucky and delivered downriver by flatboat.[106] Thirty years later, after a massive influx of art, money, and immigrants from Europe and an aggressive building campaign, the total value of Catholic church property in Hamilton County, Ohio, exceeded every other denomination's at nearly $450,000.[107] In Jefferson County, Kentucky, Catholics would also possess more property than any other denomination with the completion of their $70,000 cathedral in 1852. By 1860, a Baptist church in Kentucky carried a worth of roughly $1,130 compared to $8,430 for each Catholic edifice. While a Catholic church normally accommodated more people than a Baptist meetinghouse—on average, 540 seats versus 340—this difference in seating capacity does not account for the vast disparity in value.[108] So although Protestants in Cincinnati and Louisville could always boast of more churches than the Catholics, the Roman church made up in style and appearance what it lacked in numbers.

Rather than recoil at these costly edifices, non-Catholics felt an attraction to them.[109] Early on, curious Protestants visited Louisville's and Cincinnati's cathedrals to witness the exotic religious services. A young law student in Louisville inspected Saint Louis Church several times in the 1820s. Though convinced that the Roman Catholic faith amounted to a "Satanic spell," John Brown was awestruck by the cathedral. In a letter to his brother, Brown described the church as "one of the most splendid assemblages of ornament that can be imagined" and offered a long itemization of its opulence: "windows ornamental in the most beautiful manner"; "cross of the most brilliant gold"; "rich apparel embossed with gold from head to foot"; "golden and silver vessels"; and so on.[110] Reflecting a keen interest in Catholic devotional objects and architecture, such inventories regularly appeared in popular print publications in the 1840s.

Shortly after completion of Cincinnati's Saint Peter-in-Chains Cathedral, a Methodist magazine published a lengthy feature on the new building. With a "gentleman" companion, the feature's author attended High Mass and a musical concert at the cathedral one September Sunday in 1847. As soon as the two men entered Saint Peter-in-Chains, the author directed his friend's eye across the cathedral's expanse, taking in each sumptuous and lovely detail—columns, pedestals, recesses, fences, furniture, altars, textures, art, and cushions. The whole effect was a most "brilliant scene" compelling the men to "ruminate for a moment on the design of all this splendor." Next, the two men settled in to watch the "pageant" of the Mass, celebrated by a "mystic company" of priests and scarlet-gowned altar boys. While the author grew impatient with the "wearying repetition of prostrations, and bowings, and genuflections," the two Methodist observers appreciated the "combined and uniform effect" of Catholic worship: "With real skill have they united architecture, painting, sculpture, and music, together with the less prominent arts." "Every thing looks devout, solemn, and profound," they concluded. Nor were they the only Protestants in attendance that particular Sunday. "There are many of them here," the author observed, who "sit in mute wonder" at the magnificence of the Roman church's worship.[111] The volume of detail in these accounts reinforced a growing conviction that material beauty altered belief and behavior. According to Protestant observers, each glinting surface, vivid color, or bend of light in Catholic churches had the capacity to recondition the senses. Stepping back into their own plain meetinghouses, Protestants could hardly be blamed if they felt uninspired, even downright embarrassed.

Temple Building

As a corrective, one Protestant congregation after another undertook expensive building campaigns before the Civil War. To maintain their Reformation bona fides, Protestants would stress that Scripture, especially the Old Testament account of Solomon's temple, provided clear authority for the construction of costly and exquisite houses of worship, that such churches stimulated reverential feeling, and that beautiful churches revealed worshippers' inward grace and sanctification. This temple-building theory made fully explicit a gradual theological and devotional shift underway among radical and experiential Protestants since the eighteenth century: where American Protestants had once demeaned the things of this earth as incommensurate with Christ's sacrifice for humankind, they now saw material and earthly beauty as a means to sense God's presence and as outward symbols of an inward struggle for redemption. Although the temple-building theory elaborated during the 1840s and 1850s has the appearance of a convenient rationale for constructing fashionable churches, evangelical Protestants expected their expensive edifices to satisfy spiritual needs.

With the construction of Trinity Methodist Episcopal Church in the late 1850s, Cincinnati's white Methodists offered up a costly sacrifice to their Redeemer. Trinity's light stone building material, heavy pointed arches, and two-hundred-foot spire presented a subdued but richly textured exterior. "Carpeting, cushions, elegant lamps and chandeliers, and an organ of the finest tone and finish" adorned the interior.[112] In his dedication sermon, Rev. Davis Wasgatt Clark, editor of *The Ladies' Repository*, emphasized the "architectural magnificence" of Solomon's temple in order to establish biblical precedent for Trinity's visual and material prominence. No less than the temple in Jerusalem, Cincinnati's Trinity M.E. Church represented that *"spirit of sacrifice* which takes of our possessions and consecrates them to his service."[113] Clark here leapfrogged over the example of the Roman Catholic Church's sacred architecture to that of ancient Israel to suggest that Methodists' sacrifice glorified only God—not the institutional church on earth—in their new temple.

Baptists sounded similar themes as they began to spend small personal fortunes to replicate medieval styles precisely. In 1854, Louisville's Walnut

Street Baptist Church dedicated its new Gothic edifice, "the wonder and the pride of the city."[114] The large church was richly ornamented with delicate stained glass windows and buttresses topped by long, slender pinnacles and enhanced with finials. In their quest for a beautiful church, members spent $81,000, an amount unprecedented in Kentucky Baptist annals.[115] As one member of the building committee later recalled, "the aggregate wealth of the members of the church did not equal the amount that was finally expended upon the property."[116] The financial strain placed on Walnut Street Baptist's congregation was enormous, and members made a "heroic effort" to cancel the debt. In 1859, five years after the church's dedication and nine years after the building project was first launched, Walnut Street Baptist Church finally collected the last subscriptions for its striking cathedral-like edifice.[117]

The ornate and elegant building signified Baptists' new claims to middle-class respectability. For the first time, Louisville's Baptists had an indoor baptistery; before the dedication, Walnut Street Baptist Church had baptized converts in muddy creeks flowing into the Ohio River.[118] Although the new baptistery indicated white Baptists' rising social status, members understood their church-building project as the fulfillment of a biblical imperative. Just as the ancient Jews "were commanded to construct of the most costly materials, and after the most beautiful models," modern-day Baptists displayed their loving devotion to God and Christ in building attractive sanctuaries. "If such outlays were right then, they may be now," reasoned W. W. Everts, Walnut Street Baptist's pastor at the time of the church's dedication.[119]

An accomplished minister who had built up important congregations in New York City (including Baptist Tabernacle and Laight Street Baptist) before coming to Louisville, Everts sounded hesitant about spending so much for their new edifice. Might the $81,000 expended on their building have been better put toward Christian charities or missionary efforts? No, Everts reassured himself and the Walnut Street congregation: financial sacrifices for "fine houses" did not take away from "important charities" but rather stimulated a community's Christian benevolence through their "sacred attractions." "Avarice and parsimony" in church building were "far more to be feared than extravagance," for cheapness signaled an absence of religious feeling and ingratitude to God. By Everts's reasoning, Walnut Street Baptist's beautiful edifice constituted a capital investment that would stimulate ever-greater munificence toward "the least" of their brethren.[120]

If Old Testament accounts of temple building did not entirely appease white evangelicals' concern about the vast expenditures for beautiful churches, various pseudoscientific and philosophical theories about the relationship between physical beauty and religion—already under development since the mid-eighteenth century among English and European thinkers—helped Protestants overcome the charge of crude materialism. Writers for evangelical magazines in Cincinnati and Louisville displayed a strong desire to understand the precise relationship between beauty and emotion, and between beauty and virtue.

At *The Ladies' Repository*, Cincinnati's popular Methodist publication, articles by doctors and assorted professors posited an instinctual "love for the elegant" among humanity, "springing from the inner man, and growing out of his social nature and his affection."[121] Yet because the perception of beauty depended on an individual's feelings and affections—one's "love for the beautiful"—a distinctly circular reasoning arose when these authors attempted to pin down the emotions elicited by beauty.[122] Not surprisingly, many found that a beautiful object "awakens the intuition of love."[123] Another stated the relationship between beauty and feeling simply: "If you wish to awake the emotion of love, you must place a lovely object before the mind."[124] As a consequence, beauty and the emotion of love inevitably became one and the same, as when Rev. T. M. Griffith proclaimed: "There is nothing purer than *love*, yet nothing is more aesthetic."[125] It was a short distance to conclude that beautiful objects awakened salutary Christian feelings such as love for fellow human beings and love of virtue. "From physical to *moral* beauty the transition is easy and natural," Reverend Griffith had continued.[126] Dr. Edward B. Steven claimed that beauty promoted "a better and a kindlier atmosphere," leading to "a nature bettered, and a soul exalted."[127] According to Methodist writers, it increasingly looked like a violation of Christian ethics "to set up, in His world of order and beauty, a disproportionate and offensive building, and call it a 'house of God.'"[128] Architectural renovation even aided evangelical conversion, as when Reverend Clark assured his Methodist congregation that "in this sanctuary, the Holy Spirit [shall] polish and beautify immortal souls."[129] Though Clark seemed to make Christian "rebirth" a superficial matter of improved appearances, he drew on a wellspring of thinking about beauty's capacity to alter the moral sense in man.

Kentucky's white Baptists also melded aesthetic and religious phenomena. In his 1855 guide to church building, *Bethel; Or, The Claims of Public Worship*, the Louisville minister W. W. Everts likened a beautiful church to an art gallery: "As a connoisseur of art passing through the several departments of a gallery, lingers with fixed admiration before the work of a master, delighted with the conception, the execution . . . and the coloring," so are Christians "enamored of the beauty of the sanctuary and the loveliness of its associations."[130] In this justification for attractive churches, Everts pressed against Reformation dogma. In Everts's view, such churches offered the "brightest revelation" of God's word and person by arousing and calibrating all the human senses. Everts emphasized the aural over the visual—the faithful can "hear the voice and footsteps of the passing Deity" inside a beautiful sanctuary—but he ventured close to Catholic notions by suggesting that churches brought a personified divinity into view. Although Everts's anthropomorphizing language appeared to diminish the ambit of an illimitable and omnipresent divinity (the reader almost imagines God moving from the rear of the auditorium to the front in search of a better seat), he otherwise spoke of believers' wonder and awe in "the presence of the Holy God," a presence that was realized in special temples more than any other place on earth.[131] In *Bethel*, Everts helped to sacralize physical spaces, and especially beautiful churches, in ways that most Baptists would have deemed disturbingly Catholic just twenty years earlier. He therefore sought a scriptural basis for his aesthetic argument, quoting from Psalm 27: "One thing have I desired of the Lord . . . that I may dwell in the house of the Lord all the days of my life, to behold the beauty of the Lord."[132]

Speaking before Cincinnati's Methodists in 1859, Davis Wasgatt Clark hesitated to state unequivocally that Trinity Methodist Episcopal Church's members would "enjoy a Divine presence" in their new church. If the Holy Ghost "cease[d] to make its abode in the *sanctum sanctorum* of our hearts," Clark warned, God would no longer hallow their meeting place—however much its beauty and grandeur modeled divine glory. Clark's dedication therefore admonished members of Trinity M.E. Church to consecrate themselves to God first before expecting to find God's presence in their meetinghouse.[133]

Yet Clark nevertheless emulated Solomon's supplications to God to "dwell in the temple we have reared" when he begged, "O, thou that dwellest between the cherubim, *shine forth to-day! . . . Shine forth into this, thy temple, that it may become the house of God, and the gate of heaven to our souls!*" The ancient Jews' experience of the divine was direct, immediate, and exclusive in the Old Testament; Clark did not anticipate this same relationship for the Methodist congregation upon completion of its beautiful church (as Everts had promised his readers). But the future Methodist bishop did leave his listeners with this exhilarating possibility: while their new temple should not be taken as a "sign and symbol" of the divine, it might very well hasten the reappearance of God's "personal presence" on earth. "The promise—*I will come unto thee*—remains forever," Clark said, intimating that Trinity's congregation beckoned God to fulfill this sacred covenant now with the construction of its beautiful temple.[134]

Chosen

Aesthetically pleasing churches also allowed African Americans to realize spiritual confidence and autonomy—feelings once achieved largely through emotional conversion experiences and subsequent revivals of faith. Where before the orthodox Protestant conversion experience had provided the sole means by which individuals fell under God's sheltering love, now particular earthly spaces came to offer that same sense of regeneration and refuge. But the meanings black Protestants attributed to their new houses of worship differed from white evangelicals' temple-building theory. Unlike some whites, black Baptists and Methodists perceived no real conflict between their financial expenditures for physical buildings and their religious mission. For individuals who controlled so little of their communities' aggregate wealth, it hardly seemed a breach of Christian ethics to pool resources for an attractive, respectable meetinghouse. In contrast to white Protestants, then, the amount of money black congregations invested in their church beautification projects had significance not as an indication of their own willingness to sacrifice, but rather as a measure of God's particular love for them. Black congregations came to believe that aesthetically pleasing houses of worship offered evidence that Americans of African descent were a people chosen and favored by God.[135]

Through the 1820s and 1830s, Cincinnati's black Methodists had worshipped, at different times, in a cellar, a blacksmith's shop, a lime house, and a wood-frame meetinghouse. The distinctly profane blacksmith's shop, for instance, was "made of rough boards set on end" and "clab-board" seats without backs. Red paint coated only the front of the building. This homely setting did not dampen the religious feeling expressed inside. After the Civil War, as Rev. B. W. Arnett compiled a history of the church, an older member who had joined in 1832, Sister Sarah A. Williams, provided him with a vignette of the extraordinary preaching that went on in the "Little Red Church on the Green," as it was known to members. "The first time she ever attended church," as Arnett retold her story, the minister "went up and down the church crying that the devil was loose; and then she cryed [*sic*] and hollered so that they had to take her out of church."[136] Williams's account suggests that through the 1830s, fervency in preaching and believing mattered more to the independent black congregation than the physical structure in which it took place.

Yet sometime in the 1840s, Cincinnati's black Methodists grew concerned about their church's appearance and decided to build a more substantial and attractive brick "chapel." The Rev. Leven Gross, known as "Old Man Eloquent," persuaded church members to undertake the building project. Gross sought a more distinguished setting for his worship services, for "there was not a more polished and eloquent minister west of the mountains," Reverend Arnett later recalled of his friend. Members of the congregation evinced their own interest in the new church by distinguishing stages of the building process with carefully planned ceremonies—a fastidiousness that had not concerned them previously, even while constructing their "Bethel" wood-frame church in the mid-1830s. In 1847, the congregation held a special celebration to lay the cornerstone for Allen Chapel, a ritual that made a deep impression on the exacting Elder Gross, for he "often told me of the ceremony, and how it was conducted," Arnett related.[137]

Nearly three decades after the chapel's formal dedication, members retained a strong memory of the event. For Cincinnati's black Methodists, the chapel represented "quite a change."[138] The new church registered an architectural and stylistic departure for the black congregation. A sketch produced in the early twentieth century shows that Allen Chapel displayed a number of decorative embellishments, including Georgian-style windows with diamond-patterned cut glass. A niche stone carving of the Holy Bible and a cross, both set above the doorway, clearly denoted the building as sacred, and hence inviolable. The presence of these Protestant icons on the exterior of the church offered a strong contrast with the congregation's previous meeting places, none of which had displayed any special sanctifying features.[139] Members who had attended meetings at Father King's House, Red Church on the Green, Old Lime House, and Bethel "looked back and saw the march of the church—it was one of triumphs and victories—they could enjoy themselves."[140]

Cincinnati's black Methodists did not expect Allen Chapel to concentrate God's presence in quite the same way that white evangelicals of the 1840s and 1850s intended their newly sacralized churches to do. Where white evangelicals offered God a dwelling place on earth in order to pull Him closer to them, members of Allen Chapel stressed an opposite dynamic: by providing the black Protestant faithful with a means to build a new house of worship, God drew his favored people closer to Him. According to Arnett, members recited a familiar passage from Psalms on seeing the completed building: "The Lord is my strength and my reward, in Him will I trust." While Arnett may have inserted this verse into his 1874 history for pious effect, it suggests the meaning black Protestants attributed to their attractive chapel. In this particular chapter of Psalms, David expressed faith in God's overarching love and protection. For black Methodists in antebellum Cincinnati, the new Allen Chapel offered hope of a physical buffer between themselves and a hostile world. Reverend Arnett provided a glimpse of the relief felt by members upon the chapel's completion: "There was rejoicing among the African Methodists throughout the State, for they had to contend with the world, the flesh, and the devil."[141]

Louisville's First African Baptist Church, under the guidance of Elder Henry Adams, delivered a similar message in the 1840s and 1850s. When first organized in 1832 as a separate though not yet independent church, the black Baptist congregation resorted to an undistinguished frame building in a "swampy" part of town. A few years later, a white slaveholder offered some wooded land "beyond the city limits" to the congregation and members "put up by their own means" a new meetinghouse with donated building materials.[142] But in June 1842, Louisville's black Baptists became fully independent of their white "mother" church's oversight by adopting their own Confession of Faith, Covenant, and Rules of Decorum.[143] Just four months later, the congregation "resolved to build a house of worship" more befitting its independent status than the donated property and building located far from the center of town. For the next three years, Adams and the church's deacons looked out for a suitable lot.[144] Finding none, or lacking sufficient resources to build from scratch, the congregation decided to buy a former Christian church located "in the heart of the city."[145] That a congregation made up partly of slaves could purchase a $5,000 church once owned by whites and located in a prominent district of Louisville seems remarkable. Less than a decade later, the black congregation undertook an extensive remodeling in order to put "our House of worship in good Style."[146] The costly renovation brought the church's declared value up to $15,000 and must have been impressive, for in 1858 the local white Baptist association described it as the "finest finished of any colored church in the United States."[147]

On the eve of the Civil War, black and white Protestants insistently argued that beautiful environments remade people, rendering them pliable and susceptible to moral change. African Americans sought power in attractive churches and hoped that graceful appearances would temper racists' animus. White evangelicals wanted beauty to soothe and console troubled souls, just as traditional conversion provided a psychological ark in the unruly sea of human experience. This unusual preoccupation with architecture, though, offers additional insights into the moment in which these dedicated beauty-seekers lived. First, evangelicals' sudden commitments to striking churches reveal a certain cultural dexterity during an era of great dread about Catholic incursion. Hardly mindless in their adoption of fashionable trends and Catholic styles, Protestants in Cincinnati and Louisville made studied efforts to justify costly investments in neo-Gothic church architecture. They adroitly combined familiar evangelical language about infusions of grace with aesthetic theories arguing for beauty's power to unloose feeling. All of this cultural work suggests a second conclusion about the era: that many urban peoples accepted the notion that their moral senses, even their fundamental identities, were malleable. These great piles of stone therefore stand as monuments to a belief in the capacity of human-made environments to reshape belief and habits.

Reformation injunctions notwithstanding, Protestants claimed that beautiful churches softened resistances, allowing men and women to seek grace. In this way, sacred spaces brought humanity closer to God, very much as the evangelical conversion experience imparted new confidence to the faithful: crossing the threshold into a gorgeous temple "separates man from all that is selfish, base, and evanescent, and allies him with all that is disinterested, God-like, and immortal," Louisville's white Baptists insisted.[148] These capital projects, then, reflected an intense striving to forge bonds between the things of this earth and the divine. By definition, faith provides paths to connect with unseen things or deeper recesses of the self. In the decades before the Civil War, urban dwellers sought out more varied ways to close distances between humanity and the divine. Beauty in architecture became one such path for evangelical Protestants.

Although it is difficult to measure the cultural distances they had traveled with precision, both Protestants and Catholics in the Ohio River valley pressed their faiths into new theological terrain and experimented with new styles of persuasion—whether rhetorical or architectural—to maintain a competitive advantage in drawing urbanites into their communities. Though the era's religious strife was of no small consequence in Cincinnati and Louisville, it is important to take into account Protestants' and Catholics' concerted efforts to emulate the other's most visible, outward successes. Naturally, members of both faiths insisted they promoted change in order to protect their particular religious beliefs, and they could often find justification or precedent for new departures within their own traditions. Still, Protestants and Catholics found much that was attractive in each other's presentation of faith and, as a consequence, altered the style and appearance of their beliefs. This common religious vernacular, found in architecture and in revivals on both sides of the Ohio River, took the edge off age-old doctrinal disputes and considerably narrowed the ground on which chauvinists might stand. Though Cincinnati and Louisville have always borne reputations as provincial rather than truly cosmopolitan cities, these urban settings in the middle of the United States nevertheless encouraged residents to lower their defenses, the better to imagine bonds between unlike persons and things.

CHAPTER THREE

Devotion

As Catholics and Protestants pressed their faiths in new aesthetic and rhetorical directions to meet the demands of a competitive religious marketplace in the Ohio River valley, laypeople also recast their private devotional
practices to permit a closer, more deeply felt, personal connection to the
divine, especially God and Jesus Christ. Spiritual or mystical communion
with the divine is, of course, a central purpose of faith, and yet our studies
of nineteenth-century religion tend to focus on the nature of the moral and
social communities forged through revivals.[1] Patterns of inclusion and exclusion, as well as connections to market forces and dramatic economic change,
generally preoccupy historians of the era. But the day-to-day expressions of
faith and practices of devotion among Catholics and Protestants have garnered less attention for this particular period. What seems clear, though, is
that those men and women who animated revivals with heartfelt recognition
of their sins and entire dependence on grace for redemption also demanded
a means to cultivate feelings of ongoing closeness to the divine. The erratic
pulses of revival energy and the long stretches between periods of intense
preaching left converts uncomfortably idle during down seasons. Attendance
at churches could also be intermittent or irregular for urbanites—as much as
Protestants and Catholics may have welcomed the respite provided by a beautiful church, they craved personal access to transcendent things and spiritual
renewal in their daily lives.

Lay Catholics and Protestants therefore sought new channels to deepen
their feelings of attachment to the supernatural, and they discovered these
channels in two relatively novel forms of pious expression for general American audiences: Catholic devotional meditations and Protestant religious
poetry. To be sure, both of these forms of expression have important antecedents stretching back to the Reformation era, to medieval Christianity, and
even to the Augustinian spiritual tradition. But amid the intense competition between Catholics and Protestants in the nineteenth century for North
American preeminence, devotional meditations and religious poetry enjoyed
renewed popularity because of their apparent capacity to draw one's soul into
close union with God.

Printers, publishers, and newspaper and magazine editors in Cincinnati and Louisville raced to meet the surging demand for this literature, and soon the two Ohio River cities were awash in devotional guides, poetry gift books, and periodicals inviting readers into intimate communion with the divine. Although this kind of literature could be found in any major publishing center and, presumably, even in any small hamlet in the United States with a printing press, the Ohio River valley's authors and publishers carried on a lively discourse about the origins and purpose of religious poetry not seen elsewhere, and the devotional works published in Cincinnati and Louisville were infused with an intense piety sought out by German immigrants and then translated for English-speaking audiences. What took place in Cincinnati and Louisville, then, was a rich conversation about the bonds of union between human and divine established through an individual's emotional response to suffering and affliction. Though seemingly about private feeling—one's personal relationship with God or Christ—the sudden ubiquity of these devotional artifacts in the most public print forums suggests their broad cultural force.

Via Unitiva

As religious order priests such as Jesuits, Passionists, Redemptorists, and Franciscans arrived in American dioceses to conduct missions, they introduced native-born and immigrant Catholics to distinctive forms of devotionalism intended to bring the faithful and divine beings into union with each other. These missionary priests encouraged converts to seek out older devotional literature such as Saint Ignatius of Loyola's *Spiritual Exercises*, Saint Leonardo of Porto Maurizio's *The Hidden Treasure*, Saint Alphonsus de Ligouri's *Short Treatise on Prayer*, and Saint Francis de Sales's *Practical Piety*, all of which enjoyed new vogue among American audiences. After 1850, publishers in the Ohio River valley, including John P. Walsh in Cincinnati and Benedict Webb in Louisville, made these works available for English-speaking laypeople during missions and at local Catholic booksellers. According to Ann Taves, Ligouri's works were especially popular among mid-nineteenth-century Americans steeped in the emotional cauldron of the missions, for his guides sought "to unleash the emotions and establish a strong affective bond between the devotee and his or her supernatural patron."[2]

Liguori died in 1787, de Sales in 1622, and Ignatius of Loyola in 1556, but publishers in Louisville and Cincinnati also promoted contemporary authors who spoke to this same felt need among lay Catholics for a spiritual bond between human and divine forged in day-to-day experience to complement the sacramental rituals of the formal church. In Louisville, a widely read author of "spiritual and ascetic" works was the Reverend John M. David, the native of France whose retreats in Maryland and Kentucky gave a distinctive European stamp to early nineteenth-century Catholicism. Before his death in 1841, David wrote several manuals to the Catholic faith for the laity, including *True Piety* (1809) and *A Catechism of the Diocese of Bardstown* (1825), but his guide to devotional meditation, posthumously edited and published by Louisville's Bishop Martin John Spalding in 1864, offers insight into the spiritual aspirations of the "many pious persons" who made use of David's "Method of Mental Prayer" in their daily lives in the decades before the Civil War. Although unpublished until Spalding's edited version appeared as *A Spiritual Retreat of Eight Days*, David's style of meditation and prayer circulated widely among Kentucky's Catholics in a kind of samizdat form for many years, as the gap between David's death in 1841 and publication of the guide in 1864 suggests. In preparing *A Spiritual Retreat* for publication, Spalding pieced together David's personal writings as well as Spalding's own notes on retreats from his student days in Rome some thirty years earlier under the tutelage of the Jesuits. The entire work, by David's design and through Spalding's editing, draws heavily on the method found in the *Spiritual Exercises* of Saint Ignatius of Loyola but culminates by proffering a kind of ecstatic union with the divine that David labeled the "Via Unitiva," or "Way of Union by Love."[3] David and Spalding appear to have adapted the emotionally cooler *Spiritual Exercises* to meet the needs of priests and laypersons increasingly inclined to a "demonstrative, emotion-packed" style of faith characteristic of the nineteenth century, which the historian Jay Dolan has labeled "devotional Catholicism."[4]

Intended to complement the work of spiritual reformation undertaken by mission priests, David's guide also merited "general use" beyond revival seasons, according to Spalding's introduction. *A Spiritual Retreat of Eight Days* therefore suggests some of the ways Catholics tried to import the emotional power of the revivals into their ordinary lives. Absent here is any discussion of the rituals of the official public church; rather, David focuses on a spiritual seeker's own deliberate pursuit of a union with Christ and God as a means to salvation and, ultimately, a path to heaven. The work exhorts readers to follow a complex formula of meditations, mental prayers, exercises, aspirations, and resolutions in order to combat sin and achieve "a solid and thorough reformation of our lives." If David failed to differentiate these varied "spiritual operations" of the human "mind and heart," he did offer vivid images of the torments of hell, the Passion of Christ, and the divine love awaiting the saved in heaven for readers to fix their thoughts upon.[5] Known as "composition of place," the construction of such images is a strategy common to devotional literature.[6] For example, while contemplating "our Saviour in the garden of Olives . . . in an agony of grief covered with a sweat of blood," David urged, "beseech Him to permit you to enter into His sacred interior," to "mingle the tears of your repentance with the tears of blood He sheds for you." "Adore those wounds, that blood," David enjoined his readers. Meditation on the Passion was not for the "faint-hearted" or for "cowards," David acknowledged, but the guide did clarify the particular images on which to dwell and prescribed the right feelings and emotions for one seeking whole-hearted, compassionate empathy with Christ's suffering.[7]

Once joined with Christ in his affliction, readers could enter into the final stage of the retreat, the *Via Unitiva*, or union with the divine "by the sweet and golden bonds of love." Here one became sensible to Christ's desire to "*unite* us to Himself for ever more," and David's preparatory prayer invited readers to imagine heaven, where they would feel a "love so ecstatic that the soul goes out of itself and passes entirely into God to be consummated in unity with Him." This was, of course, the ultimate end of readers' spiritual questing, but David insisted that Catholics would experience a foretaste of the celestial feeling "in this world" through their day-to-day love of Christ. In this way, heartfelt sympathy with affliction, and acceptance of "desolation and trials" in our own lives as Christlike, constituted the foundational basis of the union between humans and God in popular Catholic devotional literature after 1840.[8]

In David's guide, the work of forging union with the divine was not reserved for priests, nor was it the exclusive province of official public worship in the church, nor even, seemingly, an adjunct to that worship. *A Spiritual Retreat of Eight Days* offered this promise of union to any individuals with the mental strength and imagination to embark on the quest for a reformation of their lives, albeit guided by Reverend David's prescribed meditations. The simple directive of his book, as he reduced it, was for the religious seeker to "retire into your heart with God, to meditate, to pray, to weep, to speak to the Lord and to listen to Him." Alone, yet in the presence of God, readers might discover grace and salvation. To his readers, David accorded full powers of insight: "Enter, then, into the disposition of the prophet," he advised, to hear and feel the divine. As a priest and a "coadjutor" bishop of Louisville, Reverend David hardly intended to launch his readers on a mystical journey without churchly oversight, but in comparison to other devotional works of the period, *A Spiritual Retreat of Eight Days* stands remarkably free of reference to the sacraments or clerical mediation.[9]

Cincinnati publishers first saw into print the devotional guides of the itinerant mission priest, Rev. Franz Xavier Weninger, who drew German-speaking immigrants into American Catholic churches through his revivals and faith manuals after his immigration to the United States in 1848. Popular among German-language readers in Cincinnati and throughout the Midwest for more than a decade, Weninger's devotional guides warranted wider audiences through English translation, in the view of both Cincinnati's and New York's leading Catholic booksellers. Weninger's *Sacred Heart Mission Book* therefore appeared in 1863, when it was simultaneously published in Cincinnati and New York.[10] More traditional than Reverend David's *Spiritual Retreat*, Weninger's guide provided instruction on performing devotions in connection with the liturgy of the church, especially Holy Communion, and assured readers that their efforts would be rewarded with papal indulgences. Weninger's devotional manual thus makes explicit connection to the official public worship and institutional authority of the church, unlike David's spiritual guide. But within Weninger's book, readers discovered an intense piety to complement the emotions aroused in revivals, and found a powerful and distinctive language of union merging human and divine realms that reacquainted English-speaking Catholics with a European mystical tradition.

A central facet of Christian spiritual practice from the seventeenth century, sacred heart devotions invited Catholics to contemplate Jesus's "pierced" body in order to "inflame" their own hearts with love and comprehension of his suffering.[11] According to Weninger, meditation on Jesus's sacred heart "*is the most perfect devotion,* because it leads so easily and safely to the highest perfection of union with Christ." The popular itinerant Jesuit offered a variety of means by which to achieve "affectionate union" with Christ, such as daily prayers, special devotions, and Holy Communion. As with David's manual, Weninger's book offered images of Christ's great suffering for devotees to contemplate as a means to deepen their religious experience: "Contemplate Jesus, his body mangled and covered with blood, his feet bare, a ragged purple garment thrown over his shoulders," begins the "Devotion of The Holy Way of the Cross." This imagery draws on standard iconography, but when the immigrant priest promised feelings of "unutterable love," "burning love," "inseparable love," and "untold bliss" through the practice of his various devotions, Weninger's guide struck a new high note, at least for Catholics of the time, in what has been termed "love mysticism" by medieval historians of religion.[12]

Weninger acknowledged and encouraged the devout reader's pantings, cravings, and desires "to become entirely absorbed in Him," and offered a language, as well as accepted Catholic practices, to give proper vent to these sentiments. For example, *The Sacred Heart Mission Book* provided a mock "dialogue" between Jesus and the "Immortal Soul," in which the voice of Jesus declares that he has "loved you with eternal love," while the soul humbly reciprocates: "My love is so tender, so ardent that no words can express it." The voice of Jesus then urges the seeker to "consider then, how I, the infinite God, fill you entirely, and how you live, move, and are entirely in me.... Consider how desirous I am, to draw you to me, to unite you with myself, and fill you with heavenly consolation." Weninger's dialogue between spiritual lovers was hardly unique: the image of Christ as bridegroom drew from erotic representations in Song of Songs and had long been a staple of the mystical tradition, going back to Saint Bernard of Clairvaux's popular sermons in the twelfth century.[13] But it did depart from the "sober piety" characteristic of English-speaking Catholics in the American colonies and represented a more emotional, demonstrative form of faith newly popular in the nineteenth century.[14] European mission priests reintroduced American audiences to this affective style of piety, thereby helping to spark the devotional revival in the United States.[15]

In providing step-by-step guides to deepen a believer's relationship with God, neither Reverend David nor Reverend Weninger invited an open-ended, or self-styled, spirituality among Catholic readers. Both manuals were intended to help Catholics maintain their devotion to the official church and its doctrines, and to ensure that the laity pursued sanctified, virtuous lives following their conversions. Their works followed in a long line of devotional manuals read by both Catholics and Protestants, whose increasing literacy since the sixteenth century had created enormous demand for personal guides to the practice of piety.[16] Religiously educated and trained in France and Austria, respectively, David and Weninger drew from rich stores of Catholic meditative practices, and these were received by an American audience—immigrant and native—eager to prolong their pious feelings beyond revival seasons. In this sense, American Catholics participated in a transatlantic devotional revival emanating from Europe and encouraged by Rome.[17] Although drawing on a tradition condoned by the institutional church, the widespread religious devotionalism speaks to a new preoccupation with forming close bonds with people and things outside the self in the United States at midcentury.

Poetry

Catholics' devotional turn in the nineteenth century had its counterpart among American Protestants; indeed, the reintroduction of an intense pietism by the thousands of Catholic immigrants after 1840 drew attention to some of the perceived deficits within an evangelicalism so dependent on re-vivalism for church growth. The Ohio River valley's great revivals of the early 1840s had highlighted these risks, with pastors exhausted by the demands of leading and calibrating the emotional highs during incessant gatherings and congregations besieged by the problems of rapidly increasing membership. As they did during the religious conflicts of the seventeenth century, when similarly confronted with a resurgent Catholicism, Protestants of varying sorts undertook their own kind of devotional turn after 1840 to reinvigorate believers' pious feelings.[18] Given a long-standing distrust of imagery and iconography among leading Calvinists, including North America's influen-tial minister Jonathan Edwards, as well as more liberal theologians of the nineteenth century, Protestants remained reluctant to dwell on images of the suffering Christ of the Passion—whether visual or textual—in their de-votions.[19] But they nevertheless relied on fairly formulaic images expressing hope in the redemptive power of suffering and loss in a newly popular form of religious writing, the devotional poem. The most moving imagery in this poetry evoked domestic scenes of loss and pain to draw readers into a close union with the divine. With kinship to scriptural verse and to hymns, in which the ear is privileged over the eye, a poetry of recognizably domestic scenes offered safe yet fertile ground for Protestant devotionalism.[20] Though starkly different in form and content, Catholic devotional manuals and Protestant religious poetry aspired to a similar end—diminishing the vast gulf between human and divine through earthly feelings of pain and loss.

The broad impulse to compose devotional poetry and the sheer pervasive-ness of printed verse treating sacred themes were new phenomena in Amer-ica. Protestants living in seventeenth- and eighteenth-century New England had by no means ignored the art: Anne Bradstreet and Edward Taylor, among several others, produced a substantial corpus of meditative poetry. But the re-ligious lyric, as historian David D. Hall has written, found few practitioners in Puritan enclaves, and little of this private and occasional poetry found its way into print before 1800.[21] In part, colonial printers lacked capital, and authors lacked patronage to assume the costs of publication.[22] But there also seems to have been little demand or perceived need for the widespread distribution or publication of devotional poetry. Composing his religious "meditations" exclusively for "secret devotions," the Puritan minister Edward Taylor never sought to have these poems published during his lifetime and asked that his heirs keep them private.[23]

Devotional or meditative verse also may have carried a taint of Roman Catholicism. The great English religious poets of the seventeenth century had imbibed Counter-Reformation devotional practices "strongly tinged with Jesuit influence," Louis Martz argued in 1954.[24] Robert Southwell belonged to the Society of Jesus; brought up as a Roman Catholic, John Donne remained partial to the Catholic Church despite conversion to Anglicanism; Richard Crashaw converted to Catholicism as an adult; and the poet George Herbert, though an Anglican, was influenced by Southwell and Donne. Moreover, Loyola's *Spiritual Exercises*, Fray Louis de Granada's *Book of Prayer and Meditation*, and de Sales's *Introduction to the Devout Life* all "enjoyed a considerable vogue" in seventeenth-century England.[25] It is difficult to establish this link between a resurgent Catholic spirituality and English Protestant expression as a cause of American colonists' tentative pursuit of devotional verse. At any event, the "metaphysical" poets' personal and figurative language appeared at odds with a radical Protestant vernacular tradition that prized a "plain" style conducive to "truth and utility."[26] Most famously, American Puritan compilers of the *Bay Psalm Book* (1640) explained that they "respected rather a plaine translation, then to smooth our verses with the sweetnes of any paraphrase, and soe have attended Conscience rather then Elegance, fidelity rather then poetry, in translating the hebrew words into english language, and Davids poetry into english meetre."[27] In keeping with this vigilant adherence to Scripture, only a small number of Protestants living in the North American colonies occupied themselves with poetic endeavors in the imaginative tradition of England's religious lyricists.[28]

Following metropolitan styles in the eighteenth and early nineteenth century, a new demand arose in America for printed verse after the style of Britain's popular "neoclassical" and "Augustan" poets, John Dryden and Alexander Pope in particular. Yet religious themes rarely surfaced in this "civic" poetry, for neoclassical poetry's dense, ornamental style and its allusions to ancient history and literature hardly conduced to expressions of pious emotion.[29] The earliest verse composed in the Ohio River valley drew from this classical vein. An early literary periodical, entitled *The Western Spy*, offered a standard poetry column called "The Parnassiad," and among the Valley's first volumes of published poetry were such titles as *The Odes of Horace in Cincinnati*

(1822) and *The Muse of Hesperia* (1823). As William Venable remarked in his *Beginnings of Literary Culture in the Ohio Valley,* "Pioneer poetry often went on stilts, and borrowed stilts at that."[30]

In provincial Ohio and Kentucky, religious verse composed in a self-consciously emotional style began to displace neoclassical poetic conventions in the 1830s.[31] By 1850, columns of verse, lengthy works of criticism, investigations into the psychology of poetry, and minutely detailed biographies of poets permeated the antebellum print media—daily newspapers as well as literary or religious periodicals. In Kentucky, the aggressive Whig newspaper, the *Louisville Journal,* acquired renown as an incubator of young authors and as a source for critical reviews and editorials on important authors and poetic conventions. Editor George Prentice (himself a poet of the most sentimental sort) helped to launch the national careers of Amelia Welby, Alice and Phoebe Cary, William Dean Howells, John Piatt, and William Ross Wallace.[32] These well-known authors did not limit themselves entirely to religious themes, but Prentice also nurtured a bevy of mostly female local poets who appeared favored with "the divine instinct—the heaven-sent intuition of poetry."[33] Through the 1840s and 1850s, these popular regional authors cleaved almost exclusively to religious themes in the pages of the *Louisville Journal.*

After 1840, Baptists and Methodists gave devotional verse new prominence in their magazines and newspapers. Poetry replaced, or competed with, wearying theological discussions of "The Fall of Man, and Universality of Human Depravity," "Generality and Guilt of Depravity," and "Objections to Inherent Moral Depravity Considered," to list a few of the more somber articles found in the *Western Christian Advocate* of the early 1840s.[34] Moreover, editors in the 1840s and 1850s went to unprecedented lengths in soliciting original verse, coaching would-be poets, commissioning articles about poetic traditions and styles, and investigating the lives of popular poets—living and dead. Davis Wasgatt Clark persuaded Alice Cary to provide regular contributions to *The Ladies' Repository* after she left Cincinnati for New York City in 1850. Cary and her sister Phoebe (according to recent critics, the more talented of the two) dominated the magazine's pages through the 1850s.[35] In an 1855 profile of Alice Cary, Clark remarked that readers insistently "inquire, 'Will she appear?' and 'when will she appear?'" in the pages of the magazine.[36]

Clark also nurtured untested authors who displayed unusual religious fervor. In 1856 and 1857, he carried on an extensive correspondence with a Mrs. C. P. Blair who believed it her "imperative duty to work in the vineyard of my Master as Writer." "With the beautiful rays of Truth and Light and Love I would if possible weave Garlands of Immortality, adapted to every brow," she wrote to Clark. After receiving the editor's encouragement and advice on how best to accomplish this great objective, Blair pursued her craft with zeal, producing some one hundred poems for the magazine.[37] By satisfying his readers' appetite for such poetry, Clark doubled his magazine's subscription list between 1852 and 1864.[38]

Readers' veneration for poets and poetry, editors' keen pursuit of the best verse by the most popular authors, and authors' missionary zeal in producing verse for their own and others' immortality were peculiar features of women's religious magazines such as *The Ladies' Repository*. Yet Methodist newspapers largely intended for a male reading audience, including the *Western Christian Advocate* and the *Nashville Christian Advocate* (read by Louisville's Southern Methodists after 1845), also offered two to three poems per issue. In these denominational newspapers, verse sometimes appeared on the front page, but readers expected to find poetry in a special left column on the third or fourth page following general news and special reports.[39] Some publishers of religious serials might have considered poetry convenient "filler," but most did not. Editors noted original contributions to their paper or took space to recommend an "exquisitely touching and beautiful" poem to readers.[40] Evidently, readers did not skip over the poetry column; rather, many felt emboldened to send in their own compositions. This was the case with John F. Jefferson, a shopkeeper and devout Methodist living in Louisville in the late 1850s. A close reader of the *Nashville Christian Advocate*, Jefferson began contributing poetry to the serial in 1857. Editors informed readers that Jefferson's sentimental poem "Summer," illuminating *"His blessings to us sent,"* had been written expressly "For the Nashville Christian Advocate."[41]

In the pages of religious periodicals, newspapers, and literary magazines, authors downplayed denominational differences, however much they identified with a particular church in their own lives. Nor did editors emphasize creedal distinctions in the poetry they published. In selecting verse to appear in the *Louisville Journal*, George Prentice did not discriminate between different types of Protestants—finding Episcopalian, Methodist, Universalist, and Baptist poets equally talented if not indistinguishable. Editors of denominational magazines also refused to discriminate: Alice Cary, a Universalist, appeared in Methodist and Baptist periodicals; John T. Swartz, a Cincinnati Methodist, published his poetry in Louisville's Baptist journals; George Prentice, an Episcopalian, appeared in both Baptist and Methodist journals; and evangelical editors liberally sprinkled poetry by Congregationalists and Unitarians through their journals. Editors and authors maximized their readership through such ecumenism and simplicity. They also stripped

their belief system to its barest, most essential elements in order to preserve Protestantism's emotional vitality in the face of Catholics' resurgent
pietism.[42]

Hebrew Muse

The novelty of poets' positions as religious spokespersons was betrayed by
extraordinary efforts to legitimize the genre's spiritual and prophetic importance. In the Ohio River valley, biblical scholars, ministers, critics, editors,
and authors themselves all advanced the heady argument that contemporary
poets had recovered a long-neglected tradition of lyrical verse found in the
Old Testament. The notion that parts of the Old Testament—most notably
Psalms, Song of Songs, Proverbs, and Ecclesiastes—took the form of poetry
was not new in 1840. Seventeenth-century English devotional poets had considered Psalms "the compendium *par excellence* of lyric poetry." Further, the
major English poets—John Donne, George Herbert, and others—drew on a
fairly systematic "biblical poetics theory," which found in Scripture—both the
Old and New Testaments—a storehouse of tropes, figures, symbols, allego-
ries, and typologies appropriate to a developing genre of Protestant religious
lyric.[43] Although American colonists had largely eschewed devotional verse
as a means to express their deepest spiritual sentiments, they too understood
the Hebraic psalms as metrical speech.

But the extent to which seventeenth- and eighteenth-century American
Protestants viewed the book of Psalms as a fully developed poetic (as opposed to musical) genre is unclear. Certainly by the early nineteenth century,
American evangelicals were well accustomed to viewing Isaac Watts's popular psalms and hymns—in use for public worship and private devotions since
their publication in 1708—as poetic adaptations of David's original songs. In
1801, Timothy Dwight, the Presbyterian minister and president of Yale College,
wrote of Watts: "As a poet, in writing a flowing happy stanza, familiar without
vulgarism, and elevated without affectation or obscurity, he has perhaps never
been excelled." Watts's versification of Psalms, Dwight added, "was one of those
happy thoughts which rarely occur," suggesting that biblical meter required
the smoothing hand of a modern poet to render it truly lyrical.[44] In Dwight's
interpretation, Isaac Watts was the genuine poet, not King David.

American Protestants thus came rather belatedly to the idea that the
"greater part of the Old Testament is poetry, and poetry too of a very peculiar and most impassioned kind." In 1829, Calvin Stowe had offered this
argument in his introduction to the first American edition of Bishop Robert

Lowth's *Lectures on the Sacred Poetry of the Hebrews,* a famous series of discourses delivered at Oxford University in the 1740s.[45] Stowe was twenty-seven years old and a year out of Andover Theological Seminary when his guide to Lowth's lectures appeared. The young scholar added nearly 160 pages of his own critical commentary and provided a useful preface describing the Oxfordian's contributions to biblical study. According to Stowe, Lowth had single-handedly rescued the study of Scripture from dull theologians and "uninspired interpreters" by showing that skilled poets had crafted the Bible. In "penetrat[ing] to the secret retirements of the Hebrew Muse," Stowe argued, Lowth had exposed the underlying "literary beauties of the Bible."[46] The critical commentaries and notes on Lowth established the budding biblical scholar's reputation: not long after the American edition of Lowth's *Lectures* appeared, the trustees of Lane Seminary in Cincinnati offered Stowe a professorship in sacred literature. And in the early 1830s, shortly after moving to Cincinnati, he also discovered a nonacademic audience for his lectures on the Bible as a poetic tour de force. In Cincinnati, these public addresses attracted the attentions of Harriet Beecher, who would become his wife in 1836.[47] In effect, Calvin Stowe launched his career by popularizing ideas that had been in circulation in England and the Continent for at least a century. But to American scholars and audiences, the idea that the Old Testament prophets spoke and wrote in verse beckoned an entirely new reading of sacred Scripture, as well as a new sense of poetry's spiritual import.

To American Protestant readers of the *Lectures on the Sacred Poetry of the Hebrews,* it was less important to understand Robert Lowth's technical theory of the unique "Hebrew metre," which he argued operated not through measured feet but through a structural "parallelism." Searching for a new means to express religious feeling, American readers and Lowth's popularizers latched onto the Oxford scholar's sweeping argument that poetry had served as the original language of faith: poetry, he asserted, constituted a sort of "primeval" or "universal" language "conceded to man by the favour of his Creator." This gift of poetic expression established the first means of communication between God and humans. The Old Testament, indeed, featured "poetry in its very beginning; not so much the offspring of human genius, as an emanation of heaven," which drew the ancient Hebrews into an intimate and exclusive relationship with the divine: "For this was the first and peculiar office of poetry, on the one hand to commend to the Almighty the prayers and thanksgiving of his creatures, and to celebrate his praises;—and on the other, to display to mankind the mysteries of the divine will, and the predictions of future events."[48]

Lowth made a further point that poetry operated as a mutually intelligible language between God and humanity because of its aesthetic qualities. In its beautiful and lyrical expression, biblical poetry most closely approached the "ineffable sublimity of its subject"—humankind's relationship to the divine and "precepts of virtue." Moreover, the Old Testament's lyrical beauty made humanity "more plastic to the artist's hand" (likening the prophets to sculptors) by stimulating human emotions and passions.[49] In this "plastic" state, humanity became more receptive to sacred teachings. Hence the Oxford scholar intimated that aesthetic experiences (the emotional reactions on hearing or reading beautiful language) enabled spiritual cognition, even knowledge of God. Americans reading the *Lectures* in the 1830s and 1840s might well have understood from Lowth that God made the poetically inspired soul a vehicle for conveying the divine message to humankind and that poets exercised special powers of divination. As a consequence, *Lectures on the Sacred Poetry of the Hebrews* helped legitimize poetic expression as a new religious calling.

Calvin Stowe emerged as the leading American popularizer of Lowth's ideas just as European romanticism came to full flower in the United States. Indeed, Lowth's almost century-old lectures had relevance to provincial Americans insofar as they addressed certain key romantic themes and ideas. As a historical "movement," romanticism is notoriously difficult to define.[50] Recent scholars describe the romantic movement as a late eighteenth-century revolt against Enlightenment reason. This intellectual, spiritual, and philosophical revolt addressed many subjects expressed in nearly as many new forms, but emphases on idealism, emotionalism, naturalism, and historicism were among the romantics' chief contributions to the arts.[51] Lowth's apparent recovery of a lost tradition of aesthetic as well as spiritual expression, his argument that Old Testament poetry operated on the "passions" and "affections" more than reason, and his characterization of poetry as prophetic art commended themselves to early romantics, especially one leading light— Johann Gottfried von Herder (1744–1803).[52] The philosopher-theologian Herder heralded emotion rather than reason as a vehicle for close communion with the divine, placed more ethical value on human sympathy than on scriptural injunction, and saw in poetry a powerful means to achieve closeness to God and stimulate moral behavior and human compassion. Advanced first by Lowth in the 1740s, and then by Herder in the late eighteenth century, these romantic themes eventually would become the hallmarks of American religious poetry in the 1840s and 1850s.[53]

In *The Spirit of Hebrew Poetry*, originally appearing in 1782–83 but not translated and published for an American audience until 1833, J. G. Herder reiterated Lowth's argument that God gave humans the "powers of poetical invention," as well as the "fountain of feeling" that inspired such invention. Yet more than Lowth, Herder emphasized the human, as opposed to divine, creativity reflected in Hebrew poetry, "for only human organs feel and utter the emotions and conceptions of the poet." Indeed, "in giving names to all, and ordering all from the impulse of [their] own inward feeling[s]," the Old Testament poets had produced an essentially "human book."[54]

Further, Herder discovered "the first development and existence of moral principle" in Old Testament poetry—found not in literal commandments and injunctions against specified behaviors, but rather in a moral circumstance unique to poetry. The descriptive requirements of poetry, he explained, established a reciprocity between humanity and the created world: "It is undeniable, that this sympathy, this transfer of one's self into the objects around us, and ascription . . . of our feelings to those objects with which we hold converse" fosters "compassion and benevolence" for things and people outside the poet. Here Herder circled back from the mundane to the sacred: by virtue of their descriptive powers, authors achieved kinship with the divine because poetic expression constituted an "imitation of that Divine agency, which creates, and gives form and determinativeness to the objects of its creation." Herder thus labeled poets "second Creator[s]." In consequence, Herder's *Spirit of Hebrew Poetry* delivered an early and important imprimatur for religious poets, whose claims to divinatory knowledge and emphasis on human emotions and relations as conduits to God now appeared in keeping with an estimable tradition extending back to the Psalms of David. Moreover, Herder helped transform mundane objects into proper subjects of sacred poetry.[55]

For nineteenth-century Protestants hesitant about poetry's value and legitimacy as a form of religious expression, Lowth's and Herder's arguments that the Old Testament prophets wrote and spoke in poetic meter, and that the intense human feeling evoked in poetry contained moral, even divine, import, removed any lingering prejudice against the art. If Roman Catholics and their fellow travelers in the Anglican Church had seemed peculiarly adept at the religious lyric in the modern era, now the original prophets in Scripture superseded them in poetic skill and religious fervor. After Lowth and Herder, it was possible to pass over a questionable English tradition and look directly to David, "the royal poet and musician of the Hebrews," whose "emotions and beauty and sublimity . . . constitute the soul of true poetry."[56]

By the 1840s in the Ohio River valley, Lowth's and Herder's religious-aesthetic theories had begun to seep into the evangelical public consciousness. In addition to Calvin Stowe's efforts to promote Lowth, both Old Testament experts entered the literary mainstream by way of *The Ladies' Repository*. For twenty-five years after its founding in 1843, the magazine offered a steady stream of articles on Old Testament poetry, with titles such as "The First Psalm," "Hebrew Minstrelsy," "Poetry of the Hebrews," "Hebrew Literature," "An Essay on Ancient Poetry," "Leading Characteristics of the Hebrew Language," and "Hebrew Poetry."[57] All written by men, mostly ministers, these articles regularly quoted Lowth on parallelism or excerpted Herder on the sublimity of Hebrew expression. The articles emphasized over and over that "the Bible is the most poetical of books."[58] In this judgment they also included the New Testament, but the minister-critics still accorded Old Testament prophets a special place as the original lyricists: "The Hebrew poets were permitted a near approach. They came directly to the fountain, and inhaled an inspiration that gave such compass and might to their thoughts, such elevation and perspicuity, that they poured forth a 'deep boiling torrent of genuine, holy song.'"[59] These ministers might have worried that poets from their own era—especially female authors—had begun to usurp the Bible's literary, spiritual, and ethical preeminence with their sentimental ministrations. But if some Protestant ministers imagined that female (and male) poets would feel intimidated by the models of poetic beauty and feeling offered by David, Job, and Isaiah, their articles had an opposite effect. Published side by side with contemporary religious lyrics, the ministerial literature on Hebrew poetry lent legitimacy to contemporary poet-prophets who "awaken[ed] the sense of the divine" in their audiences.[60]

Prophets

Thus in the 1840s, the Ohio River valley's authors, critics, anthologists, and reading audiences began to describe local poets as nothing less than prophetic. The most diffident authors only claimed divine endorsement for their poetic labors while others in the critical reading community heard directly "the voice of God" or "the breath of the Divinity" in contemporary verse.[61] Such assertions of poets' close union with the divine are legion in mid-nineteenth-century literature and verse. Addressing a fellow poet, Kentucky author Mattie Griffith wrote, "Souls like thine / Are sent by Heaven."[62] Likewise, a woman from Clermont County, Ohio, who published often in Cincinnati journals described her "young poet friend" as "half-divine."[63] An ode to "The Poet" in William T. Coggeshall's 1860 anthology, *The Poets and Poetry of the West,* declared that "God's seal doth like a star-flame glow" on an author's brow.[64] At a minimum, provincial Americans agreed with *Louisville Journal* editor George Prentice that poets enjoyed "one of the most beautiful gifts of God," as he wrote to Miss M. E. Wilson, a hopeful author.[65]

In a related but distinct interpretation of the poet's special expressive abilities, critics and authors asserted that poetry was the direct voice of the soul. The poet-critic William D. Gallagher claimed that the best compositions revealed "the deepest deep of Soul."[66] Yet in an important sense, authors—especially women—did not command the "Harp of the Soul," as Baptist minister and poet Sidney Dyer defined poetic expression.[67] When the soul spoke in poetry, it was "irrepressible," a spontaneous "outflowing" or "gushing."[68] Here the "soul" connoted something not entirely in the possession of the author—God had true proprietary rights over this prophetic voice. According to this view, only divine "*afflatus*" produced meaningful and beautiful poetry.[69] Ironically, it was the poet's peculiar responsibility "not to think of some thing to say."[70] Although critics often assigned this duty to women, it applied to men too.[71] The poet who apparently allowed his or her soul to speak without human interference drew praise for "genuineness" and spiritual authenticity.[72]

African American poets living in the Ohio River valley also claimed to have special powers of divination. One poet and Baptist minister from Zanesville, Ohio, Joshua Mc. C. Simpson (1820?–76), saw his work published in antislavery newspapers, including Frederick Douglass's *North Star* and William Lloyd Garrison's *Liberator* in the late 1840s and early 1850s.[73] African Americans in Cincinnati as well as Louisville were avid readers of both newspapers, so it seems almost certain that Simpson's poetry would have found exposure in these two Ohio River cities.[74] In 1854, Rev. Wallace Shelton, the longtime pastor at Cincinnati's Zion Baptist, heard a choir perform Simpson's songs in Columbus, Ohio, on the anniversary of Britain's abolition of West Indian slavery.[75] Simpson's poetry, normally performed as songs, apparently circulated widely, for in his 1874 collection he complained that "several of the songs have been re-published several times, under other names, and by other persons."[76] His poem "Away to Canada" even enjoyed some national fame: Sojourner Truth sang it at Harriet Beecher Stowe's house in Andover in the mid-1850s, and the author of *Uncle Tom's Cabin* later described "Away to Canada" as "an extraordinary lyric" in the *Atlantic Monthly.*[77]

A modest author who asked his readers to "excuse my simple figures and plain, undressed mode," Simpson understood his poetic gift as inborn, even

God-given, not the product of a formal education. "I did not trim the 'midnight lamp' to learn to compose verses, for this knowledge I have had from childhood," he explained.[78] Bound out to service as a young child, Simpson learned to write at the age of twenty-one while attending an "Abolition school" in Pike County (in southern Ohio, embracing the Scioto River) probably funded by a Cincinnati education society; making rapid progress as a scholar, he attended Oberlin College for a brief period.[79] Formal schooling quickened rather than curbed his "natural poetical endowments," for it seemed to be God's intent all along that he record slavery's inhumanity in verse. As a freeborn African American raised in Ohio, Simpson had no direct experience of slavery. Nevertheless, throughout his youth, Simpson's "heart secretly moaned all the time 'Lord what can be done for my people.'" The divine response to his question became clear: "As soon as I could write . . . a spirit of poetry, (which was always in me,) became revived, and seemed to waft before my mind horrid pictures of the condition of my people, and something seemed to say, 'Write and sing about it—you can sing what would be death to speak.'" Besides envisioning blacks' suffering as well as heroism under slavery, Simpson divined the future. He frequently saw "flashes of prophecies, pointing to events which came to pass." For example, before South Carolina's secession in 1860, three remarkable dreams told Simpson that civil war was on the horizon. Soon after these dreams, a "voice seemed to sing in the air 'O! there's warm times coming.'" From this mysterious warning, Simpson predicted, "slaves will soon throw off their yoke / And old America will smoke."[80] For both black and white authors, otherworldly visions, voices, dreams, and prophecies lent spiritual authority to their poetry.

In view of their elevated spiritual station, poets deliberately cultivated—or at least claimed—extrasensory powers in order to serve "as true / Interpreters of the Invisible."[81] As Christian poets, these authors envisioned events at Calvary and, more commonly, the appearance and condition of heaven. Yet the numerous poems depicting these scenes generally lacked precision. Reformation prohibitions against the veneration of images help to explain such haziness. Perhaps the most graphic vision of Christ's crucifixion offered by a popular regional author, Louisville poet Amelia Welby, briefly described "the rude cross where he suffered and died, / The gush of bright crimson that flowed from His side."[82] More typically, Protestant poets invoked an image of the cross representing Christ's sacrifice rather than depicting his bodily suffering, as in Phoebe Cary's "Strength of Sin": "When the soul / In agony for mercy calls, / Right in the shadow of that cross / The sunlight of His pardon falls."[83]

Other authors made it their specialty to describe "the heavenly shore" for readers, but these ethereal productions also provided scant detail.[84] Cincinnati author Rebecca S. Nichols offered a taste of God's promise to humankind in "A Vision" (1851). In it, the poet-narrator has a dream in which her "sight grew stronger, clearer, / Piercing hidden things, divine." In this transcendent state, she glimpses "a world of deathless beauty! / (Signed and sealed by HIM alone)."[85] Nichols, a devout Presbyterian, here gave only the briefest hint of the faithful Christian's future estate (although she certified its existence and essential promise). Otway Curry, a dreamy romantic who played his flute on the banks of the Ohio River, dwelled on heaven in virtually every poem. An index of his titles reveals his preoccupation: "The Eternal River," "Kingdom Come," "The Better Land," "The Great Hereafter," and "Lines of the Life to Come." Curry promised "rest" and "rejoicing" in the "boundless / Effulgence of Kingdom Come," but offered neither particulars about conditions in heaven nor precise directions on getting there in the first place.[86]

Evangelical poets proved more adept in describing feelings accompanying the experience of regeneration—especially anguish on realizing one's fallenness and joy on sensing Christ's nearness.[87] In "The New Birth," a poem by the Methodist minister Horatio N. Powers, the feeling of grace roused his senses—taste, sight, hearing, and touch—beyond limits of ordinary human comprehension. If Powers fell short of the sensual language of consummation found in Catholic devotional guides, he ably drew on the more chaste metaphor of an "embrace" to describe his physical closeness to divine bodies:

> But I have tasted something more divine.
>   I see a glory brighter than the May;
>   I hear what seraphs to each other say;
> A heavenly heart is throbbing against mine,
> And Love's warm arms around my spirit twine.
> . . . .
>
> O Savior, Jesus, it is all of Thee—
> This peace, this hope, this light, in which I see
> Thy perfect love and my infirmity.
>   All, all of thee—the guilt removed,
>   The joy that springs from being loved,
>   The faith that lives in one embrace,
>   And looks forever on thy face.

At this moment of rebirth, earthly and heavenly worlds enfold and the regenerate soul realizes the entire knowledge of Christ.[88] Midcentury poets used feelings of ardent love to describe grace because Scripture itself and Protestants' sermonic tradition offered precedent for such metaphors.[89] Evangelicals like Powers therefore cleaved to the familiar even though they tested new devotional forms in popular print.

Bonds

Some authors stretched the content of devotional poetry and explored in innovative ways the personal experience of religious belief. Although their poems stand at the outer edge of the genre in their originality, they nevertheless reveal a common core of thinking about faith as a particular kind of union between individuals and God. This poetry intently examined the nature of that bond in a quest to grasp its irreducible substance. One such poem appeared in an 1850 issue of the *Louisville Weekly Journal*, a popular serial from Prentice's newspaper enterprise. Entitled "To My Child," this poem appears to fall into sentimental formula, for it addresses the separation of a mother from her child through death.

Nothing quite identifies nineteenth-century cultural expression so much as its concern with death. This leitmotif was so ubiquitous that it invited ridicule even before the theme had fully played itself out by the end of the nineteenth century. For quite good reasons, relatively few modern scholars have wanted to read, sort, and analyze the vast quantity of religious verse permeating the era's publications. Unfortunate reasons have also constrained scholarly investigation: most prominently, a devaluation of female authorship, along with a related sense that the poetry offers little in the way of compelling or artful language.[90] Yet the poem "To My Child" reveals a wider authorial range than we have generally attributed to the genre. This particular poem hovers at the edge of disbelief far more than most elegiac expression from the era, and it questions the sufficiency of any outward expression to represent internal grief. Because the poem treats a human bond in extremis, at the moment of its dissolution, it functions well to identify ideas about religious belief at midcentury.

"To My Child" recounts a final private colloquy between a mother and her child before death severs their relationship. In each of the poem's stanzas, individual feelings clash with cultural imperatives, which the figure of the mother (speaking in the first person) finds utterly insufficient as a means to grasp her imminent loss. She refuses to cry, for example, asserting, "I will not lose the present hour in tears as weak as vain." The poem itself becomes the only vehicle by which she can communicate her great despair. The *"here"* in the following stanza therefore operates in a twofold manner: it suggests the last moments with her child, but also the intimate connection between author and reader through the poem's language:

> No grief shall mark my death-cold brow, no sorrow dim my eye,
> In bidding thee a last adieu when other eyes are by;
> But *here*, with none but God and thee to witness, let me tell
> How bleeds the heart, that seems so cold, in bidding *thee* farewell!

Put another way, the author of "To My Child" declares that she alone can assert meaning over the experience of loss ("let me tell"), with the consolations of poetry superseding any other means her culture offers to salve her pain.

Going further, the author of the poem questions divine intentions and, hence, the coherence and purpose of religious belief. With an insistence that conveys more doubt than certainty, the mother promises her child that God "*will* bless thee evermore, for He was sworn to be / 'A father to the fatherless'—then will He care for *thee*!" But this solace proves insufficient, for next comes the horrendous realization that this moment is truly their last together. Reeling from this knowledge, the subject recovers her conviction only in the last lines of the poem. In the end, she fathoms belief exclusively through the bond with her child:

> I leave thee with a breaking heart, a dry and aching eye,
> For none may know the thoughts that swell within my soul so high;
> I press thee in a last embrace—and *can* it be the last?
> Can all the love I felt for thee be but as shadows past?
>
> I have bent o'er thy little form, when cradled on my breast,
> Thy dark eye softly folded in its sweet unbroken rest,
> And my wild heart has gone above in gratitude to God,
> And I have bowed in spirit there, and kissed His chastening rod!
>
> My child! if in this breaking heart one feeling lingers still,
> Which anguish hath not changed to gall, nor wrong hath made an ill,
> It is the deep, redeeming love that fills my heart for thee,
> And forms the last link, yet unrent, between my God and me![91]

Faith, the author's harrowed "link" with God, reappears in the ability to feel (and poetically articulate) love for her child. No other theological assertion, imperative, or doctrine matters in the poem's concluding stanza. In contrast to the more conventional poem by Horatio Powers, where an "embrace" described a direct bond between a believer and a divine figure, here the only meaningful "embrace" is between a parent and a child. Divinity can only be felt by proxy. "To My Child" thereby makes powerful feeling for others the sole definition of religious belief.[92]

Although emphasizing the privacy shrouding her last moments with the dying child—"with none but God and thee to witness," "We are alone," "none may know"—the author/subject nevertheless shares the secret of her grief with the poem's audience, thus extending the province of feeling beyond herself and the child. Indeed, the author expected readers to recognize her subject's concealed anguish and anticipated that both she and her readers would find consolation in their sympathetic identification. In "acknowledg[ing] the shared devastation of affectional loss," "To My Child" hits a keynote in literary sentimentalism.[93] As a complex devotional poem, "To My Child" also reveals a cultural imperative, at midcentury, to discover the irreducible nature of humanity's relationship to the divine. "To My Child" strayed as far as it could from theology to describe a deepening sense among nineteenth-century Americans that the love or warmth expressed in human relations stood in for closeness to God.

In defining a new genre of religious expression, evangelicals of the nineteenth century revealed both nimbleness and uneasiness. Although none directly invoked the Catholic models of piety as sources of inspiration or apprehension, the authors of this devotional poetry, along with their ministerial allies in recovering a venerable tradition of the religious lyric, sensed a spiritual deficiency that they hoped to remedy. It is difficult to pinpoint exactly *why* this form of religious expression so swiftly filled the pages of evangelical publications and preoccupied authors, publishers, and readers alike, but the poetry gives evidence of a felt need among evangelicals for an additional, or alternative, means to achieve closeness to the divine. In the Ohio River valley, Roman Catholics appeared to have this in spades, with a ready-made tradition of devotional literature that local authors could draw on and infuse with new feeling. Partly in response to the appearance of a radical Catholic pietism, evangelicals demanded, and quickly created, a new way of cultivating faith legitimated by ministers and scholars yet practiced by a vast number of devotees. While the style of this devotional literature was deeply sentimental, both Catholics and Protestants taxed resources and intellectual energies to the utmost to achieve intimate knowledge of the divine.

The historical sources of the more intense forms of devotionalism among Catholics and Protestants are diverse, but in any event, adherents of both faiths sought new ways to achieve what they termed "*soul-union*" with the divine, and each valorized human feelings as the means to knowledge of

God.[94] This new emotive epistemology drew religious Americans' attention to the mundane scenes of this world, including suffering and loss and
beautiful sights and sounds. It therefore summoned a rich imagination. At
midcentury, this devotional culture sanctified human connection as the definition of faith itself, and then prized the ability to describe those relationships
in aesthetic form. It endowed individuals with the powers of insight and
description, as well as a sense of human plasticity. Fed by many powerful
historical antecedents, but recharged in the competitive religious environment of the Ohio River valley, this studied religious practice may have had a
kind of "priming" effect, inclining Americans to rethink social relationships
broadly. It was, in the very least, a hothouse environment highly conducive to
imagining and describing bonds of union. Together, Protestants and Catholics had produced a strikingly similar spiritual economy on both sides of the
Ohio River.

Part II
Black and White

CHAPTER FOUR

Separation

One of the most paradoxical and disheartening developments in U.S. history is the emergence of a virulent racism alongside the full flowering of democratic ideals after the American Revolution. The thorns of race hatred and the blooms of human equality grew together, as if mutually dependent, with sharp points violently protecting the fragile new growth of democracy among all white men, whether rich or poor. Between 1820 and 1860 Cincinnati and Louisville witnessed scenes of great brutality against African Americans while also propelling white men and their families toward greater economic and political possibilities. Cincinnati became infamous for some of the worst urban violence directed at African Americans the United States had ever seen by the early 1840s, while Louisvillians helped to usher in the horrific practice of lynching prior to the Civil War. Partly in consequence of this violence, some Cincinnatians and Louisvillians began to imagine (and construct the means for) divided destinies, where black and white lives would unfold more peaceably in separate geographical locales—or so the architects of new racially pure societies believed.

As with the Protestant and Catholic divide, in which Reformation and Counter-Reformation ideas galvanized religious partisans in the nineteenth-century Ohio River valley, ideologies unleashed by the Enlightenment brought fierce racial clashes to American cities. Ohio and Kentucky and especially their two leading cities—Cincinnati and Louisville—illuminate in stark ways the role of race in nineteenth-century American history. While hardly ignored in the literature considering race as a category of historical analysis, Ohio and Kentucky typically are relegated to the domain of "regional" history, while the study of racial ideas and practices in places like New York, Pennsylvania, South Carolina, or Virginia often stand in for a broader northern or southern, if not national, history. For their respective "sections," though, both Ohio and Kentucky offer powerful examples of the centrality of racial thinking even where the constitutional promise of freedom to all, as in Ohio, or a statutory limit on slavery's commercial expansion, as in Kentucky, would seemingly militate against the worst abuses in the name of race. As George Fredrickson observed, "It is uniquely in the West that we find the dialectical interaction between a premise of equality and an intense prejudice toward certain groups that would seem to be a precondition for the full flowering of racism as an ideology or worldview."[1]

In the context of the United States, the Northwest, particularly Ohio, adheres to this contradictory logic with a dubious distinction.[2] Carved out of the Northwest Territory, the "creation of Ohio was one of the great acts of the American Enlightenment," argues the historian Andrew R. L. Cayton, because its founders "were making a political community designed to exemplify a larger experiment in universal brotherhood." Admitted to the Union in 1803, Ohio's constitution "was remarkably democratic" in its efforts "to place power in the hands of the people's representatives." But although the constitution banned slavery outright and Ohio's framers rejected by an extremely narrow margin of one vote a provision to make suffrage a universal male right without consideration of race, the state's General Assembly made Ohio's laws increasingly hostile to its black residents through a series of "Black Laws" designed to curtail their rights, equality, and freedom before 1830.[3] In addition to supporting harsh statutory proscriptions, Ohio's white citizens waged a kind of continuous, low-grade race war against black Ohioans, occasionally and brutally erupting into hot conflict, as in Cincinnati in 1841.[4]

From its admission to the United States in 1792, Kentucky constitutionally protected slave property and the institution remained the basis of the state's greatest political power and wealth well into the 1850s, despite an increasingly diverse farming economy and growing manufacturing enterprises. Nevertheless, Kentucky's indigenous antislavery movement was the most visible, promising, and long-lived among slave states before 1850, and the legislature had passed a "nonimportation" law in 1833 banning the carrying of slaves into Kentucky for commercial sale.[5] Emancipationists in the state held out hope that the number of slaves in Kentucky would steadily diminish as a consequence of the Law of 1833 and slaveholders' profitable sale of slaves to the Deep South. Among the fifteen states in the Union in 1792, Kentucky also offered more white men the vote than any other state, and even briefly enfranchised free black men. A revision in 1799 expanded the number of direct popular elections, as did a new constitution ratified in 1850.[6] In short, Kentucky advanced white men's voting rights and popular control of government in the first half of the nineteenth century, and a vigorous, if conservative, antislavery movement gained adherents during the same period.

Yet, as in Ohio, such developments did not also entail a softening of ideas of race. Instead, most white Kentuckians—whether proslavery or antislavery— looked forward to a day when the state's black population would be forever removed from its boundaries, and indeed, in 1849, members of the state constitutional convention seriously debated the mass deportation of all free blacks from Kentucky. According to William Freehling, Kentucky's leading antislavery voices proved uniquely "entrepreneurial" when they "called on the white majority to outvote the propertied elite and to expel the black minority" in the 1840s. In this "most radical form of southern reform" for its time, Kentuckians such as Cassius Clay sought to combine white populism with a noxious racism to end slavery.[7] For their part, Kentucky's proslavery advocates predicted race warfare and miscegenation as the inevitable consequences of emancipation. Their positions on the slavery question notwithstanding, many white Kentuckians appeared to agree that a free society without slaves could not also be a racially mixed one. Thus, in their own ways, the histories of Ohio and Kentucky help bring into relief the harsh axiom that an implied equality among whites drew forth a virulent racism of exclusion in the nineteenth century. Indeed, the examples of Ohio and Kentucky might well be considered harbingers of national trends for the nineteenth century rather than provincial expressions of a theme already defined in older eastern states.

Great Highways

In Cincinnati and Louisville, African Americans—whether enslaved, free, or fugitive—established urban communities nourishing strong churches, schools, and social organizations prior to the Civil War.[8] They did so under the most trying of circumstances, as racially discriminatory laws, pseudo-scientific theories about skin color and intellectual or moral capacity, and political strife stemming from slavery all converged to create an environment inhospitable, to say the least, to black self-determination. Against a widening tide of hostility, free blacks flocked to cities like Cincinnati and Louisville for economic advancement, especially during the first two decades of the cities' commercial ascendancy in the West. Between 1820 and 1840, black migration to both Cincinnati and Louisville broadly tracked with white population patterns: during these early years, blacks' numbers quadrupled in Cincinnati and tripled in Louisville. Yet the black and white migration streams to western cities diverged in one crucial way. While white migrants to the cities drew broadly from eastern states as well as from Europe, black transplants came overwhelmingly from southern states. This was especially true for Louisville, but even in Cincinnati some 70 percent of the city's black population had been born in the South according to the 1850 census.[9] In 1860, just 6.8 percent of Cincinnati's black population came from northern states other than Ohio.[10]

For black working people as well as for white, the money to be earned from river commerce provided powerful economic incentive to move to western cities in the decades before the Civil War. Writing in 1897, some forty years after Cincinnati's and Louisville's economic primacy had passed, William Gibson recalled with mixed feelings the significance of river work for black westerners: "The great highway between Pittsburgh and New Orleans, the Ohio and Mississippi rivers, on whose bosom floated the palatial steamers loaded with the products of those valleys, and giving employment to thousands of free colored men and women, had its clouds and its sunshine." Among the "clouds" hanging over this work were the many physical dangers—boiler explosions, steamboat collisions, and the like. The work was often menial—blacks toiled mostly as unskilled laborers, crew members, and stewards on the boats. Black workers faced an additional hazard while plying southern rivers: the possibility that they might be kidnapped and sold into slavery. Yet according to Gibson, the dangers and detractions "did not deter these free men and women from contesting and contending for the right to make a living on these great highways."[11]

Among its advantages, river employment offered a degree of mobility that most African Americans did not enjoy in the antebellum period. Gibson reported that steamboat hands "would seek their pleasure" in the cities they visited and that "a large party or some amusement" usually awaited them portside, even in the Lower South.[12] Moreover, boatmen had occasions to assist fugitive slaves.[13] A plethora of court cases, newspaper accounts, and anecdotal evidence from the antebellum era documents the steamboat's significance for runaway slaves.[14] All things considered, Gibson viewed steamboat work as among the "few oases" for free black Americans in the antebellum era because of the modicum of freedom it provided and because of its remuneration. Steamboat stewards, he recalled, "were highly respected by the citizens generally, and most of them acquired property and lived comfortably in their homes." Gibson therefore dubbed the 1840s and 1850s "the golden age of steamboating . . . among the free colored men and women" of Louisville.[15]

Subject to Jim Crow laws and Ku Klux Klan violence after the Civil War, Gibson perhaps romanticized the independence afforded by early steamboat work, but his contention that river commerce employed free blacks more than most other occupations is borne out by city directories and census records from the period. According to census evidence, in 1840 and 1850, "boatman" was the most frequent employment for black men in Cincinnati and the occupation ranked among the most important for free African Americans in Louisville as well.[16] The 1860 census again reported blacks' high representation in river work, with one scholar's sample finding that steamboats employed 13.3 percent of black men but only 4.1 percent of white men living in Cincinnati. In Louisville, steamboat employment and "transport" work also remained significant for free blacks; only the categories of "laborer" and "wash woman" appeared with greater frequency among the occupations listed by free men and women in the city's 1860 census reports.[17]

The evidence also supports Gibson's contention that steamboat work provided a decent living for some blacks, especially stewards. In the 1850 census, the wealthiest free black man in Louisville, William Gilchrist, labored as a boatman. And in 1860, five of the twenty wealthiest free African Americans in Louisville worked on the river, all but one as stewards. Each reported owning real property worth between $2,000 and $4,000.[18] Some slaves hired out by their owners to work on steamboats earned enough to purchase their freedom. In 1863, a former slave in Louisville told the American Freedmen's Inquiry Commission that he had been able to save the high $2,100 purchase price for his freedom with wages earned as a steamboat steward.[19]

The initial attraction that river commerce held for blacks is indicated by a 421 percent increase in Cincinnati's African American population between 1820 and 1829. During the same period, white migration to the city increased by just 150 percent. By 1829, blacks accounted for more than 10 percent of the city's residents. This African American migration to the inland West did not go unnoticed by white racial purists. Regarding the "rapid increase of our Black population" with fear and hostility, some white Cincinnatians demanded that the city council restrict or reduce black migration in the late 1820s.[20] In response, city officials ordered Cincinnati's African Americans to comply with Ohio's dormant Black Laws, a series of decrees passed by the legislature between 1804 and 1807, requiring that black Americans register their names and pay a small fee to the township, provide certificates of their freedom to local courts, and secure a $500 bond to guarantee their "good behaviour."[21] But before officials could enforce these laws in 1829, at least half of the city's blacks decided to leave Cincinnati for Canada, a migration that accounts for their reduced census count the following year. Although prospective enforcement of the Black Laws had already persuaded many African Americans to abandon the city, white ruffians' violent attacks on black neighborhoods and homes added additional motivation.[22]

This mass exodus devastated Cincinnati's black community, and it would not be the last time that white hostility erupted in violence. At least three more riots and mob actions against black neighborhoods and institutions took place in Cincinnati before the Civil War, and the city acquired infamy for the sorry state of its race relations as a consequence. Already in 1830, David Walker's *Appeal ... to the Coloured Citizens of the World* used events in Cincinnati to make a case for resistance: "I dare you to show me a parallel of cruelties in the annals of Heathens or of Devils, with those of Ohio, Virginia, and of Georgia," Walker wrote, making no distinction between a northern free state and two southern slave states.[23]

Yet Cincinnati's close proximity to the South ensured its continuing significance for freed blacks and escaped slaves through the antebellum era. Moreover, in spite of recurring violence and white racism, the economic incentives offered by a flourishing river commerce continued to draw black Americans to settle in Cincinnati. Between 1830 and 1840, the city's black population returned to its pre-1829 numbers, and African Americans experienced a slightly improved economy. A small number of black entrepreneurs acquired substantial property holdings, and many others continued to find employment on steamboats.[24] Cincinnati therefore remained sufficiently attractive to black men and women who hoped the city would offer greater physical and economic independence than cities along the eastern seaboard or farther north. Indeed, Cincinnati's African American population remained the largest in Ohio throughout the antebellum period.

The institution of slavery distinguished black experiences in Cincinnati and Louisville. Before emancipation, slaves accounted for the vast majority of Louisville's black population. Yet demographic evidence suggests that free blacks viewed the southern city with some degree of favor. Although the free black population in Louisville remained small, it more than doubled every decade before 1850. In fact, through the antebellum era the free black population grew at a far higher rate than the enslaved population: between 1830 and 1850, the pace of growth among free blacks was almost three times that of slaves. And after 1850, the number of slaves in Louisville actually declined while the number of free blacks continued to grow, albeit only slightly. A more telling illustration of the increasing draw Louisville had for African Americans may be found in the proportion of Kentucky's free blacks who chose to live in the river city. This percentage steadily rose after 1820; by 1850, about 15 percent of Kentucky's free blacks lived in Louisville. By contrast, the percentage of Kentucky's enslaved blacks living in Louisville peaked at 2.6 percent in 1850.[25]

Free blacks and slaves mixed frequently in Louisville's urban environment. Slaves joined Louisville's independent black churches and openly attended schools operated by free blacks, an unusual arrangement in a slave state.[26] Free African Americans also labored to improve the lives of the enslaved, with an overriding concern to secure the free legal status of all black Kentuckians.

Much of this work was ad hoc and piecemeal, as circumstances allowed. For example, one wealthy black barber in the city named Washington Spradling purchased thirty-three slaves whom he promptly freed.[27] In the absence of financial resources, free blacks in Louisville often relied on organized vigilance to protect their legal status. In one instance, after traders "kidnapped" a slave about to gain his freedom and put him on a boat headed for the Deep South, the city's free blacks "hurried to the canal in crowds, singing and praying to God to stop the boat and deliver" the slave. As a consequence of this protest, Louisville authorities arrested the ship's captain and launched an investigation that established the slave's right to his freedom and "his chains were stricken off," according to William Gibson.[28] Moreover, the thousands of steamboats landing in Louisville in the 1830s and 1840s brought free blacks from all parts of the country through the city, and even the briefest of layovers provided opportunities to assist slaves in gaining their freedom or to share information about family members.

Slavery in Louisville had another distinctive feature: slaveholders in the city and surrounding countryside hired out an unusually high proportion of their slaves to individuals and businesses in Louisville. About 20 percent of all slaves in Louisville worked for someone who was not their owner in 1830; this figure had dipped only slightly by 1860, when 17 percent were hired out.[29] In 1828, the city made it illegal for slaves to make their own work and living arrangements and to set the terms of their contract without their owners' involvement—which suggests that some slaveholders provided little oversight of their hired-out slaves in the 1820s. As a consequence of this law, a large class of middlemen arose in Louisville to assist the contract negotiations between slave owners and potential employers, which included the city's large hotels, brickyards, tobacco manufacturers, and private households.[30] Nevertheless, the more lax practice of allowing slaves to contract their own labor continued into the 1850s. For example, a hired-out slave named Charlotte paid her owner a dollar a week but had little contact with him otherwise, "no more than if I didn't belong to him," she explained. With her earnings, she could "support myself and my two children and pay my house rent." Although her owner provided her family neither clothing nor medical care, she claimed to "get along very well and keep the hire paid up."[31] Not confined to agricultural or domestic labor, slaves in Louisville worked in virtually every one of the city's industries. Some labored in skilled trades, including bricklaying, carpentry, and blacksmithing. Combined with hiring out practices, Louisville's enslaved peoples arguably exercised some control over their labor and found more time to associate with free blacks.[32]

Against extraordinary obstacles—legal and political disfranchisement, work discrimination and racial prejudice, and close surveillance by slave patrols and city police—Louisville's free black population achieved a certain stability by 1850. Economic and institutional advancements, especially in the 1840s, even contributed to the formation of a "nascent middle-class community," one study argues. Although free blacks controlled only about 0.5 percent of all private wealth declared in the city's 1850 and 1860 census returns, they established an ineffaceable presence in Louisville through their churches, schools, and neighborhoods.[33] By 1860, the city's African Americans maintained about nine different churches—four of these largely independent of white control. Through the late 1840s and 1850s, free blacks operated at least five different common schools attended by both free and enslaved children in the city.[34]

Black labor helped Cincinnati and Louisville thrive as commercial centers in the Ohio River valley. African Americans in both cities also participated in the great institution-building projects of their time. They therefore demonstrated a "self-sufficiency as free people" entirely befitting the economic and political aspirations of their era, if not the longer history of the United States.[35] Rather than laud these achievements, some white Cincinnatians and Louisvillians heaped malice upon them.

Riots

The history of African Americans' determination to establish independent lives and claim citizenship rights in places like Cincinnati and Louisville can be overshadowed by the violence they faced in both urban enclaves. White mob violence directed against blacks in Cincinnati especially drew national, even international, scrutiny at the time, and today presents a powerful illustration of white northerners' deep racial antipathies before the Civil War. Taking place in 1829, 1836, and 1841, Cincinnati's three major riots against black homes, businesses, and institutions retain the capacity to shock. The exact sources of each of the riots varied, but typically combined conditions of economic stress for white laborers as well as the appearance of a particularly incendiary publication. For example, in public campaigns on the eve of the 1829 riots, the Ohio Colonization Society insisted that southern black migrants to Ohio harbored "schemes of blood and ruin" to be unleashed against northern whites at any moment.[36] The 1836 riot followed close on the heels of a provocative move by the abolitionist James Birney to publish his radical antislavery newspaper, the *Philanthropist*, out of Cincinnati. Before the city's

1841 conflicts, a new newspaper appeared touting antiblack and antiabolition-
ist sentiments to whip up racial fervor. With a telling redundancy, editors at
the *Enquirer* railed against African Americans who "grew more impudent in
impunity" as a result of their alliances with white abolitionists.[37]

The violence in all three of Cincinnati's riots went almost entirely un-
checked by white civil authorities, who fomented or exacerbated the rage
against black people and their property. In the first well-known act of mob
violence in 1829, rioters attempted a wholesale purge of Cincinnati's quite substantial black community, which stood at about 2,250, or close to 10 percent of
the entire city population. During a week of violence, in which white laborers
drew from an improvised arsenal of "huge stones" and guns, black residents
saw homes "demolished" and friends and neighbors "beat and driven through
the streets till beyond the limits" of the city. Intimidation and brutality by as
many as three hundred white rioters over seven days drove at least half of the
black population out of the city. Requesting but never receiving intervention
by police during the week, African Americans understood better than any
others the true sense of "impunity." The second major riot, in 1836, was in
fact a series of mob actions against both the publishers of the *Philanthropist*
and Cincinnati's black residents between April and July of that year. Here,
infamously, rioters smashed up the antislavery newspaper's press, tossing
its parts into the Ohio River. Wild, destructive ventures into districts with
a visible black presence followed. Two separate attacks left a neighborhood
of black homes "ransacked and destroyed" in 1836.[38]

Five years later, the final, and perhaps most astounding, of Cincinnati's
major antebellum riots took place. In contrast to the two previous examples
of mob violence, the 1841 riot may be properly termed a "race war," with
black and white Cincinnatians both armed to the teeth and prepared to kill
each other over a period of days in the late summer. When the poor man's
weaponry of "clubs, sticks, and stones" proved inadequate to the task of dis-
lodging the fifty or so black men armed with guns guarding homes from
rooftops, a mob of between seven and eight hundred white men dragged a
cannon, an "iron six-pounder . . . loaded with broiler punchings, &c." into the
street lined with black militia forces. Public officials watched as white men
fired this cannon "several times" into the heavily guarded neighborhood. The
well-organized black militia defended homes and residents through the night,
before giving way to the greater firepower and numbers of the white mob.
With martial law in force, police detained three hundred black men, but no
white men. As a consequence, the white mob rampaged unimpeded, once
again hurling dismantled pieces of the *Philanthropist*'s press into the Ohio

River "in malignant Satanic triumph," as one witness reported. More violence against black homes and businesses followed into yet another daybreak, until finally the governor of Ohio insisted, under threat of arms, that the bloodshed and destruction cease.[39]

This relentless terror—three major riots in a dozen years—would appear to ineluctably define antebellum race relations in Cincinnati. And yet, focusing too hard and too exclusively on white violence against African Americans misses a story of the emergence of a black community that nurtured and practiced "political self-respect and self-determination" by the early 1840s, even amid, or in spite of, such events. The historian Nikki M. Taylor has provided the closest, most contextual study of Cincinnati's racial violence and warns against narratives of "mass victimization." For example, Taylor situates the 1829 riot within a broader story of emigrationist sentiment among Cincinnati's African American population that preceded the violence. Black emigrationists who established the Wilberforce colony in Upper Canada in 1829 should not be viewed as desperate "refugees" from Cincinnati's violence, she argues, but rather as volitional actors who designed and executed an all-black settlement on their own terms. Although short-lived, Wilberforce served as an important symbol of black independence for a biracial abolitionist movement, just then bursting onto the national stage. And following the 1829 riot, a significant black population survived in Cincinnati, with notable spokespersons who built up "indigenous institutions"—churches, schools, and associational life—and connected local African Americans to a national civil rights movement originally inspired by events in Cincinnati. The 1836 riots took place amid this institution building, and the violence of that decade failed to stem black Cincinnatians' active work of petitioning and memorializing the Ohio legislature to end the state's legal discrimination against persons of African descent. The violence of 1836 had also thrown black and white antislavery activists into common cause and common defense. As Taylor explains, black Cincinnatians recognized in James Birney and Salmon Chase (who had stepped alone in front of one of the mobs in an effort to halt its destructive path) allies willing to risk their own lives for black freedom.[40]

This new biracial alliance strengthened Cincinnati's antislavery movement and independent black institution building—so much so that by 1841, black Cincinnati believed it had a great deal to defend. In consequence, as racial invective crossed into hysteria in local newspapers, African American men prepared for the violence certain to follow. At every reported engagement with white mobs and forces—however small or large—black men fought back.

In separate occasions during several days of rioting during the late summer of 1841, they beat off Irish rowdies, refused to hand over a black man sought by white thugs, and stabbed an assailant. More dramatically, with a black leader named Major James Wilkerson, they organized armed militia units and prepared for urban warfare by posting men "on rooftops, in alleys, and behind buildings" to protect homes and establishments on a predominantly black street. They also evacuated unarmed women and children prior to taking up their posts. In sum, this was not a cowering community, but rather one that "chose to stand [its] ground" and "overcame its fear" of white violence. And as Taylor documents, "the number of black institutions and aid societies established in the post-1841 era was unparalleled."[41]

Cincinnati's black experience cannot, then, stand as a mere emblem of racial violence for the antebellum era. Yet the converse argument, that African American perseverance in the face of severe inequity may be interpreted as evidence "that social conditions had improved," also does not appear warranted, in Taylor's view. Black Americans reasonably made Cincinnati their home because the city, for all of its extraordinary intolerance, enjoyed a mostly booming economy through the 1840s. Generally without resources or credit to purchase farms and land, and then without the legal recourse or standing to protect that property, black migrants to Ohio chose urban settings with the possibility of wage labor as more immediately reliable and usable livelihoods. Counterintuitively, Cincinnati also offered the benefit of proximity to slavery. In the 1830s, antislavery activists and visitors to the city observed that a majority of the city's African American population had once been enslaved, and that a super-majority, or two-thirds of black Cincinnatians, labored for cash wages they intended to use to purchase the freedom of others.[42] When fugitive slave Henry Bibb sought greater security at the shores of Lake Erie to prevent recapture by his Kentucky masters, he reported feeling insurmountable guilt because of the remoteness from his wife and child. In Bibb's view, his escape to such a distant locale bore the stigma of abandonment. Endangering his own hard-fought freedom, he several times returned to Cincinnati seeking a means of escape for his family. He also briefly worked as a hotel porter and bootblack in Portsmouth, another Ohio River city, to earn cash while still pursuing his family's reunification against greatly diminished odds.[43] By virtue of its border with slavery, Cincinnati—and southern Ohio generally—offered the promise of assisting those still in bondage. However tarnished by racial intolerance, the region held a grip on those driven to reunite with loved ones.

Conveyor of Slaves

In Louisville, white mob violence with the intent to purge the city of its black residents never appeared during the antebellum era. Nevertheless, psychological and physical mistreatment pervaded the African American experience in the Upper South city before the Civil War, and the era came to a horrific climax with the lynching of three black men found innocent of murder charges by a Louisville jury in 1857.[44] Although in decline in Louisville, slavery still provided weight and color to everyday experience, and the institution's lifeblood—the domestic slave trade—injected itself into the very arteries of the city. Along with Lexington, Louisville's central districts grew thick with slave traders and slave pens through the antebellum era, with some three hundred firms working in the business of buying and selling slaves in the Ohio River city by 1860. Thirty years earlier, fifty such operations had handled the trade. But the seemingly insatiable demand for enslaved labor in the cotton and sugar fields of the Lower South enticed hundreds of additional city dealers into the profitable business.[45] During the entire antebellum period, Kentucky's traders sold an estimated seventy-seven thousand slaves out of the state and into the Deep South's maw.[46] Hence, by the 1840s, white Louisvillians found themselves in a malignant kind of suspension: although a majority appeared to believe that slavery, as an institution and a human relation, failed to serve the broad commonweal, the city itself was entirely immersed in its essential functions as a conveyor of slaves to the Deep South.

White Louisvillians' deep entanglement in the violence of slavery elicited occasional soul-searching, especially in the 1840s. In the public press, moral complicity in a brutalizing institution came into uncomfortable view when individuals appeared to question the oft-asserted "mildness" of slavery in the Upper South state. On the basis of sheer repetition rather than any supportable evidence, most white Kentuckians hewed to the argument that "slavery assumes its best aspect" in their state.[47] Even Louisville's antislavery activists offered this remarkable assertion: "There is, in Kentucky generally, a determination on the part of masters to extend rather than curtail the privileges of the slave, and an unwavering resolution on the part of the public everywhere to enforce such humanity."[48] Thus when Edgar Needham, an English-born resident of Louisville and opponent of slavery, detailed "acts of the most revolting humanity" by Kentucky slaveholders to a Liberty Party convention in Cincinnati in 1845, he provoked a small firestorm. With characteristic bravado, George Prentice's *Louisville Weekly Journal* declared Needham's speech "the most damnable slander that ever malice, vanity, or folly led a man to utter," and the paper's denunciation goaded a mob into threatening Needham's personal safety.[49] Although Prentice took it as established fact that slavery was "pernicious" to Louisville's economic progress—"on this point there are not two opinions," he insisted—this loudest defender of Kentucky honor still denounced the "unjust imputations against the character of our fellow citizens."[50] That slavery, by its very nature, permitted barbarous acts seemed a wholly gratuitous and therefore insulting assertion to Prentice. Even without stringent laws protecting slaves, Kentuckians' ingrained moderation precluded abuse, in the *Journal* editor's view.

Despite his umbrage at Needham's disclosures, Prentice gave this "conspicuous" Englishman—as the *Journal* described him—print space to defend his views.[51] Needham first curried favor with the locals. Declaring himself a "fellow citizen" of Kentucky and of the Union, the opponent of slavery also offered this slight concession to male honor: "Men may be much better than their laws." But then Needham ventured into treacherous ground, proposing that Kentuckians' honor was of little moral account since "the law which establishes and sustains slavery" demanded so little from masters in protecting basic human relations, including a desire to love and care for a child, spouse, or parent. Under slavery, because such "great power must necessarily be placed in the hands of the owner or master," maltreatment was virtually assured. "The cupidity, avarice, or sensuality of most men will tempt them to act up to the very verge of the law," Needham wrote. Kentuckians therefore practiced a form of evasion when they rationalized slavery with this obfuscating double negative: because individual masters generally did not resort to "cruelty" and "misdeeds," the institution was not inherently iniquitous, as the familiar argument went. But such a calculation misapprehended the "evil" at slavery's core: its wrongs were not simply that it "retards the progress of [Kentucky's] commercial emporium" or "weakens the bonds which should ever hold the people of this Union together"—although both of those statements were true in Needham's view—but rather that its legal underpinnings gave quiet assent to violence.[52]

Needham's public scrum with Prentice's *Journal* did little to alter the constraints under which avowed opponents of slavery labored in Kentucky in the late antebellum era. Offering raw, uncensored accounts of masters' cruelty risked vehement condemnation, if not life and limb. Since general opinion in Kentucky so thoroughly shunned the powerful media strategy embraced by northern abolitionists, those seeking to delineate slavery's worst abuses simply left the state. But the problem of limits on speech went beyond acknowledging specific acts of brutality. White Kentuckians lacked the ability, or the will, to confront the moral costs of slavery. So concluded Louisville's antislavery reformers in the late 1840s. Though *"pecuniary loss or gain"* connected to slavery elicited enthusiastic, informed debate, any insinuation that "slavery be a curse, a wrong, a sin" left white Kentuckians "stupefied" and "stunned." Emancipationists grasped this debility in their advocacy efforts, and they lamented their own willingness to "palter with [the public's] religious or moral sense." An "undefined feeling of fear" prevented clear-eyed discussion of the "evil of slavery":

> We shrink from it as something which ought not to be discussed. The moment it is introduced in parlor, or office, or store, the voice drops to a low whisper, as if treason were lurking near; and when mentioned in the street, men go apart, and see that they cannot be overheard, lest they may draw upon their heads a horrible infliction.
>
> What it is we dread, we cannot define. It is before us, palpable as the sun; yet no one can clutch it. It is an airy phantom, seen by all—*felt* sensibly by all; yet not a man of us can fix it, or tell how it walks, or how it goes or on what it feeds.[53]

As "slaves" lacking freedom to discuss the "WHOLE TRUTH" of the peculiar institution, white Kentuckians endured their own "night-mare vision of horror," according to the state's most vocal antislavery activists.[54]

Any white southern man's pretensions to feelings of enslavement should generally be viewed as self-serving and inapt, if not delusional. Still, it seems important to observe that even those opposed to slavery and working for its demise believed they had failed to confront the full horror of the institution in Kentucky. Because of timidity and embarrassment, too much had gone unsaid. Louisville's emancipationists honed in on this internal failure even as the antislavery movement reached the height of its political influence in the state, and at a moment when genuine candor seemed most likely. Though antislavery leaders called upon Kentuckians' vaunted bravery as an antidote to concealment, they also suggested an ontological problem in recognizing the full scope of slavery's terror. "Though standing upon firm ground, the interest of man, and the appeal of heaven, beckoning us on, we stop, as if there were an abyss before, and death behind us," they wrote.[55] In this peculiar phrasing of the challenge facing Louisville's emancipationists, mortal fear gripped otherwise bold men. Perhaps this philosophical discussion operated as its own form of obfuscation, and white Kentuckians grasped the violence of slavery but would not speak against self-interest. In any event, whether proslavery or antislavery, white Kentuckians knowingly withheld from public discourse the nature of the violence they inflicted and witnessed.

Among Wolves and Vipers

Such reticence gave the lie to slavery's "mildness" in Kentucky. Superficially, this failing on the part of white men and women bears comparison to an insistent claim by former slaves from the region that the institution's brutality was, in some fundamental sense, unspeakable. Henry Bibb, a fugitive from Kentucky who survived the full horror of American thralldom, emphasized an inability to communicate the experience of enslavement. "Reader," he wrote, "believe me when I say, that no tongue, nor pen ever has or can express the horrors of American Slavery." Punctuating his narrative are acknowledgments of unavoidable failing, with resorts to these phrases: "No tongue nor pen can describe . . . ," "No tongue could express . . . ," "I can never describe . . . ," and "I find myself entirely unable to describe what my own feelings were at that time."[56] But for all of the shortcomings of language to convey the suffering, fear, despair, and loss generated by slavery, Bibb's narrative makes two ideas inescapably clear: slavery in Kentucky cannot be characterized as benign, and masters' ability and willingness to sell slaves southward constituted a kind of lifeblood of the United States' slave system. Kentucky slavery was indeed exceptional, Bibb suggested, but not because masters there proved less willing to use brutality in reinforcing bondage. For though Bibb's recurrent escapes and recaptures took him from Detroit to New Orleans and back again, white Kentuckians, and especially Louisville's slave traders, were the prime movers of American slavery. It is in this sense that Kentucky proved exceptional.

Born in 1815, Henry Bibb came into a harsh and early adulthood in the Bluegrass counties surrounding Louisville. Possibly the son of a master, he endured long separations from his mother while regularly hired out as a child to labor as a domestic servant. And although *"flogged up"* rather than "brought up," Bibb presents his childhood sufferings as a brief prelude to the defining events of his adulthood.[57] According to the narrative, his life first acquired purpose and direction with his marriage to a beloved and dangerously beautiful woman at the age of eighteen. Bibb appears to have been a devoted partner to his wife, Malinda, and father to their daughter, Frances, and his preeminent objective turned to obtaining their freedom and security in Canada. With a valiant determination, he pursued this end for the better part of a decade, from the time he was about twenty-two years old until the late 1840s. Hence

Bibb's narrative is less about bondage in situ than about enslavement in transit. The main nodes of his story as he moves both north and south of slavery are Cincinnati and Louisville, where he meets with slavery's ugliest aspects.

Whether in Cincinnati or Louisville, a fugitive from slavery confronted a similar peril: mobs of armed, angry white men who quickly banded together in pursuit of runaways. During a first attempt to bring his family out of slavery in 1838, "friends" betrayed Bibb in Cincinnati, where a "mob of ruffians who were willing to become the watchdogs of slaveholders, for a dram," captured Bibb. "Armed with weapons of death" and abetted by an even greater "crowd . . . with clubs to beat me back," this bloated mob "dragged [Bibb] through the streets of Cincinnati" until they reached a "justice office" also "crowded with spectators," although Bibb recalled that some of these spectators, African Americans, sought his release from the lawless rabble. In consequence, his Kentucky master quickly removed Bibb to Louisville and placed him in the hands of a notorious slave trader. When Bibb next ran away from the trader, a mob gotten together "in less than five minutes" pursued the fugitive, who eluded "twenty men running and looking in every direction" for him in Louisville. The slave trader imputed Bibb's escape to his "godliness," granting that only a supernatural "chariot of fire" could have rescued the desperate runaway from such a gauntlet. Bibb attempted another rescue of his family nearly a year later but once again met with a "mob of blood thirsty slaveholders, who had come armed with all the implements of death," although this time at a plantation in rural Trimble County where his family resided.[58] For all intents and purposes, the mobs in rural Kentucky and industrializing Cincinnati and Louisville sought the same ends: rigid control of people of color and defense of slave property, which they achieved through guns and threats of violence. Alone, Bibb faced three such mobs in less than a year.

Because Louisville's prosperity and growth did not directly rely on enslaved labor, the number of bondsmen and bondswomen in this industrializing city declined after 1840. Yet slaves remained valuable as trade commodities and as capital; in consequence, they constantly circled through the city, moving from wharves to slave pens, from outskirts to central trading firms, from jails to workhouses, from auction houses to homes, and from slave pens back to wharves again. Residents therefore knew the institution's signs and meanings, and dealers and jailers moving slaves through Louisville could anticipate, and play on, the locals' keen sense of the market. White Louisvillians also grasped all too well the human feelings animating runaways, and preyed on enslaved people's unwavering need and desire to protect family members.

Henry Bibb experienced transport and incarceration in Louisville on two separate occasions. On the first occasion, in 1838, the trader responsible for Bibb's keeping and sale in Louisville did not want to alienate potential local buyers by having the Kentucky fugitive "handcuffed" and "chained." Flogging a manacled slave through the city streets screamed caveat emptor to locals, and indicated (if it did not guarantee) auction in a distant market. Hoping for a quick sale in Louisville, though, the men guarding Bibb "gallant[ed]" him along the streets "with as much propriety as if I had been a white lady." "This was to deceive the people," Bibb understood, by concealing his proclivity for running away. Bibb went along with the ruse until he found himself alone with the trader, who was feeling ill. Breaking from his captor, Bibb lamented his plight in the friendless city: "To me," he recalled, "it was like a person entering a wilderness among wolves and vipers, blindfolded." Louisville appeared to hold no allies for him, until he "chanced to find by the way, an old man of color" who gave him food. This was the sole assistance he received while trapped in the city, hiding from his pursuers. Louisville thus pressed Bibb to the limits of his human senses, where "every nerve and muscle in my whole system was in full stretch." Though he escaped the city and even managed to meet with his wife at her master's Bedford plantation for a brief, terror-filled reunion, he elected to cross back over the Ohio River. Bibb's white pursuers understood the workings of his heart: "They well knew that my little family was the only object of attraction," so they too had headed toward the Bedford plantation after concluding Bibb had escaped the city.[59] For all of slavery's diminishing economic force in Louisville, then, white residents in the Upper South city possessed a rich knowledge of the institution's psychological violence and employed that knowledge to track its victims.

Although Bibb found safety once again in the Far North, at Lake Erie, his sense of "duty, humanity, and justice" propelled him back to Kentucky in a second effort to bring his family out of slavery. Caught at his wife's Kentucky plantation before he could execute his plan, Bibb and his family were transported to Louisville. This time, though, his captors took no risks with Bibb for the sake of appearances. With his feet awkwardly tied and his hands manacled, Bibb rode astride a horse into Louisville, accompanied by men armed with "loaded rifles." "We attracted much attention," Bibb remembered, and those initially drawn to the spectacle were rewarded with an even more grisly sight when the horse threw its captive. Bibb's body fell backward, but his tethered feet remained affixed to the startled beast. Kicked and trampled, Bibb barely survived. His trauma notwithstanding, Bibb "was then driven through the streets of the city" to Louisville's filth-ridden jail, "one of the most disagreeable places" he had ever seen up to that point. With his recovery assured, an enterprising dealer purchased Bibb and ferried him to the city's workhouse for safekeeping until he could be delivered to the New Orleans slave mart.[60]

Having endured Cincinnati's and Louisville's penal institutions, Bibb was not naive. Still, conditions at Louisville's workhouse proved beyond mortal comprehension: "The first impression which was made on my mind when I entered this place of punishment, made me think of hell, with all its terrors of torment; such as 'weeping, wailing, and gnashing of teeth,' which was then the idea that I had of the infernal regions from oral instruction." The crowds of men, both black and white, bent at "hard labor" provoked the correlation in Bibb's mind: "Some were sawing stone, some cutting stone, and others breaking stone." The particularly hellish aspect of this scene, though, drew from the heavy logs chained to inmates' legs, which prisoners dragged with them day and night. Bibb bore his chained weight around an ankle for three months. If this retrograde apparatus was not deterrent enough against escape, "high stone walls," surmounted by armed guards, encircled the prisoners and demonstrated the futility of imagining freedom. With its diverse inmate population of black slaves and white convicts, the workhouse surely knew infamy among Louisvillians for its harsh and desperate conditions.[61]

White Louisvillians also no doubt had vague, if not direct, knowledge of female slaves' fate at the hands of local traders. During his incarceration at the workhouse, Bibb's wife, Malinda, was held at a "private house" where traders satisfied their "basest purposes." Bibb described the residence as a "resort for slave trading profligates and soul drivers," suggesting that such houses were widely recognized through the city. Apparently without fear of censure from Louisville's residents, then, the dealer into whose hands Malinda and Henry Bibb had fallen wreaked havoc on the family. At his "resort," the dealer swore he would immediately sell their daughter, Frances, if Malinda did not submit to sex with him, and he then pretended to act on this vow when he "sent our child off to another part of the city." It appears that the trader raped Malinda in any event—the dealer's assertion of absolute power over the fate of the child seemed intended to add an extra charge of terror in the midst of regularized sexual violence against enslaved women. That the dealer could so easily move father, mother, and child into separate parts of the city as a means to maximize suffering suggests how complicit white Louisvillians were in the daily workings of the slave trade, even if not directly involved as dealers or owners. The dealer reunited the family for their trip to New Orleans, but in this instance, as in his other calculations, he demonstrated his well-practiced exploitation of familial duty and love. The Louisville trader understood that Henry would not attempt an escape while in transit if his wife and child were physically close. Brought together at Louisville's workhouse, then, the family was locked into a coffle along with other New Orleans–bound slaves and "marched off to the river Ohio to take passage on board the steamboat Water Witch," an apt, haunting name. Even Bibb's hardened workhouse inmates "appeared to be sorry to see us start off in this way."[62] White Louisvillians had not grown entirely inured to such scenes of misery in their city, but tolerated them anyway.

In their rough transit through Louisville, Henry and Malinda Bibb barely survived the city's several institutions supplying the nation's domestic slave trade, including jails, workhouses, hotels, and prisons dressed up as boarding-houses. But in this Upper South commercial metropolis, most slaves labored in private homes. Although to some extent shielded from the filth and terror of the city's various pens, slaves residing in their masters' homes endured other forms of violence and chaos, even among Louisville's self-conscious bourgeoisie. In the 1850s, the young scion of a very successful grocer, who counted himself among Louisville's wealthiest men, began keeping a diary of all manner of events in the city. In his late twenties when he began the personal journal, John F. Jefferson recorded his family's active engagement in Methodism and Democratic politics, and he had his finger on the pulse of the city, perhaps because of his family's busy store. As yet unmarried, Jefferson lived in his parents' well-appointed home and took pleasure in noting his mother's ongoing improvements, including the addition of new "rich" wall-paper, "magnificent" Brussels carpets, beautiful chandeliers, expensive furniture, and "gilt frame" portraits of the family. The Jefferson family appeared to be enjoying quite a nice run, despite the economic crisis of 1857–58.[63]

Not so the slaves living and working amid all this newly purchased finery. Through much of 1858, members of the white Jefferson family harbored fears that their black slaves wanted to poison them. Early in the year, "yeast powders" were discovered in the house, and with "some suspicion being excited concerning them," Jefferson's father employed a physician to examine the strange substance. Eight months later, slaves served "gympsum [*sic*] seed tea" to Jefferson's parents, and the nightshade plant took its predictable course: Jefferson's father first "grew delirious," next fell into a "raving" state, and finally wound up "entirely 'crazy'" by the early morning hours. A doctor was summoned and the patriarch recovered, but the Jefferson family slaves had indeed provoked a "considerable fuss" in the course of the year, so much so that on the first day of 1859, Jefferson's parents "threaten[ed] them with a sale if they don't do better."[64] By the spring, though, things had not improved:

while one slave had stolen money, another was pregnant by a white man, and still another woman fled, convinced as she was that the Jeffersons would follow through on their New Year's resolutions of punishment by auction. Louisville's watchmen searched for the runaway "in every direction," and the slave, named Susan, returned by nightfall, having concluded that escape was impossible. She remained recalcitrant in the eyes of the Jeffersons, and they had her whipped by the city watch four months later.[65]

Meanwhile, the Jeffersons sold the pregnant slave, Lisbah, to Mr. Artuburn, one of the city's most infamous slave dealers, whose vast business underpinned the domestic slave trade connecting the Upper South to the Lower South. Although the Jeffersons stipulated that Artuburn was not to sell Lisbah out of state, they knew that no law precluded him from doing so. John Jefferson's mother felt remorse at this likely eventuality, and the family raced to purchase her back. Still, the slave's situation remained insecure: "Father promised Mr. Artuburn that if sold her again, he (Mr. A.) should have her," John Jefferson wrote, a promise no doubt well known to Lisbah.[66] Though Louisville's domestic slaves avoided the physical toil of agricultural field labor, they still endured chaotic existences, with violence and sale as palpable threats. For their part, the Jefferson slaves regularly plotted escapes and physical harm to their owners. All of this took place in a city and at a time where the number of slaves was obviously declining, especially in relation to the number of free white immigrants taking up residence in Louisville. But that demographic truth obscures the degree to which Louisville's masters and slaves were fully enmeshed in a much larger story of slavery's expansion in the Lower South. No black Louisvillian could escape that reality.

Bloody Task

To be sure, white Louisvillians expressed ambivalence about slavery. In the 1840s and 1850s, voters elected into local office, including the mayoral seat, a number of emancipationist representatives. But countervailing forces pressed against the broad feeling among city leaders that slavery did not deserve a place in a forward-looking, ambitious industrial city. Tragic incidents in the first half of 1857 make these tensions evident. In mid-December 1856, three members of a rural Jefferson County family—a mother, her adult son, and her recently widowed daughter—were bludgeoned to death with hand axes and clubs as they slept in their simple "dog-trot" style, two-roomed log house. With the younger woman's two-year-old child apparently still living, the intruders set fire to the home, destroying evidence and making the log structure a crematorium for all four of the white victims. Within five days of the incident, four slaves from rural Jefferson and Bullitt Counties, just south and east of Louisville and in the vicinity of the crime, had been charged following the forced confession of a bondsman named Bill. According to reports, local whites found incriminating evidence, including $4.50 in cash, clothing, jewelry, and watches, at Bill's cabin.[67] Under mortal threat, Bill gave the names of accomplices during his initial confession: three other young male slaves, one just sixteen years old. Bill claimed that the four had planned to escape to Canada, one of the few aspects of his confession that seemed credible. In any event, constables and armed citizens transported the four slaves to Louisville in late December for legal proceedings and, ultimately, a trial for murder, arson, and robbery.[68]

The city and its hinterlands were already tense from reports of planned slave insurrections throughout the state, and just days before the four accused slaves arrived in the city, Louisville's mayor ordered an early curfew for slaves and outlawed all black gatherings except where local officials granted prior authorization.[69] From the slaves' first hearing, held on December 27, establishing their legal representation, through to grand jury proceedings, and ultimately a trial in May 1857, the city remained on edge. The case itself was both fascinating and revolting in the way that ghastly crimes are, and drew substantial attention from the press. But with the horrors of the brutality against the Joyce family attached to whites' inordinate fear about the potential for black violence, the safety of the accused was always in question. Large, uneasy crowds milled around the courts, and judges and deputies took additional precautions while transporting and housing the four slaves, once arresting an armed man threatening harm as the bound men moved from courtroom to jail. Adding to the anxiety surrounding the case was William Joyce, surviving son, brother, and uncle to the deceased victims, who kept up a vigilant presence in Louisville's courtrooms and in the streets. Inviting his own arrest at one point, Joyce disrupted formal proceedings by inciting onlookers to seize the accused and take them out for "burning." Although fiery retribution seemed impossible in the moment, one young man heeded Joyce's call to abandon the pretense of legal civility where slaves stood accused of murdering white women and a child. Rushing toward the accused with a knife, this young man was intercepted by Lovell H. Rousseau, a respected criminal lawyer for the three alleged accomplices. An infantry captain during the Mexican War, Rousseau would go on to become one of Kentucky's most successful and courageous Union generals during the Civil War.[70] To protect his enslaved clients, the agile soldier-cum-lawyer both stopped the knifeman and confined Joyce. He had an unusual ally in one of the masters to the accused, who drew a revolver to restore peace in the courtroom and thereby protect his enslaved property. This early incident gave indication of trouble to come.

Among other strange twists of the case, between January and May of 1857 the prosecution dropped murder charges against the slave Bill in order to lend credence to his confession and accusations against the other three slaves. But when the brief two-day trial in May concluded, the jury acquitted the three suspected accomplices of murder after just fifteen minutes of deliberation, having determined that Bill's confession and testimony could not be trusted. Because the other felony counts of robbery and arson had not yet been adjudicated, the four slaves were removed to Louisville's county jail by order of the judge. A large, threatening crowd soon gathered outside the jail, and a distraught William Joyce tried to get into the yard, admonishing guards, "Shoot—I have nothing left to live for." At Rousseau's urging, Louisville's mayor went among the angry men, trying to calm them. The crowd unsated, a man hurled a brick at the mayor, hitting him in the face. The politician fell back into the jail grounds, bloodied and delirious. Many attributed his death a few months later to this assault.[71]

But the mayor's injury was a footnote to the night's bloodshed. When armed rioters presented a loaded cannon and drew a lit cigar close to its charge, civil and police authorities assented to their demands for the four slaves. However, one of the accused, a man named Jack, had somehow acquired a razor. Before jailors could take him from the cell to hand over to the belligerent crowd, he had cut his throat, "nearly severing his head from his body." The other accused slaves met their fates at the hands of the mob, which hanged all three—even the sixteen-year-old—in the courthouse square that night. Newspapers revealed chilling details from the scene. Among them: the youngest slave had suffered ten minutes in an ill-fitting noose before finally dying; after the mob had dispersed, eager sightseers filled the courthouse yard where boys sold them pieces of the rope used to hang him.[72]

Recrimination swirled in the aftermath of this unprecedented vigilantism. Louisvillians variously blamed legal "technicalities," Know-Nothing rowdies, "riotous classes" from the city, "county people" from rural precincts, "turbulent youths," and incompetent police. They took several actions to prevent further violence: a grand jury was impaneled, committees were formed, resolutions were drawn up, and the Louisville Guards, a creaky organization hailing from the Mexican War, was deputized. Although the grand jury, with prominent Catholic layman Benedict Webb among its members, indicted fourteen rioters, including William Joyce, the accused men went free on bail following a judicial ruling citing irreconcilable evidence due to the riot's mayhem.[73] Whoever was to blame, Louisvillians had the dubious distinction of helping to usher in a new kind of violence wrought upon African Americans: lynching. Although truly a phenomenon of the Reconstruction and Jim Crow eras, white Louisvillians had committed one of earliest known lynchings in the Bluegrass State.[74]

Although the accused rioters eluded conviction and punishment by Louisville's justice system, the novelty of this form of violence and its sheer horror repulsed most white Louisvillians. Newspaper editors and civic leaders called for its repudiation, and its psychological toll on blacks, as well as some whites, was profound. Even John Jefferson, from the wealthy slaveholding family, was discomfited. He reported on the acquittal of the accused slaves and seemed incredulous that they might be "turned loose." While he apparently did not participate in the riot, Jefferson afterward "went down and saw the four lifeless bodies—3 hanging on trees and the fourth in the jail yard." The "horrid spectacle" seems to have made an impression, for Jefferson began recording violent nightmares in his journal. For example, early in 1858, he "dreamed of seeing a young man hung and after words [sic] of my being the condemned one." The dream continued with "an executioner who came to me after I was cut down and finding me standing up alive commenced cutting my heart out telling me in answer to a question that I would only suffer 5 minutes. When he commenced his bloody task, I awoke." In another dream, Jefferson watched his father "having the top of his head cut off."[75] Though it is impossible to prove that the lynching of the four enslaved men brought on Jefferson's mental disquiet, the journal entries do offer a glimpse into white Louisville's collective subconscious. However much slavery was in decline in the city, and however much slaveholders assured themselves of their greater humanity, Louisvillians could not easily deny or disregard their complicity in the institution's violence. John Jefferson registered his family's participation in a great evil, even if only elliptically. Nevertheless, Jefferson's own life-affirming activities—his journal keeping, poetry writing, revival attending, Sunday school teaching—went on mostly as usual in the late 1850s.

Colonization

Increasing violence against African Americans informed and shaped white and black Americans' decisions about one of the nineteenth century's most prominent and long-lived reform movements: the organized effort to remove black Americans—both legally free and the very recently emancipated—to West Africa. Established in 1816, the American Colonization Society (ACS) counted many friends among the United States' white political elite, including Henry Clay, Daniel Webster, and James Monroe, and these men pressed the federal government for support of a grandiose and, in the words of one historian, "unambiguously racist" scheme to remove free black people from the United States.[76] Initially, the organization abstained on the question of state-sponsored emancipation, deeming it too fraught for a national membership with widely varying purposes in colonization. In 1821, the United States compelled, by threat of violence, the creation of Liberia, a private colony administered by the ACS until declaring national independence in 1847. Formal U.S. recognition followed more than a decade later, in 1862.[77] Between 1820 and 1860, despite "halting and complicated" labors by ACS activists, some ten thousand free blacks and manumitted American slaves emigrated to Liberia in "what may have been the largest expatriation movement in American history," in the estimation of historian Eric Burin.[78]

For all of its high-profile backers and their improbable creation of a new West African state, colonization of free black Americans—let alone the enslaved population of the South—never presented a humane or realistic solution to the problem of slavery in the United States.[79] In consequence, the program drew vociferous opposition from black Americans. Asserting the manifest injustice of colonization in 1834, Kentuckian and future Liberty Party presidential candidate James G. Birney cited as evidence the "utter hostility to Liberian Emigration" among Cincinnati's free African Americans as well as black Louisvillians' united resistance: "Not one of them, so far as I am informed, has, at any time, emigrated to Liberia, or signified a wish to do so."[80] Black Americans' deep antipathy, slaveholder distrust of ACS motives, and legal and practical constraints on manumission in southern states together doomed the scheme. Yet despite the perverse illogic behind colonization as a means to end slavery, the idea of divided racial destinies held a close grip on the white imagination. Even as thoughtful an antislavery politician as Lincoln remained inexplicably committed to the idea up to the very eve of issuing the Emancipation Proclamation, which did not propose compensated emancipation or colonization, though preliminary versions of the radical wartime measure had done so.[81]

In the Ohio River valley, talk of colonization—and, at times, menacing threats of deportation—impinged on every imaginable discussion and polemic about race and the problem of slavery in the United States. The theme was so pervasive that it is nearly impossible to disentangle the colonization project from questions involving the very nature and stability of the Union itself. Partisans both for and against the scheme gave expression to their beliefs in the daily press, in periodicals of every stamp, in live debates, in church records, in common school readers, and in poetry and novels between 1830 and 1860. Though state and local organizations promoting colonization in Ohio and Kentucky often struggled to win financial support for their implausible undertaking, the scheme had a bizarre vitality outside of any realistic assessment of its likely success. For proponents, nearly every major event of the antebellum era gave justification for the project: the growth of visible free black communities in cities, the appearance of an abolitionist movement espousing racial equality in the 1830s, the reactionary southern position that slavery was fulfilling a "Divine appointment" to ensure the "conversion of the whole world to God," the widespread mob violence against African Americans in northern states, the spreading view of racial polygenesis—that is, the belief in the separate origins of black and white people—and even the "party strife" over slavery threatening to undo the federal union.[82] Colonization provided an apparent cure to, or derived new jolts of intellectual energy from, all of these momentous nineteenth-century developments. In Kentucky, where it was difficult to rally white proponents of the colonization cause around a coherent argument, plan, or even objective, the movement languished as a result of its "chameleonic quality."[83] But this quality also meant that the movement survived well past the point of its practical feasibility—usually on the cultural vapors of a pungent racism.

Despite its astounding impediments, colonization was hardly without real consequences in the Upper South. Slaveholders there proved the most amenable to the view of colonization as a benevolent movement, and more than in any other region of the country, they attempted to navigate daunting manumission laws in support of the cause. In fact, the Upper South provided "the seedbed of colonization," with Virginia's slave masters carrying out a third of all emancipations leading to emigration at the height of colonization activity and Kentucky serving as the place of origin for fully one-fifth of emancipated slaves attempting the rigors of resettlement in Africa.[84] In another, very different example of the movement's tangible consequences, border state legislators sought political dividends for espousing colonization as a solution to turmoil over slavery exacerbated by northern and southern extremists. As an amalgam of repugnant racism and a very gradual, voluntary system of emancipation, colonization seemed like a way to unify northern and border state white voters against the Democratic Party's zeal for slavery's expansion. At least this was the hope of Kentuckian Henry Clay, who served as a founding member and longtime president of the ACS as well as an architect of the opposition Whig Party.[85] The Ohio River valley colonization movements also had an international reach with the creation of a "Kentucky in Africa" and an "Ohio in Africa" in the 1840s and 1850s. Though these colonial outposts struggled to find settlers and to secure their survival within the newly independent state of Liberia, the fact that they existed at all demonstrates the power and will behind the movement in both U.S. states.

Arguably, though, colonization's most significant consequence was an increasingly hostile environment for free African Americans. Advocacy of black removal was never the exclusive province of high-minded patrons laboring among lawmakers, diplomats, church leaders, or wealthy benefactors. Elite perorations urging racial exclusion spread fast and furious through a sensational press to stoke violence, as in the 1829 riots in Cincinnati. For more than a year before the blunt physical attacks on black Cincinnatians, prominent men running the Ohio Colonization Society had issued public edicts predicting *"servile war"* and "schemes of blood and ruin" taking place not in the slaveholding states but in the free state of Ohio, where emancipated slaves would wreak vengeance on whites.[86] Such fantastical imagery, reinforced by state and local officials' legal sanction for expulsion, incited white laboring men in Cincinnati to brutalize the city's black residents.

Though professing to seek "the extension of the Redeemer's Kingdom," colonization advocates studded their appeals with harsh exclusionary rhetoric: "Do you love your country? Remove the free blacks," advised the Kentucky Colonization Society in 1829.[87] The following year's appeal repeated the same desire for a nation limited by color: free blacks "have here no home, and no country."[88] If at first colonization proponents saw free African Americans as "anomalous" because of their legal status—not enslaved, but also lacking the privileges and immunities of free citizens—and therefore subject to removal, the racial imperative behind the idea reached a dangerous pitch.[89] "You may change the condition of the negro, but you cannot change his colour," Kentucky's colonizationists insisted in 1833. "Degraded," yet without the care and management of their masters, the "wretched set" of freedmen would bring forth "an abyss of misery" and "national calamity and ruin."[90] A decade later, editors at the *Cincinnati Post and Anti-Abolitionist* opined: "Between the white and black man, there exists an inextinguishable difference" so that "the laws that would be sufficient to govern the white would not govern the negro." In consequence, they argued, "Our only safety depends upon holding them in slavery, and driving the free negroes out of the country."[91] In the late 1840s, a Kentuckian made a similar claim in only slightly less crude language: "The races are too distinct to be one in action, sympathy, and feeling, under one government." "The Ethiopian cannot change his skin," this writer offered as a summative argument for free African Americans' removal from the United States.[92] Colonization rhetoric thereby fostered an inherently dangerous and charged environment in both Ohio and Kentucky for persons of color who were deemed ineligible for national citizenship.

Prospecting for a Place

Even with these great provocations, black Cincinnatians and Louisvillians never accepted as just or reasonable the argument that only removal to Liberia would shelter them from white violence. They instead viewed such drastic measures as cause rather than cure for their sufferings. From the early 1830s, black Cincinnatians and Louisvillians shared an intense antipathy toward the Liberian project, and their opposition never flagged. In the earliest years of ACS activity in Kentucky, James G. Birney declared the idea a dead letter among Louisville's free African Americans after "a highly gifted agent, in behalf of colonization" offered a "very forcible appeal" to the city's black residents, but to "no effect."[93] Black Cincinnatians enjoyed fuller liberty to express hatred of the scheme. In fact, through the entire antebellum era, the city's black residents took concerted action each time agents for Liberian settlement alighted in Cincinnati soliciting money, emigrants, and goodwill. With a practiced vigilance, African Americans gathered in public meetings to draft resolutions in unequivocal opposition and printed them in leading newspapers in order to "disabuse the minds of our white fellow-citizens" that any free blacks held "the remotest idea of ever emigrating to Africa."[94] For example, in 1843, when an ACS agent spoke before the Union Baptist Church under false pretenses, the church sought "to publish as soon as practicable" their unambiguous resolve against any "scheme of expatriation." Their resolution stated simply: "That we detest colonization in every shape and form."[95] Though Cincinnati's black community relentlessly emphasized its unanimity against Liberian resettlement between 1830 and 1860, white advocates in the state proved obdurate. By 1849, as ACS agents lobbied state legislators for funds to support "Ohio in Africa," delegates to the State Convention of the Colored Citizens of Ohio expressed exasperation, having spent the better part of twenty years beating back the colonizationist threat: "We say once for all, to those soliciting us, that all of their appeals to us are in vain; our minds are made up to remain in the United States, and contend for our rights at all hazards."[96]

White Cincinnatians dominated the leadership of the state colonization society in the early 1850s, the same period during which Ohio's African colony foundered. Among the difficulties: native peoples were mounting "disturbances," and local chiefs insisted on supplying slaves to Brazilian and West Indian markets.[97] Potential settlers therefore faced risks of enslavement or warfare, conditions all but guaranteeing few, if any, takers. The "Colonization Committee of Correspondence for Ohio" acknowledged the dire situation but "assured" would-be donors that security issues demanded only "a few thousand dollars" and—ominously—"fortifications" for their resolution. The deeper problem, they believed, was black Ohioans' intransigence. No doubt familiar with black Cincinnatians' especial detestation of the Liberian project, the Ohio Committee reported that "opposition to Colonization has been more extended, and its agencies more perfectly systematized here than, perhaps, in any other State." ACS agents simply could not "obtain audiences" among black Ohioans, as "bitterly opposed to Liberia" as they were. Shunned from personal meetings, the lead agent had "to resort to his pen," bringing recruitment to a virtual standstill. The Colonization Committee's plea for private aid therefore registered a note of desperation. With no black settlers or state funds in immediate sight, the committee wondered, "Must all be lost for want of the ability to proceed?" The Ohio colony in Africa beckoned settlers with "territory enough, almost, for a kingdom," the group wrote hopefully, but its prospects were fast dimming for want of willing recruits.[98]

Though free blacks in Cincinnati and Louisville repudiated the premise of colonizing places like "Ohio in Africa" and "Kentucky in Africa," violence in the Ohio River border region did lead some African Americans to investigate other sites for emigration both inside and outside the United States. Nikki Taylor cautions against seeing emigration sentiment solely as a reaction to white people's deeds. Her analysis of the riots in 1829, for example, demonstrates that Cincinnati's African Americans considered moves to Haiti, Upper Canada, and Texas, among other sites, on their own terms, "in a context other than that of racial violence," and prior to white attacks on black persons and property.[99] While it would be inaccurate to characterize those joining the exodus from Cincinnati in 1829 as desperate refugees, many African Americans in the Ohio River valley embraced a kind of "come-outerism" from white society as a means of self-protection and self-sovereignty. Settled in the 1830s, Ohio's all-black farming communities reflected this separatist strain of thinking. The founders of one rural settlement in Jackson County wished to live "free from the looks of scorn and contempt" and enjoy a "perfect equality" among black householders. By 1840, there were at least eighteen such settle-ments in rural Ohio.[100]

Though black separatism appears to have diminished in the 1840s—despite the great violence manifested in Cincinnati's 1841 riot—discussion of mass emigration resumed in 1849, and surged following passage of the Fugitive Slave Law in 1850. At the 1849 meeting of the black state convention in Co-lumbus, several delegates, including a very youthful John Mercer Langston, proposed founding a black "nationality" outside of the United States. Just nineteen, not long from his boyhood terror during Cincinnati's riot of 1841, Langston argued that African Americans had "already drank too long the cup of bitterness and wo," and urged black Ohioans to "draw out from the Ameri-can government, and form a separate and independent one, enacting our own laws and regulations." He conditioned this undertaking upon "the event of universal emancipation" so as not to appear as if forsaking the enslaved. The more seasoned black leaders in attendance rejected Langston's vision, instead resolving to pursue rights in the United States. Nevertheless, the 1849 gathering provided a platform to a vocal minority in favor of separation and divided racial destinies.[101]

After passage of the Fugitive Slave Law and the Ohio Constitutional Con-vention's failure to provide for the elective franchise regardless of color in 1851, black emigrationist sentiment flared again. Black Cincinnatians renewed investigations into lands outside of the United States, including Canada, Central America, the West Indies, territories acquired from Mexico, and even—briefly and singularly—Liberia. In an unusual episode, Peter Clark, a young contemporary of John Mercer Langston also in his early twenties, reached out to Cincinnati's white colonizationists, having concluded that Liberia offered genuine promise of opportunity and freedom from debilitat-ing and unequal laws. Clark went so far as to travel to New Orleans to join some 140 emigrants venturing (as a condition of their manumission) to Ohio in Africa. But upon seeing the "dirty, little lumber schooner" carrying his fellow Liberian emigrants, he refused to board.[102] Returning to Cincinnati, Clark remained supportive of black emigration out of the United States (though not to Liberia), persuaded as he was that black and white peoples were fated to separate historical trajectories and distinctive nationhoods.

Clark arrived home just in time to participate in perhaps the most en-grossing and visible discussion of emigration held in Cincinnati during the antebellum period, conducted during the annual convention of "colored free-men of Ohio" in early 1852. What transpired at this meeting was a full airing of separatist feeling "pro and con" over the course of two days, with overflowing crowds drawn to hear carefully rendered speeches and impromptu debate. Though harsh experience in the United States seemed to justify claims of a "natural repellency between the two races," as John Mercer Langston argued to conventioneers, black Ohioans again voted overwhelmingly against any kind of emigration plan, with 36 of 45 votes in opposition.[103] Liberian schemes fared far worse among the delegates, with "only two men in the whole body [who] dared to record their vote in favor of the wicked system."[104]

Unmistakable militancy and broad internationalism characterized the convention's resolutions, but so too did a sense of deep commitment to the pursuit of rights and the full privileges of citizenship in "our native land—the land of our birth." Nevertheless, the resolutions resisted a reflexive patriotism based solely on birthright. Citizenship was also earned through sacrifice: "Because our ancestors and ourselves have contributed to the wealth, honor, liberty, prosperity and independence" of the United States, black Ohioans "claim[ed] our rights at the hands of this government."[105] Within the next year, the two tyros Clark and Langston had imbibed this view, both seeking in their own ways rights, equality, and opportunity in the United States. Aside from these few tumultuous years between 1849 and 1852, the mornings of their public careers, the two men never again considered racial separation as a condition of sovereign nationhood and full citizenship rights.

Though opposed to colonization schemes, Louisville's African Americans at times seriously considered emigration as a means to secure the safety of families. They did so in ways that might be described as an organizational movement. Facing white mobs while traveling through the United States and a witness to "misery and distress" caused by "negro-haters" in Louisville, William Gibson investigated settling in Canada, even purchasing land there. He was not alone. Gibson described a more general "exodus" from the city in the 1850s, following passage of the Fugitive Slave Law and the introduction of a state bill "to bind out all free negro children until they were of age." "This aroused the free families," who sought "freer soil" in Ohio, Michigan, Illinois, and Canada. Families "left in groups, prospecting for a place to settle," forming a kind of emigration "party." Though the bill failed, Gibson reveals a separatist impulse among the city's free blacks in the face of family threat.[106]

In 1854, the National Emigration Convention held in Cleveland drew eight delegates from Cincinnati and two from Kentucky, including Gibson. The guiding light of the convention, Martin Delany, delivered a stirring speech on the "Political Destiny of the Colored Race, on the American Continent," in which he reasoned, "Where there is no suffrage, there can neither be freedom nor safety for the disfranchised." He therefore recommended emigration to Canada. Immediately following this keynote, a leading minister among Cincinnati's African Methodists, the Reverend Augustus R. Green, "took the floor" to "eulogise" the speech, using his own "thrilling eloquence and masterly power" in commending Delany's arguments. Green and Gibson were both nominated to serve on state delegations for Delany's emigration movement.[107] Black Cincinnatians and Louisvillians thereby demonstrated their ongoing interest in divided racial destinies. But emigration seems to have appealed more as a hedge for men like Gibson and Green. Gibson ultimately remained in Louisville, a full "participant in the joys and sorrows of his people," and Reverend Green and his fellow Cincinnatians did not strike out for Canada.[108]

In the shorter term, Green confronted a modern-day public relations disaster on his return from the Cleveland convention. White colonizationists in Cincinnati appear to have interpreted Green's attendance at the Cleveland meeting as evidence of renewed potential for their Liberian cause, and overtures had already begun with the formation of a new Methodist organization dedicated to black removal from Ohio. Black Cincinnatians were outraged that Green had given the American Colonization Society even a speck of encouragement, and "a large number of the citizens of this community" demanded an "indignation meeting" at Green's Allen Chapel AME Church. Green moved quickly to limit damage to the church's reputation.[109]

In a passionate missive addressed to white Methodists displaying fresh colonization zeal but with black Cincinnatians also in mind as their audience, Allen Chapel's leaders asserted: "We as a people, desire all who are friendly to us to know that we hate and detest in our very soul" the Liberian project and the "robbers and assassins" who promoted it. Signed by twelve men, with Green as the lead signatory, the lengthy letter doubled down on this single point: colonization was "conceived in sin and brought forth in iniquity." The men's great anger at colonization's horrendous logic is worth reciting:

> Generation after generation shut up in this hell of despotism [enslaved people] groaned and prayed, and suffered and hoped until through the mercy of God . . . some by paying hundreds, and others thousands of dollars for their own souls and bodies, as well as their wives and children have stood forth, with those whom the bitter pangs of death made their masters release their hold; and some who [moved] of God with fear hath emancipated theirs. And now, those who had thus treated

you would come to you after all this, and you now being Free, would say to you, "now you shall not live on this Continent with us. You shall not buy lands, nor build houses, nor worship God in peace, nor go to any town or village to see your friends unless you will agree to go back from where we forced you hundreds of years ago in the loins of your ancestors, for you are degraded, ignorant and despised, and if you dont go willing we will unite in Church and State to make your lives so bitter that you will be glad to go."

Clear beyond doubt on the immorality of black removal, a critical question remained: had Green's warm reception of Martin Delany's Canadian emigration plans just two months earlier led to a misconstruing of black intentions, even suggesting possible harmony with colonizationist rationales? The church's leaders admitted, and regretted, as much. The men finally got to this confusion in the last lines of the letter: "As to the Cleveland Emigration Convention," they wrote, "we desire it to be well understood that when we shall by reason of wicked prejudice be forced to seek an asylum we will prefer any other than that of Liberia." In this phrasing, advertence to a future "when" suggests not an imminent migration out of the United States already in the offing, but one conditioned on a decision yet to come. Green did not forgo his general "object" in emigration: a "nationality," an "asylum," an end to "oppression." But in the here and now, Green and other influential Allen Chapel members would stay in Cincinnati.[110] To men like Green and Gibson, then, emigration appears more like a defense than a desire—a pull toward safety, an ark should one be needed. It was a reasonable hedge, but not one that the vast majority of Cincinnatians and Louisvillians pursued. By 1852, and certainly by 1854, they had debated and discussed separation thoroughly. They chose a different path: to seek full rights and the safeties and obligations of citizenship in the United States.

CHAPTER FIVE

Proximity

As much as whites' public discourse about race questioned the ability of black and white people to live together harmoniously on a plane of equality, a sufficient number of African Americans and whites grew to so depend upon members of the opposite race for their very subjective identities, physical well-being, and social standing that calls for their absolute separation could only be viewed as a certain posturing divorced from reality. Without question, calls for racial separation in Ohio and Kentucky had real consequences: some whites believed wholeheartedly in such claims and took legal, and extralegal, actions to lend credence to the view that a biracial society was an impossibility, as antiblack riots in Cincinnati appeared to attest. But beneath the roiling nineteenth-century debates over race and the white violence frequently used to reinforce both caste inequality and slavery in Ohio and Kentucky, black and white Cincinnatians and Louisvillians found it impossible to live without the assistance of the other in the competitive market economy of antebellum urban America.

Contemporaries who advocated the end of slavery imagined that the personal service accorded masters by their slaves constituted a kind of aristocratic luxury ill-befitting the democratic aspirations of most nineteenth-century white men. Few advocates of a liberal economy barring use of unfree labor appeared to fully appreciate the degree to which personal service would remain a critical component of class formation. In the new market economy of the early republic and antebellum eras, middle-class men and women, not to mention the upper echelons of society, seemed to require a host of personal services to establish and support their class standing. Menial housework, as well as more specialized labor such as dressmaking, barbering, and hairdressing, sustained middle-class and elite appearances and thereby established claims to belonging. In Louisville and Cincinnati, where ex-slaves filled the ranks of free black communities, African Americans tended to labor in service work for the growing white bourgeoisie of both cities. This pulled black household workers, barbers, hairdressers, and dressmakers into the orbit of aspiring professional men and their socially influential wives and families. In their turn, successful black entrepreneurs who catered to white patrons used their clients' professional and political clout to seek out protection and legal recognition of their property and civil rights. Such relationships were hardly on equal terms, and reformers like Frederick Douglass spoke critically of menial or service work as a means to racial advancement. Nevertheless, in Cincinnati and Louisville, a mutual desire to claim the prerogatives of their economic success—however disparate that success may have been—drew some blacks and whites into close, even dependent, relationships with members of the opposite race. Tethered together as they were to free African Americans, a significant number of middle-class and elite whites withdrew support for colonization schemes in Ohio and Kentucky as both impractical and unfair to black Louisvillians and Cincinnatians who had built homes, schools, and churches—visible communities, that is—through unstinting labor.

Caste Spirit

According to the historian Daniel Aaron, Cincinnati "had come of age" as a city fifty years after its founding in 1788 with the appearance of "slums, paupers, and class distinctions as well as societies, private clubs, literary magazines, parades, and epidemics."[1] With this urban complexity, a "caste spirit" arose in the Ohio River city, Aaron argued. A financial elite of merchants and bankers occupied the highest rung of society, followed by a professional middle class closely aligned to the elite. Below these groups, clerks and skilled workers possessed a somewhat less certain lower-middle-class standing, followed at the bottom by a transient lower class made up of semiskilled manual laborers. Such class divisions were not hard and fast, and movement up the economic ladder remained a possibility for the enterprising clerk or artisan who accumulated sufficient property.[2] But increasing wealth was not a guarantee of admission to Cincinnati's "private social coteries," noted Aaron, whose "snobbery" and embrace of "class distinctions" pressed against a more fluid market society.[3] Like Aaron, the historian and sociologist Walter Stix Glazer found real wealth and occupational inequality in Cincinnati by 1840, as well as an increasing consciousness of class divisions among contemporaries.[4] Notions of community changed as a consequence, becoming more exclusive and subjective. After 1840, Glazer wrote, "Cincinnatians came to define the community less in terms of the city's general progress and prosperity and more in terms of certain personal attitudes and forms of behavior."[5] "The moral criteria for inclusion in this community," he observed, "were never explicitly defined, but they clearly depended on a certain degree of ideological and behavioral conformity."[6] Rather than the circumstances of birth or origin, adherence to particular codes of etiquette and dress told the story of one's place in American society.

With Louisville's market transformations in antebellum decades, greater "social polarization" and class awareness also increased in the Upper South city after 1840.[7] Unlike Cincinnati, though, Louisville's merchants and bankers arguably joined white-collar professionals in creating a broader middle class, with slaveholding planters still constituting the most powerful "elite" in the Bluegrass State. Middle-class Louisvillians tried, above any other social ambitions, to distinguish themselves from the city's working classes, seeking out more exclusive neighborhoods, schools, shopping districts, and civic organizations to prove their higher status and reflect their distinctive values. As one of the city's historians has observed, "Louisville's middle class was not only aware of itself, but made every effort to perpetuate itself.[8]

Class in antebellum Cincinnati and Louisville was thus both a material phenomenon as measured by wealth and property, and a subjective experience governed by invented cultural codes. Of course, class identity in America was "never completely fixed," as Sven Beckert and Julia Rosenbaum argue in a recent study of the American bourgeoisie. Stressing the "active process of class formation," Beckert and Rosenbaum contend that social identity in America "was an extended and continually negotiated process" across and between class lines.[9] As a consequence, asserting and maintaining a class identity, especially within the more elite bourgeoisie and broader middle class, entailed a great deal of daily investment—whether in personal effort or in the outsourced labor of servants and other specialized workers. It surely goes without saying that the labor entailed in maintaining middle- and upper-class appearances and subjectivities was not at all akin to the "hard work of being poor" described by Seth Rockman in his study of working-class men and women "scraping by" in early republic Baltimore.[10] Nonetheless, in their own way, bourgeois and middle-class Americans worked terribly hard at defining, negotiating, promoting, and inhabiting their respective social groupings, and mustered every available personal and community resource in doing so.

In Cincinnati and Louisville, this meant that free African Americans were directly marshaled to advance white Americans' class and political ambitions, and not just in menial or household service. Some black entrepreneurs took advantage of whites' class strivings to carve out a profitable niche in what might be labeled skilled service work, including hairdressing, barbering, dressmaking, photography, and portrait painting.[11] In class-conscious Cincinnati and Louisville, this specialized labor garnered high wages and veered into the realm of artistry. It therefore seems important to consider the ways in which free blacks in Cincinnati and Louisville helped to invent, produce, and maintain the genteel appearances of both upper- and middle-class white Americans, and the degree to which whites living at this crossroads between slavery and freedom depended on African Americans for their very subjective identities and public appearances.

In nineteenth-century urban America, personal appearance and behavior mattered a great deal in the process of sorting out class identity and also in ascribing moral worth. Increasing geographic mobility and shifting class boundaries had produced a crisis in social relations in burgeoning American cities, where thousands of anonymous, deracinated individuals flocked to improve their economic standing. Here a nascent American middle class grew anxious to distinguish the truly respectable and genteel from insincere social upstarts. For Cincinnati in particular, "rapid socioeconomic change," the scholar Xiomara Santamarina argues, opened doors to wealthy new-comers but "also produced deep cultural anxiety" about this "*parvenu*" class: were these success stories morally bankrupt pretenders who might prey on the unsuspecting?[12] The aspiring members of a new middle class therefore devised an elaborate social coding system based on appearance, manners, and emotional display—a "visual language of gentility," in one scholar's words—in order to know whom to trust.[13] Without knowledge of individuals' past histories, urban Americans instead looked for the "sincere expression of right feelings"—that is, displays of authentic emotional connection with others—as well as genteel appearance and conduct when seeking business partners, friends, and spouses. To detect unscrupulous confidence men and women, these urbanites relied on a growing number of advice books and fashion guides to judge others' behavior—as well as to polish their own appearances. In arguing for a strict correspondence between an individual's outward appearance and inward sensibility, these advice manuals advanced an ideal of moral transparency.[14]

Refinement

It was one thing to read an advice book but quite another to implement its vision of modish appearances and conduct, however much fashion maga-zines like *Godey's Lady's Book* promoted "simple and unobtrusive" styles re-flecting a woman's inner worth and justifying her claims to respectability.[15] Although far less fussy than romantic dress and hair of the 1830s, women's fashions popular during the next two decades—labeled "Victorian" or "sen-timental" today—remained sophisticated, expensive, and time consuming to construct.[16] In Cincinnati and Louisville, African American hairdressers and dressmakers employed by white elite women, as well as barbers catering to a white male clientele, created prosperous businesses with the steady demand for their services after 1840. While "working class," these skilled black laborers enjoyed substantial prestige among other African Americans and became arbiters of style among whites. Even more, they coached, and sometimes admonished, white clients who failed to put together the whole package of genteel appearance and morally upright behavior suitable to their class aspirations.[17]

In Cincinnati and Louisville, the height of black dominance in personal services for a white clientele appears to have been around 1850, before skilled workers from Ireland, Germany, and other European countries began to compete in the dressmaking and barbering trades. At midcentury, fully 55 percent of all barbers in Louisville were African American, and it was the second most frequently listed occupation in the 1850 census after "laborer."[18] By 1860, the percentage of barbers who were black had dropped to 34 percent, but as a class they controlled far more wealth in real and personal property than any other occupational category among African Americans.[19] In 1860, census takers drew a finer picture of women's occupations; as a consequence, two hairdressers, both African American, appeared in Louisville's census for the first time, as did two dressmakers and a number of seamstresses.[20] In Cincinnati, 136 black men worked as barbers, a larger number than in any other occupation. The number of black barbers dropped to 118 by 1860 but was surpassed only by the number of African American steamboat workers. As in Louisville, the livelihoods to be made from skilled dressmaking and hairdressing drew Cincinnati's entrepreneurial black women into these occupational niches. Two black dressmakers appeared in the 1850 census, while nineteen African American women reported doing such work in 1860, along with close to one hundred skilled or semiskilled seamstresses. That same census year, four black women claimed the profession of hairdresser.

Clearly, this kind of skilled work remained exceptional for black women who were otherwise relegated to menial and physically demanding labor, such as "washerwoman," but the 1840s and 1850s did mark a departure for African Americans who now could claim their own kind of elite status based on successful enterprises catering to a white bourgeois and middle-class clientele.[21] This stands in marked contrast to Daniel Aaron's depiction of the place of black laborers prior to 1840: "At the bottom" of the economic scale, Aaron wrote, "forming a kind of lowest helot class and exploited by all, are the hated, disfranchised blacks."[22] Aaron's bleak assessment, as Nikki

Taylor has argued, does not reflect the deep sense of accomplishment many of Cincinnati's African Americans expressed after 1841, when they made a concerted "decision to stand and fight" for homes, schools, churches, and fledgling businesses, which they believed offered some reasonable hope of individual upward mobility and community well-being.[23]

After 1840, the most successful of Cincinnati's and Louisville's black businesses, and the source of charitable underwriting for churches and schools, were barbershops serving white male customers. Despite the service nature of the work, barbering, along with women's hairdressing and dressmaking, potentially offered African Americans steady incomes, as well as a measure of respectability.[24] In the two decades before the Civil War, Louisville's barbers were consistently among the top black wage earners, with two barbers alone owning the greatest property holdings in 1860, amounting to a combined value of $36,450.[25] In 1850, twenty-one black barbers in Cincinnati reported real estate worth over $50,000, and in 1860, a larger number of forty-three barbers still held onto real and personal property worth some $48,000, despite new competition from European immigrants.[26] Dressmakers and hairdressers were among the city's wealthiest African American women, with one dressmaker owning $2,000 in property and Eliza Potter, the city's most well-known hairdresser by virtue of her skill and the publication of a revealing professional autobiography, had an estate valued at $2,400. These service occupations were by no means guarantees of wealth, and a number of African American barbers, hairdressers, and dressmakers all earned considerably less than their highest-paid peers, but until the 1860s, African Americans maintained a professional monopoly in these fields. Those black Americans working in personal services fared much better economically than their unskilled compatriots and ultimately formed a middle-class nucleus for Cincinnati's and Louisville's African American communities.[27]

For the urban Ohio River valley, the richest source of evidence about African Americans' personal service work derives from Eliza Potter's singular autobiography, *A Hairdresser's Experience in High Life*, published in Cincinnati in 1859. Born in New York, Potter moved to Cincinnati as a young woman in 1834. She worked as a child's nurse in several wealthy white households and accompanied one family to Paris in 1841. After a dispute over wages, Potter left the family to learn the art of hairdressing. Returning to the United States after traveling and working in both France and England, she built a successful career dressing wealthy clients whom she dubbed "our aristocracy."[28] While maintaining a home in Cincinnati, Potter traveled widely—to Saratoga, New Orleans, Memphis, and New York City—earning her living.

She eventually settled in Cincinnati in the 1840s, where she contributed to humanitarian projects, including the building and running of an orphanage for black children.[29]

Skilled in her profession as a hairdresser, Potter gained access to the private dressing rooms of Cincinnati's most elite women. There, Potter established white bourgeois women's claims to beauty and instructed them in the style of femininity appropriate to their upper-class status. She was emphatic on this point: but for her labors, the entire facade of white women's beauty might well fall to pieces. As evidence, she offered this delicious bit of gossip: the "most beautiful" woman among the exclusive social set at Saratoga, Potter revealed, "was certainly the ugliest woman I ever saw, in *undress*."[30] The private boudoir was a place of physical transformation managed by professional women like Potter, and *A Hairdresser's Experience in High Life* reminds readers of her clients' dependence on her for their stylish appearances.[31] But Potter's occupation entailed much more than combing and setting hair or pulling together a fashionable look for day promenading and fancy balls. She rather aimed at the moral education of her clients, women who frequently lost sight of genuine human worth and respectability in their "anxious" quest "to get into a circle they considered a little higher than they occupied." To her disgust, status-seeking women would "crouch and bend, wire in and out, to get in" to ever more exclusive society.[32] As Potter reflected on her career in *A Hairdresser's Experience in High Life*, her real calling was to instruct troubled and hypocritical clients in the tenets of true gentility.[33]

Potter therefore did not pride herself on mere emulation of well-bred white Americans' refined standards. Early portions of *A Hairdresser's Experience in High Life* described her extended stays in Paris and London. In France she attended the Count of Paris's christening and the Duke of Orleans's funeral; she walked through exquisite gardens in Paris and Versailles; she attended "concerts, balls, hippodromes, theaters, operas, and *fetes champetre*, without number." She learned French. In England, Potter saw Prince Albert "lay the corner-stone of the Royal Exchange," participated in services at Saint Paul's Church, and witnessed the baptism of the Prince of Wales.[34] These experiences allowed Potter to trump most white Americans' social breeding by suggesting that she had learned gentility from its original practitioners: European nobility. Back in the United States, Potter deployed the polished manners and etiquette demanded in high society so well that she patrolled the borders of gentility herself, securing invitations for favored clients to parties and exposing others' violations of genteel codes.[35] In her autobiography, Potter stands as the genuine knowledge broker and white women as her undisciplined, coarsened students. "I feel sometimes like a lily in the midst of many poisonous weeds," she rued.[36]

Potter boasted, moreover, that she might well outshine white women in beauty and fashion—and hence in a certain kind of power—if she chose to do so. After a railroad fire destroyed her trunks while en route to Saratoga, Potter sought reimbursement for her expensive clothing. The railroad's officials "seemed all perfectly astonished at the list of my clothes," she wrote: "Mr. F. was aghast at the idea of my paying thirty-five dollars for a moire antique dress, and said his wife never had a dress cost so much. . . . [W]hen Mr. F. came, on the list, to a velvet basquine trimmed with deep fringe, he seemed to think it was an impossibility. . . . One of them seemed quite horrified at the very idea of my having ten silk dresses with me; but it afforded me a good deal of pleasure to let him know I had as many more at home." Concluding that these "underlings" would not offer her the settlement she deserved, Potter determined to see the railroad's president. Upon gaining entrance to his office, she "found him a perfect gentleman, in every sense of the word, and he seemed to wish to do what was right." She left his office with a fair settlement, hoping that the officials would "remember it is not the dog that is chained up the tightest, and makes the most noise, [that] does the most biting." Potter used artful diplomacy to make her way through a largely white social world: skilled in manipulating the signs of gentility and fluent in its discourse, she seldom failed to accomplish her goals when dealing with polite men and women. While Potter rejected invidious distinctions based on either race or class, she nevertheless placed enormous stock in courteous behavior as a salve for her society's ills, including slavery, giving civility nearly equal billing with Christian belief: "I like every person . . . who treat all people right, regardless of nation, station, or color; and all men and women who love their Redeemer." "Manners and principle" constituted her uncomplicated recipe for social order and harmony.[37] At least in her autobiography, she does not seem to consider whether poverty precluded participation in a social contract based, at least in part, on a particular style of behavior and appearance.

Still, Potter was a working woman, an entrepreneur in the nation's early fashion and beauty industry, and she took pride in her labor. This afforded her a certain authority to critique her female employers, whose lack of meaningful activity generated unique forms of misery. Although nineteenth-century sentimentalists typically cast the poor as the most deserving recipients of pity and compassion, Potter found an equal quotient of suffering among the rich. As she explained, "My avocation calls me into the upper classes of society almost exclusively; and there reign as many elements of misery as the world can produce. No one need go into alleys to hunt up wretchedness; they can find it in perfection among the rich and fashionable of every land and nation." With privileged access to private boudoirs, Potter discovered plenty of characters deserving of her pity. She witnessed domestic abuse, criminality, mental illness, debauchery, avariciousness, and sheer stupidity. For the victims of these misfortunes and perfidies, Potter professed genuine sympathy. When an adulterous husband committed his wife—who was also Potter's client—to an insane asylum, Potter "burst into heartfelt tears, and . . . wept freely." "I never shall forget her look, should I live a century," she wrote.[38] By weeping for the suffering rich, Potter reversed the sentimental codes of feeling. This reversal reinforced her most poignant argument: white women depended on Potter for their sense of well-being and worth far more than she on them.

To what degree did her clients and, by extension, the reading public, accept the claim of their dependence? Her clients, of course, paid her well, called on her night and day for her services, and frequently relied on her to gain entrée to higher social circles. These women implicitly understood their dependence on Potter for their gentility, beauty, and social identity. As for the broader public, a remarkable editorial exchange in the city's daily newspapers debating the merits of *A Hairdresser's Experience in High Life* allows insight into public reception of Potter's claims. Carried on over four days following the book's publication, the vituperative debate—with one editor lauding the narrative's "astonishingly acute insight" and the other dismissing it as the shoddy work of an "incompetent and vulgar person"— displayed agreement on one central point: Potter had demystified beauty's power.[39] "Before her graphic narrative," one sympathetic editor wrote, "as before the spear of Ithuriel, the illusions that becloud the common fancy, disappear like dew before the orb of day; the aroma of divinity with which, aided by imagination, art, French fabrics and perfumery, we are in the habit of investing the lovely creatures in whose sweet faces all the virtues seem to be reflected, is dissipated to return no more forever."[40] It was clear, wrote the *Daily Gazette*'s editor, that Potter was the "power behind the throne" of the city's self-appointed aristocracy and the source of its enchanting beauty.[41] A harsh and unyielding view of *A Hairdresser's Experience in High Life* appeared in the *Daily Commercial*, which attacked Potter as an "African Abigail" and her book as so much "silly and egregious trash." In Potter's regrettable "blazoning [of] private relations to the world, we are forced to take note of [her book] as an impertinence and an imposition." This editor did not generally dispute the veracity of Potter's claims, only that her book "amounted to a wanton violation" for having exposed "private" affairs to a scandal-seeking audience. Taken as a whole, the editorial debate lays bare a public recognition of the artifice of white femininity. Yet that a black woman was so obviously and centrally "behind the scenes" in generating white women's beauty and social influence was a point taken with no little controversy. Potter's own claims to respectability were thus impugned by the *Daily Commercial*. Labeling her an "impudent pretender," the paper's editor takes Potter to task for her imagining more than a purely service role for herself: "To have been elevated to the high honor of dressing a lady's hair, is here made a license for publicly assuming the office of the arbiter of her character, the critic [of] her person, and the censor of her morals." Potter failed to recognize her "place" and true dependence on white women for her position, and more fundamentally, she lacked the right to determine the nature of her own labor, according to the *Daily Commercial*.[42] That Potter had earned enough wealth to place her squarely within the middle, if not upper-middle class well before publishing her controversial book in 1859 seemed to contradict this point. Whether or not she anticipated such a backlash in publishing *A Hairdresser's Experience in High Life*, Potter apparently felt secure enough in her indispensability to white women's beauty project to offer a revealing portrait of her employers' dependence on her for their appearance and prestige.

While less visible today than Eliza Potter, Cincinnati's and Louisville's black barbers enjoyed local renown as the most prominent and wealthy men of their day, and community histories from the second half of the nineteenth century detailed the enormous financial, legal, and social contributions of these men toward the building of schools, churches, and other voluntary organizations before the Civil War. As service workers catering to a white clientele, they endured scorn from men like Frederick Douglass who were at the forefront of the abolitionist and civil rights movements of the nineteenth century. Yet for men who hoped to provide a modicum of a living for their families, and with little realistic hope for paths into more independent professions or skilled crafts, the barbering trade proved something of a boon, especially in the Upper South. In this regard, Cincinnati looks more like an Upper South city than a typical northern metropolis such as Philadelphia, New York, or Boston. With negligible competition from whites, black barbers fostered a certain trade protectionism, and they made the most of the economic opportunity.[43] Recognizing the powerful class forces at work in the cities, with appearance and deportment rather than birth used as markers of status, barbers became skilled practitioners of the genteel arts and, like Eliza Potter, instructed white Americans in the fashions appropriate to their social class.

With their virtual monopoly on the business of male shaving and grooming, African American men invented both "first-class" barbershops as well as commercial bathhouses, thus setting standards for middle- and upper-class men's habits of personal care.[44]

As with Eliza Potter's hairdressing, far more than simple grooming took place in barbering establishments in Louisville and Cincinnati. A distinctive kind of human exchange took place here, with black barbers subtly teaching white men genteel social arts and extending the reach of respectability to include African Americans. Beginning in 1840, John Mercer Langston, then just eleven years old, spent a little over two years boarding at the homes of Cincinnati's most prominent and wealthy barbers. The son of a Virginia planter and his enslaved mistress, Langston was orphaned at the age of four. Friends of his father, as well as Langston's two older brothers, wanted to ensure John's formal education, and so the young boy was sent to Cincinnati to attend a rigorous school run by two white "men of high scholarly attainments" for children of color at the city's leading black Baptist church.[45] While distinguishing himself at the school and earning a spot at Oberlin College, Langston worked every Saturday at the barbershop of William W. Watson, one of the city's wealthiest black men.[46] Langston considered his time at Watson's barbershop and bathhouse nearly equal in importance to the formal schooling he received in Cincinnati. Gaining an appreciation of business acumen and untiring effort during long workdays lasting even until midnight, he also came to understand the far-reaching nature of "service" work. Conducting a business "upon the highest moral principles," Watson's enterprises stood as models of "perfect order and decorum" that elicited clients' respect. Beyond earning white men's esteem, Watson's businesses wrought a subtle psychological transformation among clients: "Every customer and visitor," Langston recalled, "was entirely pleased and won" by the men laboring in the shops. From Langston's perspective, this ability to draw out clients' sense of well-being was the most significant work accomplished by Watson and his employees, and it achieved a double end: while demonstrating African Americans' keen understanding of good manners and fashionable taste, the barbershops softened white men's sense of racial superiority. Almost incidentally, Langston noted that the businesses' ostensible purpose, barbering, "was done in the most skillful and satisfactory manner."[47]

To the youthful Langston, barbering did not, of necessity, demand ingratiating or subservient behavior on the part of black men toward their white clients. Instead, Langston observed that a combined "spirit of accommodation, politeness and industry" yielded significant pecuniary rewards for black barbers.[48] Attached here to middle-class practices of diligent labor, genteel values offered a path to upward mobility. In no way demeaning, hard work in his enterprises allowed William Watson, a former slave, to create a refined life for his family on par with any upper-class white citizen. As Langston recalled, Watson's "pleasant and attractive" home "was one to whose well-furnished and pleasant rooms and parlors, the very best and most highly educated and cultured young colored persons were wont to come; and where, by reason of the generous hospitality and kindness of the whole household, they were always at ease." Respectable men like Watson created "wholly agreeable" homes and businesses in which polite values amplified every visitor's sense of self-worth. Home and work were therefore extensions of the same genteel values embodied by the thriving entrepreneur. At least here, Cincinnati in 1840 presented an ideal world to the young Langston, one in which black "families possessing a reasonable amount of means . . . bore themselves seemingly in consciousness of their personal dignity and social worth."[49] Middle-class African Americans exemplified these desirable traits, and in patronizing businesses such as Watson's, white men gained an appreciation for black respectability. They were also compelled to practice civility in a new kind of interracial setting designed by African Americans for the mutual benefit of client and proprietor.

Even a young John Mercer Langston very well grasped that the world outside Watson's barbershop was a menacing one, having survived Cincinnati's 1841 "race war," as Nikki Taylor has labeled the several days and nights of violent attacks by some seven or eight hundred white rioters against African Americans.[50] Overhearing that a hastily assembled white militia was at work seizing and detaining *all* of the city's black men, Langston ran to find his older brother Gideon Q. Langston, also a respected barber with his own shop, to warn him of the impending arrests. A chilling scene in Langston's autobiography describes the boy's desperate race to his brother: with white officers hard on his heels and "ordering him to stop," Langston "ran with all his might" across an open bridge toward a hidden entrance into his brother's business. Once inside the "fortified" barbershop, he immediately fainted, "as if dead." Writing more than a half century later, Langston reflected that the "horrid character" of Cincinnati's racial conflicts had "forever [stood] impressed upon the memory of the lad who witnessed, as he was terrified by them!"[51]

In celebrating black-owned enterprises as bright spots in an otherwise "malignant" world, Langston may have diminished the racial strain within Cincinnati's barbershops, where "unspoken resentments and barely concealed snobbery float[ed] in the background," as one historian has characterized the atmosphere surrounding black service work. Because black barbers "had to project a cheerful subservience and repress any anger they felt over how they were treated," historian Douglas W. Bristol writes, the special nature of personal service work "magnified their experience of racism."[52] But Langston's portrait of Cincinnati's African American businesses reinforces Bristol's broader argument that opportunities for black independent proprietorship countered the menial aspects of barbering and, further, that the wealth and influence accorded black barbers should not go unheeded because earned amid such unequal circumstances. Until 1860 in the Upper South, barbering provided one of the surest routes to economic independence and, in some instances, to considerable personal wealth, which helped to foster the development of Cincinnati's and Louisville's nascent black middle class.[53] Along with hairdressing and other skilled service work, barbering provided another sort of satisfaction: grudging recognition on the part of some white patrons that their personal sense of self as well as class standing depended on African American artistry, skill, and refinement, a recognition evidenced by whites' willingness to make the work lucrative.

Nevertheless, black barbers appear to have viewed their work in instrumentalist terms: their livelihoods provided for a greater good, which was their families' and communities' well-being and improvement. Barbers overwhelmingly sent their children to primary schools, which, at the time, were privately funded by wealthier African Americans, since any public monies supported schools for white children only.[54] Black barbers' educational aspirations for their children indicate that they wanted to see the next generation possess a wider range of economic opportunities, and in this ambition they proved successful. John Mercer Langston's experience reinforces this point. Although boarding among prominent barbers and with an older brother in the same field, Langston was carefully groomed for college by the black men in his life. He would graduate from Oberlin College, study law, and become Ohio's first African American lawyer in 1854.

African Americans who pioneered other fields of work in close relationship with whites derived more personal satisfaction from the inherent artistry and independence of their professions. James Presley Ball, a photographer, and Robert S. Duncanson, a painter, both established successful careers in antebellum Cincinnati catering to white patrons, yet each left behind a substantial body of work demonstrating their creative talents as well as a sense of pride in their respective enterprises. As with the barbering trade, the powerful class aspirations of white Americans—whether upper or middle class—lent black artists and artisans openings to practice their craft. "Ball's

Great Daguerrean Gallery of the West," as it was known, met with remarkable economic success by using the latest technology in photography as well as creating a new kind of commercial studio to elicit and display his clients' middle-class status in paper prints known as *cartes de visite*, which could be easily reproduced and circulated.[55] Duncanson, a landscape painter, benefited from and made use of Cincinnatians' civic ambitions to advance his artistic career.[56] Boosters who sought to make Cincinnati the leading commercial and industrial city of the Midwest patronized the arts in a bid to demonstrate the region's elevated cultural sensibilities, and Duncanson's highly stylized works with literary themes delivered a certain cachet.

White Cincinnatians depended on Ball and Duncanson to envision, create, and represent their respectability. They therefore paid respectable sums for the men's services. Ball's strategies to capture his patrons' class status photographically were sophisticated and labor intensive, and they reflect his familiarity with the most advanced trade practices. In 1851, Ball opened his second photography studio in Cincinnati, having already achieved success with a small business opened just two years earlier.[57] The second studio proved something of a visual marvel, drawing extensive attention in a high-toned literary magazine published out of Boston, *Gleason's Pictorial Drawing-Room Companion*, in 1854. Occupying several floors of a large building, Ball's new enterprise offered fantastic attractions in his "great gallery," where the goddesses of Poesy, Music, Science, Religion, Purity, and Beauty graced the walls and ceiling. Aside from the *cartes de visite* patrons might ultimately purchase, the "delicately drawn, and very beautiful" goddess of Purity, with "her spotless hands press[ing] a dove to her heaving bosom, with whose sinless spirit she is now communing," might alone have been worth a visit. "From her angel face," the magazine profile went on, "the expression of every evil thought is driven." A stunning Venus appeared on the ceiling, "recumbent on a splendid throne," with seven cupids surrounding "the blooming goddess" and the three graces "adorning her noble person." Robert Duncanson's landscapes also hung on the gallery's walls, and with modish furniture and carpet, Ball's gallery "present[ed] you a scene replete with elegance and beauty." "To cap the climax," a musician played a "noble piano," according to *Gleason's*.[58] In this Sistine Chapel of American middle-class tastes, Ball placed his patrons in the most elevating atmosphere in order to elicit a similarly poised and elegant appearance from his sitters once before the camera.[59] The gallery also established Ball's own proficiency in gentility, thereby gaining the confidence of white clients who would soon have to relinquish control over their image to a relative stranger.

With his patrons at ease, having basked in the gallery's elegance, Ball next ushered them into an "operating room," where photographers closely studied the visage and body of their sitters in order to place them at the greatest advantage.[60] Here the photographer employed a number of props, such as pedestals, curtains, chairs, and balustrades, and what was known as a "posing stand," a device used to hold neck and body in an upright position during long exposure times, to situate patrons in the constrained yet gracious stances characteristic of Ball's work. The men employed by Ball thus made a number of calculations and judgments about the white patrons they needed to photograph, and they could only facilitate the presentation of class status and individual character with an expert knowledge of the conventions of middle-class culture. J. P. Ball and his employees also necessarily touched, arranged, smoothed, and disciplined white bodies, according them a respectability intended to fulfill their clients' class pretensions.[61] Because Ball's studio proved so popular, his photography codified a certain style of middle-class refinement in the Ohio River valley. For their idealized display of that refinement, white patrons depended on Ball's professional eye and artistry.

Coined by the historian George Frederickson to describe a pre–Civil War belief in African Americans' moral superiority as exemplary Christians, "romantic racialism" may help explain the success of black artists, artisans, and service workers laboring to soften and refine their white clients' appearances.[62] Patrons' sense of African Americans as embodying the finer, yet gentler, values of sympathetic feeling in an otherwise callous, hurly-burly world gave black artists and personal service workers license or permission to reform white bodies and souls. But to make black service work exclusively a function of white needs and perceptions may miss an opportunity to see how African Americans turned an arguably more benign racism to advantage. In both Cincinnati and Louisville, barbers, hairdressers, artists, and photographers all worked a demanding double shift, so to speak, altering both the physical appearances and subjective racial views of their white clients with a reformist agenda in mind. Without the political clout of the vote, black Americans necessarily turned to white allies to gain basic civil rights, access to public schools, legal support for fugitives, and, ultimately, emancipation on the soil. In close personal contact with powerful whites, Cincinnati's and Louisville's black barbers and men like J. P. Ball and Robert Duncanson were well situated to persuade white men to assist the Ohio River valley's black communities in achieving political power.

Alliances

Romantic racialists such as Harriet Beecher Stowe and Alexander Kinmont—both long-term residents of Cincinnati—breathed new life into the stalled colonization movement through their expressed belief that black and white Americans were fundamentally different and therefore socially incompatible, even if, as in Stowe's and Kinmont's literary and theological schemas, African Americans occupied a higher moral ground than whites through their self-effacing Christian values. This view seemingly left black Americans at great personal risk in a heartless, individualistic society such as the United States, since, in George Fredrickson's words, "it also implicitly deprived the Negro of the inherent ability to compete on equal terms with the ruggedly aggressive Anglo-Saxons, for he was denied the very qualities necessary in such a competition. Hence it indirectly encouraged a fatalistic attitude toward any failure of freed Negroes to rise to white levels of practical competence and worldly success."[63] In the view of sentimental abolitionists such as Stowe, colonization seemed the most humane solution to an apparently foreordained and ineradicable inequality, whether under slavery or freedom. Joined with overtly racist propagandists, these antislavery moderates gave fresh impetus to the idea of black emigration in the 1850s.[64] The two groups were not entirely strange bedfellows, as Fredrickson noted in his analysis of their racial ideologies, thereby demonstrating the obstacles to imagining a truly biracial society imposed by even those who viewed African Americans as moral paragons.

Thus in Cincinnati and Louisville, the personal relationships between black service workers and middle-class whites arose in a context in which even the most sympathetic white Americans harbored deep suspicions about the possibility of a biracial society and in which whites brought any number of hoary stereotypes, paternalist views, and condescending feelings—usually in some unruly combination—into their dealings with African Americans. What seems clear, though, is that black service workers, and particularly those in regular contact with white patrons, grew savvy in discerning which of their clients might offer the most tangible aid to black communities and which might serve as useful allies in beating back the colonizationist impulse, with all of its presumptions about the incompatibility of the races. In both Cincinnati and Louisville, barbers especially became ambassadors to powerful white men, often lawyers, who could be called on to look out for the legal interests of black individuals in the protection of their person and property. But above and beyond the legal protection of a single individual or church property, barbers and others acting on the authority of a broader black community crafted public relations campaigns—often, but not always, in tandem with organized abolition or antislavery reform efforts—to establish a firm place for respectable middle-class African Americans within Ohio and Kentucky. In this effort, black leaders created alliances with white men who, in disavowing colonization, begged the question of what a biracial society might look like. In the Ohio River valley's cities, middle-class blacks and whites placed extraordinary emphasis on the power of refinement to negate racism and its attendant maltreatments in a postemancipation society. In doing so, they took advantage of what the historian Richard Bushman argues was the most powerful cultural current in antebellum America.[65]

As these black and white reformers recognized, gentility could serve to obscure a more rigid and injurious color line by substituting a class line of genteel behavior that some African Americans could cross. At the least, the "visual language of gentility" provided a clear coding system by which to communicate across racial barriers.[66] These particular blacks and whites believed that manners, emotional display, and material goods could signify their "right feelings" toward each other.[67] Entailing fewer political risks than a race strategy for group uplift, genteel spokespersons blended evangelicals' emphasis on moral sensibility with a nonracial system of class discrimination. Middle-class blacks thereby challenged the use of race to inhibit class conflict among whites. In this effort, they sought out white allies willing to expand gentility's "magic circle" to include refined African Americans and repudiate rude white racists' claims to inclusion.[68]

Having emerged from Cincinnati's 1841 race riots with renewed determination to protect as well as build upon their community's resources, African Americans belonging to the city's most prominent black church, the Union Baptist Church, worked to establish close ties with sympathetic whites possessing political influence. In 1845, members of the church wanted to recognize the legal work of Salmon P. Chase, by then a prominent lawyer, antislavery advocate, and aspiring third-party politician. The ostensible occasion for planning a formal ceremony to present "a testimonial of their grateful appreciation" to Chase was his recent legal defense of the fugitive slave Samuel Watson. But the event was actually part of a long-standing and concerted effort by the city's black community to engender a firm bond between the Liberty Party leader and African Americans. Some weeks before the ceremony acknowledging his legal defense of fugitive slaves, for example, Union Baptist Church had invited Chase to watch academic exercises performed by students attending Cincinnati's Colored High School. Chase was duly impressed by the scholars' "intelligent countenance" and "generous aspiration," and he made public note of their accomplishments, as the church no doubt had hoped. Chase's formal visits to the black church in 1845 capped a longer, albeit less visible, relationship in which the white lawyer had provided various "professional services" to black Cincinnatians. "During a period of many years," the city's leading black church had looked on Chase's career as an advocate for African Americans "with silent admiration." Now, in the spring of 1845, the church wanted to properly honor Chase's "public services in behalf of the oppressed," and they did so with close attention to the politics of refinement.[69]

The church wagered that the careful presentation of black Americans' own economic success and irreproachable moral standing despite Ohio's severe legal disabilities would prod Chase on to still greater effort "to correct that unmanly and wicked public sentiment which crushes us to the earth, and which has no foundation in the naturally just and generous emotions of the human heart, but is the mere creature of a vicious education."[70] In the view of Union Baptist Church's leaders, the stakes for this gathering of black church members and white political leaders must have seemed incalculably high: black Cincinnatians had already striven as far as anyone might reasonably imagine without the help of political influence or the protection of even basic civil rights. Although they had survived the 1841 riots, memory of those recent horrors propelled the most economically well off in Cincinnati's black community to seek the immediate overturning of Ohio's debilitating "Black Laws." To do so, they turned to white allies like Chase who might one day have the wherewithal to strike them down. The Union Baptist Church here made a shrewd choice in its political associations.

The Union Baptist Church's planning for the May occasion began in early 1845 with the creation of an event committee and the commissioning of a special engraved gift, a silver pitcher, inspired by "a fine antique model," to be fabricated by Cincinnati's most esteemed silversmiths. "With little ornament beyond the slight chasing of the borders and handle," the pitcher's beautiful design and "elegance of finish" offered evidence of that "refinement of sentiment, which every lover of the well-being and progress of society must regard with peculiar and cordial interest." The event itself was orchestrated to a fare-thee-well. The audience was "very large" and pleasing, the gift a beautiful token, the speeches eloquent, and the well-chosen hymn celebrating America "sung with great taste and feeling." A published booklet memorializing the evening and its speeches also displayed a quiet elegance in its cover and spacious typeface.[71]

The speaker selected by Union Baptist Church to present the engraved pitcher and deliver the address praising Chase's work was A. J. Gordon, a Cincinnati barber and renowned black orator. Gordon's speech blended historical, constitutional, and moral arguments against slavery based upon the Declaration of Independence, the American Revolution, the Northwest Ordinance of 1787, and Scripture. He quoted Shakespeare's *Henry VI* to fortify Chase for further struggle against the slave power: "Thrice is he armed, who hath his quarrel just."[72] But Gordon also manipulated the codes of gentility in praising Chase's "deep and heart felt sympathy" for arguing the unconstitutionality of the 1793 fugitive slave law during Watson's trial. Though the argument had failed to persuade the court and Watson was remanded back to slavery, in Gordon's opinion the "irrepressible applause" and the "gushing sympathy of approving hearts" shown Chase at the conclusion of the trial "attested [to the public's] appreciation of your efforts, and their sympathy with the oppressed." So powerfully and publicly expressed in the courtroom by audience members, these "right feelings" demonstrated the "naturally just and generous emotions of the human heart." According to Gordon, Chase's efforts on behalf of Watson had repudiated a "perverted public sentiment" characterized by prejudice and violence against black people.[73] More than a legal argument or juridical exercise, Watson's trial had been a performance of genteel conduct by both Chase as attorney and his black and white allies as spectators in the courtroom drama. Watson's case had sealed a sympathetic bond between the white lawyer and a black public.

While offering thanks to Chase for his "high moral daring" in arguing the fugitive slave cases, Gordon's address and the ceremonial presentation of the silver pitcher also exhorted the aspiring politician to attack "the wrongs inflicted upon the free colored people of this country." "You have not been unmindful of the deprivation of rights endured," Gordon affirmed, but the antislavery cause was not won until "every vestige of oppression and prejudice" had been wiped out. Here, in a real sense, was the purpose of the Union Baptist Church's public honoring of Chase's antislavery labors: to reinforce to Chase and his white political friends the fundamental relationship between southern slavery and northern prejudice. Gaining basic rights for Ohio's African Americans, including the vote, was necessarily of a piece with eliminating "all invidious distinctions founded on color."[74] Crucially, Gordon's address assumed an antislavery goal of emancipation on the ground without African American emigration. This too counted as a form of prodding on Gordon's part: colonization would have no place in this staged conversation between black Cincinnatians and Chase. Chase was thus drawn into a fight for northern black rights and against racial prejudice. Gordon acknowledged black Cincinnatians' dependence on Chase for the political ways and means toward a truly biracial society, but his church wanted to generate the conditions and terms of that equality.

In response to Gordon's speech and gift of the silver pitcher, the future Supreme Court justice twice noted the "novel position" he now found himself by enjoying the liberality of an African American church. While reiterating familiar constitutional and legal arguments from his several fugitive slave trials, Chase's speech contained its own novelty: here, for the first time, Chase publicly advocated the vote for black Ohioans.[75] He reasoned, "The moment the law excludes a portion of the community from its equal regard, it divides the community into higher and lower classes, and introduces all the evils of the Aristocratic principle. Henceforth, in that community, rights, in the proper sense of that word, cease to exist."[76] Though insisting on a sincere sympathy with the "oppressed," Chase admitted to self-interested motives in his antislavery advocacy, "since our rights . . . are involved in the struggle in which we are engaged."[77] Yet Chase's address was foremost an examination of the wrongs stemming from Ohio's Black Laws, and especially the exclusions from voting, attending public schools, and testifying in courts. He further lambasted Ohio's requirement that African Americans provide bonds for good behavior in order to permanently reside in the state. In forceful terms, Chase "demand[ed] in the name of our common manhood, and our common Christianity, and our common destiny, the reversal of this policy, and the abrogation of this legislation."[78] This represented a shift in his thinking away from an exclusive focus on slavery as the nation's singular evil.[79] Before the end of the decade, in 1849, Chase would make good on this pledge by crafting the legislation finally repealing the state's Black Laws.[80] Plausibly, the Union Baptist Church's public advocacy and concerted pressure had pushed Chase toward a more determined opposition to Ohio's racist statutes and a newfound support for full manhood suffrage.

In his address to the black congregation, Chase also strayed from constitutional arguments to consider the significance of refined behavior in changing public sentiment on black rights. He insisted that African Americans' "good conduct" provided "ample refutation of the base and vulgar calumny that the colored people are incapable of refined sentiment or grateful feeling," and he emphasized the evidence of refinement already vouching for full black citizenship. In his audience, Chase observed "conscience, reputation, personal interest, social and domestic ties," a nearly perfect catalog of middle-class values. Here he found the essential ingredients for a truly biracial society, and Chase appeared hopeful that courtesy, grace, and good manners would dissolve prejudice and invite harmony. "The cordial reciprocation of benefits, not the mutual infliction of injuries," he argued with no little understatement, would allow for "the peaceful dwelling together of different races." Such an assertion would have appeared grossly simplistic but for his prior appreciation of the systemic violence and legalized oppression generating hardship for African Americans in Ohio. And to an audience fully steeped in gentility as a strategy for group uplift, his social equation might not have seemed outlandish. Even so, Chase's address asked far more of individual black Cincinnatians in his vision for racial justice, for any single African American's "unworthy vices ... gives ground for sweeping charges against the race, and holds back his fellows from the career of advancement," he warned audience members.[81] In any event, Chase viewed refinement as a kind of a priori condition for full legal equality, and this was a view encouraged by members of Union Baptist Church. To both Chase and the black church, a common gentility or middle-class refinement did seem to offer one means to imagine a biracial world in the United States. Christian Scripture lent itself to problematic, if inchoate, arguments about separate racial destinies, and legal equality in northern states remained politically elusive; in contrast, black and white allies in the antislavery movement could immediately seize upon gentility as a means to racial harmony.

Although Chase had offered support for colonization well into the 1830s, and while serving in the U.S. Senate in the early 1850s he briefly did so again, the Democratic-turned-Republican politician rejected any form of compulsory emigration. As a cabinet member in Lincoln's administration, he opposed colonization as part of the Emancipation Proclamation.[82] He also labored to overturn Ohio's discriminatory laws and to advocate for black suffrage through the 1850s, believing that race prejudice was "inhuman and unjust."[83] Personal contact with Union Baptist Church in 1845—a critical moment in Chase's political career and evolution of his abolitionist thinking, and a point at which black Cincinnatians' determination to remain in southern Ohio was indisputable—set Chase on a unique course to undo Ohio's legalized discrimination, advocate suffrage, combat racial prejudice, and reject colonization at a decisive moment in the Civil War.

Ripest for Emancipation

In Louisville, a similar story played out between the city's leading black Methodist congregation and prominent white men who would also disavow colonization as a precondition for slaves' emancipation in the state and nation. According to William Gibson, the most "prominent" African Americans of that time were typically barbers, including Washington Spradling and David Straws, who appeared to have among the best books of business in town, both in the shaving trade and in the legal sense of that phrase. Spradling's "customers were the first judges and lawyers of the State, and from long and constant contact with them he seemed to have acquired their inspiration." Among Louisville's African Americans, Spradling had a reputation as "one of the best lawyers to plan or prepare a case for the court." "Nearly every colored person who was in trouble (more or less) first consulted" Spradling. Working with white members of the bar, Spradling "selected the lawyer" but "prepared the case." As Gibson noted, he rarely lost his cases, yet stood ready to appeal any decisions disadvantageous to his "clients." Besides his legal acumen, Spradling became wealthy through real estate development, which he accomplished "in connection with his shaving." By his death, Spradling had built an estate worth $135,000 and, though affluent, refused to conform to genteel styles, choosing instead "very common" dress, "as he exhibited no pride in that direction," Gibson remembered.[84]

Spradling's unique career suggests the kinds of extensive business and legal ties that developed in Louisville between black personal service workers and their white clients, ties that African Americans parlayed into other lucrative ventures. The barber David Straws, a slave who purchased his freedom, provides another example, and his legal contacts may have had greater political import than even Spradling's real estate wealth. According to Gibson, Straws was "an honored citizen" who "figured very prominently in the lawsuits against the white Methodist South" as a member of the black Fourth Street Methodist Episcopal Church.[85] Gibson thus offers intriguing evidence of a personal connection between Straws and a white judge, most likely Samuel S. Nicholas, who would assist the black church in establishing its legal independence from white control and at the same time, striking a blow against colonization, a perennial cause among Kentucky's white antislavery conservatives. Chancellor of Louisville's Chancery Court between 1844 and 1850, Nicholas was a Kentucky native, born into a slaveholding family. He nevertheless supported conservative antislavery measures throughout the late 1830s and 1840s.[86]

The 1848 tract *Slave Emancipation in Kentucky*, largely written by Nicholas and signed by ten other Louisvillians connected with organized antislavery in the city, voiced conservative proposals for gradual emancipation, convinced as the authors were that anything more radical or immediate would not be supported by Kentuckians statewide. The proposed plan for emancipation outlined in the pamphlet echoed economic arguments made by Kentucky's most famous antislavery advocate, Cassius Clay, by insisting that slavery had "thus far been a curse, a withering blight on [Kentucky's] growth and prosperity." And although the authors sought, by the elimination of slavery, "the increase of [Kentucky's] white population, and of that wealth and industry which ever accompany an exclusive white population," they rejected "the driving off or carrying off the emancipated blacks" through colonization or other removal schemes. The committee suggested that "a very exaggerated estimate of the evils to be felt from having a free black population" made colonization popular in Kentucky and diminished the prospects of emancipation. They therefore sought to reassure readers that free blacks, "with their previous training for freedom, will not be a very heavy burthen to a white population," which they projected to grow much more rapidly than the black community following emancipation. Although by no means a paean to biracialism, the committee's tract did claim that its gradual plan for emancipation benefited "the permanent interests and welfare of the white population equally with justice to the blacks."[87]

Advocating against colonization upended precedent set in the two previous decades of agitation over the slavery question in Kentucky. Voices decrying the injustice and racism of colonization, including those of native sons James G. Birney, Cassius Clay, and John G. Fee, could be heard before 1850, but among the state's far more numerous antislavery gradualists, propounding emancipation without also advancing some scheme for colonization or deportation of free blacks amounted to a kind of heresy.[88] Louisville's white antislavery activists of the late 1840s, nearly all of whom remained gradualists, took tentative steps to sever this linkage between emancipation and colonization. In a signed article first appearing in the *Louisville Journal* in early 1849, Judge Nicholas insisted that his own "pertinacious refusal" to support colonization had led Louisville's advocates to question conventional thinking in *Slave Emancipation in Kentucky*. In a rare advertence to the sentiments of free black Kentuckians, Nicholas explained that his "unbelief is based upon the idea that the negroes themselves will be unwilling to be removed to Africa, and, if so, their removal is therefore not practicable." Though he also railed against "blind, popular prejudice" leading poorer whites to vote contrary to their interests on the slavery question, Nicholas's editorial nevertheless reinforced white bigotry. Since the "menial offices of house servants" were best "performed by a distinct and inferior class," he argued, a small free black population would always be desirable among white Kentuckians.

Nicholas's beliefs thus represented no break with caste inequality, yet his doubts about colonization did help to set Louisville's organized white anti-slavery movement apart from conservative emancipationists outside of the state's largest city.[89] It seems possible that Judge Nicholas's experience with the Fourth Street Methodist Church informed his antislavery activism. Witnessing the church's desire for autonomy in his courtroom in 1845, as well as the congregation's tenacity in holding onto its property and independence, he would have apprehended the folly of colonization.

Personal connections between Gibson's Fourth Street Methodist Church and the city's leading white emancipationists also appear in the pages of the city's antislavery newspaper, the *Examiner*, which began publication in 1847. The editors almost never spoke of the doings of Louisville's African American community, but they did describe visiting the Fourth Street Church, where they listened to choral performances directed by William Gibson. "Here was a large church," the editors of the *Examiner* gushed, "brilliantly lighted with gas and situated in the very heart of the city, a church owned entirely by the blacks." The congregation, "mostly composed of slaves," they wrote, demonstrated "the capacity of improvement in the colored population." The beauty of the church and its music, along with the "elegance" of the audience, the editors went on, "would fill with gladness and gratitude . . . every soul which glows with the love of freedom."[90] In the newspaper's very first issue, the editor at the time, John Vaughan, had explained his reasons for establishing an antislavery paper in Louisville: "Of all the slave states," Kentucky seemed "the ripest for emancipation" because of the "improvement of the negroes" and their preparation for freedom. Contact with the Fourth Street Church validated that view and may have helped move the editors of the *Examiner* to pointedly declare colonization "unjust" in 1849.[91] Thus, the Fourth Street Church had sought out and courted powerful men with emancipationist sympathies like Nicholas and the editors of the *Examiner*, and their gambit paid off in at least two ways: they ensured the protection of their church's independent standing, and they led some of Louisville's conservative white emancipationists to abandon schemes for colonization as both impractical and absurd given the permanence of black churches and the communities they represented.

The 1850s were perhaps the high-water mark of the cultural power of refinement in the United States. Certainly after the Civil War, genteel styles and behavior came in for withering satire. But until then, refinement had the power to draw black and white Americans into common cause, whether that was in pursuit of a middle-class or elite status or in imagining the conditions for a biracial society. Pursuit of middle-class status on the part of blacks and whites also created unique kinds of dependencies, with whites dependent on black service workers for their very appearance and sense of subjective well-being and black Cincinnatians and Louisvillians reliant on white allies for legal and political advocacy in state legislatures. Black Americans bore the greater burdens in these dependent relationships—the work necessary to maintain associations with white clients or white political allies fell to men and women like Eliza Potter, A. J. Gordon, James P. Ball, and David Straws, who over and over again had to prove their social value and insist on their equal rights to enjoy the fruits of their labor in the United States. But some whites who came into extended contact with African Americans in Cincinnati and Louisville recognized the folly of colonization schemes and took steps to disavow the necessity of racial separation. They also began to imagine a common bond in the pursuit of refinement and the security of middle-class homes and families.

CHAPTER SIX

Enlightenment

Discriminatory laws, mob violence, and damaging cultural presumptions produced unaccountable suffering and loss for African Americans living in the Ohio River valley. Yet as the historian Dana Weiner writes, "this difficult region always had a counter-narrative" in its antislavery activists who pursued racial equality and civil rights against extraordinary odds through the antebellum era.[1] Recent histories of abolitionism in the Old Northwest as well as the border states show that black and white reformers in the region invested in tactics and ideas distinctive from antislavery radicals in Boston or New York. Both pragmatic and inventive, the Ohio River valley's abolitionists waged a sweeping rights campaign for full civic equality.[2]

Though often depicted as conservative, abolitionist groups in the Old Northwest attracted greater numbers of members, pursued a wide geographical reach in their organizing, and collaborated far more across ideological and partisan lines than their eastern counterparts. Facing daunting legal strictures designed to preclude their civic participation, black activists in Ohio nevertheless led "the most aggressive and sustained" movement for rights in the North, holding annual conventions with a "record of frequency and longevity unmatched in any other state."[3] In this effort black Ohioans had support of white allies, who grasped slavery's influence in the state through its "Black Laws" and worked to overturn them. Their work altered Americans' understanding of the nature of rights by pressing for greater freedom of speech, press, and assembly. South of the Ohio River, Kentuckians "consciously adhered to an ideology that constantly reminded them that freedom for all people, whether black or white, was a primary moral and civil value," Harold Tallant argues. In consequence, a "genuine, native antislavery movement" always claimed at least some adherents in antebellum Kentucky, and "radicals" espousing racial equality exerted their greatest authority in the state in the 1850s.[4]

Antislavery movements in the Old Northwest and Kentucky might still be described as moderate or conservative because their members pursued mainstream political alliances with Democrats and Whigs and lobbied for legal revisions using the incremental, frustrating processes of state and local government and courts. Yet activists' innumerable gatherings—their weeklong conventions, twenty-four-hour debates, monthly prayer meetings and sewing circles, and annual fair work, among other activities—offered ample space and time in which to consider the deeper implications of their work: that is, the conditions necessary for a fully biracial society. Their urgent collaborations assisting fugitive slaves also demanded trust across racial lines and provoked examination of the ways people of color lacked the equal protection of the law in Ohio.

Beginning in the 1830s, antislavery reformers in Cincinnati and Louisville pursued far-reaching efforts to eradicate prejudice and foster feelings of respect and belonging in daily life. The solutions they arrived at—equal educational opportunity and literacy for all children regardless of color—may not have been entirely original for an era in the grip of a reading revolution, but activists in Cincinnati and Louisville who sought to end educational inequity formed the nation's vanguard. Through the antebellum era, they fought for the resources to build state-of-the-art schools and employ well-trained teachers for African American children. Black leaders in the two cities worked zealously for full classical and practical instruction for their children and established unique "Education Societies" to fund this broad aim in the absence of public monies.[5] Black Cincinnatians also led the statewide drive for common schools by lobbying the Ohio legislature and pursuing successful lawsuits decided by the state's supreme court. Cincinnati's white abolitionists joined these efforts in "unprecedented" ways, most notably by paying black and white teachers and petitioning the state for funding of common schools serving black children.[6]

In the 1840s and 1850s, an especially dedicated corps of ambitious educators made Louisville their home. These forward-thinking men and women provided an enriched curriculum for free and enslaved children in day schools that would become the education model for Kentucky's postbellum era. Though white antislavery moderates do not appear to have involved themselves in the day-to-day operations of Louisville's black schools, as was sometimes the case in Cincinnati, they offered moral support in the city's antislavery press and touted the transformative power of education as a means to ease the path toward emancipation. In this way, Louisville's African Americans and whites used education and literacy as forms of antislavery persuasion.

Building schools and garnering public support for African American children's well-rounded education were profound achievements before the Civil War. But the story goes further, for Cincinnatians and Louisvillians also produced a unique body of fictional literature, plumbing the deeper meaning of widespread literacy and creating the grounds for cross-race identification through the act of reading—an activity freighted with the very essence of what it meant to be human in the first part of the nineteenth century.[7] This literary vanguard, which included Harriet Beecher Stowe, grasped that the emergent genre of fiction offered one of the most powerful means to forge a sense of identification across human difference. From such unlikely settings as Cincinnati and Louisville, these educational activists and literary innovators thereby broadened the antislavery movement. While continuing to advance humanitarian arguments against the extreme forms of human suffering caused by slavery, they began to construct the foundation for a particular kind of biracial society, one heavily invested in middle-class modes of expression and feeling. Their schools and literature illuminated ways that the noxious weeds of prejudice might be rooted out of northern free states and face-to-face exchange among diverse people might flourish in the region. Publicly funded schools also forged bonds between African Americans and the state, which now invested directly in black lives.

By the 1850s, these activists offered a consistent vision of self-determination and full equality for black Americans in the United States—not in Canada, not in Central America, and not in Liberia. To be sure, elements of their plan demanded pragmatic politics, for they involved such basic challenges as funding and operating actual brick-and-mortar schools. But these reformers were also guided by genuine idealism to see in every child the fullest humanity and to foster enlightenment. That they did so in a region exhibiting some of the worst examples of race-based hate in the nineteenth century makes their work seem all the more significant. What they glimpsed prior to the Civil War became a template for national reunion after emancipation.

Universal Education

In the first half of the nineteenth century, Cincinnati and Louisville drew their fair share of dreamers, zealots, and worriers who threw their energies into the cause of education. Among the most passionate of this special class of migrants was the Beecher clan, led by Lyman, the patriarch, and Catherine, his indefatigable daughter. In all, nine Beechers decamped en masse from the East and headed west in 1832, many bearing plans for one kind of educational scheme or another. Lyman trained ministers at Lane Seminary in Walnut Hills, Catherine established a school for young women in Cincinnati, and son Edward educated young men in a liberal curriculum at Illinois College in Jacksonville. Although not keen to join the exhausting work of building schools, Harriet chose a complementary trade: she planned to become a children's book author. A Cincinnati press brought out her first publication, a geography primer, in 1833. When Lyman Beecher insisted that "there is at the West an enthusiastic feeling on the subject of education," he knew whereof he spoke.[8]

Beecher offered a fervid explanation for his family's educational mission to Cincinnati in fund-raising speeches on behalf of Lane Seminary. Published as a *Plea for the West* in 1835, Beecher's speeches can be read in several ways— as anti-immigrant and anti-Catholic screeds, as paranoid manifesto—but at their most strenuous, the speeches thundered out a basic message: "We must educate! We must educate!" In the absence of schools, "a poor, uneducated, reckless mass of infuriated animalism" would "rush on resistless as the tornado," or, in Beecher's whipsawing turn of metaphor, "burn as if set on fire of hell." Though his speeches mostly forecast horrors to come, he insisted that the West had already "reached an appalling crisis" with fast-multiplying numbers of settlers lacking any connection to cultured society. His proposed remedy: "cheap and effectual education," as well as professional teachers, to foster "an enlightened public sentiment." For all of its hyperbole about foreign and domestic dangers—indeed, its veritable call to Armageddon in the Ohio River valley—Beecher's *Plea* was at bottom a program for "universal education" through public schools.[9]

Although Harriet Beecher tried to keep a safe distance from the grand schemes of her father and siblings, her life was both taxed and enriched by this mission for universal education. Her first children, twins, were born while her husband Calvin Stowe traveled abroad under a special commission by the Ohio legislature to research public schools in Europe that the state might emulate. Though he left shortly after Lyman Beecher's fulsome "dreams about Rome, and Vienna, and Metternich" appeared, Stowe found much to admire in state schools designed by enlightened autocrats.[10] He esteemed the Prussian system most of all, arguing that it best implemented the "proper object of education," which he defined in universalist terms as "a thorough development of all the intellectual and moral powers—the awakening and calling forth of every talent that may exist, even in the remotest and obscurest corner of the State, and giving it a useful direction."[11] Stowe praised the breadth of European common school education: it drew in children of all ranks and educated them in an "extensive and complete course of study" at once practical and attentive to the finer arts. In his travels he met enthusiastic, well-trained instructors. Though Stowe questioned whether some children were "actually incapable of learning to draw and to sing," teachers dismissed his concern, insisting that every student—regardless of family wealth or background—could discover latent talents with proper encouragement and discipline. He was awed to find all manner of children thriving amid a rich curriculum, "respected and happy" in their sense of belonging and purpose. "If it can be done in Prussia, I know it can be done in Ohio," he urged brightly to legislators.[12] Following its appearance in 1837, Stowe's *Report on Elementary Public Instruction in Europe* enjoyed "an important influence on the development of common school education."[13]

For all of their cultural chauvinism, then, the Beechers and their kin offered an encompassing vision of education, one that was inclusive and equal, with children of varied economic backgrounds receiving the same broad-minded curriculum, guided by thoughtful, sympathetic instructors. In *Uncle Tom's Cabin*, written more than a decade later, Harriet Beecher Stowe extended this vision to include African Americans by describing "the figure of the black reader" in order "to ask whether barriers to learning are natural, just, and irrevocable" in an enlightened society. In 1850, when installments of Stowe's wildly popular and politically explosive novel first appeared in the *National Era*, hers was an original representation of black literacy, capacity, and subjectivity within the genre of sentimental fiction.[14] Her father and husband had provided some of the cultural and evidentiary grounds for this literary innovation.

Other educational projects in Cincinnati had also encouraged Stowe to think expansively about race and intellectual ability. Her fictional depiction of the radical significance of literacy among enslaved peoples was surely informed by dramatic events shaping her first years in the West. In 1834, Lyman Beecher and Calvin Stowe together made a fatal decision to disband Lane Seminary's student abolition society because members had undertaken an unusual social experiment testing their own feelings toward Cincinnati's black community—an experiment that drew the ire of local whites. Beecher was then serving as the college's president, and Stowe as its professor of theological studies. After seventeen nights of debate on whether to strike out for an immediate end to slavery or to adhere to the American Colonization Society's gradualist black removal program, seminary students drew an unequivocal conclusion: colonization constituted a perverse charade. Although draped in the language of benevolent moral reform, colonization advanced slaveholders' interests in a poisonous social program intended to undermine free blacks' achievements in the United States and slow the course of emancipation. Armed with this new certitude, and with a burning desire to upend colonization logic, the white students plunged themselves into unprecedented collaboration and personal relationships with black Americans. Their objective was to expose the folly of white prejudice by demonstrating black intellectual ability. In creating a "spectacle of free black cultivation," Theodore Dwight Weld and other student leaders expressed a desire to disrupt unexamined and deeply damaging ideas about black inferiority.[15]

As the Lane Seminary students wished, all eyes in Cincinnati watched the unprecedented enterprise unfold. For a time, a rich educational program drew in hundreds of black students thirsty for fresh currents of intellectual stimulation and knowledge. Popular lyceum lectures by Lane Seminary students offered insights into science and literature to the black public, and day and night schools enrolled about one hundred students. The seminarians dedicated a special library for black students to follow their own scholarly inclinations.[16] To advance this academic program, Lane Seminary's white students also "associated with the colored people upon terms of equality," had "visited and eaten with them," and, in several instances, "boarded with colored people." To "associate intimately with the people they instruct" was "essential to success," the seminarians argued. It mattered that Cincinnati's African American students imbibed their lessons well, and the young teachers believed that disproving erroneous ideas about black intellect depended, in part, on having real knowledge of their students' lives. In seeking more genuine personal relationships with black people, the white students had wanted to illuminate an idea, as well as to test themselves personally: "It is fundamental to our principles to treat men according to their character without respect to condition or complexion. Thus we have learned the law of love. Thus we would act against the pride of caste. Thus we would practice as we preach—the only mode to get credit for sincerity or to influence others." Through this individual effort, the seminarians wanted to demolish a seemingly self-evident colonization argument that white bigotry was ineradicable in the United States. The students mocked as "unintelligent" a prejudice based on something as arbitrary as skin color, as though individuals could "absorb the rays of the sun" by some kind of moral "volition."[17] In sum, it was impossible to narrowly construe students' ambitions, for black education here served as means to dramatically rethink deeply rooted causes of inequality in American life. Rather than search for answers in black ability, the seminarians had turned the mirror back upon themselves, and upon white Americans generally, as the source of inequity. For this reason, the students encountered hostility.

Some white Cincinnatians concluded that this work fostered a dangerous and illicit "scheme of equalization."[18] To undermine the seminarians' ambitious social project, these Cincinnatians insinuated that the students encouraged (or had already instigated) sex across racial lines. That a white male student had boarded with a black family was true enough, but this supposed carnal proof, along with other circumstantial evidence, illustrates the nineteenth century's contradictory and hypocritical views of interracial sex. Ohio's unique "visible admixture" eligibility test in voting—where state and local officials did a visual once-over of men's skin color to measure degrees of whiteness—acknowledged the complex ancestry of many Americans at the time.[19] Nevertheless, interracial marriage and sex remained anathema by convention and law, if not in actual practice, and such accusations usually doubled as a threat of violence against those appearing to blur the boundaries of race. In the case of the Lane Seminary education project, evidence of illicit activity included the following: a white male student and a black woman were seen walking together to the college and then back to Cincinnati again following an event, and a few black women rode "in a carriage" to a lecture at the seminary, drawing the "marked attention" of the male students. Lyman Beecher and Calvin Stowe provided an awkward but provocative label for the principle behind students' behavior: these incidents were, in their words, fruits of the "doctrine and practice of immediate intercourse irrespective of color." Beecher and Stowe predicted a violent "reaction that nothing could resist" and grew convinced that the abolition society's work imperiled Lane Seminary's financial solvency by scaring off both donors and students with their radical "doctrine."[20] They disbanded the abolition society and halted their educational work among Cincinnati's blacks.

As advocates of universal education, Beecher and Stowe endorsed students' limited goal "to extend intellectual and moral culture to the colored population of the city."[21] But Beecher had cautioned the radicalized seminarians to move slowly with their public display of respect and friendship with black people: "If you want to teach colored schools, I can fill your pockets with money; but if you will visit in colored families, and walk with them in the streets, you will be overwhelmed."[22] The students did not heed these strictures. In the aftermath, Beecher and Stowe criticized students' calculated decision to pursue "some action, in advance of public opinion," in order "to put it down." In other words, the students acted provocatively to draw out the public's ire, the better to identify and diffuse its error. In their formal defense, the students' never confessed to this strategy but instead offered as explanation a thoughtful insight into the special nature of education: that teaching was inherently personal, demanding students' "confidence" in their instructors.[23] Social distance, rigid presumption, and misunderstanding lessened a teacher's facility, threatening to wreck even the most limited educational goals. At stake here was not mere ciphering, though. With the slave system gaining new potency from its close cousin and ally, colonization, education had been called heavily into service to end these evils. The white students hoped to avoid failure with a close understanding of black needs and wishes and a greater sense of equality inhering in the conventions of teaching. For its hard-line stance in stunting this work, Lane Seminary's own educational ambitions suffered. Enrollments fell to dangerous lows after 1836, and not a single student was in attendance by 1845.[24] Neighboring Oberlin College, by contrast, appeared to thrive with the arrival of the Lane "Rebels," who had insisted on the admission of students of color on equal terms with whites in exchange for their matriculation.[25]

Exclusion

Even with the radical students' abrupt departure from Lane Seminary, Cincinnati remained Ohio's front line for black educational advocacy and school building in the decades before the Civil War. Risks and public outcry notwithstanding, the close collaboration modeled by Lane Seminary students and Cincinnati's African Americans persisted and expanded over the next decade. With greater organization and more charitable interest, diverse white and black antislavery advocates in Cincinnati allied with Oberlin students to provide instruction to black children and adults in the city and its agricultural hinterlands. Advocates' social goals also grew more ambitious. Rather than shrink from greater personal identification between student and teacher, advocates prized the affective style of instruction pioneered by Lane seminarians. Moreover, advocates deepened their sense of education's inextricable connection to the larger community, offering rich sociological reports of the legal, cultural, and economic impediments to decent schools.

Without state or local tax support for schools serving African American children, education activists drew new lessons while experimenting with private funding strategies to ensure that poor as well as better-off children had access to schools. Enraged that black Ohioans' tax money supported white children's educations while their own children fell subject to the whims of unpredictable donors, African Americans lobbied the legislature for their rightful share of common school funds. Winning this campaign at the state capital in 1849, they next waged uphill legal and public battles to ensure that allocated money flowed, students enrolled, and school buildings opened through the 1850s. In all, theirs was a formidable effort yielding profoundly important shifts in black Ohioans' connection to the state in the span of a decade. By 1860, seven thousand African American children were enrolled in state-funded schools.[26] To be sure, great impediments to equal, comprehensive, and racially integrated education remained. Cincinnatians, though, had forged a significant new bond between black Americans and the state involving the care and instruction of their children.

In the aftermath of Lane Seminary's imbroglio, a remarkable collaboration between white women in Cincinnati and black and white teachers, many of them students or graduates of Oberlin, intensified the drive for comprehensive schooling among black Ohioans. A number of women's antislavery organizations involved themselves in this work after 1835, with the Ohio Female Anti-Slavery Society and the Ohio Ladies' Society for the Education of Free People of Color serving as central clearinghouses of information and funds. Oberlin's energetic, idealistic young students and graduates worked in the field as agents and teachers. While a number of black and white teachers had continued to work in Cincinnati's private black schools in the mid-1830s, formation of the Ohio Ladies' Society for the Education of Free People of Color in 1840 brought new organizational strength, with greater geographical reach, to Cincinnati's maturing education movement. Established by white evangelical women opposed to colonization, the society sent black and white teachers into Ohio's numerous all-black agricultural "settlements."[27] Mostly freed or escaped slaves, men and women in these settlements labored under enormous hardships attempting to build prosperous, independent farms. While a few achieved notable successes, most settlements eked out a bare subsistence.[28]

As Lane Seminary students had done, the new organizations fastened upon a broad view of education. They insisted that the overall context in which schools operated—that is, whether the community validated or withheld support for them—determined success. Moreover, the new advocates demanded much of teachers, believing that only the well trained should take up the cause of "intellectual and moral elevation."[29] Cincinnati's activists also continued to believe that classrooms were coextensive with home life. Under this new and energetic leadership, then, teachers labored mightily, guarding students and buildings from hostile whites, learning about families' struggles, and illuminating connections between educational opportunity and social context. It was, without question, daunting labor.[30]

An offshoot of the local Cincinnati Ladies' Antislavery Society, the Ohio Ladies' Society for the Education of Free People of Color elected each year an executive board made up mostly of women from Cincinnati's prominent white abolitionist church, the Sixth Presbyterian. Although directed by women from Cincinnati, the group drew financial support from various local female antislavery societies around the state. Women's antislavery fairs, sewing circles, and cent-a-week societies provided most of the funding. Official expenditures each year hovered around $250, although the women believed they needed $300 to $400 to accomplish their "plans for the elevation of colored children throughout the State."[31] Ohio's public school laws excluded black children from common instruction, so except for the few private subscription schools found in cities and towns, most black children had few opportunities for formal learning. During the years for which we have reports, the society supported on average twenty teachers and visited thirty settlements.[32]

As the society's leadership grasped, significant education projects are inseparable from the larger context in which they exist. The Cincinnati women therefore conceived their work as political, in the broadest sense. Teaching and advocacy blended together in pursuit of an ambitious goal: repeal of Ohio's discriminatory Black Laws. With ears and eyes close to the ground, teachers would be able to supply state legislators with "well authenticated" facts showing the injurious effect of the Black Laws. Each year, the Education Society asked that teachers "send *full* and *accurate* reports" describing "the condition of the people among whom they labored."[33] Demonstrating the seriousness with which they pursued their work, teachers prepared reports resembling modern-day sociological studies based on fieldwork. Using teachers' observations, the leadership in Cincinnati crafted petitions, circulated them throughout the state for signature, and presented them to Ohio's legislators in the form of memorials.[34] At least until 1845, the Ohio Ladies' Education Society sent memorials to the legislature asking for repeal of exclusionary school laws that tacitly condoned violence against black people.[35]

In their reports, teachers identified a new social type: the vulgar white racist. Defined above all by his prejudice, the vulgar white endangered African Americans and threatened society generally. Teachers commonly represented this white social type as poorly educated, if not illiterate, to draw greater attention to black intellectual achievement and respectability. The greater community threat in these reports was white racism, not black degradation. For example, the mannerly and poetic George Vashon, an African American teacher laboring in Pea Pea Creek, quoted threatening notes posted by whites to harass blacks. Vashon carefully transcribed the terrible grammar and spelling in one note ordering black farmer John Woods "to take them cattle away from her, or . . . you will be tore up." Another notice from the same "Black Hock Comp'y"—a white vigilance committee that could not spell its own name—Vashon claimed was too "profane" for insertion into the report.[36] Teachers described "profane and uncivil" treatment, including mob violence, terrorism, and economic betrayal, in unrelenting detail.[37] Like Vashon though, teachers found some "meanness . . . beyond the power of description on paper."[38]

Reports from the front lines of this education movement drew bitter conclusions. Teachers and agents came to recognize the way exclusion from the common school fund and the absence of state legitimacy particularly incited hostility toward black education. By insisting that black children enjoyed no relationship to the state, Ohio's legislators created conditions that left private schools vulnerable and dangerously exposed, however well intentioned, funded, and staffed with dedicated teachers those independent schools might have been. The great unfairness of the exclusionary school law—that black Ohioans paid taxes to elevate white children—meant that any privately supported black school bore the stamp of illegality. Ohio state law had not condoned such schools and had actively discouraged their creation by withdrawing money earned by black people and placing those resources into white hands. This tax swindle became clear enough.[39] Yet Cincinnati activists realized that "the operation of this law is not merely to prevent colored youths from attending schools with whites, but to prevent colored people from establishing schools among themselves" as well. Writing in palpable anger laced with sarcasm, agents explained that state lawmakers had fostered these "distinguished patterns" of exclusion with their 1831 law barring black children from state-supported schools. In consequence, an easily wrought up "populace following in the wake" of legislators' decrees used blunt force to reinforce paper laws enacted in Columbus. Viewing black schools as illegitimate, this white constituency felt entitled, quite simply, to "burn down colored people's school houses." "No less than five school houses have been burned to ashes within the last four years, to prevent colored schools," an agent grimly reported in 1840.[40]

Teachers also faced cruel ostracism. Echoing events at Lane Seminary, white female teachers endured barely disguised accusations of prostitution, with labels such as "straggling stranger" applied to them. Although whites in Big Bottom, in Pike County, claimed to "have no objection to your educating your children or yourselves . . . by your own colored teachers," they demanded that black school managers end their white teacher's "*female stroll as your preceptress*," or she would suffer a "coat of tar and feathers." Reports made evident that white women especially faced "all manner of vile and slanderous reports" while working in black schools.[41]

Some of this antipathy may have been in response to the close connections forged among teachers, students, and their families. In addition to their daily duties in the classroom, teachers tried to refashion the subjective identities and outward behaviors of settlement residents, which teachers found wanting. Encouraging the founding of temperance societies, Sabbath schools, and churches, teachers aimed at nothing less than a revolution in "customs, habits, and appearances" among black settlers.[42] Teachers' expectations of their young students also ran impossibly high: they wanted to see children "possessed of informed and disciplined minds . . . powerful to control and regulate the whole being at *all* times and under *all* circumstances."[43] Though this entailed a high level of intrusion into settlers' personal lives, residents seemed to endorse the program. "Anxious for schools" and "anxious to improve themselves," settlers boarded teachers, built schoolhouses, and sometimes helped pay teachers' salaries.[44] Teachers reported that settlers readily adapted to "mental culture."[45] "When a friend comes among them," one teacher wrote, "they rouse up and make a struggle to overturn the mountains that lie in their way."[46]

Oberlin College and the Ohio Ladies' Education Society sent persuasive models of "mental culture" to the settlements. The teacher at Pea Pea Creek, George Vashon, was Oberlin's first black graduate in 1844. As a young man with "handsome endowments of manner and address," Vashon idolized Lord Byron, wrote epic poetry, and would later become a professor of belles lettres.[47] Another African American teacher, W. C. Whitehorn, frequently spoke at black celebrations because of his fine oratorical skills.[48] "Of gentlemanly demeanor," teacher John M. Brown would later serve as a bishop in the African Methodist Episcopal Church.[49] Even if settlement work was a cross-class experience for such men of refinement, these teachers "easily governed." Most described miraculous feats of learning among their "quick" and "intelligent" students. One five-year-old child "came to the school not knowing the alphabet, but by the end of five months" could read the Bible to his grateful parents.[50]

Going further, reports of the Education Society described affectionate relationships between teachers and students.[51] In one instance, an older student (who was also an ex-slave) decided to give a wedding dress to her betrothed teacher. An agent reported that the woman "made an arrangement with a friend of hers, and uniting their funds, they purchased [their teacher] a valuable dress, which they presented her, as a testimony of their affection and gratitude."[52] Teachers also detailed tearful leave-takings from their schools and settlements. As one woman wrote, "It was truly painful to witness the farewell scene. So long, and loud, was their weeping, that some persons pass-ing by, came [in to] know what was the cause."[53] "Nearly all wept" for William Coleman when he left his school.[54] Through such gestures and emotional displays, students demonstrated their true sympathy and "right feelings" for their teachers.[55] Depicting education in personal, affective terms, the Cincin-nati organizations tried to diminish social distance and forge intimate bonds between white and black people in otherwise hostile environments.

Compared to its hinterlands, Cincinnati offered greater resources for en-tirely black-run schools and, after 1841, more security for private institutions operated cooperatively by blacks and whites. The first independent black school opened in 1826, and more appeared in the 1830s following the 1829 riot. In a sign of the serious commitment black Cincinnatians had made to formal education, those who removed to Wilberforce, Canada, established a school as their first act of institution building. Among those who remained in Cincinnati following the 1829 violence, great effort went into fostering education among children representing all economic classes. After 1836, an Education Society pooled resources to fund the tuitions of poorer children in three different schools overseen by the black organization. In the absence of dedicated buildings, educators sought out churches and private homes to host these earliest schools.[56]

In the 1840s, a number of whites again helped to establish notable educa-tional institutions for black students in Cincinnati, including an elementary school run by two white ministers at the black Union Baptist Church and a high school founded by a radical antislavery Methodist minister, Hiram S. Gilmore. The curricula at both schools sought to meet black parents' hopes for full and rich courses of study. In pursuit of "broad-based enlightenment," students studied history, philosophy, science, ancient languages, algebra, music, rhetoric, elocution, and gymnastics. Students at Cincinnati High School enjoyed well-appointed facilities and excellent teachers, especially in music. Frequent exhibitions placed students' accomplishments on display to white and black audiences in Cincinnati, and those in the musical program trav-eled through Ohio, New York, and Canada offering acclaimed performances at antislavery gatherings. Graduates of these programs pursued distinguished public careers: Following his attendance at the Union Baptist Church school in the early 1840s, John Mercer Langston undertook rigorous studies at Ober-lin and then gained admittance to the state bar as its first African American member. In its short five-year existence, Cincinnati High School enjoyed some fame, with students coming from afar to attend, including the Georgia-born, future Louisiana politician P. B. S. Pinchback. Cincinnati's promising youth enrolled at this high school, Ohio's only educational institution serving black students in upper-level grades. Among the most well-known today is Peter H. Clark, a radical educator who ushered Cincinnati's black public schools through the tumultuous Civil War and Reconstruction eras.[57]

Though sincere, white support for such schools could be quixotic. Gilmore, the philanthropist behind Ohio's first black high school, turned his attention to building a utopian community in rural Clermont County. Late one night in 1847, an Ohio River flood tragically killed seventeen black and white members of Gilmore's "Universal Brotherhood" as they slept together in their communal "phalanstery." In the aftershock of this great loss, Gilmore left behind the dream of a racially integrated utopia and his prestigious Cincinnati High School in 1849.[58]

The other profound problem for schools without public support was space. In crowded Cincinnati, black schools resorted to "converted pork shops, rooms in abandoned buildings, or parlors in people's homes."[59] For ambitious teachers who wanted to instruct more than a handful of students, churches offered a possibility. But black worship houses already served many community purposes, and even the better-off congregations could not accommodate large numbers of energetic children safely or easily. When teachers sought out use of Cincinnati's Union Baptist Church rooms, for example, trustees justifiably worried about appropriate fencing and privies for the children. Day schools also competed with the missionary, prayer, and antislavery meetings filling church calendars, as well as the singing and Sunday schools occupying precious space. And although a few dedicated teachers took on such challenges for longer stretches of time, many proved flighty: Union Baptist Church expressed due frustration with one instructor who lasted just a month under the rigors of running a day school.[60] In sum, the spectacular dream black and white educators held in the antebellum era—to use enlightened schools to dispel prejudice, overthrow slavery, and uplift the struggling—faced all manner of small, daily difficulties and nearly insuperable barriers of racial animosity in the absence of general, consolidated public support for strong institutions dedicated to learning and open to every child.

Privileges in Common with Others

Without the elective franchise, black Cincinnatians had long petitioned for public support for schools serving their children. The petition to elected officials was a critical tool for political effect employed by antislavery women and African Americans who lacked the vote. "Petitioning," Ohio's African

Americans once declared, was "the straw which may save us from drowning." Black Cincinnatians addressed their first petition for a share in public education to city officials in 1830, writing, "The people of colour in the First Ward pray that a school may be opened in it for the benefit of their children."[61] Although an 1829 state law provided some discretion to local trustees to direct tax money toward "the education of black or mulatto persons," a revision in 1831 restricted school funding to "white youth of every class and grade, without distinction."[62] Black residents in Cincinnati nevertheless presented frequent petitions for schools to the city council through the mid-1840s.[63]

At this point, with the black convention movement in high gear, Cincinnatians directed their school advocacy energies to the Ohio state legislature. By 1849, black Ohioans were driving hard toward their rightful share of common school funds. Gathering in Columbus in January, the "Colored Citizens of Ohio," women included, secured permission to meet as a convention in the Hall of the House of Representatives. With the symbolic cover of state authority, they would deliver in person to legislators and other interested citizens the case for common school fund inclusion and repeal of Ohio's discriminatory laws. In staging this historic event, black delegates "march[ed] in order to the State House" from their church meeting place, bearing a "framed" petition. With the heightened anticipation given to such "unusually interesting" moments, a "large audience of both colored and white citizens" at the statehouse gathered to hear black Ohioans present their cause. The evening's speakers walked a careful rhetorical line, condemning the state's discriminatory laws for fostering "degradation to the black and disgrace to the white man" while also insisting on black Americans' "patriotic devotion to their country and race." Newspapers marked the unprecedented meeting as either "the most cheering state of progress in the public mind" or further evidence that "the blacks have already assumed high airs," depending on editors' views of black rights.[64]

The 1849 black convention proceedings exhibited a kind of whirlwind tempo. The day following the newsworthy statehouse meeting of black men and women calling for equal citizenship rights, a Columbus barber and printer named David Jenkins, "with much haste," burst into a floor discussion of colonization to report that he had just come from a meeting with the state auditor. The official had informed Jenkins "that the colored people were taxed for the support of schools, whether there were any colored children in them or not." Incensed, and with lingering disbelief, Jenkins announced "that he had just paid for the support of *white* children."[65] Confusion ensued as delegates attempted to make sense of a recent revision to the common school law taxing "black or colored persons" to fund "a separate account" for their children's schooling. But these funds were subject to a host of restrictions. The 1848 amendments delimited separate provisions for when districts held "twenty or more black or colored children," or "more than fifty black or colored scholars," or "three or more of the black or colored taxpayers," or "less than twenty black or colored children."[66] The new law was confounding. Previously, lacking access to common schools, black property owners had been legally exempt from school taxes (though actual practice varied through the state). Now, state and local assessors had admittedly failed to establish the "separate account," yet they levied the taxes in any event. Jenkins's meeting with the auditor therefore confirmed what black delegates suspected: Ohio "takes money out of our pockets to school the other class" of white children. At first view, those in attendance considered this an utterly maddening step backward.[67]

Over the course of their four-day meeting, however, black delegates sensed the ground shifting and new justifications for change arising from this injustice. Clearly, there was the manifest unfairness of "separate" taxes collected by the 1848 amendments without any mechanism to see those funds disbursed to black children's schools. The black representatives therefore "ask[ed] for school privileges in common with others" for the simple reason that "we pay school taxes in the same proportion."[68] But delegates pressed their arguments further, calling for integrated rather than separate black schools.[69] In doing so, they echoed arguments made several years earlier by Oberlin students and Cincinnati education activists, revealing a keen sense of the legitimacy conferred on children by equal laws and an iniquitous education system's deeper relationship to prejudice: "In children thus divided by [the common school] law, the most Satanic hate is likely to be engendered. This, no one who has studied human nature will deny. . . . What children are in the school room, they are when manhood has come over them, and what feeling the school-room fosters appears in after life in the shape of a monster called law."[70] For all of the despair registered in this insight, delegates to this particular state black convention intuited that Ohio's legislature might soon be pressed to do away with the instruments of racial hatred and inequity. A perception of imminent change gathered force. Delegates' alert, sharpened energies are captured in the relentless staccato em-dash breaks bringing their convention address to a close:

> To the Colored Citizens of Ohio, we would . . . say, come out, as soon as possible, from situations called degrading—encourage education—be

temperance men and women—resist every species of oppression—serve
God and humanity. . . . Inform our opposers that we are coming—
coming for our rights—coming through the Constitution of our
common country—coming through the law—and relying upon God and
the justice of our cause, pledge ourselves never to cease our resistance to
tyranny, whether it be in the *iron* manacles of the *slave,* or in the unjust
written manacles for the *free.*[71]

Just four weeks after the black delegates' convention, the Ohio legislature
indeed passed a new common school law to publicly fund the establishment
of institutions of learning for black children. The 1849 law allocated money
from a single state source, according to the population census. Although local
governments could tax black-owned property separately for local district
schools to supplement state monies, some notions of fair representation came
into play since the legislature required the election of black school boards or
directors to administer funds, teachers, enrollment, curriculum, and buildings
with this local and state money.[72]

In consequence of the new common school law, black male property
owners now enjoyed a limited right to vote to oversee the governance of
black children's schools. In the same common school enactment, Ohio state
legislature repealed nearly all of the Black Laws, excepting those restricting
juries and poor relief. Though black men's full enfranchisement remained
elusive in the 1849 legislation, and separate rather than integrated schools
for black and white children received some codification, black Ohioans were
encouraged. More than ever before, "the universal education of our people,"
a foremost desire of black Ohioans, seemed in reach.[73]

Power of Intellect

Under the leadership of a remarkable man, John Isom Gaines, black Cincinnatians immediately set to the work of establishing schools for their children
following passage of the 1849 legislation. Born in 1821 to a formerly enslaved
woman, Elizabeth, and a free man residing in Cincinnati, Gaines had exposure to the rich educational curriculum in an encouraging setting while
attending one of the schools run by Lane Seminary's radical students.[74] His
father Isom also inspired John, for the elder Gaines attended a night school in
order to learn to read at the age of forty-five. The Gaines family owned their
home and labored, with "practical common sense," to provide a secure life to
their children.[75] The younger Gaines perhaps came to associate his father's

quest for literacy with this relative safety and independence. He surely contrasted this stability against his mother Elizabeth's anguished enslavement in Kentucky, where she bore at least three children with a man who was also her master, John Clarke. Her first pregnancy took place when she was fourteen and Clarke nearing forty years old. Though Clarke manumitted Elizabeth and her children at his death in 1814, and left resources for their care in his will, one child, Elizabeth's youngest, remained enslaved. Elizabeth and her older children removed to Cincinnati in 1816 to chart free lives. The youngest child, Elliot, would finally join his mother, her new Gaines family, and his siblings by John Clarke in 1827 after a decade-long separation. John Gaines would have been approximately six at the time, old enough to begin to grasp the personal suffering and fragility of family ties under slavery.[76] His mother's history and Gaines's half siblings readily told that story.

Tragedy struck the Gaines family in 1832 when Isom, John's father, died of cholera.[77] Not yet in his teens, John still enjoyed brief schooling with the progressive Lane seminarians, but afterward worked to help support his family. Over the next twenty years, John Isom Gaines established himself as an independent grocer, or "stevedore," at the Cincinnati waterfront, catering to steamboat workers. Although the grocery business provided Gaines with a measure of prosperity—in 1850 he reported personal property worth $3,000—work on the levee was grueling and not conducive to intellectual pursuits.[78] Gaines nevertheless hungered for learning and swiftly grew into a forceful scholar by dint of his own serious study, reflection, and writing. His attention to education and enlightenment proved unswerving, without the slightest intemperate diversion. He famously rejected all drink, declining a small tumbler of "sparkling Catawba" wine once mischievously set before him by Cassius Clay while the men dined together at a "social party" in Cincinnati.[79] Gaines used his very short, purposeful life—he died at the age of thirty-eight after a crippling illness—to establish universal, public schooling of the highest intellectual caliber for black children in Cincinnati.

Just a few years after his brief education with the Lane Seminary abolitionists, Gaines participated in a black state convention, probably in 1837. Gaines was sixteen years old and acquiring fame as a wunderkind.[80] At the meeting, the first of its kind in Ohio, "he showed clearly his mental powers, and men, many years his senior, listened with respect to the sage counsel which even then he was capable of giving."[81] Moving at a breakneck speed in life, Gaines displayed great erudition as he approached his thirties. In 1849, though still about twenty-eight years old, Gaines delivered an oration to a Columbus audience celebrating West Indian emancipation. Perhaps revealing his deepest intellectual love, this narrative revealed the work of a skilled, "impartial Historian."[82] Offering a condensed but fine-grained account of the antislavery movement from the Declaration of Independence through to the drama of the moment—the possibility of constitutional emancipation in Kentucky— Gaines wove connections between humble antislavery petitions and high politics, and between the domestic slave trade and an ascendant Free Soil Party. He made black Americans' political and military accomplishments central to the history of abolition, and their patriotism a key to the movement's future success. His forward-looking account drew attention to international influences on the United States' antislavery movement. In reviewing this complicated history, Gaines saw antislavery forces gaining ground. In the late summer of 1849, following the momentous shifts in Ohio's law and with Kentucky "now on the eve of changing her Constitution," Gaines's oration delivered an insistent message: "Yes, it is written in indelible characters on the tablet of the American heart, that slavery shall & must die." "Colored Americans awake," he cried out, "for the days of that hydra-headed monster that has made us aliens in the land of our birth are numbered."[83]

In the two weeks following this address, Kentucky's voters would go to the polls to select delegates to draft a new state constitution that many hoped would begin the gradual process of emancipation in Kentucky, and Cincinnati's African American men would exercise the franchise for the first time in Ohio's history since statehood. On August 13, 1849, black men elected a slate of "school visitors and trustees" to establish Cincinnati's very first state-funded schools for children of color, which now looked imminent. The two prospective votes, and the funding of common schools for black children, must have seemed like harbingers of change for John Isom Gaines when he spoke to the Columbus audience. Elected to the board of school trustees on August 13, Gaines was named board president. Gaines and his fellow trustees swiftly established two schools and employed four talented teachers to instruct Cincinnati's children of color. The common schools were up and running at the beginning of 1850.[84] To be sure, the summer of 1849 had presented severe tests, with Asiatic cholera raging through the Ohio River valley. But Gaines sensed a new historical arc late that summer.

Instead, 1850 proved one of the meanest years. Kentucky strengthened rather than diminished its protections for slavery, blighting hopes for gradual, constitutional emancipation. White officials in Cincinnati fought the new common school law by refusing to disburse the tax money already collected to support schools for children of color on the grounds that black Ohioans were not citizens of the state. In September of that year, Congress stunned Americans with passage of the Fugitive Slave Law. Border violence over slavery that had long smoldered in the West ignited into warfare between proxy armies for northern and southern states in the territories.[85] The Fugitive Slave Law also sparked renewed interest in colonization and emigration schemes among black Ohioans. John Isom Gaines now faced two crises: wavering support among black Americans to remain in the United States, and a legal and constitutional battle to ensure Cincinnati's compliance with the 1849 common school law. These two battles were not unrelated, and for the next five years Gaines redoubled his energies to see black Americans firmly planted in the United States, with hopes for the future inhering in their children's lives.

Gaines first of all waged a legal battle, raising funds and hiring prominent attorneys in Cincinnati to challenge city officials who had blocked disbursement of the common school tax money. One of these attorneys, the unfortunately named Flamen Ball, was Salmon P. Chase's law partner. Ball represented Gaines and the other school trustees. The Ohio Supreme Court found in favor of Gaines, asserting that "the establishment of separate schools for the education of colored children . . . is constitutional" and ordering the public fiscal support of those schools by the city of Cincinnati. They further established that the black trustees were "entitled to all the rights and privileges" enjoyed by white school boards.[86] Because this decision accorded power and autonomy to black educators to govern schools for children of color, historian Nikki Taylor has called the order a "monumental victory."[87] John Gaines's nephew and a leading educator in Cincinnati in his own right, Peter Clark, later wrote of his diminutive uncle's achievement: "At last the little black man triumphed over the city of Cincinnati."[88]

With Gaines at the forefront, black leaders attempted to educate black parents across the state about the 1849 school law, their rights under it, and the supreme court decision mandating city and state funding for their children's schooling. They made a special effort to publicize the main points of the court decision, emphasizing the language of equality. The 1849 act, the court had written, "places colored youth, in Ohio, upon an equal footing with white youth, in respect of Common Schools." Gaines wanted to see parents "guided by" this basic principle "in the formation of School Districts."[89] Yet Gaines also presented an ambitious vision of education to black parents, insisting it was "the glory of any people" and the "foundation" of the "beautiful and judicious structure of their politics, their wise and comprehensive diplomacy and the durability of their institutions."[90] This appears to have been one of

Gaines's foremost ambitions: to see black intelligence an attribute of state and national "glory." Black leaders like Gaines therefore deemed the public nature of common schools inherently significant. Private subscription schools did not lend the air of legitimacy and did not form mutually reinforcing bonds between black families and the state. The 1851 supreme court decision thus marked a pivotal moment. If black parents left public school monies unused, white Ohioans would surely view such an omission as evidence of black incapacity. Gaines could not step back from the effort he had set in motion with his suit. Following the 1851 decision, he and his education allies seemed to be everywhere at once speaking to black families.

Though many black Ohioans already sent their children to private schools, gaining access to the public funds now constitutionally available and building the infrastructure of a common school system were formidable undertakings, as Cincinnatians had learned. Advocates like Gaines encouraged other high aims, such as "convenient school houses," "well qualified teachers," and institutions that expressed "a deep interest in the welfare of the communities" they served.[91] This was the view of education long advocated by Ohio Valley education and antislavery activists to counter prejudice and invalidate proslavery arguments. Needless to say, Gaines's enlightenment project could seem intimidating to families struggling to meet basic needs. Black leaders were not insensitive to this, and launched public relations campaigns. Gaines's lieutenant in this operation, John Mercer Langston, traveled by "horse and buggy across the state from the lake country to the Ohio River" to educate parents about their children's rights to schools and the mechanics of funding and governance. As an Oberlin graduate, Langston also connected black communities to top teaching talent coming out of that progressive institution. Over time, this energetic effort paid dividends: During the 1852–53 school year, just 939 of 6,862 children reportedly attended Ohio's 22 black common schools. By 1860–61, 7,000 students of a total school-age population of 14,247 had enrolled in 159 publicly funded schools.[92]

Profoundly important in principle because it established a right to state-supported common schools, the 1851 supreme court decision arrived at a moment of great turmoil because of the Fugitive Slave Law. Constitutionality and mandated public funding of schools hardly mattered if black people chose to decamp to Canada, the unorganized western territories, or, in Gaines's opinion, the worst of such options, Liberia. Such schemes had attracted renewed interest in 1851 and 1852 due to the Fugitive Slave Law's passage. In convention after convention through the mid-1850s, Gaines worked to stanch such thinking among black Ohioans, earning fame as "the most ultra anti-emigrationist in the West" for his unrelenting stance.[93] Refusing to distinguish between black resettlement plans and white-designed schemes such as "Ohio in Africa," Gaines deemed proposals by men like Martin Delany as "nothing more nor less than the 'old coon' colonization."[94] When Gaines spoke before the 1853 Cincinnati antislavery convention, he gave no ground: "We are not Africans, . . . but we are colored Americans. We claim no other soil than this—no other home than this—no other altar where we can kneel to venerate the memory of our fathers; and he who denies it, be he black or white, is a monomaniac and should be immediately indited and sent to the Lunatic Asylum."[95] Not surprisingly, when Gaines and Langston appeared at Delany's Cleveland convention in 1854 hoping to block the famous emigrationist's inroads among Ohioans, Delany refused to allow Gaines to speak from the floor, although delegates made repeated requests to hear him.[96] Despite Delany's rebuff, Gaines and his allies were surely relieved to find just fifteen black Ohioans in attendance at the convention, a sign that emigrationist sentiment in their home state was abating. Gaines could not risk a mass exodus of black people from the state, especially among those with the wherewithal to do so. Such leave-taking would signal a loss of hope in Ohio's opportunities and future, and would forsake those African Americans with the fewest resources to resettle their families. By 1854, Gaines had wielded enough influence to deal a strong blow to the emigration movement in Ohio.

His enlightenment project still hung in the balance, though. Gaines had the Ohio Supreme Court behind him and a black constituency willing to invest in his plan for universal, public education, but he met new obstacles at the local level. In Cincinnati, the black board of trustees lost authority to manage the common schools when city officials persuaded the state legislature to undo the board's power in 1853. White administrators also launched a concerted effort, it seemed, to alienate black Cincinnatians from their own schools with the appointment of a deeply racist superintendent overseeing daily affairs. Gaines and John Mercer Langston returned to Columbus, and sympathetic assembly members belonging to the new Republican Party eventually passed a law reinstating the power of Cincinnati's black school board. By 1857, a board more truly representing African American voters again wielded authority. In addition to his election to the new board, John Gaines assumed the office of superintendent of Cincinnati's black common schools and the more than six hundred children registered in them.[97] He immediately undertook the construction of two spacious new buildings, thus bringing children out of church basements and cramped parlors for their intellectual growth.[98]

By 1859, when John Gaines died, the struggle to establish decent common schools for children of color, with genuine oversight by black Cincinnatians and supported by Ohio's public funds, had proved herculean. In his last years, Gaines suffered a debilitating condition that left him physically immobile. But he never tired of working on behalf of the public schools he had inaugurated. Eager to weigh in on an important school issue one evening, he asked friends to carry him to a board meeting. He died within days of this exertion.[99]

In 1860, on the eve of the Civil War, Cincinnati's common schools offered black families their surest means to increase their children's economic security and opportunity, in spite of the many injurious ways white Ohioans had tried to stymie the public funding of such schools.[100] Gaines had always viewed the purpose of common schools in the most ambitious terms, as a mode of delivering enlightenment, dispelling prejudice, and quickening emancipation. In furthering these great goals, he despaired at times. In 1853 he conceded, "American prejudice has a woolfish [*sic*] appetite." Freedom for black Americans, wherever they lived, "is a lie—a cruel, unmitigated lie," he wrote bitterly.[101] At the moment of his writing, emigrationists had drawn the attention of black Ohioans, and Cincinnati's black school board had just lost its elective authority. Speaking before an antislavery convention in Cincinnati, Gaines was enraged at these setbacks to his education ambitions and blamed slavery as their cause. Seeing few options, he predicted a violent end to human bondage in America. "I warn Southern men of their danger. . . . If poor human nature having been long outraged, should resolve to throw off the yoke and assert her own rights, who, in the wildness of his imagination can picture the result." History provided the model: "A black Cato or Brutus will yet arise (unless Heaven decree otherwise), in America, as Toussaint L'Overture did in Hayti, and then wo to your ill gotten possessions."[102]

But embedded in this same speech about the "strong arm of the sword" and "brother's blood," Gaines presented an alternative image, that of students in resolute pursuit of a broad education—of enlightenment, really.[103] Before white Cincinnatians undid his elected authority as a board member, Gaines visited the schools under his watch in an effort "to see if there was any difference in the progress of youths arising out of color." "Diligently engaged" in answering this question, he observed classes and spoke to teachers. The students in Cincinnati's black common schools presented a bewildering array of "all complexions—Black, White, Mulatto, Sambo, Mungroo, Quadroon and Mestic." From such schoolrooms, Gaines drew a firm conclusion: "I declare that I was never able to make out a single leading fact" about a relationship between skin color and aptitude. "In Grammar, Geography, Arithmetic,

Reading, Spelling, United States history and Composition, colored children are as forward as white." The "power of intellect," he insisted, "does not grow out of their complexion." If the sheer diversity of students in Cincinnati's black schools rendered spurious any effort to assign capacity to color, Gaines nevertheless brought attention to a single student "who has always struck me with peculiar force" in his thinking about education. In physical appearance, she exhibited what Gaines described as "the leading traits of African character" with her "black skin" and "short hair." To anyone willing to give her due attention, it was "clear as noonday" that this particular girl was "the best reader, speller and thinker in her class." This student served as a lodestar to Gaines. White Americans refused to acknowledge her existence.[104]

Gaines named his culprit for this willful blindness: Thomas Jefferson, and his pronouncements on race in *Notes on the State of Virginia.* " 'Never could I find a black had uttered a thought above the level of a plain narration,' " Gaines quoted from Jefferson's Enlightenment treatise.[105] For Gaines, the way to dislodge this prejudice, articulated so tersely by the United States' foremost statesman, was to prove that enlightenment did not respect color. Gaines faced a formidable antagonist. He could point to "a Frederick Douglass, C. L. Remond, Garnett, Langston, Day, Clark, and last, though not least, of all that black—jet black tower of eloquence, Samuel R. Ward," to demonstrate that "colored persons, like white, are capable of the highest degree of civilization."[106] But Gaines sensed white Americans might deem these men exceptional. He had therefore plotted his course to extend enlightenment and opportunity broadly, to the poorest quarters of urban life, and to Ohioans living under the worst afflictions of prejudice in nineteenth-century America. He also wanted the power of the state behind his education project. Pursuit of enlightenment seemed the only way to demonstrate the fallacy of Jeffersonian prejudice. At the end of his life, this was his deeper commitment, not "the strong arm of the sword."[107]

Saved Educationally

Louisville's African Americans knew John Isom Gaines fairly well. William Gibson, the Kentucky city's leading educator before the Civil War, heard Gaines speak at First of August celebrations in Cincinnati and recalled these important black gatherings in his 1897 memoir.[108] Henry Adams, the long-time minister of Louisville's largest black Baptist church, supervised the city's largest schools before 1860. While he pastored Cincinnati's Union Baptist

Church in the 1850s, Gaines's publicly funded schools operated out of the congregation's building.[109] These two towering figures in Louisville's antebellum history therefore had a close understanding of black Cincinnatians' pursuit of state-funded schools and the significance they attached to rich, broad educations rather than vocational or trade preparation.

Though Gibson and Adams proved exceptional education leaders in their own rights, before extensive contact with the Ohio movement, they nevertheless drew important lessons from the Cincinnati experience. Foremost among these lessons was the need for state and locally funded schools so that children of color enjoyed Kentucky's investment in their advancement. Far more than any other locale in the commonwealth, Louisvillians pursued access to public funding with tremendous energy immediately following the Civil War. And like black Cincinnatians, they closely monitored the tax monies to ensure their expenditure on behalf of Louisville's African American children. Moreover, as in Cincinnati, black Louisvillians wanted oversight of their children's schools and fought for the right of separate governance of the segregated schools in the 1860s and 1870s. Their advocacy for public money came more than a decade after the great effort by advocates like Gaines in Cincinnati, but the Louisvillians saw swift change. By the fall of 1873, nearly two thousand African American children were enrolled in publicly funded common schools in Louisville. That same year, black educators dedicated Central School, a new $25,000 three-story building with ten "recitation rooms" and office space for its new principal. White elected officials from the city and state and Louisville's black school board members participated together in the ceremonial exercises. These were important accomplishments in a former slave state in the immediate aftermath of the Civil War.[110]

One figure at the 1873 school dedication was African Methodist Episcopal Bishop Daniel A. Payne who had contributed indirectly to black Louisvillians' strong culture of education in Louisville before the Civil War. In the 1840s, he had tutored a very young William Gibson in Baltimore. Gibson must have shown a strong intellectual bent, for after attending "select schools," prominent black religious leaders, including Payne, provided "private instructions" to him. The precocious youth was being groomed for important work. When the minister at Louisville's Fourth Street Colored Methodist Church announced a call for a teacher, Gibson responded. The Louisville minister had specifically requested a teacher who was "desirous of benefiting his race."[111] Well educated by his private tutors, Gibson proved a perfect match for the church-based school, for as he later wrote, the "wishes and desires of our hearts" was to see that "our people might be saved educationally, and at the same time be the recipients and participants in the redemption of others in this great work."[112] A dreamer and a visionary, the young Gibson brought with him a deep commitment to intellectual life as a means to freedom.[113]

In early 1848, Gibson established the first of several highly regarded schools in Louisville, and he did this unabashedly before the city's slaveholders. Undaunted by warnings to remain discreet in his educational projects or face "city authorities," Gibson placed his first school "in the heart of the city."[114] In contrast, the three other schools operated by African American teachers at the time stayed "on the outskirts of the city" so as not "to be so objectionable."[115] And although he had direct "instructions to teach no slaves without a written permit from their master or mistress," Gibson overcame this intended deterrent to educating enslaved children in schools. "Of these permits we had hundreds on file," Gibson remembered with satisfaction.[116] He operated day and night schools, with between fifty and one hundred students enrolled at a time. His schools pushed beyond the rudiments of math and language literacy to offer a highly regarded music program and advanced algebra and geometry, as well as Latin language studies. For these rigorous programs, Gibson had financial support from the "Quaker Friends of Indiana," who "visited the school and inspected the work" in the mid-1850s, finding all to their satisfaction.[117]

Gibson saw education in the double sense that black Cincinnatians also advocated: education promised broad enlightenment, what Gibson described as "the thirst for light," but it was also a powerful form of antislavery persuasion. Though still a very young man, just in his twenties, Gibson grasped this double sense, and seemingly all of his varied educational pursuits operated with a twofold agenda. Even music bore antislavery messages in Louisville. At the Fourth Street Methodist Church, Gibson introduced music and singing schools upon his arrival. An avid violinist, Gibson established an orchestra with African American and German immigrant musicians in the city; they called themselves the Mozart Society of Louisville.[118] Because of this classical musicianship, Gibson invited the attention of prominent white Louisvillians who came away from his church's choir performances persuaded of "the capacity of improvement in the colored population." When a group of white emancipationists visited the church in 1848, they "were not prepared for the correctness of style, the excellence of modulation" in the choir. What struck the white visitors as especially remarkable was the forty-member choir's use of "note-books" through the performance and their obvious "acquaintance with the language of letters and of music, which could be the result only of good instruction, well applied." Since the Fourth Street Church was "mostly composed of slaves," undoubtedly the choir included some individuals still subject to masters.[119]

Many southerners, including even proslavery advocates, had long advocated teaching enslaved people to read the Bible. White evangelicals in Louisville generally supported Sunday school work among children of color, according to Gibson, and Louisville's emancipationists often urged the churches "to teach colored people to read the word of God."[120] This did not appear to be controversial, at least not in Louisville. Although a committed Methodist, Gibson wanted to stretch beyond Bible literacy. As he put it, "We were feeling our way, aiming for a higher plane of civilization."[121] Original musical compositions, classical orchestration, and formal choirs lining out their notes offered a novel way to insinuate new ideas about black intellectuality among white Kentuckians. Such musical performances offered an indirect means to argue for "the religious and intellectual education of the blacks generally" and black Kentuckians' particular readiness for freedom.[122] Some white Louisvillians became persuaded of this idea in the late 1840s through Gibson's calculated artistry.

Though he and his fellow education advocates sought the "general improvement of the mind" with zeal and energy, Gibson viewed this objective as a piece with his abolitionist work.[123] While he could not safely advocate abolition, even in Louisville, Gibson longed to be part of the national movement. In addition to joining black gatherings in Cincinnati, he attended a Free Soil Convention in 1852 wishing to hear Frederick Douglass. Writing in 1897, Gibson remembered many of the details of Douglass's speech and bearing at that meeting. He immediately subscribed to Douglass's paper, but had to do so secretly. Sent first to New Albany, Indiana, the papers were ferried over the Ohio River, and closely "read by us," with "the subject-matter discussed" among black Louisvillians. To prevent discovery by white authorities, Gibson concealed Douglass's papers inside his piano "among the music"—art and abolition inseparable.[124]

White emancipationists also began to draw close connections between slavery in Kentucky and the degree of education among the state's people, and in particular undertook a rich discussion of the common schools in Louisville. "Public schools," wrote the editors of the Louisville *Examiner*, had enlarged purposes, far beyond practical training in mechanical trades or business. Their purpose was to cultivate "the infinite value of the love of truth, of justice, of integrity, of fidelity in contracts, of industry, of charitableness, [of] judgment." Good common schools instructed children in managing social relations and encouraged "improving all one's faculties."[125] But they were also intended to bring all classes together, making education universal, rather than the privilege of the wealthy or the last resort of the poor. Louisvillians sharply rebuked Kentucky's leadership on this point, arguing that "the State has not dealt fairly with her *poor* children."[126] The city of Louisville also came in for stinging criticism. Although the city had established a free public school system early, in 1829, almost a decade ahead of the state, Louisville's common schools enrolled few students, probably because a tuition requirement had been imposed to pay for buildings. Enrollment in 1850 was at a lowly 691 students for the entire city, and close to 20 percent of those went to school for only three months of the year.[127] For a time, scholarships gave "poor lads" a chance to attend more advanced grades, depending on merit, but that encouragement had fallen away by 1850. Teachers were not paid well, and buildings were in an embarrassing state of disrepair. Parents even failed to come to their children's public examinations. Louisville's emancipationists staked out their theory of decline: "The institution of slavery, and a good practical system of public education *never have* and *never can* co-exist together."[128]

Support for universal free education proved one of the most significant arguments of the emancipationist movement in Louisville, where nonslaveholders, mostly working class, held sway in elections. Louisville counted more working and laboring men than any other southern city in 1850.[129] With these voters in mind, antislavery advocates repeatedly offered a vision of "common schools bringing light and liberty to the poor man's cabin" in the run-up to elections for delegates to the Kentucky Constitutional Convention in 1849.[130] At a mass meeting of "mechanics and laboring men" in 1849, emancipationists promised "common schools, adequate to the wants of a nation of freemen, drawing their nourishment from the bosom of the State, nestling in every valley, and lifting their sunny fronts on every mountain top."[131] If this sounded impossibly utopian, Louisville's antislavery activists insisted that voters need only look for proof in Ohio, which had "dotted her whole surface with schoolhouses!" By contrast, Kentucky "left her children without the means of acquiring an education."[132] The Louisvillians raised a terrifying specter of "poorer boys" without schooling, whose "ignorance" brought them to "social degradation," including crime and intemperance. The worst off "sank into utter depravity, and breathed their last as outcasts." By its "very nature at war" with education, slavery had made poor families' children a "sacrifice."[133] Although Louisville's emancipationists stressed the ways slavery demeaned white working men's labor, they made calls for universal public education visceral.

The city's voters responded at the polls. Sometimes called the "Free White Laborers" coalition, white emancipationists and working men regularly sent antislavery men to Congress from Louisville through the 1840s, and three times elected an antislavery candidate to the office of mayor. Nearly half of the Louisville city council was made up of antislavery advocates in 1848. In the 1849 elections for the constitutional convention, emancipationist candidates drew approximately 45 percent of the city's votes.[134] Although Louisville's antislavery working men did not have enough electoral clout to overcome proslavery advocates at the state constitutional convention in 1849, they did compel one smaller, significant change at the local level: in 1851, Louisville's city council made its public schools entirely free, eliminating the tuition hampering poorer children from gaining access to education. In consequence, enrollment in the city's public schools surged into the thousands.[135]

In the state of Kentucky, Louisville was distinctive in its manufacturing and commercial economy, its large number of European immigrants, its diminishing reliance on slavery, and its political antipathy to slavery. Louisvillians' assertion of the value of common schools and public support for free education also proved unusual in antebellum Kentucky. In the immediate aftermath of the Civil War, black Louisvillians sought to capitalize on this broad support to secure public funding for the private schools already serving children of color in the city.

In 1865, at the close of the Civil War, black Louisvillians conducted approximately eight private schools serving nearly one thousand children. Demand for schools was at an all-time high, with large numbers of children—as many as forty at one popular school—sitting outside classroom doors awaiting vacancies.[136] As Louisville's African American women grouped together to raise money to pay the tuition required for their children's education, leading men sent petitions urging the state legislature to provide common schools for black children. As in the Cincinnati example, they also wanted to ensure black oversight of funds, teachers, and buildings.[137] Although the state passed several laws theoretically supporting common schools for black Kentuckians in the late 1860s, none required the building of schools, and the legislation perversely required that separate school funds first go toward the support of paupers. This impossible condition meant that black Kentuckians annually paid taxes toward a school fund that met with all manner of misuse and confusion at the local level. In consequence, state money almost never made it to black schools until the legislature established a segregated system in 1874.[138]

Between late 1866 and the summer of 1870, the Freedmen's Bureau in Kentucky injected tens of thousands of dollars into black schools operating in the state, supplementing what black families were already paying privately in tuition. In 1868–69, Kentucky's freed people paid $26,000 toward the schooling of approximately thirteen thousand children. The Freedmen's Bureau primed this pump with more than $40,000 of additional support for the approximately 267 schools then operating in the state.[139] As important as Freedmen's Bureau money was, especially for rural districts, Kentucky's African Americans still supported 87 schools entirely on their own, with no public subsidies. As Marion Lucas has observed for these immediate postwar years, "Overall, Kentucky blacks contributed larger sums for education of their children than did those of any southern state except Louisiana."[140]

The states' most well-established black schools remained in Louisville, and education leaders like Gibson resided there. The city's voters had also demonstrated strong public support for free universal education. Freedmen's aid groups chose Louisville when they wanted to establish an institution to train black teachers, dedicating a school there in 1868.[141] In consequence, when the Freedmen's Bureau declared its intentions to leave Kentucky, thereby withdrawing its support to black schools, efforts to seek public funding largely fell to Louisvillians. In the summer of 1869, a "Colored Educational Convention" in the city drew more than 250 delegates and white supporters of black education from across Kentucky. Though lacking official sanction, they established a "Kentucky State Board of Education," drew up school districts, agreed to a system of management, and determined conditions for teacher certification. Delegates approved a constitution and bylaws and elected its board, with William Gibson named as its first president. A "Board of Examiners" also had a black Louisvillian at its helm.[142] Education leaders thus took matters into their own hands to ensure school organization and support. At this meeting they enjoyed the guidance of one veteran from the education front, John Mercer Langston, who in 1851 had served as a preacher of black education in Ohio, itinerating across the state to convince parents to join the public school movement. Almost twenty years later, Kentuckians borrowed this example, selecting their own "Traveling Agent and Organizer of County and District Schools." According to Gibson, "Many schools were organized and teachers employed" through the agent's labors.[143] Although this group once again petitioned the state legislature for "equal taxes and equal education," the city of Louisville became the first public entity to create a common school fund for black children, just eight months after the Colored Education Convention took place.[144] The Louisville fund brought forward the taxes black residents had been paying since 1866 and added an appropriation from the city. These public funds immediately went to support three black schools.

The Fifth Street Baptist Church's private school converted into Louisville's first public school for African Americans, known as "No. 1." Through the antebellum era, Henry Adams had conducted a large school at his Louisville church without interruption, and the designation as school "No. 1" gave modest recognition of that achievement.[145] Adams was part of another public education first in the Ohio River valley: when John Gaines established his initial two common schools in Cincinnati, one was located at Union Baptist Church, where Henry Adams served as the minister.

The schools established in the Civil War era in Cincinnati and Louisville segregated black and white students and gravely underfunded most black school districts. Black school trustees were encumbered by racism in their efforts to oversee educational quality and ensure a close connection between the institutions and the people they served. State and local officials in both Ohio and Kentucky also used criminal malfeasance in budgets and levies to both underfund and overtax African Americans for their children's educations. These inequities have required vigilance, advocacy, and legal battles into the twenty-first century.

This should not take away from what people like William Gibson believed they had achieved. As Gibson looked back from 1897, he marked the transformation from his arrival in Louisville fifty years earlier. In 1847, four tuition-based schools enrolled two hundred black children, but as he wrote at the end of his life, "we have thousands in attendance in the schools of this city, over one hundred teachers, nine buildings, and a high school." "County and district schools" now educated children of color "all over the State." Gibson wanted this remembered as an important revolution at a moment of faltering hopes among black Kentuckians still struggling against intractable inequity and exclusion. Although Gibson's purpose in writing his memoir was to provide a very human history of the past fifty years and he rarely placed this in a sacred framework, in this instance he followed his sharply drawn statistical comparison with an immediate hallelujah: "Praise God from whom all blessings flow," he wrote.[146]

Of course, human advocacy charted this transformation, and in particular historical ways, as Gibson wanted to recount. John Isom Gaines and Gibson petitioned, lobbied, and organized to reap equal public tax dollars for black common schools. Private tuition-based and subscription schools were simply out of financial reach for most black families in Ohio and Kentucky. The public schools opened their doors to all comers, though, to be sure, in ways that often reinforced many whites' prejudices. For all of the shortcomings of this relationship, black families now had a formal bond to the state that was circuited through their children. Though imperfect, public investment stated clearly that black intellectual expression and cultivation mattered, and it mattered to the fullest workings of the state and representative democracy. This was at least in part because men like Gaines and Gibson had insisted on such a breathtaking sense of enlightenment by way of common schools.

Fictions

Most white Americans living in the Ohio River valley had not anticipated the advent of black public education nor, perhaps especially, the African American pursuit of enlightened curricula—that is, something greater than functional knowledge to get by in the world. A good number of white Ohioans and Kentuckians fought these developments, unable to harmonize the idea of black intellectual ambition with pervasive claims of black people's likely, if not inevitable, degradation outside of slavery. But by the late antebellum era, publicly funded schools and private colleges graduating African American students were a hard-won reality in Ohio, and black Louisvillians offered ample evidence of educational ambition and accomplishment.

In both Cincinnati and Louisville, antislavery activists endlessly made the argument that, in freedom, ex-slaves would not fall into dependency and recklessness, thereby endangering white freedom and security. Free blacks' educational attainments in Cincinnati and Louisville provided powerful evidence disproving proslavery ideas of black incapacity. Antislavery advocates regularly pointed to these achievements—cataloging example after example of significant personal success even in the face of nearly insurmountable barriers. John Isom Gaines sought to do so in Cincinnati in 1853 by listing the many impressive black scholars, doctors, and public figures known throughout the northern states. But Gaines also recognized that many white Americans had yet to fully reckon with, and make sense of, black intellectual equality as a general proposition. By their inherent structure, universal public schools assumed intellectual promise, if not equality, among all children. Yet the legislature in Ohio (and later in Kentucky) tried to diminish the radical significance of public education for African Americans by first establishing segregated schools with visibly unequal resources allocated for their support. In sum, a welter of ideas—many of them inconsistent if not mutually exclusive—about black ability, readiness for freedom, and capacity for full inclusion in the state as citizens—competed for attention in the Ohio River valley on the eve of the Civil War.

In the 1850s, an unusual literature emerged from the region that attempted to make sense of the proposition of black intellectual equality and its concomitant argument for full inclusion in the American body politic. Written by white authors sympathetic to—even entirely committed to—immediate abolition, this fictional literature came from both Cincinnati and Louisville, where local authors and publishers witnessed clashing examples of slavery's inherently demeaning practices and free blacks' efforts to establish their essential humanity and equality through the pursuit of literacy and education. The literature these authors and publishers produced dwelled on black literacy especially, as in the case of Stowe's *Uncle Tom's Cabin* and in a fictional slave narrative by a white Kentucky native, Mattie Griffith, entitled *The Autobiography of a Female Slave*. Acquiring some fame through her poetry, which often appeared in George Prentice's *Daily Journal*, Griffith lived in Louisville in the early 1850s before moving to Boston, where she joined radical Garrisonian antislavery social and literary circles. Published in 1857, her pseudo–slave narrative takes place in Kentucky, with nearly half of the novel devoted to fictional events in Louisville. As in Stowe's earlier blockbuster novel, *The Autobiography of a Female Slave* makes black readers pivotal to its story—indeed, the plot itself could not progress without the lead character's depth of humanity, which is revealed by her literacy. These two singular novels were not the only publications treating such themes. In Cincinnati, an organization of white antislavery activists formed a high-volume publishing house for antislavery children's literature in the early 1850s. The Cincinnati board solicited, edited, and distributed stories that in every instance showcased black readers, intellectuality, and personal subjectivity. Nearly all of the narratives also made schools the settings for plot development and key shifts in white children's attitudes toward people of color and toward slavery more generally. The Cincinnati and Louisville fictional literature shows, collectively, a sustained effort on the part of some whites to grasp just how far black Americans' literacy and full intellectual equality had altered the landscape of racial relations in the Ohio River valley.

But important distinctions arise in looking at this fiction together—that is, by comparing Stowe's disruptive novel, Griffith's inferior and lesser-known work, and Cincinnati's robust enterprise in antislavery children's stories. *Uncle Tom's Cabin* proved distinctive in two significant ways. Most obviously, the novel offered a striking narrative due to Stowe's longer experience and serious thinking about the importance of compelling dialogue and realistic detail. Her fast-paced plotting also riveted readers. Stowe represents, by far, the best writer of the group, for all of the common sentimental tropes employed across this body of literature. These stylistic issues are significant, for they meant that Stowe's serialized novel quickly drew a mass readership. While not ignored, the other narratives never approached *Uncle Tom's Cabin*'s powerful sway. But a second contrast is nevertheless important. While Stowe's novel famously concluded with an unequivocal colonization argument that African Americans seeking full command and direction over their lives would never enjoy equality or satisfaction in the United States, the other fictional accounts insisted on the opposite: that black Americans deserved lives entirely equal to whites in northern free states. Nearly every story published by the Cincinnati advocates, and even Griffith's Louisville drama, concludes with black Americans, many of them ex-slaves, establishing self-determining lives in the United States. For readers, and especially for children, the authors made black characters' lives in places like Ohio appear natural and inevitable once whites had been purged of their errant racism. Though Stowe's novel was far more consequential, its advocacy of colonization did not represent a consensus among white residents of the Ohio River valley. Lesser writers and publishers from the region adopted and revisited her fictional representations of black subjectivity through literacy but arrived at entirely different conclusions. Together, the literature reveals both the imaginative constraints and freedom giving shape to Americans' beliefs about the viability of a biracial society on the eve of the Civil War.

Acts of Reading

Harriet Beecher Stowe resided just outside of Cincinnati, in Walnut Hills, for eighteen years, from 1832 until the spring of 1850. In the West, she married, gave birth to six children, managed a complex household, faced financial insolvency, and began a literary career. Her full life in Cincinnati contained both joy and great travail.[147] Nearly forty years old when she left Ohio for Brunswick, Maine, she had acquired some familiarity with black Cincinnatians' lives, appreciation for slaveholders' great power and violence, and warm antislavery sentiments while living in Walnut Hills. Enraged by the Fugitive Slave Law of 1850, she drew on her western experiences to write installments of *Uncle Tom's Cabin*, which appeared in Gamaliel Bailey's Washington, D.C., antislavery newspaper, the *National Era*, for nearly a year beginning in June 1851. Though readers and critics questioned whether *Uncle Tom's Cabin* offered a "fair representation of slavery," Stowe insisted that her experiences "on the frontier-line of slave states" allowed her to offer "sketches drawn from life." "Some of the most deeply tragic and romantic, some of the most terrible incidents, have also their parallel in reality," she wrote.[148]

Romantic racialism, evangelical Christianity, and sentimentality operated as heavy filters on Stowe's narrative, yet her skillful storytelling maintained a "surface texture of convincing realism."[149] Before writing *Uncle Tom's Cabin*, Stowe had grown convinced of the power of fiction to foster understanding, to "make real and vivid on every mind" ideas that might otherwise fall victim to abstraction.[150] For Stowe, imaginative stories enmeshed in "historic verisimilitude" had the greatest potential to animate feeling, which in turn activated knowledge. In fiction, feeling was inseparable from reasoning. She characterized such narrative work as "combined imagination and critical ingenuity."[151] In short, fiction operated on the reader's imagination to stimulate feeling, thereby producing understanding.[152] She applied this thesis to the moral problem of slavery. By 1851, when Stowe began to write, Americans had grown familiar with antislavery arguments and premises, and representations of enslaved peoples in fiction and poetry had become conventional, even "perfunctory"; thoughtful people seemed "inured" to slaves' suffering. As Barbara Hochman has argued, "Stowe was determined to break through what she saw as the defenses of readers who could hear about slavery every day, and never 'listen.'"[153] Upon passage of the Fugitive Slave Law, Stowe felt "perfect surprise and consternation" that "humane people" had resigned themselves to aid in the capture and delivery of fugitive slaves to authorities, as the new law demanded. To Stowe, this morally bankrupt response demonstrated that "men and Christians cannot know what slavery is." With her formidable narrative skills, Stowe believed she could upset complacency by describing slavery's great wrongs as "a *living dramatic reality*."[154]

Though she had wanted to supply enlivening detail and description, Stowe nevertheless relied on the conventions of her era, deploying the strategies of sentimentality to prepare white readers to "*feel right*" about the sufferings of others. She also presented race as a fixed, inborn quality: the "Anglo-Saxon" in her rendering was "stern, inflexible, energetic," while people of African descent were "affectionate, magnanimous, and forgiving."[155] Coaxing an appropriate white sympathetic response to black distress, Stowe's novel worked to "objectify" and thereby "dehumanize" her black characters, as many critics and scholars have observed. Of course, this was precisely what Stowe hoped to avoid in *Uncle Tom's Cabin*, but it is impossible to read the novel today without seeing the ways sentimentality and romantic racialism circumscribed the very people she sought to characterize with greater individuation.[156]

Yet *Uncle Tom's Cabin* remains a complex text, made all the more refractory to analysis with its many secondary derivations, illustrations, and abridgements that quickly appeared in print, stage, and song. Stowe provided depth and subjectivity to the enslaved figures in her story when she described them as readers. To be sure, the way Stowe presented the act of reading itself, and recognizable social practices around reading, reflected middle-class habits of mind. Stowe made reading an essential feature of secure families and religious faith, a part of the nineteenth century's veneration of domesticity. While many southerners viewed literate black people—whether enslaved or free—with suspicion, as sources of unrest or slave flight, Stowe generally characterized them as "pious and peace-loving." Even so, according to Barbara Hochman, these same "scenes of reading harbored radical implications," for they gave her audience enduring images of "black privacy, subjectivity, and moral autonomy." By depicting enslaved peoples (and former slaves) in private study of a book, in discussions about the meaning of texts, and in spaces physically dominated by books, Stowe showed black characters thoughtfully immersed in the ascendant culture of reading. As Hochman explains, "The very association of reading with contemplation—with moral and spiritual qualities rather than professional or commercial activities—made it a perfect vehicle for representing interiority, the very thing white readers regularly denied black people." "Literacy," she writes, "could facilitate citizenship, self-improvement, or worldly success only for a person with a heart, mind, and soul."[157] In this way, Stowe used the images of reading to signal and describe that deepest personhood of her black characters to her own readers. These representations encouraged white readers' identification with black figures in her narrative and would seem to have provided a basis for a more harmonious biracial society, for they suggested agreement on sources of subjectivity.

But Stowe sent her narrative in an unexpected direction: to Africa, Liberia specifically, where the character of George Harris, along with his family, chooses to settle in order to satisfy the ex-slave George's desire for "an African *nationality*." Self-educated under slavery, university trained in freedom, George has developed all of the values and habits of independence. An emblem of his depth of character and self-possession is his regular practice of reading "well-selected books," which he examines carefully by "making notes." His "study" is set apart within his family's modest but warm "tenement" in Canada. Sitting at his writing desk and "table covered with a green cloth," a small library attached, George Harris looked the part of Saint Jerome in his study, after van Eyck. George is scholarly, contemplative—a practitioner of the "coveted arts of reading and writing." But still, in Stowe's rendering, his reading and "self-cultivation" is in service of his family, to which he is fiercely attached, and of an active Christian life. It is just in this moment of recognition and identification, of relief and satisfaction that white readers would have had in Harris's life, that Stowe redirects him to Africa. In Stowe's explanation, Harris wants a "tangible, separate existence" from either the United States or Canada, where he can "form part of a nation, which shall have a voice in the councils of nations." From such a position he can better achieve the abolition of slavery in the United States, for, as Stowe has Harris argue, "A nation has a right to argue, remonstrate, implore, and present the cause of its race,—which an individual has not." In a strange inconsistency with the image of Harris as contemplative, Stowe indicates that he wants to go to Liberia in order to "work with both hands," as a kind of physical nation-builder rather than a philosophical one.[158]

In January 1851, six months before the first installments of *Uncle Tom's Cabin* appeared, Stowe explained her initial purpose in undertaking her narrative in a letter to her husband, Calvin Stowe. She explained that her envisioned "sketch for the Era" would treat "the capabilities of liberated blacks to take care of themselves," and she requested that Calvin, still residing in Cincinnati, gather information from the city's black community: "Cant you find for me how much Willie Watson has paid for the redemption of his friends—& get me any items in figures of that kind that you can pick up in Cincinnati."[159] He dutifully gathered this information, and his brief, notarized survey of black self-purchase, family redemption, and economic success in Cincinnati appears in her "Concluding Remarks" to the novel. In addition to this community survey, Stowe drew on her limited knowledge of Cincinnati's free blacks to demonstrate, she wrote, that "the first desire of the emancipated slave, generally, is for *education*." She explained: "There is nothing that they are not willing to give or do to have their children instructed." Stowe claimed to have even labored as a teacher herself, having taught the children of her black servants "in a family school, with her own children."[160] Several of Stowe's servants had escaped from slavery. Combined, Calvin's sociological evidence and Harriet's firsthand experiences revealed an extraordinary effort toward achieving freedom, and then self-made success and education, among those in Cincinnati's black community. Stowe believed she had fulfilled one of her original purposes in writing *Uncle Tom's Cabin*.

Yet, oddly, these achievements did not suggest to Stowe that residence and citizenship in the United States might also be ex-slaves' goals. William Watson, known to Harriet and included in Calvin's canvass, achieved eminence and a measure of wealth in Cincinnati; he also served as a longtime deacon of

Union Baptist Church. No evidence exists suggesting that Watson condoned colonization or even emigration, and Calvin Stowe's synopsis did not reveal if any of the men for whom he collected information supported Liberian removal. In fact, all indications are that Cincinnati's black community rejected colonization, and meetings held in Watson's very own Union Baptist Church strenuously advocated against such schemes.[161] Moreover, the drive toward public-funded education, at least theoretically achieved in 1849 legislation and just underway in Cincinnati as she left, eluded Stowe's sight. Though she mentions private schools for African American children established "by benevolent individuals" and her own home schooling efforts, she did not foresee the state of Ohio having a stake in black education. Stowe therefore could not grasp black parents' understanding of schools and education as a piece with their commitment to place and to citizenship in the United States. Colonization did not make sense within the context of that bond.[162]

Vivid Narratives

Stowe's Liberian argument was immediately apparent to readers, who understood *Uncle Tom's Cabin* as "distinctively a Colonization book."[163] Especially in the immediate aftermath of the Fugitive Slave Law, many whites sympathetic to antislavery and to black rights evinced frustration with Congress and the great impediments to change. If voluntary, colonization or emigration schemes did not appear out of the question. This seems to have been the case with Salmon Chase, who privately advised black Ohioans to consider the West Indies and Liberia in the late fall of 1850, just weeks after passage of the act.[164] But most sympathetic whites in Cincinnati did not flinch on colonization, as Chase appeared to do in 1850 from his perch in the U.S. Senate and as Stowe did from her new home in Brunswick, Maine. In fact, leading antislavery activists in Cincinnati affirmed strong commitments to emancipation on the soil and to black rights just six months before Congress passed the Fugitive Slave Law in September 1850. In consequence, they proved less susceptible to renewed calls for colonization amid the furor that followed the Fugitive Slave Law's enactment.

In the immediate aftermath of the Ohio state legislature's repeal of the Black Laws, antislavery activists in Cincinnati appeared emboldened. In late 1849, a group of religious abolitionists began to organize anew in the city, calling for a "Christian Anti-Slavery Convention" to be held in the spring of 1850. Prominent ministers, politicians, and educators from across the Old Northwest states attended the meeting, with Cincinnatians predominating.

John Fee, the Presbyterian minister from Kentucky, attended along with ministers from Methodist, Baptist, Episcopal, and Quaker churches in the North. Asserting without qualification that "slavery directly contravenes the laws of God," the men called for urgent, ongoing advocacy in churches and civil society to end slavery. They asked ministers to "instruct their congregations in the duties of citizens, of voters, of legislators, and of administrative and judicial officers" so as to be more effective agents of legal or constitutional emancipation. They also threatened electoral repercussions against candidates for office who continued to support discriminatory Black Laws, insisting that "Christians have no moral right to help into office men who disregard the rights of any class of their fellow men." Though the men stressed legal avenues of change, in a more radical vein they gave evangelicals permission to disobey "laws which contravene the laws of God." They clearly sensed momentum for change and wanted church members, of whatever denominational stripe, to continue to agitate against slavery and prejudice in the public sphere. Using pulpits and churches, these evangelicals would flex their electoral might for political ends. A final resolution adopted by the convention, at the last day's last hour, came from John B. Vashon, a prominent African American leader, war veteran, and educator from Pittsburgh. Without amending Vashon's proposed language, the conventioneers declared "that the American Colonization Society is a twin sister to Slavery, and has done incalculable injury to the free colored man, and should not be countenanced by the Christian Churches."[165] In the spring of 1850, then, Cincinnati's evangelicals had taken on a mighty task of persuading the public and its elected representatives of the justness of immediate emancipation without colonization. Passage of the Fugitive Slave Law a few months later did not stem their ambitions, nor were they inclined to renege on their resolutions against colonization.

In 1851, a number of men who had been active participants in the Christian Anti-Slavery Convention formed a publishing society, deeming the press "one of the most powerful influences which can be employed to form a correct public sentiment."[166] Established in Cincinnati in late 1851, the group called itself the American Reform Tract and Book Society (ARTBS) and named evangelical Congregationalists and Presbyterians from the city to its board of directors. John Rankin, friend to the fugitive slave in Ripley, Ohio, served as the group's first president. The organization maintained a regular newspaper, known as the *Christian Press*, and published close to one hundred antislavery and religious tracts for adults, including John Fee's argument against colonization (and in favor of "amalgamation") and powerful works decrying racism, such as Benjamin Aydelott's *Prejudice Against Colored People* (1852). Neverthe-less, the ARTBS made a strategic decision to focus on children, deeming them likely converts and lifetime voters or activists for emancipation without colonization.[167]

Because national publishing societies like the American Tract Society and the American Sabbath School Union strictly avoided reference to the national sin of slavery in their publications, the ARTBS board believed it had discovered an "almost universal vacuum" in the nation's influential market for Sabbath school literature. The proposed ARTBS literature would offer "vivid narratives" so that children might understand "American Slavery as it is," and "their hearts be made to feel for the down-trodden sons of Africa in our own beloved country."[168] By "children," the ARTBS seemed to mean girls and boys between the ages of eight and thirteen, old enough for conflicts of consequence to occur, yet young enough to enjoy malleable minds. Children at that age were more likely to attend Sunday school and perhaps also com-mon schools or private academies, so many of the narratives begin in formal school settings, especially if the story takes place in the North. If in the South, private tutoring or some kind of surreptitious instruction among slaves often drives plot development. Familiar with schools, young readers would have had an expectation of intellectual development and cultivation—by white as well as black characters—because of the inherent nature of the settings. Sabbath schools looked to even greater transformations among students in pursuit of "changes of heart." Anticipating that children would naturally link schools with cultivation and radical transformation, ARTBS authors and publishers hoped to prime readers for more flexible thinking about their own future interactions with people of color. Persuaded of emancipated people's right to self-determining lives within the United States and the justness of aboli-tion, children reading these books would exert important influence in their families, among friends, and, as adults, in politics and governance, so the ARTBS board hoped.

By the time of the Civil War, the ARTBS advertised more than one hun-dred titles in its catalog of publications; in 1859 alone, the society distributed some four million pages of antislavery and religious literature.[169] While in most cases it is difficult to determine where the authors of this literature lived (although at least two children's stories are set in Ohio), the ARTBS's Cincinnati publishers shaped the stories' content. For example, in 1855 the so-ciety offered a $100 prize "for the best manuscript for a religious Anti-Slavery Sunday School Book, showing that American chattel slaveholding is a sin against God, and a crime against man, and that it ought to be immediately repented of and abolished." Forty-eight authors from across the country entered the contest.[170] Awarding their prize to Maria Goodell Frost's manuscript, "Gospel Fruits," the Cincinnati publishers also asked her to revise the ending of the story.[171] After selecting and reshaping their children's stories, the ARTBS then sought a broad distribution for its sentimental literature. The officers of the ARTBS had close ties to the American Missionary Association, whose missionaries and colporteurs sold the Cincinnati society's evangelical and antislavery literature throughout the West.[172] Through their close connection to Rev. John Fee, officers claimed that ARTBS "tracts have already been circulated to some extent in Kentucky, and more are called for from that State." "Even there, they are beginning to read," Charles Boynton wrote hopefully to potential Congregationalist supporters.[173]

The ARTBS published at least twelve original antislavery stories and novels designed to teach children that prejudice and slavery were twin evils.[174] These stories are unique in their depiction of friendships between black and white children and their representations of cross-race identification among both children and adults.[175] While a shared evangelical Protestantism makes these friendships and identifications possible, the relationships are also intensely sentimental: black and white tears flow together, black and white hearts pulsate in harmony, and white people react physically to black suffering. In the ARTBS's literature, authors linked blacks and whites in remarkable physical and emotional intimacy and made community harmony dependent on blacks' and whites' social responsibility toward one another. Though sentimentally bound together, fictional blacks and whites redressed the problem of prejudice and confronted the terrors of slavery in unequal ways. Generally speaking, authors encourage white characters to feel for black suffering and to render aid to people of color in situations of severe crisis. As in other sentimental works, including *Uncle Tom's Cabin*, white readers might draw the conclusion that they were safely unlike black people, whose anguish merited readers' pity and sympathy, but perhaps little more than that. In this way, sentimental fiction helped "to police the boundaries of the self" rather than "break down barriers by extending the category of the human."[176] However well intentioned, such literature potentially reinforced a sense of difference between black and white people.

But as in *Uncle Tom's Cabin*, images or storylines within a sentimental text can work against the genre's tendency to impose distance between sufferer and savior. Because audiences had wide familiarity with sentimentality as a mode of discourse by the time Stowe's book appeared, readers may have sought out elements of "surprise" in *Uncle Tom's Cabin*. As Hochman explains,

"Sympathy for 'the lowly' was only one of many responses to her tale, even in the 1850s."[177] Though Cincinnati's ARTBS literature also encouraged sympathy, even pity, on the part of white readers for slaves' or free blacks' tribulations, the stories invited other considerations, including the pursuit of reading and literacy among black Americans. These representations demanded responses from white readers beyond sympathy alone.

Several major themes related to education appear in ARTBS children's fiction. One profoundly important theme is the desire among people of color for literacy as part of a systematic education. This holds true if the story takes place in the North or the South, but the separate narratives stress the very different kinds of conditions under which enslaved people of the South and free blacks in the North might acquire an education. Even for stories set in the South, though, the best educations derived from semiformal instruction by teachers or tutors, usually white instructors. In either scenario, though, ARTBS narratives emphasized independent initiative and self-taught skills among black children and adults to depict literacy as a kind of innate human activity. A second related theme is that slavery and white prejudice seek to impede this universal striving for knowledge—and that these twin pillars of racial inequality damage white psyches too. White racists in the narratives demean themselves, bring dissension into their communities, and inhibit the spread of evangelical faith. Other ubiquitous themes are that white prejudice can be eradicated and that children can elicit reformations in feelings among adults. The stories empowered young white readers to identify with black protagonists seeking safety, autonomy, and freedom and to lead adults to similar considerations. Finally, the stories bore an inclusive message, as nearly all of them end with the incorporation of black people and families into northern society. Colonization is never an option, although in one instance a man of color chose to serve as a missionary in "distant lands."[178] But in the vast majority of the narratives, black families discover enough security and satisfaction to express hope for their futures in northern states.

Maria Goodell Frost's *Gospel Fruits: Or, Bible Christianity Illustrated* (1856) announces its sentimental and evangelical arguments early in the narrative. "True religion" demands "sympathy for the oppressed," the narrative begins, and the "salvation of the soul includes a salvation from the sins of selfishness and prejudice."[179] As Stowe had done, Frost translated these abstract ideas into a powerful narrative with vivid sketches of children's lives and language. The plot begins with the arrival of a black girl, Jane Brown, at an all-white Sunday school in a northern city. Jane is pious and respectable, but her appearance at the school is nonetheless a powerful test of her classmates'

Christian feelings. At first, a number of socially influential girls reject Jane's presence among them. Their teacher, an abolitionist, gently guides her students in self-examination of their hearts and leads them to love Jane Brown. A message here is that Christianity is love, so white people's sympathy for Jane represents the measure of their religious belief.

The children who espouse racist ideas in this story do so because erring parents have taught them that black people are inferior. In *Gospel Fruits*, a girl named Adeline represents the perversity of racial prejudice. Adeline is a selfish, arrogant child whose "heart was far from right, so full was it of prejudice and hate, toward the slave and all colored people." When Jane Brown joins Adeline's Sunday school class, Adeline treats her with contempt. A scriptural lesson on the Second Epistle of John intended to teach the class that Christians should "love everybody" leads Adeline to protest, "Some persons are so disagreeable that no one could love them," directing her comment at Jane. Later in the story, during a class picnic, Adeline announces, "I don't eat with niggers!" This naturally prompts Jane to "burst into tears," and the other girls (and by extension, the reader) identify with Jane's plight. But after self-examination, Adeline undergoes a religious conversion and finally comes to love Jane, "because Christ does."[180] In *Gospel Fruits* and in other ARTBS fiction, the message was clear: "[God] loves black children just as well as He does you."[181]

A religious revival started among the children next spreads to the adults in Frost's story. Black and white people worship in the same church and together launch crusades against slavery and prejudice. Tears and melting hearts signify the end of racial antipathies, as when Jane's father John participates in the revival at the white church. When John Brown weeps at learning that Jesus Christ's compassion and love are also intended for him, a white deacon who had formerly expressed proslavery views "knelt down beside that colored man, and prayed as he had never prayed before." Weeping and praying together, John Brown and the white deacon illustrate the combined power of evangelical religion and sentimental love. "Where were the prejudice and hate now?" Frost asked.[182]

Gospel Fruits identified for white children how racism looked and sounded, and illuminated how it hurt and diminished black children's sense of well-being. The narrative coached children on ways to overcome distance and establish identification across racial lines. Although such interracial contact remained improbable in Ohio's segregated school settings, these relationships did pertain in the adult realms of work, politics, and reform. The ARTBS's white publishers and authors wanted to explore this interpersonal realm and imagine contexts and settings in which black and white people discovered common ground. They focused on reading and education, broadly understood, as sites of exchange and shared aims. The publishers assumed, though, that most white readers had not really seen, let alone comprehended the import of, the black pursuit of education. This had been John Gaines's concern in 1853: the invisibility of the black scholar or student, fully equal in intellect to white students. The ARTBS literature proved absolutely insistent on this point, reiterating through their fiction the depth and seriousness of this pursuit among people of color, and the firm stake it lent to African American lives in northern communities. *Gospel Fruits* exemplifies this strategy.

Members of Jane Brown's family are objects of white sympathy in *Gospel Fruits*, but they are also the architects of their own futures through education. Jane Brown directs *Gospel Fruits'* plot development with her unrelenting pursuit of knowledge and edification. Her father, a fugitive slave laboring as a barber, cannot read, nor can her freeborn mother, a laundress. But both want educations for their children, and their desire is the initial impetus for Jane's attendance at a white Sabbath school close to their home. Though Jane already enjoys basic literacy at the outset of the book, once in school she quickly immerses herself in a deeper enlightenment project. One of the first signs Jane might gain acceptance at her school is another girl's gift of a bookmark with the motto, "God is Love." Jane is thrilled that she can "keep my place" in her books, an indication of systematic reading over time. Next, the other girls in her Sabbath school undertake to tutor Jane in appropriate grammar and speech so that she can "use words properly." This grows into an informal program "to lend her books to read and study, for her amusement and instruction." The Sabbath school teacher soon sees that Jane is an extraordinary student: "The child had herself improved astonishingly, she never knew a scholar do better in the same length of time." "I never saw any thing like it in my life," she tells skeptical women, who wonder why their church has been enlisted in this biracial experiment in education.[183]

One consequence of Jane's presence in the class is the white church's deeper awareness of, and connection to, the African American community, which wants its own church. Though white women in the congregation have committed to help raise funds for the black church building effort, there are problematic holdouts. One white woman cannot "see what under the sun the *niggers* wanted of a Church. . . . [T]he blacks never could be elevated, they were such a low, vicious degraded set."[184] Compressed into a very few words, this despairing view of black ability was the single greatest barrier to antislavery and emancipation, according to Cincinnati's ARTBS publishers. Stark and simple, pervasive and wounding, such prejudice had produced "that flood of calamities which now threatens to overwhelm us in one common ruin," Rev. Benjamin Aydelott argued in an early ARTBS tract, *Prejudice Against Colored People* (1852). He insisted that "till this most unreasonable and unjust prejudice be abjured, there can be no true, permanent peace to our country."[185]

Then-president of Cincinnati's Woodward College, Aydelott walked readers through a crisp philosophical exegesis invalidating racial distinctions. The fundamental *"sameness"* of all people inhered in the fact that "we are all moral creatures," he argued. According to Aydelott, a "moral being" uses understanding, discernment, conscience, and free will to carry out "moral agency." In this sense of things, being human approximated the pursuit of enlightenment, combined with action. The color of one's skin had no bearing on this essentially human work. And just as John Isom Gaines marveled at the many shades of color in Cincinnati's black common schools, Aydelott celebrated the "endless variety" among people. Diversity in color, he wrote, was "one of the great means of interest and enjoyments in the present world," a wondrous display "of God's creation" on earth. He relished the thought of even *more* "amazing variety" among saints in heaven, available to "the gaze and admiration of all holy beings" for an "eternity." Such diversity, Aydelott further argued, made racial classifications—especially those asserting a connection to intellect—utterly futile. ARTBS tracts sought to dispel white prejudice by explaining its philosophical, religious, and logical error. Yet authors like Aydelott also saw black elevation as the single greatest antidote to white bigotry. He therefore advised Americans to "encourage schools, and every other means of education, and of moral and religious culture among colored people." Use "all in your power," he wrote, to assist black Americans "to become more enlightened, virtuous, useful, happy!"[186]

In *Gospel Fruits*, white characters display a range of responses to the Brown family's appearance in their lives. Some are overtly racist; others appear uncertain and suspicious; though a few seem exceptionally welcoming and sympathetic, they often have selfish reasons for doing so. This great assortment notwithstanding, the Brown family remains steadfast in its own course of action. Midway through the novel, Jane grows independent of the support and encouragement given to her by classmates for her education. She even begins her own weekly school, teaching young girls of color, who are described as "Jane's scholars." Her family, including her father, also makes rapid advances in the pursuit of literacy, seeking out books and tracts to read. In their "snug little home," they maintain a small library of religious texts and sermons, "and quite an assortment of school books." This security and happiness is interrupted when slave hunters capture John and whisk him back to slavery, never to be heard of again. John's wife and children are devastated, but remain undaunted in their pursuit of knowledge. By the end of the novel, Jane devotes "all her leisure hours" to "reading and study." In the final scenes, she marries "one of our best educated young colored men, a college graduate," and they offer financial support to Jane's young brothers so that they can also attend formal schooling and college.[187] With Jane's educational achievement as a mainspring of strength, the family settles into middle-class lives in a northern state. *Gospel Fruits*' insistent, almost urgent emphasis on reading, education, elevation, and security surely seems heavy-handed today. But given John Isom Gaines's sense that white Americans had great difficulty recognizing intellectual possibility in children of color, the prewar antislavery literature coming out of Cincinnati worked doubly hard to correct that failing.

Black Cincinnatians tacitly endorsed the ARTBS's enlightenment project in the 1850s. In 1853, the society's newspaper, the *Christian Press*, included a letter from the Zion Baptist Church, a black congregation, seeking assistance with "forming a Library for the church" containing "suitable books." The letter emphasized that among the black church's members and supporters were some dozen subscribers to the *Christian Press*.[188] In 1854, the Union Baptist Church expressed a desire to "make the pastor a life Member of the American Reformed Book and Tract Society at Some future time."[189] The *Christian Press* also wanted "to make public such evidence" of "improvement" among black Cincinnatians, so editors attended various community events and celebrations.[190] In late 1852, in an anniversary service for the Sunday school at the Union Baptist Church, invited editors witnessed a "most touchingly interesting scene." Students presented Mr. Joseph Emery, their white superintendent, with the gift of "a massive and superbly bound Bible, which had been purchased by the subscriptions of the whole school." The "female scholars" who presented the Bible also delivered a lovely speech in which they asked Emery to "bind it as a choice treasure to your heart; may it ever be your guiding-star, directing you in the way of all truth." Emery received his gift "with a voice faltering with emotion."[191]

The evangelicals who formed the American Reform Tract and Book Society insisted that black and white people enjoyed "the same mental, moral, and social natures."[192] Fictional representations (as well as real evidence) of the shared pursuit of reading and education seemed the most powerful means to demonstrate "black intellectual potential, moral depth, and meaningful interiority," as the literary critic Barbara Hochman has argued.[193] This sense of sameness, that blacks and whites "possess the same susceptibilities of improvement," fostered bonds of union among Cincinnatians and held out promise for an enlightened, biracial society with emancipation.[194] The organization did so at a moment of great despair in such a possibility.

Momentum of Mind

To a degree, Louisville's printers, publishers, and editors also fostered an environment in which a radical antislavery vision found voice through fiction. For the better part of the antebellum era, literature served as one of the great battlegrounds for proslavery and antislavery perspectives, especially following the appearance of Stowe's *Uncle Tom's Cabin*. Though Louisvillians condoned the existence of antislavery newspapers in the Civil War era, the city's publishers never got into the business of fictionalizing slavery. Nevertheless, the city of Louisville—both as a complex racial setting and as Kentucky's most important publishing center—helped to produce one singular abolitionist writer, Mattie Griffith. Born sometime between 1825 and 1830 in Owensboro, Kentucky, Martha Griffith lost both parents before the age of five. Her father willed six enslaved people to Mattie (as she was known) and her only sister.[195] At some point in her childhood, Griffith moved to Louisville to live with extended family. By 1851, while in her early twenties, Griffith regularly published poetry in Prentice's *Louisville Weekly Journal*. Though she may have resided in several northern Kentucky towns before leaving the state permanently in the mid-1850s, Louisville's unusual significance as a nurturer of poets ensured Griffith some national acclaim and served as a key setting for her most ambitious antislavery novel, *The Autobiography of a Female Slave*, published in 1857. Griffith knew the city and its most important publishing forum for women writers very well.

Throughout her life, Griffith defied social convention. Grand juries in Kentucky called her and her sister to task for failing to supervise their slaves adequately. She converted from Catholicism to Protestantism in remonstrance against her native church's failure to criticize slavery. After moving to Philadelphia in 1854–55, she and her sister Catherine lived in apparent penury, worried that hostile relatives would take away Catherine's children with an estranged husband. Under these stressful conditions, Griffith wrote *The Autobiography of a Female Slave*, a compendious, studied attack on Kentucky slavery while assuming the persona of an enslaved black woman. Griffith returned to Kentucky in 1858 to emancipate the six slaves bequeathed to her and

Catherine, then relocated them to Cincinnati. With this transformation from slaveholder to emancipator, she became a darling to New England abolitionists, with whom Griffith most closely identified because of their radicalism and high-minded intellectuality. They apparently saw in her a bright light. Encouraged with this reception, Griffith soon turned to organized activism in New York City and Boston, first in pursuit of universal emancipation as a condition of peace during the Civil War and then in an effort to secure women the right to vote. In 1866, at around forty years of age, she married Albert Gallatin Browne, a man with an appreciation for radicalism. A dedicated abolitionist, Browne faced murder charges in 1854 connected to his effort to secure the fugitive slave Anthony Burns's freedom. Browne later served the Union military cause as an agent of the Treasury Department in the occupied South. With an encouraging spouse, and childless, Griffith remained committed to activism well into her seventies, offering support to black women laboring to improve their children's educations and to halt violence against people of color in the South in the late 1890s. In appearance, Griffith cut an eccentric if not gaudy figure, with a predilection for the color red, unafraid to wear the eye-catching hue from head to toe through Harvard Square. At her death in 1906, she owned some five thousand pieces of jewelry, much of it declared worthless by her executor.[196]

Though Boston and New York City proved more hospitable to such a fierce individualist, Louisville gave Griffith her start as a writer in a forum that suited, and even encouraged, her ardency. This forum was Prentice's newspaper, the *Louisville Daily Journal*, and its weekly variant. From the early 1830s, Prentice encouraged women to submit poems to the paper for publication, and for three decades before the Civil War they did so in such stunning profusion as to constitute an identifiable tradition within the history of American poetry. Although outwardly adhering to the contours of genteel expression, some of the better-known poets nurtured by Prentice pressed hard against convention. Prentice gave women a uniquely uninhibited space in which to express individual feeling and subjectivity, what one scholar has labeled "confessional poetry."[197] A number of these poems are remarkable for their time. An 1843 poem by Amelia Welby, publishing as "Leila," for example, gave voice to extramarital desire while acknowledging its emotional toll and destructiveness. "I've striven to hate thee," the poem's subject admits, recognizing that she can "never sleep upon thy bosom / Nor bear thy name." Nor does the woman's volatile feelings seem safely contained when she settles for "the languid blisses / Of soft desire; I ask but Love's pure flame—/ Thy thoughts, thy sighs, thy warm delicious kisses / Are all I claim."[198] In the 1850s, the *Louisville Daily Journal* published the work of Sarah Morgan Bryan, who married Ohioan John James Piatt in 1861 following an introduction by Prentice. Recently, Sarah Piatt has been compared to Emily Dickinson because of her poetry's "complex subjectivity and startling originality," as Paula Bennett has written. Some of Piatt's "deviant poetics" first appeared in the pages of the *Louisville Daily Journal*.[199] "A Poet's Soliloquy" from 1859 begins starkly:

> Yon cloud is bathed in blood—whence can it start?
> Ah, some Dark Power has stabbed the heart of Heaven!
> No—'tis the rising moon—but mine own heart is stabbed—
>   most deeply—and its wounds have given
> My spirit's glimmering sight a dim, red haze
> That lends all things it sees a gory hue:
> And so but now, in agonized amaze
> Because my bosom bled I thought the skies bled too.
> . . . .
> And are the glittering things that sometimes start
> From my dark bosom, in so wild a way,
> But sparks struck by the clash of *fragments* of a heart?[200]

A later poem, her most anthologized today, displays Piatt's "figural power" and political sensibility. Its first line reads: "She has been burning palaces." With that, Piatt signals a full-stop break with her era's limits on women's expression.[201]

Mattie Griffith immersed herself in this experimental writer's "workshop" in the early 1850s.[202] In 1851 and 1852, her poetry regularly appeared in the *Louisville Weekly Journal,* and she participated in the unusual circularity of nineteenth-century poetry publication, in which authors addressed each other in supportive and adoring language within their verse. Prentice's female authors took part in this ongoing reinforcement for some thirty years, so certain internal conventions emerged over time, especially a "passionate, alienated psyche," as one literary scholar characterizes the *Louisville Journal* poetry's defining aspect.[203] With its lush emotionalism, Griffith's poetry fit well in this expressive tradition. She quite possibly represented an extremity within the genre, as this poem of unrequited love from 1852 suggests:

> Ha! What wild power is this that fills my soul,
> Holding thought, feeling, ay, my very life,
> In its resistless thrall? 'Tis strangely sweet,
> Yet there is madness in its influence,

And with a trembling soul and frame I bow
To its mysterious mystery. Oh, unchain
Thy victim, strong and beauteous spirit, take
Thy magic fetter from my soul; unbind
My wing and leave me free, as I have been,
To wander with the birds, the waves, the winds,
The clouds, the stars, where'er I list, o'er earth
And through the blue and boundless cope of Heaven.

Dwelling on stricken orphans, dying girls, and abandoned lovers, Griffith sought subjects in profound distress, the better to explore the linguistic limits of the *Journal's* emotive verse style. In 1852, the New York publishing firm of D. Appleton & Company believed Griffith's reputation sufficiently strong to print a collection of her poetry in both the United States and London. Not yet exiled from her native state, she dedicated the volume "To the Great People of Kentucky" and declared herself "the humblest and most devoted of Kentucky's daughters."[204]

Soon thereafter, though, Griffith's loyalties faltered, as she undertook a close study of the moral problem of slavery in her home state. By the fall of 1856, roughly four years after the appearance of her poetry collection, Griffith had completed *The Autobiography of a Female Slave.*[205] A lengthy work, verging on political treatise as opposed to moral fiction, the novel offered a scathing attack on Kentucky slavery, argued for immediate emancipation, declared colonization criminally unjust, and insisted upon absolute human equality. What brought her to such a studied opposition to slavery remains murky from Griffith's personal letters, but this first novel indicates that conditions in Louisville—the ready availability of antislavery publications, a literate and organized free black population, and urban spaces where African Americans held a certain leverage—helped move Griffith toward a visceral as well as informed opposition to slavery and to any temporizing in its favor.

The Autobiography of a Female Slave is almost entirely set in Kentucky, with the first half taking place on rural plantations and the second half directed toward events in Louisville, to which the central character, Ann, moves in order to serve as a domestic slave—primarily in the capacity of hairdresser and personal maid—for a recently betrothed daughter of her master. Though she enjoyed a relatively calm childhood, Ann's sale away from her mother's plantation at about the age of thirteen jolts the novel into action. Ann arrives at the Peterkin farm and survives her adolescence in the midst of unremitting terror and violence. The other slaves on the Peterkin plantation seem almost lost to humanity, traumatized by the "ferocious" whims of the master and his socially ambitious but cruel daughters. In no way mild, Kentucky slavery broke human psyches, with the smallness and loneliness of it all intensifying suffering. From this deranged world, Ann is taken to Louisville, which beckons a very different set of circumstances. In Griffith's narrative, slaves on the rural plantation hold important information about free blacks in the city: Louisville's African Americans consider themselves the equal of white gentlemen, and in dress and speech cannot be distinguished from "quality men." Working as waiters and independent barbers, Louisville's free black men enjoyed a certain ease with whites, who lingered at barbershops for conversation and rapport. The Peterkin slaves marveled at this state of affairs. Leaving rural Kentucky for Louisville therefore presents the possibility of a rebirth for Ann, who swears she will "ever remember" her break with a "dark and fearful" past. "In the distance loomed up the city and freedom," and Ann "felt half-emancipated" even before setting foot in Kentucky's largest city.[206]

Ann's first residence, with her mistress, is at Louisville's Galt House, a hotel with a long list of esteemed guests through the nineteenth century, including Charles Dickens in 1842 and William Tecumseh Sherman twenty years later.[207] While her mistress threw herself into Louisville's fashionable social scene, Ann revels in a newfound autonomy at the Galt House. Growing close to the many free and enslaved servants laboring at the hotel, she joins a supportive black community. Moreover, the hotel offers intellectual vibrancy, with books, literature, and newspapers in abundance and entirely accessible to African Americans in service to the Galt House's white guests. Ann learns about radical movements and politics from "the leading Anti-slavery journals" available in reading rooms, uncensored conversations among proslavery and antislavery travelers, and even surreptitious chats with northerners.[208] Griffith's account has a ring of authenticity here: at the time of her own residence at Louisville, slaveholders often stayed at the Galt House, and some occasionally sent notes to editors of the city's antislavery newspaper, indicating that they had read the journal while staying at the hotel.[209] Louisville contains its own grave perils, though, tethered as the city was to the domestic slave trade. Griffith's narrative therefore presents a somewhat knowing picture of Louisville's slave traders, jails, and pens, and reveals an understanding of the role urban bankers played in financing slaveholders' purchase of human property. As in rural Kentucky, the city also harbors abusive masters, whose wealth and finer cultivation is no sure indication of their ethics. Nevertheless, for Griffith's fictional heroine Ann, Louisville lent the possibility of intellectual growth, economic aspiration, and genuine community among free as well as enslaved blacks thrown into common cause. In this way, the novel illuminates a basic truth about Louisville—tragically ensnared in slavery, yet with an African American population compelling attention to its own pursuits of happiness.

For all of its radicalism and the author's about-face toward her native state, *The Autobiography of a Female Slave* stands as a deeply flawed work today. There is first of all Griffith's deception in seeking to write an "auto-biography" on behalf of an imagined enslaved woman—a means for Griffith to explore through language the outer limits of human suffering that she herself would never endure. Though she quickly revealed her identity as the author and the narrative as fictional (even if, as Griffith claimed, based on real incidents she had witnessed), the presumption smacks of a violation or usurpation for personal advantage. Griffith never profited from her antislav-ery writings, yet she did enjoy brief renown accompanied by modest financial support from abolitionists following publication of *The Autobiography of a Female Slave*. More damaging is Griffith's reinforcement of white Americans' unexamined assumptions about skin color in her era: that lighter skin repre-sented greater sensitivity as well as intellectual capacity, while darker-toned skin reflected the meanest debasement by slavery. Very light in coloration, Griffith's heroines could pass into white society. While her novels insisted, with no little vehemence, on genuine human equality, Griffith nevertheless undercut her own argument with a kind of racial determinism based on de-grees of whiteness or blackness. She seemed, for the most part, unable to recognize beauty or comeliness in darker-hued individuals. Though Griffith squarely lays blame for slavery's evil on morally degraded whites (especially women), she found it difficult to render black individuals held in conditions of profound stress as legible and sympathetic. The book therefore registers a failure of understanding, and a resort to stinging caricature.

Still, *The Autobiography of a Female Slave*'s numerous lengthy asides about religion, politics, society, and law show one white woman's genuine effort to grasp how slavery deformed American life. Griffith knew quite a lot about the abolition movement in the North and free blacks' leadership in it, sug-gesting that her political education began before she left Kentucky. "Show me the men, like that little handful at the North, who are willing to forfeit everything for the maintenance of human justice and mercy," she wrote, identifying Theodore Parker, Charles Sumner, and William Seward in her short list. Demonstrating a close knowledge of these men's political work, she revealed their direct influence on her: "Theirs is no ordinary gift of speech; it burns and blazes with a mighty power!" Her "great reformers" included

Frederick Douglass and other free black "defenders of Abolition."[210] But as in the Cincinnati antislavery fiction, the greatest agent of change in *The Autobiography of a Female Slave* is Ann's pursuit of knowledge—basic literacy as a child, and then genuine education in her adulthood. Already by the second page of Griffith's novel, Ann reads well. She is fully literate by the age of ten. Thereafter, her ability to read and study depends on circumstances beyond her control. Yet Griffith's narrative is very much about a particular kind of reader, one whose mind cannot be sated without the freedom to pursue knowledge on her own terms. To indicate Ann's "aspirings" for broad education, Griffith provides unusual detail about her intense reading habits. Early in the novel, we learn that Ann "read long and late," and that "love of study taught me seclusive habits." Before her sale to the Peterkin farm and while still attached to an encouraging mother, she "eagerly read every book that fell in my way." Upon her removal to Louisville, she becomes a "furious reader of newspapers," and "borrowed interesting books, compends of history, bible-stories, poems, &c."[211] Here is an indication of some transference at work in the narrative, for Griffith personally amassed a huge library in her lifetime. Indeed, her executor gave up counting the number of books in Griffith's Boston home, simply listing a collection "running into the thousands."[212]

In Griffith's novelistic treatment of slavery, the withholding of knowledge and the institution's "stultifying influences" were the deepest human rights violations. A "thirsty spirit . . . that craveth so madly the food and drink of knowledge" defined the heroine's character. Here she asserted an entire equality in "momentum of mind," and declared any human categorization by the accident of complexion as both mortal and political sin. Griffith examines this intellectual equality in a bond shared between a dying mistress and Ann, whose sole employment is to read books aloud as a means to alleviate the woman's physical suffering. Willed her freedom and a substantial bequest following the mistress's death, Ann moves to New England where she establishes a school for children of color. Unmarried, and entirely content in her life as a teacher, Ann states by way of the novel's conclusion: "I am calm and self-possessed." Unstinting pursuit of education had brought Ann to such a satisfying point—as near a statement of human happiness as any.[213]

Even with her literary deficiencies, racial misapprehensions, and personal eccentricities, Griffith carried important symbolic value to the abolition movement following publication of *The Autobiography of a Female Slave*. Here was a slaveholding Kentuckian who underwent a thoroughgoing conversion to the policy of immediate emancipation without colonization, who advocated a fully integrated society, and who expressed favor toward inter-racial marriage since all persons are "the direct descendants from the great progenitor of the human family, old Adam."[214] Though Kentuckians had abjured emancipation in 1849, Griffith offered concrete evidence that a native antislavery sentiment in the state had not entirely perished. Lydia Maria Child's narrative, "How a Kentucky Girl Emancipated Her Slaves," appeared in newspapers and antislavery journals, including Horace Greeley's New York *Tribune* and Henry Ward Beecher's *Independent* magazine in 1862, a year in which some Republican plan for emancipation appeared imminent. Griffith's personal story reassured on two counts: that Kentuckians, even without northern prodding, could see logic and justice in abolition and that on-the-ground emancipation could be achieved peacefully. "In view of these facts," Child wrote, "I would ask any candid person what reason there is to apprehend danger in emancipating the slaves. It is surely time for us to stop repeating stereotyped falsities, invented for the convenience of slavehold-ers."[215] In practically every facet of her life, including her manumission of six enslaved people, Griffith presented an exceptional case. But in the late 1850s and first years of the war, abolitionists and Republican Party architects seized on Griffith's example as a means to diffuse hysteria over general on-the-ground emancipation, which they argued was the only just and practicable means to end the Union's thrall to slavery. In microcosm, she exemplified mainstream Republican policy by 1862.

In our own moment, Griffith's other insistent arguments—contained in her fiction—that organized pursuits of enlightenment fostered close bonds between diverse Americans and that such pursuits, if universalized, would mark a sharp break with the horrific history of slavery, can yield a contra-dictory response: the idea seems at once unassailable and naive. "Let but the schoolmen breathe upon" children's minds, "let the architect of learning fashion" youthful perception, Griffith argued, and prejudice and ignorance would cease.[216] By 1857, when her novel appeared, black residents in the Ohio River valley had already weathered hard battles in establishing actual brick-and-mortar schools for their children. To these veterans of the first public school movement for children of color, Griffith would have surely sounded glib. But her more general proposition that literacy, reading, and universal common schooling offered the antidote to slavery's maladies was not auto-matically accepted in the 1840s and 1850s. Organized movements for edu-cational equality in the Ohio River valley, and in Cincinnati and Louisville in particular, had brought this argument to the fore. In refracting the idea through fiction, Griffith and the other antislavery writers in the Ohio River valley helped to make enlightenment a bond of union at a pivotal moment. It seems important that activists and writers from this Civil War borderland urged this idea so fiercely in the 1840s and 1850s, and had gained some ground on the point before the formal outbreak of hostilities in 1861. With public schools operating throughout Ohio and private schools attended by enslaved and free Louisvillians, and with popular fictional authors offering earnest support for the idea of universal enlightenment as a strength of union, the argument began to assume its unassailability.

Part III
Section and Nation

CHAPTER SEVEN

Alienation

Because Cincinnati and Louisville served as entrepôts for the entire Ohio and Mississippi Valleys—an inland region bounded by the Great Lakes and Gulf Coast and the Allegheny and Rocky Mountains—the two cities fastened together disparate regional economies and diverse peoples at the nation's most significant geographical and cultural divide, the Ohio River. Early on, residents celebrated this pivotal role in the nation's trade by assigning patriotic, near-mythical meanings to their interstate commerce. In 1826, Cincinnatian Benjamin Drake delivered an Independence Day oration proclaiming that "our steam-boats, apparently annihilating time and space, have joined in one social circle, those who dwell upon the tributary streams of the Ohio, Mississippi, and Missouri, with those who brave the scorching sun-beams, where the congregated waters of these mighty rivers are commingled with the ocean."[1] Writing more than a dozen years later, another booster's poetic flourish suggests contemporaries' sense of Cincinnati's centrality to national unity: from the city's riverfronts "the products of the south will fly as by magic to the north," and at its yet-to-be-built railroad depots, he predicted, "the east and the west will be joined together by bars of iron."[2] Less lyrically, but no less pointedly, one Louisvillian claimed that his city stood as the "half-way house between North and South."[3]

When far-flung trade goods, agricultural products, and credit and cash flowed through Cincinnati and Louisville, these Middle West cities diluted distinctive regional origins. Even in 1852, when "North" and "South" had come into regular use as shorthand labels suggestive of the specific interests held by the nation's two "sections," Louisvillians celebrated their role as intermediaries. The "most distinguishing feature of this society," wrote Ben Casseday, "is the readiness with which it receives and swallows up all those sectional differences which in other cities remain intact." In Louisville, he insisted, "the Northern, Eastern, or Southern man, as well as the native of another country, seems to lose all identity of manner, and becomes only an integral part of one great circle."[4] According to such views, Louisville and Cincinnati had come into being for the very purpose of saving the Union by blunting the force of northerners' and southerners' divergent interests through the mysterious workings of commerce.

Effusive claims about "the puritan and the planter" casting off their "inwoven tissue of sentiments" to "meet half way, and embrace" in places like Cincinnati and Louisville invite ridicule, but wishes for the happy intermingling of very different regional types reveal Americans' genuine anxieties about whether their strangely divided nation, held together by constitutional patchwork, could persist. Such visions also spoke to a common argument that economic ties forged in the Ohio River valley, and especially in its commercial cities, diminished the force of sectional extremism. This argument carries serious weight among historians today and often underpins explanations for Cincinnatians' hostility to abolitionism, for example.[5] Yet even in tradedependent Cincinnati and Louisville, residents did not always act in their immediate economic self-interest, and they often staked out political positions or acted in ways that strained rather than strengthened the profitable commercial ties holding together North and South.

In fact, individual Cincinnatians and Louisvillians presided over the creation of institutions and organizations—the Free Soil and Republican political parties and the new southern denomination of the Methodist Episcopal Church most significant among them—that stoked tension between free and slave states. Cincinnatians and Louisvillians generally avoided the most provocative disunion rhetoric of their era, that which deemed the Constitution hopelessly proslavery or, on the other side, called for nullification of federal laws. Both of those arguments raised the specter of a swift dissolution of the nation. Cincinnatians and Louisvillians rarely incited such direct hostility to the national government or Constitution in the abstract. However, in their church life and in their very structures of government, Ohioans and Kentuckians helped to cordon off slave and free sections to prevent a kind of moral cross-contamination across state lines after 1845. Louisvillians and Cincinnatians were very often at the front lines of these events, manning the barricades.

Fractured Faiths

Two decades after the start of the Civil War, a Protestant minister recalled that "the fall of 1845 witnessed the 'beginning of sorrows'" for Methodism in Cincinnati.[6] The minister here quoted a weighty phrase from Matthew 24 in which Jesus foretells the "great tribulation" preceding his second coming.[7] In the minister's view, only the torments of end times could begin to convey what followed from Americans' religious schisms over slavery. In 1845, the Methodist Episcopal Church, as well as the national association of Baptist churches, split into separate southern and northern denominations. A few years earlier, Presbyterian congregations in the North began to sever their relationships with southern churches, a division that was all but complete by 1850. Provoked by the moral question of slavery, the sectional crisis in the churches prefigured and contributed in profound ways to the national political impasse over slavery and the coming of the Civil War.[8] Laypersons, editors, and politicians expressed grave forebodings about the future of the nation in the wake of sectional schisms. Just before southern Baptists met to consider the formation of a separate denomination, one Baptist editor in Louisville asked all Protestants to weigh carefully the political consequences:

> Let the three great denominations of Christians be divided, by State lines, upon the subject of abolitionism, and who does not see that all social intercourse between the parties will be sundered, and the parts continually recede? . . . Who does not see . . . that if the religious and consequently the social interests of the country are divided by State lines, that more than half of the bonds which hold the political compact in harmony are dissolved, and that the ground work is laid for the ultimate dissolution of the Union, and the destruction of the fairest fabric of civil and religious liberty the world ever saw?[9]

Religious ruptures along the line separating slave and free states undermined Americans' sense of their nation's durability and appeared to lay out a process or template for the creation of rival sectional governments at best, or civil anarchy at worst. Contemporaries thus sensed the hazards involved in their divisions.

The fracturing of faith at the border of freedom and slavery also imperiled evangelicals' sense of united purpose in animating Christian belief among a habitually roving people. Native-born and immigrant Americans often sought new frontiers of opportunity at the expense of organized faith. But missionaries usually traipsed close behind, supported by congregations in long-settled areas. As Presbyterians, Methodists, and Baptists severed their national governing councils into northern and southern bodies, they reluctantly aborted bold missionary programs to evangelize throughout the western United States. Where nationwide religious organizations had once drawn a dispersed population into a "common sense of nationhood" via evangelical Protestantism, their northern and southern offshoots (especially those in the South) promoted a diminished sense of evangelical identity tied inextricably to region and the ability to own and control slaves.[10] As historian Richard Cawardine argues, and as many contemporaries themselves realized, these divisions "bequeathed a legacy of bitterness and sectional stereotyping that seriously corroded evangelicals' sense of belonging to a political and ecclesiastical Union based on common values."[11]

Nowhere was this bitterness more evident than in border cities like Cincinnati and Louisville.[12] Since both cities stood at the natural geographical divide between the sectional churches, Protestants in Cincinnati and Louisville bore an additional burden to choose their affiliations, and considerable confusion arose as a consequence. This was especially the case with Methodists, whose ill-conceived "Plan of Separation" allowed "border conferences" the right to vote to belong to either the northern or southern church.[13] Hence a congregation in Cincinnati affiliated with the M.E. Church, South, in order to establish a southern "beachhead" in Ohio, while northern Methodists created a "Kentucky District" within the Ohio Conference and later delimited a smaller "Cincinnati and Kentucky Conference" in 1852.[14] Adding to the confusion, black and German Methodists in Louisville asserted their right to remain in the "mother" church, now designated the M.E. Church, North.[15]

Rather than blunting the sharp edges of the slavery debates in Cincinnati's and Louisville's churches, this ecclesiastical messiness pressed evangelicals into strident assertions of sectional loyalty. In both cities, church members and leaders with already strong perspectives on the issue of slavery took the institutional division as a kind of sanction or sign to swiftly imprint their views on local churches and associations. In their view, a unique historical moment had arrived: with bright light cast on a matter of profound importance, time had come to clarify allegiances. Though Cincinnatians and Louisvillians never perfectly demarcated their church affiliations along the Ohio River's political border, a number of groups in each city became vociferous proponents of what should be labeled sectional arguments. So in Louisville, white Baptists and Methodists threw their loyalties to southern institutions with surprising zeal. In the 1840s, they embraced the southern church's "mission" cause, whose essential premise was the spiritual and social inequality of whites and blacks, which white evangelicals wished to preserve rather than lessen through their redemptive work among the enslaved. In stark contrast, Cincinnati's evangelicals codified antislavery planks in their churches and associations, and they began to create new alliances to pursue greater racial equality as an adjunct to the work of emancipation. Cincinnati also became home to one of the most significant archives of Methodist antislavery literature before the Civil War.

By 1845, white evangelicals had come to view Louisville, and northern Kentucky more broadly, as a great battlefield in the fight against the "aggressive spirit of Abolitionism" fomented by northern agitators. Kentucky's white evangelicals conceived abolitionism as a sort of foreign intrigue bent on the destruction of southern slavery by unleashing race warfare, and the very term raised a terrifying specter of anarchic violence against whites. The region's urban and rural ministers therefore saw it as their peculiar duty to defend against abolitionism's incursions into the South. The Reverend A. D. Sears, pastor at Louisville's First Baptist Church, stressed that he and his fellow church leaders "occupy a more extended border line upon the free States than any other Association of Baptists." Along the Ohio River, the single most important boundary between North and South, "the struggle upon the slavery question has to be met," he urged in 1845.[16] With these fighting words, Sears incited ministers in Louisville and its hinterlands to join the newly formed southern branch of the Baptist church, dedicated in no small part to bringing bondsmen and bondswomen under the watch of the evangelical church through the establishment of slave missions. Such missions would serve the dual purpose of inculcating subservience in slaves and demonstrating the righteousness of American slavery. Indeed, church objectives and proslavery arguments merged seamlessly in the mission to the slaves. Evangelization of the peoples of African descent was now, in the minds of white denominational leaders, the blessed purpose of slavery. White Baptist and Methodist ministers in Louisville found these arguments irresistible, and they took practical as well as ideological steps to advance the mission in the state's largest city.[17]

Although responsibility for the church schisms over slavery during 1844 and 1845 is mostly assigned to firebrands in New England and the Deep South, Louisville's white ministers proved early and staunch supporters of separation, and they enthusiastically embraced the idea of missions. But given that white Louisvillians had generally paid scant attention to the spiritual doings of African Americans in the city before 1845, their new exertions on behalf of "missions" to redeem slaves carried a false ring, to say the least, and in fact looked entirely out of touch with the reality of black church independence in the Upper South city. In consequence, white missionary activity among African Americans in Louisville after the southern church secessions bore the marks of a reactionary movement attempting to counter religious developments that had moved well beyond their control.

Independence

The case of Louisville's Fifth Street Baptist Church furnishes insight into the local dynamics of church separation and the possible causes of whites' outward enthusiasm for missions. By 1840, the Reverend Henry Adams already enjoyed renown as a preacher in black Baptist circles, and he was a highly sought speaker at religious meetings throughout the Ohio River valley. Testimony to Adams's gifts as a minister and revivalist is best seen in his Kentucky labors. According to the white-led Long Run Association's membership statistics, Adams's Fifth Street Church met with spectacular success in converting new members and retaining old ones through the entire antebellum period. In 1839, when the association first mentioned Adams's "African Church," the congregation numbered 300 while its white parent church, First Baptist, consisted of 232 members. Over the next five years, during a remarkable revival season, Adams baptized converts at more than twice the rate of his white brethren. While Fifth Street's congregation grew 161 percent, white membership at First Baptist increased by just 77 percent. A member of the white Baptist church offered faint praise in his letter to the Long Run Association in 1840: "It is useless to say, that this African Church is prospering" and "is a standing reproof to many of our Churches of another color." William Gibson later remembered that the famed revivals at Fifth Street Baptist Church lasted "for weeks, and some times for months" while "anxious seekers for redemption in Christ" sought Adams's encouragement and sanction.[18] By 1842, Adams's church represented the largest congregation of the Long Run Association's twenty-three mostly rural churches. Although the white association admitted Louisville's Colored Baptist Church as an independent governing body in that year, it refused to allow the congregation to send its own delegates. "Our colored brethren," the white ministers declared, "are advised to place themselves under the supervision" of Louisville's First Baptist Church, whose own delegates would also provide the black church's official representation at Long Run Association meetings.[19]

Several months before this condescending induction into the regional Baptist Association, Adams's Colored Baptist Church, with "the hearty consent" of Louisville's First Baptist Church, had been formally constituted with its own confession of faith, covenant, and rules of decorum. Before an audience of several hundred black and white Baptists in the city, the Colored Baptist Church's members asserted their desire to "win . . . souls, remembering that God hath not given us the spirit of fear, but of power and of love." "We are the light of the world, and the salt of the earth, and . . . a city, set upon a hill, cannot be hid," they announced.[20] This language of spiritual covenant, however standard among Baptist churches, may have struck observers as remarkable, given the large proportion of enslaved members in the congregation—perhaps as high as 80 percent.[21] But at least before 1844, white Baptists seemed amenable to such claims to religious self-determination among their black brethren, so long as the Fifth Street Baptist Church nominally remained under the supervision of its white mother church, First Baptist Church of Louisville.

Yet Adams's church pressed its case for autonomy further, seeking the right to send its self-selected representatives to annual meetings of the Long Run Association of Baptists. In the year following their constitution as an independent church, the Fifth Baptist Church complied with the Long Run Association's instruction that the black congregation appoint white delegates to association meetings. But this obligation to remain dependent on white representation exasperated the pastor and members of Louisville's first independent black church, especially given the congregation's growth from 513 to 745 converted souls under Reverend Adams's revival preaching. Indeed, the black congregation now dwarfed every other Baptist church in the Long Run Association. So in September, bearing news of his congregation's remarkable spiritual growth as well as $115.50 (a large contribution, by Kentucky standards) for missionary work in Africa, Adams traveled to the association's annual meeting of ministers at Floyd's Fork, Kentucky, to make known his church's sentiments. At least initially, to avoid overstepping racial proscriptions against his speaking to white delegates as an equal, Adams went through the cumbersome process of presenting a letter from his church requesting that "their pastor be received as a messenger to the Association." Despite a seconded motion to grant the request, followed by "much discussion," the white ministers in attendance rejected the church's appeal.[22] Disappointed, but sensing tractability among the white members given the favorable motion and debate, Adams pressed his church's case through direct, personal entreaty. Hoping that his persuasive skills and agreeable mien might alter the delegates' disposition, Adams "requested permission to make some remarks, and to ask whether the Association considered the Colored church a member of their body." The white ministers "unanimously granted" Adams's wish and listened to the black minister. Their response slipped on the shoals of race: yes, the Fifth Street Baptist Church was fully constituted as an independent member of the association, but it could only be represented through letter and white Baptists at Louisville's First Church. With that, they rejected Adams's bid to join on equal terms the Long Run Baptist Association of Kentucky. Poignantly, Adams had also brought contributions of $4.00 from his church (again, more than any other church's contributions that year) to help defray costs for printing the association's unyielding resolutions that year.[23]

Adams never again attended the Long Run Association's annual meetings, nor did his congregation ever again formally appoint delegates from Louisville's

First Church to represent them. They also did not direct any more money for missionary enterprises through the Long Run Association. Adams had tried without success to integrate the Long Run Association and establish a role for African Americans within the larger structure of the church. By 1843, Adams would also have been well aware of the brewing struggles within the Baptist denomination over slaveholding. Even in the absence of direct proof, it seems likely that he sought to have a voice and equal footing in an important association of ministers in order to influence—or, at the very least, bear witness to—its discussions about slavery and the church. Adams's boycott of the Long Run Association began in 1844, just as a majority of Louisville's white ministers affirmed their support for a separate Southern Baptist Convention.[24]

With white Baptists' shrill proslavery crusade now taking official form, Adams and other leading church members at the Fifth Street Church also began to ignore entirely the old oversight arrangements with Reverend Sears's First Baptist Church. They redoubled efforts to build or purchase their own meetinghouse for the growing congregation. In 1845, Adams's church moved into a centrally located building vacated by the city's First Christian Church. This autonomous effort immediately drew the scrutiny of First Baptist Church's "Standing Committee," who believed they should "be consulted on all important business relative to the [Colored Baptist Church]." When the standing committee tried to interfere with the black congregation's real estate dealings, the Colored Baptist Church produced a strongly worded set of resolutions clarifying their relationship to Louisville's so-called mother church: "We wish the continuance of a standing comm. from the First Church if it will be so kind as to continue one . . . for the special object of protecting the colored Church [from] molestation and injustice; and with this *express understanding that the existence of such a committee shall in no way whatever impair the independence and right of the Colored Baptist Church*, as legally Constituted, as a Regular Baptist Church." Three weeks later, the standing committee reported to the congregation at First Baptist that "it would have been courteous on the part of the coloured Church to have consulted with said committee, relative to the appointment of Trustees to hold property for the benefit of said Church," but relented on the issue.[25]

Louisville's white Baptists do not appear to have insinuated themselves into the daily affairs of Adams's church after this assertion of independence. Beginning in 1845, though, the very same whites who had denied Adams's personal representation of his church at their associational meetings, and who, at least theoretically if not practically, claimed oversight of the Fifth Street Baptist Church, began to wage a high-stakes rhetorical war calling for disunion with the free states in the realm of faith. In that year, Reverend Sears of Louisville's First Baptist Church would warn "against the aggressive arm of misrule" as he decried abolitionism's influence in "our own beloved Commonwealth" and lamented the "season of gloom" that had descended on Kentucky's Baptist churches. To Sears, even the "milder aspect of *gradual* emancipation" then gaining political traction in Louisville was proving "subversive of the rights of the churches in the slaveholding States," and he advocated a spiritual raising of the barricades to prevent the flow of anti-slavery ideas into Kentucky from Ohio.[26]

No direct evidence suggests that Sears associated Henry Adams with such cross-contamination along the Ohio River, although the famous black preacher had been playing a dangerous game. Through the 1840s and 1850s, Adams maintained close connections with Cincinnati's Union Baptist Church and even served as the church's minister between 1850 and 1853. Soon after his move to Kentucky, he had created a buzz among black Baptists in Louisville and beyond, and the Union Baptist Church of Cincinnati began to court him to become their minister. His talents also captured attention at the Chillicothe meeting of the "Regular Baptist Churches of Color in Ohio" during the summer of 1840. Even before Adams had preached to the black brethren at this gathering, they invited him to deliver the opening sermon at the following year's meeting. Such was his celebrity as a speaker. Although Adams likely had many suitors, the Union Baptist Church never gave up hope that the charismatic preacher would become its minister. The congregation considered his candidacy several more times through the early 1840s and then finally secured his services in the pulpit in 1850. This bond of admiration and labor afforded Adams intimate knowledge of the northern church's abolitionist activity in the city and in the state of Ohio. Later, in the 1850s, Adams tried to protect the Union Baptist Church's antislavery strategy when it came under attack from other Cincinnati blacks for its allegedly conciliatory alliances with white abolitionists.[27]

With care and shrewdness, Adams managed to keep this long history of complicity with antislavery radicals out of the earshot of white Louisvillians. The popular black preacher never came under personal scrutiny by white authorities in the city, and he evaded the violence of white ruffians who normally acted on the slightest rumor and innuendo. In Louisville, at least, Adams took a conservative approach to his antislavery activity, for in his view, acting "injudiciously and illegally" on behalf of enslaved church members "would have destroyed his influence, and made their condition worse." Adams first and foremost preached "power and love" through gospel tenets, and he invested his prodigious energies in institutions, education, and uplift. He does not appear to have knowingly incited slaves in his congregation to direct resistance of their bondage.[28] Nevertheless, the Fifth Street Baptist Church's assertion of spiritual independence constituted an element of the perfect storm white Baptists believed they faced at the time of the great church divisions. Moreover, because the porous border between Ohio and Kentucky so alarmed white evangelicals in Louisville, Adams's frequent river crossings no doubt added to their anxiety—which by 1845 approached a panic—however much the black Baptist minister concealed his Ohio antislavery connections.

The leading light of Louisville's white evangelicals at the time of the Baptist church separation, Reverend Sears, declaimed against Kentucky's permeable border with Ohio. Dangerous ideas and people had now become "insinuated" into the commonwealth's churches. Though northern abolitionist activity spawned this contamination, in Sears's view the consequences for Kentucky's Baptists were manifold. According to Sears, the drift of antislavery ideas produced "iniquity," "spiritual declension," "gloom," and "other evils" within congregations. The situation was nothing short of dire: "The love of many has waxed cold," he reported, and "the effect of all these combined evils . . . has been most paralyzing." Presented to the ministers attending Kentucky Baptists' annual meeting and published in their official minutes, Sears's manifesto for church separation captured white evangelicals' sense of crisis in 1845 and underscored the sectional nature of Baptist church divisions. To stop the flow of antislavery crusaders with their pernicious ideas about race equality and to delimit the unfortunately fluid "border line" between free and slave states, Sears advocated a somewhat surprising antidote: he proposed joining in "common cause upon the subject of missions with our brethren of the South." Ending his circular on a note of can-do optimism, he urged: "Let us become missionaries" and fan out to " 'preach the gospel to every creature.' "[29] In the context of the great church divisions, this exhortation to his Baptist colleagues meant evangelizing to slaves and free blacks. If safely (back) in the fold of southern Baptist churches, Sears reasoned, Kentucky's people of color would evince little interest in the seditious whisperings of northern abolitionists, and the tribulations of the moment would soon waft away.

Of course, Sears's plan contained a hitch. By 1845, white Baptists in the city enjoyed few institutional channels of religious influence among people of color, given the past decade of growing church independence among African Americans. Given his church's special relationship to the Fifth Street

Baptist Church, Sears suggested a work-around: white Baptists would pursue informal missionary work in "neighborhoods," "families," and private "associations of life."[30] To say the least, it was a flimsy plan during this moment of high resolve to establish a separate southern church on the grounds that slaves needed white missionaries to redeem their souls.

In any event, it appears that Louisville's white evangelicals now recognized the implications of independent black churches led by free people. They stood as testimony against the assertion that black people required whites to manage their salvation and that slavery presented the most conducive environment for missionary work among people of color. In truth, Louisville's black churches mocked the conceit that the newly formed southern churches were unselfishly and disinterestedly intended for the redemption of black people. At least for Louisville, establishing a separate denomination for the purpose of evangelizing slaves seemed a backward-looking attempt to check the growing autonomy and authority of black congregations like Henry Adams's Fifth Street Baptist Church. However out of touch with the reality of black spiritual independence in Louisville, though, white evangelicals in the Upper South pressed on with their new allegiances to southern churches, and they did so with remarkable zeal.

Committee on Division

South Carolina or Georgia would have seemed likely sites for the first formalized divisions among Methodists, but in fact Kentuckians spearheaded southern church secession by creating the first "Committee on Division" in the fall of 1844, in advance of the region's other Methodist conferences. At that influential meeting of Kentucky's ministers, the state's most famous divine, the Reverend Henry Bidleman Bascom, then president of Transylvania University, made a stirring call for secession from the national conference of Methodists. Bascom's five-hour speech insisted that separation alone would "save the Church in the south from utter extermination." Bascom's arguments, and the conference's report based on them, furnished the intellectual "groundwork for all the other southern conferences," according to northern Methodist editor and historian Charles Elliot, a resident of Cincinnati and perhaps the closest student of the church's division. Upper South divines, particularly Bascom, thus helped to articulate a distinctive identity and mission for the southern church at its inception. In chronicling these events, Elliott would later accuse Kentuckians of leading "the work of revolution with a thorough good-will."[31]

Elliott singled out Bascom as a chief insurgent for persuading southern churchmen to cut their ties to the General Conference with his book *Methodism and Slavery*, published on the eve of the meeting to form the Methodist Episcopal Church, South. In this breathless defense of the southern position (not a single chapter division appears in 165 pages of argument), Bascom made evangelization among southern slaves the raison d'être of the new denomination. "We regard ourselves as involved in a great providential movement," he wrote, "connected with the destinies of the African race, here and elsewhere." As a former agent of the American Colonization Society, which he declared a "God-like cause," Bascom wanted to "arrest the vandal inroads of abolitionism, so as to allow the 'gospel free course' among the slaves of the South." If slavery made possible the Christianization of African Americans and their eventual emancipation and resettlement in Africa as missionaries themselves, then the South's peculiar institution was self-evidently "the design of Heaven." Were southern Methodists to remain members of a church that disciplined slaveholders, as the General Conference of Methodists insisted on doing in 1844, northern abolitionists might eventually gain access to slaves and incite them to rebellion. Slavery's sacred cause would obviously be lost. And because of their proximity to the free North, Kentucky's slaves would be among the first to fall into the hands of abolitionists.[32]

Kentucky's Methodist ministers worried so much about the fate of the missions that they hastened separation by providing ideological as well as logistical support to the formation of the southern church. In addition to Bascom's case for separation and the advance work of Kentucky's Committee on Division, the state's conference eagerly invited southern delegates to Louisville to deliberate the formal creation of the new church, and the city played host to the convention forming the Methodist Episcopal Church, South, in May 1845. As a consequence, Louisville's churches were put on early alert about the potential for separation, and had, in effect, the best seats in the house to witness the fracturing of a national church. Some three hundred delegates, future apostles of the M.E. Church, South, descended on Louisville, where they received a "kind reception and hearty welcome" by the city's white churches—churches, it may be noted, with the largest African American congregations under their presumed ecclesiastical control. Members of one of these white churches, Louisville's Fourth Street Church, believed that the South's Methodist leadership had followed "the letter and spirit of the discipline" in advancing separation, and seemed to relish national attention as hosts of the 1845 meeting.[33]

In spite of this resolve from both ministers and the rank and file, the 1845 gathering in Louisville proved dramatic. Because severing the denominational connection was anathema to Methodists, southern ministers "wept in heaviest sorrow" at the prospect of separation, and the meeting to form the new southern church was a scene of "agonizing prayer," according to one historian of the event. But with a constellation of star preachers in attendance, including William Capers, the recognized founder of the slave missions from South Carolina, doubts fell away as speakers took the podium. One Georgia minister, the Reverend George F. Pierce, then "in the blossoming-time of his genius and fame," delivered a rousing speech in which he "besought the Convention to . . . give free scope to [the Methodist church's] energies, that in her errands of love and compassion she might go to the bedside of the dying Negro and point his fading eye to the brightening glories of the cross and immortality beyond." "Untrammeled" by abolitionist interference, he predicted, southern churchmen would go among the slaves doing the "godlike work of blessing and saving the souls of men of all conditions and in all circumstances of human life." Pierce's vision for Methodist missionaries was deeply affecting, and in the end, only 3 of the 293 delegates in attendance at the Louisville meeting voted against the establishment of the new southern church.[34] Southern ministers were thus nearly unanimous in their belief in the justness of separation, and in order to realize Pierce's hopes for slaves' redemption at the hands of white missionaries, they immediately embarked on building up new slave missions, augmenting those already in existence, and recalibrating their delicate relationships with slaves and free blacks to assume greater control over the separate churches dotting the South.

Remove an Evil

Strikingly different developments took place in Cincinnati between 1844 and 1848. Whereas Henry Adams exerted little influence on Kentucky's regional Baptist association and white Baptists there struck out for separation and slave missions with fervor, Cincinnati's black Baptists had much greater success steering the most powerful Baptist association in southern Ohio toward a clear antislavery position and support of repeal of prejudicial state laws. By the late 1840s, Cincinnati's white Baptists, as well as leading Methodist church leaders, adopted or reinforced the antislavery planks in their church organizations. Although white Baptists and Methodists in Cincinnati would hardly be considered "disunionists," even modest statements against the institution of slavery or in favor of racial equality before the law appeared hostile to southern partisans, and especially to those former brethren building up the new southern denominations. By midcentury, the landscape of faith and race looked remarkably different in Louisville and Cincinnati, and white evangelicals on either side of the Ohio River had moved toward antagonistic positions on the morality of slavery.

In the early 1840s, the Union Baptist Church made a bid to press the local Miami Baptist Association toward a visible and vocal antislavery position. In 1842 the Union Baptist Church had become the first independent black congregation to join the association, made up of seventeen white-led churches throughout southwestern Ohio. After two years of membership in the Miami Baptist Association and emboldened by sustained growth in their church (from 263 members in 1840 to 385 in 1844), the congregation began to consider antislavery resolutions to present to the September 1844 meeting in Middletown, Ohio.[35] The leadership of the Union Baptist Church must also have sensed new urgency to test white Baptists' feelings on the subject since the planning for a separate Southern Baptist Convention was already underway in the fall of 1844. Internal discussions among black Cincinnatians reveal considerable stress and dissension over how best to approach the white Baptist association. In fact, one consequence of the church division over slavery at midcentury was a fracturing of black Baptists over strategy, with leading members of Union Baptist Church insisting on careful, deliberate advocacy among white Ohioans and a minority desiring direct confrontation and action.

Thus, three days before the Middletown meeting, Brother William E. Walker introduced a set of powerful resolutions to the Union Church's congregation demanding that the Miami Baptist Association declare "slavery . . . a great moral and physical evil and that it is exerting a very pernicious and deleterious influence through the churches." In consequence, Walker's resolution stated, "it is the duty of the association to lift up its voice or in other words show its opposition to slavery by example as well as precept." More controversially, Walker's resolutions asked member churches to "withhold fellowship and communion from all persons who are guilty of the crime of slaveholding or are proslavery in their principles" and asked the association's ministers "to preach and lecture against slavery." For Baptists who jealously guarded their independence, such resolutions could be interpreted as unjust intrusions into congregational decision making about fellowship and ministerial rights and duties. Nevertheless, Walker's resolutions added an ultimatum that the association accept the proposals or see the Union Baptist Church withdraw from its organization.[36]

The congregation promptly adopted Walker's resolutions but then just as quickly rescinded them the next day. The church's cautious pastor, Charles Satchell, who viewed Walker's ultimatum as reckless, persuaded the congregation to redraft the resolutions. After lengthy debate over whom to empower with this task, the church adopted a far less controversial strategy for the Middletown meeting. Within the standard letter presented to association meetings about a church's spiritual and financial states, the congregation decided to insert the following questions: "They enquire whether the Bible any where sanctions or recognises American Slavery as a Divine institution? If so where? If not, can churches or Associations hold fellowship with pro-slavery bodies without being involved in their guilt?"[37] In response to these queries, yet without opening the Middletown meeting to debate on the subject, the Miami Baptist Association passed a broad resolution opposing slavery: "*Resolved*, That we deem American Slavery a sin against the law of love of God and man, and as such should be opposed in the spirit of the gospel by all Christians."[38]

Because this resolution attached no practical, political, or ecclesiastical sanctions to its declaration, some in the Union Baptist Church, including William Walker, found it too tepid. Indeed, Walker, author of the more radical set of resolutions rescinded by the congregation in favor of a more conciliatory approach, shot off a highly critical letter to the *Disfranchised American*, Cincinnati's local African American newspaper. Walker's letter, "over the signature of Justice," implied that the Union Baptist Church and its pastor "were proslavery in principle."[39]

Elder Satchell and the other brothers identified in Walker's letter were livid at the impugning of their antislavery principles, and they moved quickly to protect their congregation's standing among Cincinnati's blacks. While disavowing Walker's "base slanders upon the brethren and upon the church," the congregation's statement included an ad hominem attack denouncing Walker as a "private and obscure member" who acted "through the very worst of motive[,] as he has but little regard for the truth." In conjunction with this public statement, William Watson, a member of the congregation closely allied with Elder Satchell, also counterattacked by "publicly accusing [Walker] of attempting to violate by fource the virtue of a sister in the church."[40]

The Union Baptist Church never had a chance to investigate the merit of this charge against one of its members because, at its next meeting, William Walker "was excluded from the fellowship of the church for fighting" after "striking [William Watson] with his cane."[41] One consequence of these public disputes and physical altercations with Walker appears to have been the departure of a number of members from Union Baptist Church. Like William Walker, more militant African Americans who could not stomach an association with white Baptist churches turned instead to Cincinnati's Zion Baptist Church for fellowship.[42]

It appears, indeed, that Union Baptist Church never entirely shook the "proslavery" stigma for its formal associations with white Baptists belonging to the Miami Association. Former members leveled the charge in 1846, and again in 1853.[43] Union Baptist Church's members felt profoundly aggrieved at this "slander," especially after Elder A. E. Graham scored an important triumph within the Miami Baptist Association in late 1846.[44] Just before the meeting at Jonas Run, Ohio, the congregation unanimously passed two resolutions for Graham to present before the association's all-white ministerial and lay leadership. The resolutions again sought to prevent any churches in the Miami Baptist Association from allowing slaveholders into their fellowship, and to preclude "correspondence with any other association or convention" that did not exclude slaveholders. Further, members of Union Baptist Church sought to address political means to end slavery, as more radical voices like Walker had advised in 1844: "Resolved, that this association would most earnestly recommend all the churches of which this body is composed to exert to the fullest extent all their influence and means for the over through [throw] of American slavery." "If these resolutions are not heard or [are] treated with contempt," they added, Graham was instructed to "enter . . . [the church's] most solomn protest against the association."[45]

In response to Graham's resolutions, the association's ministers passed a strong statement denouncing slavery and "pledg[ing] . . . to use all lawful and prudent measures, effectually to remove an evil of such magnitude from our beloved country." While the ministers stopped short of offering specific means and did not pass any measures declaring fellowship with slaveholders a sin, as the Union Baptist Church had hoped, they did offer several other resolutions addressing racist laws in Ohio. Declaring the state's Black Laws "oppressive and unjust," the association "recommend[ed] to all christians and philanthropists, to petition the next Legislature for their repeal."[46]

Elder Graham remained at the Jonas Run meeting of Baptists and delivered a sermon on the last evening. Before the assembly of white ministers from southwestern Ohio, Graham preached from Isaiah 24:11–12, which describes the suffering following God's judgment. "The Lord maketh the earth empty, and maketh it waste," this chapter begins. Graham's selections describe the devastation that accompanies judgment: "All joy is darkened, the mirth of the land is gone. In the city is left desolation, and the gate is smitten with destruction."[47] It seems fair to infer from this selection that Graham wanted to call his white audience to repentance for the nation's sin of slavery and Ohio's hostile climate toward African Americans. It is not clear that the Union Baptist Church felt a sense of triumph here, especially given its internal turmoil over their strategy, but the Miami Baptist Association's adoption of a powerful antislavery statement and the call to its nearly two thousand, mainly white members to work toward the repeal of the state's Black Laws revealed, at the very least, a stark contrast between the northern and southern branches of the Baptist church, and it may have assisted Ohio's and Kentucky's white Baptists in clarifying those differences.

Though neither the Miami Baptist Association nor the Long Run Association of Baptists in Kentucky sought the nation's disunion, these two leading Baptist associations nevertheless represented irreconcilable positions on the place of slavery in American life in 1845 and 1846. Black Americans in Cincinnati and Louisville had done much to shape these two positions—even if inadvertently in the case of Kentucky—and had propelled white evangelicals in their respective states along radically different trajectories. Whether Ohioans or Kentuckians, evangelicals now surely grasped the significance of their divisions.

The General Subject of Slavery

More than Baptists, American Methodists entered into a decades' long, bitter antagonism between their northern and southern churches in 1845. When Bishop Leonidas L. Hamline arrived back in Cincinnati after the Louisville meeting in favor of separation, he "found war and wickedness" among the city's church members.[48] Following the division, Cincinnati became one of several flash points in the M.E. Church's border disputes.[49] The M.E. Church, South, had selected Cincinnati to test an "aggressive . . . interpretation of the Plan of Separation," and in 1845, Bishop Andrew of the southern church recognized a society there.[50] The establishment of a southern church in a northern city caused no end of wrangling among Cincinnati's Methodists and church officials, in part because it pointed out the broad room for interpretation in the Plan of Separation. Northerners worried that the meaning of "border" society, as described in the Plan of Separation, could be a continually shifting line if the M.E. Church, South, recognized congregations farther and farther north. Referring to the southern church's actions, Bishop Hamline wrote in his diary that "grievous wolves have entered in not sparing the flock."[51] While this battle over borders raged, Cincinnati's Western Book Concern emerged as another source of contention between the northern and southern churches. Southern Methodists sued for half of the value of the Cincinnati publishing house, but their claims would not be settled until 1854 when the U.S. Supreme Court declared in favor of the M.E. Church, South.

One of the closest witnesses to these events was the Reverend Charles Elliott, who had a pastoral charge in Cincinnati while also editing the *Western Christian Advocate*. Born in Ireland, Elliott had an insatiable passion for scholarship, evidenced in his first major work, entitled *Delineation of Roman Catholicism, Drawn from the Authentic and Acknowledged Standards of the Church of Rome: Namely, Her Creeds, Catechisms, Decisions of Councils, Papal Bulls, Roman Catholic Writers, the Records of History, Etc. Etc.: In Which the Peculiar Doctrines, Morals, Government, and Usages of the Church of Rome are Stated, Treated at Large, and Confuted* (1841). At nearly one thousand pages, in two volumes, this treatise set forth Elliott's style: exhaustive in its use of original sources and frankly partisan. He was therefore a logical person to prepare an official history treating "the last four years" of the ecclesiastical crisis, as leading churchmen outlined the scope of their charge to Elliott in 1848.[52]

This might have seemed a mere toss-off work, hardly on the scale of a history of the Roman Catholic Church, except for what Elliott quickly discovered: his true subject was slavery, which "presented in every step of his progress" to comprehend the church divisions of the 1840s. So Elliott embarked on a quest to describe "the general subject of slavery . . . as thoroughly as he could," but with a careful determination to reveal the institution's inhumanity.[53] Within two years, he had produced a two-volume study, weighing in at over seven hundred pages, with this definitive title: *Sinfulness of American Slavery: Proved from Its Evil Sources; Its Injustice; Its Wrongs; Its Contrariety to Many Scriptural Commands, Prohibitions, and Principles, and to the Christian Spirit; And from Its Evil Effects; Together with Observations on Emancipation, and the Duties of American Citizens in Regard to Slavery* (1851). Yet another major book project spun out from his original mandate, prospectively examining ancient slavery and the primitive church. Before committing to that perilous labor ("If life be spared this may be presented to the public," he hedged), Elliott returned to the immediate task at hand: a history of the Methodist Church divisions between 1844 and 1848.[54]

Even with a seemingly discrete topic, his exhaustive research "task[ed] him to the utmost." To complete his *History of the Great Secession* (1855), Elliott amassed a remarkable archive of materials connected to the study of

Methodism and slavery. His *History* drew on three major collections in his possession. First, he compiled "eighty or one hundred unbound volumes of newspapers" covering events between 1844 and 1854, the year he ultimately concluded his history. From these, he "cut" articles, pasting his selections into eight volumes of "Historical Scrap-Books." By his none-too-precise counting, these clippings made up "6,727 columns of fourteen inches long." Next, supplementing the newspapers, Elliott possessed "over fifty volumes, comprising all the pamphlets treating slavery that issued from the press in Europe and America for eighty years past." Third, "a valuable collection of bound books and periodicals" added yet more bulk. Elliott's index to these printed materials alone took up "350 pages foolscap." Surely he did not exaggerate when he gazed over this mass of material and ventured the following: "It may be difficult to find a more ample collection any where on the subject of slavery." A scrupulous historian, he hoped to place the volumes with the Methodist Book Concern of Cincinnati as a permanent archive for those wanting to check his claims against original sources.[55]

Cincinnati's Methodists must have had some inkling of the Irish-born minister's growing magnum opus. There was the public nature of his official charge to write the history coming from the Methodist Episcopal Church in the first place, and during the work of researching and writing, Elliott enjoyed no monkish seclusion but rather had the "ordinary duties of a district or station to perform."[56] At the same time, he maintained his editorship of the *Western Christian Advocate*. Elliott also could not easily mask the nature of his project, given the challenges of storing and maintaining his unwieldy library over many years. Nevertheless, he proceeded in his partisan work, eviscerating claims for slavery's divine origins, and he did so unmolested by Cincinnati's skittish mobs. For by the time Elliott took up this ambitious project in 1848, his views about slavery and the radical danger presented by exclusive southern institutions had become entirely mainstream in Cincinnati.

Elliott did not endorse abolitionism, viewing it as a form of "ultraism" not unlike the extreme proslavery positions staked out by southern ministers.[57] But he did present persuasive, overwhelming evidence that the Methodist Episcopal Church, South, was founded "to continue and protect slavery." In consequence, the schism represented a "revolutionary" movement "to support a wrong system."[58] Through much of the one thousand pages making up his *History of the Great Secession*, Elliott labored to demonstrate the essential fallacy of southern claims—namely, that the founders of the M.E. Church, South, undertook their secession to promote continued conversions among slaves and, as a corollary, that slavery was, in its essence, a missionary enterprise. Elliott countered this by insisting that effective missionaries, "whose duty it is to carry the Gospel to all, whether bond or free," explained any gains among slaves prior to 1844.[59] Put simply, slavery itself should not be credited with accelerating Christian conversions among the enslaved. "Slavery can have no more pretension to a missionary character," Elliott asserted, "than drunkenness, theft, and idolatry can have to be good, moral, and religious."[60] Nor could he find evidence that the long-standing antislavery discipline of the Methodist church had dissuaded planters from accepting missionaries' labors among slaves prior to 1844, ostensibly a mainspring for separation. Far more likely, Elliott predicted, enslaved people would reject missionaries insisting on divine sanction for their suffering. The "Southern church, by their proslavery principles and action, in time, will be shut out from access to the slaves and colored people of the south," he reasoned.[61] In casting church "secession" as a scandalizing breach of moral and religious principles, Elliott reinforced the growing power of antisouthern sentiments in Ohio politics.

In the 1840s, leading white Baptists and Methodists in Ohio and Kentucky steered congregations into separate denominations and toward radically different positions on the morality of slavery. Moreover, relations between black and white evangelicals shifted dramatically by 1850 on either side of the Ohio River. Greater antagonism between white and black congregations ensued in Louisville, where white Kentuckians wanted to prove slavery's Christianizing influence. The city's African Americans resisted these new intrusions into their spiritual and congregational lives and sought to protect their independence from white oversight, which had seemed well enough established before 1845. In Cincinnati, by contrast, black evangelicals met with important successes in persuading local white Baptists in southern Ohio to declare their opposition to slavery and to the state's unequal treatment of black and white people under the law. Moreover, the leading Baptist association in the region had encouraged its thousands of white members to petition the Ohio state legislature to repeal unequal laws. White Methodists in Cincinnati also emphasized the legacy of antislavery in their church, thereby undermining justifications for the new southern Methodist denomination. These actions stood in marked contrast to white Kentuckians' effort to invigorate slavery by assigning it new sacred significance as a missionary enterprise. So while antislavery sentiments gained traction in Cincinnati's religious institutions, proslavery arguments found strong proponents among Louisville's leading white churchmen. The faithful on either side of the Ohio River also encouraged new organizations to clarify and articulate their particular beliefs about the morality of slavery. Intended to block the flow of contaminating ideas across the Ohio River, these organizations reinforced growing sectional alienation in politics and law.

Rich Chapters in Political Diplomacy

In the mid-1840s, just as northern and southern branches of the national churches were assuming their new sectional guises as antislavery and proslavery denominations, politics in both Ohio and Kentucky underwent dramatic shifts, threatening long-standing Whig and Democratic alignments. Through the 1830s, Jackson-era political parties had held dilemmas over slavery in check as most voters found banking and economic development decisions more immediately relevant to their day-to-day lives. Comfortable assumptions that the slavery question operated at the political margins, while persuasive for the 1830s, lost credibility as the United States annexed Texas and pursued fevered dreams of expansion into Mexico's northern borderlands. As economic juggernauts, Cincinnati and Louisville had wielded significant political power within their states, and residents of both cities had reliably supported the Whig Party's economic proposals through the 1830s. But over the next decade, the two cities proved pivotal in realigning national politics around the slavery question, and residents in both Cincinnati and Louisville played critical, if at times unintentional, roles in determining the way new political parties spoke about and debated slavery in American life. By 1850, Kentucky's and Ohio's elected representatives had legislated their states into recognizably sectional positions—with Kentuckians guaranteeing inalienable property rights for slave holders and Ohioans making freedom for African Americans more secure—though not without great political controversy.

Beginning with the 1844 elections, but most obviously in the 1848 state and national elections, Ohioans placed slavery at the heart of their politics, and they did so in a way that reflected the peculiar history and more conservative influence of Cincinnati. Rather than the abolitionist immediatism emanating from Ohio's radical Western Reserve, Cincinnati's new Democratic majority of the 1840s shaped the state's antislavery coalitions and ultimately left its ideological imprint on the new national Free Soil and Republican parties of the late 1840s and 1850s. The Ohio River city's great population wielded unusual force in the politics of the state, but Cincinnati's sordid history of antiblack sentiment and violence, and its hard-money Democratic partisans drawn from the ranks of Irish and German Catholics, hardly seem conducive to any broadly national antislavery politics or even northern sectionalism in the state. And yet it was a "Cincinnati Clique" of political organizers, led by Salmon Chase, Gamaliel Bailey, and Thomas Morris, who "officiated at the marriage between Jacksonian egalitarianism and antislavery" sentiment.[62] Seeking an alliance with Democrats rather than Whigs in the late 1840s, this influential group advocated a constitutional solution to the national division over slavery, which the historian Jonathan Earle labels "Antislavery Unionism." In the view of Chase, Bailey, and Morris, the federal government could and should act to "Relieve itself from all Responsibility for the Existence or Continuance of Slavery wherever that Government possess Constitutional Power to Legislate on that Subject, and is thus Responsible for its Existence."[63] This constitutional approach insisted that the federal government retained the power to restrain slavery's growth and thereby slowly legislate the institution out of existence. The view drew support among Ohioans perturbed by slaveholding politicians' pursuit of western lands through aggressive policies of annexation and war.

By the 1848 elections, the appeal of moderate antislavery politics among Ohio's voters was clear even in Cincinnati, where Free Soil candidates and ideas ruptured some Democrats' hard-and-fast loyalties to their party.[64] With success in the fall elections, Salmon Chase's Free Soil advocates wielded eleven swing votes in the Ohio legislature, enough to determine whether evenly divided Democratic or Whig partisans held sway over the state.[65] A newspaper promised "some rich chapters in political diplomacy for the wonder of the people," and the state legislature's Free Soil and Democratic representatives indeed delivered great drama during "the winter's plotting" of 1848–49.[66] Barely contained chaos—which included legislators absconding to a nearby hotel to prevent a quorum—produced one of the more astounding political feats of the antebellum era as Free Soil legislators brokered a complex settlement with the state's Democrats to seat their party's elected representatives from Cincinnati, where they had been victims of Whig gerrymandering. In exchange, Democrats repealed nearly all of Ohio's prejudicial Black Laws and elected the antislavery Chase to the U.S. Senate. In the aftermath, contemporaries confronted two remarkable, intertwined consequences of this partisan ingenuity: first, that antislavery sentiment now exerted a "controlling influence over Ohio politics," and second, that an incipient "civil rights revolution" was underway in this most racist of northern states.[67]

Passed in February 1849, the legislation repealing Ohio's Black Laws did away with special residency requirements such as surety bonds and written proof of freedom intended to make it more difficult for black Americans to settle in the state. Now, people of color could take up residence in Ohio without threat of official inquiry into their legal status. Drafted by Chase, the repeal legislation also advanced black Ohioans' access to fair trials in the state's courts by allowing their testimony in criminal or civil cases involving white people. The 1849 law further provided public funding for black children's schooling and did not prohibit integrated classrooms. Severe legal disabilities remained in place, including prohibitions against voting and jury service. Black Ohioans could not partake of poor relief either, although they paid taxes that aided the state's financially distressed white residents. Nevertheless, Ohioans "understood the magnitude of the change" wrought by the 1849 legislation, as Paul Finkelman argues.[68]

The legislation reflected Chase's political acumen and deep personal attachments to racial justice, but it also capped a fifteen-year petitioning effort by a broad swath of antislavery Ohioans who recognized that the state's unequal laws diminished their moral authority and made freedom and personal security illusory for emancipated slaves.[69] By the 1840s, the Ohio legislature sensed enough political pressure to appoint special committees to investigate and review the Black Laws. Courtroom restrictions drew the most scrutiny, and the state senate narrowly repealed limits on black testimony in 1845, only to see the Democratic-controlled house block this hard-won effort.[70] Lawyers, Chase included, pursued a parallel effort in the courts to find antitestimony laws unconstitutional. Ohio jurists revealed growing impatience with the legal absurdity of restrictions on sworn statements by persons of color where whites were a party.[71] In addition, back-to-back governors in the 1840s, Mordecai Bartley and William Bebb, viewed the Black Laws as manifestly unfair and called on the Ohio legislature to consider their modification or abrogation.[72] Thus, when Free Soil representatives arrived at the Ohio statehouse in late 1848 ready to exert their new political clout, they entered a well-trod "battlefield over civil rights reform" in the legislature.[73] The 1849 repeal legislation represented both the culmination of a long, steady advocacy effort as well as a beckoning for further change.

When delegates gathered in Columbus in the spring of 1850 for the first state constitutional convention since 1802, advocates for racial equality hoped that the vote for black men would be forthcoming. It was not. Although a proposal for black enfranchisement reached the floor for a vote, it met with overwhelming defeat, with just fifteen votes in favor and seventy-five against. Alarmingly, delegates also presented petitions calling for reinstatement of the Black Laws and advocated proposals for black removal from the state, either through colonization to Liberia or stark banishment. In the end, petitions favoring equal rights greatly outnumbered such removal schemes, and delegates never allowed a full vote on proposals to limit or exclude black residency in Ohio. They also refused the American Colonization Society's requests for funding and approbation of their scheme for Liberian resettlement. In context, Ohio's rejection of any kind of limits on black settlement and disavowal of colonization is significant, given that three other western states along with Kentucky affirmed the illegality of black migration into their jurisdictions in the 1840s and 1850s.[74]

Freedom Proposition

In the first part of the 1850s, mainline political parties incurred voters' enmity after Congress passed their two infamous acts, the Fugitive Slave Law and the Kansas-Nebraska Act. Instead of dampening the crisis over slavery, both laws quickly spawned new violence over fugitive slaves and the territories. They also spurred development of a major political party drawing together disaffected Whigs, Democrats, and third-party Free Soil and nativist members of the new "American," or "Know-Nothing" organization. Just as the Free Soil Party met with notable political success in Ohio between 1848 and 1854, so the Republican Party had its coming of age in the state with Salmon Chase's election to the governorship in 1855. Winning the executive office in one of the nation's most populous states demonstrated the Republic Party's viability and accorded Ohioans a prominent role in shaping the new national organization.[75]

Tumultuous events in Cincinnati once again played a role in the ascent of antislavery office seekers. Following nativist violence against immigrants during the city's mayoral election in the spring of 1855, the state's Know-Nothing Party fell into disrepute. Branded "knaves and asses" for alienating rather than enticing voters with their rioting, Know-Nothings "suffered a failure of nerve" and did not endorse their own candidate for governor. Chase secured their nomination for the state's highest office by co-opting Know-Nothing support for his candidacy through a "dazzling mixture of conciliation and intimidation."[76] Chase won his statewide bid, though not with the support of Hamilton County electors, who divided their votes among three candidates. However inadvertently, Cincinnatians dampened support for narrowly nativist office seekers and provided an opening for the savvy Chase to fill a political void.

Yet Salmon Chase was also very much a product of Cincinnati's unique history, and he cultivated his thoughts about the possibility of racial equality and constitutional emancipation while living there in the 1830s and 1840s.[77] From the early 1840s, Chase helped to pull Ohio into the politics of antiextension and to promote his constitutional theory of "Freedom National, Slavery Sectional." While governor, he presided over Ohioans' deepening attachment to the idea that slaveholders' power should not extend into states where the institution was illegal and that the federal government had no constitutional duty to protect or encourage slavery where it did not already exist. In fact, the federal government's true role was to discourage slavery's expansion beyond its original confines and to promote the progress of freedom.[78]

This view drew at least in part from the peculiarities of Ohio's history and law. From its earliest years of statehood, Ohio law revealed "ambivalence" about black residents. In its most starkly racist provisions, state law placed unusual burdens on would-be black settlers to prove their freedom and independence (although these were almost never enforced in practice). The white men who crafted these provisions intended to make it more difficult, if not impossible, for people of color to settle and enjoy freedom in the state. On the other hand, in the very same provisions, the architects of state law levied heavy fines on those who attempted to drag legally free people into southern bondage. The state legislature increased these penalties several times in the first half of the nineteenth century. Although the Ohio legislature passed a runaway slave law at the behest of Kentucky in 1839, the new provisions set out "an elaborate state system for regulating the return of fugitive slaves."[79] In consequence, lawmakers doomed the law to failure, and ultimately repealed it. When Congress passed the new Fugitive Slave Act of 1850, Ohioans were incensed, and the state legislature drew up resolutions reflecting popular opposition. For half a century, then, laws and popular sentiment expected the state to ensure the freedom of black residents who met Ohio's stringent, race-based residency requirements.

Chase's political work carved away at both sides of this legal equation: first, by reducing the special legal burdens borne by black Ohioans and, second, by extending the freedom proposition already seeded in Ohio law. With Chase controlling the state's highest office and the Republican Party in ascendancy, Ohio embarked on a remarkable freedom project. For one, Ohio's courts and legislature declared that slaves coming into Ohio with their masters automatically became free. The legislature even imposed criminal penalties on masters who knowingly brought their slaves into Ohio. These masters imperiled their own freedom as well as the property in the person of their slave.

Personal liberty laws passed by Ohio Republicans added harsh penalties for kidnapping free blacks and precluded the use of Ohio's jails to detain alleged fugitives. More dramatically, Ohio refused to assist Kentucky in prosecuting those who abetted fugitives coming into the northern state and, in one instance, retrieved the children of a free black Ohioan who had been abducted and then sold into slavery in Kentucky. Ohioans thus enlisted their courts, laws, and public resources to maintain a "safe haven" for African Americans after 1855.[80]

Higher Law

The year 1849 began auspiciously for black rights in the Ohio River valley, with Ohio repealing prejudicial laws and ensuring state support for black education. Many Americans also entertained hopes for the adoption of a gradual emancipation scheme during Kentucky's constitutional convention, scheduled for the fall of 1849. Both of these developments seemed to beckon a peaceful, legal way out of the slavery crisis. Albeit slowly, and with notable setbacks, Ohioans moved their state toward more equitable laws and state protection of black freedom under the helm of antislavery politicians after 1849. Kentucky, though, tacked in the opposite direction, insisting on an inviolable right to own slaves that neither state nor federal law could limit or diminish. In suggesting that veritable marauders preparing to unleash race warfare stood by, awaiting just the right moment to cross into Kentucky, slaveholders sought to stamp out the emancipationist movement in the state. At the state constitutional convention, held in October, delegates tried to punish Louisvillians for their modest antislavery sympathies and banned free black migration into the state. Drafters of the new state constitution were not subtle about their purposes, arguing that the time had arrived to declare Kentuckians' sympathy with other slave states. In 1849, Kentuckians battened down the hatches and curtailed moderate antislavery hopes that the state would be the first to pursue gradual emancipation.

Antislavery advocates in Louisville inadvertently helped to provoke this reactionary state constitution. At midcentury, the city formed the nerve center of Kentucky's emancipation movement. The state's only dedicated antislavery newspaper at the time, the *Examiner*, was published weekly out of Louisville, and the city's voters had elected emancipationist politicians into significant offices, including mayor and Congress. Antislavery activists exulted that "four-fifths of the people are for emancipation" in Kentucky's "commercial metropolis" after only a few years of advocacy. Six months before the state's controversial convention to reconstitute its government in 1849, they vowed that Louisville's citizens were "ready and willing to use all honorable means to procure the extinction of slavery." Despite its invocation of southern honor, this vow exacerbated fears in the Bluegrass of an abolitionist plot to wreak havoc in slave-rich sections of the state.[81] That Louisville's most vocal emancipationists also questioned Kentuckians' long-standing advocacy of colonization while apparently in league with the city's free blacks added an extra charge of danger to the antislavery activism emanating from the Upper South city and ran counter to the powerful strain of exclusionist racial thinking held by the majority of white Kentuckians at the time. To proslavery and antislavery conservatives alike, Louisville thus increasingly looked like a "beachhead" for abolitionism and, by extension, slave insurrection or racial amalgamation.[82]

Antislavery agitators had established their foothold in Louisville and appeared poised to move into rural districts. In Kentucky's slave heartland, these agitators would lure bondsmen and bondswomen into rebellion. This was at least the view held by Kentucky's proslavery delegates to the constitutional convention in 1849, and troubling evidence of alliances between free blacks and white emancipationists, as well as the violent run-up to the convention, confirmed their worst fears. During the unprecedented statewide discussion Kentuckians held about the future of slavery between 1847 and 1849, the assertiveness of free blacks and their white emancipationist allies became political fodder for those who wanted to maintain the status quo or enhance slavery's protections in the new framework for government. In time, Louisville functioned as a kind of shorthand for all that seemed to threaten Kentucky's attachment to slavery, and to the South generally. But the accusations proslavery ideologues leveled against Louisville were not without some basis, and they helped to determine key provisions in the new state constitution.

While antislavery advocates looked to Louisville's white emancipationists for leadership in organizing and publishing, differences between the city's reformers and activists statewide jeopardized their efforts to elect antislavery delegates to the constitutional convention. Although otherwise in accord with Kentucky's conservative antislavery sentiment, which emphasized gradual schemes for emancipation, the *Examiner*'s editors and a number of its contributors began to write more earnestly against colonization in late 1848 and early 1849 in preparation for the election of delegates to the constitutional convention. Many white Kentuckians had questioned the practicality and cost of colonization, but the *Examiner*'s editors were exceptional in their continued support for emancipation despite their opposition to blacks' forced removal from the state. "We frankly confess that we have no sympathy with any plan of expatriation, any plan that will drive the black man, however great his reluctance, to the shore of Africa," the editors wrote in 1849, four days before a convention of the states' leading emancipationists, scheduled to take place in Frankfort. As inheritors of Cassius Clay's antislavery paper, the *True American*, the *Examiner*'s editors were among the most radical in the state, and were in regular consultation with white immediatists in the North and Kentucky's John G. Fee, who advanced racial egalitarianism as part of his abolition work. But the questioning of colonization in Louisville had extended beyond the editors of the *Examiner* to include conservative men like Samuel Nicholas, who took the "initiatory step" in "presenting the subject of emancipation" without also advancing the compulsory removal of freed people in late 1848. Along with Cassius Clay and John Fee, Louisville's emancipationists voiced the strongest white opposition to colonization on the grounds of racial justice; by contrast, other state antislavery leaders remained committed to the complete separation of the races following emancipation, whether through freed slaves' forced colonization to Africa or deportation to other states.[83]

When the state's emancipationists gathered in Frankfort in April 1849 to develop a unified platform for candidates to the constitutional convention, this difference nearly derailed their meeting. Representing Louisville and Jefferson County, respectively, William L. Breckinridge and W. P. Thomasson both presented resolutions that would have made inclusion of a constitutional provision for "gradual prospective emancipation with colonization" a part of the Emancipation Party's platform. Despite appearances of agreement on colonization, delegates from rural Kentucky balked at this, since the resolutions would have required "each candidate to present his plan for emancipation" and would have put on display the divisions within the state's antislavery movement. "The truth is," said Judge Ben Monroe of Franklin County, president of the Kentucky Colonization Society, "we have now no general or special plan upon which we can agree." Monroe, who had served as chair of the "grand committee" to devise the Emancipation Party's platform, feared that the differences over colonization, if aired during the canvass for delegates to the constitutional convention, "would destroy us." "The gentlemen of Louisville or Jefferson [County], may be far in advance of us," Monroe warned. But "*I am for emancipation with colonization, and not otherwise*—nor will I vote for any man or advocate any plan which contemplates emancipation without colonization," he made emphatically clear. In Monroe's view, the Louisville advocates could not be counted on to affirm this necessary relationship between black freedom and deportation. Kentucky's antislavery delegates managed to keep this dispute simmering quietly by adopting compromise language affirming the "complete power in the people of Kentucky to enforce and perfect, in or under the new constitution, a system of gradual prospective emancipation of slaves," thereby obviating the need for a specific plan for the voters to accept prior to the election of delegates the following August. Even among like-minded conservative emancipationists, then, Louisville's antislavery voices appeared tinged by radicalism.[84]

Cognizant of emancipationists' superior organization and publishing capacities in Louisville, antislavery conservatives nevertheless called on the city's leadership to form a "Central Committee," with responsibility "to use all proper means to promote the views of this convention on the subject of emancipation" throughout the state. As a consequence, by late 1849, Kentucky's Bluegrass politicians had branded Louisville the "headquarters of abolitionism and emancipation" in the state, a phrase redolent of northern fanaticism rather than the conservative antislavery thinking common to Kentucky. This recognition of Louisvillians' leadership thus came at a political price, since "abolitionists" in the city would be blamed for the violence plaguing the state prior to the August election for delegates to the constitutional convention. With advocates for proslavery and antislavery positions stumping throughout the state, passions flared: real and imagined slave insurrections in the Bluegrass, gun battles between voters in Louisville, and Cassius Clay's knife slaying of a proslavery advocate's son in Madison County all revealed an "atmosphere of desperate anxiety" by the summer of 1849. Selecting their delegates amid a raging cholera epidemic in August, Kentucky's voters signaled their apprehension about tampering with slavery, sending just two candidates who advocated emancipation to the convention. Even Louisville's voters fell shy of electing reformers to the convention.[85]

Cholera's appearance during polling, emancipationists' divisions over when and how slavery should meet its peaceful end in Kentucky, fears of local slave insurrection, and national disputes over slavery's fate in the territories probably all contributed to the Emancipation Party's nearly across-the-board losses. In any event, proslavery delegates elected to the constitutional convention would insistently remind their fellow delegates of the "fire and brimstone" they had passed through to get to Frankfort and would blame Louisville's emancipationists for the violence preceding the election. Kentucky's rural politicians looked on Louisville with "holy horror" for the city's leadership in the statewide emancipation movement, its troubling free black population, and its foreign-born residents with little stake in slavery. The state's "northern frontier," insinuated these representatives, was "teeming with abolitionism," raising fears of racial amalgamation and slave insurrection along with illegitimate free-state interference in southern institutions. Other delegates would diminish the numbers of antislavery supporters in Kentucky while heightening their effect: "The few emancipationists in this State had produced an excitement that alarmed the whole South," complained Beverly Clarke, a lawyer from Simpson County, early in the convention proceedings. Whether a "few" in number or "teeming," emancipationists seemed a genuine threat to Kentucky's well-being and to the South's corporate unity, according to the proslavery majority elected to redesign the state's government.[86]

The prolonged process for calling and seating a convention had thus illuminated one urgent task for delegates to take up during the meeting itself: since Kentuckians had obviously failed to halt the flow of fanaticism into the state through its northern border, and incendiaries in Louisville appeared poised to make mayhem in the slave-rich Bluegrass, proslavery representatives wanted to halt any further "agitation" by making slave property very nearly sacrosanct in the new legal framework for government. Summoning a "higher" law beyond that of "constitutional sanction," delegates would adopt a new provision stating that the "right" to own slaves was "inviolable" by Kentucky's voters and legislators. Arguably, Kentucky's 1799 slave article as adopted into the new constitution already guaranteed that consideration of any emancipation scheme would have to reckon with slaveholders' property interests, but the added provision affirmed Kentuckians' will to protect the peculiar institution from legislative infringement, if anyone was uncertain on that point. Convention delegates thus sent a powerful signal to state and national audiences that Kentucky would shield the South's most distinctive form of property from abolitionist assault. The state's own antislavery gradualists, who had insistently disavowed anything to do with abolitionism but had failed to offer white Kentuckians a clear plan for a postemancipation society, also appeared hamstrung by the new provision making slaveholding a fundamental or natural right. In the view of Abraham Lincoln, who had closely followed the state's constitutional convention, the "signal failure" of Kentucky's emancipationists in 1849 had made the "peaceful extinction of slavery" a hopeless cause.[87]

 Convention representatives would further try to punish Louisvillians for the heresy of abolition by weakening the city's influence in the state. Hoping to "seal up the mouths of the abolitionists" there, Philip Triplett of Daviess

County proposed limiting the city's representation in the state senate. Samuel Nicholas's Chancery Court in Louisville, the only such court in the state, also caught the attention of proslavery delegates, who proposed its elimination. During the convention, Nicholas, along with Cassius Clay and Henry Clay, were named as "the prime movers of emancipation in Kentucky." Placing Nicholas's courtroom on the chopping block was surely payback for his support of emancipation and perhaps also his connections with Louisville's free blacks. Above all other groups, though, free blacks in Kentucky endured the greatest scorn in lawmakers' debates about the future of the state. David Meriwether, representing rural Jefferson County, proposed nothing less than the banishment of "all free negroes and mulattoes now in this state." While lawmakers would pull back from disfranchising Louisville in state government, eliminating its Chancery Court, and removing all free blacks from the state, they would insert a new provision in the constitution that made any person of color who immigrated to Kentucky, or who was manumitted there and remained in the state, "guilty of a felony, and punished by confinement in the Penitentiary." Delegates contended that "the free negro population among us is conceded by all to be worthless, and highly detrimental to the value of our slaves, as well as the security of the owner," alluding to the previous summer's hysteria in the Bluegrass counties of Mason, Fayette, and Bourbon over several attempted large-scale slave escapes. In addition to criminalizing free blacks, the new provisions in the slave article required the removal of any emancipated slaves from the state, thus setting a precedent for deportation and restricting population growth among the state's free blacks.[88] Kentucky's delegates thus reassured slaveholders that the Upper South state would protect the peculiar institution through new constitutional mandates.

Louisville's white emancipationists and free blacks sustained a blow with voters' ratification of the new state constitution. With little hope for pursuing gradual emancipation in the state, antislavery activists ceased publication of the *Examiner* in 1850. A year later, Louisville's elected officials amended the city charter to assert impossibly broad control over black gatherings, requiring "visitation of the police" at "all meetings or assemblies of colored persons" and licenses for any future "place or house" in which African Americans met "for any ... purpose whatever." City officials also retained the explicit power to "silenc[e] any preacher or teacher of colored persons." The new government provisions, along with passage of the national Fugitive Slave Law in 1850, meant that free blacks in Louisville faced "perilous" threats to their freedom and safety. It is no wonder that the free black population in the city saw little growth through the 1850s and that William Gibson and

Henry Adams devised strategies to ensure their families' security after 1850. As hedges against the risks in residing in a slave state, Gibson purchased land in Canada while Adams held a dual position as minister to both Louisville's Fifth Street Baptist Church and Cincinnati's Union Baptist Church for several years in the early 1850s.[89]

By 1850, white Ohioans and Kentuckians had articulated starkly different purposes for their religious organizations and laws. With Cincinnatians sometimes at the forefront and at other times in tow, Ohioans had rendered their faiths and constitution into notably antislavery positions and had begun to undo prejudicial laws afflicting free persons of color. As Ohioans injected a "freedom national" philosophy into their most powerful institutions, Kentuckians sensed risk. In reaction, slaveholders there tried to purge the state of its emancipationist sentiments by diminishing Louisvillians' electoral influence and by restricting the growth of a free black population. And though Ohioans insisted on the immediate rupture of property rights in persons upon contact with its soil, Kentuckians gave new divine clout to those same property rights. Before 1849, these sectional positions had not needed to be staked out so clearly. After that year, Ohio and Kentucky risked increasing sectional alienation to further their positions on the morality of slavery.

CHAPTER EIGHT

Allegiances

Kentucky's 1849 constitution gave property rights the force of "higher law," thereby deadening hope for even the most gradual or limited steps toward emancipation in the state. At nearly the same time, under Salmon Chase's leadership, Ohio refused to recognize any right of property in persons and began to strip the state constitution of prejudicial laws impinging on black freedom. This stark difference begged the question of federal power and law. Could both states claim the authority of the Constitution to support its local laws? How could the federal government reconcile these two understandings of property in persons? The answer, of course, is that it could not, and the nation fractured over the right to own humans in 1860–61.[1] This irreconcilability seems clear enough, but allegiances in the Ohio-Kentucky borderland did not easily align with such sharp divisions in thinking.

One of the more vexing historical questions related to the Civil War is this: How did the Union pull Kentucky along in its orbit during the Civil War, given the state's argument that a sacred right of property in persons stood above any earthly authority?[2] Secessionists argued that the Constitution, properly interpreted, protected slaveholders' rights to carry their enslaved property anywhere they wished within the borders of the United States. Lincoln, and the Republican Party generally, endangered that right, they further claimed. Slaveholders' only option, secessionists insisted, was to establish a government where property rights in persons would be sacrosanct, beyond the reach of misguided fanatics. Given its recent state constitutional history, Kentucky seemed likely to agree with this logic.

But Kentucky's allegiances, tested as they may have been, remained with the Union through the Civil War. This outcome might suggest a fatal ethical compromise with Kentucky's slaveholding commonwealth by Republicans like Chase and Lincoln. Did they conciliate slaveholders in the state in order to preserve loyalties, and thereby diminish the moral force of their anti-slavery convictions in waging a war for the Union? Arguably, they did not. The evidence for "conciliation" as a Republican policy in Kentucky appears complicated by at least two circumstances. First, Chase in particular, and Lincoln's civilian and military leadership in general, used forceful diplomacy very early in the war, arming Kentucky's "Unconditional Unionists" in the summer of 1861 and thereby hastening the end of the state's dubious "neutrality." Second, over time, some Louisvillians contended powerfully for a Union without slavery and insisted that the federal government had the constitutional authority to abrogate property rights in persons in their state.[3]

From his work on behalf of fugitive slaves in Cincinnati, Chase established a legal foundation to argue that the Constitution did not recognize property rights in persons. Accordingly, the federal government was obliged to ban slavery where the Constitution held exclusive force, such as in western territories. Yet Chase also hewed to the view that the federal government could not interfere with slavery where it already existed. In other words, the Constitution accorded no clear authority to the federal government to abrogate property rights in persons where state law positively defined those rights. Chase's constitutional thinking here accords with what James Oakes calls the "federal consensus." This consensus view held that the federal government could not interfere with slavery in the states, because the Constitution, as drafted in 1787, provided no specific authority for it to do so.[4]

The federal consensus appeared to place slaveholding beyond the reach of the federal government, secure until a state chose, of its own volition and by its own legislative processes, to emancipate any persons held in bondage there. But the federal consensus did not promise unassailable protection. This was because Republicans, and in particular Chase, undertook an "unabashed" attack on slavery, and slavery's malignant effects, in places where positive state law defining property rights in persons did not operate. This explains Chase's work in Ohio to negate slavery's contaminating reach into free state soil and the Republican Party's insistence that western territories remain free. According to Chase, the Constitution endowed the federal government with the "power to spread freedom everywhere" outside of the states where slavery had the force of positive law. Over time, free states would outnumber and surround slave states, whose power would diminish proportionally, thereby "cordoning slavery off." Slaveholders "themselves would realize that slavery was holding them back economically, disrupting the social order, and promoting political instability." As rational actors, they would begin to undo laws recognizing property in persons in their states. This theory of slavery's inevitable demise through a combination of external and internal pressure stood behind Republican Party policies to undermine the institution in the Civil War era.[5]

From the late 1840s Chase advanced this theory of applied political abolitionism in both Ohio and Kentucky, and in broad outline, the process for undermining slavery unfolded as Republicans thought it would. More precisely, the story line played out in Louisville, whose residents argued for slavery's immediate end in the state after the chaotic conditions of the war. Certainly by 1864, if not earlier, prominent Louisvillians insisted that the federal government could, and should, abolish slavery in Kentucky. This stood in contrast with the Kentucky state legislature's "warfare" with Republican policies in the state, including the Thirteenth Amendment.[6]

That Kentucky remained loyal to the Union through the war, even despite the Republican assault on slavery there, may be partly attributable to the work of Chase and George Prentice. Both developed powerful views of constitutional union in the decades before the Civil War, and they applied their thinking in astute ways during the secession crisis and in wartime to maintain Kentucky's allegiances. Though both stressed the federal consensus argument, they also realized (albeit at different times) that Republican antislavery policies in peace and in war rendered slaveholding in Kentucky unenforceable under state law. The Emancipation Proclamation may have exempted Kentucky, but this was very nearly a moot point by 1863.[7] From their deep attachments to the value of union, Chase and Prentice drew the same conclusion that federal power rightly abolished slavery in Kentucky. Chase and Prentice thereby made emancipation a just constitutional means to hold the Union together.

New Englanders by birth, Chase and Prentice were well into their fifties as the Civil War began. As young men, cutting their teeth as opinion makers, both wrote significant books in direct response to the nullification crisis of 1832. Both thought deeply about the crisis and became powerful spokesmen on behalf of union in that moment, yet with special reference to the unique histories of their adopted states, Ohio and Kentucky. By the time of the Civil War, Chase and Prentice were hardened veterans of the political strife of the 1840s and 1850s, but they enjoyed credibility and influence. Neither man needed to recant or revise previously held views or statements; both remained fairly true to their Unionist identities, forged thirty years earlier in the nullification crisis. Their attachments to the federal government—their powerful belief in its capacity to do well by its people by fostering both order and freedom—helped Louisvillians navigate the chaos brought on by the war.

Less visibly, African Americans in Kentucky, and especially free blacks in Louisville, adhered to a vision of union with consequences for Kentucky's sympathies with, and similarities to, the states that ultimately joined the Confederacy. In the late 1840s and 1850s black Kentuckians fought hard against a central premise of the new southern religious denominations: that the purpose of slavery was sacred. African Americans in Louisville refused to be any party to the white "mission" churches established in the name of this argument. Because slave missions were such a clear failure in Louisville, Kentucky's evangelicals could not as easily claim, let alone pursue, the righteous purpose of slavery as they saw it. Black rejection of a central premise for the founding of the southern evangelical churches therefore reveals a vulnerability of proslavery religion in the Upper South on the eve of the Civil War. By 1861, white evangelical Kentuckians had less in common with their religious brethren in seceded Confederate states. In consequence, arguments for the sacred nature of slavery—a powerful justification for secession, in fact—could not easily draw Kentuckians away from their political allegiances to the Union.

Northwest Ordinance

Born in Cornish, New Hampshire, in 1808, to a prosperous and civic-minded farming family, Salmon Chase enjoyed a comfortable childhood until the death of his father in 1817, when Chase was six months shy of his tenth birthday. A bright child, Chase then began a peripatetic course toward acquiring a rigorous classical education, with his financially straitened mother taking advantage of better-off relatives to provide schooling for her son. By 1820, Chase was living with his uncle, the Episcopal bishop Philander Chase, on a farm in rural Ohio, and he would briefly attend Cincinnati College before returning to New Hampshire in 1823 to complete his education at Dartmouth. Family connections next took Chase to Washington, D.C., where he labored as a schoolmaster to children of the city's political elite, including the sons of William Wirt, attorney general in John Quincy Adams's administration. Seeking a profession more suited to his serious temperament, Chase arranged to study law under Wirt. The busy attorney general provided little formal instruction to Chase, whose studious habits enabled him to read Blackstone independently and with sufficient intellectual command to join the bar in 1830. Although relatives had facilitated Chase's education, he also worked diligently and relied on his own initiative. And despite the haphazard nature of his schooling, Chase acquired a broad erudition by dint of strenuous personal effort combined with admirable curiosity. As a young lawyer, for example, he "read widely and well" in a number of subjects, including, in one impressive stretch of study, Galileo's scientific contributions, machinery's relationship to society, English common law, and the Old Testament's book of Psalms.[8]

Chase carried this voracious intellectual energy and professional ambition with him to bustling Cincinnati, where he launched his legal career in

1830. While building his law practice (and recovering from a near-fatal case of cholera), Chase took on an ambitious side project: a legal analysis of Ohio statutes and important local ordinances since 1803, along with a full treatment of Ohio's unique territorial and statehood history, to be published within one accessible reference work. The book project bore the hallmarks of many of Chase's subsequent endeavors. Though serving the public good, the work also had the potential to advance Chase's personal career, draw attention to his substantial scholarly gifts, and persuade a wide audience of a particular view of the past as a means to shape the political future.[9]

Just two months before Chase left Washington, D.C., for Cincinnati, Daniel Webster delivered his famous reply to Senator Robert Hayne of South Carolina in which he argued for the supremacy of the general government and insisted on the fallacy of state nullification of federal law. Chase had been struck by Webster's discussion of the Northwest Ordinance and Ohio's special relevance to the debates about the nature of the federal union and to the worsening sectional antagonisms over slavery. Not long after settling in Cincinnati, Chase embarked on his compilation of Ohio's statutes, with a keen interest in the state's development from colony to territory and then to statehood under the auspices of the newly formed United States. The young lawyer sensed that his interpretation of Ohio's settlement and organization under the terms of the Northwest Ordinance, as well as its history of statehood, would be the book's most significant contribution to the politics of the moment, viewed in light of the heated debates over nullification taking place as he was writing. Despite the topic's timeliness, the challenges of writing such a comprehensive history looked daunting in the summer of 1833. To his close friend Hamilton Smith, Chase complained that he "[found] this a work of great labor" since no one had yet produced such a survey of Ohio's unique development. "I almost regret I ever attempted this work," Chase confessed, given the challenges of gathering disparate sources together.[10]

The Ohio country's history was, in truth, a dizzyingly complex one: native peoples, European colonizers, and new American states had all competed viciously for sovereignty over the region. The bright spots in Chase's account occur when congressional or federal power was asserted, as with the Northwest Ordinance, which rescued the region from "various pretentions" to sovereignty that "for a long time darkened the prospects of the American union." Federal power over the Ohio country began auspiciously with the Ordinance of 1787, "the last gift of the congress of the old confederation to the country," and was reinforced by Ohio's admission to the Union in 1803, which allowed settlers to "escape from a rule which they thought harsh and oppressive" under the undemocratic territorial government. While national power favored "the genuine principles of freedom" and the "great doctrine of equal rights," localism bred disorder and despotism. Thus, in Chase's telling, federal claims to the Ohio country appeared "rational and just," the Northwest Ordinance embodied "the true theory of American liberty," and the democratic and liberal institutions of governance inhering in the state's constitution and bill of rights fulfilled the vision of the ordinance's enlightened congressional authors. The greater bulk of the book, his extensive review of Ohio's statutes and local codes since statehood, would reinforce the central point of his historical narrative: Ohioans, whose enjoyment of prosperity and liberties seemed illimitable as he wrote in 1833, owed their success to federal power, principles, and institutions. Further, as the first state within the Northwest Ordinance's geographical bounds, Ohio bore a special relationship to the federal union. Chase's newly adopted state would therefore "cleave fast to the national constitution and the national union," he predicted, and "her growing energies will, on no occasion, be more willingly or powerfully put forth, than in the support and maintenance of both, in unimpaired vigor and strength."[11]

Chase applied this thinking to his work on behalf of fugitive slaves, which he undertook for the better part of a decade after 1836. Although his clients were nearly always remanded back to slavery, Chase's unstinting legal work to establish the Constitution as an antislavery force brought him to political prominence. By the mid-1840s he actively sought election to national office. Yet it was difficult to find a congenial political home for his "antislavery unionism," as Jonathan Earle has described the distinctive brand of pragmatic and legalistic reform logic that emerged from Cincinnati.[12] Over yet another decade, Chase labored within all the leading and third-party organizations, and helped to found two new major political affiliations, the Free Soil Party and the Republican Party, in order to make antislavery unionism a major party plank palatable to diverse voters in both the North and South. His political pragmatism paid great electoral dividends: by 1860, Chase had served in the U.S. Senate, and he was also twice elected to Ohio's governorship after 1855. In 1861, he resigned from a second appointed term in the Senate to serve as secretary of the treasury under Lincoln.

Although something of a political changeling during the tumultuous shifts in party alignments during the late 1840s and 1850s, Chase held consistent antislavery views throughout his long career in public service. Ohio's unique history and the Ordinance of 1787 remained touchstones for him as he argued against the extension of slavery into new American territories and insisted that the Declaration of Independence, Constitution, and Bill of Rights together fostered a "national political faith" that was, at its core, opposed to slavery.[13] Judging the actions of the Founding Fathers in crafting the Northwest Ordinance and in designing the Constitution and its Bill of Rights, Chase inferred that the United States' first generation of statesmen intended to end slavery by preventing its expansion. Errant interpretations of the founders' vision for a nation fully committed to freedom had led to compromises, such as that over Missouri in 1819 and, most criminally, the Kansas-Nebraska Act of 1854 authorizing the use of "popular sovereignty" to determine the place of slavery in new western states. He deemed these actions subversions of the nation's creed of freedom. Confounding founders' expectations, slavery had been allowed to extend into new territories in spite of Congress's obvious power to ban the institution, as evidenced in the Northwest Ordinance and its subsequent enforcement under the U.S. Constitution. The few indirect references to slavery in the Constitution, Chase further asserted, indicated that the institution was not actuated by federal power but rather was "the creature of State law, and dependent wholly upon State law for its existence and continuance."[14] Chase insisted, then, that he only wanted to rescue the first animating political principles of the founders from the illicit power of a small cabal of slaveholders. "We would not invade the Constitution; but we would have the Constitution rightly construed and administered according to its true sense and spirit," he argued in 1845.[15] A powerful writer, Chase offered these arguments eloquently in a steady stream of party platform statements, campaign speeches, public appeals, and inaugural addresses for almost two decades before Lincoln appointed him to serve as secretary of the treasury.

Because he grew impatient with single-issue third parties and wanted to place antiextension and antislavery planks within the major political parties' platforms, Chase may be viewed as a pragmatist or moderate in comparison to abolitionists who resisted any kind of temporizing in the suppression of a moral evil such as slavery. On the other hand, he has also been grouped with the "radical" Republicans because of his support for African American citizenship rights. While a Liberty Party and Free Soil candidate, Chase spoke fervently about "the brotherhood of the Human Family," perhaps more so than he would as a Republican Party leader seeking national office.[16] But he continued to insist that a broad conception of human freedom and rights had animated the Founding Fathers as they designed the U.S. system of government. Simply put, "the basis of American Institutions is the democratic principle of equality of men," Chase argued in his inaugural address as governor of Ohio in 1856.[17]

As he labored to woo Democratic Party voters to Free Soil and Republican candidates and principles, he would also draw on egalitarian rhetoric, demanding "Exact Justice to all men!" and "Equal Laws guarding Equal Rights."[18] And though Chase opportunistically courted American Party voters, he rejected Know-Nothings' nativism and intolerance of immigrants. "The rights of all my fellow-citizens, native or naturalized, are as dear to me as my own," Chase averred at a campaign stop in Cincinnati, worried as he was about alienating a significant voting block of German-born immigrants in southern Ohio.[19] Despite Chase's legalism and vote chasing, then, a current of radical egalitarianism ran through his public statements that drew its power from both the Declaration of Independence and the Christian command "to behold in every man a brother."[20] Genuine moral sentiment, albeit inseparable from his political ambition, animated Chase's career in public service as he sought, through his antislavery activism, "the happy result of a more perfect Union, established upon the solid foundation of exact justice, and equal rights."[21]

Best Theatre for Political and Military Genius

For all of his radicalism, Chase never disavowed the federal consensus on slavery. He consistently asserted that the general government lacked constitutional authority to abolish slavery in states where the institution had existed at the creation of the federal compact, or where slavery had gained a foothold by virtue of political concession, as in the Missouri Compromise. While insisting that extending slavery any further into federal territories violated the founders' original intent, he would not claim that the U.S. government had the authority to emancipate bondsmen and bondswomen within existing slave states. As James Oakes writes, "Chase in particular was convinced that it was both constitutionally incorrect and politically suicidal for an antislavery party to deny that the Constitution protected slavery in the states where it already existed."[22] Counterintuitively, this position gave Chase a certain leverage as he attempted to test Republican policies encouraging slavery's eventual abolition in Kentucky.

From the early 1840s Chase manifested a keen political interest in Kentucky because his legal antislavery work involved fugitives from the neighboring slave state. Until 1850, Kentucky also stood as the only southern slave state with a reasonably active and indigenous antislavery movement, led early on by the voluble Cassius Clay. In 1842 Clay stroked Chase's ego by writing to the young antislavery lawyer and aspiring politician, "The ground upon which you stand is immovable, the cause which you advocate is our country's, the fights which you vindicate belong to mankind—all are akin to immortality, they cannot perish."[23] Thus personally encouraged, Chase took a long-standing interest in the state as promising ground for the development of a southern antislavery movement.

Chase's close involvement with the emancipation movement in Kentucky began with Cassius Clay's overture to the young Cincinnatian in 1842. Though heaping praise on Chase for his antislavery advocacy, Clay warned against direct action in Kentucky, writing, "I love my own native land touch not her honor," and counseled Chase to avoid pitting the sections against each other in his quest for office: "I love the Union 'tis my shield and sword the ark of my political safety." "Preserve it—and I am with you," Clay pledged.[24] Although Chase once chastised him for antiblack views and criticism of the Liberty Party appearing in the *True American*, Clay's antislavery newspaper, the Ohio politician remained a firm supporter of Kentucky emancipationists through the 1840s and by and large followed Clay's admonitions to tread carefully in the commonwealth's affairs.[25]

When Clay decided to serve in the Mexican American War, causing a stir among abolitionists and consternation among his paper's subscribers for leaving it in the care of his financially distressed wife, Chase intervened. To ensure the continuity of the *True American*, he selected a capable editor, solicited subscriptions and endorsements among leading northern abolitionists, supported the paper financially, and aided in the paper's relocation from Lexington to Louisville. In an 1846 letter to Gerrit Smith, the wealthy New York abolitionist, Chase defended Clay's military service as "sincere" and driven by political conditions unique to Kentucky. He also enjoined Smith to renew his subscription to the paper based on editorial changes and the "very great influence" the paper would soon have in Kentucky. "Now, my dear sir, will you not renew your efforts in favor of the paper?," Chase implored the wealthy benefactor. "The aspect of the anti slavery cause was never so promising in the West as now," he averred.[26]

Chase's financial support of the paper continued at least through 1848, and in 1849 he believed he saw Free Soil principles gaining ground in Kentucky as emancipationists there rallied to elect antislavery candidates to the approaching constitutional convention.[27] "The prospects of emancipation are, also, brightening in Kentucky; and the Emancipationists are all anti-extensionists," Chase wrote to Ohio Democrat Jacob Brinkerhoff in 1849, expressing optimism that Kentucky's senators, Henry Clay and Joseph Underwood, would "vote with us"—that is, the Free Soil voices in Congress. The two senators were "already well inclined" to do so, given that "the state of public opinion" in the slave state appeared to be shifting in favor of emancipation.[28] Chase was not alone in placing great hope in Kentuckians to pioneer state-sponsored antislavery in the South. These optimists endured great disappointment. The new state constitution reinforced rather than weakened slaveholders' property rights. Although chastened, Chase kept a close eye on events in Kentucky, and he remained a strong supporter of Cassius Clay.[29]

Through the 1850s Chase threw his prodigious energies into the complex machinations necessary to build a new major political party with antislavery as a central plank, even as he occupied increasingly visible offices as U.S. senator and Ohio governor. His correspondence during this time, however, does reveal an abiding concern to advance his antislavery politics in Kentucky, one that did not impugn his commitment to the Union or cast him as a narrowly "sectional" politician. While representing Ohio in the U.S. Senate in the early 1850s, Chase projected a reputation as an antislavery politician with crossover appeal to slave-state voters. In 1851, for example, he wrote to his close friend from college, Hamilton Smith, then a resident of Louisville, seeking assistance in a public relations campaign in Kentucky to "improve my position before the country by shewing that in a slave state . . . justice can be done me, and personal regard manifested." He therefore wanted Smith to draft a statement recounting his private knowledge of Chase's decent character and moderate politics for publication in one of Louisville's leading papers, and he hoped to have the piece favorably blurbed by a prominent editor. In sum, Kentucky newspapermen would vouch for Chase's "consistency with myself following out my ancient opinions to my present position." Smith was the perfect vehicle for this kind of public promotion: "You know how early I entertained and avowed antislavery opinions. . . . You know, also, that while I have maintained my own opinions on slavery with firmness & decision I have never quarreled with any one on account of adverse opinions and have never manifested any wish to interfere with slavery in any of the states; but have simply claimed the right and asserted the duty of the General Government to restrict it within state limits." If Kentucky's leading newspapers offered validation that Chase was admirably "firm" in his views but "not rabid or intolerant," he stood to gain politically as a candidate worthy of consideration in the state.[30]

Newspaper blurbs were one prong in Chase's Kentucky public relations campaign. As a senator, he also supported legislation directly benefiting voters in the southern slave state. Having secured funding for the construction of federal buildings in Cincinnati and Saint Louis, Chase endorsed the same for Kentucky's leading city, and he made sure others knew that his vote in these allocations mattered. "When the proposition for Louisville was before the Senate," Chase wrote to Edward Hamlin, an Ohio representative to Congress and later a prominent newspaper editor, "I spoke for it & voted for it when my single vote would have defeated it, the Senate being almost equally divided." To Chase, the greater point was that he had "aimed to be liberal & just to all sections of the country" as a legislator.[31] Here was the work of an ambitious, savvy politician seeking to prove his appeal among a wide range of voters in a moment of shifting party allegiances. But if placed in the light of his long-standing antislavery advocacy, his outreach does not seem quite so self-serving. Chase kept up pressure in the state and often took the pulse of antislavery opinion there, especially in Louisville. His antislavery bona fides were already well known by the 1850s; he did not diminish or minimize them for a Kentucky audience.

Yet Chase might still be charged with placating Kentucky's slaveholders as secretary of the treasury in Lincoln's cabinet. Chase directed the administration's military and political action on the ground in Kentucky through the summer and fall of 1861, thus helping to secure the critical slave state's Union loyalty after an unusual four-month stint in the constitutional no-man's-land of "strict neutrality."[32] To Lincoln and Chase, this period of time was one of the most uncertain of the Civil War. Although Kentucky had abandoned neutrality in favor of union in August, two nearly simultaneous events threatened that renewed allegiance. First, John Frémont's August 30 proclamation empowered Union troops to liberate the slaves owned by rebellious masters and imposed martial law in Missouri. Then, on September 3, Confederate forces invaded Kentucky. If Kentuckians took the assault on slavery in Missouri as reason to bolt from the Union, the Confederacy would quickly reap victory and an independent nationhood. At this juncture Lincoln opined on the state's significance: "I think to lose Kentucky is nearly the same as to lose the whole game." He reasoned this way: "Kentucky gone, we can not hold Missouri, nor, as I think, Maryland. These all against us, and the job on our hands is too large for us. We may as well consent to separation at once, including the surrender of this capitol."[33] This logic was persuasive, if terrifying, and Chase threw himself into the work of preserving allegiances in Kentucky.

In the immediate aftermath of Frémont's martial law proclamation, Kentuckians besieged Chase with letters expressing disbelief and betrayal. From Louisville, the prominent Unionist Joshua Speed demanded retraction of the proclamation, for Kentucky's loyal slaveholders could not endure two enemies: their slaves and disloyal Confederates: "Do not allow our wives & children to be murdered" by unleashed slaves, as Speed predicted would be the effect of Frémont's proclamation, "while we are willing to give our lives, if need be to our country—Give us a chance & Ky will soon have 25 @ 30,000 men in the field—But for God sake dont suffer our love of the Union & the Govt to be crushed out by these foolish & wicked proclamations."[34] Writing from Frankfort, where he was deliberating with Kentucky's state legislators on "movements and measures" to uphold the Union, Garrett Davis told Chase that "the proclamation fell amongst us with pretty much the effect of a bomb shell." Although Davis, a U.S. senator from Bourbon County, had personally supported emancipation as a lawmaker, he warned Chase that "there is a very general, almost universal feeling in this State against this war being or becoming a war against slavery."[35] In response to Kentuckians' "grt. apprehension," Chase urged a "restrict[ed]" interpretation of the proclamation, to conform to congressional Confiscation Acts already in place. Moreover, to Green Adams, his treasury representative in Kentucky, Chase emphasized the prewar federal consensus on slavery: "The question whether a person is Slave or Free is a question to be determined by State law as applied & enforced by State Courts."[36]

To Kentuckians worried about Republican Party intentions in the loyal slave states, Chase denied radical sympathies. Responding to Garrett Davis, Chase wrote: "That I have been much misunderstood does not at all surprise me." Late in August 1861, on the eve of the Confederate invasion of Kentucky, Chase insisted that he was not a closet abolitionist seeking the "immediate & unconditional emancipation, without much regard to means or consequences." Chase then took pains to explain the constitutional process by which slavery would meet its end, according to Republican theory and practical policy: "I have wished to see Popular Government vindicating itself & accomg. itself by its demonstrated capacity to probe & redress so great an evil as Slavery, first by the Constitutional action of the National government within its appropriate sphere, & then by the unconstrained action of the States within their several jurisdictions."[37] Although this might be read as conciliatory on the question of Republican intentions in Kentucky, it struck a surprisingly activist note in a moment of fear and trembling as the state awaited Confederate invasion. Descriptions of a government seeking to "vindicat[e]," "probe," and "redress so great an evil as Slavery" were perhaps not quite the words white Kentuckians wanted to hear in the first days of September 1861.

In fact, Chase was fostering conditions for the "redress" of slavery in the state. Military planning and strategy would seem odd responsibilities for a secretary of the treasury, but war minister Simon Cameron's ineptitude provided an opening for Chase to exert influence in a region he viewed as "the best theatre for political and military genius" in the war's early months. So he enthused to George B. McClellan, then in command of Ohio's troops, while proposing that McClellan "march down" from Kentucky, "through the mountain-region . . . then reach the Gulf at Mobile . . . thus cutting the rebellion in two." "Perhaps you will laugh," Chase demurred to McClellan in this July 7, 1861, letter, "and ask, 'What does the Secretary of the Treasury so far from the money-bags?' "[38] It was an overreaching letter, to be sure, but it does reveal Chase's aggressive work to arm "the frds. of Unconditional Union" in Kentucky.[39] While exercising his regulatory powers over trade and customs, Chase also directed the distribution of munitions, calling up of troops, and establishment of camps for Union forces in Kentucky through the summer of 1861. His agents from the treasury bureau had already organized five regiments in Kentucky, two of which were near Louisville under the command of Colonel Lovell Harrison Rousseau. Promising "arms and guns" and "rapid enlistment," Chase placed these all at McClellan's disposal. "Just as soon as circumstances will allow, you can yourself take the open command of the regiments" now raised in Kentucky, Chase wrote. The letter indicates no little exhilaration at his swift orchestration of this military work.[40]

Commanders in the field, as well as treasury agents traveling through the state at Chase's behest, also kept him apprised of Union sentiment through the summer and fall of 1861 as Kentuckians voted in critical elections and faced down Confederate invasion. From his operatives in the field, including William Nelson, a former Navy lieutenant working as a secret Union agent (despite weighing a conspicuous three hundred pounds and standing well above six feet), and Green Adams, a special treasury emissary and native of Kentucky, Chase received detailed portraits of popular sentiment, county by county, during the tense summer of 1861.[41] His intelligence described the activities of Kentucky's leading Union politicians and their reactions to arming and raising federal troops in the state. In late July 1861, on the eve of the legislative elections to determine the state's loyalties, Nelson reported that the embarrassing losses at Bull Run had not irreparably damaged Union feeling among political leaders. He promised Chase, "You can count on Kentucky, she is true as steel."[42] As Chase's eyes and ears in Kentucky, Green Adams wrote, "I assure you all is right—the people are ready, & anxious to meet the crisis & go into the fight for the Government."[43] Chase raised regiments and monitored loyalties in Kentucky to protect the state from Confederate invasion. But he was also creating conditions entirely inhospitable to slavery by organizing Union forces in the state. As a consequence, the old federal consensus would not stand for long in Kentucky. Chase's work constituted an aggressive form of antislavery diplomacy, not a temporizing with slaveholders. Many Louisvillians accepted this forceful use of federal power to end slavery by 1864.

Mystical Union

Following South Carolina's secession from the Union in December 1860, Kentuckians began a tortuous struggle to determine their state's allegiances in the fight over slavery and union—a struggle that, in truth, would last well into the postwar period. The bitter contests over loyalties initially centered on control of state elected offices, moved on to the battlefield early in the military conflict, slipped into smaller-scale raids and guerrilla actions until the war's close, and continued to swirl in struggles over African American civil rights and questions of identity and region in the era of Reconstruction.[44] George Prentice's *Louisville Journal* would have its say in all of these events, but its most prominent contribution to ensuring Kentuckians' Union allegiances would be in 1861 as the state legislature first pursued a singular course of neutrality and then abandoned this policy in favor of union by September 1861. Through the teeming activity of 1861, with multiple conferences convened to try to avoid war, elections held to control state offices, and troops organized and armed to command the state's loyalties, the *Journal* "indignantly spurned" the rebellion against the United States and labored to ensure that Kentuckians had "soul enough" to "preserve and not to destroy" the Union.[45]

In broad outline, Prentice's childhood and early adulthood resembled Chase's New England upbringing. Six years older than Chase, Prentice was born in 1802 to a well-regarded, although not wealthy, farming family in Preston, Connecticut. Like Chase, Prentice was a precocious child, even drawing visitors to his home curious to see a three-year-old reading entire Bible chapters aloud. Later, as a youth, Prentice required just six months' study to have full command of both Greek and Latin. He taught in local schools to earn money before enrolling at Brown University, from which he graduated in 1823 at the top of his class.[46] Like Chase, Prentice tried the law after college to escape a dreary career in the schoolhouse. But a literary penchant drew him away from law and into journalism, a fate sealed when he became editor of the *New England Weekly Review* in Hartford in 1828.

Earning acclaim as a spirited partisan on behalf of political candidates, Prentice was solicited by Henry Clay's presidential campaign backers to write a biography of the Kentucky statesman. Prentice traveled south to meet the famed legislator in the spring of 1830, and by the fall of that year, he had published a glowing—to say the least—account of Clay's life and accomplishments, moved permanently to Louisville, and launched a Whig newspaper, the *Journal*. In short order, his life had taken a dramatic southern turn. While Prentice never shook his sobriquet as the "Yankee schoolmaster," he became an unrelenting advocate of the worldview codified by Henry Clay.[47] Seen through the gauze of Prentice's poetic and literary sensibilities, though, Clay's particular politics became a kind of sentimental creed in support of union.

Although more properly categorized as a work of hagiography, Prentice's *Biography of Henry Clay*, published in Hartford in 1831, lays out political themes that would pervade the pages of the *Louisville Journal* for some three decades, with renewed salience during the secession crisis of 1860–61. There was, of course, a ringing endorsement of Clay's integrated commercial vision for an "American system" providing federal government support for domestic manufacturing and transportation improvements. Prentice endorsed Clay's view of broad constitutional powers for Congress and Congress's importance itself as an instrument of national "cohesion" through commerce. Writing amid the brewing crisis over slavery and South Carolina's assertion of state sovereignty within the federal union (and at nearly the same moment a youthful Chase was puzzling over Ohio's relevance to the same crisis), Prentice disavowed, speaking through Clay, the South's "right to claim that the policy of the union should be established in sole reference to the condition of the blacks—in other words, that the whole country should become the slave of slaves." Although Prentice argued Clay's position that South Carolina could never have the power to nullify the federal tariff in service of its own state interests—that is, slavery—Clay nevertheless "believed that the constitution had withheld from congress all power over the subject" of slavery. Abolitionism as a movement was anathema to Clay, as it would be to Prentice, both favoring instead a "slow and certain process" of emancipation over the very long run, with each state pursuing its own separate and unique course. In Prentice's inimitable phrasing, "the abolition of slavery at once" portended a "tide of death," unleashing a "dark and thundering torrent . . . over the country."[48] All of these economic, political, and racial perspectives received ongoing and ample coverage in the *Louisville Journal* through the antebellum period, and with urgency in 1861.

Yet Prentice's *Biography of Henry Clay* offers not so much a political treatise as perhaps a poetic or even religious meditation on the meaning of union. Readers discovered, on the one hand, the unreserved hyperbole of an exuberant partisan: any number of references in the book depict Clay as very nearly a deity himself, a "saviour of his country," an "ancient patriarch," and a "superior being commissioned by Heaven."[49] But more deeply, the biography displayed what Prentice considered the means to unity, or union, in a polity seemingly on the brink of division in 1830. For one, Prentice literally envisioned bodies melding and melting together in the presence of Clay's person and rhetoric. Although war with Britain in 1812 had produced bitter controversy in Congress, political adversaries "forgot their antipathies, and wept together" while listening to Clay, who vigorously endorsed the military conflict. Prentice loosely quoted poets Milton and Cowper to convey Clay's powers as an orator:

> He is such a perfect master of the language, tone, and look of passion, he
>   addresses himself to the deeper feelings with such mysterious skill,
> "Untwisting all the chains that tie
> The hidden soul of sympathy,"
> That opposing spirits feel the influence of his power, and, "like kindred
>   drops, are mingled into one."[50]

According to Prentice, his numerous speeches in Congress drew forth physical responses in his listeners: tears fell copiously, blood "thrill[ed] through the veins," and "electrick flash[es]" pulsed through hearts, so that enmity dissolved.[51]

Prentice also exalted the Kentucky statesman's glorious "systems" of political and commercial union. The Constitution presented one such system, which alone enjoyed "the power . . . of diffusing intelligence, affluence, and happiness, throughout the nation—the power of twining still more closely the silver cords of Union around the whole of our mighty and almost limitless territory." And Clay's "American system" of commerce, by linking manufacturers, farmers, and consumers through new infrastructure, or "internal improvements," would regenerate souls along with the nation: "The desert will blossom as the rose, and new streams will start into being, as at the voice of Omnipotence, bearing wealth and beauty upon their tide, ministering to the noble commerce of mind, and, our whole country will, as it were, be created anew, with greater powers and enlarged capacities." Here Prentice drew on the familiar evangelical language of the "new birth" so that the political and economic meanings of union stood as proxies for faith. It is certainly possible to argue that Prentice waxed poetic about a political ideology serving the interests of a particular segment of the American population and that not all would enjoy the "prosperity and happiness of the Union" promised by Clay, or by Prentice as his backer and biographer.[52] But this nearly mystical sense of union, with its capacity to remake individuals as new moral beings and bind adversaries together, found ongoing expression in Prentice's *Journal,* most pressingly in 1861.

While George Prentice gained some fame as a man of letters, the *Louisville Journal* acquired most of its large readership because of Prentice's biting humor and vituperative style as an editor.[53] In a highly partisan era, his withering jabs at political opponents sold newspapers. In seeking an editorial assistant, Prentice once laid out his job criteria: "Have you conscience enough to write for Clay and go the whole hog, from tail to snout?"[54] Within six months of launch, the *Journal's* editor boasted of fifteen hundred subscribers for three different editions of his newspaper, including a "tri-weekly" version, and the paper cultivated a devoted readership among Louisvillians, who were said to have "rather done without their breakfast than the morning *Journal.*"[55] The paper also grew to have considerable appeal beyond Kentucky, enjoying the largest circulation for a daily paper published west of the Appalachians.[56]

Henry Clay's ghost loomed large in the pages of the *Louisville Journal* through 1861. Although Clay had died nearly a decade earlier in 1852, his words "should sink deeply into every Kentucky heart," Prentice wrote, to stave off "the heresy of secession."[57] "Now, as in 1832, it devolves upon Kentucky to shield the people of South Carolina from the penalty which they had madly provoked, and thereby save the nation from utter desolation of civil war," he contended, looking back to Clay's rejection of the policy of nullification.[58] In following Clay's example through previous national crises, Kentucky would hold fast to its historical role and serve as a "mediator" or "pacifica- tor" diminishing the extremes of northern abolitionism and southern rights fanaticism.[59] "Let Kentucky speak, and she will be heard respectfully, alike by the North and the South."[60] This mediating role made more sense before hostilities had erupted in April 1861, but well into the summer of that year, the voice of Clay, rousting the "slumbering patriotism of the country" and "seeking the salvation of the Union," rang forth in the *Journal.*[61]

In late July 1861, with Confederate and Union troops fighting in earnest, the tide of conversation turned in the pages of the *Journal* to comprehend- ing the purpose of the federal government in its military campaigns against the rebellious states.[62] The "object of the war" was emphatically not to free slaves. The *Journal* insisted, "There is not one deed of the United States in the present or prospective prosecution of the war against the Southern rebel- lion that shows that the *status* of the negro has any more to do with this war than it had to do with the American Revolution." Prentice argued that Kentuckians could better protect the status of slaves under the Union banner, but armed conflict in the border slave states reignited concerns about the safety of enslaved human property. To assert that the war itself would have no impact on the status of slaves required a bit of legerdemain on Prentice's part, and he resorted to race baiting to ensure Kentuckians' loyalty to the Union: "Intelligent freemen," he wrote, should not "permit political demagogues to darken their minds by covering them with the skin of the negro." That the United States would emancipate slaves—whether as a contingency of war or through deliberate policy decision—was a "*colored* lie," Prentice editorialized on the eve of Kentucky's August elections.[63]

Unionism and its opposite, secessionism, took on a discernable corporeality in the *Louisville Journal*. In editorials, Prentice wrote of secession "as a dead body [that] sinks in the sea," and viewed neutrality as a "quiescent" bodily state akin to a disabling paralysis.[64] By contrast, Union loyalty he conceived, not surprisingly, as vital and pulsing with life. Articles in the *Journal* routinely employed standard turns of phrase here: "The sentiment of loyalty . . . yet burns in the hearts of her sons," one editorial pledged on behalf of Kentucky's men.[65] With his sentimental bent, Prentice extended this vitality to the state of Kentucky itself, viewing it as the "heart and soul of the Union," and the border states together as a "GREAT CENTRAL BODY" that "shall not be broken or weakened" in its commitment to union.[66] And "nobody, who knows how loyally the heart of Kentucky has always beaten, will doubt its decision," Prentice confidently predicted in July 1861.[67] If Kentucky was the "heart" of the Union, Henry Clay was, although dead and buried for nearly a decade, the still-throbbing heart of Kentucky. The state's "patriotic impulses seem like the very pulsations of the great heart which too soon ceased to beat for his country," one editor wrote about Clay's unique longevity within the bodies of all loyal Kentuckians on July 4, 1861.[68] Prentice's sentimental impulses lent power to his belief in a mystical union binding together the nation through Kentucky's unique political history.

Warranted by the Constitution

Chase and Prentice had helped to shore up Unionist allegiances in 1861, each arguing that Kentuckians should feel assured that the federal government would not undertake emancipation in loyal states. This constitutional view prevailed in the Emancipation Proclamation, but the very exigencies of the military conflict and enslaved people's pursuit of liberation amid wartime conditions brought about slavery's undoing. This was as true in the loyal border state of Kentucky as in the rebellious states.

Chase and Prentice both grasped the import of these historical events, and thus supported the use of federal power and executive authority in the Constitution to ratify and further the war's indubitable assault on slavery. As a member of Lincoln's cabinet, Chase gave encouragement to the Emancipation Proclamation in late 1862. Notably, he proposed adding language to the final draft of the proclamation affirming that emancipation and black enlistment in the rebellious states were "sincerely believed to be an act of justice, warranted by the Constitution, upon military necessity." Lincoln accepted the wording.[69] In September 1862, the *Louisville Journal* had declaimed against the Preliminary Emancipation Proclamation as "wholly unwarrantable" and "wholly pernicious."[70] Three years later though, Prentice argued for the use of federal power to end slavery and encouraged acceptance of the Thirteenth Amendment.

In May 1865, he prepared a lengthy "Open Letter to the People of Kentucky," which appeared in the *Louisville Journal*. This summative statement offered a history of secession and war, a primer on the original intent of the drafters of the U.S. Constitution with regard to slavery, and a vision of future progress and prosperity for Kentuckians with the elimination of the "disturbing element" of human bondage. Though Prentice claimed that secession and war of themselves provoked the "utter demoralization of slavery," even absent federal policies or specific measures advancing emancipation, he nevertheless contended that the national government had rightly aided slaves' liberation and enlistment in "the spirit of self-defence." But if Prentice viewed "the new exigencies which had arisen" in wartime as the proximate cause of slavery's demise, he did not comprehend emancipation merely as the product of historical accident and battle confusion.[71] To do so would have diminished the very meaning and power of union in 1865.

Prentice now insisted that the federal government properly exercised legal authority to terminate slavery in Kentucky and that such action was indeed "warrantable" according to the original intent of the framers of the U.S. Constitution. Practically speaking, during the war, when local law enforcement in slave states broke down and Union authority ensued, slavery met with "inevitable" collapse since "the Federal Government had nothing to do with the maintenance of the relations of slavery *within* the States." Though Prentice had once insisted on the theory of state precedence, he now negated local authority over slavery by way of constitutional principle.

Delving into debates at the Constitutional Convention and the history of the Northwest Ordinance of 1787, he concluded that the federal government possessed the power of amendment to end slavery and that this eventuality was the founders' original hope. "It is but fair to infer," Prentice reasoned, "that they intended that the country should ultimately get rid of that evil by a resort to the power of amendment." He validated this assertion by adverting to "the instructions of the great commoner Henry Clay, who true to the teachings of the founders of the Republic . . . wisely foresaw the inevitable tendency of coming events and advocated emancipation." It was urgent, Prentice insisted, for Kentuckians to "cement more closely the bands that unite her to the loyal States," given the state's precarious allegiances. That meant immediately acknowledging the power of the national government to forever ban slavery by ratifying the Thirteenth Amendment. With its passage, he predicted "a new era of enlightened thought and action" and a "magnificent destiny" for Kentuckians and the nation. Newfound "prosperity, happiness, and wealth" would follow the abolition of slavery.[72]

Prentice's recognition of federal authority over slavery and the status of people of color departed from views held by most white Kentuckians, even those holding Unionist sympathies. In May 1865, Kentucky was the last southern state with significant numbers of enslaved people still subject to legal bondage, at least theoretically. From late 1862, when Confederate armies invaded Kentucky with the intention of occupying Louisville and Cincinnati, Union armies protecting the state had slowly chipped away at slavery through impressment, enrollment, and enlistment of enslaved and free black Kentuckians. Union military and civilian leaders saw this as a means to undermine slavery even without the constitutional authority of the Emancipation Proclamation or Kentuckians' assent to the Thirteenth Amendment. In consequence, military recruitment extended well into June 1865 in Kentucky, with black men of almost any physical description and age accepted into service because it would ensure their emancipation. In Kentucky, Union armies mustered more African Americans than in any other slave state excepting Louisiana.[73]

Yet the state's white political leadership fought black recruitment to the brink of nullification and military resistance. Writing to the president in early 1864, the state's governor, Thomas Bramlette, threatened to arrest and convict federal recruiters on state felony charges. The penalty, he cautioned, could be twenty-years imprisonment for violating state fugitive slave laws.[74] This was somewhat better than the "summary justice" he had promised to anyone enlisting black recruits a few months earlier.[75] In March 1864, Bramlette informed a provost marshal that "if the President does not upon my demand stop the Negro enrollment I will."[76]

Within days of this brash assertion, a small group of Unionists, including Theodore S. Bell of Louisville, rushed to Frankfort to confer with the governor, who was readying what some later deemed a "nullification proclamation" for the people of Kentucky because it called for the use of force to stop black military enrollment. Over seven hours of negotiation, concluding at three o'clock in the morning, the four Unionists talked Bramlette down from the dangerous ledge he had climbed. But Bramlette's resistance still exacted its damage: provost marshals and enlisting black Kentuckians faced appalling violence, some of it by whites from the state in service to the Union. Seven provost marshals lost their lives during this moment of great tension between Kentucky leaders and the federal government.[77]

Nonetheless, black enlistment proceeded apace in the state, assisted by the imposition of martial law in July 1864. By the first days of 1865, some twenty-five thousand enslaved men had gained their legal freedom through enlistment in Union service, and their families, also legally emancipated by federal authority, swelled that number considerably.[78] Slavery clearly was at its end, for no legal authority—including the state—could enforce the provisions necessary for its maintenance. As Congress and the nation debated the Thirteenth Amendment in the first part of 1865, slaves headed for Louisville and other Kentucky towns to learn what might come next for them.

George Prentice thus wrote his justification for federal authority over emancipation in this context. By May 1865, when he issued his "Open Letter to the People of Kentucky," the fate of slavery was all but clear, and few demanded its restoration. But questions about the authority to legally end slavery, and, more importantly, to shape the lives of freed people, ensured discord between proponents of state sovereignty in these areas and the advocates of federal union. To men with strong Unionist feeling like Prentice, the Thirteenth Amendment represented a means to finally resolve the constitutional crisis surrounding slavery and enjoy the fruits of free labor. Prentice wanted to see former slave states like Tennessee, Kentucky, and Missouri "united as free commonwealths" with Ohio, Indiana, and Illinois for their mutual prosperity.[79] By dividing the region and demeaning labor, slavery had blighted Kentucky. With those antagonisms removed by the power of the federal Union, Kentucky would reap new wealth and exhibit greatness in the way Henry Clay had predicted.

But even avid Unionists like Prentice contended that national powers with respect to slavery extended no further than to declare and enforce emancipation. Beyond that clear directive, delineating freed people's enjoyment of rights, freedoms, and duties still resided within the express powers of the state. Here Prentice clearly broke from Chase and the Republican Party, as did the vast majority of white Kentuckians, in thinking about the nature of union. Prentice had undergone a revolution in thinking about the power and authority of the federal government to end slavery in the state, yet he still promoted the state as arbiter of citizenship rights, including the right to suffrage. He vehemently rejected the "idea of social and political equality between negroes and white men" as "not less absurd than odious."[80] For Prentice, the benefits of emancipation mainly flowed to white Kentuckians, who could now fully enjoy the commerce, prosperity, and civilization attaching to free labor and national harmony.

Secession

In Louisville, black Americans pressed against the rising sectional tide in Kentucky. Beginning in the mid-1840s, the city's African Americans staged a dramatic fight against the newly created sectional churches among white Methodists and Baptists by refusing fellowship or affiliation with them. Having already established precedents for their spiritual independence, black congregations in Kentucky's northernmost city were not about to give these up. But in rejecting white churchmen's bids for greater control over their spiritual affairs, black Louisvillians did more than protect the status quo. Departing from patterns established elsewhere in the South, African Americans shunned the mission churches in Louisville and orchestrated their own "secession" from white ecclesiastical structures. In league with white emancipationists in the city, their congregations were emboldened to cast off the last vestiges of spiritual authority maintained by white churches, and they declared their intentions to "enter the conflict for church freedom from the slaveholding power."[81] As a consequence, the white-led slave missions in Kentucky, and especially in Louisville, never got off the ground, and rank-and-file black church members severed their connections with white denominational structures in the months and years following the formation of the southern Baptist and Methodist churches in 1845.

In rejecting white oversight, Louisville's black Protestants undercut white churchmen's argument for the sacred basis of slavery. Faced with a defiant black population, Kentucky's church leaders could not fulfill their divine charge, which they understood to be the salvation of people of color through the loving ministrations of benevolent white Christians and the maintenance of gospel order through slavery. In the longer run, church leaders failed to make the critical Upper South state a religious buffer zone between abolition-ism and slavery by building up the missions.[82]

Although Donald Mathews suggests that the missions had more ideologi-cal import than numerical significance, recent studies have argued for their greater success in drawing slaves and free blacks into the churches. Janet Cornelius finds that "slave missions were important symbolically in the late 1850s, but their expansion was also a reality." Charles Irons's study of the Virginia missions reinforces Cornelius's view. Through a complicated give-and-take between white and black evangelicals, Virginia's African Americans joined the mission churches in striking numbers in the antebellum period, but they also won significant concessions from white church leaders. Above all other kinds of missions, black converts in Virginia sought out semiau-tonomous churches, where white supervision did not prohibit black mem-bers from prescribing the manner of worship and, in some cases, hearing black preachers. Nevertheless, in Irons's argument, the outward success of the missions in Virginia served white evangelicals' broader purpose, which was to demonstrate "that God intended to use slavery for good." By joining the mission churches, Virginia's African Americans "inadvertently abetted the development of proslavery evangelicalism." Irons's argument thus re-inforces Eugene Genovese's earlier political assessment of proselytization to the slaves in *Roll, Jordan, Roll*. "Religious instruction," in his view, "formed part of the swelling demand to make slavery safer for the masters by making it more tolerable for the slaves—a demand that implicitly deepened the South's commitment to slavery as a permanent social order."[83]

At the least, it would seem that enough black southerners elected to nur-ture their religious communities and faith within the evolving slave missions in Virginia and the Deep South to give the movement political credence. But in Louisville, considerable unrest surrounded the mission cause, and it proved a failure there. Between approximately 1844 and 1848, persuaded as they were of the essential responsibility of the new southern churches to provide for the religious instruction of slaves and free blacks, white evan-gelicals in Louisville attempted to increase or reassert their supervision of the separate black churches in the city. Some of these efforts at reclaiming authority were crude and violent, other tactics more subtle, but at all events, the city's free and enslaved blacks bluntly refused to accept white oversight of their religious affairs and struck back with whatever tools or resources they had, including the strategic use of white emancipationists in the city. One of the by-products of denominational schism in Louisville, indeed, was the almost wholesale loss of spiritual control over black worshippers in the southern churches in the city. Louisville's black Methodists and Baptists were well aware of the ideological and spiritual significance of the slave missions to proslavery Christianity, and they sought to minimize their influence in the Upper South city at every turn.

Methodist statistics reveal a striking black exodus from white ecclesiastical control between 1845 and 1850. In these five years, the number of black members of the white-controlled "colored charge[s]" declined a precipitous 60 percent (from 860 to 336), while numbers of white Methodists in Louisville held steady, increasing a slight 4 percent (from 1,322 to 1,386). Even by 1860, the number of African Americans considered members of the mission churches stood at just 755, only slightly higher than the 625 black members reported in 1840. And given white Methodists' complaints about blacks' absence from the churches and their "frequent disorders" in the 1850s, it appears likely that the M.E. Church, South, overstated Louisville's black membership statistics in the decade following the church schism. Especially for the 1840s, when the African American population increased by some 70 percent, the rapid falling away of black members in Louisville after the 1845 schisms stands out as a statistical anomaly for Methodist churches in the South.[84]

The black exodus from white spiritual control is most evident in the "stirring scenes" following the Fourth Street Colored Methodist Church's decision to "sever [its] connection from the white Southern Methodist Church." From the fall of 1844, "after the division of the Methodist Episcopal Church . . . a large number of colored members were anxious to leave the Southern branch," reported William Gibson, a former congregant at the Fourth Street Church, which in 1845 consisted of 410 black members, making it the largest black Methodist church in Louisville at the time. Free African Americans deemed membership in the proslavery M.E. Church, South, to be repugnant, and they immediately began to plan their exit from its ecclesiastical control. In early 1845, the black membership at Fourth Street acquired church property at a Chancery Court sale and ensured that they had clear title with a judge's certification. As a consequence, the trustees of the church would be black, not white, as had formerly been the case.[85]

The conspicuous brick churches so sought after by black congregations in the 1840s were not guarantees of security or freedom from interference, particularly with the new zeal for slave missions among Kentucky's white evangelicals so in evidence in Louisville after 1844. Quick to recognize the import of the church schisms among whites, as well as the excited rhetoric about the missions accompanying formation of the southern churches in 1845, black leaders moved to protect their churches' separate standings and distance themselves from the self-appointed apostles to the slaves. With their unique property deed won in the city's Chancery Court in 1845, the Fourth Street Colored Methodist Church was well poised to achieve both of these ends, and the congregation quietly initiated contact with the African Methodist Episcopal Church. By the time of the AME Church Conference meeting at Madison, Indiana, in 1848, the Fourth Street Church had prepared resolutions declaring its independence from the M.E. Church, South, and had elected delegates to attend the Madison conference. Received into "full connection" by Bishop Paul Quinn, the Fourth Street Colored Methodist Church was wary of the anticipated reaction by Louisville's white Methodists. As Gibson later wrote, "This bold secession, by a Negro church, in the heart of slavery, in the very city where the division of the North and South Church took place, and only a square from the locality of that memorable event of 1845, which shook the Christian denominations of this country from center to circumference, was a striking coincident." "The news created a sensation in Methodist circles," Gibson recalled, and the independent black congregation prepared for trouble.[86]

Indeed, the city's "white masters," as Gibson called them, immediately charged the congregation's black elder, Rev. James Harper, with "rebellion." Harper refused to stand trial, asserting that he was no longer a member of the M.E. Church, South's connection. After the city's white Methodist officials tried Harper (in absentia) and expelled him, they moved to take control of the black congregation's church property. Gibson and other leaders of the black church had anticipated this move and made sure that an "eminent judge was employed to be present and witness the proceedings" when white officials attempted to persuade rank-and-file members of the Fourth Street Colored Church to remain with the M.E. Church, South.[87]

When white officers appeared at the black congregation's services the Sunday following Reverend Harper's exclusion, Harper and the unnamed judge were prepared to defend the church's independence. Reading the property deed aloud to the southern church officials, the judge promised to "enter suit against them for disturbing religious worship, for they were not colored Methodists." Finding declarations of black spiritual and ecclesiastical autonomy obnoxious, white Methodist officials moved to take physical control of the pulpit. Gibson, who was present, described this "graphic" moment:

> The white presiding elder ascended the pulpit; also the colored elder. One seized the Bible and the other the hymn-book.

The colored brother read "Jesus, Great Shepherd of the Sheep, to Thee for help we fly," etc., which was sung with great power by the vast congregation. He prayed such a prayer as only he could pray, with responses from all the members over the house. At the close, the white elder announced his text: "Servants, be obedient to your masters." The argument was unheeded, for they had concluded to come out of Egypt, though Pharaoh and his host pursued them.

Eventually, Louisville's courts would decide in favor of the black congregation, and its members only then felt confident to celebrate their independence. When Bishop Quinn arrived in Louisville to admit the new AME church, "a great jubilee" accompanied the formal reception. "For some time this event was a matter of rejoicing among the colored people," Gibson wrote. In the aftermath of the M.E. Church, South's organization, black members of the new Louisville Conference (carved out of the former Kentucky Conference) had reconsidered their church affiliation and successfully orchestrated their very own "secession."[88]

Not all black Methodist congregations were as well situated as the politically connected Fourth Street Colored Methodist Church, renamed Asbury Chapel after its admission to the AME connection. But even if a black Methodist congregation could not secure its own property by legal title, as William Gibson's Asbury Chapel had, members took whatever actions they could to make a mockery of the slave missions in Louisville. As a consequence, after 1845 white officials of the Louisville Conference of the M.E. Church, South, had considerable difficulty organizing and overseeing the district's black "charges," and by 1860 they declared their efforts a failure.

Conference minutes in the first years following the denominational schism provide evidence that officials tried to refashion the relationships between white and black Methodist congregations. In 1845, the Methodist conference's minutes list black congregations under the auspices of white churches. Although contemporary city directories and later church histories indicate that each black Methodist congregation had a distinctive name (usually for the street or location of its church edifice), the Louisville Conference's minutes do not list these particular names, but instead fold black memberships into their white supervisory churches. During two years (1846 and 1848), white officials in the Louisville Conference created a special category for the "Colored Mission," or the "Colored City Mission," and simply combined figures for separate black Methodist churches into a single line item in their records.[89] Thus immediately after 1845, the M.E. Church, South's official records sought to convey two ideas: first, that they would still oversee and control the several separate black Methodist congregations, and second, that black members required the ministrations of white missionaries, as if Louisville's African Americans remained essentially unchurched. On both of these counts, the southern church's official records made false representations. William Gibson's Fourth Street Church obviously did not fit into the category of a "mission," even though for several years, until 1848, it was considered such.

Other congregations also rejected the label of "mission" and their association with the proslavery M.E. Church, South. For example, black members of the Brook Street Church had worshipped on their own since 1832, when they began to meet in a "small frame structure over a pond" known distinctively as Old Frog Pond Church. Sometime in the early 1840s, the black congregation moved into a new building on Jackson Street and, beginning in 1848, was listed in Louisville's city directories as the Jackson Street Church. It would be easy to miss the significance of this church since church officials counted Jackson Street's membership as part of the white-led Brook Street Church each year until 1859, when the Jackson Street congregation first appeared as a separate entity in minutes for the M.E. Church, South.[90] Importantly, though, black members of the Jackson Street Church never accepted the legitimacy of the new southern Methodist denomination, nor their affiliation with it, and they have handed down a different understanding of their ecclesiastical history to succeeding generations in the church. A "historical account" produced in 1992 (on the 160th anniversary of the church's organization) proudly asserts that Jackson Street Church never joined the M.E. Church, South, but rather "remained in the Mother church as the only Methodist Episcopal Church in Louisville" until 1865.[91] The notable factual disparity between the Louisville Conference's official representations to the M.E. Church, South, and the historical knowledge and experience handed down by members of the Jackson Street Church suggests that white Methodists did not succeed in exercising spiritual or ecclesiastical authority over their black "charges" after 1845.

White Methodists had also failed in a bid to gain spiritual control over the oldest separate black Methodist congregation in Louisville just weeks before southerners gathered in the city to establish their separate church in 1845. A decade earlier, free African American members of the Center Street Church (as it was later known) had leased property in their own names and constructed a new frame church building. White Methodists tolerated this arrangement for a decade and even allowed their slaves to attend what became known as a "free church" because of Center Street's property arrangement and leadership by free blacks. But in 1845, according to an 1897 community history of Louisville's African Americans, "the slaveholders became somewhat alarmed and thought it unwise for their slaves to attend a church of this description."[92]

Sensing restlessness within their black Methodist "charge" as the meeting to form the M.E. Church, South, drew near, the city's white church officials purchased ground and quickly threw up a new one-story frame church with a "natural earth" floor and "ordinarily built" pews. The white trustees of the property then bade the enslaved as well as free members of Center Street Church to its rough new quarters. The property under lease by the black congregation apparently lapsed back to its wealthy free black owner, Washington Spradling, who "sever[ed] his membership with Centre-street." Rank-and-file members appear to have followed this example, for between 1845 and 1850, black membership at the crudely built church fell off considerably.[93] Once again, white Methodists' efforts to assert spiritual control over black members backfired.

Little if Any Progress

As a consequence of black Methodists' overt disaffection, the Louisville Conference of Methodists ultimately provided few resources—financial or otherwise—after 1850 to evangelize in Louisville's black community at large or even to assist those free blacks who might consider a missionary undertaking in Liberia. In fact, by 1858 the Louisville Conference admitted its spiritual failures among the "people of color" living within their charges, and they formed a Committee on Missions to investigate. "It is the opinion of the Committee that but little if any progress has been made of late years, in bringing the colored people among us under the influence of Christianity—we fear, indeed, that there has been a retrograde movement," several ministers warned. By this neglect, the ministers lamented, they had failed to "meet the high responsibility we assumed in separating from the M.E. Church in 1844." The Louisville Conference at once "resolved that the preachers . . . make arrangements . . . for the employment of Missionaries to the people of color." But even with this official instruction, the conference's ministers exerted scant effort to provide special ministration to the African Americans within the Louisville Conference. A year later, the ministers revealed their limited knowledge of and interest in blacks' spiritual doings by complaining that "they have no means at hand to report the col'd population within our bounds" and by delegating their responsibilities to a special agent, Richard Deering, who would "organize missions to the colored people."[94]

After a year of traveling within the Louisville Conference's boundaries, Deering offered a despairing report of black Methodism in 1860. "For many years the tendency of the Colored people in Kentucky has been to indepency," he wrote, "and the employment of preachers of their own color, to serve them." To white Methodists, such independence appeared "disordered," and "a growing distrust and uneasiness of the public mind in refference to this class of people" had become manifest. He especially singled out Louisville for its "frequent disorders at the black people's meetings." And despite "preaching a great many sermons, and witnessing a good many conversions," Deering "labour[ed] nearly all the time under a depressing feeling, that I had been intrusted with a most important work, and had made a failure." By 1860, Methodist conferences elsewhere in the South would be able to point to "thriving" black congregations under their auspices, and they documented with pride the growing accessions to the mission churches in both urban settings and rural enclaves. With just two black "charges" remaining under their care and overwhelming evidence of these two congregations' disapprobation of the M.E. Church, South, Louisville's white Methodists could make no such claims, much to their disappointment.[95]

In the case of both Baptists and Methodists, the missionary cause so closely associated with separate southern churches found few takers among African Americans in Louisville. Leading black congregations in the city instead made dramatic and overt breaks with the newly formed southern churches in the mid-1840s in order to either preserve or enhance their freedom from white evangelicals' supervision. Their actions gave lie to a fundamental assumption of southern evangelicals' missions to the slaves—namely, that both free and enslaved black people required the benevolence and philanthropy of white people for their moral elevation in this life, and their salvation in the next. If this was the purpose of slavery according to white evangelicals, then black Louisvillians' rejection of the missions negated the proslavery gospel's central tenet.

Independent black churches also stood as the most obvious symbols of the advancements and aspirations of people of color—both free and enslaved—and so when Baptists and Methodists in Kentucky allied with the southern churches and dedicated themselves to the slave missions, autonomous African American churches seemed starkly incongruous within the emerging proslavery gospel. Subsuming Louisville's black churches within the southern Baptist and Methodist denominations had therefore been a foremost objective of white evangelicals in the city, but their efforts to reinstate old arrangements or impose new forms of oversight met with powerful resistance from the state's most troubling and anomalous demographic group, urban free blacks. As a consequence, the slave missions proved a failure in the most populous region of the state and, more alarmingly, along the porous border with the free states of Ohio, Indiana, and Illinois. In other regions of the South, by contrast, the slave missions validated the proslavery gospel and affirmed the role of southern churches in maintaining social order.[96]

Rejecting any and all fellowship with the newly created "southern" denominations of the Baptist and Methodist churches, black Christians in Louisville asserted their desire to remain connected to associations in the North. Tethering their political identity to faith, black Unionist sentiment worked against church-based sectionalism among white Kentuckians. In consequence, the Confederate nation-building enterprise had fewer ideological sources of allegiance to call upon in Kentucky. In Kentucky's most populous city, proslavery faith was a nonstarter. Lincoln and his cabinet had astutely, if aggressively, pursued military and constitutional emancipation in Kentucky while maintaining the state's allegiances. Yet black Louisvillians had also shaped allegiances by diminishing Kentuckians' sense of common cause with proslavery evangelicals advancing the Confederacy's nation-building project. The view that American slavery held a special world destiny to fulfill could not realistically claim adherents in Kentucky in 1861. Arguably, the most consequential group of "secessionists" in Louisville were black Christians who broke from southern proslavery churches and maintained their loyalties to the national denominations. Their work, combined with Unionists' forceful political and military pressure in the state, spelled slavery's end in Kentucky.

CHAPTER NINE

War

As Confederate forces drew close to the Ohio River in 1862, fear, disorder, and violence gripped the civilian populations of Louisville and Cincinnati. The Union army commander charged with defending Louisville, General William "Bull" Nelson, made extraordinary contingency plans should the city fall to the rebels: If compelled to retreat, Nelson's troops would ignite Louisville in flames before transporting their artillery into Indiana. Once across the Ohio River, Union soldiers would bombard the city, leaving nothing of worth to incoming Confederate forces. Had Louisvillians known of this endgame strategy, they might have felt more relief than alarm at Nelson's untimely murder at the Galt Hotel as the city prepared for war in September. By an uncanny coincidence, Nelson's murderer bore the name of Jefferson Davis, provoking panic among residents about an elaborate conspiracy.[1] Confederate forces by this time were within fifty miles of the Ohio River, and authorities in both Louisville and Cincinnati imposed martial law and provoked "alarm and terror" among local African Americans, who endured mass arrests and forcible impressment to construct their cities' fortifications.[2]

The deepening military crisis produced another stunning turn of events: the collapse of slavery throughout Kentucky. Although Lincoln's Preliminary Emancipation Proclamation—issued at the height of the Confederate siege in Kentucky—indicated the border state's exclusion from its provisions, slaves fled to Union camps and troops in their own bid for freedom without presidential sanction. At the same moment, political dissenters in Cincinnati and Louisville grew vociferous in their critique of the war and its prosecution by Republicans. After 1862, Kentuckians with deep attachments to Whiggery fell in with the Democratic Party, and a vociferous band of antiwar partisans hailing from Cincinnati "turned upon the president like a mad dog," throwing their support to Clement Vallandigham, the political foe of Lincoln.[3] In 1863 and 1864, Cincinnatians and Louisvillians grappled with emancipation's reality on the ground, and Kentucky fell into bitter guerrilla warfare as former slaves enlisted in Union forces in the Bluegrass.

In response to these confusing events, diverse Cincinnatians and Louisvillians—Unionists, soldiers, and relief workers—began to imagine and practice new forms of allegiance to the Union. Their creative efforts to advance the Union cause through relief, service, and advocacy helped to defend Kentucky and Ohio from Confederate invasion, and their mobilization ensured Kentucky's loyalty to the federal government. "Kentucky has been the saddest and yet most hope-inspiring episode in this fratricidal war," observed John S. Newberry, a relief agent working in Louisville through the course of the war.[4]

Western Central Office

During the war, Louisville presented a study in contradictions. Visitors to the city gleaned very different impressions of loyalty. When Andrew Phillips arrived in Louisville late in 1862 to tend to his ill son, a Union soldier apparently suffering from both pneumonia and dysentery, the family with whom he boarded drew a sharp map of the state's wartime fault lines: "Since the emancipation proclamation," they explained, "the people of Kentucky are all secesh except at Louisville & along the river at Covington."[5] Nearly three years later, during a tour through the immediate postwar South, Ohio journalist Whitelaw Reid found just the opposite, discovering "more loyalty in Nashville than in Louisville, and about as much in Charleston as in either" Upper South city. Dining among "the last collection of men from the midst of a Rebel community" in Louisville, Reid realized that the African American men serving his party remained enslaved and noted their historical significance: "They were the last any of us were ever to see on American soil."[6]

These apparently shifting loyalties in Civil War–era Louisville, and Kentucky more generally, have perplexed and fascinated historians ever since.[7] In the most recent scholarship, historians argue that wartime emancipation and ex-slaves' pursuit of an equal political voice in postwar years account for white Kentuckians' "ex post facto" Confederate sympathies and the racial violence that accompanied this embrace of Lost Cause mythology. But even these latest histories continue to emphasize complexity and geographical variation. As Anne Marshall writes, "there was no *one* memory of the war in Kentucky but rather divergent memories belonging to many Kentuckians, which competed with one another over time for cultural primacy."[8] To understand Kentucky's "belated Confederates," Aaron Astor focuses on the violent unraveling of slavery in the Bluegrass section of the state.[9]

It is possible to trace the practical workings of union amid the pressures and contingencies of the war in the Ohio River valley's urban enclaves. Union sentiment among Louisvillians and Cincinnatians did not entail devotion to the Republican Party, although a vocal minority in both cities passionately endorsed "Unconditional Union," emancipation, and Lincoln's reelection bid in 1864. Nor did loyal citizens always invoke self-government and liberty as the foundation of political union. Civilians in the Ohio River valley's largest cities instead generated distinctive ideas of "union" to respond to the direct crises posed by the Civil War's astounding violence. Especially through their relief work, Louisvillians and Cincinnatians put into practice unique forms of loyalty on behalf of Union soldiers.

As the "Western Central Office" for the U.S. Sanitary Commission, Louisville collected financial donations and civilian-made goods intended for soldiers' relief from all points north and distributed them to western armies. With its depot serving as the heart of a "systematic and cooperative beneficence," the city permitted loyal citizens well beyond Kentucky to aid Union soldiers.[10] Lodging wounded and discharged soldiers coming from western battlefields, Louisville also maintained the largest "Hospital Directory" in the country, centralizing information about casualties throughout the vast western theater. By the end of the war, civilian clerks in Louisville had gathered exclusive information about the fate of nearly eight hundred thousand soldiers and responded with care and alacrity to families' queries from all over the Mississippi Valley.[11] Kentucky's northernmost city therefore became the vital link reconnecting northern families and sons, fathers, and spouses in Union armies.

With the help of the U.S. Sanitary Commission's western secretary, Dr. John S. Newberry, Louisville's leading political Unionists formally established a local branch of the civilian relief work agency in October 1861, just as Confederate troops occupied Bowling Green and smaller-scale warfare began to grip the southern and central parts of the state.[12] The branch's board included George Prentice and Joseph Holt, Lincoln's future appointee to the position of judge advocate general for the Union army.[13] Sick Union soldiers had "accumulated very rapidly in our city," John H. Heywood later reported, prompting the need for a well-organized agency to care for them. From the Green River region of Kentucky, upward of one hundred men began to arrive "every evening," in immediate need of attention, and messengers knocked at commission members' homes at all hours of the night seeking medical care and bedding in the fall of 1861.[14] These numbers quickly grew to the thousands as fierce fighting engaged great armies at Fort Donelson and Perryville, close to the Ohio River city. Through the course of the war, soldiers needing hospital care or trying to get home after discharge came to Louisville from small and large battles taking place all across the western theater, including Mill Springs, Shiloh, Corinth, Stones River, and Vicksburg. By the fall of 1863, Louisville's local branch of the Sanitary Commission maintained twenty-two hospitals in the city for the wounded or sick and, on any given night, could lodge as many as one thousand soldiers in transit to northern states. In just eight months' time, between January and August 1863, Louisville's Soldiers' Home had housed 17,000 soldiers, making it the "most extensive and complete establishment of the kind which exists in the country."[15] By November 1865, the city's "homes" had fed and housed a total of 268,114 Union troops through three years of intense relief service.[16] In addition to providing aid within the city, agents of the Louisville commission traveled to battlefields to gather the sick and distribute medicine, clothing, food, and varied supplies—what commissioners collectively labeled "stores."

Through 1861 and part of 1862, local branches of the U.S. Sanitary Commission in the Mississippi Valley worked somewhat haphazardly at getting their donated "stores" to soldiers in need, hiring their own steamboats and transportation and seeking to direct items to specific regiments and companies. Following the battle at Perryville, though, John Newberry concluded that he had to move his western Sanitary Commission headquarters from Cleveland to Louisville in order to systematize relief. He chose the Kentucky city because of its connection "to the home field at the North, and to the theater of important military operations at the South." As Newberry later reflected, "Every subsequent day's experience confirmed the wisdom of this choice of location for the Western Central Office," as the headquarters in Louisville came to be called. The depot at Louisville received stores from nearly all of the northern states, including Ohio, Indiana, Michigan, Wisconsin, Illinois, New York, Pennsylvania, Connecticut, and Massachusetts, and it served as a record-keeping center for warehouses at Cincinnati, Cairo, and Memphis. The value of medical and hospital supplies, clothing, and food passing through these major depots, including Louisville, amounted to more than $5 million.[17]

Louisville's relief agents worked most closely with Cincinnati's branch of the U.S. Sanitary Commission, in part because of proximity, but also because Ohio's soldiers' aid societies donated more in the way of money and supplies than those in any other western state. After federal troops met with hard fighting at Fort Donelson, on the Cumberland River, Cincinnatians took the lead in bringing relief to soldiers in the field in February 1862.[18] Sanitary Commission members there swiftly gathered medical supplies and hired surgeons and nurses. As they rushed to board a chartered steamboat, concerned citizens "accosted [them] in the streets," pressing cash into their hands. This spontaneous "blaze of enthusiasm" raised three thousand dollars for the expedition.[19] Stopping in Louisville, they invited Newberry and his Kentucky associates to accompany them to the war's front, and relief agents from Indianapolis and Columbus also boarded the crowded steamer headed toward Fort Donelson. Newberry deemed this joint venture "gratifying proof of the vigor and value of our organization, now spread over all the loyal States," and he appreciated seeing the men "harmonized by their humane and patriotic mission."[20] Similarly satisfied by this model of cooperation, Cincinnatians soon after called on "the people," and especially the women, of Ohio, Indiana, and Kentucky to join together to provide for the "immediate relief of our sick and wounded soldiers."[21] They would have another opportunity for cooperation at the battle of Perryville, some eighty-five miles from Louisville.

By the fall of 1862, Newberry had relocated the headquarters for his western field operations to Kentucky, just in time to witness the Confederacy's boldest advance in the western theater as E. Kirby Smith took control of Lexington and Frankfort and Braxton Bragg's troops occupied Bardstown, within a stone's throw of Louisville. Federal forces under Don Carlos Buell distracted Bragg's troops from their goal of taking the Union's logistical center at Louisville and compelled them to move southward. But Confederates quickly turned on Federals "with the desperation of Demons," as one soldier from Ohio characterized the attack at Perryville. Although the battle proved something of a draw, the historian Earl J. Hess writes that Union forces were "crushed," "worn down," and "mangled" in the engagement, producing "one of the more vicious battles of the war." Total casualties from both sides amounted to nearly 8,000 out of 72,000 troops in the field.[22] Overwhelmed and shocked at these losses, Louisville's corps of relief agents labored alongside a Cincinnati delegation in trying to lessen the "great suffering" at Perryville by distributing supplies from Illinois, Ohio, and Kentucky and removing the wounded and ill to hospitals at Louisville.[23]

With the soldiers from the battle at Perryville recovering in Louisville, and hard warfare in Tennessee and Mississippi, the Western Central Office of the U.S. Sanitary Commission undertook new measures to address the needs of Union armies and the families connected to them. Along with the main Washington office, Louisville began to keep a "Hospital Directory," which gathered vital information about the fates of military hospital patients for families. Studying reports from forty-three hospitals in ten different states (five southern and five northern), clerks amassed information about some 76,000 soldiers, exceeding even the Washington Office's figures by February 1863. "We are sometimes called upon to answer a hundred or more inquiries in a day, coming from residents of all parts of the West," Newberry reported, with growing concern about the scale of the work.[24] Six months later, Louisville's Directory contained 186,433 names, with 102 hospitals sending frequent reports to the Sanitary Commission's western headquarters. With a newly hired "corps of clerical assistants," the Louisville office responded to 4,016 inquiries about soldiers, still leaving an apparent backlog of some 2,000 letters.[25] In 1864, Newberry characterized the work of the Hospital Directory as "immense," and by the war's end, Louisville's clerks had collected vital data on 799,317 soldiers, had fielded close to 19,000 personal inquiries, and had written over 12,000 letters to families in twenty-nine different states and six foreign countries.[26]

As the Hospital Director's superintendent in Louisville later wrote, the sheer weight of these statistics masked the "labor, patience, and feeling" that attended every inquiry and case. Although charged with maintaining an inordinately complex system of books, "unbound sheets," "bound volumes," "regimental packs," and portfolios, clerks recognized the "peculiar and painful" nature of their labors. "Each name is the name of a man dear to a circle of kindred and friends; each inquiry bears the interest, anxiety, and earnestness of some relative." Louisville's superintendent explained the relationship forged by his office: "Between the parties stood the Hospital Directory, with its records and helpful agents."[27] This remarkable work bound Louisvillians in sympathetic relationships with families throughout the North and beyond.

Louisville's Western Central Office and its local branches were at pains to describe these unique bonds between relief agents, soldiers, and families through imperfect language. Not surprisingly, Hospital Directory clerks used more organizational terminology. From "scattered" stories, the Western Central Office had established with their record keeping a "wide relationship," a "connecting link," and a "central point" between the Kentucky city and "all sections of our own country."[28] But the branch offices in Cincinnati and Louisville recognized a more satisfying and locally appropriate metaphor for their labors: their relief work sustained "a river of life" running between soldiers and families, carried along on "the rills of kindness flowing from generous hearts in far away Maine, [and] blended with kindred rills flowing from loyal hearts in Wisconsin and Kentucky and its sister States."[29] From Cincinnati, Charles Boynton explained that the Sanitary Commission "has laid down . . . the costly aqueduct by which the waters of relief, gathered from every hillside in the loyal States, and accumulated in the reservoirs of the Branches, are at length distributed in the hospitals and in the camps and battlefields of the army."[30] Here was a form of union naturalized through human bonds and waterways (even those man-made). Imagining relationships flowing via tearful expressions of sympathy and movements of rivers, these metaphors immersed Kentucky, Ohio, and the rest of the loyal states in a kind of fluid union.

Home Influence

Sanitary Commission agents in Louisville and Cincinnati worked incessantly at forging bonds between civilians and soldiers, home and war fronts, and women's relief aid and men's logistical administration. They built these relationships through the collection and distribution of soldiers' stores at branch offices as well as through "sanitary fairs" held throughout the North after 1863.[31] In Cincinnati and Louisville, agents of the Sanitary Commission used the press to reinforce these bonds. In addition to the commission's regular reports from branch offices and myriad circulars, notices, and pamphlets, between 1863 and 1865 the Western Central Office published a small magazine out of Louisville, entitled the *Sanitary Reporter*, which was primarily intended for women. Within about five months, the *Reporter* circulated to six thousand subscribers, and eventually reached seventy-five hundred by 1864.[32] With ambitious hopes at the outset, Newberry and his associates "aimed to make it as catholic and national as possible."[33] Reflecting later on this work, Newberry stressed the importance of the publication for generating "harmony and cordiality" between a female-dominated "home field" of charity and the commission's male relief agents on the battlefield.[34] Newberry's Western Central Office hoped to direct "the loving hand of the people extended to the soldier of the nation," as the *Sanitary Reporter* explained its work.[35]

To demonstrate the necessary union between civilian and war fronts, the Ohio River valley's commission agents frequently invoked the horror of a soldier detached from his home. The Reverend F. H. Bushnell, a hospital visitor employed by the Louisville Branch of the U.S. Sanitary Commission to provide succor to soldiers, reported a distressing incident in the *Sanitary Reporter*. While at a hospital in Jeffersonville, Indiana, a young soldier "was brought in speechless, and no one could tell where the home was which he had thus vainly struggled to reach." Both soldiers and civilians suffered in this crisis: on the one hand, Bushnell wondered "who would mourn" for the unidentified, dying soldier, and on the other, he raised the specter of a family eternally anxious about "where his poor body was lying."[36] From Cincinnati, the Reverend Charles Boynton understood the central purpose of the Sanitary Commission was to "bind the soldier back to his distant home" through a "web of living sympathy." But his concerns were not so much psychic and religious as political: in war, among soldiers whose "memories of home grow dim" and where "the power of home influence . . . [is] diminished," "isolation begets estrangement, and what was intended only as the country's defense, becomes a terror and a scourge." Thus, the Sanitary Commission arose "to prevent the isolation of the soldier from home" and the growth of large standing armies at odds with "a free people."[37] Although women's relief aid to soldiers appears to have predated the creation of the U.S. Sanitary Commission, male agents nevertheless urgently appealed to women's "service" to soldiers and country, as though their voluntary labors might cease at any moment.[38] This suggests that the commission's ongoing appeals had less to do with women's actual aid and support, which remained forthcoming, than with a sense of rupture and crisis caused by the war's violence.

In consequence, men preparing narrative reports and filling out the columns of the *Sanitary Reporter* sought to lessen the great geographical and psychological distance between the home and war fronts and between civilians and soldiers by presenting pictures of soldiers physically touched by relief workers' hands and objects and garments prepared by women's hands. For example, John Newberry's report describing relief work at Fort Donelson offered unusual detail about the washing and dressing of wounded soldiers' bodies: "Each was placed in a clean and comfortable bed; their soiled and bloody clothing removed; they were washed with warm water throughout, including their feet; new and clean underclothing, with socks, and when needed, slippers were furnished to all. . . . In short, in all things they were nursed and served as though they had been our brothers and sons."[39] Here the male relief agents performed a kind of vicarious service that women might normally have provided at home, but the amount of space Newberry devoted to the scene suggests a desire to assure civilians, and particularly women, that proper care, indeed a kind of home care, had been provided. Attempting to describe relief activity at a field hospital, the Cincinnati Branch of the Sanitary Commission addressed women more directly: "You have been thinking, my sisters, where is *our* work, in all these scenes?" The answer was obvious: "Your work is every where." The author then offered a picture of a soldier enwrapped in the objects "*your* fingers wrought, *your* heart conceived." As examples, "that snowy roll of linen; that little pillow beneath the sufferer's head; that soft fold across the gashed breast" all provided relief.[40] If not physically present at hospitals or fields to touch, wash, dress, and nurse soldiers, women nevertheless intimately cared for soldiers through the workings of the Sanitary Commission.

The literature produced by the Sanitary Commission in Cincinnati and Louisville forged another kind of bond when it emphasized that civilians offered religious salvation through their relief aid. In one metaphor, the Sanitary Commission represented "the hand of 'the People,' filled with bread and wine," and "reached out in such manner as not to be refused" by soldiers.[41] Poetry appearing in Louisville's *Sanitary Reporter* embraced the view that succor to suffering Union soldiers did more than physically heal. The stanzas for a poem dedicated to the Sanitary Commissions' work alternated between these first lines: "How They went forth to die!" and "How Ye went forth to save!"[42] With greater subtlety, a Louisvillian depicted women's aid as redemptive in an original poem submitted to the *Sanitary Reporter*. Even something so mundane as a pair of knitted "blue woolen socks" contained "dreams and prayers / Wove in like a mystic, golden thread—/ Dreams that may stir a soldier's heart / And prayers to bless a dying head."[43] In a similar vein, the Louisville magazine offered poetic instruction to hospital relief workers among the "sick and dying." "Go speak to him words of comfort, and teach him the way to die," one poem counseled. Remind soldiers that their service ensures salvation: "Tell him to call it not grievous, but joyous to fall by the sword."[44] The literature of the Sanitary Commission therefore reversed a conventional portrayal of military service. Here, rather than Union soldiers offering their lives to a nation to save civilians from harm or oppression, civilians instead metaphysically saved soldiers suffering the trauma of war. In sum, Louisville's and Cincinnati's Union relief workers presented powerful relationships between civilians and soldiers through physical or vicarious touch and by way of religious counsel and even sacred transcendence.

Good Genius of the War

The work of the Sanitary Commission in the Ohio River valley, and in Kentucky in particular, gave unusual force to meanings of union while avoiding the more divisive politics of loyalty and patriotism. They did this by arguing that the experience of war exalted its participants, whether soldier or civilian. War and "human civilization" were not antithetical, but rather fused together to improve humankind during the American Civil War. The proposition that war had ultimately "drawn out the good" among those loyal to the Union enjoyed strong, even enthusiastic support in Louisville and Cincinnati by 1865.[45]

The war's first years had not encouraged this view. At Fort Donelson, John Newberry found a battlefield covered with "unburied dead, strewn with arms, clothing, and accouterments," the aftermath of a "death storm." On hospital boats he met men "smeared with filth and blood" still four days after the battle. This suffering hardly appeared ennobling. Fort Donelson nevertheless presented scenes that Newberry and the other relief workers had already "pictured in our minds," and so it did not shock as much as reinforce the urgent need for their services.[46] The battle of Perryville in October 1862 was altogether another matter. Reports coming from Louisville's agents described "peculiarly distressing" anguish by wounded men abandoned on the battlefield and questioned whether "war can be so softened down and Christianized as to be otherwise than unutterably hideous in all its aspects." That "refined humanity" could "mitigate in great measure some of the darkest horrors of war" did not appear evident in the war's increasing violence. Louisvillians at the scene drew even harsher conclusions from soldiers' exposure and neglect after battle: these unfortunate men had in truth been "*tortured* to death." According to these aid workers, the greatest evils in war followed from leaving wounded men unattended, so they die "when the simplest succor might restore them to life and health."[47]

But by 1864, and even more with the war's end, such overt criticism largely disappeared from commission writings. "Human Civilization" now appeared vindicated through war. "If the blood of the boldest and bravest flowed in battle, so did the love of the good and noble stanch their wounds," Charles Boynton enthused from Cincinnati. He insisted that "it was reserved for America to prove that in the darkest calamities of war there could be exhibited the highest qualities of human nature, ennobled by the peaceful attributes of Christianity."[48] Given the dark turn of events in Kentucky, with the rise of guerrilla warfare in 1864, and the state's difficulty meeting Union recruitment quotas, the notion that war "elevates, improves, and ennobles humanity" seemingly failed to inspire white men to service.[49] Nevertheless, Sanitary Commission agents writing from Louisville insisted on "the good genius of the war" stemming from relief work in "comforting the afflicted" and "in all ways strengthening the hands of those who hold up the liberties of the world."[50] Recognizing that Kentuckians' loyalties to the Union often rested upon "aching hearts," the Louisville press argued that civilian aid to soldiers, especially that provided by local women, "exhibits fallen human nature in a new light" and "give[s] a zest and purpose and value to life."[51] Although white men often withheld their military service in Kentucky, other forms of Union sentiment took shape, especially in Louisville, helping to prevent the state's formal secession amid the crises of war.

The Louisville and Cincinnati branches of the U.S. Sanitary Commission fostered intense emotional bonds between civilians and soldiers through print. Distributing "many millions of pages" of reports and association news, Louisvillians and Cincinnatians crafted a literary version of their relief work that imagined a powerful union between the home and war fronts.[52] Through these relationships, civilian relief agents insisted they made war humane. Violence and civility, in their minds, fused in a kind of transcendent union that ennobled rather than cast doubt on patriotism. Interstate relief work on behalf of soldiers in the field and in hospitals formed a critical arena in which Louisvillians and Cincinnatians expressed their allegiances to the wartime Union.

Great Western Sanitary Fair

Through most of 1863, Union allegiances in and around Cincinnati appeared deeply frayed. Having lost the fall 1862 election for his seat in the U.S. House of Representatives, Clement Vallandigham left Washington, D.C., bitterly opposed to Lincoln's Emancipation Proclamation and antagonized by Republicans' unwillingness to consider peace terms with southern states. Arriving home to Ohio in early 1863, he stirred the pot of Democratic opposition, insisting that Republicans had turned vicious despots not unlike Robespierre and his followers during the French Revolution's most reactionary violence. Other events also cast a gloom over the state in the first half of 1863: Union generals had not fared well in their most recent western battles, a slew of provost marshals charged with enrolling young men in Union armies brought home the grim reality of a draft, and Lincoln and his commander in the Department of Ohio, General Ambrose E. Burnside, appeared bent on destroying civil liberties, at least in the eyes of Democrats. After one incendiary speech too many, Vallandigham suffered the wrath of Burnside, who sent 150 soldiers to seize the former congressman in the dead of night at his home in Dayton. Imprisoning Vallandigham in Cincinnati, Burnside put this troublesome civilian to a military tribunal, which found him guilty of treasonous disloyalty. Hoping to avoid Vallandigham's martyrdom if locked away in a federal prison, Lincoln ordered him banished to the Confederacy. The wily Vallandigham managed to elude this fate and made his way by ship to Canada. From there, he commenced an improbable run for the office of governor of Ohio, anticipating a groundswell of Democratic support.[53]

These extraordinary events kindled hope among Confederate leaders that Ohio was slipping away from the Republican administration's grasp and that Union loyalties were at the breaking point. As John Hunt Morgan's men undertook raids across the Ohio River, General P. G. T. Beauregard began to envision a renewed Confederate drive into Ohio to assist "Vallandigham's 'friends'" in forming a separate political alliance of midwestern states. This new confederacy might feasibly threaten a second secession from the United States. Faced with such a dire possibility, according to Beauregard, the Lincoln administration would broker a truce confirming Confederate independence, thereby securing the future of slavery.[54]

Though Cincinnatians had no direct knowledge of Beauregard's scheme, those with Unionist allegiances grasped their military and political vulnerabilities in the middle of 1863. These Unionists felt keenly the need to rally southern Ohio's loyalties, and embarked on a two-pronged campaign for the hearts and minds of Cincinnatians especially. First, not wishing their allegiances to suffer questioning, Unionists organized to ensure War Democrat John Brough's landslide victory over Vallandigham in the fall 1863 gubernatorial election.[55] Second, inspired by an exhibition of patriotic feeling among Chicagoans while raising funds to care for soldiers, these Unionists staged their own massive "Sanitary Fair" to support the local Cincinnati Branch of the U.S. Sanitary Commission in late 1863. This voluntary "branch" organization labored to provide basic medical services as well as comfort and care to thousands of sick or wounded fighting men from the western military campaigns. By the time of the fair, Cincinnati's branch-sponsored surgeons and nurses had served soldiers in dire situations following engagements at Fort Donelson, Perryville, and Shiloh. Loaded with essential medical supplies and food from Ohio donors, thirty-two steamers plied western rivers destined for camps and field hospitals. Eight hospitals serving soldiers operated in Cincinnati, and between May 1862 and late 1863, more than eighty thousand troops had passed through the city's Soldiers' Home. To meet these great needs, Cincinnati's fair could not be a trifling event. Organizers printed and distributed two hundred thousand "patriotic circulars" inviting donations and participation from across loyal states, including Kentucky. In the final tally, the Great Western Sanitary Fair exceeded all expectation by raising some $234,000 dollars, with "ten thousand gifts and precious memorials," agricultural and horticultural displays, and fine art bringing thousands of visitors to six large halls during the December holidays. Organizers achieved this even amid an "arctic winter burst" carrying freezing temperatures to the city and leading to a "terribly severe coal panic."[56]

In their dedication to the fair's success, despite great logistical and me-teorological challenges, promoters appeared driven by more than an objec-tive to fulfill soldiers' desperate physical and material needs. They sought to prove that "Cincinnati is a great center of patriotism and instrumentalities" to any who doubted that fact in the aftermath of Vallandigham's embarrass-ing run for office from government-imposed exile. Organizers also asserted their wish to "infuse a spirit among the people" to "sustain the Government in putting down a wicked rebellion." These purposes offered inconsistent perspectives on allegiances at the end of a deeply troubling year: positively stated, loyalties had held firm through the political and military crises of 1863; from a less confident perspective, fair organizers appeared worried that southern Ohioans' patriotism was flagging.[57] In all likelihood, as promoters inadvertently acknowledged, both claims carried truth. Such complexity was often the reality in this Ohio River borderland throughout the Civil War era.

Focusing on soldiers' sufferings and sacrifices was a palpable way to bolster support for the Union government's successful prosecution of the war and to demonstrate Cincinnatians' steadfastness in the face of great human losses. Only the most hard-hearted—disloyal Copperheads and "invulnerable old bachelor[s]" in the estimation of fair promoters—could not but feel for the "glorious defenders of our Union" on viewing the "Case of Blood-stained Flowers, from the battle-field of Gettysburg," or the war-torn flags of fallen color-bearers from the Fifth Ohio, as tens of thousands of Cincinnatians had an opportunity to do during the Great Western Sanitary Fair.[58] Yet promoters and fairgoers also understood these great sacrifices on behalf of the nation in specific frameworks, stemming from bonds of union forged in antebellum decades. For Cincinnatians, soldiers' travails bore meaning only insofar as residents could view their miseries and casualties alongside other impor-tant commitments. At the Great Western Sanitary Fair, Cincinnatians gave context to soldiers' sufferings by stressing other key ideas: religious har-mony, emancipation, and black inclusion in the body politic.

All Creeds

Fair organizers and promoters sent out their circulars inviting contributions without consideration of political or religious differences. As organizers explained—somewhat redundantly—they designed their appeal "to be as broad as it is universal." These invitations "ask[ed] for *something* from all, of all creeds, and all professions," emphasizing ecumenism. At least twelve Catholic parishes participated in the fair, alongside the many Protestant and evangelical churches represented.[59] Major exhibitions took place at the "Catholic Institute," a new, spacious building in central Cincinnati dedicated to "mutual improvement" and "social recreation" among the city's Roman Catholic faithful.[60] Unusual juxtapositions appeared in the course of the fair: At the German Catholic parish display in the "Ladies Bazaar," a statue of the Madonna stood close beside images of George and Martha Washington. In the exhibition halls at the Catholic Institute, viewers could gaze upon a sixteenth-century Psalter possessed by two different popes, Leo X and Gregory XVI, not far from fragments of Plymouth Rock. An "ancient sermon manuscript" carried to North America by the Puritans on the Mayflower lay near a papal bull. A "large painting of the Crucifixion" hung alongside a portrait of Cincinnati's most famous nativist, the evangelical minister Lyman Beecher. Perhaps most remarkably, General William S. Rosecrans, an Ohio-born convert to Catholicism, served as president of the fair, while a rabidly nativist minister, the Reverend Charles B. Boynton, helped to prepare a lengthy history of the Great Western Sanitary Fair and his church, the Vine Street Congregational Church, held a prominent place at the bazaar.[61]

As recently as 1855, Reverend Boynton, a preacher of "magnetic eloquence," had avowed in an Independence Day Oration to Cincinnatians that "an army of the Catholic population of Europe has been systematically directed upon us, marshalled by Jesuits and Priests." "Subverting our Republic government and our Protestant faith" were their dual purposes in the Ohio River valley. In short, "Papal power" conspired to destroy the United States.[62] This oration capped a decade-long spiritual war against Catholicism led by Boynton, a native of Massachusetts and adult evangelical convert who settled in Cincinnati in 1846. True to his origins, shortly after his arrival in Ohio, Boynton had argued that "Puritanism" stood as Americans' one true faith. Lest he appear parochial or hopelessly old-timey in his new bustling and diverse western home, Boynton insisted that "Puritanism belongs not to New England only: it is found wherever a heart throbs with genuine American feeling." In further proof of Puritanism's global significance, Roman Catholics bore special spite toward them, Boynton contended. In an interesting historical argument, Boynton offered this assertion: "From the moment the Papacy was born it declared war against Puritanism, for Puritanism is older than Rome."[63] With these fulminations, Boynton picked up the torch of anti-Romanism from Lyman Beecher, who had migrated to Cincinnati in 1832 for the express purpose of saving the American West from Roman Catholic cultural invasion and political subversion.

Though the two New England warriors stoked old Reformation and Counter-Reformation ideological battles in Cincinnati for three decades before the Civil War, violence erupted only in 1853 and 1855, as the relative stability of the national two-party system gave way to narrower third parties such as the nativist "American," or "Know-Nothing" organization. In 1855, anticipating attacks by nativists, Cincinnati's Germans formed themselves into militia units and barricaded bridges into their "Over-the-Rhine" neighborhood. Meanwhile, their would-be attackers dragged a cannon loaded with boulders around the city, threatening German press offices, private homes, and ward officials charged with counting votes for elections, which were the original flashpoint of violence.[64] Eight years later, in the middle of the Civil War, these same German Catholics and New England Protestants—"Papists" and "Puritans"—sat side by side at the Sanitary Fair's "Ladies Bazaar" and viewed Lyman Beecher's portrait hanging in the city's well-finished Catholic Institute.[65]

It was not just that the Civil War had suddenly dissipated ancient antipathies. The riots of the 1850s and conspiratorial New Englanders notwithstanding, Protestants and Catholics in Cincinnati had pursued compromises and alterations to their faiths for three decades in the highly competitive religious environment of the Ohio River valley. Holding onto the faithful or claiming new converts often demanded adjusting the look and feel of belief to resemble religious adversaries. In the zealous atmosphere of "Great Awakening" revivalism—of which both Catholics and Protestants partook—evangelists and converts practiced similar modes of religious expression across divides of faith and sought the same ends—radical union with the divine—regardless of their opinions of the Reformation. Resemblances forged in antebellum decades thus aided the cause of political union at a moment of some despair in the middle of the Civil War. The religious détente established before 1860 made it possible to hold a massive fair to ensure Cincinnatians' loyalties to the United States in a building carved with the name "Catholic Institute" in its masonry facade.

Permanent Freedom

Cincinnati's white fair organizers also invited African American participation. Although the city's long-standing and prominent black churches do not seem to have hosted display tables in the Ladies Bazaar, during the fair week black Cincinnatians held an exhibition and sponsored a supper, both intended to raise funds for the fair. The city's Union Baptist Church organized African Americans' participation in the fair, "actuated by a deep-seated desire to prove that we earnestly sympathize with our country in her hour of trial" and wishing to support "our noble heroes, white and black, who are offering their breasts as a rampart to check the steps of those who would destroy our Constitution, and trample the banner of beauty and glory in the dust." Black supporters of the fair urged the "earnest co-operation of all," believing that "the cause in which we labor is the cause of liberty, of humanity, of God." For their exhibition, the African American Executive Committee decided to present a concert by students attending the city's public schools for children of color.[66] This decision was of great symbolic importance, for black Cincinnatians had waged a three-decade battle for common schools for their children, and only in the mid-1850s had their victory been assured through state law, Ohio Supreme Court decisions, and tireless, statewide advocacy by African Americans. The children who performed in the exhibition therefore represented black Americans' attachments to the state and white Ohioans' shared investment in black intellectual accomplishment.

A black Cincinnatian, Robert S. Duncanson, enjoyed pride of place in the fair's art gallery as a "fine proof of the swift progress of American civilization . . . in a city almost a thousand miles from the ocean, and on the spot which so many foreigners think of as the 'backwoods' of America." Duncanson displayed four major works at the fair, two of which took their themes from Tennyson's poetry. One offered arresting, if oblique, commentary on the American Civil War. In his *Land of the Lotus Eaters* (1861), Duncanson found inspiration in Tennyson's verse describing Ulysses's soldiers, lured away from the brutal work of war to an earthly paradise. In Duncanson's rendering, white soldiers have departed the battlefield to repose alongside a tropical river. Dark-skinned natives tend to men, who "gaze into the blank air," as a reviewer from the Cincinnati *Commercial* observed. These unfortunate soldiers "smile only with the dreamy contortion of one who is ready to despair, or of one whose reason has deserted its throne." They "wander, sad and lonely," in the verdant landscape.[67] The contemporary art historian Joseph Ketner interprets Duncanson's 1861 painting as a critique of the Confederacy's wayward, inhumane pursuit of war in protection of slavery.[68] The *Commercial* reviewer appeared to grasp in the painting a depiction of the moral costs to people participating in a corrupting venture.

Duncanson's other paintings on display at the fair revealed a range of artistic concerns, including the power of nature to impart spiritual insight and the suffering caused by human treachery. In representing the anguish of Tennyson's Oenone, Duncanson created a "subtile cord of sympathy" between himself and the paintings' viewers, who could enter into "the train of his own thought" to understand another person's sorrow. To Cincinnatians, Duncanson represented a painter "true to his calling" and in full command of the "animating genius" within his art. By 1863, white Cincinnatians accepted the idea of black artistry and "genius," and sought their own spiritual uplift and immersion in an African American conception.[69]

Although organizers of the Great Western Sanitary Fair labored a mere six weeks to prepare for their massive event, they took precious time to ensure that one singular theme received ample consideration by fairgoers: the historical significance of emancipation. To understand this event, they sought out evidence and insight from participants in the nation's abolitionist movement. Preprinted circulars went out to many white antislavery luminaries and radicals, including William Lloyd Garrison, Gerrit Smith, and Wendell Phillips. Garrison provided handwritten copies of poems written while held in prison in Baltimore on account of his radical abolitionism. A small committee of men and women in Cincinnati went further to collect the original artifacts of emancipation. They addressed special letters and importuned figures with close connections to the process of emancipation during the course of the war. For example, Cornelia Williams of Cincinnati corresponded with General John C. Frémont, hoping that he might be able to supply his original declaration liberating slaves in Missouri in 1861 for display and auction at the Great Western Sanitary Fair. Not surprisingly, he no longer possessed the original. However, on behalf of the fair organizers Frémont tried to secure its return from its current possessor, E. M. Davis, but Davis contended he had other plans for the proclamation's "exhibition and sale . . . for the benefit of those made free January 1, 1863, and those yet in bondage."[70]

The unprecedented declaration by a United States' general would not be going to Cincinnati, then, but fair planners did score one coup: a handwritten copy of Lincoln's "Proclamation of Amnesty and Reconstruction" from December 8, 1863, offering "full pardon" and "restoration of all rights" to rebellious persons (excepting officers in the Confederacy) if they swore an oath of loyalty to the United States and, in the same pledge, guaranteed the emancipation of any enslaved persons in their possession.[71] The proclamation further indicated Lincoln's Reconstruction plans, which included slaves' "permanent freedom" and "education," and adverted to the need for legal protection for the "laboring, landless, and homeless class" among emancipated peoples. Upon learning of the Great Western Sanitary Fair, the two senators from Ohio, John Sherman and Benjamin Wade, immediately "waited on the President" to see if they might be able to obtain the original Amnesty Proclamation, just issued, which the two men deemed "of the highest historical interest." Lincoln "cheerfully" complied, although he copied, in his own hand, the proclamation from a "somewhat defaced" original. The proclamation still resides with the Cincinnati Historical Society Library and Archives today.[72] In undertaking this artifact quest, white Cincinnatians sought to understand the significance of emancipation and to connect their own humanitarian work to the unfolding historical event. In the context of the Great Western Sanitary Fair, emancipation breathed meaning into Cincinnatians' philanthropy and sacrifice, and secured deeper loyalties to the Union cause.

Although limited, the representations of African Americans at the fair reveal sources of union between blacks and whites, and between black Americans and the state, cultivated over nearly thirty years in Cincinnati. For one, a powerful education movement involving blacks and their white allies had established publicly funded schools for children of color just on the eve of the Civil War, connecting black enlightenment to the well-being of a representative democratic government. In addition, black artistry, expressed in Robert Duncanson's paintings, had the capacity to refine and ennoble whites, an idea long in circulation by 1863. In Cincinnati, blacks and whites labored together, often in close proximity, in one of the nineteenth century's great social projects: the creation and refinement of the middle classes. Recognition of black intellectuality, expression, and respectability helped to disenthrall white Cincinnatians of the appeal of colonization schemes calling for—if not legally demanding—racial separation. Cincinnati's biracial projects therefore enabled growing numbers of Ohioans to imagine an inclusive, biracial democracy. These shifting ideas about community and identity made the practical work of emancipation seem less formidable and allowed white Ohioans to see black freedom as a worthy and logical Union undertaking during the Civil War. As with the Catholic and Protestant resemblances and attractions, the bonds of union between black and white Cincinnatians forged before 1860 reinforced loyalties during the war itself.

Unconditional Union

If the Confederate invasion of Kentucky and threatened attack on Ohio in 1862 compelled men and women in Louisville and Cincinnati to imagine new kinds of allegiances through their relief aid, Lincoln's Emancipation Proclamation produced more convulsions in the region demanding still greater imaginative efforts in behalf of union. In Ohio, antiwar Democrats discovered a congenial home among discontented voters, and elections in the fall of 1862 and spring of 1863 carried powerful dissenting voices from Cincinnati into Congress and the city's mayoral office.[73] Although Democratic outcry against the Republican administration's conduct of the war stemmed from several sources, including unhappiness about the suppression of anti-Lincoln sentiment by federal authorities, the Emancipation Proclamation brought dissent to "high tide" in the six months after its issue on January 1, 1863, and inspired the exiled Clement Vallandigham's run for Ohio governor. His running mate for lieutenant governor, George E. Pugh, hailed from Cincinnati, and the Chicago Democratic Convention chose another Cincinnatian, George H. Pendleton, as General George B. McClellan's vice presidential running mate. Cincinnati was also home to an unusual band of extremists headed by Alexander Long, a congressman, and William M. Corry, who found even McClellan too tepid in his criticism of the Lincoln presidency. These "true-blue Democrats" railed against the Emancipation Proclamation, insisted on slavery's constitutionality, and demanded an immediate peace with the Confederacy. As Long pronounced in Congress,

> If there ever was a time when the Union could have been restored by war (which I do not believe), it has long since been dispelled by emancipation, confiscation, amnesty, and like proclamations. . . . It is the object of the sword to cut and cleave asunder, but never to unite. . . . [T]he Union is lost, never to be restored . . . and I now believe that there are but two alternatives, and they are either an acknowledgment of the independence of the South as an independent nation, or their complete subjugation and extermination as a people; and of these alternatives I prefer the former.

For this disunion speech, Republicans very nearly expelled Long from Congress.[74]

Among white Kentuckians, the Emancipation Proclamation smacked of betrayal. Although exempted from its provisions because of the state's loyalty, Kentucky's slaveholders could hardly expect to maintain slavery for very long as the institution disintegrated around them. They were incensed. A white Union soldier from Louisville, Andrew Pirtle, wrote to his father upon learning of the proclamation: "To us that are fighting the battles of the Union, it seems as if we had been deceived and that we are fighting the battles of a party and not of a great people."[75] Lincoln worried deeply about such sentiments. As he and his cabinet deliberated the final shape of an emancipation proclamation, they acknowledged the problem of Kentucky's loyalties directly. In August 1862, Lincoln's advisors discussed "a report that the Louisville Democrat had come out openly for disunion, saying that it was now manifest that the Government was in the hands of the Abolitionists." Lincoln interpreted such a view as "a declaration of hostility by the entire Douglas Party of Kentucky, and manifested much uneasiness."[76] The historians Aaron Astor and Anne Marshall attribute white Kentuckians' "disenchantment" with the Union to both Lincoln's issuance of the proclamation and African Americans' subsequent enrollment in federal forces in striking numbers.[77]

Cincinnatians and Louisvillians thus served as lead witnesses in the war's new dramatic unfolding, with rising dissent, bitter partisanship, and slavery's collapse proving uniquely divisive in the Ohio River valley. In both urban enclaves, though, vocal associations arose to promote the rechristened Republican Party, known as the "Union" Party after the elections of 1861, and to advance an abolitionist interpretation of the war. In Cincinnati, a National Union Association formed in early 1863 "to sustain the Federal Government in all its measures for putting down the rebellion."[78] They labored through both the gubernatorial race of 1863, pitting Clement Vallandigham against War Democrat John Brough, the Union Party candidate, and the presidential contest in 1864. In Louisville, a "Union executive committee" began publishing a newspaper called the *Daily Union Press* in April 1864 "to represent and advocate the views of Unconditional Union men," and they sponsored meetings and conventions to promote the "Union Electoral Ticket" in Kentucky.[79] While Cincinnati's National Union Association could claim greater electoral success, with Brough and Lincoln victories in Ohio, Louisville's Union advocates believed they gained important ground for Lincoln in the 1864 presidential canvass, and they labored to see acceptance of emancipation, black military service, and the idea of civic equality among white Kentuckians through 1864 and 1865.[80]

In fact, both organizations helped to advance a radically novel idea among most white Cincinnatians and Louisvillians: that emancipation would bring peace and order to the union, while continued slavery guaranteed political strife, treason, and violent disorder both in Kentucky and the Union at large. Of course, Lincoln, his commanders, and Union soldiers had for some months accepted the view that only slavery's demise would end the Civil War, but for white Kentuckians accustomed to believing that emancipation would in all likelihood spark race war, black freedom appeared anathema to peace. The Union advocates in Louisville therefore artfully argued the need to reverse this view, insisting instead that slavery was the essence of anarchy and that guerrilla warfare plaguing the state in 1864 would cease with acceptance of emancipation and its two corollaries, black military service and equal rights. While Cincinnati's National Union Association grappled with a somewhat different adversary in 1863—the Vallandigham and McClellan men—the organization's speakers made political hay of "Peace Democrats" who advocated an armistice by guaranteeing the protection of slavery. Local organizations such as the National Union Association in Cincinnati and the Union Executive Committee in Louisville endorsed Lincoln's wartime policies and vigorously argued for emancipation, black enlistment, and equality in the Ohio River valley through 1863 and 1864. The arguments made from both urban centers illuminate the rich and fascinating ways emancipation came to be viewed by some as a bond of union.

Arch-enemy of Our Peace

Founded early in 1863, the National Union Association maintained its headquarters in Cincinnati and was under the direction of John D. Caldwell, its general secretary, who also served a critical role in the Cincinnati Branch of the U.S. Sanitary Commission's relief and fund-raising efforts. The ostensible reason behind the group's organization was an "appeal from Ohio soldiers," who drafted resolutions "to maintain the honor and integrity of our Government" while still on the battlefield at Stones River, Tennessee. They had survived bitter fighting there at the start of the new year in 1863, just as the Emancipation Proclamation took effect and Democratic criticism of the war's course reached a fevered pitch. Gathering word of Ohioans' dissatisfaction, the soldiers grew infuriated: "Why should the brave, true men of the great army of the United States, war-broken, toil-worn and battle-stained, be left without sympathy or aid from you, men of Ohio, now enjoying the blessings of peace, careless of dangers of invasion and war's dread terrors, only because we, your brothers and sons, stand 'between your loved homes and war's desolation?'" "Stop your wild, shameless, political strife," they demanded, and "put an end to covert treason at home, more dangerous now to our national existence than the presence of armed hosts of misguided rebels in the field." Leading Unionists in Cincinnati responded to this appeal by organizing the National Union Association, passing a constitution and declaration of principles, as well as adopting an obligatory oath. The group called for a "vigorous prosecution of the war" and promised to "bear true faith, allegiance and loyalty" to the government.[81] Toward these ends, the association invited powerful speakers and held public meetings in Cincinnati to encourage support for the Union and the war. The group published these speeches for a wider impact on public opinion.

Among the association's first speakers was Rev. Charles G. Ames, who delivered a rousing entreaty to Cincinnatians to "Stand By the President!" in March 1863. Punctuated by "deafening and long-continued applause," the speech he delivered sounded many of the same themes articulated by Ohio's soldiers at Stones River. "We have at last touched bottom," Ames began, what with growing attacks on the president by seemingly loyal northerners, "snakes in the grass" who would in truth "assassinate the government by stabbing it in the back" with their "unscrupulous and malignant system of slander." Ames insisted on "unfaltering support of the present [p]resident . . . in whatever war policy his convictions may require him to adopt," fearing that any perceived lack of unity would benefit the Confederacy. Although Ames heaped criticism on Democrats for lambasting Lincoln, he did not view loyalty as an end in itself, disconnected from any particular action undertaken by the president's administration. Ames reserved his most powerful language for support of emancipation as an imperative war objective. Praising Lincoln's "strength" and "conviction," Ames drew "thunderous applause" from his audience with this striking interpretation of the Emancipation Proclamation's origins and purpose: "[Lincoln's] eye sweeps over the vast territory of the Union and down the nation's future. He sees that *slavery* is the arch-enemy of our peace; that *slavery* is the arch-traitor to the Constitution . . . that *slavery* is the viper which the Republic has warmed into life, and which has stung its unwise benefactor . . . and then, he 'puts the foot down firmly,' on that viper's neck! God bless him! And God blast the viper!" Should northerners abandon the president in this mortal combat against slavery, they faced "general ruin" and victory for "bloody treason," according to Ames.[82]

Other speeches sponsored by the National Union Association advanced the same view that slavery fomented war and that emancipation would restore the Union. From St. Louis, Charles D. Drake, a Radical Republican at the time of the war, traveled to both Cincinnati and Louisville in 1864 to stir the locals to greater support for Lincoln's reelection and his emancipation policies.[83] In his Cincinnati speech, just on the eve of the election, Drake insisted that slavery had initiated the war against the Union and that the Peace Democrats, along with presidential candidate McClellan, would perpetuate slavery, and hence "at once denationalize America" and "break its Union into formless ruins," producing "warring confusion" and "irretrievable anarchy." The speech's scorching conclusion, delivered to "tremendous applause" and "great cheers," declared that the admonition to "'STRIKE THE SHACKLES

OFF THE LAST SLAVE IN THE REPUBLIC!' is the only watchword of real peace."[84] Through 1863 and 1864, the National Union Association had moved beyond Lincoln's stated reasoning for the Emancipation Proclamation as a "military necessity" to defeat the Confederacy to argue that ending slavery was an absolute condition of union.

In Louisville, the rhetorical shift evident in Union speeches and publications was striking. Advocates for Lincoln's emancipation policies gathered at a "Freedom Convention" in Louisville in February 1864, and the fiery, eccentric Charles Drake was a keynote speaker. Here he painted a picture of slavery's far-reaching violence: "Everywhere [slavery] is an aristocrat; everywhere the foe of the poor. . . . It is written in blood all over this land, that Slavery is a PUBLIC ENEMY; and the whole mass of loyal Americans proclaim, in a voice like mighty thunderings, that Slavery shall be destroyed," adding with emphasis, "*and in Kentucky, too.*" When Drake described slavery's essential temperament as "cruel, blood thirsty, and treacherous" before his Louisville audience, he offered an obviously abolitionist interpretation of the war and its causes.[85] The Lincoln supporters and Sanitary Commission agents hearing Drake's speech were hardly unfamiliar with such arguments, but for the first time in the war, these Louisvillians embarked on a wide-ranging organized effort to represent slavery as the epitome of violence and to make the institution cause for Kentucky's descent into race warfare in the Bluegrass, where white men loyal to slavery waged attacks on black Union enlistees through the summer and fall of 1864. Primarily in their newspaper, the *Daily Union Press*, these "Loyal Men" offered careful and sustained arguments that only emancipation "on the soil," without colonization, and civil rights for freed people would form the basis of a peaceful nation in the aftermath of war.[86]

National Progress

Louisville's Unionists launched their daily newspaper in the spring of 1864 to advocate for Lincoln's reelection, and they couched his opponents in the Democratic Party as stand-ins for slaveholders, "deliver[ing] over the nation, bound hand and foot, to its open, armed and vindictive enemy."[87] By September, the publishers had embarked on a weekly edition of their paper for readers outside the city and listed agents for the *Union Press* with residences in Kentucky, Indiana, Tennessee, Georgia, and New York.[88] Judging from notices for meetings and conventions, the Union Executive Committee appeared both ambitious and deeply concerned about Kentucky's ability to retain its influence over "the national progress" should they resist emancipation: following the "Freedom Convention" in February 1864, the committee sponsored an "Unconditional Union Convention" in May of that year, and it was planning yet another "State Convention" by December.[89] In between these events, "Magnificent Demonstrations," "torchlight processions," courthouse meetings, and speeches sought to generate enthusiasm for Lincoln.[90] This concerted effort to alter Kentucky's political dynamics on the question of slavery demanded no little resolve. In October, just weeks before the November presidential election, Unionists from Indiana visited Louisville and were "set upon with stones and street boulders" and "badly injured" by "rowdies." Editors at the *Daily Union Press* expressed outrage. But two days later, they consoled themselves with the long view: just "four years ago," their press would have suffered "the destruction of our office by a pro-slavery mob, any day of the week, to say nothing of the Sabbath," given the current "charges of Abolitionism heap[ed] upon us daily" by the *Louisville Journal*.[91] In the fall of 1864, Louisville's Unionists believed they were moving Kentuckians toward a new perception of slavery's dangers. "Slavery is a dead cock in the pit," the editors pronounced after Lincoln's reelection, and they presented the hopeful claim that this "profound revolution in sentiment" supporting emancipation "is now extending with rapidity and power through the State of Kentucky."[92]

Before the Civil War, Kentucky's moderate antislavery voices mostly relied on an economic argument in calling for an end to the use of enslaved labor. The argument appeared self-evident to its supporters: the slave state's prosperity simply had not matched that of free-labor Ohio, typically invoked as Kentucky's economic alter ego. To counter this point, proslavery advocates in the state insisted that slavery provided stability and order to Kentuckians' biracial world, and absent the social controls of the institution, violence and anarchy would ensue. Louisville's radicals rejected this line of reasoning. The stated purpose of their Union political party was to realize "the earliest practicable extirpation ... of the anarchic, discordant, dangerous and strife-producing institution of negro slavery, that apple of discord at the National Feast, which has always been, and always must be the source of incessant and infinite turbulence and confusion."[93] In article after article, editors cataloged an exhaustive list of harms, arranged in a drumbeat of horrors: "Slavery bewilders, blinds, and perverts every heart that loves it," causing "tumult, ruin, and immeasurable terror."[94] Louisville's Unionists also charted a long and sordid history in the pages of the *Daily Union Press*. First the institution had "stained and poisoned" the nation through war, next it produced a "carnival of treason" with the likes of Vallandigham and his fellow Peace Democrats, and finally it drove "the thieving band of guerillas," or "home rebels," to attack black and white Unionists in Kentucky's interior.[95] Their conclusion seemed inescapable: violence and disloyalty were slavery's foul fruits.

Although more than certain of slavery's train of abuses, editors of the *Daily Union Press* seemed to have more difficulty expressing, in positive terms, the benefits to flow from emancipation. They sought to establish, at the very least, that emancipation alone would reestablish the bonds of union. Toward that end, the editors took great pains to write a history of the Emancipation Proclamation in two lengthy articles entitled "Mr. Lincoln and Slavery." "Restoration of the Union," Lincoln's clear and unequivocal objective, had finally demanded emancipation, given the course of the war, and the editors walked readers through a close examination of unfolding events after 1861, "which none could control," they insisted. Driven by these contingencies, but without abandoning the principle upon which he had waged the war, Lincoln arrived at "the conviction that slavery stood in the way of national existence."[96] Yet "national existence" appeared somewhat featureless as a purpose for emancipation. From the *Daily Union Press*'s many articles, readers needed to infer that if slavery produced some evil, emancipation would confer its opposite. So when editors declared that slavery "is not a lovely institution even here," in Kentucky, and that "it is not a promoter of purity, manliness or the Christian graces," one could draw the conclusion that emancipation might coax greater humanity out of white Kentuckians.[97] Because Henry Clay loved "law and order," he would have embraced emancipation for Kentuckians, editors argued.[98] Obliquely, then, readers were to understand that greater security should follow from the abolition of slavery. So although Louisville's editors pictured emancipation "building the goodly structure of justice, freedom and prosperity" atop the "unsightly ruin" of slavery, readers needed to undertake a fair amount of conjecture to imagine the broad benefits of emancipation.[99]

In contrast to these inferred advantages, white Louisvillians as well as Cincinnatians recognized one immediate consequence of Lincoln's Emancipation Proclamation: black enlistment in Union forces. In both Ohio River cities, those advocating for acceptance of the Emancipation Proclamation and prospective abolition of slavery could point to black military service as evidence of renewed loyalty and allegiance to the Union. In this sense, Lincoln's proclamation not only ensured continued "national existence" but also inspired sweeping examples of bravery and fidelity to a national union. Louisville's white Unionists wrote often and admiringly of black service in 1864, after African Americans in Kentucky began to enlist in striking numbers.

As the historian Aaron Astor has recently shown, though, black enlistees faced chilling violence at the hands of white Unionists in the Bluegrass.[100] Louisville was not immune to such resistance, as William Gibson discovered when he attempted to enroll volunteers in the Fifty-Fifth Massachusetts Colored Regiment. As a Kentucky recruiting sergeant in 1863, Gibson received "hundreds of applicants," but "so-called Union" men undermined African Americans' enlistment. As a consequence, he "failed to get a man enrolled in Louisville."[101] Yet by late 1864, Louisville's white Unconditional Unionists sought to vindicate Lincoln's Emancipation Proclamation and its direct encouragement for former slaves' military service. On the one hand, they offered a patently unjust argument: black enlistment relieved white men of duty. "There are to-day five thousand men in the city of Louisville—stout, able-bodied men—pursuing the avocations of civil life and enjoying the comforts of home, who, but for the emancipation proclamation and the arming of blacks, would have been forced into service and now be undergoing the dangers and hardships of military life," they reasoned.[102] For their white readership, this relief from service may well have served as a compelling, albeit racist and self-interested, reason to embrace Lincoln's wartime policies.

Yet this argument hardly ennobled white readers. Perhaps in recognition of this dilemma, the Louisville *Daily Union Press* appeared to use black military service as both a real and figurative proxy for white men's duty to the Union. The editors categorically rejected "Copperhead" claims that black troops "wouldn't stand fire" by carefully reviewing evidence from the Petersburg campaign and setting the unfortunate events there in a larger context of service at Fort Wagner, Port Hudson, Milliken's Bend, and Fort Pillow. Presenting details from Grant's advance toward Richmond, the editors cited the "conspicuous bravery and efficiency" of black troops belonging to the Tenth and Eighteenth Corps. Their "splendid exploits" and "heroism" had yet to receive proper notice in Democratic papers, a lacuna that Louisville's white Unionists characterized as "the gangrene of meanness."[103] The editors at the *Daily Union Press* began to speak more regularly about black rights after November's presidential election, and in view of widening African American service. In "fierce and gallant" fighting at Decatur, Georgia, black Union troops had "exhibited obedience, fidelity, and valor," according to the newspaper. Such bravery invited recognition that "the fate of this great nation" rested with former slaves and free blacks in service to the Union.[104] While calling colonization schemes a "delusion," the newspaper for the first time spoke of African Americans in reference to the Declaration of Independence, avowing that until white Kentuckians "acknowledge the negro as a *man*, 'endowed with certain inalienable rights,' . . . the Lord will hold us fast to our afflictions, as erst, he did the incorrigible King of Egypt."[105] Going beyond this rhetoric, the newspaper endorsed tangible benefits for the families of Kentucky's black soldiers. George D. Blakey, Lincoln's assistant provost marshal general in the state, argued that the "hundreds and thousands" of black servicemen from Kentucky "fighting for Union and Liberty" had "paramount claims" to proposed state compensation to the families of soldiers. Blakey considered this an "act of justice" on behalf of "black citizens" now in military service.[106]

For all of their limits, Louisville's white Unionists advanced novel concepts of allegiance and citizenship in the aftermath of Kentucky's distinctive self-emancipation process. Emancipation forged new relationships, fostering African American allegiances to the Union. While these relationships were implicit in the Emancipation Proclamation itself, Kentucky had been exempted from its provisions. African American enlistment in military service made emancipation an on-the-ground reality in Kentucky, but Louisville's loyalist press provided ideological and rhetorical support to black freedom as a bond of union.

Archives of the State

In Cincinnati, the National Union Association urged emancipation as the only means to sectional reconciliation, but this argument emerged in the context of Democrats' powerful challenge to Republican policies as well as worries about Union military losses. Debates about emancipation in Cincinnati therefore often revolved around questions of loyalty and allegiance to the Union. As in Louisville, though, Cincinnatians grasped the war's full import for the status of African Americans through black military service.

Immediately following the fall of Fort Sumter, black residents offered to defend Cincinnati as a self-organized unit of "Home Guards," but white city officials and residents rejected their services, arguing that "this is a white man's war, and you d—d niggers must keep out of it" while also threatening violence, as Peter Clark later recounted. In late 1862, the city's black residents remained circumspect when the mayor called able-bodied men to duty in order to protect the city from advancing Confederate forces. An inquiry put to a policeman about whether African Americans should appear for the muster drew a racist, albeit confusing answer: "You know d—d well [the mayor] doesn't mean you. Niggers ain't citizens." To which the black inquirer responded that the mayor had requested both citizens and aliens to appear for duty. Apparently perplexed, the policeman retorted that the mayor merely wanted Cincinnati's black residents "to keep quiet" during the crisis. That very night, military authorities began to violently conscript black men into fatigue duty. According to Clark, men were "dragged out, and amidst shouts and jeers, marched like felons to the pen" in a "saturnalia of ruffianism." Clark's history offered a sharp and stinging account of this callous "impressment for a work in which [black Cincinnatians] would have proudly volunteered."[107]

Two days after these midnight arrests, an antislavery Republican attorney, William Dickson, was placed in command of Cincinnati's black forces, which he named the "Black Brigade." Cincinnati's African American community must have known Dickson well because, within hours, men "came forward to aid in the city's defense." "Glowing with enthusiasm," Clark reported, "they were ready for any thing." Dickson immediately demonstrated a shared under-standing of the meaning of their service by proclaiming that "Slavery will soon die; the slaveholders' rebellion, accursed of God and man, will shortly and miserably perish." He and members of the Black Brigade would then enjoy "one country, one flag, and one destiny," he promised. Although assigned to "fatigue duty," their service proved invaluable to Cincinnati's safety. In a short period of approximately three weeks, they accomplished astonishing feats, having "made miles of military roads, miles of rifle-pits, felled hundreds of acres of the largest and loftiest forest trees, [and] built magazines and forts." In Dickson's view, this work turned back the Confederate siege of the city.[108]

They also faced grave risk. Placed "far in advance" of Union troops on the Kentucky side of the Ohio River, the Black Brigade faced the impending invasion "with nothing but spades in their hands," and their fortifications "deterred the enemy from attacking." Out of regular sight of white Union forces, the men "were once mistaken for the enemy" and fired upon, only escaping injury because of a Union officer who, sensing something amiss, disobeyed the order by using blank cartridges. Despite this exposure (to both Union and Confederate troops), black men flocked to the fortifications to enlist. "Colored men singly," then "in squads and companies, from every part of Southern Ohio" arrived at the Black Brigade's camp. In all, some one thousand men enrolled in the unit, the very first military organization of African Americans in the West. Denied the ability to carry arms by the state of Ohio, though, many members of the Black Brigade would go on to serve in the famous Massachusetts Voluntary Infantry Regiments.[109]

Both white and black Cincinnatians recognized the value of the brigade's service. At the conclusion of their duties, the unit prepared a grand procession back into Cincinnati. After presenting Dickson with the gift of a sword, the men marched "in order," with music and banners, through Cincinnati's "principal streets." Clark wrote that the brigade met with "kindly enthusiasm" throughout its procession. Yet in 1864, he remained disconsolate about the prospects for equality. The men who served in the brigade "wish to be numbered among the children of the nation, ... to say with proud joy: we too are American citizens! Is this too much to hope for?" Clark asked his readers. "Slavery, social and political proscription, these were [the] gifts" given to black servicemen, he argued, rather than honor and full enjoyment of the state's privileges and immunities. Clark hoped that his history of the Black Brigade, appearing in 1864, would bring recognition of African American service and claims to full citizenship.[110]

While the precise nature of the relationship between Clark and the brigade's commander, William Dickson, is not clear from his history of the unit, it seems possible that Clark prevailed upon the Republican attorney to prepare a narrative of the Black Brigade to draw official attention to African American sacrifice on behalf of Cincinnati and the state of Ohio. Clark's history includes an extensive account of the brigade's service prepared by Dickson, which he submitted to the governor of Ohio and the legislature, where it was read and "ordered to be placed on the record." Although the Black Brigade formed a unit of the U.S. forces, Dickson argued that Ohio should recognize its service: the brigade's "labors were in the defense of her soil, and it seems but proper that some memory of it should be preserved in her records." He therefore wanted the history of the West's first black military unit placed "in the archives of the State."[111] Black Cincinnatians had undertaken the hazards of service to the state during the war, and as Clark's history illustrates, they also pressed for full acknowledgment of that allegiance.

Military service among black Ohioans and Kentuckians demonstrated loyalty to the Union in the most palpable form. Their white allies in both states, and especially in Cincinnati and Louisville, took notice and attempted to provide rhetorical support to black sacrifice during the war. These fervent nationalists went beyond the Emancipation Proclamation as a practical point of military necessity to make black allegiance and sacrifice exemplary and inspiring. Although unequal in their demands, the physical and rhetorical expressions of this allegiance cemented new bonds of union.

Following the crisis of secession, the American Civil War presented Cincinnatians and Louisvillians with formidable tests of loyalty. Allegiances remained precarious in both places as the challenges of rapid mobilization, political dissent, and emancipation pressed against fragile bonds of union. But in both cities, residents practiced forms of allegiance through their relief work to Union soldiers. If white military service from Louisville, and Kentucky more generally, remained limited, this relief work helped border state residents establish bonds with those in northern states who suffered and sacrificed. Rhetorically, the relief work also fashioned powerful identities between civilians and soldiers to repair the violent ruptures of war. And in both cities, black and white Unionists pressed for an abolitionist interpretation of the conflict, making emancipation a means of national reunification and opposition to black freedom an act of disloyalty or, worse, treason. Yet black military service proved the most conspicuous example of the war's new allegiances. Whites in Cincinnati and Louisville scrambled to make sense of this great sacrifice, and in 1863 and 1864 began to see African American enlistment as a new means of national redemption and the most stunning example of loyalty wrought by the war. In Louisville, black service and white ideological support helped to make emancipation and the hope of citizenship rights a reality in Kentucky, even if still a bitterly contested one. At a minimum, their physical and rhetorical work on behalf of the Union prevented Kentucky's departure from the national fold. These overlapping groups of citizens—white Unionists, relief agents and volunteers, and black soldiers and their families—had invented and deployed novel forms of allegiances to express the bonds of union.

Epilogue

In the spring and early summer of 1865, after Lee laid down his arms at Appomattox Court House, Louisvillians helped pull Kentucky back from the brink of anarchy. Over the prior twelve months, the Bluegrass had descended into chaos—a civil war within the Civil War. This was because the Union army had begun to enroll, enlist, and even aggressively recruit black Kentuckians into its ranks starting in the spring of 1864—regardless of their legal status as free or enslaved individuals. The state's governor had very nearly delivered a "nullification proclamation" calling for armed resistance to black enlistment in March 1864. With martial law imposed in July, recruitment of black soldiers had proceeded apace, with some fourteen thousand enlisted by August. Even with constitutional emancipation on the horizon in early 1865, white Kentuckians remained recalcitrant. In the spring of 1865, the Union army stepped up black enlistment in Kentucky as the only means to undermine the institution of slavery in the state, and continued with this strategy into July, well after recruitment had ended in the rest of the country. Most white Kentuckians remained apoplectic. In the Bluegrass, south of Louisville, guerrilla warfare to thwart emancipation through black military service had begun in spring of 1864, and still raged in early 1865.[1]

In February 1865, Lincoln assigned a new commander, General John M. Palmer, to the District of Kentucky, over his protestations, with these words: "Go to Kentucky, keep your temper, do as you please, and I will sustain you." When Palmer assumed his office at the Louisville headquarters, he entered into a dystopian atmosphere. Palmer's predecessor, General Stephen G. Burbridge, had filled the state's prisons to overflowing with guerrillas, Confederates, and rebel sympathizers. Infamously, Burbridge attempted to reinforce Union loyalty through terror, executing guerrillas by an arbitrary "lot" system.[2] On his arrival, Palmer discovered all manner of disturbing conditions in Kentucky's prisons stemming from the Burbridge era, including regularized sex between incarcerated women and guards at a Louisville jail. He quickly moved to "break up" that government humiliation and ensured the release of small-time offenders swept up in Burbridge's injudicious dragnet throughout the state. Next, Palmer confronted the numerous guerrilla bands roaming through rural Kentucky. But his conundrum here reveals the confused, unclear loyalties in the state in early 1865. To catch a notorious irregular fighter known as "Marion," Palmer deputized a former Confederate, Edwin Terrill, whose qualifications for this undercover police work included that had "killed an officer in his regiment." Though Terrill caught and summarily killed "Marion," Palmer considered his accessory "an exceedingly dangerous man" and "never let [Terrill] enter my quarters without keeping a revolver at hand."[3] Such was the nature of allegiances in Kentucky's rural districts in early 1865. In confronting irregular warfare in the Bluegrass, Palmer could not trust even avowed Unionists.

In addition to dealing with Burbridge's messes and guerrilla warfare in Kentucky's interior, Palmer had to contend with the state legislature, a true hornet's nest for Republican administrations in Washington. In speaking with the state's elected representatives immediately upon his arrival, Palmer acted the part of a foreign emissary: "Suffice it to say, I come among you as a representative of the National Government," he stated by way of introduction to the state legislature. Born and raised in Kentucky until the age of eleven, when his father moved the family to the free state of Illinois to avoid slavery's contaminating atmosphere, Palmer abjured a heavy-handed summons to loyalty with the wary legislators. Employing frankness intended to disarm his audience, he contrasted his earlier military service with the new responsibilities he faced in Kentucky:

> In the field, the duties of the commander, though onerous, and dangerous, are comparatively simple—not so here. To the military duties are added those of a semi-civil character, rendering the position complex and most delicate. Your state is regarded by the government and myself as loyal, and her people entitled to the enjoyment of all private and public rights and immunities of a loyal people. These rights are threatened and obstructed by those who are enemies, not so much of the government, in the abstract, as of the general good order and quiet of the people—desperadoes and marauders whose object is spoliation and plunder. It is to protect you against these men that I am here.

In this odd statement, Union and Confederate allegiances barely made an appearance, and Kentucky occupied a distinct universe of fleeting, uncertain loyalties—or, more dangerously, no loyalties whatsoever. Palmer did not try to sort all of this out in his first meeting with Kentucky's legislators; he merely acknowledged that "you are divided into parties, and that deep feeling and some degree of bitterness exists between the parties." Palmer therefore emphasized a central, if modest, purpose for his appointment—"that of giving protection to your people." If we "each attend to [our] own business," Palmer proposed, "all will work well." Little of political principle or common cause beyond "protection" entered into this federal government parley with the Kentucky state legislature.[4]

Though intended to mollify, Palmer's "cooling off" approach late in February 1865 was overtaken by other fast-moving events in Kentucky. On March 3, Congress approved a resolution declaring that the wives and children of all men mustered into U.S. military service were henceforth "forever free."[5] According to Palmer, black enlistments in the state had grown to nearly 29,000 men by the time of the March 3 resolution, so he estimated that the congressional act had freed somewhere between about 72,000 and 101,000 family members.[6] In the hinterlands, masters stormed against the March 3 act and promised reenslavement once federal troops left Kentucky. Considering their options, Kentucky's enslaved peoples fled these angry masters, heading to locales with secure federal presences, and especially to Louisville.[7] By May 11, Louisville was so crowded with refugees from the interior that the mayor and council called on Palmer to address the crisis, insisting that conditions presented a grave health risk to the city. Though Louisville's white elected officials hoped Palmer would "cooperate with them in ridding the city of the evil," the federal commander seems to have recognized the part he might play in this emancipation drama. According to his autobiography, Palmer appeared genuinely moved to extend his idea of "protection" to Kentucky's ex-slaves to ensure their safety and freedom. In addition, he did not want to force the newly emancipated from the state, insisting to white authorities, "These people and their ancestors for generations are, and have been, natives of [the] State of Kentucky, and have all as strong local attachments as other natives of the state."[8]

In consequence, Palmer undertook an entirely novel approach to undermining the legality of slavery in the state. In Louisville, he ordered that his provost marshals begin to issue "passes" to any applicants, enabling black Kentuckians to move freely, seek employment, and establish residences. He also required that operators of public conveyances, including railroads, steamboats, and ferries, provide transportation services to those bearing his official seal of freedom.[9] Palmer's "curious system of passes," as John Mercer Langston described it, enabled freed people to move about the state—or beyond—without fear of arrest and incarceration for being a fugitive or for vagrancy, which was the only real strategy left for Kentucky slaveholders to maintain the institution of slavery after the near elimination of patrols by the spring of 1865.[10] By early June, Palmer's Louisville office had issued some 3,000 of these passes, and the provost marshals grew accustomed to drafting out between 150 and 300 each day. To black Kentuckians, the passes served as the equivalent of legal freedom papers.[11]

Palmer did not remain aloof from Louisville's African American residents during this critical period. In late March, a short time after Congress passed its freedom resolution for the benefit of enlisted men's families, he visited a black church in the city and announced to the congregation that slavery had ended in Kentucky and that masters and slaves no longer owed legal obligation toward each other.[12] Over the next three months, Palmer was preoccupied with the humanitarian crisis in the city, and he inaugurated his pass system. But the city's black leaders appear to have begun planning and making arrangements to engineer a "general emancipation" proclamation for Kentucky's slaves.[13]

How much of this advance work Palmer knew about is unclear, for he claimed surprise at the extraordinary events that would come to pass on July 4, 1865. Palmer insisted in his autobiography that the first he heard of slaves' anticipation of a proclamation of their freedom was a few days before the holiday, when a man residing some sixty miles from Louisville made the long trip to see the commander in person at his headquarters. The man urgently demanded explanation: "What in the h-ll do you mean by telling the negroes to come to Louisville on the Fourth of July and you will set them free?" The distressed visitor reported that "the whole negro population in his part of the state were in motion for Louisville, where they expected to be declared free by me." Palmer protested his ignorance, but he appears to have been at the mercy of greater forces. On July 3, a "committee" of African Americans "waited on me at my headquarters to know 'at what hour and at what place I would declare their freedom.' " To the delegation, Palmer claimed to lack authority for such a declaration and, in his memoir, seemed to think he had corrected black Louisvillians' misapprehensions.[14]

We have conflicting accounts of what happened next from Palmer and John Mercer Langston, a participant in black Louisvillians' historic Independence Day. Palmer explains that he was invited by a traveling circus ring master to visit his nearby fairgrounds to hear a famous Methodist evangelist, the Reverend C. B. Parsons, read the Declaration of Independence. For this trip to the fair, Palmer enjoyed use of the circus leader's "gilded chariot" and four "piebald," or black-and-white mottled, horses on the morning of July 4. While Parsons spoke, fleet "messengers" began appearing at the fairgrounds to alert the commander that "the city was full of negroes who were waiting for me to set them free." By his account, Palmer ignored the first few notices of crowds amassing in Louisville but finally consented to leave the Independence Day observances at the insistence of his adjutant-general and white city leaders. He flew back to the city in the borrowed golden carriage. There he joined with Louisville's prominent black Baptist minister, the Reverend Henry Adams, and Ohio's John Mercer Langston, by now a lawyer and advocate investigating conditions among newly freed people of the South. The party traveled together to a large "grove" outside of the city where tens of thousands of people had assembled to hear of their universal emancipation. Langston reported seeing "a hundred thousand men and women" gathered, while Palmer believed the audience stood closer to twenty thousand.[15] In any case, people had come from far and wide to hear Palmer deliver a pronouncement "in the name of the national government, of the utter overthrow of slavery in the State, and the full and complete freedom of the slave."[16]

The arriving commander and his associates could not be missed in the gleaming chariot drawn by four rare horses, and the crowd grew electric in its anticipation. Finding it impossible to move through the crush of men, women, and children, Palmer "was lifted over their heads" and moved hand to hand onto the stage. "A storm and flood of applause" welcomed the emancipator, who spoke briefly but concluded dramatically: "Now, by the Declaration of Independence, by the Constitution of the United States, by that law of our country which makes all of its inhabitants free, since our government is a democracy; as commanding officer of this Commonwealth, by the power and authority invested in me and upon the instruction and approval of the president of the United States, I do declare slavery forever abolished in this State." According to Langston, the exultant reaction that followed "came like the dashing of contending floods, in hottest, wildest contest." A national figure by 1865, Langston was no stranger to public orations at mass meetings, so when he asserted that "no speech heretofore made by any orator in the United States of America, had ever had such close and climax," he had wide basis for comparison. Palmer next introduced Langston, who sought to "inspire" his listeners "with the hope of a glad future," a profound message in a moment of great revolution. Langston was nearly overwhelmed by the magnitude of the occasion, believing that he must "in no wise tend to abate the enthusiasm" of a people so joyous now, but faced with such daunting challenges ahead. At hearing their "deafening applause" for his remarks, he felt tremendous relief that he had established a fast connection to this unusual audience.[17]

The Reverend Henry Adams spoke last. Even to such a large audience, Adams was a well-known figure, having moved to Kentucky some thirty-five years earlier. In his more than four decades serving as pastor of Louisville's first independent black church, Adams enjoyed legendary successes, converting an estimated ten thousand people in his lifetime. "Verily he was a lover of his people," observed Rev. Charles Parrish, Louisville's most prominent black minister in the early twentieth century. In 1865, Adams was in his sixties, and his compatriot on that day, John Langston, was about half his age. They made an exceptional pairing, the beloved local minister and youthful leader with a growing national reputation. Adams seemed grateful to have such a powerful model of black achievement and education at the event, and he "dwelt with emphasis" upon Langston's "matchless, eloquent address" in his own complimentary remarks to the audience. If the Kentucky audience had not grasped this already, Adams emphasized that the "young colored orator" spoke with "truth and power to instruct this vast gathering of former slaves, just now made free." Langston was Adams's exemplar for black freedom: the son of a manumitted woman and her former master in Virginia, Langston had earned a college education at Oberlin and became the first black Ohioan to join the state's bar. The minister surely did not speak to these precise details of Langston's life at such an emotional moment, but Adams nevertheless sought to link the accomplishments of a free black Ohioan to the transformations wrought among enslaved Kentuckians that day.[18]

Adams knew Langston well. For several years in the 1850s, the Louisville minister served as pastor of a Cincinnati church to which members of Langston's family and close friends belonged. Beyond a common evangelical faith, the Cincinnati congregation shared with Adams a great interest in public education for children of color. It was not at all a coincidence that the two Baptist churches Adams served—the one in Cincinnati and the other in Louisville—housed the first publicly funded schools in their respective cities. Langston was also a fervent advocate of common schools, and he would return to Louisville in 1869 to provide guidance for the establishment of a statewide system in Kentucky. Like the Ohioans with whom he affiliated, Adams was an advocate and an institution builder. Yet he had chosen to make Louisville his home and the headquarters for ambitious denominational work on behalf of black Baptists. A native of Georgia, Adams had the opportunity and financial wherewithal to leave the slave South: he married a free black woman from Chillicothe, Ohio, in 1842 and might have agreed to serve any number of northern black Baptist churches. But he had decided to remain in Louisville through the course of his career "for the cause's sake." Adams nurtured black Baptist congregations throughout the region and raised up a powerful organizational base ready to assist African Americans in the transition from freedom to slavery. In 1865, his Louisville church would host the formation of the State Convention of Colored Baptists in Kentucky, the first such organization in the American South, and his First African Baptist Church would later be celebrated as the "mother church" to the state's powerful black Baptist movement.[19]

Given these personal histories, it does not seem credible that the two black leaders' presence in Palmer's borrowed carriage and their pointed speeches were accidental—the impromptu decisions of a frantic morning that also somehow involved a circus ringmaster. Although Palmer's published memoir gives the appearance of an entirely spontaneous event, evidence of black Louisvillians' advance planning for the "general emancipation" of Kentucky's slaves on July 4, 1865, is apparent in details from both Palmer's and Langston's memoirs. First, Langston had visited Louisville earlier in the year on his way to make a "general trip of observation of the colored people of the South." Black Louisvillians therefore knew he was somewhat close at hand, traveling through Tennessee and Kentucky. This helps to explain why Langston had been "specially invited" to address black Kentuckians alongside Palmer, as he later noted. Second, the Ohioan offered a precise recollection of the Union commander's demeanor on the morning of July 4. Palmer did not give the appearance of a harried commander, besieged by messengers at a fairground to attend to a crisis. Instead, according to Langston, as the three men traveled "through the streets of the proud city of Louisville, he displayed no other feelings than those of confidence and satisfaction." Palmer had just returned from a brief trip to Washington, "where he seemed to have gained special inspiration for his matchless task," Langston wrote. Perhaps some psychological transference was at work here, but Langston insisted that Palmer understood "the dignity and glory of the task" at hand, which was the "work of general emancipation." Moreover, Langston recalled that a "band of music" and an "imposing array of military and popular characters" led their four horses and glinting chariot into the grove where the three men would speak to the amassed thousands on a stage "erected for the occasion," as Palmer noted. In addition to this lively procession, "negro regiments" and "a great unbroken negro artillery company" stood around the whole grove to "guard and protect this gathering," Langston remembered. Maybe C. W. Noyes, the circus leader, had not so much offered to lend the grand carriage as Palmer had importuned him to borrow it for the day. However that may be, it was with fanfare and attention to grand entrances and spectacle that John Palmer and his black allies declared the official end to Kentucky slavery on a singular day, July 4, 1865.[20]

Louisville was the setting for the extraordinary event not only because the Union commander of the District of Kentucky had made his headquarters there, and not only because martial law remained in force in the state in July 1865, a point at which the Civil War was technically over. Nor was it the happenstance of a single day or the few months of John Palmer's command in Kentucky. That the July 4 gathering took place at all reflects a longer history in Louisville, stretching back to the 1830s. Long-standing black organization in Louisville—centered mostly around religious and educational pursuits— meant that African Americans in Kentucky were activated and ready to pursue the fruits of universal freedom. Langston said as much in his memoir, arguing that the "many colored people who had been free for a long time, born so or emancipated" provided an "incalculable advantage to those who were just leaving their slavery." He explained that "they had, notwithstanding their hard condition socially, made some progress in earnest life. They had built for themselves churches; in some communities they had established schools for their children; they had in some cases accumulated considerable property and made for themselves small but desirable homes." Here Langston especially cited the achievements of Louisvillians, including Henry Adams.[21]

Although Langston wrote from his experiences touring Kentucky and Tennessee, he might have cited such community building for any number of southern cities, especially those situated in border states. Yet Louisville's black institutions were also attached to an entirely unique antebellum history that contributed to the July 4, 1865, "general emancipation" declaration. Black Louisvillians had a history of dramatic, flagrant breaks with the "slaveholding power," as they termed it before the Civil War, in order to take full possession of their lives and dissociate themselves from proslavery institutions and ideas. As in the case of John Palmer in 1865, they often declared independence with the assistance of carefully selected white "front men" who had exhibited some sympathy for the idea of black freedom and autonomy. In the two decades before the Civil War, black Louisvillians had forged these important alliances with men of influence and had charted an unusual course away from formal affiliation with slaveholding institutions and ideologies. Thus, well before 1865, Louisvillians had made it eminently clear that their bonds of union were with northern free institutions—whether those were educational, religious, or political. African Americans in Kentucky's leading city were therefore ready to play a role as powerful agents of union during the Civil War itself. The unusual events of July 4, 1865, make greater sense within this longer context of antebellum black activism in Kentucky's largest city.

Louisville had long stood apart from its Kentucky home. In 1849, states-men drafting a new constitution railed against the dangers to slavery emanat-ing from the city, where the slave South's most significant emancipationist movement before the Civil War had discovered a relatively hospitable environment. Persuaded by local African Americans, Louisville's white emancipationists had also made a striking break with the colonization move-ment, whose main premise held that black and white people could never create a society of mutual benefit for both races. This idea claimed the loyal-ties of most whites in the state and even infused the state's antislavery cam-paigns. But Louisvillians labored to refute that premise. By the time of the Civil War, residents in the city had a longer history to draw upon to imagine a new basis for a racially inclusive society following emancipation.

Moreover, Louisvillians—both black and white—maintained stronger ide-ological bonds with the federal union through antebellum years, and dwelled upon Kentucky's unique history within the context of a larger constitutional whole. When secession and the Confederacy beckoned, Louisvillians cleaved to the Union and became a major center for the relief and care of its soldiers during the Civil War. Witnesses to the unfolding brutality and disorder in the Bluegrass region later in the war, Louisvillians urgently argued that slavery was, in its very essence, a form of violence and that for peace and order to resume, the institution required immediate dismantling. The idea drew additional force from historical experience: during the 1840s, white Louisvillians had carried on a significant, if limited, discussion of slavery's deeper psychological and physical harms.

For all that we now know about emancipation's violent aftermath and the stubborn persistence of inequality today—even still with lethal, harrowing consequences—giving close attention to some Americans' efforts to dimin-ish racial divides before 1865 might appear misplaced, if not naive. That we have not fully reckoned with slavery's profound toll, nor grasped its entire entanglement in U.S. history, may make Cincinnatians' and Louisvillians' bonds of union seem like so many broken reeds.[22] Yet it is also the case that Americans today often cannot describe the human connections supporting their polity, that many people with means or influence seem to lack even a basic curiosity about the causes of nearly inescapable poverty, and that civilians know little of wars now fought in their name. In light of these con-temporary lacunae, it seems worthwhile to investigate a time when some Americans closely examined, and tried to express, what held people with distinctive historical experiences together in union.

Living along a unique borderland, the Americans examined here pursued knowledge of the daily life and struggle of very differently situated people. They did so with zeal and energy, rendering visible real, and hoped-for, bonds between disparate peoples and places. These particular individuals desperately wanted to lessen divides in experience and understanding—divides that helped to sustain an abhorrent racial caste system—because they believed their own lives depended on doing so. By their lights, disunion, or some kind of anarchic disintegration, appeared imminent if they did not close gaps in their understanding. When secessionists severed the polity in late 1860 and early 1861, enough Cincinnatians and Louisvillians ensured the Union's continued existence by securing Kentucky's allegiance, and they did so while also arguing for slavery's immediate end in that loyal state as well as in the rebellious Confederacy. Their argument arose from a keen sense of the bonds of their union together.

The people highlighted in this book were predisposed by religious faith to acknowledge suffering as a universal human condition. But they suggested that affliction might be lessened if described and shared. Reading about—and vicariously experiencing—others' hardships acquired a devotional cast in this hypersensitive environment. Kentucky and Ohio also offered perspective on extreme forms of unequal standing caused by legalized prejudice and slavery. Some Americans living in the region made sincere efforts to grasp slavery's gravest harms to individuals and to the wider society. With an enviable sophistication, they came to view enlightenment through universal public education as the antidote to ills produced by slavery and as the basis for a biracial society. This was at least in part because they understood "union" in a capacious way, as self-government predicated upon affective bonds among diverse people. That we now have such a narrow, paltry sense of our government's relationship to its citizens, and have no little difficulty expressing "community" as a function of government, indicates a diminution of our sensibilities. For these reasons, the cautious hope expressed on that exceptional July Fourth in Louisville might not be discounted.

Notes

Preface

1. Lincoln, "Repeal of the Missouri Compromise and the Propriety of Its Restoration," in Basler, *Abraham Lincoln*, 283; Foner, *Fiery Trial*, 65.

2. Lincoln, "Repeal of the Missouri Compromise," 309–10; Foner, *Fiery Trial*, 64, and 63–72 generally.

3. See Colossians 3:14 in the Weymouth New Testament.

4. Gallagher, *Union War*, 3–4.

5. Lincoln, "Mr. Lincoln's Reply in the Ottowa Debate," in Basler, *Abraham Lincoln*, 446.

6. First Orthodox Congregational Church, *Manual of the First Orthodox Congregational Church, in Cincinnati*, 16.

7. [American Reform Tract and Book Society], *Walter Browning*, 21.

8. Chase, *Address of the Southern and Western Liberty Convention*, 9.

9. Lincoln, "Repeal of the Missouri Compromise," 309.

10. Whether the Constitution protected slavery was the central question facing political abolitionism. James Oakes reviews the Republican Party leaders' development of an "antislavery constitutionalism" in *Freedom National* to recover the "antislavery origins of the Civil War." See Oakes, *Freedom National*, xvi–xvii and ch. 1, 1–48, generally. For the phrase "antislavery constitutionalism," see ibid., 29.

11. Lincoln, "Mr. Lincoln's Reply in the Ottawa Debate," in Basler, *Abraham Lincoln*, 446–47.

12. Ibid., 446.

13. Stanley Harrold treats the region's violence over slavery in *Border War*, and Luke Harlow examines the Ohio Valley as an ideological "battleground" in *Religion, Race, and the Making of Confederate Kentucky*, 2.

14. Foner, *Fiery Trial*, 168–69, 177. For helpful discussion of the immediate context surrounding Lincoln's claims about Kentucky's importance, see Oakes, 159–66.

15. For this argument, see Freehling, *South vs. the South*.

16. Important recent studies of the region include Taylor, *Frontiers of Freedom*; Taylor, *America's First Black Socialist*; Cheek and Cheek, *John Mercer Langston and the Fight for Black Freedom*; Lucas, *A History of Blacks in Kentucky*; Trotter, *River Jordan*. J. Blaine Hudson examines the African American experience in Louisville in the Civil War era in articles cited here. My book could not have been written without this scholarship.

17. Antislavery activists used this phrase as an animating precept for their work. For an example from fiction, see "M. A. F.," *Gertrude Lee; Or, The Northern Cousin*, 11.

18. Abruzzo, *Polemical Pain*, 48.

19. Kersh, *Dreams of a More Perfect Union*, 103; Varon, *Disunion!*, 1.

20. Kersh, *Dreams of a More Perfect Union*, 2, 6, 77, 122.

21. Kersh, *Dreams of a More Perfect Union*, 108, 78.

22. Varon, *Disunion!*, 1–2.

23. On fear as a driving force of disunion, see Taylor, *Internal Enemy*.

24. *OED Online*, s.v. "Union, n. 1," http://www.oed.com/view/Entry/214678 (May 2, 2015).

25. See Appleby, *Inheriting the Revolution*.

Chapter One

1. Dolan, *Catholic Revivalism*, 17–18; Billington, *Protestant Crusade*, 119.

2. Venable, *Beginnings of Literary Culture*, iii.

3. Ibid., 219, 225.

4. Ibid., 226, 221.

5. Western Baptist Education Society, "First Annual Report," in General Convention of Western Baptists, *Proceedings of the Second Anniversary of the General Convention of Western Baptists*, 38.

6. Mahan, *Autobiography*, 223.

7. Jonathan Blanchard to Mary Avery Bent, May 12, 1838, and Jonathan Blanchard to Mary Avery Bent, March 28, 1838, Jonathan Blanchard Collection.

8. Clarke, *Autobiography, Diary and Correspondence*, 50.

9. Jackson, *Memoirs of the Rev. William Jackson*, 218–20.

10. On domestic missionary societies, see Ahlstrom, *Religious History*, 423, 858–60. Although outdated, Miyakawa's *Protestants and Pioneers* provides an overview of early Presbyterian, Baptist, Methodist, and Society of Friends activities in the Ohio River valley.

11. Ninth Street Baptist Church, *Semi-Centennial*, 7.

12. "Sixth Street Baptist Church, Cincinnati," *Atkinson's Casket; Or Gems of Literature, Wit and Sentiment* (Philadelphia), 12 (December 1832), 565.

13. Miami Baptist Association, *Minutes of the Miami Baptist Association* (1829).

14. Miami Baptist Association, *Minutes* (1829 and 1834).

15. Miami Baptist Association, *Minutes* (1834), 4; Ahlstrom, *Religious History*, 859–60. These divisions are treated in Dunlevy, *History of the Miami Baptist Association*, 66–81.

16. Lynd, "Circular Letter," in Miami Baptist Association, *Minutes* (1832), 6.

17. Miami Baptist Association (Anti-Mission), *Minutes of the Miami Baptist Association held at Dry Fork Whitewater Church, Hamilton County, Ohio* (1836); Miami Association of Regular Baptists (Anti-Mission), "General Corresponding Letter," in *Minutes of the Forty-Ninth Anniversary of the Miami Association of Regular Baptists, Held with the West Lebanon Church* (1848). I have provided full bibliographic information for the anti-mission Baptists in order to prevent confusion with the missionary Baptists, who went by the same association name.

18. Miami Association of Regular Baptists (Anti-Mission), "Circular Letter of the Miami Baptist Association," in *Minutes* (1848), 6; Miami Association of Regular

Baptists (Anti-Mission), "Circular Letter," in *Minutes of the Fifty-Third Anniversary of the Miami Association of Regular Baptists, held with the Church at Fairfield* (1852), 5–6.

19. Miami Association of Regular Baptists (Anti-Mission), "Circular Letter," in *Minutes of the Fifty-Eighth Anniversary of the Miami Association of Regular Baptists, held with the Mt. Pleasant Church* (1856), 5–6; Miami Baptist Association of Primitive Baptists, "Statistical Table," in *Minutes of the One Hundred-Seventeenth Annual Session of the Miami Baptist Association of Primitive Baptists,* 1917.

20. Ninth Street Baptist Church, *Semi-Centennial,* 8.

21. Lynd, "Circular Letter," 6–7.

22. Minutes of the Ninth Street Baptist Church, December 11, 1838, Lakewood Baptist Church, Cincinnati, Ohio.

23. Western Baptist Education Society, "First Annual Report," in General Convention of Western Baptists, *Proceedings of the Second Anniversary,* 38. For discussion of the "Village Plans," see Miami Association of Regular Baptists, *Minutes* (1841–46).

24. Miami Association of Regular Baptists, *Minutes* (1842), 8.

25. Western Baptist Education Society, "First Annual Report," 38.

26. Miami Association of Regular Baptists, *Minutes* (1844), 11.

27. Kimbrough, *History of the Walnut Street Baptist Church,* 42; DeBow, "Table XIV," in *Seventh Census of the United States: 1850,* 633–41.

28. Minutes of the First Baptist Church of Jesus Christ [Disciples of Christ], October 24, 1830, Nashville, Tenn.: Southern Baptist Historical Library and Archives, n.d., microfilm 1062.

29. Kimbrough, *History of the Walnut Street Baptist Church,* 34–40.

30. Willson's name is variously spelled "Willson" and "Wilson" in the primary and secondary literature. Pendleton, "Condition of the Baptist Cause in Kentucky in 1837," in General Association of Baptists in Kentucky, *Memorial Volume,* 4–5; Kimbrough, *History of the Walnut Street Baptist Church,* 35–36.

31. "Revival in Shelbyville (Ky.) and Vicinity," *Baptist Advocate* 1, January 1835, 19.

32. "Obituary," *Baptist Advocate* 1, September 1835, 216.

33. Pendleton, "Condition of the Baptist Cause," 6.

34. Ibid., 9.

35. Sears, "Baptists of Kentucky and Benevolence," in General Association of Baptists in Kentucky, *Memorial Volume,* 55.

36. Kimbrough, *History of the Walnut Street Baptist Church,* 42.

37. Gibson, "Semi-Centennial of the Public Career," 4.

38. Green, quoted in Peter Clark, "Developing Power of African Methodism," in Arnett, *Proceedings of the Semi-Centenary Celebration,* 101.

39. Gibson, "Semi-Centennial of the Public Career," 3–5, 32, 34–35, 39.

40. Smith, *Biography of Rev. David Smith,* 68, 71–72.

41. Arnett, *Semi-Centenary Celebration,* 16–18. On the number of members reported in 1824 to the General Conference, see Payne, *History of the African Methodist Episcopal Church,* 44.

42. Arnett, *Semi-Centenary Celebration,* 12.

43. On the introduction of African Methodism into Louisville, see Smith, *Biography of Rev. David Smith*, 82–84.

44. Weeden, *Weeden's History of the Colored People of Louisville*, 11.

45. Smith, *Biography of Rev. David Smith*, 83–84. Also see Gibson, "Semi-Centennial of the Public Career," 11.

46. Quinn, quoted in Payne, *History of the African Methodist Episcopal Church*, 171.

47. Although Allen Temple's records previous to 1854 are now lost, church minutes from the late 1850s confirm that Allen Temple's members regularly housed fugitives and raised funds for their conveyance. Financial Records of Allen Chapel, August 1, 1859, Allen Temple African Methodist Episcopal Church, Cincinnati, Ohio. On this entry, the church reported collecting $32.56 for the Underground Railroad. On October 6, 1861, the church reported $13.30 raised for fugitives. Other entries in this record book suggest indirectly that the church aided fugitives. For example, on December 13, 1860, the clerk reported: "A destitute Sister being at Bro. L. S. Lewis with several children, and required some aid to assist her in her journey." For the church's relationship with Levi Coffin, see Quarterly Conference Minutes for A. M. E. Church Conference, Cincinnati Station, December 27, 1860, Allen Temple African Methodist Episcopal Church, Cincinnati, Ohio. When Rev. Benjamin Arnett wrote his 1874 history of Allen Temple, he apparently had in his possession the entire set of church records. He relied on these documents and oral histories from longtime members to write the church's history. Arnett, *Semi-Centenary Celebration*, 16, 18, 20.

48. Gibson, "Semi-Centennial of the Public Career," 11–12.

49. Clark, "Developing Power of African Methodism," in Arnett, *Semi-Centenary Celebration*, 101.

50. Page, *History of Union Baptist Church*, 6.

51. Ibid., 9; Regular Baptist Churches of Color, *Minutes of the Second Annual Association* (1837), 3–5.

52. Regular Baptist Churches of Color, *Minutes of the Second Annual Association*, 5.

53. See "Report" and "Summary of Letters from Churches" on Shelton and Satchell's activities on behalf of the newer churches, in Regular Baptist Churches of Color, *Minutes of the Fifth Annual Association*, 4–6. On Shelton's success in founding churches, see also Page, *History of Union Baptist Church*, 9.

54. Regular Baptist Churches of Color, *Minutes of the Fifth Annual Association*, 4.

55. Satchell, "Circular Letter," in ibid., 7–8.

56. Blanchard, *Perfect State of Society*, 5, 16.

57. Lamott, *History of the Archdiocese of Cincinnati*, 98, 77.

58. Purcell, "Documents: Bishop Purcell's Journal," 241, 246, 248, 250, 252–53.

59. *The Catholic Almanac: Or, Laity's Directory* (1833), 38, in *American Catholic Directories, 1817–1879*, microfilm (hereafter cited as *ACD*).

60. Crews, *American Holy Land*, 101–4.

61. Crews writes that this 35,000 figure "may have been a little high." Ibid., 106.

62. Lamott, *History of the Archdiocese of Cincinnati*, 77; *Metropolitan Catholic Almanac, and Laity's Directory* (1842), 163, in *ACD*. These increases largely track with

nationwide statistics for Catholic growth. In 1807, just 70,000 laypersons and seventy priests represented the whole of Catholicism in the United States in a total population of nearly 7 million people. Yet by 1830, the Catholic Church counted approximately 318,000 adherents served by 232 priests, and by 1841, 1.3 million adherents and 541 clergy. For these numbers, see Billington, *Protestant Crusade*, 37; Carey, *Roman Catholics*, 31, 24; *Metropolitan Catholic Almanac* (1842), 171, in ACD.

63. *Metropolitan Catholic Almanac, and Laity's Directory* (1840), 146, in ACD. The "Recapitulation" on this page fails to list one of the convents described on 142–45.

64. Fr. William Untertheiner to Fr. Arbogast Schöpf, April 1845, in McCloskey, *Letters ... (1844–46)*, 78–79.

65. Fr. Francis Louis Huber to Minister General Joseph Mary Maniscalco, July 2, 1840, in Wuest, *Materials for a History*, 4:3.

66. Monsignor Purcell to James F. Wood, May 31, 1840, in ibid., 4:5.

67. See Dichtl, "She Stalks Abroad," 347–73. Dichtl argues that Kentucky's Catholics "exercised an aggressive, traditional religious drive" and "displayed distinctive religious practices with the hope of reaching the minds and hearts" of non-Catholics. Ibid., 348.

68. Otis, *Louisville Directory*, 139.

69. "Preaching and Practice," *Catholic Telegraph*, November 19, 1831; "Cincinnati Revival," *Catholic Telegraph*, June 23, 1832. Here the editors excerpted a description of local revivals by Frances Trollope in her *Domestic Manners of the Americans*.

70. *Catholic Telegraph*, October 22, 1831, and November 5, 1831.

71. "Conversions," *Catholic Telegraph*, December 3, 1831.

72. For an overview of this event, see Billington, *Protestant Crusade*, 67–92.

73. For an analysis of the role played by gender and class in the treatment of Rebecca Reed, who wrote an infamous exposé of the Charlestown convent, see Cohen, "Respectability of Rebecca Reed," 419–61.

74. Roemer, *Leopoldine Foundation*, 152.

75. Ibid., 155.

76. Rt. Rev. Frederic Résé, quoted in ibid., 160.

77. Metternich to Bishop Edward Fenwick, April 27, 1830, in Leopoldine Foundation of Vienna, *Berichte* (Leopoldine Reports) 1:7, quoted in ibid., 153.

78. Morse, *Foreign Conspiracy*, 10, 22, 23, 45, 32.

79. Anbinder, *Nativism and Slavery*, 9–10.

80. Beecher, *Plea for the West*.

81. Ibid., 12, 113, 110.

82. For a brief discussion of both of these societies, see Billington, *Protestant Crusade*, 121.

83. McGann, *Nativism in Kentucky*, 2–3n4.

84. Beecher identified Flaget's quotes as coming from the *Annales de la Propagation de la Foi*, the annual reports for the Society for the Propagation of the Faith (Lyons, France), but Beecher actually relied on a periodical entitled the *Quarterly Register* (he cites vol. 2 [1830]: 194, 197), which reprinted quotes from Flaget. This may have been the *American Quarterly Register* of the American Education Society, a Boston

organization with which Beecher probably had ties. Beecher, *Plea for the West*, 100. For Beecher's worries about Catholic schools, see 95–99. On Metternich, see 165.

85. Beecher, *Plea for the West*, 12.

86. On the difficulties faced by Kentucky's three Catholic colleges in the 1820s and 1830s, see Crews, *American Holy Land*, 94–98. For Ohio's colleges and seminaries, see Lamott, *History of the Archdiocese of Cincinnati*, 280–82, 287–90.

87. [James Hall], "Critical Notices: A Plea for the West," in *Western Monthly Magazine* 3, May 1835, 323.

88. For a brief biography of James Hall and a bibliography of his writings, see Coyle, *Ohio Authors and Their Books*, 265–67. For additional discussion of Hall's reaction to Beecher's *Plea for the West*, see Aaron, *Cincinnati, Queen City of the West*, 180–81.

89. James Hall, "The Catholic Question," *Western Monthly Magazine* 3, June 1835, 385.

90. [Hall], "Critical Notices," 324.

91. Hall, "Catholic Question," 377, 385.

92. Ibid., 381, 386, 376; [Hall], "Critical Notices," 324.

93. "The Controversy," from the *Republican* newspaper, in *Debate on the Roman Catholic Religion*, x.

94. Beecher, *Plea for the West*, 10.

95. Ibid., 19–20.

96. Ibid., 12.

97. On Roman Catholic predominance in Hamilton County, Ohio, and Jefferson County, Kentucky, see Gaustad and Barlow, *New Historical Atlas*, figures C.3 and C.4, 359–60.

98. Cist, *Sketches and Statistics of Cincinnati in 1851*, 83.

99. Cist's estimate places Catholic numbers at more than 40,400 in a total population of 115,438, which seems improbably high. Yet this figure may not have been too far-fetched, given Purcell's 1847 report. Also in 1847, 12,000 Cincinnatians received Communion in celebration of the jubilee proclaimed by the pope. Lamott, *History of the Archdiocese of Cincinnati*, 170. See also Stritch, "Nativism in Cincinnati." Stritch gleaned his number from the *Catholic Telegraph*, January 8, 1846.

100. Crews, *American Holy Land*, 109.

101. Lamott, *History of the Archdiocese of Cincinnati*, 224–64.

102. In the Diocese of Cincinnati, sixty-one parish schools were in operation by 1860. Lamott, *History of the Archdiocese of Cincinnati*, 278. It is not clear how many parish schools existed in the Diocese of Louisville in 1860.

103. Crews, *American Holy Land*, 107, 126. Most of the religious communities were located in the vicinity of Bardstown, the original see city of the American West.

104. See Franchot, *Roads to Rome*.

105. Boynton, *Oration*, 19.

106. Beecher, *Plea for the West*, 60; Boynton, *Oration*, 11.

107. Boynton, *Oration*, 22.

108. Lamott, *History of the Archdiocese of Cincinnati*, 247–48. For confirmation that this was the same property, compare Lamott with the address for the "Western Female

Institute" listed in *Cincinnati Directory for the Years 1836–37*. The Sisters of Charity school, called "St. Peter's Orphan Asylum and Free School," is briefly described in *Catholic Almanac* (1846), 98, in *ACD*.

109. Boynton, *Oration*, 22–23.

110. Billington's survey of anti-Catholic thought and literature, *Protestant Crusade*, mainly relied on material published in Boston, New York, Philadelphia, and Baltimore. According to the historian Bryan Le Beau, "anti-Catholic activity was less pronounced and less violent in the West than in the East." Le Beau, "Saving the West from the Pope," 112.

111. Kelso, *Danger in the Dark*. The thirty-first edition was also published in Cincinnati, by H. M. Rulison, in 1855.

112. A Presbyter, *Weighed in the Balance*, 79.

113. Elliott, *Delineation of Roman Catholicism*, 1:5, 303.

114. *Louisville Journal*, August 5, 1855, quoted in Crews, *American Holy Land*, 143.

115. *Louisville Journal*, August 6, 1855, quoted in Baldwin, "George D. Prentice," 490. According to Baldwin, Prentice may not have caused the riots, but his inflammatory rhetoric was "irresponsible." See 494. Betty Congleton argued that Prentice was a political opportunist in his anti-Catholicism, but not a true advocate of its prejudices. See Congleton, "George D. Prentice and Bloody Monday."

116. On May 20, 1852, Unterthiner wrote to Venantius of Celano, "It is true that the religious habit cannot be worn outside the house because it would do more harm than good. But we do wear it at home and in the church and at all the services." Wuest, *Materials for a History*, 4:57.

117. Fr. Unterthiner to Fr. Arbogast Schopf, July 23–26, 1844, McCloskey, *Letters . . . (1844–46)*, 47.

118. Archbishop John B. Purcell to Archbishop Francis Patrick Kenrick, Baltimore, Baltimore Cathedral Archives, 31 C 13, quoted in McGann, *Nativism in Kentucky*, 55. McGann does not provide a date for this letter.

119. Marianne Reilly, journal, April 3, 1853, Archives of the Archdiocese of Cincinnati.

120. Dannenbaum, *Drink and Disorder*, 158. For a fuller discussion of Bedini's troubled visit to the United States, see Anbinder, *Nativism and Slavery*, 27–30.

121. Dannenbaum, *Drink and Disorder*, 158; Stritch, "Nativism in Cincinnati," 45.

122. Dannenbaum, *Drink and Disorder*, 158.

123. Anbinder, *Nativism and Slavery*, 29.

124. For a survey of "ethnic rioting" between 1800 and 1860, see Gilje, *Rioting in America*, 64–69.

125. *Louisville Journal*, August 8, 1855, quoted in McGann, *Nativism in Kentucky*, 94. For a chronology of events during the course of the riot, see ibid., 92–98. See also Crews, *American Holy Land*, 144–45.

126. Gienapp, *Origins of the Republican Party*, 56–58. In the 1852 elections, the Free Soil Party only carried 1 percent of the vote in Cincinnati. See Dannenbaum, *Drink and Disorder*, 110.

127. James C. Klotter, "Whig Party," in Kleber, *Encyclopedia of Louisville*, 936–37. Also, Burckin, "Formation and Growth of an Urban Middle Class," 495, 505. J. Stoddard Johnston, "Political History of Louisville," in Johnston, *Memorial History of Louisville*, 1:130.

128. Dannenbaum, *Drink and Disorder*, 106–8.

129. "James Stephens Speed," in Kleber, *Encyclopedia of Louisville*, 843.

130. For a detailed account of this brief alliance, see Dannenbaum, *Drink and Disorder*, 157–66.

131. Anbinder, *Nativism and Slavery*, 103–26.

132. Stritch, "Nativism in Cincinnati," 49–53.

133. Dannenbaum, *Drink and Disorder*, 166.

134. Rhonda Abner, "Know-Nothing Party," in Kleber, *Encyclopedia of Louisville*, 487–88.

Chapter Two

1. Studies exploring these similarities and attractions include Smith, *Gothic Arches, Latin Crosses*; Franchot, *Roads to Rome*; Dolan, *Catholic Revivalism*.

2. Hatch, *Democratization of American Christianity*, 133–39.

3. Dolan, *Catholic Revivalism*, 203.

4. Trollope, *Domestic Manners*, 71. For extended discussion of these revivals, see Ford, "Beyond Cane Ridge."

5. Mahan, *Autobiography*, 215.

6. Gaddis, *Foot-Prints*, 246.

7. Church association records provide membership statistics. The following Baptist, Methodist, and Presbyterian records were consulted: Long Run Association (Kentucky), *Minutes* (1815–1860); Miami Baptist Association (Ohio), *Minutes* (1820–1836); Miami Association of Regular Baptists (Ohio), *Minutes* (1837–1860); Regular Baptist Churches of Color, *Minutes* (1837 and 1840); Methodist Episcopal Church, *Minutes* (1820–1860); Methodist Episcopal Church, South, *Minutes* (1845–1860); General Assembly of the Presbyterian Church in the USA, *Minutes* (1821–1837); General Assembly of the Presbyterian Church in the USA (Old School), *Minutes* (1838–1860); General Assembly of the Presbyterian Church in the USA (New School), *Minutes* (1838–1860). Because of the split in the Presbyterian Church, membership statistics for Cincinnati and Louisville are spotty in official minutes. I therefore relied on additional sources, including the Presbytery of Cincinnati and the Ministerial Association of Cincinnati, *Presbyterianism in Cincinnati: Its History, Position and Duty.*

8. Ninth Street Baptist Church, *Semi-Centennial*, 15.

9. Gaddis, *Foot-Prints*, 252.

10. Maffitt, *Pulpit Sketches, First Series*, 26, 30–31.

11. Gaddis, *Foot-Prints*, 242–44, 246.

12. Ibid., 251–52.

13. Wesley Chapel Methodist Church (Cincinnati), Member Records, Book One, 1834–1867, microfilm 1987643. Church clerks maintained four separate membership

lists during the period under consideration for this study: (1) 1834–44, (2) 1845–50, (3) 1851–52, and (4) 1859–61. These lists provide the member's name, along with the date on which the member was either "received into full connection" (indicating a conversion experience and a six-month probation period) or "received by certificate" (from another Methodist church). The 428 members noted here were "received into full connection" in July 1840 after their probationary period. These particular church membership lists do not indicate the names of those who converted during the revival but then failed to meet the requirements of the six-month probationary period. Given anecdotal evidence from Gaddis, however, it would seem likely that many more claimed to be converted at the height of the revival than actually joined Wesley Chapel six months later.

14. Gaddis, *Foot-Prints*, 272, 275, 281.

15. Crawford, *Seasons of Grace*, 81–90; Brekus, *Strangers and Pilgrims*, 36–44. On historians' debates over the legitimacy of the label "Great Awakening," see Jon Butler, "Enthusiasm Described and Decried," and Lambert, *Inventing the "Great Awakening."* For an alternative interpretation stressing religious pluralism and institutional authority, not revivalism, in the eighteenth century, see Jon Butler, *Awash in a Sea of Faith*, 98–128, 164–93.

16. Isaac Watts, "The Inward Witness of Christianity" (1721), in Crawford, *Seasons of Grace*, 89.

17. Crawford, *Seasons of Grace*, 97.

18. Hatch, *Democratization of American Christianity*, 134–35 and 133–40.

19. Dichtl, *Frontiers of Faith*, 181–84.

20. Spalding, *Sketches of the Early Catholic Missions of Kentucky*, 250.

21. Dolan, *Catholic Revivalism*, 16–17; M. J. Spalding, "Biographical Notice of the Right Rev. John B. David, Bishop of Mauricastrum," in David, *Spiritual Retreat*, 12, 14–15.

22. Spalding, "Biographical Notice," 12–13.

23. Ibid., 16–17.

24. Dolan, *Catholic Revivalism*, 17–18.

25. Quoted in Webb, *Centenary of Catholicity*, 105.

26. Webb, *Centenary of Catholicity*, 149. On Abell's early speaking gifts, see 108–9.

27. Ibid., 148, 270–71, 300–302, 317, 306, 507.

28. Ibid., 105, 301, 316–17.

29. While Webb was nurtured in the Catholic Church from his birth in Bardstown in 1814, his family's connections to Catholicism were somewhat tangled: His father, Nehemiah, converted to Catholicism (rejecting his parents' Quakerism) at the age of eighteen and married into a prominent Protestant clan in Kentucky, the Waller family of Cartwright's Creek. This first wife of Nehemiah became a convert to Catholicism upon her marriage, a "match . . . bitterly opposed by the father from motives of pure bigotry," while Benedict's mother, his father's third wife, was born into a Catholic family from Maryland. See Webb, *Centenary of Catholicity*, 59, 69, 201. So although Webb's attachment to the Catholic Church remained firm through his lifetime, his family's roots in the church were arguably shallow.

30. Ibid., 307–8.

31. Ibid., 295, 316–18, 395–96, 477, 560.

32. Ibid., 514, 535.

33. William Unterthiner to Schopf, May 9, 1845, in McCloskey, "Letters . . . (1844–46)," 117–18.

34. Ibid., 118.

35. See Smith, *Gothic Arches, Latin Crosses*, 9–10.

36. Francis Huber to Joseph Mary Maniscalco, July 2, 1840, in Wuest, *Materials for a History*, 4:3.

37. Miller, *Experience of German Methodist Preachers*, 65, 84, 79–80, 87, 65.

38. Nast to Rev. N. Callender, April 22, 1839, MSS 873, Box 3-63, Folder 2, Nippert Collection; *Minutes of the Annual Conferences of the Methodist Episcopal Church* (1837), 499; ibid. (1838), 584.

39. Nast quoted in Miller, *Experience of German Methodist Preachers*, 422–26.

40. *Minutes of the Annual Conferences* (1864), 157–59; ibid. (1865), 177–80.

41. Charles Elliott, "Introduction," in Miller, *Experience of German Methodist Preachers*, 5–9. William Nast worried about the "prejudice of the Emigrants against the M.E. Church," and hoped his work in the press would allow that prejudice to be "torn down." Nast to Rev. N. Callender, April 22, 1839.

42. Miller, *Experience of German Methodist Preachers*, 112–13.

43. Ibid., 292–93.

44. Ibid., 388.

45. Nast to Rev. N. Callender, May 31, 1839; July 9, 1839, MSS 873, Box 3–63, Folder 2, Nippert Collection.

46. Nast to Rev. N. Callender, May 31, 1839.

47. Miller, *Experience of German Methodist Preachers*, 121–22, 225–26, 249, 292, 329.

48. George H. Buck, "Class Book of the First German Society of Episcopal Methodists formed in the city of Cincinnati" (1835), MSS 873, Box 3–55, Folder 17, Nippert Collection.

49. Miller, *Experience of German Methodist Preachers*, 232, 104, 325.

50. Buck, "Class Book of the First German Society"; Miller, *Experience of German Methodist Preachers*, 232.

51. Robson, *Franciscans in the Middle Ages*, 19.

52. Ibid., 1, 18, 48–51.

53. Roemer, *Ludwig-Missionsverein*, 81–83; McCloskey, "Letters . . . (1844–46)," 17.

54. Salzbacher quoted in Roemer, *Ludwig-Missionsverein*, 43.

55. McCloskey, "Letters . . . (1844–46)," 10–12.

56. Ibid., 181–82.

57. *Catholic Telegraph*, January 24, 1857, cited in McCloskey, *1846–54 Letters*, 188.

58. Francis of Jerome Holzer to John Capistran Sojer, November 15, 1857, in Wuest, *Materials for a History*, 2:113.

59. Unterthiner to Lucas Rauth, August 1, 1850, in McCloskey, *1846–54 Letters*, 86.

60. Unterthiner to Schopf, April 1845, in McCloskey, "Letters . . . (1844–46)," 79.

61. Unterthiner to [Arbogast?] Schopf, November 29, 1844, in ibid., 62.

62. Unterthiner to Arbogast Schöpf, June 24, 1851, in McCloskey, *1846–54 Letters*, 115; Unterthiner to Lucas Rauth, August 1, 1850, in ibid., 86.

63. Unterthiner to Joseph Cupertino Friedl, May 17, 1852, in ibid., 134; Unterthiner to Venantius of Celano, May 20, 1852, in Wuest, *Materials for a History*, 4:57–58.

64. As examples, while on missions and conducting parish business, the friars wanted to wear "linen undertunic[s]" and "femoralia" with their distinctive habits, along with shoes. Outside the churches and residences, the men sometimes wore "entirely secular clothes which are proper to priests," to avoid inviting violence or harm. See Unterthiner et al., "Rules for Religious Life," July 10, 1850, in McCloskey, *1846–54 Letters*, 83. Traveling in the United States also placed a particular strain on Franciscan rules against handling money, riding horseback, eating meat, and fasting. Unlike in Europe, it proved impossible for the friars to move about without money, begging for "support of life," and because American roadways were often "impassable on foot, at one time because of dust, at other times because of mud," the men wanted to ride horses on their missions. And Americans' "custom of eating meat and other by no means light" foods led the friars to relax rules about avoiding heavy fare, and long trips into rural settlements made fasting too wearying for the friars, who wanted to "remain freed from the obligation" where "the danger of scandal is absent." See "Municipal Statutes of the Custody of St. John the Baptist, United States, North America, August 1, 1859," in Wuest, *Materials for a History*, 4:98; and Unterthiner et al., "Rules for Religious Life," 82.

65. Antonio da Rignano to Monsignor D. Alessandro Barnabo, June 15, 1852, in Wuest, *Materials for a History*, 4:60.

66. John B. Purcell to Bernardine Trionfetti, September 8, 1858, in ibid., 4:68.

67. McCloskey, *1846–54 Letters*, 11; Mentag, "Catholic Spiritual Revivals," 33.

68. Unterthiner to Joseph Cupertino Friedl, December 31, 1851, in McCloskey, *1846–54 Letters*, 120; Unterthiner to Arbogast Schöpf, June 24, 1851, in ibid., 116.

69. Unterthiner to [Arbogast?] Schopf, May 9, 1845, in McCloskey, "Letters . . . (1844–46)," 112.

70. Unterthiner to Lucas Rauth, November 17, 1845, in McCloskey, "Letters . . . (1844–46)," 147–48. See 1 Corinthians 1:19–22.

71. 1 Corinthians 1:23; Unterthiner to [Arbogast?] Schopf, July 23–26, 1844, in McCloskey, "Letters . . . (1844–46)," 53.

72. See Unterthiner and Edmund Etschmann to Lucas Rauth, May 29, 1847, section of letter labeled "Private Information," in McCloskey, *1846–54 Letters*, 38; Unterthiner to Lucas Rauth, November 17, 1845, in McCloskey, "Letters . . . (1844–46)," 147.

73. Unterthiner to Joseph Cupertino Friedl, May 17, 1852, in McCloskey, *1846–54 Letters*, 136; Unterthiner to Lucas Rauth, May 17, 1850, in ibid., 75.

74. Unterthiner to Lucas Rauth, November 15, 1849, in ibid., 67–68; Unterthiner to Joseph Cupertino Friedl, May 17, 1852, in ibid., 136.

75. Unterthiner and Edmund Etschmann to Aloysius of Loreto, August 23, 1847, in McCloskey, *1846–54 Letters*, 43; Unterthiner and Edmund Etschmann to Lucas Rauth, May 29, 1847, in ibid., 35.

76. Unterthiner to Lucas Rauth, January 9–13, 1846, in McCloskey, "Letters . . . (1844–46)," 166; Unterthiner to Definitor Marcus Vergeiner, April 10, 1854, in McCloskey, *1846–54 Letters,* 159.

77. Arsacius Wieser to Lucas Rauth, undated, in Wuest, *Materials for a History,* 2:178. McCloskey suggests that Wieser wrote the letter sometime between February 1846 and September 1846. See 2:195n1.

78. David Widmann to Joseph C. Friedl, April 27, 1853, in ibid., 2:53.

79. John B. Purcell to [Arbogast?] Schopf, December 17, 1844, in McCloskey, "Letters . . . (1844–46)," 73.

80. Unterthiner to Lucas Rauth, January 12, 1848, in McCloskey, *1846–54 Letters,* 50; Widmann to Friedl, April 27, 1853, in Wuest, *Materials for a History,* 2:53. Easter attendance figures may be found in Unterthiner and Edmund Etschmann to Lucas Rauth, May 29, 1847, in McCloskey, *1846–54 Letters,* 35–36.

81. Unterthiner to Lucas Rauth, November 17, 1845, in McCloskey, "Letters . . . (1844–46)," 155.

82. David Widmann to Joseph C. Friedl, September 9, 1855, in Wuest, *Materials for a History,* 2:73–74. On Unterthiner's style, see also McCloskey, "Letters . . . (1844–46)," 182.

83. See appendix 2, "Missionaries from the Province of St. Leopold," in Wuest, *Materials for a History,* 2:197–200; *American Catholic Directory* (1855), 113, 137–39.

84. *Catholic Telegraph,* September 25, 1841; Mentag, "Catholic Spiritual Revivals," 51.

85. Mentag, "Catholic Spiritual Revivals," 62, 168–70.

86. Dolan, *Catholic Revivalism,* 105.

87. *Catholic Telegraph,* December 7, 1861, quoted in Mentag, "Catholic Spiritual Revivals," viii; 136.

88. Arnold Damen to [Father General], June 12, 1863, quoted in Conroy, *Arnold Damen,* 227.

89. Conroy, *Arnold Damen,* 226, 49, 208.

90. Ibid., 208, 225; Mentag, "Catholic Spiritual Revivals," 252.

91. *American Catholic Directory* (1945), 184; *American Catholic Directory* (1860), 64, 163; DeBow, *Seventh Census,* 875–76; Statistics of the United States, 443, 445.

92. "A Day with the Catholics," *Ladies' Repository* 7 (September 1847): 281.

93. On Baptists' countercultural status in the South, see Isaac, *Transformation of Virginia.*

94. Trollope, *Domestic Manners,* 51–52.

95. Louisville's first Catholic chapel, constructed in 1811, was also "in the Gothic style, but small and plain." Otis, *Louisville Directory,* 140.

96. Bushman, *Refinement of America,* 313, 335–49.

97. Lamott, *History of the Archdiocese of Cincinnati,* 185–86.

98. A city guide later declared Murillo's work "one of the chief glories of art in America." Kenny, *Illustrated Cincinnati,* 102.

99. "Ohio," *U. S. Catholic Miscellany* 7, May 3, 1828, 342–43, quoted in Lamott, *History of the Archdiocese of Cincinnati,* 60–61.

100. Otis, *Louisville Directory*, 139, quoted in Crews, *Presence and Possibility*, 21. According to several sources, no illustration of this church exists today.

101. Crews, *Presence and Possibility*, 38.

102. Cist, *Cincinnati in 1851*, 326; Kenny, *Illustrated Cincinnati*, 101.

103. Cist, *Cincinnati in 1851*, 326; Williams, *Houses of God*, 161. See also Clubbe, *Cincinnati Observed*, 49.

104. Kenny, *Illustrated Cincinnati*, 102. Cist, *Cincinnati in 1851*, 326–27.

105. Crews, *Presence and Possibility*, 38–39.

106. Lamott, *History of the Archdiocese of Cincinnati*, 37.

107. Yet Catholics had half as many churches as the Methodists and Presbyterians, denominations with the first- and second-largest numbers of churches in the county, respectively. See DeBow, *Seventh Census*, 875–76.

108. "Churches in Kentucky," *Statistics of the United States . . . in 1860*, 395–400.

109. Franchot's *Roads to Rome* provides the most comprehensive study of this Protestant fascination with Catholicism. On the appeal of Catholic church architecture for Protestants, see Ryan K. Smith, "Cross: Church Symbol and Contest," 716–17, and Smith, *Gothic Arches, Latin Crosses*.

110. John Brown, Louisville, to William N. Brown, October 20, 1821, copy in Brown, Diary. For further discussion of Brown's impressions, see Dichtl, "She stalks abroad," 347–73.

111. "A Day with the Catholics," 281–83.

112. "Trinity Methodist Episcopal Church, Cincinnati," *Ladies' Repository* 19 (November 1859): 694.

113. Clark, *Temple Built*, 5, 8.

114. Eaton, *History of the Walnut Street Baptist Church*, 11.

115. Kimbrough, *History of the Walnut Street Baptist Church*, 85.

116. Eaton, *History of the Walnut Street Baptist Church*, 11.

117. Kimbrough, *History of the Walnut Street Baptist Church*, 82, 85.

118. Eaton, *History of the Walnut Street Baptist Church*, 12, 14.

119. Everts, *Bethel*, 159, 161.

120. Ibid., 161; Matthew 25:40 (KJV).

121. Edward B. Stevens, MD, "The Government of Taste," *Ladies' Repository* 7 (October 1847): 301. These ministers and medical doctors were not original thinkers; rather, they popularized the works of Francis Hutcheson, Edmund Burke, and John Ruskin, among others.

122. Rev. T. M. Griffith, "Loving the Beautiful," *Ladies' Repository* 25 (September 1865): 556.

123. Professor R. C. Merrick, "The Beautiful," *Ladies' Repository* 11 (May 1873): 378.

124. Rev. Joseph Alden, "Culture of Our Emotive Nature," *Ladies' Repository* 7 (March 1871): 176.

125. Griffith, "Loving the Beautiful," 557.

126. Ibid.

127. Stevens, "Government of Taste," 302.

128. "Church Architecture; Or, the Duty of Man to Consecrate His Best Works to the Service of God," *Ladies' Repository* 16, no. 11 (November 1856): 690.

129. Clark, *Temple Built*, 15.

130. Everts, *Bethel*, 36–37.

131. Ibid., 144, 140, 143, 183.

132. Ibid., 41, 112.

133. Clark, *Temple Built*, 16, 13.

134. Ibid., 12, 14.

135. Among black Americans in antebellum Cincinnati and Louisville, church-building therefore acquired significance as a symbolic manifestation of the Exodus story. See Raboteau, *A Fire in the Bones*, 17–36.

136. B. W. Arnett, "Historical and Semi-Centennial Address, Delivered in Allen Temple A. M. E. Church . . . ," in Arnett, *Semi-Centenary Celebration*, 18, 19, 24. Arnett may have delivered this historical address with the Rev. Daniel Alexander Payne's discriminating tastes in mind, for Payne—a chief architect of the African Methodist Episcopal Church's campaign for respectability—was in attendance at Allen Temple's semi-centenary celebration. For more on Payne, see Walker, *Rock in a Weary Land*, 21–24.

137. Arnett, "Historical and Semi-Centennial Address," 20–23.

138. Ibid., 23–24.

139. Sketches of all the congregation's meeting places may be found Allen Temple AME Church, *Centennial Guide*, 13, 15, 21.

140. Arnett, "Historical and Semi-Centennial Address," 23–24.

141. Ibid., 24. The passage is probably from Ps. 28:7.

142. Long Run Association, *Minutes* (1839), 291; Weeden, *Weeden's History*, 38–39.

143. Weeden, *Weeden's History*, 39; Minutes of the Fifth Street Baptist Church, September 28, 1842.

144. Minutes of the Fifth Street Baptist Church, July 23, 1843, September 24, 1843, September 25, 1843, March 24, 1844, March 1845.

145. Weeden, *Weeden's History*, 39; Gibson, "Semi-Centennial of the Public Career," 19.

146. Minutes of the Fifth Street Baptist Church, June 8, 1853.

147. Long Run Association, *Minutes* (1858), 15.

148. Ibid., 122.

Chapter Three

1. Perrin, "Mysticism," 442–58.

2. Taves, *Household of Faith*, 81.

3. David, *Spiritual Retreat*, iii, vi, 53, 248–49.

4. Dolan, *Catholic Revivalism*, 218–19.

5. David, *Spiritual Retreat*, vi, 40, 36.

6. Hambrick-Stowe, *Practice of Piety*, 30–31.

7. David, *Spiritual Retreat*, 224–29, 240. Morgan, *Visual Piety*, 62–71. It is not clear when Catholics in the Ohio River valley may have seen a visual representation of the Passion, or the Stations of the Cross. In 1852, the Franciscan priest William Unterthiner requested of his Roman superiors that the friars in the Ohio River valley be able "to attach the indulgences of the Way of the Cross to the crucifix since this is really necessary," suggesting that a crucifix substituted for a proper physical representation of the fourteen stations making up the Way of the Cross. Unterthiner to the Minister General, Venantius of Celano, May 20, 1852, in McCloskey, *1846–54 Letters*, 144. As Morgan argues in *Visual Piety*, Catholic devotionalism from the late medieval until the modern era relied heavily on visual representations of the Passion and the bodily sufferings of Christ, which were intended to invite viewers' empathy. But in the absence of such art, devotional literature such as that published in Cincinnati and Louisville relied on textual descriptions of the Passion rather than visual representations.

8. David, *Spiritual Retreat*, 249, 270, 257. See "The Affective Bond," in Taves, *Household of Faith*, 71–87.

9. David, *Spiritual Retreat*, 79–80. For David's appointment as "coadjutor," see Spalding, *Sketches*, 246–48.

10. Citations here will be to the New York edition. The 1863 Cincinnati edition was published by John P. Walsh.

11. Weninger, *Sacred Heart*, 2, 6; Hambrick-Stowe, *Practice of Piety*, 23.

12. Weninger, *Sacred Heart*, 11, 20, 30, 187, 103, 113–16; Wiethaus, "Christian Spirituality," 115.

13. Weninger, *Sacred Heart*, 12, 211–13, 285; Wiethaus, "Christian Spirituality," 115.

14. Dolan, *Catholic Revivalism*, 94.

15. Taves, *Household of Faith*, 88, and elsewhere.

16. See Hambrick-Stowe, *Practice of Piety*.

17. Taves, *Household of Faith*, 6, 89–102, 114–18.

18. For commonalities between Catholic and Protestant devotionalism during the seventeenth century, see Hambrick-Stowe, *Practice of Piety*.

19. Morgan, *Visual Piety*, 65–66, 74–77, 87; Fox, *Jesus in America*, 12–13, 226–30. A helpful overview of the complex questions surrounding the Reformation's impact on the arts may be found in Hart, "Protestantism and the Arts," 268–86.

20. Hart, "Protestantism and the Arts," 278, 281.

21. Hall, "Readers and Writers," 146.

22. Ibid., 142, 147–48. As a result, London publishers and British patrons brought out the first editions of Anne Bradstreet's *The Tenth Muse Lately Sprung up in America* (1650) and Phillis Wheatley's *Poems on Various Subjects, Religious and Moral* (1773). Written in an epic rather than meditative style, Michael Wigglesworth's *The Day of Doom* (Cambridge, 1662) was a popular exception. Hall, "Readers and Writers," 147–51. See also Shields, "Eighteenth-Century Literary Culture," 471; and Reilly and Hall, "Customers and the Market for Books," 387.

23. Hambrick-Stowe, *Early New England Meditative Poetry*, 53, 158. Taylor's poetry would not appear in print until the twentieth century. Hall, "Readers and Writers,"

145–46. See also Reilly and Hall, "Customers and the Market for Books," 387–99; and Hall and Martin, "Note on Popular and Durable Authors and Titles," 519–21.

24. Martz, *Poetry of Meditation*, 6, 13. Barbara Kiefer Lewalski downplays this influence in favor of "contemporary, English, and Protestant" poetic influences. See Lewalski, *Protestant Poetics*, 5. The differences in Martz's and Lewalski's arguments might stem from their selection of poets. Lewalski considers the poetry of Donne, Herbert, Vaughan, Traherne, and Taylor, but not Crashaw or Southwell. For recent reiteration of Martz's argument, see Hambrick-Stowe, "Introduction," in *Early New England Meditative Poetry*, 7–62.

25. Martz, *Poetry of Meditation*, 3, 5–6.

26. Hall, "Readers and Writers," 142–44.

27. "The Preface," *The Whole Booke of Psalmes Faithfully Translated into English Metre*. In the online World Digital Library edition used here, this passage appears on page 11, at the conclusion of "The Preface." The original volume cited here is unpaginated.

28. Jantz's *Bibliography of Early New England Verse* lists the names of 169 known poets (found either in print or in manuscript), 96 of whom were pastors. Merchants, government officials, physicians, schoolmasters and teachers, and booksellers and printers also wrote poetry. These authors generally wrote public elegies, the most popular form of verse in seventeenth-century New England. While religious, the public elegy was not considered a form of meditational or devotional verse. Jantz, *First Century of New England Verse*, 175–286. On the prominence of Harvard-educated men among Jantz's list of elegists, see Shields, *Civil Tongues*, 220.

29. Some authors did attempt to yoke evangelical Christianity to neoclassical poetry. Shields, *Civil Tongues*, 219–43, esp. 236, where he discusses the "tensions" and "contradictions" involved in "Christian belletrism." See also Shields, "Eighteenth-Century Literary Culture," 442–43, 447–49.

30. Venable, *Beginnings of Literary Culture*, 269, 275–76, 272; Coyle, *Ohio Authors*, 491.

31. For a definition of sentimentalism, I have relied on Dobson, "Reclaiming Sentimental Literature." Dobson defines literary sentimentalism as "an emotional and philosophical ethos that celebrates human connection, both personal and communal, and acknowledges the shared devastation of affectional loss. . . . Sentimentalism envisions the self-in-relation; family (not necessarily in the conventional biological sense), intimacy, community, and social responsibility are its primary relational modes." Ibid., 266–67. Halttunen discusses the "crisis in social relations" that gave rise to sentimentality in *Confidence Men and Painted Women*, 51–55.

32. Piatt, "Biographical Sketch," in Prentice, *Poems*, xxii.

33. Mrs. Mary E. Nealy, "M. Louisa Chitwood," *Ladies' Repository* 9 (January 1872): 58. George Prentice edited Chitwood's poetry for publication before the Civil War. See Chitwood, *Poems*.

34. *Western Christian Advocate*, June 30, 1843, July 7, 1843, and August 4, 1843.

35. Bennett, *Nineteenth-Century American Women Poets*, 95–96.

36. Davis Wasgatt Clark, "Literary Women of America: Alice Cary," *Ladies' Repository* 15 (August 1855): 449–51.

37. C. P. Blaire to Davis Wasgatt Clark, November 2, 1856; May 15, 1857; and September 16, 1857, Davis Wasgatt Clark Papers.

38. Biographical note, Clark Papers.

39. Kete, *Sentimental Collaborations*, 25.

40. In this case, the editor referred to Rev. John Pierpont's poem "My Child," reprinted in the *Nashville Christian Advocate*, December 2, 1858.

41. John F. Jefferson, "Summer," *Nashville Christian Advocate*, July 23, 1857.

42. Anne C. Rose argues that "Victorians fell back on a few simple religious truths to circumvent the hard task of adapting traditional Christian doctrines to a changing world." Rose, *Victorian America and the Civil War*, 52. While nineteenth-century Protestant poets generally dwelled on core Christian themes, they did so in novel and intellectually ambitious ways. They also confronted the problem of religious doubt. See Kete, *Sentimental Collaborations*, 5–6, 32, 182.

43. Lewalski, *Protestant Poetics*, 39, 253, 4–5.

44. Watts, *Psalms of David*, 6.

45. Lowth's Oxford lectures were originally published in Latin in 1753. An English translation first appeared in 1787. Lowth, *Lectures*, xv. All subsequent citations are to this edition.

46. Stowe, "Preface," in Lowth, *Lectures*, iv–v, xvi.

47. Hedrick, *Harriet Beecher Stowe*, 96.

48. Lowth, *Lectures*, 156–57, 29, 15, 28, 27.

49. Ibid., 22, 13.

50. Shriver, "Romantic Religion," 1103.

51. Standard studies of "romanticism" include Ahlstrom, *Religious History of the American People*, 583–614; Reardon, *Religion in the Age of Romanticism*; Chai, *Romantic Foundations*; and Abrams, *Natural Supernaturalism*. On the relationship between Methodism and Romanticism, see Prickett, *Romantics*, 115–63. On British romantic poetry and its religious aspects, see Ryan, *Romantic Reformation*. On romanticism and American poetry, see New, *Regenerate Lyric*. Kete examines the "articulation of a particularly American expression of romanticism" in *Sentimental Collaborations*, 26, 14–30, passim.

52. Robert Ryan writes: "One has little difficulty accumulating evidence of this tendency of the Romantic poets to ordain themselves ministers of the world, charged with the task of bringing the means of redemption to a community that had lost its way morally and spiritually." Ryan, *Romantic Reformation*, 37.

53. On the close relationship between romanticism and sentimentality in the American context, see Kete, *Sentimental Collaborations*, xiv.

54. Herder, *Spirit of Hebrew Poetry*, 2:6–7; Herder, "Author's Preface," in ibid., 1:22. According to Herder, the "giving vent to [human] feeling" constituted "the spirit of the Hebrew language." Ibid., 1:35. Many historians and literary critics view James Marsh, the translator of Herder's work, as a crucial figure in the introduction of German romanticism to American readers, especially the Transcendentalists. Rejecting Unitarianism, Marsh himself remained orthodox in his religious views. See Ahlstrom,

Religious History, 599–600; Gura, *Wisdom of Words,* 39–51; and Bratt, "Reorientation of American Protestantism," 68.

55. Herder, *Spirit of Hebrew Poetry,* 2:12, 7–8.

56. George Waterman Jr., "The First Psalm," *Ladies' Repository* 3 (December 1843): 371.

57. Ibid., 371–73. The following citations are from *The Ladies' Repository*: "Hebrew Minstrelsy" 4 (December 1844): 362–63; Professor Waterman, "Poetry of the Hebrews" 7 (February 1847): 36–39; Rev. L. D. Stebins, "Hebrew Literature" 11 (June 1851): 217–19; Lewis Freeman, "An Essay on Ancient Poetry" 19 (May 1859): 280–81; Henry Craik, "Leading Characteristics of the Hebrew Language" 21 (February 1861): 81–85; [J. G. Herder], "Hebrew Poetry. From the 'Spirit of Hebrew Poetry' " 27 (September 1867): 524–25.

58. Rev. B. F. Tefft, "Holiness," *Ladies' Repository* 6 (October 1846): 301.

59. Stebins, "Hebrew Literature," 217.

60. Perkins, quoted in Coggeshall, *Poets and Poetry,* 157.

61. Perkins, quoted in ibid.; Prentice, quoted in Wilson, *Poems by Lizzie,* 33.

62. Griffith, "To J. R. Barrick," in *Poems, By Mattie Griffith,* 121.

63. Eulalie, "Stanzas—To My Young Poet Friend," in *Buds, Blossoms, and Leaves,* 87. Her preface is signed "Eulalie, Cincinnati, June, 1854."

64. Benjamin T. Cushing, "The Poet," in Coggeshall, *Poets and Poetry of the West,* 494–95.

65. George D. Prentice to Miss M. E. Wilson, May 14, 1852, Prentice Papers.

66. William D. Gallagher, "Amelia's Poems; Or, the Western Poetess, Mrs. Amelia B. Welby. Biographical Sketch," in *Gems of Poetry,* 45.

67. Dyer, *Voices of Nature,* 145.

68. "Frances Dana Gage," in Coggeshall, *Poets and Poetry of the West,* 393; Davis Wasgatt Clark, "Literary Women of America. No. VI," *Ladies' Repository* 15 (September 1855): 558.

69. "Amelia Welby," in Coggeshall, *Poets and Poetry of the West,* 209.

70. Venable, *Beginnings of Literary Culture,* 480.

71. In 1860, William Coggeshall wrote that Coates Kinney's poetry "seems not to have been labored at all, but to have come itself, like a shower in April, or to have grown wild, like blossoms in the woods." Coggeshall, *Poets and Poetry of the West,* 528. Coates Kinney was a prominent male poet in Cincinnati.

72. See, for example, Griswold, *Female Poets of America,* 372.

73. Sherman, *Invisible Poets,* 36. See J. C. Mc Simpson, "A Voice from Jamaica on the First of August," *North Star,* July 28, 1848; and J. Mac C. Simpson, "The Slaveholder's Rest," *North Star,* December 7, 1849. Simpson's name appears in several variations.

74. For evidence of the regular smuggling of Douglass's paper into Louisville, see Gibson, "Semi-Centennial of the Public Career," 33–34.

75. "Emancipation Celebration," *Frederick Douglass' Paper,* August 18, 1854. Information about Rev. Wallace Shelton may be found in Page, *History of the Union Baptist*

Church, 9–10. After the Civil War, at an 1866 meeting of the Equal Rights State League in Columbus, Ohio, several prominent black advocates from Cincinnati, including Peter H. Clark, heard Simpson sing his poem, "Let the Banner Proudly Wave." "Every person in the house seemed to appreciate the sentiment of this verse," a reporter wrote. "A Letter from Columbus, O.," *Christian Recorder,* February 10, 1866.

76. Simpson, "Note to the Public," in *Emancipation Car,* VI. Under a Zanesville, Ohio, imprint, a book of Simpson's poetry appeared sometime in the late 1840s or early 1850s. Sherman, *Invisible Poets,* 36.

77. Sherman, *Invisible Poets,* 36. Harriet Beecher Stowe, "Sojourner Truth, the Libyan Sibyl," *Atlantic Monthly* 11 (April 1863): 479. A brief discussion of Truth's visit to Stowe's house may also be found in Hedrick, *Harriet Beecher Stowe,* 270.

78. Simpson, "Note to the Public," V, and "How I Got My Education," in *Emancipation Car,* 132–33.

79. Simpson, "How I Got My Education," 137. On the probable links between the Ohio Female Anti-Slavery Society and the Ohio Ladies' Education Society (both based in Cincinnati) and the "Big Bottom" abolition school, see Ohio Female Anti-Slavery Society [Mr. Barber, Agent], "Report on the Condition of the Colored People in Ohio," *Philanthropist,* July 14, 1840; and Ohio Ladies' Education Society, "Second Annual Report of the Ladies' Education Society," *Philanthropist,* June 22, 1842. Simpson wrote his first poem, "Hail Thou Sweet and Welcome Day," for an 1842 exhibition held at the Big Bottom school. Simpson, "Note to the Public," IV.

80. Simpson, "Note to the Public," III–V; Simpson, "Warm Times Coming," *Emancipation Car,* 141.

81. C. P. Blair, "Poetry and Her Priests," *Ladies' Repository* 23 (December 1863): 750.

82. Welby, "Pulpit Eloquence," *Poems by Amelia,* 181. This collection was first published in 1845. See *Poems by Amelia* (Boston: A. Tompkins, 1845).

83. Phoebe Cary, "Strength of Sin," in Alice and Phoebe Carey [Cary], *Poems of Alice and Phoebe Carey* [sic], 245. Ryan Smith explains Protestants' preference for images of the cross as opposed to the bodily suffering of Christ. He writes that Protestant "discomfort arose from an understanding of worship as commemorating rather than reenacting Jesus's passion, as well as from traditional taboos involving raw bodily displays." Smith, "Cross: Church Symbol and Contest," 719.

84. Phoebe Cary, "Otway Curry," *Ladies' Repository* 21 (March 1861): 165.

85. Nichols, "A Vision," in *Songs of the Heart,* 138.

86. "Otway Curry," in Coggeshall, *Poets and Poetry,* 95–107. See Curry's poems, "The Eternal River," "The Better Land," "Kingdom Come," in Coggeshall, *Poets and Poetry,* 99–103.

87. Elisa New discusses these themes, found in the poetry of Hart Crane, Emily Dickinson, and Walt Whitman, in *Regenerate Lyric.*

88. H[oratio] N. Powers, "The New Birth," *Ladies' Repository* 17 (May 1857): 280.

89. See Caldwell, *Communion of the Spirit,* for a discussion of the concept of union in Jonathan Edwards's theology.

90. Bennett, "Introduction," *Nineteenth-Century American Women Poets,* xxxiv–xxxvii.

91. "To My Child," *Louisville Weekly Journal* (1850), quoted in Bennett, *Nineteenth-Century American Women Poets,* 419–20.

92. "To My Child," in Bennett, *Nineteenth-Century American Women Poets.* According to sentimentalists, Dobson writes, "human connection is the genesis, in this life, of the divine." Dobson, "Reclaiming Sentimental Literature," 266.

93. "To My Child," in Bennett, *Nineteenth-Century American Women Poets;* Dobson, "Reclaiming Sentimental Literature," 266.

94. Stebins, "Hebrew Literature," *Ladies' Repository* 11 (May 1851): 217–18.

Chapter Four

1. Frederickson, *Racism: A Short History,* 12.

2. Foner, *Free Soil,* 261–62.

3. Cayton, *Ohio: The History of a People,* 2, 6–10.

4. See Taylor, *Frontiers of Freedom,* 117–37.

5. Harrison and Klotter, *New History of Kentucky,* 174–79; Freehling, *Road to Disunion,* 464–69.

6. Harrison and Klotter, *New History of Kentucky,* 63–64, 77–79, 118.

7. Freehling, *Road to Disunion,* 465.

8. This section generally follows recent scholarship by J. Blaine Hudson for Louisville and Nikki M. Taylor for Cincinnati. See Hudson, "'Upon this Rock'" and Taylor, *Frontiers of Freedom.*

9. Horton and Flaherty, "Black Leadership in Antebellum Cincinnati," 76.

10. "Nativity of the Population of the City of Cincinnati, Ohio," in *Population of the United States in 1860,* 612.

11. Gibson, "Semi-Centennial of the Public Career," 30.

12. Ibid., 31.

13. Trotter, *River Jordan,* 29. An examination of free blacks' assistance to fugitives in Louisville may be found in Hudson, "Crossing the 'Dark Line.'"

14. Among the most famous cases is *Strader v. Graham* 51 U.S. (10 How.) 82 (1850). See Finkelman, *Slavery in the Courtroom,* 35–38. One celebrated trial in Cincinnati occurred in 1853 before the U.S. commissioner. In this case the escaped slave Lewis had been missing for three years during which time he had "been to New Orleans, and all up and down the river and at Cincinnati." When asked by a marshal "if he was not afraid his master would get him by being on the river," Lewis responded that "he was not." "Fugitive Slave Case before U.S. Commissioner Carpenter, Yesterday," newspaper clipping, n.d., in a scrapbook kept by Thomas Foraker, Cincinnati History Library and Archives. See also Middleton, "Fugitive Slave Crisis in Cincinnati," 26. Coffin, *Reminiscences of Levi Coffin,* discusses Lewis's case, as well as his own frequent use of steamboats to hide runaways. On the difficulties fugitives faced and the high rate of slaves' recapture, even on steamboats, see Franklin and Schweninger, *Runaway Slaves,* 118–19, 168. Nevertheless, steamboats seem to have been a preferred means of escape, according to Franklin and Schweninger (ibid., 133).

15. Gibson, "Semi-Centennial of the Public Career," 30–32.

16. Riley, "Negro in Cincinnati," 58, cited in Koehler, *Cincinnati's Black Peoples*, 25; Bertaux, "Structural Economic Change," 135; Burckin, appendix 7 in "Formation and Growth of an Urban Middle Class," 641–42. River work may well have been the most important labor for free blacks in Louisville, but the U.S. census did not offer separate categories for steamboat stewards, laborers, cooks, and barbers. According to Burckin's chart, 6.9 percent of free blacks in Louisville worked on steamboats. This was well below the figures for barbers and laborers, but still ranked third in numerical significance. For further anecdotal evidence about the significance of river work for western African Americans, see Malvin, *North into Freedom*, 59–62. Malvin, an African American who made his home in Cleveland, provided a firsthand account of his work on steamboats. In 1839, he served as captain of a boat plying the Ohio Canal, which connected Cleveland and Chillicothe. Of his six-person crew, three were white and three black.

17. Bertaux, "Structural Economic Change," 135–37; Burckin, appendix 8 in "Formation and Growth of an Urban Middle Class," 643.

18. Burckin, appendix 1 and appendix 12 in "Formation and Growth of an Urban Middle Class," 649–52; Koehler, *Cincinnati's Black Peoples*, 40.

19. O'Brien, "Slavery in Louisville," 45.

20. *Liberty Hall* (Cincinnati), June 28, 1825, quoted in Wade, *Urban Frontier*, 7–8.

21. Wade, "Negro in Cincinnati," 48.

22. Ibid., 50–55.

23. Walker, *Walker's Appeal*, 56. Anger over the 1829 violence also prompted black citizens to organize the first national political convention for the promotion of civil rights, held in Philadelphia in 1830. Litwack, *North of Slavery*, 235.

24. Koehler, *Cincinnati's Black Peoples*, 16, 25–26, 28, 30.

25. Burckin, "Formation and Growth of an Urban Middle Class," 168–70; Hudson, "'Upon this Rock,'" 297–99, 305.

26. The state of Kentucky never legally prohibited literacy among enslaved people. O'Brien, "Slavery in Louisville," 96, 124.

27. Ibid., 85.

28. Gibson, "Semi-Centennial of the Public Career," 36–37.

29. O'Brien, "Slavery in Louisville," 55; Burckin, "Formation and Growth of an Urban Middle Class," 171–72. On the high number of slaves hired out in Louisville, see also Eaton, "Slave-Hiring in the Upper South," 674.

30. O'Brien, "Slavery in Louisville," 51.

31. American Freedmen's Inquiry Commission Interviews, 1863, Record Group 94, National Archives, Washington, D.C., quoted in ibid., 23.

32. Wade, *Slavery in the Cities*, 48–54. See also Wade, *Urban Frontier*, 222–23.

33. Burckin, "Formation and Growth of an Urban Middle Class," 165, 199.

34. O'Brien, "Slavery in Louisville," 122–26; Hudson, "'Upon this Rock,'" 310–15.

35. Hudson, "'Upon this Rock,'" 325.

36. Quoted in Taylor, *Frontiers of Freedom*, 56.

37. Quoted in ibid., 119.

38. Ibid., 50, 64, 112.

39. Ibid., 121–25. Taylor cites the *Cincinnati Daily Gazette* (September 6, 1841) for the quote beginning with "iron six-pounder," in ibid., 121. The quote, "in malignant, Satanic triumph," may be found in Langston, *From the Virginia Plantation to the National Capital*, 66, and quoted in ibid., 123.

40. Ibid., 2, 50, 72, 105–7, 112–15.

41. Ibid., 119–26.

42. Ibid., 126, 82.

43. Bibb, *Narrative of the Life*, 83, 170. He says that he removed to Lake Erie, but does not indicate whether Detroit or another locale.

44. Wright, *Racial Violence in Kentucky*, 5.

45. Lucas, *History of Blacks in Kentucky*, 346n18. See also 84–100 for Lucas's full discussion of Kentucky's slave trade.

46. Ibid., 99.

47. "Edgar Needham Again," *Louisville Weekly Journal*, June 25, 1845. For a helpful discussion of the perceived benignity of Kentucky slavery, see Lucas, *History of Blacks in Kentucky*, 42–50.

48. "There is Progress," *Louisville Examiner*, June 19, 1847.

49. "Edgar Needham Again," *Louisville Weekly Journal*, June 25, 1845; and "Case of Edgar Needham," *Louisville Weekly Journal*, July 2, 1845.

50. "Case of Edgar Needham," *Louisville Weekly Journal*, July 2, 1845.

51. Ibid.

52. Needham, "To the Editors of the Louisville Journal," *Louisville Weekly Journal*, July 9, 1845.

53. "Difficulties," *Louisville Examiner*, August 7, 1847.

54. "How Shall They Be Overcome?," *Louisville Examiner*, August 14, 1847.

55. Ibid.

56. Bibb, *Narrative of the Life*, 15, 75, 130, 89, 147, 126.

57. Ibid., 13.

58. Ibid., 60–61, 64, 79, 86

59. Ibid., 71–72, 75–76, 79.

60. Ibid., 83, 88, 90–91.

61. Ibid., 92.

62. Ibid., 98–99.

63. Jefferson, diary entries for May 16, 1858, October 18, 1858, April 27, 1859, September 14, 1859, May 4, 1859, and March 5, 1859.

64. Jefferson, diary entries for March 15, 1858; November 5, 1858; and January 1, 1859.

65. Jefferson, diary entries for May 18–20, 1859, and September 17, 1859.

66. Jefferson, diary entries for May 21–23, 1859.

67. Observers failed to note any discrepancy between the humble cabin owned by the victims and the relatively fancy items found with Bill.

68. Baker, "Joyce Family Murders," 357–59. Also see Jefferson, diary entries for May 13–20, 1857.

69. Baker, "Joyce Family Murders," 362–63; Lucas, *History of Blacks in Kentucky*, 59–61.

70. Quoted in Baker, "Joyce Family Murders," 365, and 365–66 generally; Kleber, *Encyclopedia of Louisville*, 771

71. Quoted in Baker, "Joyce Family Murders," 370. For details of these events, see 367–71.

72. Quoted in ibid., 371–72. Also see Jefferson, diary entries for May 13–20, 1857.

73. Quoted in Baker, "Joyce Family Murders," 373–80.

74. Wright, *Racial Violence in Kentucky*, 5n6. Wright cites the date for this event as 1858, although 1857 is the correct year. Even so, it is the earliest recorded lynching in Kentucky cited by Wright, whose book provides most comprehensive study of the practice for the state.

75. Jefferson, diary entries for January 1, 1858, and July 12, 1859.

76. Tallant, *Evil Necessity*, 32.

77. A comprehensive treatment of the founding and work of the American Colonization Society is Burin, *Slavery and the Peculiar Solution*. For the establishment of Liberia, see 13–15.

78. Ibid., 21, 29–30. See table 2, "ACS emigration by period, 1820–1860," found on 170 in the unpaginated "Tables" section. Burin labels the late 1840s and 1850s as African colonization's " 'golden age.' "

79. Ibid., 21.

80. Birney, *Letter on Colonization*, 33–34.

81. Foner, *Fiery Trial*, 221–47.

82. See Buck, *Slavery Question*, 24; records of the Louisville Annual Conference (1847); and Bullock, "Address before the Kentucky Colonization Society . . . Frankfort," *Louisville Examiner*, June 26, 1847.

83. Tallant, *Evil Necessity*, 32.

84. Burin, *Slavery and the Peculiar Solution*, 46.

85. Ibid., 1.

86. Quoted in Taylor, *Frontiers of Freedom*, 56.

87. "Address of the Kentucky Colonization Society," *African Repository and Colonial Journal*, March 1829, 29.

88. "Kentucky Colonization Society," *African Repository and Colonial Journal*, May 1830, 82.

89. "Memorial of the Kentucky Colonization Society," *African Repository and Colonial Journal*, January 1830, 348.

90. Kentucky Colonization Society, "Fourth Annual Report of the Kentucky Colonization Society, with an Address, . . . by Rev. John C. Young," 20.

91. "The Difference," *Cincinnati Post and Anti-Abolitionist*, February 26, 1842.

92. A Colonizationist, "African Colonization—No. 1," *Louisville Examiner*, October 2, 1847.

93. Birney, "Letter on Colonization," 33–34.

94. "Colonization," from the Cincinnati *Chronicle*, reprinted in *Philanthropist*, November 10, 1842.

95. Union Baptist Church, "Proceedings of the Colored People in Cincinnati," *Philanthropist*, March 15, 1843.

96. *Minutes and Address of the State Convention of the Colored Citizens of Ohio, Convened at Columbus* (1849), 17.

97. [McIlvaine et al.], "Address of the Ohio Colonization Committee, to the Clergymen of Ohio," [1853?], 59, African Colonization Pamphlets, Cincinnati History Library and Archives. Six of nine members of the "Colonization Committee of Correspondence for Ohio" resided in Cincinnati. See ibid., 63, and [McIlvaine et al.], "Ohio in Africa," 7, for residences of the committee members.

98. "Address of the Ohio Colonization Committee," 59–63.

99. Taylor, *Frontiers of Freedom*, 60.

100. Cheek and Cheek, *John Mercer Langston and the Fight for Black Freedom*, 27–28n60; Ohio Female Anti-Slavery Society, "Report on the Condition of the Colored People in Ohio," *Philanthropist*, July 14, 1840.

101. *Minutes and Address of the State Convention of the Colored Citizens of Ohio, Convened at Columbus* (1849), 8, 11, 17.

102. Quoted in Taylor, *America's First Black Socialist*, 51. For Clark's views on emigration, see 42–60.

103. Cheek and Cheek, *John Mercer Langston and the Fight for Black Freedom*, 190.

104. *Proceedings of the Convention of the Colored Freemen of Ohio, Held in Cincinnati . . .* (Cincinnati: Dumas & Lawyer, 1852), 5, African Colonization Pamphlets.

105. Ibid., 9, 7.

106. Gibson, "Semi-Centennial of the Public Career," 77, 40, 35.

107. *Proceedings of the National Emigration Convention of Colored People; Held at Cleveland, Ohio . . .* (Pittsburgh, Pa.: A. A. Anderson, 1854), 12–14, African Colonization Pamphlets.

108. For this phrase, see Gibson's subtitle to "Semi-Centennial of the Public Career."

109. Allen Chapel Officers, "Letter to the Bishop and Conference of the M. E. Church for the Cincinnati District, now in session," October 21, 1854, Samuel Williams Collection (MSS qW727 Box 3, Folder 17), Methodist Church Papers.

110. Ibid.

Chapter Five

1. Aaron, *Cincinnati, Queen City*, 49.

2. Ibid., 53–66.

3. Ibid., 67, 49, 78.

4. Glazer, *Cincinnati in 1840*, 108–10.

5. Ibid., 77.

6. Ibid., 78.

7. Burckin, "Formation and Growth of an Urban Middle Class," 8.

8. Ibid., 7, 13.

9. Beckert and Rosenbaum, *American Bourgeoisie*, 2–3.

10. See Rockman, *Scraping By*.

11. Santamarina, "Introduction," in Potter, *Hairdresser's Experience*, xix.

12. Ibid., xviii–xix.

13. Cohen, "Respectability of Rebecca Reed," 455.

14. Halttunen, *Confidence Men and Painted Women*, xv–xvi, 28–32, 118, 193–94.

15. Ibid., 89.

16. On the artisanship involved in women's clothing, see Amneus, *Separate Sphere*.

17. Santamarina, "Introduction," in Potter, *Hairdresser's Experience*, xix–xxii.

18. Burckin, appendix 7 and appendix 2 in "Formation and Growth of an Urban Middle Class," 641–42, 634.

19. Burckin, appendix 12 in ibid., 650–52.

20. Aubespin et al., *Two Centuries of Black Louisville*, 58.

21. Taylor, *Frontiers of Freedom*, 132–34, appendix 5, 209.

22. Aaron, *Cincinnati, Queen City*, 55.

23. Taylor, *Frontiers of Freedom*, 117.

24. Ibid., 103–4.

25. Burckin, appendix 12 in "Formation and Growth of an Urban Middle Class," 650.

26. Taylor, *Frontiers of Freedom*, 133–35, appendix 18, 221.

27. On the regional dimensions of barbering, and the somewhat more hospitable environment of the upper South for black barbers, see Bristol, *Knights of the Razor*, 71–79, 105–6.

28. Santamarina, "Introduction," in Potter, *Hairdresser's Experience*, xiv–xvii; Potter, *Hairdresser's Experience*, 55.

29. For evidence of her work in social reform circles, see Managers of the Colored Orphan Asylum, *Eleventh Annual Report*. This report listed Eliza Potter as both a manager and a solicitor for the asylum.

30. Potter, *Hairdresser's Experience*, 35.

31. Santamarina, *Belabored Professions*, 103–5.

32. Potter, *Hairdresser's Experience*, 170.

33. Santamarina, *Belabored Professions*, 112–20.

34. Potter, *Hairdresser's Experience*, 10–14.

35. Santamarina, "Introduction," in ibid., xx. Santamarina provides an analysis of Potter's "inside outsider" status.

36. Potter, *Hairdresser's Experience*, 124.

37. Ibid., 57, 63, 150, 163.

38. Ibid., 1, 156.

39. Santamarina, "Appendix B," in ibid., 184 and 194, and 183–97 generally.

40. Ibid., 184.

41. Ibid., 187.

42. Ibid., 194, 196–97, 192.

43. Bristol, *Knights of the Razor*, 71–79.

44. Ibid., 41–42, 63–65.

45. Langston, *From the Virginia Plantation*, 59.

46. Taylor, *Frontiers of Freedom*, 133–34.

47. Langston, *From the Virginia Plantation*, 72.

48. Ibid., 71.

49. Ibid., 61–62.

50. Taylor, *Frontiers of Freedom*, 125.

51. Langston, *From the Virginia Plantation*, 65–66.

52. Bristol, *Knights of the Razor*, 52, 3. On the unequal relations between white clients and black barbers, see 41–53 generally.

53. Trotter, *River Jordan*, 38–40.

54. Taylor, *Frontiers of Freedom*, 167–68.

55. Volpe, "Cartes de Visite," 158.

56. Katz, *Regionalism and Reform*, 90.

57. Willis, *J. P. Ball*, xiii–xvii.

58. "The Daguerian Gallery of the West," *Gleason's Pictorial Drawing-Room Companion*, April 1, 1854, 208. See also Ball, *J. P. Ball's Splendid Mammoth Pictorial Tour*, 8–10, reprinted in Willis, *J. P. Ball*, 250–52.

59. Katz, *Regionalism and Reform*, 117–18.

60. "The Daguerian Gallery of the West."

61. Volpe, "Cartes de Visite," 161. In every one of Ball's images of standing male patrons, the posing device is visible, but in photographs of women, the apparatus is disguised by their dress.

62. Fredrickson, *Black Image in the White Mind*, 101–2.

63. Ibid., 126.

64. Ibid., 110–26.

65. On gentility's "spreading across the land," see Bushman, *Refinement of America*, 402.

66. Cohen, "Respectability of Rebecca Reed," 455.

67. The significance of "feeling right" to nineteenth-century sentimentalists is discussed in Halttunen, *Confidence Men and Painted Women*, 40–43, 51–55, 118–19, and also June Howard, "What is Sentimentality?," 69–73.

68. Wexler, "Tender Violence," 17. She observes, "Any meaningful enlargement by sentimentality of the percentage of the population who can come 'inside' this magic circle still leaves behind the vast number who cannot qualify for entry under moral standards determined by arbiters who remain in power."

69. Chase, *Address and Reply*, 10–12, 34.

70. Ibid., 17.

71. Ibid., 10–11, 3. Although attributed to Chase's authorship, the pamphlet's printer, A. G. Sparhawk, was well known to the black community. In 1846, Sparhawk would also publish a songbook used by students at Cincinnati's black high school.

72. Ibid., 15.

73. Ibid., 13, 16–17.

74. Ibid., 17–18.

75. Foner, *Free Soil*, 282–83.

76. Chase, *Address and Reply*, 19–20.

77. Ibid., 21.

78. Ibid., 27.

79. Blue, *Salmon P. Chase*, 20.

80. Foner, *Free Soil*, 283.

81. Chase, *Address and Reply*, 34, 33, 26, 33, 35.

82. Blue, *Salmon P. Chase*, 187–89.

83. Quoted in ibid., 83.

84. Gibson, "Semi-Centennial of the Public Career," 25–26.

85. Ibid., 26.

86. Kleber, *Encyclopedia of Louisville*, 657. From the evidence, it does not appear that other judges served in Louisville's Chancery Court, so Nicholas almost certainly presided over the drafting of the unique deed in the chancery proceedings in 1845. Given his familiarity with the deed, it seems likely that the church would have called on him to be present in 1848. For Nicholas's involvement in antislavery activities in the late 1840s, see Tallant, *Evil Necessity*, 139, 144. The "Convention of the Friends of Emancipation in Kentucky," now known as the Frankfort Convention, met in April 1849, and Nicholas played a role in the proceedings. See "Convention of the Friends of Emancipation in Kentucky," *Louisville Examiner*, May 5, 1849.

87. [Nicholas et al.], *Slave Emancipation in Kentucky*, 3–6, 8. Tallant states that Nicholas's pamphlet appeared in December 1848, although *Slave Emancipation in Kentucky* has an 1849 publication date. See Tallant, *Evil Necessity*, 139. On Cassius Clay's economic arguments against slavery, see Tallant, *Evil Necessity*, 116–18, and Freehling, *Road to Disunion*, 462–65.

88. Harrison, *Antislavery Movement in Kentucky*, 30–37; Tallant, *Evil Necessity*, 27–57; Harlow, "Religion, Race, and Robert J. Breckinridge," 7–12. On the colonization movement in the upper South generally, see Berlin, *Slaves without Masters*, 199–213. James Birney's antislavery work is treated in Harrison, *Antislavery Movement in Kentucky*, 39–45. Cassius Clay's opposition to colonization is discussed in Harrold, *Abolitionists and the South*, 132–35. On John G. Fee, see Tallant, *Evil Necessity*, ch. 7.

89. Nicholas, "Emancipation," *Louisville Examiner*, March 17, 1849.

90. "Concert at the Fourth Street Methodist Church," *Louisville Examiner*, June 17, 1848.

91. "There is Progress," *Louisville Examiner*, June 19, 1847; "African Colonisation," *Louisville Examiner*, April 21, 1849.

Chapter Six

1. Weiner, *Race and Rights*, 33.

2. See Robertson, *Hearts Beating for Liberty*.

3. Cheek and Cheek, *John Mercer Langston*, 133–34.

4. Tallant, *Evil Necessity*, 12, 3, 161.

5. Taylor, *Frontiers of Freedom*, 97–98, and 162. See ch. 8, generally.

6. Robertson, *Hearts Beating for Liberty*, 13, 28.

7. Hochman, *Uncle Tom's Cabin and the Reading Revolution*, 51–52. See ch. 2, generally.

8. Beecher, *Plea for the West*, 43.

9. Ibid., 30, 37, 41, 164, 84.

10. James Hall, "Critical Notices," *Western Monthly Magazine*, May 1835, 323.

11. Stowe, *Report of Elementary Public Instruction in Europe*, 27.

12. Ibid., 19, 53.

13. Hedrick, *Harriet Beecher Stowe*, 112.

14. Hochman, *Uncle Tom's Cabin and the Reading Revolution*, 72, 53.

15. Weld to Louis Tappan, March 18, 1834, in Theodore Dwight Weld, *Letters of Theodore Dwight Weld, Angelina Grimké and Sarah Grimké, 1822–1844*, 2 vols., edited by Gilbert H. Barnes and Dwight L. Dumond (Gloucester, Mass.: Peter Smith, 1965), 1:135, quoted in Cheek and Cheek, *John Mercer Langston and the Fight for Black Freedom*, 53.

16. Cheek and Cheek, *John Mercer Langston and the Fight for Black Freedom*, 53; Taylor, *Frontiers of Freedom*, 47.

17. [Lane Theological Seminary], *Fifth Annual Report of the Trustees of the Cincinnati Lane Seminary*, 39–40.

18. Ibid., 37.

19. For a discussion of Ohio's laws related to voting, see Taylor, *Frontiers of Freedom*, 177.

20. [Lane Theological Seminary], *Fifth Annual Report*, 37.

21. Ibid., 34.

22. Beecher quoted in Hedrick, *Harriet Beecher Stowe*, 103.

23. [Lane Theological Seminary], *Fifth Annual Report*, 37.

24. Hedrick, *Harriet Beecher Stowe*, 104.

25. Cheek and Cheek, *John Mercer Langston and the Fight for Black Freedom*, 85.

26. Ibid., 184.

27. Executive Committee of the Ohio Ladies' Society, "The Call of the Ladies' Committee," *Philanthropist*, October 6, 1840. In 1842, the society reported, "There are about 45 colonies or settlements of free colored people in this State. The smallest in numbers containing about 50 people, and the largest from three to four thousand." Ohio Ladies' Education Society (hereafter, OLES), "Second Annual Report of the Ladies' Education Society," *Philanthropist*, June 22, 1842.

28. For information on two relatively prosperous settlements, the Mercer County and Jackson County settlements, see Cheek and Cheek, *John Mercer Langston and the Fight for Black Freedom*, 22, 54.

29. Mr. [Amzi D.] Barber, "Report on the Condition of the Colored People in Ohio," *Philanthropist*, July 14, 1840.

30. Robertson, *Hearts Beating for Liberty*, 15–24.

31. Executive Committee of the Ohio Ladies' Society, "The Call of the Ladies' Committee," *Philanthropist*, October 6, 1840.

32. OLES, "First Annual Report of the O.L.E.S.," *Philanthropist*, June 9, 1841.

33. Mary A. Blanchard, "Notice to Teachers of Colored Schools," *Philanthropist*, April 20, 1842.

34. In 1841, the society first devised a memorial "praying for the repeal" of the law exempting the property of African Americans from the common school law and memorializing the legislature to provide for black children's education "in a way which the wisdom of the legislature may seem proper to direct." OLES, "Proceedings of the Ohio Ladies' Society for the Education of the Free People of Color," *Philanthropist*, June 9, 1841. Thereafter, the *Philanthropist* regularly reprinted the memorial, advising readers to copy and circulate the form. See John O. Wattles, "Request to the Friends of Colored People throughout the State," *Philanthropist*, December 7, 1842. In 1843, an agent of the society, William W. Wright, "circulated petitions to Congress and our state Legislature in more than forty towns. OLES, "Third Annual Report of the O.L.E.S.," *Philanthropist*, August 9, 1843.

35. In 1841, an agent of the OLES participated in an Ohio State Anti-Slavery Society convention (Garrisonian) that resolved to solicit a meeting with the Ohio State Legislature's House Judiciary Committee to discuss the Black Laws and their effect on Ohio's black residents. Ohio State Anti-Slavery Society, "Convention Proceedings," *Philanthropist*, February 2, 1841. Although the society apparently continued its activities through 1844, the *Philanthropist* did not publish an annual report that year.

36. OLES, "Second Annual Report of the Ladies' Education Society," *Philanthropist*, June 22, 1842.

37. John O. Wattles, "Heroism," *Philanthropist*, February 8, 1843.

38. Barber, "Report on the Condition of the Colored People in Ohio."

39. Taylor, *Frontiers of Freedom*, 163.

40. Barber, "Report on the Condition of the Colored People in Ohio."

41. Ibid.

42. OLES, "Second Annual Report," *Philanthropist*, June 22, 1842.

43. OLES, "Annual Report of the Ladies' Education Society (Concluded)," *Philanthropist*, June 29, 1842.

44. Executive Committee of the Ohio Ladies' Society, "The Call of the Ladies' Committee," *Philanthropist*, October 6, 1840; OLES, "Annual Report of the O.L.E.S.," *Philanthropist*, June 29, 1842. The agent H. W. Cobb reported in 1841 that the OLES desperately needed money and stated that "many" schools for black children "are now supported wholly by the colored people." "To the Friends of the Education of the Colored People Through the State," *Philanthropist*, November 10, 1841.

45. OLES, "Second Annual Report," *Philanthropist*, June 22, 1842.

46. OLES, "Third Annual Report," *Philanthropist*, August 9, 1843.

47. Langston, *From the Virginia Plantation*, 74–75, quoted in Cheek and Cheek, *John Mercer Langston and the Fight for Black Freedom*, 88, 89, 121–22n28.

48. Ibid., 88, 110, 126n81.

49. Ibid., 126n86.

50. OLES, "Second Annual Report," *Philanthropist*, June 22, 1842.

51. Cincinnati Women's Antislavery Society, "Third Annual Report of the Cincinnati Women's Antislavery Society," *Philanthropist*, November 4, 1840.

52. OLES, "Second Annual Report," *Philanthropist*, June 22, 1842.

53. Ibid.

54. OLES, "First Annual Report of the O.L.E.S.," *Philanthropist*, June 9, 1841.

55. Halttunen, *Confidence Men and Painted Women*, 118–19, and generally.

56. Taylor, *Frontiers of Freedom*, 46–48, 68–70, 93–98.

57. Taylor, *Frontiers of Freedom*, 96, 162–63; Shotwell, *History of the Schools in Cincinnati*, 453–55; Check and Check, *John Mercer Langston*, 58–59, 70–71, and generally.

58. Taylor, *America's First Black Socialist*, 29–33.

59. Ibid., 29.

60. For examples of the Union Baptist Church's many discussions of schools in their building, see the following minutes: November 21, 1839; April 13, 1846; February 24, 1847; March 10, 1847; April 26, 1847; November 15, 1848; November 26, 1852.

61. "Address to the Colored Men of the State of Ohio," in *Minutes and Address of the State Convention of the Colored Citizens of Ohio, Convened at Columbus, . . . 1849*, 6; Quoted in Shotwell, *History of the Schools of Cincinnati*, 447.

62. Middleton, *Black Laws*, 34–35.

63. Cheek and Cheek, *John Mercer Langston and the Fight for Black Freedom*, 77n31.

64. *Minutes and Address of the State Convention of the Colored Citizens of Ohio, Convened at Columbus . . . 1849*, 9, 15, 5, and "Extracts from Newspapers," in ibid., 27–28.

65. Ibid., 14.

66. Middleton, *Black Laws*, 36–37.

67. *Minutes and Address of the State Convention of the Colored Citizens of Ohio, Convened at Columbus . . . 1849*, 14.

68. "To the Citizens of Ohio," in ibid., 24.

69. "Resolutions," in ibid., 18. See resolution 15.

70. "To the Citizens of Ohio," in ibid., 23.

71. Ibid., 25.

72. Taylor, *Frontiers of Freedom*, 165.

73. Ibid. Cheek and Cheek, *John Mercer Langston and the Fight for Black Freedom*, 180–81; Taylor, *Frontiers of Freedom*, 165; "Resolutions," in *Minutes and Address of the State Convention of the Colored Citizens of Ohio, Convened at Columbus . . . 1849*, 17.

74. Taylor, *America's First Black Socialist*, 39.

75. Quoted in Cheek and Cheek, *John Mercer Langston and the Fight for Black Freedom*, 150.

76. Elizabeth's history and genealogy has been reconstructed by Taylor, *America's First Black Socialist*, 18–21.

77. Ibid., 20.

78. Ibid., 39. Cheek and Cheek, *John Mercer Langston and the Fight for Black Freedom*, 51.

79. Cheek and Cheek, *John Mercer Langston and the Fight for Black Freedom*, 151. The "sparkling Cawtaba" story may also be found in Brown, *Rising Son*, 452.

80. Cheek and Cheek place the convention in 1837 while Taylor suggests the year was 1838. See Taylor, *America's First Black Socialist*, 39. The date of 1837 seems likely, since it was the very first such black Ohio Convention, attended by leaders in the education movement. See Cheek and Cheek, *John Mercer Langston and the Fight for Black Freedom*, 145, 151, and 163n12.

81. Brown, *Rising Son*, 450.

82. Gaines, "Oration, Delivered on the First of August, 1849, before the Colored Citizens of Columbus, Ohio," in Gaines and Perkins, *Orations*, 6.

83. Ibid., 11–12.

84. The State, on Relation of the Directors of the Eastern and Western School Districts of Cincinnati, v. The City of Cincinnati and Others, in *Reports of Cases Argued and Determined in the Supreme Court*, 179, 183. See also Taylor, *Frontiers of Freedom*, 165.

85. See Harrold, *Border War*.

86. The State, on Relation of the Directors of the Eastern and Western School Districts of Cinicnnati, v. The City of Cincinnati and Others, in *Reports*, 178

87. Taylor, *America's First Black Socialist*, 63.

88. Quoted in Cheek and Cheek, *John Mercer Langston and the Fight for Black Freedom*, 181.

89. *Proceedings of the Convention, of the Colored Freemen of Ohio* (Cincinnati: Dumas & Lawyer, 1852), 12, in African Colonization Pamphlets.

90. Ibid., 8.

91. Ibid.

92. Cheek and Cheek, *John Mercer Langston and the Fight for Black Freedom*, 182–84.

93. Ibid., 231.

94. Ibid., 192.

95. Gaines, John [I.], "Speech of John [I.] Gaines, of Cincinnati, at the Late Convention in that City," *Anti-Slavery Bugle*, May 21, 1853. This article's authorship is listed as John J. Gaines, who was a relation of John I. Gaines. However, based upon the biographical information provided in the speech, and other corroborating evidence related to the 1853 antislavery convention, this speech was clearly the work of John Isom Gaines.

96. Cheek and Cheek, *John Mercer Langston and the Fight for Black Freedom*, 232.

97. These events are covered in ibid., 181, and Taylor, *Frontiers of Freedom*, 166–67; see also Taylor, *America's First Black Socialist*, 63–64, 85. Cheek and Cheek lists enrollment figures for Cincinnati on 184, and Taylor on 167 (in *Frontiers of Freedom*).

98. Samuel Matthews, "John Isom Gaines," 45.

99. Cheek and Cheek, *John Mercer Langston and the Fight for Black Freedom*, 151; Taylor, *America's First Black Socialist*, 85.

100. On the significance of Cincinnati's schools, see Taylor, *Frontiers of Freedom*, 168–74. Her study of Peter S. Clark reinforces Taylor's argument that Cincinnati's schools were the primary means of "black upward mobility" in the Civil War and Reconstruction eras. See Taylor, *America's First Black Socialist*, 86.

101. Gaines, "Speech of John [I.] Gaines, of Cincinnati, at the Late Convention in that City" *Anti-Slavery Bugle*, May 21, 1853.

102. Ibid.

103. Ibid.

104. Ibid.

105. Ibid.

106. Ibid.

107. Ibid.

108. Gibson, "Semi-Centennial of the Public Career," 67–68.

109. For example, see minutes for Union Baptist Church, November 26, 1852.

110. According to Lucas, only Louisiana's African Americans offered greater financial support to schools for children of color following the war. See Lucas, *History of Blacks in Kentucky*, 234. On Central School and statistics in Louisville for public school enrollment, see 247–48.

111. Gibson, "Semi-Centennial of the Public Career," 3.

112. Ibid., 83.

113. Ibid., 4, 32, and 6. "Joys and Sorrows" comes from the title of his memoir, which follows Gibson's *History* in the same volume. For more on Gibson's life and work in Louisville, see Lucas, *A History of Blacks in Kentucky*, 142–44.

114. Gibson, "Semi-Centennial of the Public Career," 4–5.

115. Ibid., 38.

116. Ibid., 5.

117. Ibid., 12–13.

118. Ibid., 69, 38, 55–56.

119. "Concert at the Fourth Street Methodist Church," *Louisville Examiner*, June 17, 1848.

120. Gibson, "Semi-Centennial of the Public Career," 23; "The Gospel in Kentucky," *Louisville Examiner*, July 31, 1847.

121. Gibson, "Semi-Centennial of the Public Career," 78.

122. "Concert at the Fourth Street Methodist Church," *Louisville Examiner*, June 17, 1848.

123. Gibson, "Semi-Centennial of the Public Career," 13.

124. Ibid., 33–34.

125. "Public Schools," *Louisville Examiner*, February 26, 1848.

126. "Common Schools," *Louisville Examiner*, December 18, 1847.

127. "Public Schools," *Encyclopedia of Louisville*, 735.

128. "Corresponding and Executive Committee" on Emancipation, *Address to the Non-Slaveholders of Kentucky*, 5–6.

129. Tallant, *Evil Necessity*, 130–31.

130. "Population," *Louisville Examiner*, February 5, 1848.

131. "Corresponding and Executive Committee" on Emancipation, *Address to the Non-Slaveholders of Kentucky*, 8.

132. Cleros, "Shall Kentucky Continue a Slave State?," 14, in ibid.

133. "The Town, or the Poorer Boys in it," *Louisville Examiner*, September 11, 1847. "[V]ery nature at war" comes from "Corresponding and Executive Committee" on Emancipation, *Address to the Non-Slaveholders of Kentucky*, 6.

134. On the power of laborers and working men in Louisville, and their coalitions with conservative emancipationists, see Tallant, *Evil Necessity*, 130–31, 149.

135. "Public Schools," *Encyclopedia of Louisville*, 735.

136. Lucas, *History of Blacks in Kentucky*, 236–37.

137. Ibid., 229.

138. Ibid., 231–32, 255.

139. Ibid., 233–43.

140. Ibid., 234.

141. Ibid., 238.

142. Ibid., 245.

143. Gibson, "Semi-Centennial of the Public Career," 69–70.

144. Quoted in Lucas, *History of Blacks in Kentucky*, 245.

145. Lucas, *History of Blacks in Kentucky*, 246.

146. Gibson, "Semi-Centennial of the Public Career," 83.

147. On Stowe's Cincinnati years, see Hedrick, *Harriet Beecher Stowe*, esp. 143–201.

148. Stowe, *Key to Uncle Tom's Cabin*, in Hedrick, *Oxford Harriet Beecher Stowe Reader*, 411, 403, 399.

149. Hedrick, *Harriet Beecher Stowe*, 214.

150. Mrs. Harriet Beecher Stowe, "Jesus," *New-York Evangelist*, February 19, 1846, 29.

151. Stowe, "Introductory Essay," in Beecher, *Incarnation*, vi.

152. For the argument that feeling essentially resides in fiction or narrative, and is "a substantive mode of understanding," see Bell, *Sentimentalism*, 4–8. For a discussion of Stowe's "Introductory Essay," see Hochman, *Uncle Tom's Cabin and the Reading Revolution*, 29–31, 94–97.

153. Ibid., 44, 27.

154. Stowe, *Uncle Tom's Cabin*, in Hedrick, *Oxford Harriet Beecher Stowe Reader*, 400–401.

155. Ibid., 402, 394–95.

156. On sentimentality's tendency to render "formulaic" others' "individuated experiences," see Ahern, *Affect and Abolition*, 8–13. Quotes are on 8.

157. Hochman, *Uncle Tom's Cabin and the Reading Revolution*, 51–55, 72.

158. Stowe, *Uncle Tom's Cabin*, in Hedrick, *Oxford Harriet Beecher Stowe Reader*, 390–96; Hochman, *Uncle Tom's Cabin and the Reading Revolution*, 64.

159. Stowe, quoted in Hedrick, *Harriet Beecher Stowe*, 206.

160. Stowe, *Uncle Tom's Cabin*, in Hedrick, *Oxford Harriet Beecher Stowe Reader*, 403.

161. Cheek and Cheek provide a useful overview of colonization and emigration discussions among black Ohioans through the figure of John Mercer Langston. See Cheek and Cheek, *John Mercer Langston and the Fight for Black Freedom*, chs. 5 and 6.

162. On Stowe's limited view from the domestic sphere, see Hedrick, *Harriet Beecher Stowe*, 209.

163. Hochman, *Uncle Tom's Cabin and the Reading Revolution*, 261–6n74.

164. Cheek and Cheek, *John Mercer Langston and the Fight for Black Freedom*, 174.

165. Christian Anti-Slavery Convention, *Minutes of the Christian Anti-Slavery Convention*, 19–20, 22–23.

166. Ibid., 21.

167. "Catalogue of Publications," *Christian Press*, June 1862, 428.

168. "Vine Street Congregational Church of Cincinnati, to the Natick Congregational Church," broadside, August 11, 1854, American Antiquarian Society.

169. McKivigan, *War against Proslavery Religion*, 121.

170. "Premium Offered," in Frost, *Gospel Fruits*, v. On the contest, see "Circular" printed at the end of Frost, *Gospel Fruits*, 190.

171. The ARTBS's corresponding secretary and treasurer, George L. Weed, wrote a letter to Frost "suggest[ing] your adding another chapter, feeling that it closes too abruptly." He wanted the story "to follow Deacon Brown in his bonds, doing good to those in darkness & thus show the providence of God in calling his chosen to suffer in order to bring about a greater good." George L. Weed, Cincinnati, to M. G. Frost, December 20, 1855, Maria Goodell Frost Papers, Special Collections. Ultimately, Weed published the manuscript with Frost's original ending. George L. Weed, Cincinnati, to M. G. Frost, January 16 [?], 1856, in ibid.

172. The most complete list of publications may be found in "Catalogue of Publications," *Christian Press*, June 11, 1862, 428; McKivigan, *War against Proslavery Religion*, 121.

173. "Vine Street Congregational Church of Cincinnati, to the Natick Congregational Church."

174. The society also published tracts for adults decrying slavery. See "Catalogue of Publications," *Christian Press*.

175. For an examination of the ARTBS's publications as part of a larger body of children's antislavery literature produced by women authors, see De Rosa, *Domestic Abolitionism and Juvenile Literature*.

176. Ahern, *Affect and Abolition*, 13. Ahern here draws on Lynn Festa's scholarship.

177. Hochman, *Uncle Tom's Cabin and the Reading Revolution*, xi, 2.

178. Mrs. M. J. P. Smith, *Little Robert and His Friend*, 110.

179. Frost, *Gospel Fruits*, ix.

180. Ibid., 50, 24, 61, 133.

181. Lois, *Harriet and Ellen*, 11.

182. Frost, *Gospel Fruits*, 80.

183. Ibid., 36, 57, 63, 72, 93.

184. Ibid., 92.

185. Aydelott, *Prejudice against Colored People*, 18.

186. Ibid., 6–7, 20–21.

187. Frost, *Gospel Fruits*, 136, 160–61, 182, 184.

188. *Christian Press*, April 8, 1853.

189. Union Baptist Church, *Minutes*, June 30, 1854.

190. *Christian Press*, May 20, 1853.

191. "Bible Presentation," *Christian Press*, November 5, 1852.

192. "Letter of a Colored Girl," *Christian Press*, May 20, 1853.

193. Hochman, *Uncle Tom's Cabin and the Reading Revolution*, 51–52.

194. "Letter of a Colored Girl," *Christian Press*, May 20, 1853.

195. Lockard, "Griffith Brown, Mattie," *American National Biography Online.*

196. Ibid.; Lockard, "Afterword," in Griffith, *Autobiography of a Female Slave,* 416. See also Ceplair, "Mattie Griffith Browne."

197. Hall, "From Voice to Persona," 225.

198. Welby, "To—," *Louisville Daily Journal,* September 22, 1843, quoted in Hall, "From Voice to Persona," 225–26.

199. Bennett, *Palace-Burner,* xxxix, xxx.

200. Piatt, "A Poet's Soliloquy," *Louisville Daily Journal,* March 9, 1859, in Hall, "From Voice to Persona," 238–39.

201. Bennett, *Palace-Burner,* xxxix. For Piatt's full poem, see 39.

202. For the argument that the *Daily Journal* formed a "poetry workshop," see Hall, "From Voice to Persona," 228 and 234.

203. Ibid., 234.

204. Griffith, "To—," *Poems,* 114–15.

205. On the misleading publication dates, see Lockard, "Griffith Browne, Mattie," and Lockard, "Afterword," 407–8.

206. Griffith, *Autobiography of a Female Slave,* 141, 103, 212, 252.

207. "Galt House," *Encyclopedia of Louisville,* 327.

208. Griffith, *Autobiography of a Female Slave,* 257–58.

209. "Stick to the Right," *Louisville Examiner,* August 7, 1847.

210. Griffith, *Autobiography of a Female Slave,* 128, 79, 60.

211. Ibid., 125, 12, 257.

212. Lockard, "Afterword," 416.

213. Griffith, *Autobiography of a Female Slave,* 356, 125, 79, 400.

214. Ibid., 79.

215. Lydia Maria Child, "How a Kentucky Girl Emancipated Her Slaves," *Independent,* March 27, 1862.

216. Griffith, *Autobiography of a Female Slave,* 86.

Chapter Seven

1. Drake, *Public Oration,* 8.

2. Cist, *Cincinnati in 1841,* 254.

3. Casseday, "Sketch of the Annals of Louisville," *Louisville City Directory,* 12.

4. Casseday, *History of Louisville,* 212–13.

5. Flint, *Condensed Geography,* 206–7. See, for example, Gruenwald, *River of Enterprise,* and Salafia, *Slavery's Borderland.* Salafia offers a careful and sophisticated argument about the Ohio River valley's moderating influences upon politics and culture.

6. Hibbard, *Biography of Rev. Leonidas L. Hamline,* 196.

7. Matt. 24:8 (KJV).

8. For this argument, see Goen, *Broken Churches,* and Snay, *Gospel of Disunion.*

9. *Baptist Banner and Pioneer* (Louisville), May 1, 1845, quoted in Goen, *Broken Churches,* 98.

10. Goen, *Broken Churches*, 19; Snay, *Gospel of Disunion*, esp. 53–109. See also Heyrman, *Southern Cross*, 206–52. Heyrman argues that southern evangelicalism developed in ways distinct from the North before 1830, but she makes slavery and "mastery" crucial to these regional distinctions.

11. Carwardine, *Evangelicals and Politics*, 171.

12. Ibid., 162–66.

13. Jones, "Years of Disagreement," 159–67.

14. Ibid., 160; Methodist Episcopal Church, "Ohio Conference" in *Minutes of the Annual Conferences of the Methodist Episcopal Church* (1851), 663; Methodist Episcopal Church, "Cincinnati and Kentucky Conference," in *Minutes of the Annual Conferences* (1852), 119–25.

15. R. E. Jones United Methodist Church, "Historical Account of R. E. Jones United Methodist Church," in *Our Heritage Past and Present*, 7. Methodist Episcopal Church, "Ohio Conference," in *Minutes for the Methodist Episcopal Church* (1845), 647. The Louisville City Directory for 1859 listed two German churches as members of the "Methodist German Episcopal Church, North." See Tanner, *Louisville Directory and Business Advertiser for 1859–60*, 312.

16. A. D. Sears, "Circular Letter," *Minutes of the Long Run Association of Baptists* (1845), 9–10. On Kentuckians' perceptions of northern abolitionists, see Harrold, "Violence and Nonviolence in Kentucky Abolitionism," 22; and see, generally, Harlow, *Religion, Race, and the Making of Confederate Kentucky*.

17. On the relationship between the slave missions and the establishment of the separate southern churches, see Irons, *Origins of Proslavery Christianity*, 195–200; Snay, *Gospel of Disunion*, 94–97; and Sernett, *Black Religion and American Evangelicalism*, 47–58.

18. *Minutes of the Long Run Baptist Association* (1839), 1, 6; ibid. (1839–1845); ibid. (1840), 1, 8; ibid. (1841), 1, 16; ibid. (1842), 4, 13; ibid. (1843), 4–5; ibid. (1844), 3; Gibson, "Semi-Centennial of the Public Career," 17.

19. *Minutes of the Long Run Association of Baptists* (1842), 4, 9.

20. Minutes of the Fifth Street Baptist Church, April [1842].

21. "Coloured Sunday Schools in Louisville, Ky.," *Bible Society Record*, February 1, 1855, 127–28.

22. Minutes of the Fifth Street Baptist Church, August 27, 1843; *Minutes of the Long Run Association of Baptists* (1842), 4; ibid. (1843), 4–5, 7, 13.

23. *Minutes of the Long Run Association of Baptists* (1843), 7, 10.

24. Sears, "Circular Letter," 9–10. See also Birdwhistell, *Gathered at the River*, 44–46.

25. Minutes of the Fifth Street Baptist Church, September 28, 1842, September 24, 1843, February 25, 1844, and March 20, 1845; Hampton, *Historical Sketch*, not paginated; Minutes of the Walnut Street Baptist Church (original name, First Baptist Church), February 17, 1844, and March 15, 1844. See minutes for February 17, 1844, for the first mention of these troubles with the Fifth Street Baptist Church.

26. Sears, "Circular Letter," 9–10.

27. Evidence of Adams's relationship with Ohio's leading black Baptist churches first appears in 1840, when he attended the annual meeting of the Regular Baptist Churches of Color in Ohio, held in Chillicothe. See *Minutes of the Fifth Annual Association of the Regular Baptist Churches of Color* (1840), 2–3. Through the 1840s and 1850s, the Union Baptist Church of Cincinnati maintained close ties with Adams and invited him to be its pastor several times before 1850, when he agreed to help the Cincinnati congregation straighten out its troubled finances. Adams did not relinquish his post at Louisville, however, and for nearly three years he ministered to both the Union Baptist and Fifth Street Baptist Churches. Stretching across the Ohio River, this pastoral relationship between leading black Baptist churches reveals the close ties between Cincinnati's and Louisville's African American evangelicals throughout the antebellum period. Evidence for this relationship may be found in the Minutes of the Union Baptist Church, April 17, 1840, April 24, 1840, May 27, 1842, December 31, 1847, October 18, 1850, and November 25, 1850.

28. Adams, "To the First Colored Baptist church of Louisville," quoted in Mohon, "First African Baptist Church of Louisville," 11–12.

29. Sears, "Circular Letter," 9–10.

30. Ibid., 10.

31. Elliott, *History of the Great Secession*, 411–16. On the role of the Kentucky Conference in the division of the Methodist Church, see also Harmon, "Organization of the Methodist Episcopal Church, South," 99–100.

32. Elliott, *History of the Great Secession*, 466–69; Bascom, *Methodism and Slavery*, 78, 125, 65. On Bascom as a leading polemicist of the southern church, see Donald G. Mathews, *Slavery and Methodism*, 275, and Snay, *Gospel of Disunion*, 129–31, 134.

33. Elliott, *History of the Great Secession*, 412; [Eighth Street and Fourth Street Churches, Louisville], [petition], September 5, 1844, Kentucky Annual Conference Papers (Kentucky United Methodist Heritage Center, Kentucky Wesleyan College, Owensboro); *Minutes of the Annual Conferences of the Methodist Episcopal Church, South* (1845). For a description of the Methodist ministers in attendance at the Louisville meeting, see Fitzgerald, *John B. McFerrin*, 177–81.

34. Fitzgerald, *John B. McFerrin*, 175–76, 187–88, 191.

35. Miami Association of Regular Baptists, *Minutes of the Miami Association of Regular Baptists* (1840–44).

36. Minutes of the Union Baptist Church, September 3, 1844.

37. Ibid., September 4, 1844; Miami Association of Regular Baptists, *Minutes* (1844), 13.

38. Miami Association of Regular Baptists, *Minutes* (1844), 6.

39. Walker sent the letter sometime between September 7, 1844, when the Middletown meeting concluded, and November 8, 1844, when mention of Walker's article first appeared in the Union Baptist Church's minutes. Minutes of the Union Baptist Church, November 8, 1844, and November 12, 1844. Unfortunately, there are no extant copies of the *Disfranchised American* today.

40. Minutes of the Union Baptist Church, November 8, 1844, and November 12, 1844.

41. Ibid., November 19, 1844.

42. For the suggestion that Zion's founding members left because of Union Baptist Church's membership in the white Miami Baptist Association, see the *Philanthropist* (Cincinnati), May 31, 1843, and July 12, 1843. For the sources of the dispute between Union and Zion Baptist Churches, see also Minutes of the Union Baptist Church, October 30, 1846.

43. See, for example, Minutes of the Union Baptist Church for July 31, 1846, which reported that a member charged with absenteeism "Decried this Church a Pro Slavery Church." See also minutes for February 25, 1853.

44. Minutes of the Union Baptist Church, February 25, 1853.

45. Ibid., September 11, 1846.

46. Miami Association of Regular Baptists, *Minutes* (1846), 5.

47. Isa. 24:1–2, 4, 11–12 (KJV).

48. Hamline, quoted in Hibbard, *Biography of Rev. Leonidas L. Hamline*, 157.

49. Norwood, *Schism*, 132. Other local conflicts emerged in eastern Virginia, western Virginia, St. Louis, and Maysville, Kentucky.

50. Ibid., 139.

51. Hamline, entry for February 27, 1846, quoted in Hibbard, *Biography of Rev. Leonidas L. Hamline*, 224.

52. Elliott, *History of the Great Secession*, iii.

53. Ibid.

54. Ibid., iv.

55. Ibid., iv–v.

56. Ibid, v.

57. Ibid., vi.

58. Ibid., 568.

59. Ibid., 260.

60. Ibid., 821.

61. Ibid., 569.

62. Earle, *Jacksonian Antislavery*, 144.

63. Quoted in ibid., 162.

64. Maizlish, *Triumph of Sectionalism*, 117.

65. Ibid., 124.

66. Ibid., 121.

67. Ibid., 145; Finkelman, "Race, Slavery, and Law in Antebellum Ohio," 751.

68. Finkelman, "Race, Slavery, and Law in Antebellum Ohio," 751.

69. Maizlish, *Triumph of Sectionalism*, 137.

70. Middleton, *Black Laws*, 127–29.

71. Ibid., 130–33.

72. Ibid., 141.

73. Ibid., 142.

74. Cheek and Cheek, *John Mercer Langston and the Fight for Black Freedom*, 160–61. On exclusionary laws and their demographic impacts, see Weiner, *Race and Rights*, 42–45.

75. Maizlish, "Ohio and the Rise of Sectional Politics," 133; Gienapp, "Salmon P. Chase," 5.

76. Gienapp, "Salmon P. Chase," 28. See also Blue, "Moral Journey of a Political Abolitionist," 224.

77. Blue, "Moral Journey of a Political Abolitionist," 216–23.

78. On this point, see Oakes, *Freedom National*, especially the preface and ch. 1.

79. Finkelman, "Race, Slavery and Law in Antebellum Ohio," 756–57, 764.

80. Ibid., 769.

81. "Convention of the Friends of Emancipation in Kentucky," *Louisville Examiner*, May 5, 1849. On slave escapes and fears of slave revolts in the Bluegrass instigated by abolitionists prior to the Constitutional Convention, see Harrison, *Antislavery Movement in Kentucky*, 58, 83–84; Tallant, *Evil Necessity*, 146–47; and Lucas, *History of Blacks in Kentucky*, 59, 73.

82. Matthews, "Beleaguered Loyalties," 19; Berlin, *Slaves without Masters*, 184–85, 199–201. On the connection between antislavery conservatives' racism and support for colonization in Kentucky, see Harlow, "Religion, Race, and Robert J. Breckinridge," 1–24, and Harlow, "Neither Slavery nor Abolitionism," 367–89.

83. Tallant, *Evil Necessity*, 125–32 and 138–45; Harrold, *Abolitionists and the South*, 131; "African Colonisation," *Louisville Examiner*, April 21, 1849; Nicholas et al., *Slave Emancipation in Kentucky*, 1. On other prominent antislavery advocates' continued endorsement of colonization, see Harlow, "Religion, Race, and Robert J. Breckinridge," 19, and Harlow, "Neither Slavery nor Abolitionism," 378.

84. "Convention of the Friends of Emancipation in Kentucky," *Louisville Examiner*, May 5, 1849.

85. Ibid.; Kentucky, and Richard Sutton, *Report of the Debates*, 105, 117; Tallant, *Evil Necessity*, 137, 145–49. Nevertheless, Tallant finds that in counties whose returns are available, the Emancipation Party earned an average of 35.1 percent of the vote; in some districts, including Louisville, antislavery candidates failed to win seats but still garnered over 40 percent of voters' support. Extrapolating statewide, Tallant estimates that, at a minimum, close to 10 percent of voters supported candidates holding antislavery views. While giving credit to emancipationists for a "respectable showing . . . in a slave state," Tallant attributes their losses to the absence of a practical plan for freeing Kentucky's slaves. Tallant, *Evil Necessity*, 149–51.

86. Tallant, *Evil Necessity*, 145–51; Harrison, *Antislavery Movement in Kentucky*, 56–59; Kentucky, and Richard Sutton, *Report of the Debates*, 90, 459, 83.

87. For concerns about "agitation" of the slavery question during the convention debates, see as an example the speech of Albert G. Talbott, of Boyle Co., in the Bluegrass section of the state, in Kentucky, and Richard Sutton, *Report of the Debates*, 948–52; ibid., 1100; Abraham Lincoln to George Robertson, August 15, 1855, in Basler, *Collected Works of Abraham Lincoln*, 2:317–19, quoted in Tallant, *Evil Necessity*, 158. See also Harrison and Klotter, *New History of Kentucky*, 117–19, and Tallant, *Evil Necessity*, 155–58.

88. Kentucky, and Richard Sutton, *Report of the Debates*, 117, 743, 70, 1100–1101, 1088.

89. Tallant, *Evil Necessity*, 159–60; Strattan and Vaughan, *Collection of the State and Municipal Laws*, 90; Gibson, "Semi-Centennial of a Public Career," 34–37, 43.

Chapter Eight

1. For the central question of "property in man," see Oakes, *Freedom National*, 8–14, and 1–48 generally.

2. William C. Harris argues that Lincoln's adept "management" secured border state loyalties in *Lincoln and the Border States*, 8, and passim. Harris's book offers the most careful recent treatment of Lincoln's responses to rapidly shifting events in the border states.

3. For a review of the historiography surrounding the idea of "conciliation," and compelling evidence countering this thesis, see Phillips, "Lincoln's Grasp of War." For Kentucky in particular, see 186–87, 191–93, and 200–202.

4. On Chase's antislavery constitutionalism, see Oakes, *Freedom National*, 15–17. Discussion of the "federal consensus" can be found in ibid., 2–8.

5. Ibid., xii, 7, 4, 26, 33–34.

6. Ibid., 366.

7. For the Emancipation Proclamation's "exemptions," see ibid., 362–67.

8. Niven, *Salmon P. Chase*, 29–33.

9. Ibid., 36–37.

10. Chase to Hamilton Smith, August 7, 1833, in Niven, *Chase Papers*, vol. 2, *Correspondence, 1823–1857*, 55.

11. Chase, *Sketch of the History*, 5, 10, 22, 40.

12. Earle, *Jacksonian Antislavery*, 151–54.

13. On the Northwest Ordinance as a "touchstone" for political abolitionists, see Oakes, 12–13; Chase, *Address of the Southern and Western Liberty Convention*, 2.

14. Chase, *Address of the Southern and Western Liberty Convention*, 3.

15. Ibid., 14.

16. Ibid., 10.

17. Chase, *Inaugural Address*, 9.

18. Chase, *Speech of Hon. Salmon P. Chase*, 17.

19. Ibid., 16; Varon, *Disunion*, 262.

20. [Chase et al.], *Appeal of the Independent Democrats*, 7.

21. Chase, *Inaugural Address*, 15.

22. Oakes, *Freedom National*, 28.

23. Cassius Clay to Salmon P. Chase, March 1842, in Niven, *Chase Papers*, vol. 2, *Correspondence, 1823–1857*, 90.

24. Ibid.

25. Niven, *Salmon P. Chase*, 93.

26. Salmon Chase to Gerrit Smith, September 1, 1846, in Niven, *Chase Papers*, vol. 2, *Correspondence, 1823–1857*, 129–30.

27. Chase diary, January 3, 1848, in Niven, *Chase Papers*, vol. 1, *Journals, 1829–1872*, 195.

28. Chase to Jacob Brinkerhoff, April 7, 1849, in Niven, *Chase Papers*, vol. 2, *Correspondence, 1823–1857*, 242.

29. Chase successfully promoted Clay as minister to Russia early in the Lincoln administration. Blue, *Salmon P. Chase*, 139.

30. Chase to Hamilton Smith, September 15, 1851, in Niven, *Chase Papers*, vol. 2, *Correspondence, 1823–1857*, 337.

31. Chase to Edward S. Hamlin, June 6, 1853, in ibid., 353–55.

32. Harrison, *Civil War in Kentucky*, 9.

33. Quoted in Oakes, *Freedom National*, 162–63. For Lincoln's statement in the context of fast-moving events, see ibid., 159–66.

34. Joshua F. Speed to Salmon P. Chase, September 2, 1861, in Niven, *Chase Papers*, vol. 3, *Correspondence, 1858–March 1863*, 93–94.

35. Garrett Davis to Chase, September 3, 1861, in ibid., 94.

36. Chase to Green Adams, September 5, 1861, in ibid., 95–96.

37. Chase to Garrett Davis, August 24, 1861, in ibid., 87.

38. Chase to George B. McClellan, July 7, 1861, in Niven, *Chase Papers*, vol. 3, *Correspondence, 1858–March 1863*, 75.

39. Chase to Garrett Davis, August 24, 1861, in ibid., 87.

40. Chase to McClellan, July 7, 1861, in ibid., 75.

41. Harrison and Klotter, *New History of Kentucky*, 190; Niven, *Chase Papers*, vol. 3, *Correspondence, 1858–March 1863*, xx.

42. Nelson to Chase, July 23, 1861, in Niven, *Chase Papers*, vol. 3, *Correspondence, 1858–March 1863*, 80.

43. Green Adams to Chase, July 31, 1861, in Niven, *Chase Papers*, vol. 3, *Correspondence, 1858–March 1863*, 82.

44. See Marshall, *Creating a Confederate Kentucky*, and Harrison, *Civil War in Kentucky*.

45. *Louisville Journal*, July 31, 1861.

46. Congleton, "George D. Prentice and Bloody Monday," 94–98.

47. John James Piatt, "Biographical Sketch," in Prentice, *Poems of George D. Prentice*, xiii.

48. Prentice, *Biography of Henry Clay*, 21, 149, 187, 196.

49. Ibid., 212, 137, 208.

50. Ibid., 98. In another example, during Clay's defense of common law as a fount of individual rights, one listener finally gave in to his emotion and "suffered [his tears] to flow uncontrolled, for he saw that he wept not alone." Ibid., 42.

51. Ibid., 155, 137.

52. Ibid., 119, 149, 160–61.

53. His humor today would seem nothing short of appalling in its assumptions about women, African Americans, and various ethnic groups, although he had a keen regard for female poets who expressed appreciation for his patronage.

54. Prentice to Asa Bolles, December 31, 1831, quoted in Congleton, "George D. Prentice and Bloody Monday," 102–3.

55. Congleton, "George D. Prentice and Bloody Monday," 101, 115.

56. Congleton, "Prentice, George Denison," in Kleber, *Kentucky Encyclopedia*, 736.

57. *Louisville Journal*, July 16, 1861. Betty Congleton contends that Prentice's editorials appeared without titles, as in this case, helping to identify his own writing from that of his assistants.

58. *Louisville Journal*, January 8, 1861.

59. Ibid.

60. Ibid.

61. *Louisville Journal*, July 16, 1861.

62. *Louisville Journal*, July 29, 1861, and July 31, 1861.

63. *Louisville Journal*, July 31, 1861.

64. Ibid., and *Louisville Journal*, January 4, 1861.

65. *Louisville Journal*, January 17, 1861.

66. *Louisville Journal*, January 8, 1861.

67. *Louisville Journal*, July 16, 1861.

68. *Louisville Journal*, July 4, 1861.

69. Blue, *Salmon P. Chase*, 188.

70. Quoted in Foner, *Fiery Trial*, 232.

71. Prentice, "Open Letter."

72. Ibid.

73. Howard, *Black Liberation*, 82. Howard notes that Kentucky had the highest number of men mustered. See 195n38.

74. Howard, *Black Liberation*, 53–54.

75. Quoted in ibid., 51.

76. Quoted in ibid., 59.

77. Quoted in ibid., 59–60, 64.

78. Ibid., 67, 71.

79. Prentice, "Open Letter."

80. Ibid.

81. Gibson, "Semi-Centennial of the Public Career," 6.

82. On the connection between the slave missions and a growing argument for the sanctity of slavery, see Snay, *Gospel of Disunion*, ch. 3. On the relationships between the slave missions and the church schisms, see Sparks, "To Rend the Body of Christ," 273–95; Touchstone, "Planters and Slave Religion," 99–126; Mohr, "Slaves and White Churches," 153–72; Irons, *Origins of Proslavery Christianity*, 195–200; Sernett, *Black Religion and American Evangelicalism*, 47–58; Carwardine, *Evangelicals and Politics*, 153–74; Mathews, *Slavery and Methodism*, 62–87. On the schisms within the major evangelical denominations generally, see Snay, *Gospel of Disunion*, and Goen, *Broken Churches*.

83. Mathews, *Religion in the Old South*, 137–50; Cornelius, *Slave Missions*, 178; Irons, *Origins of Proslavery Christianity*, 170; Genovese, *Roll, Jordan, Roll*, 190. On the "vitality" of the slave missions, see also Sernett, *Black Religion and American Evangelicalism*, 55–58. Albert J. Raboteau questions the success of the plantation missions in *Slave Religion*, 175–77.

84. *Minutes of the Annual Conferences of the Methodist Episcopal Church, South* (1845–1850), quotation in 1846 minutes; "Report of Richard Deering, Agent to Organize Missions to the Colored People" (1860), Louisville Annual Conference, Papers; Burckin, "Formation and Growth of an Urban Middle Class," 168.

85. Gibson, "Semi-Centennial of the Public Career," 5–6; *Minutes of the Annual Conferences of the Methodist Episcopal Church, South* (1845). The Fourth Street Methodist Episcopal Church's white branch had hosted the 1845 convention where Methodists met to form the M.E. Church, South. See Harmon, "Organization of the Methodist Episcopal Church, South," 112.

86. Gibson, "Semi-Centennial of the Public Career," 6–7. For additional information about the Fourth Street Colored Methodist Church's unusual property arrangement, see Weeden, *History of the Colored People of Louisville*, 42–43.

87. Gibson, "Semi-Centennial of the Public Career," 7.

88. Ibid., 6–8.

89. *Minutes of the Annual Conferences of the Methodist Episcopal Church, South* (1846), 61; ibid. (1848), 164. However, in 1847, official minutes again listed black Methodists as members of white churches. See *Minutes of the Annual Conferences of the Methodist Episcopal Church, South* (1847), 109. Louisville's city directories began to provide the distinctive names of black Methodist congregations in 1848. See Collins, *Gabriel Collins' Louisville*, 244. The *Minutes of the Annual Conferences of the Methodist Episcopal Church, South*, did not begin to do so continuously until 1859 (with one exception in 1854 for the "Centre Street Colored Church").

90. R. E. Jones United Methodist Church, "Historical Account," 7; Weeden, *History of the Colored People of Louisville*, 41–42; Collins, *Louisville and New Albany Directory and Annual Advertiser*, 244; Jegli, *Louisville Directory for 1848–49*, 31; *Minutes of the Annual Conferences of the Methodist Episcopal Church, South* (1859).

91. The church history states that Jackson Street Church "remained . . . the only Methodist Episcopal Church in Louisville until Trinity was founded some years later." R. E. Jones United Methodist Church, "Historical Account," 7. The first quotation comes from the title of the source. Trinity Methodist Episcopal Church does not appear in city directories before the Civil War, and the *Encyclopedia of Louisville* dates its founding to 1865. See entry under "Methodists," in Kleber, *Encyclopedia of Louisville*, 614. Louisville's two German churches were technically affiliated with the independent "Methodist German Episcopal Church, North," so R. E. Jones's "Historical Account" accurately asserts that no other Methodist Episcopal Church congregations remained in Louisville before Trinity's founding in 1865. In 1992, at the time of the drafting of the "Historical Account," six current members of the (renamed) R. E. Jones United Methodist Church had worshipped at the Jackson Street location. One older member, Hazel Green, even recalled stories from her childhood about "an aunt who attended the 'Old Frog Pond' Methodist Church," so it is possible that oral history contributed to members' understanding that Jackson Street Church always remained northern in its ecclesiastical affiliation. See R. E. Jones United Methodist Church, *Our Heritage Past and Present*, 22.

92. Weeden, *History of the Colored People of Louisville*, 52.

93. Ibid., 52, 42; *Minutes of the Annual Conferences of the Methodist Episcopal Church, South* (1845–50).

94. Loose notes (1858), Louisville Annual Conference, Papers; [Report by Committee on Missionary Charges] (1858), Louisville Annual Conference, Papers; [Committee on Missions] (1859), Louisville Annual Conference, Papers; Deering, "Report of Richard Deering." At its 1859 meeting, the Louisville Conference's Committee on Missions had "deem[ed] the appointment of an exclusive agent to this work for the present inexpediant [*sic*]," but the conference nevertheless decided to hire a missionary to work among black Methodists, for Deering's 1860 report states that he was "appointed" the previous year.

95. Deering, "Report of Richard Deering"; Irons, *Origins of Proslavery Christianity*, 201. Both of the two remaining black congregations considered mission "charges" by the M.E. Church, South, the Jackson Street Church and Centre Street Church, had troubled histories with white Methodists, as described above.

96. Cornelius, *Slave Missions*, 177–80; Irons, *Origins of Proslavery Christianity*, 170–74; Snay, *Gospel of Disunion*, ch. 3.

Chapter Nine

1. Rockenbach, "Border City at War," 40, 48.

2. Clark, *Black Brigade of Cincinnati*, 16. William H. Gibson described African Americans' impressment into "the spade and shovel brigade" to defend Louisville in late 1862. He numbered the men who served in the "thousands." Gibson, "Semi-Centennial of the Public Career," 47.

3. Klement, "Sound and Fury," 102.

4. J. S. Newberry, "Report on the Condition of the Troops and the Operations of the Sanitary Commission in the Valley of the Mississippi, for the Three Months Ending Nov. 30, 1861," 16, in United States Sanitary Commission, *Documents of the U.S. Sanitary Commission*, vol. 1, No. 36.

5. Andrew Phillips from Hospital No. 10, Louisville, Kentucky, October 19, 1862, http://www.kyhistory.com/cdm/compoundobject/collection/MS/id/194/rec/11. This letter is cited by Marshall, *Creating a Confederate Kentucky*, but she provides 1863 as its date of authorship. See 29–30. The more likely date appears to be 1862, since Phillips discusses the Battle of Perryville.

6. Reid, *After the War*, 294. For this incident, see also Marshall, *Creating a Confederate Kentucky*, 35.

7. The most recent scholarship directly engages with this complexity while charting white Kentuckians' "belated" or "ex post facto" secession from the Union after 1865 by means of racial violence and an imagined Confederate past. See Marshall, *Creating a Confederate Kentucky*; Astor, *Rebels on the Border*; and Dollar et al., *Sister States, Enemy States*. Two notable treatments of Kentucky's postwar sympathy for the Confederacy include Coulter, *Civil War and Readjustment in Kentucky*, and Woodward, *Origins of the New South, 1877–1913*. See Astor, *Rebels on the Border*, 5, and Marshall, *Creating a*

Confederate Kentucky, 34. For the situation in Louisville, see Rockenbach, "Border City at War," 50.

8. Marshall, *Creating a Confederate Kentucky*, 4.

9. Astor, *Rebels on the Border*.

10. Kentucky Branch of the U.S. Sanitary Commission, *Report* (1866), 8–9.

11. Newberry, *U.S. Sanitary Commission*, 434.

12. Harrison and Klotter, *New History of Kentucky*, 196–98.

13. A brief biography of Holt may be found in Kleber, *Encyclopedia of Louisville*, 395.

14. Kentucky Branch of the U.S. Sanitary Commission, *Report* (1866), 6.

15. J. S. Newberry, "Report on the Operations of the U.S. Sanitary Commission in the Valley of the Mississippi, Made September 1st, 1863," 19 in U.S. Sanitary Commission, *Documents of the U.S. Sanitary Commission*, vol. 2, No. 75.

16. Kentucky Branch of the U.S. Sanitary Commission, *Report* (1866), 17.

17. Newberry, *U.S. Sanitary Commission*, 68, 205, 217.

18. Hess, *Civil War in the West*, 36–39.

19. Dr. J. S. Newberry, "A Visit to Fort Donelson, Tenn. For the Relief of the Wounded of Feb. 15, 1862," 2–3, in U.S. Sanitary Commission, *Documents of the U.S. Sanitary Commission*, vol. 1, No. 42.

20. Newberry, "Visit to Fort Donelson," 1–3.

21. Cincinnati Branch of the U.S. Sanitary Commission, *For the Immediate Relief of our Sick and Wounded Soldiers* and *To the People of Ohio, Indiana, and Kentucky*.

22. Hess, *Civil War in the West*, 101–2. Quoted in Hess, 102.

23. United States Sanitary Commission, *Reports from the Western Department*, 6, 8.

24. J. S. Newberry to W. P. Sprague, February 16, 1863, "What the U.S. Sanitary Commission is Doing in the Valley of the Mississippi," 4–5, in U.S. Sanitary Commission, *Documents of the U.S. Sanitary Commission*, vol. 2, No. 64.

25. J. S. Newberry, "Report on the Operations of the U.S. Sanitary Commission in the Valley of the Mississippi, Made September 1st, 1863," 9, in U.S. Sanitary Commission, *Documents of the U.S. Sanitary Commission*, vol. 2, No. 75.

26. J. S. Newberry, "Report on the Operations of the U.S. Sanitary Commission, in the Valley of the Mississippi, for the Quarter ending Oct. 1st, 1864," 5, in U.S. Sanitary Commission, *Documents of the U.S. Sanitary Commission*, vol. 2, No. 84.; Newberry, *U.S. Sanitary Commission*, 442–43.

27. Newberry, *U.S. Sanitary Commission*, 433–35, 443.

28. Ibid., 431–43.

29. Kentucky Branch, *Report*, 9.

30. Boynton, *History of the Great Western Sanitary Fair*, xx.

31. Lawson, *Patriotic Fires*, 14–39.

32. Newberry, "Report . . . September 1st, 1863," 9; Newberry, "Report . . . Oct. 1st, 1864," 5.

33. Newberry, "Report . . . September 1st, 1863," 9.

34. Newberry, *U.S. Sanitary Commission*, 102, 68.

35. "The Mission of the Reporter," *Sanitary Reporter*, June 1, 1863.

36. Bushnell, "Report of the Rev. F. H. Bushnell," *Sanitary Reporter*, April 1, 1864.

37. Boynton, *History of the Great Western Sanitary Fair*, x–xii.

38. Cincinnati Branch, *For the Immediate Relief of our Sick and Wounded Soldiers*, 1.

39. Newberry, "Visit to Fort Donelson," 7.

40. Cincinnati Branch of the United States Sanitary Commission, "The Wounded and their Friends," *Monthly Bulletin of the Operations of the Cincinnati Branch*, October 1863, 16–17.

41. F. N. K., "Plain Answers to Plain Questions," *Sanitary Reporter*, April 1, 1864. The *Sanitary Commission Bulletin* originally published this article.

42. "To the Sanitary Commission," *Sanitary Reporter*, April 1, 1864. The poem originally appeared in *Harper's Weekly*.

43. M.R.B., "At the Aid Society," *Sanitary Reporter*, May 1, 1864. The column indicates that the author was from Louisville.

44. "In the Hospital," *Sanitary Reporter*, April 15, 1865.

45. Newberry, *U.S. Sanitary Commission*, 104. This language originally appeared in the *Sanitary Reporter* on August 15, 1865, and was reprinted in Newberry's history.

46. Newberry, "Visit to Fort Donelson," 3–4.

47. United States Sanitary Commission, *Reports from the Western Department* (1862), 1–2, 5.

48. Boynton, *History of the Great Western Sanitary Fair*, 574, 568.

49. Ibid., 578. On Kentucky's low rates of service, see Marshall, *Creating a Confederate Kentucky*, 20.

50. "Blowing our Trumpet," *Sanitary Reporter*, April 15, 1864.

51. Newberry, *U.S. Sanitary Commission*, 104–5.

52. J. S. Newberry to W. P. Sprague, February 16, 1863, "What the U.S. Sanitary Commission is Doing in the Valley of the Mississippi," 5, in U.S. Sanitary Commission, *Documents of the U.S. Sanitary Commission*, vol. 2, No. 64.

53. Klement, *Copperheads in the Middle West*, 73–106.

54. The word "friends" comes from P. G. T. Beauregard to Charles J. Villere, May 26, 1863, *Official Records of the Union and Confederate Armies* (128 vols., 1880–1901), Ser. 1, XIV:995, quoted in ibid., 124.

55. Ibid., 130–32.

56. Boynton, *History of the Great Western Sanitary Fair*, xii, 533.

57. Ibid., 34, 37.

58. Ibid., 248, 45, 378.

59. Ibid., 47–48, 240, 116.

60. *History and Organization of the Catholic Institute of Cincinnati, O.*, 16.

61. Boynton, *History of the Great Western Sanitary Fair*, 283, 355, 360, 376, 392, 412, 407.

62. Thalheimer, "History of the Vine Street Congregational Church of Cincinnati," 49; Boynton, *Address Before the Citizens of Cincinnati*, 11–12.

63. Boynton, *Oration, Delivered on the Fifth of July, 1847, Before the Native Americans of Cincinnati*, 11.

64. See Baughin, "Bullets and Ballots: The Election Day Riots of 1855," 267–72.

65. Boynton, *History of the Great Western Sanitary Fair*, 403.

66. Ibid., 93, 108.

67. Ibid., 403–10.

68. See Ketner, *Emergence of the African American Artist*, 90–92.

69. Boynton, *History of the Great Western Sanitary Fair*, 409–10; Katz, *Regionalism and Reform*, 90, 117.

70. Boynton, *History of the Great Western Sanitary Fair*, 226.

71. Oakes, *Freedom National*, 457–58.

72. Lincoln, "Proclamation of Amnesty and Reconstruction," in United States, *Statutes at Large*, 737–39. Boynton, *History of the Great Western Sanitary Fair*, 212–13.

73. Klement, "Sound and Fury," 105. See also Lawson, *Patriot Fires*, 71–74.

74. Klement, "Sound and Fury," 105–9. Congressional Globe, 38 Cong., 1st sess., 1501–3.

75. Pirtle, quoted in Marshall, *Creating a Confederate Kentucky*, 25.

76. Chase, journal entry for August 3, 1862, in Niven, *Chase Papers*, vol. 1, *Journals*, 357.

77. Astor, *Rebels on the Border*, 5, 122–26; Marshall, *Creating a Confederate Kentucky*, 24–30.

78. Klement, *Copperheads in the Middle West*, 207–10. Klement writes that the "Union" Party emerged "in those states where the political contests were in doubt." Ibid., 208. See also Lawson, *Patriot Fires*, 67–79. National Union Association, "To the Citizens of Ohio," 1863.

79. "Our Paper," *Louisville Daily Union Press*, September 1, 1864.

80. See "Kentucky's Vote" and "Then and Now," in which the editors of the *Louisville Daily Union Press* cite large increases in the numbers of voters selecting Lincoln in the 1864 election relative to the negligible number of votes from 1860. *Louisville Daily Union Press*, November 9, 1864.

81. National Union Association, "To the Citizens of Ohio." It is not clear that the association had ties to more widely known Union Leagues or clubs established throughout the North. See Klement, *Copperheads in the Middle West*, 210–13. For a discussion of the Stones River battle, see Hess, *Civil War in the West*, 126–33.

82. Ames, *Stand By the President!*, 5, 3, 8, 11, 14–15, 58.

83. On Drake's complex politics and wartime activities, see Arenson, *Great Heart of the Republic*, 138–39.

84. Drake, *Speech of the Hon. Charles Drake*, 7, 14.

85. Drake, *Union and Anti-Slavery Speeches*, 407.

86. "Necessity of Emancipation," *Louisville Daily Union Press*, November 26, 1864.

87. "Prospectus of the Louisville Weekly Union Press," *Louisville Daily Union Press*, September 7, 1864.

88. "Our Agents," *Louisville Daily Union Press*, September 10, 1864.

89. "Our Creed," *Louisville Daily Union Press*, September 2, 1864; "To the Loyal Men of Kentucky," *Louisville Daily Union Press*, December 9, 1864.

90. See, for example, "Union Meeting at the Court House," *Louisville Daily Union Press*, October 4, 1864, and "Great National Union Demonstration," *Louisville Daily Union Press*, October 4, 1864.

91. "Rowdyism Saturday Evening," *Louisville Daily Union Press*, October 17, 1864; "Then and Now," *Louisville Daily Union Press*, October 19, 1864.

92. "The New Order of Things," *Louisville Daily Union Press*, November 14, 1864.

93. "Prospectus of the Louisville Weekly Union Press," *Louisville Daily Union Press*, September 7, 1864.

94. "The Slave Power and the War," *Louisville Daily Union Press*, October 3, 1864; "Choose Ye this Day," *Louisville Daily Union Press*, November 8, 1864.

95. "Union Men of Kentucky," *Louisville Daily Union Press*, September 19, 1864; "The Slave Power and the War."

96. "Mr. Lincoln and Slavery," *Louisville Daily Union Press*, September 2 and 3, 1864.

97. "The Slave Power and the War."

98. "Henry Clay," *Louisville Daily Union Press*, October 25, 1864.

99. "Necessity of Emancipation."

100. Astor, *Rebels on the Border*, 126.

101. Gibson, "Semi-Centennial of the Public Career," 47–48.

102. "Mr. Lincoln and Slavery," *Louisville Daily Union Press*, September 3, 1864.

103. "Copperhead Comments on Negro Troops," *Louisville Daily Union Press*, October 7, 1864.

104. "The Importance of Negro Enlistments," *Louisville Daily Union Press*, November 9, 1864.

105. "The Colonization Scheme," *Louisville Daily Union Press*, December 24, 1864.

106. "A Reply to Gov. Bramlette," *Louisville Daily Union Press*, December 12, 1864.

107. Clark, *Black Brigade of Cincinnati*, 4–10.

108. Ibid., 9, 13.

109. Ibid., 10, 15, 19–21.

110. Ibid., 11–13.

111. Ibid., 14–15.

Epilogue

1. Howard, *Black Liberation in Kentucky*, 51–60, 67.

2. Palmer, *Personal Recollections*, 267; Harrison and Klotter, *New History of Kentucky*, 204–5.

3. Palmer, *Personal Reflections*, 268. Palmer spells his name "Terrell." On Terrill, see Harrison and Klotter, *New History of Kentucky*, 204–5. They describe him as "a leader of Union guerrillas in Spencer County."

4. Palmer, *Personal Recollections*, 228–29.

5. United States Congress, "A Resolution to encourage Enlistments and to promote the Efficiency of the military Forces in the United States," in United States, *Statutes at Large*, 571.

6. Palmer, *Personal Recollections*, 254.

7. Ibid., 238–39.

8. Ibid., 237.

9. Ibid., 244.

10. Langston, *Virginia Plantation to the National Capital*, 238.

11. Howard, *Black Liberation in Kentucky*, 80–86.

12. Ibid., 79.

13. Langston, *Virginia Plantation to the National Capital*, 238.

14. Palmer, *Personal Recollections*, 240.

15. Langston, *Virginia Plantation to the National Capital*, 237; Palmer, *Personal Recollections*, 241.

16. Langston, *Virginia Plantation to the National Capital*, 237.

17. Ibid., 237–40.

18. Parrish, *Golden Jubilee of the General Association of Colored Baptists*, 196–97; Langston, *Virginia Plantation to the National Capital*, 239–40.

19. Henry Adams, "To the First Colored Baptist church of Louisville, on 5th street," *Western Recorder* (Louisville), April 29, 1871, 2, quoted in Mohon, "First African Baptist Church," 11; Parrish, *Golden Jubilee*, 281; Lucas, *History of Blacks in Kentucky*, 123–26, 211–12. Paul Harvey states that North Carolina black Baptists were the first to form a state organization, in 1866, but black Baptists in Kentucky trace the origins of their association to the previous year. Harvey, *Redeeming the South*, 62.

20. Langston, *Virginia Plantation to the National Capital*, 232–39; Palmer, *Personal Recollections*, 242.

21. Langston, *Virginia Plantation to the National Capital*, 234–35.

22. See Baptist, *The Half Has Never Been Told*. Also, Taylor's *Internal Enemy* provides new dimension to the grip and violence of slavery.

Bibliography

Primary Sources

MANUSCRIPT AND ARCHIVAL SOURCES

African Colonization Pamphlets. 5 vols. Cincinnati History Library and Archives, Cincinnati Museum Center, Cincinnati, Ohio.

African Methodist Episcopal Church Conference, Cincinnati Station. Quarterly Conference Minutes. Allen Temple African Methodist Episcopal Church, Cincinnati, Ohio.

Allen Chapel. Financial Records. Allen Temple African Methodist Episcopal Church, Cincinnati, Ohio.

Allen Chapel Officers. "Letter to the Bishop and Conference of the M. E. Church for the Cincinnati District, now in session" (October 31, 1854). Samuel Williams Collection, Methodist Church Papers. Cincinnati History Library and Archives, Cincinnati Museum Center, Cincinnati, Ohio.

Asbury Chapel (Cincinnati). Minutes of the Board of Trustees. Salt Lake City, Utah: Genealogical Society of Utah, 1995. Microfilm 1987642.

Banks, Daniel Chapman. Diary, Letters, and Papers. Filson Historical Society, Louisville, Ky.

Blanchard, Jonathan. Correspondence and Journals. Jonathan Blanchard Collection. Buswell Memorial Library Archives and Special Collections, Wheaton College, Wheaton, Ill.

Booth Family Papers. Correspondence. Filson Historical Society, Louisville, Ky.

Brown, John. Diary, 1821–1822, 1852. Filson Historical Society, Louisville, Ky.

Campbell, Arthur Lee. Papers. Filson Historical Society, Louisville, Ky.

Central Christian Church. Records. Cincinnati History Library and Archives, Cincinnati Museum Center, Cincinnati, Ohio.

Clark, Davis Wasgatt. Papers. Cincinnati History Library and Archives, Cincinnati Museum Center, Cincinnati, Ohio.

Covenant-First Presbyterian Church. Minutes of the Vestry. Cincinnati History Library and Archives, Cincinnati Museum Center, Cincinnati, Ohio.

Fifth Street Baptist Church. Minutes. University Archives and Records Center, University of Louisville, Ky.

First Baptist Church of Jesus Christ (Louisville). Church Minutes. Nashville, Tenn.: Southern Baptist Historical Library and Archives. Microfilm 1062.

First Unitarian (Congregational) Church. Correspondence and Records. Cincinnati History Library and Archives, Cincinnati Museum Center, Cincinnati, Ohio.

Foraker, Thomas. Scrapbook. Cincinnati History Library and Archives, Cincinnati Museum Center, Cincinnati, Ohio.

Frost, Maria Goodell. Papers. Special Collections, Hutchins Library, Berea College, Berea, Ky.

Irwin, John. Letters. Filson Historical Society, Louisville, Ky.

Jefferson, John F. Diaries. Filson Historical Society, Louisville, Ky.

Kentucky Annual Conference. Papers. Kentucky United Methodist Heritage Center, Kentucky Wesleyan College, Owensboro, Ky.

Louisville and Vicinity Bible Society. Records. Filson Historical Society, Louisville, Ky.

Louisville Annual Conference. Papers. Kentucky United Methodist Heritage Center, Kentucky Wesleyan College, Owensboro, Ky.

Mason, Johnson, Jr. Journal. American Antiquarian Society, Worcester, Mass.

Ninth Street Baptist Church. Records. Lakewood Baptist Church, Cincinnati, Ohio.

Nippert Collection of German Methodism. Cincinnati History Library and Archives, Cincinnati Museum Center, Cincinnati, Ohio.

People's Church. Session Records. Cincinnati History Library and Archives, Cincinnati Museum Center, Cincinnati, Ohio.

Prentice, George Dennison. Papers. Filson Historical Society, Louisville, Ky.

Reilly, Marianne. Journal. Archives of the Archdiocese of Cincinnati, Mount St. Mary's, Cincinnati, Ohio.

St. Paul's Episcopal Church. Minutes of the Vestry. Archives of the Diocese of Southern Ohio, Cincinnati, Ohio.

Union Baptist Church. Records. National Underground Railroad Freedom Center, Cincinnati, Ohio.

United States Sanitary Commission. *Documents of the U.S. Sanitary Commission.* 2 vols. New York, 1866. Huntington Library, San Marino, Calif.

Vine Street Congregational Church (Cincinnati). Broadside Collection. American Antiquarian Society, Worcester, Mass.

Walnut Street Baptist Church (Louisville). Records and Minutes. Nashville, Tenn.: Southern Baptist Historical Library and Archives. Microfilm 6395.

Wesley Chapel Methodist Church (Cincinnati). Member Records. Salt Lake City, Utah: Genealogical Society of Utah, 1995. Microfilm 1987643.

OFFICIAL PAPERS

DeBow, J. D. B. *The Seventh Census of the United States: 1850. . . .* Washington, D.C.: Robert Armstrong, 1853.

[Griswold, Hiram]. *Reports of Cases Argued and Determined in the Supreme Court of the State of Ohio, in Bank.* Vol. 19. 2nd ed. Cincinnati: Robert Clarke and Company, 1860. http://babel.hathitrust.org/cgi/pt?id=mdp.35112103922359;view=1up;seq=10. May 4, 2015.

Kentucky, and Richard Sutton. *Report of the Debates and Proceedings of the Convention for the Revision of the Constitution of the State of Kentucky, 1849.* Frankfort, Ky.: A. G. Hodges, 1849.

Statistics of the United States, (Including Mortality, Property, &c.,) in 1860. . . .
  Washington, D.C.: Government Printing Office, 1866.
Strattan, Oliver H., and John M. Vaughan. *A Collection of the State and Municipal
  Laws, in Force, and Applicable to the City of Louisville, Ky.* Louisville, 1857.
Stowe, C. E. *Report of Elementary Public Instruction in Europe, Made to the
  Thirty-Sixth General Assembly of the State of Ohio, December 19, 1837.* Boston: Dutton
  and Wentworth, 1838. https://archive.org/details/reportonelementoogoog. May
  4, 2015.
United States. *Statutes at Large, Treaties, and Proclamations of the United States of
  America.* Vol. 13. Boston, 1866. Freedmen & Southern Society Project. http://
  www.freedmen.umd.edu. May 6, 2015.
United States Congress. *Congressional Globe.* Washington: Blair and Rives,
  1834–1873. http://memory.loc.gov/ammem/amlaw/lwcg.html. May 6, 2015.

CHURCH MINUTES AND ANNUAL REPORTS OF RELIGIOUS ASSOCIATIONS

American Catholic Directories, 1817–1879. Washington, D.C.: Catholic University of
  American Press, 1950–1974. Microfilm.
Cincinnati Bible Society. *The First Annual Report of the Cincinnati Bible Society.*
  Cincinnati: Looker & Reynolds, 1830.
Cincinnati Miami Bible Society. *Fifth Annual Report of the Cincinnati Miami Bible
  Society.* Cincinnati: Mason and Palmer, 1819.
General Assembly of the Presbyterian Church in the USA. *Minutes of the General
  Assembly of the Presbyterian Church in the United States of America, 1821–1837.*
General Assembly of the Presbyterian Church in the USA (New School). *Minutes
  of the General Assembly of the Presbyterian Church in the United States of America,
  1838–1860.*
General Assembly of the Presbyterian Church in the USA (Old School). *Minutes
  of the General Assembly of the Presbyterian Church in the United States of America,
  1838–1860.*
General Convention of Western Baptists. *Proceedings of the Second Anniversary of
  the General Convention of Western Baptists. . . 1835.* Cincinnati: N. S. Johnson,
  1835.
Long Run Association (Kentucky). *Minutes of the Long Run Association of Baptists,
  1815–1860.*
Methodist Episcopal Church. *Minutes of the Annual Conferences of the Methodist
  Episcopal Church, 1820–1860.*
Methodist Episcopal Church, South. *Minutes of the Annual Conferences, 1845–1860.*
Miami Association of Regular Baptists (Ohio). *Minutes of the Miami Association of
  Regular Baptists, 1837–1860.*
Miami Association of Regular Baptists [Anti-Mission] (Ohio). *Minutes of the Miami
  Association of Regular Baptists, 1840–53, 1856.*
Miami Baptist Association (Ohio). *Minutes of the Miami Baptist Association,
  1820–1836.*

Miami Baptist Association [Anti-Mission] (Ohio). *Minutes of the Miami Baptist Association, 1836–39.*

Miami Baptist Association of Primitive Baptists (Ohio). *Minutes of the One Hundred-Seventeenth Annual Session of the Miami Baptist Association of Primitive Baptists,* 1917.

Regular Baptist Churches of Color. *Minutes of the Annual Associations of the Regular Baptist Churches of Color in Ohio,* 1837 and 1840.

NEWSPAPERS, MAGAZINES, JOURNALS, AND PERIODICALS

The African Repository and Colonial Journal (Washington, D.C.)

Anti-Slavery Bugle (New-Lisbon, Ohio)

Atkinson's Casket; Or, Gems of Literature, Wit, and Sentiment (Philadelphia)

The Baptist Advocate (Cincinnati)

Bible Society Record (New York)

The Catholic Telegraph (Cincinnati)

The Christian Press (Cincinnati)

The Christian Recorder (Philadelphia)

The Christian Repository (Louisville)

Cincinnati Post and Anti-Abolitionist

The Examiner (Louisville)

Ford's Christian Repository (Louisville)

Frederick Douglass' Paper (Rochester)

Gleason's Pictorial Drawing-Room Companion (Boston)

The Independent (New York)

The Ladies' Repository (Cincinnati)

Louisville Daily Journal

Louisville Daily Union Press

Louisville Journal

The Louisville Weekly Journal

Monthly Bulletin of the Operations of the Cincinnati Branch, United States Sanitary Commission (Cincinnati)

Nashville Christian Advocate

New-York Evangelist

The North Star (Rochester)

The Philanthropist (Cincinnati)

The Sanitary Reporter (Louisville)

Watchman of the Valley (Cincinnati)

Western Christian Advocate (Cincinnati)

Western Monthly Magazine (Cincinnati)

PUBLISHED PRIMARY SOURCES

Allen Temple AME Church. *Centennial Guide: Allen Temple A. M. E. Church, Organized February 4, 1824....* Cincinnati: Centennial Commission of the Allen Temple AME Church, 1924.

American Colonization Society. Ohio Committee of Correspondence. *Ohio in Africa. Memorial to the Honorable, the Senate and House of Representatives of the State of Ohio.* Cincinnati[?], 1851.

[American Reform Tract and Book Society]. *Walter Browning; or, The Slave's Protector; Founded on Fact.* Cincinnati: American Reform Tract and Book Society, 1856.

Ames, Rev. Charles G. *Stand By the President! An Address Delivered Before the National Union Association, of Cincinnati, March 6, 1863.* Philadelphia: King & Baird, 1863.

Arnett, Rev. B. W., ed. *Proceedings of the Semi-Centenary Celebration of the African Methodist Episcopal Church of Cincinnati, held in Allen Temple. . . 1874.* Cincinnati: H. Watkin, 1874.

Aydelott, Rev. B. P. *Prejudice Against Colored People.* Cincinnati: Western Tract and Book Society, 1852.

A Baptist [Silas J. Evans]. *A History of Persecution, for the Truth's Sake, in Louisville, KY., by a Baptist.* Louisville: Printed for the Author, 1858.

Bascom, H[enry] B. *Methodism and Slavery: With Other Matters in Controversy Between the North and the South. . . .* Frankfort: Hodges, Todd & Pruett, 1845.

Basler, Roy P., ed. *Abraham Lincoln: His Speeches and Writings.* Cleveland: World Publishing, 1946.

———. *The Collected Works of Abraham Lincoln.* Vol. 2. New Brunswick, N.J.: Rutgers University Press, 1953.

Beecher, Lyman. *Plea for the West.* Cincinnati, 1835. Reprint, New York: Arno, 1977.

Bibb, Henry. *Narrative of the Life and Adventures of Henry Bibb, An American Slave Written by Himself.* Introduction by Lucius C. Matlack. New York: Published by the Author, 1850. https://archive.org/details/narrativeoflifeaoobibb. May 4, 2015.

Birney, James Gillespie. *Letter on Colonization: Addressed to the Rev. Thornton J. Mills, Corresponding Secretary of the Kentucky Colonization Society.* New York: American Anti-Slavery Society, 1838.

Blanchard, Jonathan. *A Perfect State of Society: Address before the "Society of Inquiry," in Oberlin Collegiate Institute.* Oberlin, Ohio: James Steele, 1839.

Boynton, Charles B. *Address Before the Citizens of Cincinnati; Delivered on the Fourth Day of July, 1855.* Cincinnati: Cincinnati Gazette Company Print, 1855.

———. *History of the Great Western Sanitary Fair.* Cincinnati, Ohio: C. F. Vent, 1864.

———. *Oration, Delivered on the Fifth of July, 1847, before the Native Americans of Cincinnati.* Cincinnati: Tagart & Gardner, 1847.

Brisbane, William H. *Church Abolitionism; Or, The Legitimate Tendency of the Doctrines of Modern Abolitionism; Practically Illustrated, in the Recent Disruption of the First (Late Enon) Baptist Church of Cincinnati.* Cincinnati, 1841.

Brown, William Wells. *The Rising Son; Or, The Antecedents and Advancement of the Colored Race.* Boston: A. G. Brown, 1882. https://archive.org/details/risingsonorantecoobrow. May 4, 2015.

Buck, William C. *The Slavery Question.* Louisville: Harney, Hughes & Hughes, 1849.

Cary, Alice. *Poems.* Boston: Ticknor and Fields, 1855.

Carey [Cary], Alice and Phoebe. *Poems of Alice and Phoebe Carey* [*sic*]. Philadelphia: Moss and Brother, 1850.

Casseday, Ben. *The History of Louisville from its Earliest Settlement till the Year 1852.* Louisville: Hull and Brother, 1852.

Chase, Salmon P. *The Address and Reply on the Presentation of a Testimonial to S. P. Chase, by the Colored People of Cincinnati, with some account of the case of Samuel Watson.* Cincinnati: Henry W. Derby, 1845.

———. *The Address of the Southern and Western Liberty Convention held at Cincinnati, June 11 & 12, 1845. With Notes by a Citizen of Pennsylvania.* New York: William Harned, 1845.

———. *Inaugural Address of Salmon P. Chase, Governor of the State of Ohio: Delivered Before the Senate and House of Representatives.* Columbus: Statesman Steam, 1856.

———. *A Sketch of the History of Ohio.* Cincinnati: Corey and Fairbank, 1833.

———. *Speech of Hon. Salmon P. Chase, Delivered at The Republican Mass Meeting, in Cincinnati, August 21, 1855; Together with Extracts from His Speeches in the Senate on Kindred Subjects.* Columbus: Ohio State Journal, 1855.

Child, Lydia Maria. "How a Kentucky Girl Emancipated Her Slaves." *Independent,* March 27, 1862. Emory Women Writers Resource Project. http://womenwriters .library.emory.edu/content.php?level=div&id=child_kentucky_001&document =child_kentucky. May 6, 2015.

Chitwood, M. Louisa. *Poems.* Edited by George Prentice. Cincinnati: Moore, Wilstach, Keyes, 1857.

Christian Anti-Slavery Convention. *Minutes of the Christian Anti-Slavery Convention.* Cincinnati: Ben Franklin Book and Job Rooms, 1850.

Cincinnati Branch of the United States Sanitary Commission. *For the Immediate Relief of our Sick and Wounded Soldiers. To the Women of Ohio, Indiana, and Kentucky.* Cincinnati, 1862. https://archive.org/details/101206067.nlm.nih.gov. May 6, 2015.

———. *To the People of Ohio, Indiana, and Kentucky.* Cincinnati, [1862?]. https:// archive.org/details/101180711.nlm.nih.gov. May 6, 2015.

Cincinnati Directory for the Year 1829. . . . Cincinnati: Robinson and Fairbank, 1829.

Cincinnati Directory for the year 1831. . . . Cincinnati: Robinson and Fairbank, 1831.

Cincinnati Directory for the Years 1836–37. . . . Cincinnati: J. H. Woodruff, 1836.

Cist, Charles. *Cincinnati in 1841: Its Early Annals and Future Prospects.* Cincinnati, 1841.

———. *Sketches and Statistics of Cincinnati in 1851.* Cincinnati: Wm. H. Moore, 1851.

———. *Sketches and Statistics of Cincinnati in 1859.* Cincinnati, 1859.

Citizen. *The Cincinnati Directory. . . .* Cincinnati: Oliver Farnsworth, 1819.

Clark, Davis Wasgatt. *The Temple Built and the Temple Blessed: A Dedication Sermon Preached at the Opening of the Lecture and Sunday School Rooms at Trinity Methodist Episcopal Church, Cincinnati. . . .* Cincinnati: Methodist Book Concern, 1859.

Clark, Peter H. *Black Brigade of Cincinnati: Being a Report of Its Labors and a Muster-Roll of Its Members; Together with Various Orders, Speeches, Etc. Relating to It.* Cincinnati, 1864.

Clarke, James Freeman. *Autobiography, Diary and Correspondence*. Edited by Edward Everett Hale. 1891. Reprint, New York: Negro Universities Press, 1968.

Cleros. *Address to the Non-Slaveholders of Kentucky, Read and Adopted at a Meeting of the Mechanics and Laboring-Men of Louisville, Held at the Court-House, April 10, 1849*. Louisville: Published for the Corresponding and Executive Committee on Emancipation, 1849.

Coffin, Levi. *Reminiscences of Levi Coffin, The Reputed President of the Underground Railroad*. 1876. Reprint, New York: Arno, 1968.

Coggeshall, William T. *The Poets and Poetry of the West: With Biographical and Critical Notices*. Columbus: Follett, Foster, 1860.

Collins, Gabriel. *Gabriel Collins' Louisville and New Albany Directory and Annual Advertiser, for 1848. . . .* Louisville, 1848.

——. *The Louisville Directory, for the Year 1836. . . .* Louisville: Prentice & Weissinger, 1836.

——. *The Louisville Directory, for the year 1841. . . .* Louisville: Henkle Logan, 1841.

"Corresponding and Executive Committee" on Emancipation, *Address to the Non-Slaveholders of Kentucky*. Louisville: April 1849.

Craik, James. *Historical Sketches of Christ Church, Louisville*. Louisville: John P. Morton, 1862.

Dana, E. *Geographical Sketches on the Western Country: Designed for Emigrants and Settlers*. Cincinnati: Looker, Reynolds, 1819.

David, John M. *A Spiritual Retreat of Eight Days*. Louisville, 1864.

A Debate on the Roman Catholic Religion, Held in the Sycamore-Street Meeting House, Cincinnati. . . 1837. New York: Benziger Brothers, 1837.

Dixon, James. *Personal Narrative of a Tour through a part of the United States and Canada: With Notices of the History and Institutions of Methodism in America*. New York: Lane & Scott, 1849.

Drake, Benjamin. *A Public Oration, Delivered by Appointment, before the Phi Alpha Theta Society, July 4, 1826*. Cincinnati: Morgan, Lodge and Fisher, 1826.

Drake, Charles D. *Speech of Hon. Charles D. Drake, Delivered Before the National Union Association, at Cincinnati, October 1, 1864*. https://archive.org/details /speechofhoncharloodrak. May 6, 2015.

——. *Union and Anti-Slavery Speeches, Delivered During the Rebellion*. Cincinnati, Ohio: Applegate, 1864.

Dunlevy, A. H. *History of the Miami Baptist Association; From its Organization in 1797 to a Division in that Body on Missions, etc., in the Year 1836. . . .* Cincinnati: G. S. Blanchard, 1869.

Dyer, Sidney. *Voices of Nature, and Thoughts in Rhyme*. Louisville: J. V. Cowling & G. C. Davies, 1849.

Easton, L. D. "The Colored Schools of Cincinnati." In *History of the Schools of Cincinnati and Other Educational Institutions, Public and Private*. Edited by Isaac M. Martin. Cincinnati, 1900.

Eaton, Thomas Treadwell. *History of the Walnut Street Baptist Church, 1815 to 1900.* Louisville, 1900.

Elliott, Rev. Charles. *Delineation of Roman Catholicism, Drawn from the Authentic and Acknowledged Standards of the Church of Rome. . . .* 2 vols. New York: Published by George Lane, for the Methodist Episcopal Church, 1841.

———. *History of the Great Secession from the Methodist Episcopal Church in the Year 1845, Eventuating in the Organization of the New Church, Entitled the "Methodist Episcopal Church, South."* Cincinnati: Swormstedt & Poe, 1855.

Emerson, Ralph Waldo. *The Collected Works of Ralph Waldo Emerson.* Edited by Joseph Slater, Alfred R. Ferguson, and Jean Ferguson Carr. Vol. 3. Cambridge, Mass.: Belknap Press of Harvard University Press, 1983.

Eulalie [Mrs. Mary Eulalie Fee Shannon]. *Buds, Blossoms, and Leaves: Poems.* Cincinnati: Moore, Wilstach & Keys, 1854.

Everts, W. W. *Bethel: Or The Claims of Public Worship.* Louisville: Hull and Brother, 1855.

First Orthodox Congregational Church. *Manual of the First Orthodox Congregational Church, in Cincinnati.* Cincinnati: Cincinnati Gazette Company Steam Printing House, 1856.

Fitzgerald, O. P. *John B. McFerrin: A Biography.* Nashville, Tenn.: M.E. Church, South, 1889.

Fitzhugh, George. *Cannibals All! Or, Slaves without Masters.* 1857. Reprint, edited and with an introduction by C. Vann Woodward. Cambridge, Mass.: Belknap Press of Harvard University Press, 1988.

Flint, Timothy Flint. *A Condensed Geography and History of the Western States, or the Mississippi Valley.* Cincinnati: E. H. Flint, 1828.

Frost, Maria Goodell. *Gospel Fruits: Or, Bible Christianity Illustrated; A Premium Essay.* Cincinnati: American Reform Tract and Book Society, 1856.

Gaddis, Maxwell Pierson. *Foot-Prints of an Itinerant.* Cincinnati: Printed at the Methodist Book Concern, for the Author, 1855.

Gaines, J. I., and J. H. Perkins. *Orations, Delivered on the First of August, 1849, before the Colored Citizens of Columbus and Cincinnati.* Cincinnati, 1849. http://babel .hathitrust.org/cgi/pt?id=hvd.hx4q3r. May 4, 2015.

Gems of Poetry; Containing the Poems of Samuel Woodworth, the Biography and Poetry of "Amelia," the Western Poetess. Lancaster, Pa.: James H. Bryson, 1844.

General Association of Baptists in Kentucky. *Memorial Volume Containing the Papers and Addresses that were Delivered at the Jubilee of the General Association of Baptists.* Louisville: John P. Morton, 1888.

Gibson, W. H., Sr. "Semi-Centennial of the Public Career of W. H. Gibson, Sr.: Fifty Years' Experience and a Participant in the Joys and Sorrows of His People, From the Year 1847 to 1897." In *History of the United Brothers of Friendship and Sisters of the Mysterious Ten. . . .* Louisville: Bradley & Gilbert, 1897.

Griffith, Mattie. *Autobiography of a Female Slave* (New York, 1856). Jackson: University Press of Mississippi, 1998.

———. *Poems, By Mattie Griffith. Now First Collected.* New York: D. Appleton, 1852.

Griswold, Rufus, ed. *Female Poets of America.* Philadelphia: Carey and Hart, 1849.

Hamline, Mrs. Melinda. *Memoirs of Mrs. Angeline B. Sears, with Extracts from Her Correspondence.* Cincinnati: Swormstedt and Power, for the Methodist Episcopal Church, 1850.

Hampton, George A. *Historical Sketch of the Fifth Street Baptist Church of Louisville, Kentucky.* Louisville: American Baptist, 1969.

Hedrick, Joan. ed. *The Oxford Harriet Beecher Stowe Reader.* New York: Oxford University Press, 1999.

Herder, Johann Gottfried. *The Spirit of Hebrew Poetry.* Translated by James Marsh. 2 vols. Burlington, Vt.: Edward Smith, 1833.

Hibbard, Rev. F. G. *Biography of Rev. Leonidas L. Hamline, D.D., Late One of the Bishops of the Methodist Episcopal Church.* Cincinnati: Hitchcock and Walden, 1880.

History and Organization of the Catholic Institute of Cincinnati, O. Cincinnati: Wahrheits-Freund Job Office, 1860. https://archive.org/details/historyoforganizoocinc. May 6, 2015.

Hopkins, John Henry. *Essay on Gothic Architecture, with Various Plans and Drawings for Churches, Designed Chiefly for the Use of the Clergy.* Burlington, Vt.: Smith & Harrington, 1836.

Hord, B. C. *History of the Baptist Church Difficulties.* Louisville, 1858.

Jackson, Margaret A. *Memoirs of the Rev. William Jackson, First Rector of St. Paul's Church, Louisville.* New York: Protestant Episcopal Society for the Promotion of Evangelical Knowledge, 1861.

Jegli, John B. *John B. Jegli's Louisville Directory for 1848–49.* . . . Louisville: John C. Noble, 1848.

Johnston, J. Stoddard, ed. *Memorial History of Louisville from its First Settlement to the Year 1896.* 2 vols. Chicago: American Biographical Publishing, 1896.

Kelso, Isaac. *Danger in the Dark: A Tale of Intrigue and Priestcraft.* Cincinnati: Published for the author by Moore, Anderson, Wilstach & Keys, 1854.

Kenny, D. J. *Illustrated Cincinnati: Pictorial Hand-Book of the Queen City.* Cincinnati: Robert Clarke, 1875.

Kentucky Branch of the U.S. Sanitary Commission. *Report.* Louisville, Hull & Brother, 1866.

Kentucky Colonization Society. *Fourth Annual Report of the Kentucky Colonization Society, with an Address . . . by Rev. John C. Young.* Frankfort, Ky.: Albert G. Hodges, 1833.

King, Margaret R. *Memoirs of the Life of Mrs. Sarah Peter.* Cincinnati: Robert Clarke, 1889.

Lakewood Baptist Church (Ninth Street Baptist Church). "Our Church History." Cincinnati: Lakewood Baptist Church, n.d. Photocopy.

[Lane Theological Seminary]. *Fifth Annual Report of the Trustees of the Cincinnati Lane Seminary....* Cincinnati: Corey & Fairbank, 1834. https://archive.org /details/fifthannualreporoolane. May 4, 2015.

Langston, John Mercer. *From the Virginia Plantation to the National Capital; Or, The First and Only Negro Representative in Congress from the Old Dominion.* Hartford, Conn.: American Publishing, 1894. https://archive.org/details /fromvirginiaplanoolangiala. May 4, 2015.

Lois. *Harriet and Ellen: Or, The Orphan Girls.* Cincinnati: American Reform Tract and Book Society, 1865.

Louisville City Directory and Business Mirror; for 1858–59.... Louisville: Hurd & Burrows, 1858[?].

Lowth, Robert. *Lectures on the Sacred Poetry of the Hebrews.* Translated by G. Gregory. 1753. Reprint, with new introduction and notes by Calvin E. Stowe. Andover, Mass.: Crocker and Brewster, 1829.

M. A. F. ["By a Lady."] Revised by the Committee of Publication. *Gertrude Lee; Or, The Northern Cousin.* Cincinnati: American Reform Tract and Book Society, 1856.

Maffitt, John Newland. *Poems.* Louisville: Prentice and Weissinger, 1839.

———. *Pulpit Sketches, First Series.* Louisville: W. Harrison Johnston, 1839.

Mahan, Asa. *Autobiography: Intellectual, Moral, and Spiritual.* London: For the author, T. Woolmer, 1882.

Malvin, John. *North into Freedom: The Autobiography of John Malvin, Free Negro, 1795–1880.* Edited by Allan Peskin. Cleveland: Press of Western Reserve University, 1966.

Managers of the Colored Orphan Asylum. *Eleventh Annual Report of the Managers of the Colored Orphan Asylum for 1855–56.* Cincinnati: Henry Watkins, 1855–56.

McCloskey, Patrick, ed. *The 1846–54 Letters of Fr. William Unterthiner, O.S.F. Founder of St. John the Baptist Province.* Cincinnati: St. Clement Friary, 1982.

———. "Letters of Fr. William Unterthiner, O.S.F. (1844–46): Founder of St. John the Baptist Province." Master's thesis, St. Bonaventure University, 1979.

McMurtrie, H[enry]. *Sketches of Louisville and its Environs.* Louisville: S. Penn, 1819.

A Memorial on the Present State of the Presbyterian Church. Cincinnati: James M'Millan, 1833.

Miller, Rev. Adam, ed. *Experience of German Methodist Preachers.* Cincinnati: Methodist Book Concern, 1859.

Miller, Shackelford. *Historical Sketch of the First Presbyterian Church of Louisville.* Louisville, 1916.

M'Ilvaine, Charles Pettit. *The Chief Danger of the Church in These Times: A Charge Delivered to the Clergy of the Diocese of Ohio.* New York: Harper and Brothers, 1843.

Minutes and Address of the State Convention of the Colored Citizens of Ohio, Convened at Columbus, ... 1849. Oberlin, Ohio: J. M. Fitch's Power Press, 1849.

Morse, Samuel Finley Breese [Brutus, pseud.]. *Foreign Conspiracy Against the United States: The Numbers of Brutus, Originally Published in the New York Observer.* 1835. Reprint, New York: Arno, 1977.

National Union Association. Circular, "To the Citizens of Ohio." Cincinnati, 1863.

Newberry, J. S. *Report on the Operations of the U.S. Sanitary Commission in the Valley of the Mississippi, for the Quarter ending Oct. 1st, 1864.* Washington, D.C., 1864. https://archive.org/details/reportonoperatiooonewb. May 6, 2015.

———. *The U.S. Sanitary Commission in the Valley of the Mississippi, During the War of the Rebellion, 1861–1866.* Cleveland, Ohio: Fairbanks, Benedict, 1871.

[Nicholas, Samuel S., et al.] *Slave Emancipation in Kentucky.* [Louisville], 1849. Samuel J. May Anti-Slavery Collection, Division of Rare and Manuscript Collections, Cornell University Library. http://ebooks.library.cornell.edu/cgi/t/text/text-idx?c=mayantislavery;idno=27892710. May 4, 2015.

Nichols, Rebecca S. Reed. *Songs of the Heart and the Hearth-Stone.* Cincinnati: J. F. Desilver, 1851.

Ninth Street Baptist Church. *Semi-Centennial of the Ninth Street Baptist Church of Cincinnati, November 7, 8, and 9, 1880; Historical Discourse and Other Papers.* Cincinnati, 1880.

Niven, John, ed. *The Salmon P. Chase Papers.* 5 vols. Kent, Ohio: Kent State University Press, 1993–1998.

Norton, John N. *The Duty and Privilege of Building and Adorning Churches: A Sermon Preached at the Re-Opening of Christ Church, Louisville.* Louisville: Hulls & Shannon, 1850.

Otis, Richard. *The Louisville Directory. . . .* Louisville: Richard W. Otis, 1832.

Palmer, John. *Personal Recollections of John M. Palmer: The Story of an Earnest Life.* Cincinnati, Ohio: Robert Clarke, 1901.

Parrish, C. H., ed. *Golden Jubilee of the General Association of Colored Baptists in Kentucky. The Story of Fifty Years' Work from 1865–1915.* Louisville: Mays Printing, 1915.

[Parsons, Charles Booth]. *The Pulpit and the Stage; or, The Two Itinerancies. An Historic, Biographic, Philosophic Miscellany.* Nashville: Southern Methodist Publishing House, 1860.

Payne, Daniel. *History of the African Methodist Episcopal Church.* Edited by Rev. C. S. Smith. Nashville: Publishing House of the AME Sunday-School Union, 1891.

Perrin, William Henry, J. H. Battle, and G. C. Kniffin. *Kentucky: A History of the State. . . .* 8th ed. Louisville: F. A. Battery, 1888.

Poor, N. Peabody, comp. *Haldeman's Picture of Louisville, Directory and Business Advertiser, for 1844–45; Containing an Historical Sketch of the Town from 1778 to the Present. . . .* Louisville: W. H. Haldeman, 1844.

Population of the United States in 1860. . . . Washington, D.C.: Government Printing Office, 1864.

Potter, Eliza. *A Hairdresser's Experience in High Life.* 1859. Edited with introduction by Xiomara Santamarina. Chapel Hill: University of North Carolina Press, 2009.

Prentice, George D. *Biography of Henry Clay*. Hartford, Conn.: Samuel Hammer Jr. and John Jay Phelps, 1831.

———. *The Poems of George D. Prentice*. Edited by John James Piatt. Cincinnati: Robert Clarke, 1876.

A Presbyter. *Weighed in the Balance and Found Wanting*. Cincinnati: Printed for the Author, 1853.

[Presbytery of Cincinnati and the Ministerial Association of Cincinnati]. *Presbyterianism in Cincinnati: Its History, Position and Duty*. Cincinnati, 1871.

Purcell, John. "Documents: Bishop Purcell's Journal, 1833–1836." *Catholic Historical Review* 5 (July/October 1919): 239–56.

Redford, Rev. A. H. *The History of Methodism in Kentucky*. Nashville: Southern Methodist Publishing House, 1870.

Reid, Whitelaw. *After the War: A Tour of the Southern States, 1865–1866*. New York: Harper & Row, 1965.

Shaffer, David Henry. *The Cincinnati, Covington, Newport and Fulton Directory for 1840*. Cincinnati: J. B. & R. P. Donogh, 1840.

Simpson, J. Mc. C. [Joshua McCarter]. *The Emancipation Car, Being an Original Composition of Anti-Slavery Ballads, Composed Exclusively for the Under Ground Rail Road*. 1874. Reprint, Miami, Fla.: Mnemosyne, 1969.

A Sketch of the Life of Rev. John Collins, Late of the Ohio Conference. Cincinnati: Swormstedt and Power, for the Methodist Episcopal Church, at the Western Book Concern, 1849.

Smith, Benjamin Bosworth. *The Blessedness of the Sacraments, Aside from Their Immediate Efficacy*. Louisville: Morton and Griswold, 1850.

Smith, David. *Biography of Rev. David Smith of the A.M.E. Church; Being a Complete History, Embracing over Sixty Years' Labor in the Advancement of the Redeemer's Kingdom on Earth. . . .* Xenia, Ohio: Xenia Gazette Office, 1881.

Smith, Mrs. M. J. P. *Little Robert and His Friend; Or, The Light of Brier Valley*. Cincinnati: American Reform Tract and Book Society, 1861.

Spalding, M. J. *Sketches of the Early Catholic Missions of Kentucky; From Their Commencement in 1787, to the Jubilee of 1826–7. . . .* Louisville, 1844.

Stowe, Harriet Beecher. *Uncle Tom's Cabin*. 1852. Reprint, edited with an introduction and notes by Jean Fagan Yellin. New York: Oxford University Press, 1998.

Stowe, Mrs. H[arriet] E. B. "Introductory Essay." In *The Incarnation; Or, Pictures of the Virgin and Her Son*, by Charles Beecher. New York: Harper & Brothers, 1849.

Tanner, Henry, comp. *The Louisville Directory and Business Advertiser for 1859–60. . . .* Louisville: Maxwell, 1859.

Thalheimer, Miss M. E. "History of the Vine Street Congregational Church of Cincinnati." *Papers of the Ohio Church History Society* 9 (1898): 41–56.

Trollope, Frances. *Domestic Manners of the Americans*. 1832. Reprint, with an introduction by Herbert Van Thal. London: Folio Society, 1974.

United States. Congress. *Appeal of the Independent Democrats in Congress to the People of the United States: Shall Slavery be Permitted in Nebraska?* [U.S.], [1854?]. https://archive.org/details/ASPC0005194100. May 6, 2015.

United States Sanitary Commission. *Reports from the Western Department.* https://archive.org/details/101525064.nlm.nih.gov. May 6, 2015.

Venable, W. H. *Beginnings of Literary Culture in the Ohio Valley: Historical and Biographical Sketches.* Cincinnati: Robert Clarke, 1891.

Walker, David. *Walker's Appeal, in Four Articles; Together with a Preamble, to the Coloured Citizens of the World. . . . 1830.* Reprint, with an introduction by Peter P. Hinks. University Park: Pennsylvania State University Press, 2000.

Walnut Street Baptist Church. *Testimony in Full in the Case of Ford Against Everts for Slander, and in the Case of Hord Against Ford for Immoral Conduct. . . .* Louisville: Walnut Street Baptist Church, 1859.

Watts, Isaac. *The Psalms of David, Imitated in the Language of the New Testament, and Applied to the Christian Use and Worship.* 1801. Reprint, edited by Timothy Dwight. New Haven, Conn.: Durrie & Peck, 1837.

Webb, Benedict J. *The Centenary of Catholicity in Kentucky.* Louisville: Charles A. Rogers, 1884.

Weeden, Henry Clay. *Weeden's History of the Colored People of Louisville.* 1897. Reprint, compiled by Juanita Landers White, Louisville, 1986.

Welby, Amelia Ball (Coppack). *Poems by Amelia.* New York: D. Appleton, 1856.

Weninger, Rev. F. X. *The Sacred Heart Mission Book: A Guide to Christian Perfection.* New York: P. O'Shea, 1863.

The Whole Booke of Psalmes Faithfully Translated into English Metre. Cambridge, Mass., 1640. http://www.wdl.org/en/item/2834/. September 19, 2015.

Williams' Cincinnati Almanac, Business Guide and Annual Advertiser, 1850. Cincinnati: C. S. Williams, 1850.

Williams' Cincinnati Directory, City Guide, and Business Mirror, for the Year 1859. Cincinnati: C. S. Williams, 1859.

Wilson, Lizzie. *Poems by Lizzie.* Louisville: Hull & Brothers, 1860.

Wuest, John B. *Materials for a History of St. John the Baptist Province, II: The 1850–74 Letters of Twelve Tyrolese Friars in the U. S.* Translated by Aldric Heidlage and edited by Patrick McCloskey. Cincinnati: St. George Friary, 1984.

Wuest, John B., ed., with Patrick McCloskey, and Cyprian Berens, trans. *Materials for a History of St. John the Baptist Province, IV: The 1840–68 Letters in the General Archives of the Order of Friars Minor.* Cincinnati: St. Clement Friary, 1983.

Secondary Sources

Aaron, Daniel. *Cincinnati, Queen City of the West: 1819–1838.* Columbus: Ohio State University Press, 1992.

Abrams, M. H. *Natural Supernaturalism: Tradition and Revolution in Romantic Literature.* New York: W. W. Norton, 1971.

Abruzzo, Margaret. *Polemical Pain: Slavery, Cruelty, and the Rise of Humanitarianism.* Baltimore: Johns Hopkins University Press, 2011.

Abzug, Robert H. *Cosmos Crumbling: American Reform and the Religious Imagination.* New York: Oxford University Press, 1994.

Ahern, Stephen, ed. *Affect and Abolition in the Anglo-Atlantic, 1770–1830.* Farnham, England: Ashgate, 2013.

Ahlstrom, Sydney E. *A Religious History of the American People.* New Haven: Yale University Press, 1972.

Albanese, Catherine L. "Transcendentalism." In *The Encyclopedia of American Religious Experience: Studies of Traditions and Movements,* edited by Charles H. Lippy and Peter W. Williams. 3 vols. New York: Charles Scribner's Sons, 1988.

Amneus, Cynthia. *A Separate Sphere: Dressmakers in Cincinnati's Golden Age.* Cincinnati: Cincinnati Art Museum; Lubbock: Texas Tech University Press, 2003.

Anbinder, Tyler. *Nativism and Slavery: The Northern Know-Nothings and the Politics of the 1850s.* New York: Oxford University Press, 1992.

Andrews, Dee. *The Methodists and Revolutionary America, 1760–1800: The Shaping of an Evangelical Culture.* Princeton, N.J.: Princeton University Press, 2000.

Appleby, Joyce. *Inheriting the Revolution: The First Generation of Americans.* Cambridge, Mass.: Belknap Press of Harvard University Press, 2000.

Arenson, Adam. *The Great Heart of the Republic: St. Louis and the Cultural Civil War.* Cambridge, Mass.: Harvard University Press, 2011.

Astor, Aaron. *Rebels on the Border: Civil War, Emancipation, and the Reconstruction of Kentucky and Missouri.* Baton Rouge: Louisiana State University Press, 2012.

Aubespin, Mervin, Kenneth Clay, and J. Blaine Hudson. *Two Centuries of Black Louisville: A Photographic History.* Louisville: Butler Books, 2011.

Ayers, Edward L., et al. *All Over the Map: Rethinking American Regions.* Baltimore: Johns Hopkins University Press, 1996.

Baker, David L. "The Joyce Family Murders: Justice and Politics in Know-Nothing Louisville." *Register of the Kentucky Historical Society* 102 (Summer 2004): 357–82.

Baldwin, Thomas P. "George D. Prentice, the *Louisville Anzeiger,* and the 1855 Bloody Monday Riots." *Filson Club History Quarterly* 67 (October 1993): 482–95.

Ballinger, Franchot. *The Way to Community: A History of Community Monthly Meeting of the Religious Society of Friends, Cincinnati, Ohio.* Cincinnati: Community Monthly Meeting of the Religious Society of Friends, 1998.

Baptist, Edward E. "'Cuffy,' 'Fancy Maids,' and 'One-Eyed Men': Rape, Commodification, and the Domestic Slave Trade in the United States." *American Historical Review* 106 (December 2001): 1619–50.

———. *The Half Has Never Been Told: Slavery and the Making of American Capitalism.* New York: Basic Books, 2014.

Baughin, William A. "Bullets and Ballots: The Election Day Riots of 1855." *Bulletin of the Historical and Philosophical Society of Ohio* 21 (October 1963): 267–72.

Baym, Nina. *Woman's Fiction: A Guide to Novels by and about Women in America, 1820–1870.* 2nd ed., with new introduction and supplemental bibliography. Urbana: University of Illinois Press, 1993.

Beckert, Sven, and Julia B. Rosenbaum. *The American Bourgeoisie: Distinction and Identity in the Nineteenth Century.* New York: Palgrave Macmillan, 2010.

Bell, Michael. *Sentimentalism, Ethics and the Culture of Feeling.* Houndmills, England: Palgrave, 2000.

Benedict, Philip. "Calvinism as a Culture? Preliminary Remarks on Calvinism and the Visual Arts." In *Seeing Beyond the Word: Visual Arts and the Calvinist Tradition,* edited by Paul Corby Finney. Grand Rapids, Mich.: William B. Eerdmans, 1999.

Bennett, Paula, ed. *Nineteenth-Century American Women Poets: An Anthology.* Malden, Mass.: Blackwell, 1998.

———. *Palace-Burner: The Selected Poetry of Sarah Piatt.* Urbana: University of Illinois Press, 2001.

Berlin, Ira. *Slaves without Masters: The Free Negro in the Antebellum South.* New York: New Press, 1974.

Bertaux, Nancy. "Structural Economic Change and Occupational Decline among Black Workers in Nineteenth-Century Cincinnati." In *Race and the City: Work, Community, and Protest in Cincinnati, 1820–1970,* edited by Henry Louis Taylor Jr., 126–55. Chicago: University of Illinois Press, 1993.

Billington, Ray Allen. *The Protestant Crusade, 1800–1860: A Study of the Origins of American Nativism.* New York: Macmillan, 1938. Reprint, Gloucester, Mass.: Peter Smith, 1963.

Birdwhistell, Ira V. *Gathered at the River: A History of the Long Run Association.* Louisville: Long Run Baptist Association, 1978.

Blue, Frederick J. "The Moral Journal of a Political Abolitionist." *Civil War History* 57 (September 2011): 210–33.

———. *Salmon P. Chase: A Life in Politics.* Kent, Ohio: Kent State University Press, 1987.

Bratt, James. "The Reorientation of American Protestantism, 1835–1845." *Church History* 67 (March 1998): 52–82.

Brekus, Catharine. *Strangers and Pilgrims: Female Preaching in America, 1740–1845.* Chapel Hill: University of North Carolina Press, 1998.

Bristol, Douglas Walter, Jr. *Knights of the Razor: Black Barbers in Slavery and Freedom.* Baltimore: John Hopkins University Press, 2009.

Buell, Lawrence. *Literary Transcendentalism: Style and Vision in the American Renaissance.* Ithaca, N.Y.: Cornell University Press, 1973.

Buggeln, Gretchen Townsend. "Elegance and Sensibility in the Calvinist Tradition: The First Congregational Church of Hartford, Connecticut." In *Seeing beyond the Word: Visual Arts and the Calvinist Tradition,* edited by Paul Corby Finney. Grand Rapids, Mich.: William B. Eerdmans, 1999.

Burckin, Alexander Irwin. "The Formation and Growth of an Urban Middle Class: Power and Conflict in Louisville, Kentucky, 1828–1861." PhD diss., University of California, Irvine, 1993.

Burin, Eric. *Slavery and the Peculiar Solution: A History of the American Colonization Society*. Gainesville: University Press of Florida, 2005.

Bushman, Richard. *The Refinement of America: Persons, Houses, Cities*. New York: Vintage Books, 1993.

Butler, Diana Hochstedt. *Standing against the Whirlwind: Evangelical Episcopalians in Nineteenth-Century America*. New York: Oxford University Press, 1995.

Butler, Jon. *Awash in a Sea of Faith: Christianizing the American People*. Cambridge, Mass.: Harvard University Press, 1990.

———. *Becoming America: The Revolution before 1776*. Cambridge, Mass.: Harvard University Press, 2000.

———. "Enthusiasm Described and Decried: The Great Awakening as Interpretive Fiction." *Journal of American History* 69 (September 1982): 305–25.

Caldwell, Robert W. *Communion in the Spirit: The Holy Spirit as the Bond of Union in the Theology of Jonathan Edwards*. Eugene, Ore.: Wipf & Stock, 2007.

Carey, Patrick. *The Roman Catholics*. Westport, Conn: Greenwood, 1993.

Carwardine, Richard. *Evangelicals and Politics in Antebellum America*. New Haven: Yale University Press, 1993.

Cayton, Andrew R. L. *Ohio: The History of a People*. Columbus: Ohio State University Press, 2002.

Ceplair, Larry. "Mattie Griffith Browne: A Kentucky Abolitionist." *Filson Club History Quarterly* 68 (April 1994): 219–31.

Chai, Leon. *The Romantic Foundations of the American Renaissance*. Ithaca, N.Y.: Cornell University Press, 1987.

Charvat, William. *Literary Publishing in America, 1790–1850*. 1959. Reprint, with an afterword by Michael Winship. Amherst: University of Massachusetts Press, 1993.

Cheek, William, and Aimee Lee Cheek. *John Mercer Langston and the Fight for Black Freedom, 1829–65*. Urbana: University of Illinois Press, 1989.

Clubbe, John. *Cincinnati Observed: Architecture and History*. Columbus: Ohio State University Press, 1992.

Cohen, Daniel A. "The Respectability of Rebecca Reed: Genteel Womanhood and Sectarian Conflict in Antebellum America." *Journal of the Early Republic* 16 (Fall 1996): 419–61.

Congleton, Betty Carolyn. "George D. Prentice and Bloody Monday: A Reappraisal." *Register of the Kentucky Historical Society* 63 (1965): 218–39.

Conkin, Paul K. *Cane Ridge: America's Pentecost*. Madison: University of Wisconsin Press, 1990.

Conroy, Rev. Joseph P. *Arnold Damen, S.J.: A Chapter in the Making of Chicago*. Cincinnati: Benziger Brothers, Printers to the Holy Apostolic See, 1930.

Cornelius, Janet Duitsman. *Slave Missions and the Black Church in the Antebellum South*. Columbia: University of South Carolina Press, 1999.

Coulter, E. Merton. *The Civil War and Readjustment in Kentucky*. Gloucester, Mass.: P. Smith, 1966.

Coyle, William, ed. *Ohio Authors and Their Books: Biographical Data and Selective Bibliographies for Ohio Authors, Native and Resident, 1796–1950.* Cleveland: World Publishing, 1962.

Crawford, Michael J. *Seasons of Grace: Colonial New England's Revival Tradition in Its British Context.* New York: Oxford University Press, 1991.

Crews, Clyde F. *An American Holy Land: A History of the Archdiocese of Louisville.* Wilmington, Del.: Michael Glazier, 1987. Reprint, Mt. Vernon, Ind.: Windmill, 1999.

———. *Presence and Possibility: Louisville Catholicism and Its Cathedral: An Historical Sketch of the Louisville Catholic Experience as Seen through the Cathedral of the Assumption.* 1973. Reprint, Louisville: Lost Cause, 1983. Microfiche.

Dannenbaum, Jed. *Drink and Disorder: Temperance Reform in Cincinnati from the Washingtonion Revival to the WCTU.* Urbana: University of Illinois Press, 1984.

Davis, David Brion. *The Slave Power Conspiracy and the Paranoid Style.* Baton Rouge: Louisiana State University Press, 1969.

De Rosa, Deborah. *Domestic Abolitionism and Juvenile Literature, 1830–1865.* Albany: State University of New York Press, 2003.

Dichtl, John R. *Frontiers of Faith: Bringing Catholicism to the West in the Early Republic.* Lexington: University Press of Kentucky, 2008.

———. "'She stalks abroad displaying her splendid trappings': Transplanting Catholicism to Kentucky, 1793–1830." *Register of the Kentucky Historical Society* 97 (Autumn 1999): 347–73.

Dobson, Joanne. "Reclaiming Sentimental Literature." *American Literature* 69 (June 1997): 263–88.

Dolan, Jay P. *Catholic Revivalism: The American Catholic Experience, 1830–1860.* Notre Dame: University of Notre Dame Press, 1978.

Dollar, Kent T., Larry H. Whiteaker, and W. Calvin Dickinson, eds. *Sister States, Enemy States: The Civil War in Kentucky and Tennessee.* Lexington: University Press of Kentucky, 2009.

Douglas, Ann. *The Feminization of American Culture.* New York: Avon Books, 1978.

Earle, Jonathan H. *Jacksonian Antislavery and the Politics of Free Soil, 1824–1854.* Chapel Hill: University of North Carolina Press, 2004.

Eastman, Carolyn. *A Nation of Speechifiers: Making an American Public after the Revolution.* Chicago: University of Chicago Press, 2010.

Eaton, Clement. "Slave-Hiring in the Upper South: A Step toward Freedom." *Mississippi Valley Historical Review* 46 (March 1960): 663–78.

Fahs, Alice. *The Imagined Civil War: Popular Literature of the North and South, 1861–1865.* Chapel Hill: University of North Carolina Press, 2001.

Finkelman, Paul. "Race, Slavery, and Law in Antebellum Ohio." In *The History of Ohio Law,* edited by Michael Les Benedict and John F. Winkler, with a foreword by Hon. Thomas J. Moyer, 2:748–81. Athens: Ohio University Press, with the Ohio State Bar Foundation, 2004.

———. *Slavery in the Courtroom: An Annotated Bibliography of American Cases.* Washington, D.C.: Library of Congress, 1985.

Foner, Eric. *The Fiery Trial: Abraham Lincoln and American Slavery*. New York: W. W. Norton, 2010.

———. *Free Soil, Free Labor, Free Men: The Ideology of the Republican Party before the Civil War*. 1970. Reprint, with a new introductory essay. New York: Oxford University Press, 1995.

Ford, Bridget. "Beyond Cane Ridge: The 'Great Western Revivals' in Louisville and Cincinnati, 1828–1845." *Ohio Valley History* 8, no. 4 (Winter 2008): 17–37.

———. "Black Spiritual Defiance and the Politics of Slavery in Antebellum Louisville." *Journal of Southern History* 78, no. 1 (February 2012): 69–106.

Fox, Richard Wightman. *Jesus in America: Personal Savior, Cultural Hero, National Obsession*. San Francisco: HarperSanFrancisco, 2004.

Franchot, Jenny. *Roads to Rome: The Antebellum Protestant Encounter with Catholicism*. Berkeley: University of California Press, 1994.

Franklin, John Hope, and Loren Schweninger. *Runaway Slaves: Rebels on the Plantation*. New York: Oxford University Press, 1999.

Fredrickson, George M. *The Black Image in the White Mind: The Debate on Afro-American Character and Destiny, 1817–1914*. Hanover, N.H.: Wesleyan University Press, 1971.

———. *Racism: A Short History*. Princeton: Princeton University Press, 2002.

Freehling, William W. *The Road to Disunion: Secessionists at Bay, 1776–1854*. New York: Oxford University Press, 1990.

———. *The South vs. The South: How Anti-Confederate Southerners Shaped the Course of the Civil War*. New York: Oxford University Press, 2001.

Gaustad, Edwin Scott, and Philip L. Barlow. *New Historical Atlas of Religion in America*. New York: Oxford University Press, 2001.

Gellman, David N. "Race, the Public Sphere, and Abolition in Late-Eighteenth-Century New York." *Journal of the Early Republic* 20 (Winter 2000): 607–36.

Genovese, Eugene D. *Roll, Jordan, Roll: The World the Slaves Made*. New York: Vintage Books, 1976.

Gienapp, William E. *The Origins of the Republican Party, 1852–1856*. New York: Oxford University Press, 1987.

———. "Salmon P. Chase, Nativism, and the Formation of the Republican Party in Ohio." *Ohio History* 93 (Winter/Spring 1984): 5–39.

Gilje, Paul A. *Rioting in America*. Bloomington: Indiana University Press, 1996.

Glazer, Walter Stix. *Cincinnati in 1840: The Social and Functional Organization of an Urban Community during the Pre–Civil War Period*. With a foreword by Carl Abbott and an afterword by John D. Fairfield. Columbus: Ohio State University Press, 1999.

Goen, C. C. *Broken Churches, Broken Nation: Denominational Schisms and the Coming of the American Civil War*. Macon, Ga.: Mercer University Press, 1985.

Goodman, Paul. "The Manual Labor Movement and the Origins of Abolitionism." *Journal of the Early Republic* 13 (Fall 1993): 355–88.

———. *Of One Blood: Abolitionism and the Origins of Racial Equality*. Berkeley: University of California Press, 1998.

Gruenwald, Kim M. *River of Enterprise: The Commercial Origins of Regional Identity in the Ohio Valley, 1790–1850*. Bloomington: Indiana University Press, 2002.

Gura, Philip F. *The Wisdom of Words: Language, Theology, and Literature in the New England Renaissance*. Middletown, Conn.: Wesleyan University Press, 1981.

Hackenberg, Michael, ed. *Getting the Books Out: Papers of the Chicago Conference on the Book in 19th-Century America*. Washington, D.C.: Center for the Book, Library of Congress, 1987.

Hall, David D. "Readers and Writers in Early New England." In *The Colonial Book in the Atlantic World*, edited by Hugh Armory and David D. Hall. Vol. 1 of *A History of the Book in America*. Cambridge: Cambridge University Press, in association with the American Antiquarian Society, 2000.

———. "The Uses of Literacy in New England, 1600–1850." In *Cultures of Print: Essays in the History of the Book*. Amherst: University of Massachusetts Press, 1996.

Hall, David D., and Russell L. Martin. "A Note on Popular and Durable Authors and Titles." In *The Colonial Book in the Atlantic World*, edited by Hugh Armory and David D. Hall. Vol. 1 of *A History of the Book in America*. Cambridge: Cambridge University Press, in association with the American Antiquarian Society, 2000.

Hall, Susan Grove. "From Voice to Persona: Amelia Welby's Lyric Tradition in Sarah M. B. Piatt's Early Poetry." *Tulsa Studies in Women's Literature* 25 (Fall 2006): 223–46.

Halttunen, Karen. *Confidence Men and Painted Women: A Study of Middle-Class Culture in America, 1830–1870*. New Haven: Yale University Press, 1982.

Hambrick-Stowe, Charles, ed. *Early New England Meditative Poetry: Anne Bradstreet and Edward Taylor*. New York: Paulist, 1988.

———. *The Practice of Piety: Puritan Devotional Disciplines in Seventeenth-Century New England*. Chapel Hill: University of North Carolina Press, 1982.

Hardy, Daniel W. "Calvinism and the Visual Arts: A Theological Introduction." In *Seeing beyond the Word: Visual Arts and the Calvinist Tradition*, edited by Paul Corby Finney. Grand Rapids, Mich.: William B. Eerdmans, 1999.

Harlow, Luke E. "Neither Slavery nor Abolitionism: James M. Pendleton and the Problem of Christian Conservative Antislavery in 1840s Kentucky." *Slavery & Abolition* 27 (December 2006): 367–89.

———. "Religion, Race, and Robert J. Breckinridge: The Ideology of an Antislavery Slaveholder, 1830–1860." *Ohio Valley History* 6 (June 2006): 1–24.

———. *Religion, Race, and the Making of Confederate Kentucky, 1830–1880*. New York: Cambridge University Press, 2014.

Harmon, Nolan B. "The Organization of the Methodist Episcopal Church, South." In *The History of American Methodism*, edited by Emory Stevens Bucke. Vol. 2. New York: Abingdon, 1964.

Harris, William C. *Lincoln and the Border States: Preserving the Union*. Lawrence: University Press of Kansas, 2011.

Harrison, Lowell H. *The Antislavery Movement in Kentucky*. Lexington: University Press of Kentucky, 1978.

———. *The Civil War in Kentucky*. Lexington: University Press of Kentucky, 1975.

Harrison, Lowell, and James C. Klotter. *A New History of Kentucky*. Lexington: University Press of Kentucky, 1997.

Harrold, Stanley. *Abolitionists and the South, 1831–1861*. Lexington: University Press of Kentucky, 1995.

———. *Border War: Fighting over Slavery before the Civil War*. Chapel Hill: University of North Carolina Press, 2010.

———. *Gamaliel Bailey and Antislavery Union*. Kent, Ohio: Kent State University Press, 1986.

———. "Violence and Nonviolence in Kentucky Abolitionism." *Journal of Southern History* 57 (February 1991): 15–38.

Hart, Trevor. "Protestantism and the Arts." In *The Blackwell Companion to Protestantism*, edited by Alister E. McGrath and Darren C. Marks, 268–86. Malden, Mass.: Blackwell, 2004.

Harvey, Paul. *Redeeming the South: Religious Cultures and Racial Identities among Southern Baptists, 1865–1925*. Chapel Hill: University of North Carolina Press, 1997.

Hatch, Nathan. *The Democratization of American Christianity*. New Haven: Yale University Press, 1989.

Hedrick, Joan D. *Harriet Beecher Stowe: A Life*. New York: Oxford University Press, 1994.

Hemphill, C. Dallett. *Bowing to Necessities: A History of Manners in America, 1620–1860*. New York: Oxford University Press, 1999.

Hendler, Glenn. *Public Sentiments: Structures of Feeling in Nineteenth-Century American Literature*. Chapel Hill: University of North Carolina Press, 2001.

Hess, Earl J. *The Civil War in the West: Victory and Defeat from the Appalachians to the Mississippi*. Chapel Hill: University of North Carolina Press, 2012.

Heyrman, Christine Leigh. *Southern Cross: The Beginnings of the Bible Belt*. New York: Alfred A. Knopf, 1997.

Higginbotham, Evelyn Brooks. *Righteous Discontent: The Women's Movement in the Black Baptist Church, 1880–1920*. Cambridge, Mass.: Harvard University Press, 1993.

Higham, John. *From Boundlessness to Consolidation: The Transformation of American Culture, 1848–1860*. Ann Arbor, Mich.: William L. Clements Library, 1969.

Hillerbrand, Hans J., ed. *The Oxford Encyclopedia of the Reformation*. 4 vols. New York: Oxford University Press, 1996.

Hochman, Barbara. *Uncle Tom's Cabin and the Reading Revolution: Race, Literacy, Childhood, and Fiction, 1851–1911*. Amherst: University of Massachusetts Press, 2011.

Hofstadter, Richard. "The Paranoid Style in American Politics." In *The Fear of Conspiracy: Images of Un-American Subversion from the Revolution to the Present*, edited by David Brion Davis. Ithaca, N.Y.: Cornell University Press, 1971.

Horton, James Oliver, and Stacy Flaherty. "Black Leadership in Antebellum Cincinnati." In *Race and the City: Work, Community, and Protest in Cincinnati, 1820–1970*, edited by Henry Louis Taylor, Jr., 70–95. Chicago: University of Illinois Press, 1993.

Howard, June. "What is Sentimentality?" *American Literary History* 11 (Spring 1999): 63–81.

Howard, Victor B. *Black Liberation in Kentucky: Emancipation and Freedom, 1862–1884*. Lexington: University Press of Kentucky, 1983.

———. "The Kentucky Presbyterians in 1849: Slavery and the Kentucky Constitution." *Register of the Kentucky Historical Society* 73 (July 1975): 217–40.

Hudson, J. Blaine. "Crossing the 'Dark Line': Fugitive Slaves and the Underground Railroad in Louisville and North-Central Kentucky." *Filson History Quarterly* 75 (Winter 2001): 33–83.

———. " 'Upon This Rock' "—The Free African American Community of Antebellum Louisville, Kentucky." *Register of the Kentucky Historical Society* 109 (Summer/Autumn 2011): 295–326.

Hutchinson, John. "Cultural Nationalism and Moral Regeneration." In *Nationalism*, edited by John Hutchinson and Anthony D. Smith. New York: Oxford University Press, 1994.

Irons, Charles F. *The Origins of Proslavery Christianity: White and Black Evangelicals in Colonial and Antebellum Virginia*. Chapel Hill: University of North Carolina Press, 2008.

Isaac, Rhys. *The Transformation of Virginia, 1740–1790*. Chapel Hill: University of North Carolina Press, 1982.

Jantz, Harold S. *The First Century of New England Verse*. New York: Russell & Russell, 1962.

Jeffrey, Julie Roy. *The Great Silent Army of Abolitionism: Ordinary Women in the Antislavery Movement*. Chapel Hill: University of North Carolina Press, 1998.

Johnson, Paul E. *A Shopkeeper's Millennium: Society and Revivals in Rochester, New York, 1815–1837*. New York: Hill and Wang, 1978.

Jones, Arthur E., Jr. "The Years of Disagreement, 1844–1861." In *The History of American Methodism*, edited by Emory Stevens Bucke, 114–205. Vol. 2. New York: Abingdon, 1964.

Kane, Paul. "Ralph Waldo Emerson." In *Encyclopedia of American Poetry: The Nineteenth Century*, edited by Eric L. Haralson, with advisory editor John Hollander. Chicago: Fitzroy Dearborn, 1998.

Katz, Wendy Jean. *Regionalism and Reform: Art and Class Formation in Antebellum Cincinnati*. Columbus: Ohio State University Press, 2002.

Kelly, Catherine E. "'Well Bred Country People': Sociability, Social Networks, and the Creation of a Provincial Middle Class, 1820–1860." *Journal of the Early Republic* 19 (Fall 1999): 451–79.

Kersh, Rogan. *Dreams of a More Perfect Union.* Ithaca, N.Y.: Cornell University Press, 2001.

Kete, Mary Louise. *Sentimental Collaborations: Mourning and Middle-Class Identity in Nineteenth-Century America.* Durham, N.C.: Duke University Press, 2000.

Ketner, Joseph. *The Emergence of the African-American Artist: Robert S. Duncanson, 1821–1872.* Columbia: University of Missouri Press, 1993.

Kilby, Clyde S. *Minority of One: The Biography of Jonathan Blanchard.* Grand Rapids, Mich.: Wm. B. Eerdmans, 1959.

Kimbrough, B. T. *The History of the Walnut Street Baptist Church, Louisville, Kentucky.* Louisville: Press of Western Recorder, 1949.

Kinzie, Mary. *A Poet's Guide to Poetry.* Chicago: University of Chicago Press, 1999.

Kirby, James E., Russell E. Richey, and Kenneth E. Rowe. *The Methodists.* Westport, Conn.: Greenwood, 1996.

Kleber, John E., ed. *The Encyclopedia of Louisville.* Lexington: University Press of Kentucky, 2001.

———. *The Kentucky Encyclopedia.* Lexington: University Press of Kentucky, 1992.

Klement, Frank L. *The Copperheads in the Middle West.* Chicago: University of Chicago Press, 1960.

———. "Sound and Fury: Civil War Dissent in the Cincinnati Area." *Cincinnati Historical Society Bulletin* 35 (1977): 99–114.

Koehler, Lyle. *Cincinnati's Black Peoples: A Chronology and Bibliography, 1787–1982.* Cincinnati: Cincinnati Arts Consortium, in association with the Center for Neighborhood and Community Studies, University of Cincinnati, 1986.

Laderman, Gary. *The Sacred Remains: American Attitudes toward Death, 1799–1883.* New Haven: Yale University Press, 1996.

Lambert, Frank. *Inventing the "Great Awakening."* Princeton, N.J.: Princeton University Press, 1999.

Lamott, John H. *History of the Archdiocese of Cincinnati, 1821–1921.* New York: Frederick Pustet, 1921.

Lancaster, Clay. *Antebellum Architecture of Kentucky.* Lexington: University Press of Kentucky, 1991.

Lawson, Melinda. *Patriotic Fires: Forging a New American Nationalism in the Civil War North.* Lawrence: University Press of Kansas, 2002.

Le Beau, Bryan. "'Saving the West from the Pope': Anti-Catholic Propaganda and the Settlement of the Mississippi River Valley." *American Studies* 32 (Spring 1991): 101–14.

Lewalski, Barbara Kiefer. *Protestant Poetics and the Seventeenth-Century Religious Lyric.* Princeton, N.J.: Princeton University Press, 1979.

Litwack, Leon. *North of Slavery: The Negro in the Free States, 1790–1860.* Chicago: University of Chicago Press, 1961.

Lockard, Joe. "Griffith Browne, Mattie." *American National Biography Online.* October 2007. http://www.anb.org/articles/16/16-03522.html. May 6, 2015.

Long, Kathryn T. "The Power of Interpretation: The Revival of 1857–58 and the Historiography of Revivalism in America." *Religion and American Culture* 4 (Winter 1994): 77–105.

Lucas, Marion B. *A History of Blacks in Kentucky.* Vol. 1: *From Slavery to Segregation, 1760–1891.* Frankfort: Kentucky Historical Society, 1992.

Maizlish, Stephen E. "Ohio and the Rise of Sectional Politics." In *The Pursuit of Public Power: Political Culture in Ohio, 1787–1861,* edited by Jeffrey P. Brown and Andrew R. Clayton, 117–43. Kent, Ohio: Kent State University Press, 1994.

———. *The Triumph of Sectionalism: The Transformation of Ohio Politics, 1844–1856.* Kent, Ohio: Kent State University Press, 1983.

Marcus, Alan. *The Allen Temple (formerly Bene Israel Synagogue, 1852–1979).* Cincinnati: Procter & Gamble, 1980.

Marcus, Alan, with Gale E. Peterson and Daniel Hurley, eds. *Allen Temple.* Cincinnati: Cincinnati Historical Society, in association with Procter & Gamble, 1979.

Marshall, Anne E. *Creating a Confederate Kentucky: The Lost Cause and Civil War Memory in a Border State.* Chapel Hill: University of North Carolina Press, 2010.

Martz, Louis L. *The Poetry of Meditation: A Study in English Religious Literature of the Seventeenth Century.* 1954. Rev. ed., with a new preface. New Haven: Yale University Press, 1962.

Mathews, Donald G. *Religion in the Old South.* Chicago: University of Chicago Press, 1977.

———. *Slavery and Methodism: A Chapter in American Morality, 1780–1845.* Princeton, N.J.: Princeton University Press, 1965.

Matthews, Gary R. "Beleaguered Loyalties: Kentucky Unionism." In *Sister States, Enemy States: The Civil War in Kentucky and Tennessee,* edited by Kent T. Dollar, Larry H. Whiteaker, and W. Calvin Dickinson, 9–24. Lexington: University Press of Kentucky, 2009.

Matthews, Samuel. "John Isom Gaines: The Architect of Black Public Education." *Queen City Heritage* 45 (Spring 1987): 41–48.

McCoy, Drew R. *The Elusive Republic: Political Economy in Jeffersonian America.* New York: W. W. Norton, 1982.

McDannell, Colleen. *The Christian Home in Victorian America, 1840–1900.* Bloomington: Indiana University Press, 1986.

———. *Material Christianity: Religion and Popular Culture in America.* New Haven: Yale University Press, 1995.

McGann, Sister Agnes Geraldine. *Nativism in Kentucky to 1860.* Washington, D.C.: Catholic University of America Press, 1944.

McKivigan, John R. "The Sectional Division of the Methodist and Baptist Denominations as Measures of Antislavery Sentiment." In *Religion and the*

Antebellum Debate over Slavery, edited by John R. McKivigan and Mitchell Snay, 343–63. Athens: University of Georgia Press, 1998.

———. *The War against Proslavery Religion: Abolitionism and the Northern Churches, 1830–1865*. Ithaca, N.Y.: Cornell University Press, 1984.

McLoughlin, William G. *Revivals, Awakenings, and Reform: An Essay on Religion and Social Change in America, 1607–1977*. Chicago: University of Chicago Press, 1978.

Mentag, John V. "Catholic Spiritual Revivals, Parish Missions in the Midwest to 1865." PhD diss., Loyola University, Chicago, Ill., 1957.

Miami Baptist Association. *A Bicentennial History of the Miami Baptist Association, with Roster of Churches and Ministers. . . .* Cincinnati: Edge Graphics, 1998.

Middleton, Stephen. *The Black Laws: Race and the Legal Process in Early Ohio*. Athens: Ohio University Press, 2005.

———. "The Fugitive Slave Crisis in Cincinnati, 1850–1860: Resistance, Enforcement, and Black Refugees." *Journal of Negro History* 72 (Winter–Spring 1987): 20–32.

Mintz, Steven. *Moralists and Modernizers: America's Pre–Civil War Reformers*. Baltimore: Johns Hopkins University Press, 1995.

Miyakawa, T. Scott. *Protestants and Pioneers: Individualism and Conformity on the American Frontier*. Chicago: University of Chicago Press, 1964.

Mohon, Timothy. "First African Baptist Church of Louisville, Kentucky, 1842–1872: A Preliminary Study." Unpublished research paper, Southern Baptist Theological Seminary, Louisville, 1996.

Mohr, Clarence L. "Slaves and White Churches in Confederate Georgia." In *Masters and Slaves in the House of the Lord: Race and Religion in the American South, 1740–1870*, edited by John B. Boles. Lexington: University Press of Kentucky, 1990.

Moore, R. Laurence. *Religious Outsiders and the Making of Americans*. New York: Oxford University Press, 1986.

Morgan, David. *Visual Piety: A History and Theory of Popular Religious Images*. Berkeley: University of California Press, 1998.

Morris, J. Wesley. *Christ Church Cincinnati, 1817–1967*. Cincinnati: Episcopal Society of Christ Church, 1967.

Morrison, Michael A. *Slavery and the American West: The Eclipse of Manifest Destiny and the Coming of the Civil War*. Chapel Hill: University of North Carolina Press, 1997.

Murphy, Teresa Anne. *Ten Hours Labor: Religion, Reform, and Gender in Early New England*. Ithaca, N.Y.: Cornell University Press, 1992.

New, Elisa. *The Regenerate Lyric: Theology and Innovation in American Poetry*. New York: Cambridge University Press, 1993.

Niven, John. *Salmon P. Chase: A Biography*. New York: Oxford University Press, 1995.

Noll, Mark A. *A History of Christianity in the United States and Canada*. Grand Rapids, Mich.: Wm. B. Eerdmans, 1992.

Nord, David Paul. "The Evangelical Origins of Mass Media in America, 1815–1835." *Journalism Monographs* 88 (May 1984): 1–30.

———. "Religious Reading and Readers in Antebellum America." *Journal of the Early Republic* 15 (Summer 1995): 241–72.

———. "Systematic Benevolence: Religious Publishing and the Marketplace in Early Nineteenth-Century America." In *Communication and Change in American Religious History*, edited by Leonard I. Sweet, 239–69. Grand Rapids, Mich.: Wm. B. Eerdmans, 1993.

Norwood, John. *The Schism in the Methodist Episcopal Church, 1844: A Study of Slavery and Ecclesiastical Politics*. Alfred, N.Y.: Alfred University Press, 1923.

Nutt, Rick. *Contending for the Faith: The First Two Centuries of the Presbyterian Church in the Cincinnati Area*. Cincinnati: Presbytery of Cincinnati, 1991.

Oakes, James. *Freedom National: The Destruction of Slavery in the United States, 1861–1865*. New York: W. W. Norton, 2013.

O'Brien, Mary Lawrence. "Slavery in Louisville during the Antebellum Period: 1820–1860." Master's thesis, University of Louisville, 1979.

Page, Wilber Allen. *History of Union Baptist Church*. Cincinnati: Selby Service/Roxy Press, 1978.

Perrin, David B. "Mysticism." In *The Blackwell Companion to Christian Spirituality*, edited by Arthur G. Holder, 442–58. Oxford: Blackwell, 2005.

Phillips, Christopher. "Lincoln's Grasp of War: Hard War and the Politics of Neutrality and Slavery in the Western Border States, 1861–1862." *The Journal of the Civil War Era* 3, no. 2 (June 2013): 184–210.

Prickett, Stephen, ed. *The Romantics*. London: Methuen, 1981.

Rabinowitz, Richard. *The Spiritual Self in Everyday Life: The Transformation of Personal Religious Experience in Nineteenth-Century New England*. Boston: Northeastern University Press, 1989.

Raboteau, Albert J. *A Fire in the Bones: Reflections on African-American Religious History*. Boston: Beacon, 1995.

———. *Slave Religion: The "Invisible Institution" in the Antebellum South*. New York: Oxford University Press, 1978.

Rael, Patrick. *Black Identity and Black Protest in the Antebellum North*. Chapel Hill: University of North Carolina Press, 2002.

Ramage, James. *Kentucky Rising: Democracy, Slavery, and Culture from the Early Republic to the Civil War*. Lexington: University Press of Kentucky, with the Kentucky Historical Society, 2011.

Reardon, Bernard M. G. *Religion in the Age of Romanticism: Studies in Early Nineteenth-Century Thought*. New York: Cambridge University Press, 1985.

Reilly, Elizabeth Carroll, and David D. Hall, "Customers and the Market for Books." In *The Colonial Book in the Atlantic World*, edited by Hugh Armory and David D. Hall, 387–98. Vol. 1 of *A History of the Book in America*. Cambridge: Cambridge University Press, in association with the American Antiquarian Society, 2000.

R. E. Jones United Methodist Church. *Our Heritage Past and Present at R. E. Jones United Methodist Church from 1832–1992*. Louisville, 1992.

Reynolds, David. *Faith in Fiction: The Emergence of Religious Literature in America*. Cambridge, Mass.: Harvard University Press, 1981.

Richards, Leonard L. *The Slave Power: The Free North and Southern Domination* Baton Rouge: Louisiana State University Press, 2000.

Robertson, Stacey M. *Hearts Beating for Liberty: Women Abolitionists in the Old Northwest*. Chapel Hill: University of North Carolina Press, 2010.

Robson, Michael. *The Franciscans in the Middle Ages*. Woodbridge, UK: Boydell, 2006.

Rockenbach, Stephen J. "A Border City at War: Louisville and the 1862 Confederate Invasion of Kentucky." *Ohio Valley History* (Winter 2003): 35–52.

Rockman, Seth. *Scraping By: Wage Labor, Slavery, and Survival in Early Baltimore*. Baltimore: Johns Hopkins University Press, 2009.

Roemer, Theodore. *The Leopoldine Foundation and the Church in the United States (1829–1839)*. United States Catholic Historical Society Monograph Series 13. New York: United States Catholic Historical Society, 1933.

———. *The Ludwig-Missionsverein and the Church in the United States (1838–1918)*. Washington, D.C.: Catholic University of America, 1933.

Rose, Anne C. "Interfaith Families in Victorian America." In *Moral Problems in American Life*, edited by Karen Halttunen and Lewis Perry, 223–43. Ithaca, N.Y.: Cornell University Press, 1998.

———. "Some Private Roads to Rome: The Role of Families in American Victorian Conversions to Catholicism." *Catholic Historical Review* 85 (January 1999): 35–57.

———. *Victorian America and the Civil War*. New York: Cambridge University Press, 1992.

Ross, Steven J. *Workers on the Edge: Work, Leisure, and Politics in Industrializing Cincinnati, 1788–1890*. New York: Columbia University Press, 1985.

Roth, Randolph. *The Democratic Dilemma: Religion, Reform, and the Social Order in the Connecticut River Valley of Vermont, 1791–1850*. New York: Cambridge University Press, 1987.

Rush, Dorothy. "Early Accounts of Travel to the Falls of the Ohio: A Bibliography with Selected Quotations, 1765–1833." *Filson Club History Quarterly* 68 (April 1994): 232–66.

Ryan, Mary P. *Cradle of the Middle Class: The Family in Oneida County, New York, 1790–1865*. New York: Cambridge University Press, 1981.

Ryan, Robert M. *The Romantic Reformation: Religious Politics in English Literature, 1789–1824*. New York: Cambridge University Press, 1997.

Salafia, Matthew. *Slavery's Borderland: Freedom and Bondage along the Ohio River*. Philadelphia: University of Pennsylvania Press, 2013.

Sánchez-Eppler, Karen. *Touching Liberty: Abolitionism, Feminism, and the Politics of the Body*. Berkeley: University of California Press, 1993.

Santamarina, Xiomara. *Belabored Professions: Narratives of African American Working Womanhood.* Chapel Hill: University of North Carolina Press, 2005.

Schantz, Mark S. *Piety in Providence: Class Dimensions of Religious Experience in Antebellum Rhode Island.* Ithaca, N.Y.: Cornell University Press, 2000.

Schmidt, Martin F. "The Early Printers of Louisville, 1800–1860." *Filson Club History Quarterly* 40 (October 1966): 307–34.

Schneider, Carl E. *The German Church on the American Frontier: A Study of the Rise of Religion among the Germans of the West. . . .* St. Louis: Eden, 1939.

Shotwell, John B. *A History of the Schools of Cincinnati.* Cincinnati: School Life, 1902.

Seeman, Erik R. *Pious Persuasions: Laity and Clergy in Eighteenth-Century New England.* Baltimore: Johns Hopkins University Press, 1999.

Sellers, Charles. *The Market Revolution: Jacksonian America, 1815–1846.* New York: Oxford University Press, 1992.

Sernett, Milton C. *Black Religion and American Evangelicalism: White Protestants, Plantation Missions, and the Flowering of Negro Christianity, 1787–1865.* Metuchen, N.J.: Scarecrow, 1975.

Sherman, Joan R. *Invisible Poets: Afro-Americans of the Nineteenth Century.* 2nd ed. Urbana: University of Illinois Press, 1989.

Shields, David S. *Civil Tongues and Polite Letters in British America.* Chapel Hill: University of North Carolina Press, 1997.

———. "Eighteenth-Century Literary Culture." In *The Colonial Book in the Atlantic World,* edited by Hugh Armory and David D. Hall, 434–76. Vol. 1 of *A History of the Book in America.* Cambridge: Cambridge University Press, in association with the American Antiquarian Society, 2000.

Shriver, George H. "Romantic Religion." In *The Encyclopedia of American Religious Experience: Studies of Traditions and Movements,* edited by Charles H. Lippy and Peter W. Williams, Vol. 2, 1103–15. 3 vols. New York: Charles Scribner's Sons, 1988.

Sizer, Sandra. *Gospel Hymns and Social Religion: The Rhetoric of Nineteenth-Century Revivalism.* Philadelphia: Temple University Press, 1978.

Sklar, Kathryn Kish. *Catharine Beecher: A Study in American Domesticity.* New York: W. W. Norton, 1976.

Smith, Ryan K. "The Cross: Church Symbol and Contest in Nineteenth-Century America." *Church History* 70 (December 2001): 705–34.

———. *Gothic Arches, Latin Crosses: Anti-Catholicism and American Church Designs in the Nineteenth Century.* Chapel Hill: University of North Carolina Press, 2006.

Smith, Timothy L. "The Ohio Valley: Testing Ground for America's Experiment in Religious Pluralism." *Church History* 60 (December 1991): 461–79.

Snay, Mitchell. *Gospel of Disunion: Religion and Separation in the Antebellum South.* Chapel Hill: University of North Carolina Press, 1993.

Sparks, Randy J. " 'To Rend the Body of Christ': Proslavery Ideology and Religious Schism from a Mississippi Perspective." In *Religion and the Antebellum Debate over Slavery,* edited by John R. McKivigan and Mitchell Snay, 273–95. Athens: University of Georgia Press, 1998.

Stanton, Phoebe. *The Gothic Revival and American Church Architecture: An Episode in Taste*. 1968. Reprint, Baltimore: Johns Hopkins University Press, 1997.

Stewart, James Brewer. *Holy Warriors: The Abolitionists and American Slavery*. New York: Hill and Wang, 1976.

Stout, Harry S. *The Divine Dramatist: George Whitefield and the Rise of Modern Evangelicalism*. Grand Rapids, Mich.: Wm. B. Eerdmans, 1991.

Stritch, Alfred. "Nativism in Cincinnati, 1830–1860." PhD diss., Catholic University of America, 1935.

Sutton, Walter. *The Western Book Trade: Cincinnati as a Nineteenth-Century Publishing and Book-Trade Center*. Columbus: Ohio State University Press, for the Ohio Historical Society, 1961.

Tallant, Harold D. *Evil Necessity: Slavery and Political Culture in Antebellum Kentucky*. Lexington: University Press of Kentucky, 2003.

Taves, Ann. *The Household of Faith: Roman Catholic Devotions in Mid-Nineteenth-Century America*. Notre Dame: University of Notre Dame Press, 1986.

Taylor, Alan. *The Internal Enemy: Slavery and War in Virginia, 1772–1832*. New York: W. W. Norton, 2013.

Taylor, Henry Louis, Jr., ed. *Race and the City: Work, Community, and Protest in Cincinnati, 1820–1970*. Urbana: University of Illinois Press, 1993.

Taylor, Nikki M. *America's First Black Socialist: The Radical Life of Peter H. Clark*. Lexington: University Press of Kentucky, 2013.

———. *Frontiers of Freedom: Cincinnati's Black Community, 1802–1868*. Athens: Ohio University Press, 2005.

Thomas, John L. "Romantic Reform in America, 1815–1865." *American Quarterly* 17 (Winter 1965): 656–81.

Tompkins, Jane P. *Sensational Designs: The Cultural Work of American Fiction, 1790–1860*. New York: Oxford University Press, 1985.

Touchstone, Blake. "Planters and Slave Religion in the Deep South." In *Masters and Slaves in the House of the Lord: Race and Religion in the American South, 1740–1870*, edited by John B. Boles, 99–126. Lexington: University Press of Kentucky, 1990.

Trotter, Joe William Jr. *River Jordan: African American Urban Life in the Ohio Valley*. Lexington: University Press of Kentucky, 1998.

Troutman, Phillip Davis. "Slave Trade and Sentiment in Antebellum Virginia." PhD diss., University of Virginia, 2000.

Varon, Elizabeth. *Disunion! The Coming of the American Civil War, 1789–1859*. Chapel Hill: University of North Carolina Press, 2008.

Volpe, Andrea. "Cartes de Visite Portrait Photography and the Culture of Class Formation." In *The Middling Sorts: Exploration in the History of the American Middle Class*, edited by Burton J. Bledstein and Robert D. Johnston, 157–69. New York: Routledge, 2001.

Wade, Richard C. "The Negro in Cincinnati, 1800–1830." *Journal of Negro History* 39 (January 1854): 43–57.

———. *Slavery in the Cities: The South, 1820–1860*. New York: Oxford University Press, 1964.

———. *The Urban Frontier: The Rise of Western Cities, 1790–1830*. Cambridge, Mass.: Harvard University Press, 1959.

Walker, Clarence E. *A Rock in a Weary Land: The African Methodist Episcopal Church during the Civil War and Reconstruction*. Baton Rouge: Louisiana State University Press, 1982.

Weiner, Dana Elizabeth. *Race and Rights: Fighting Slavery and Prejudice in the Old Northwest, 1830–1870*. DeKalb: Northern Illinois University Press, 2013.

Weisert, Anita Boss. "German Protestants on the Urban Frontier: The Early History of Louisville's St. John's Evangelical Church." Edited by Carl E. Kramer. *Filson Club History Quarterly* 72 (October 1998): 379–418.

Wexler, Laura. "Tender Violence: Literary Eavesdropping, Domestic Fiction, and Educational Reform." In *The Culture of Sentiment: Race, Gender, and Sentimentality in Nineteenth-Century America*, edited by Shirley Samuels, 9–38. New York: Oxford University Press, 1992.

Wiethaus, Ulrike. "Christian Spirituality in the Medieval West (600–1450)." In *The Blackwell Companion to Christian Spirituality*, edited by Arthur G. Holder, 106–20. Oxford: Blackwell, 2005.

Williams, Peter W. *Houses of God: Region, Religion, and Architecture in the United States*. Urbana: University of Illinois Press, 1997.

———. "The Iconography of the American City: Or, A Gothic Tale of Modern Times." *Church History* 68 (June 1999): 373–97.

———. "Metamorphoses of the Meetinghouse: Three Case Studies." In *Seeing beyond the Word: Visual Arts and the Calvinist Tradition*, edited by Paul Corby Finney, 479–505. Grand Rapids, Mich.: William B. Eerdmans, 1999.

Willis, Deborah, ed. *J. P. Ball: Daguerrean and Studio Photographer*. New York: Garland, 1993.

Woodward, C. Vann. *Origins of the New South, 1877–1913*. Baton Rouge: Louisiana State University Press, 1951.

Wright, George C. *Life behind a Veil: Blacks in Louisville, Kentucky, 1865–1930*. Baton Rouge: Louisiana State University Press, 1985.

———. *Racial Violence in Kentucky, 1865–1940: Lynchings, Mob Rule, and "Legal Lynchings."* Baton Rouge: Louisiana State University Press, 1990.

Yellin, Jean Fagan. *Women and Sisters: The Antislavery Feminists in American Culture*. New Haven: Yale University Press, 1989.

Index

Note: Illustrations are indicated by page numbers in *italics*.